Edition ZfE

Volume 3

Series editor
I. Gogolin, Fakultät für Erziehungswissenschaft, Universität Hamburg
Hamburg, Deutschland

Die Reihe ‚Edition ZfE' wird von den Herausgeber(innen) der Zeitschrift für Erziehungswissenschaft verantwortet. In der Reihe werden Originalbeiträge publiziert, die den strengen Qualitätsmaßstäben für die Publikation von Manuskripten in der Zeitschrift standhalten. Veröffentlicht werden von Expert(innen) begutachtete erstklassige Beiträge zu aktuellen Befunden und Entwicklungen der Erziehungswissenschaft und Bildungsforschung. Die Zahl solcher Beiträge übersteigt die Möglichkeiten der Publikation in der Zeitschrift für Erziehungswissenschaft. Mit der ‚Edition ZfE' wird hier Spielraum eröffnet. Durch die Auswahl von Herausgeber(innen) und die Themenwahl stehen die Beiträge zur Buchreihe ebenso wie die ZfE selbst für den interdisziplinären Charakter einer umfassenden Erziehungswissenschaft, deren Gegenstand der gesamte Lebenslauf des Menschen ist. Die gezielte Aufnahme internationaler Beiträge gewährleistet den Anschluss an erziehungswissenschaftliche Entwicklungen außerhalb Deutschlands. Die Leser(innen) der ‚ZfE-Edition' verfügen somit über eine zusätzliche Informationsquelle, die ihnen die für Erziehung und Bildung wichtigen internationalen und interdisziplinären Entwicklungen in weiten Bereichen der Erziehungswissenschaft zuverlässig, nüchtern und nachvollziehbar präsentiert.

More information about this series at http://www.springer.com/series/13862

Hans-Peter Blossfeld · Hans-Günther Roßbach
Editors

Education as a Lifelong Process

The German National Educational Panel Study (NEPS)

Second Revised Edition

 Springer VS

Editors
Hans-Peter Blossfeld
Otto-Friedrich-Universität Bamberg
Bamberg, Germany

Hans-Günther Roßbach
Otto-Friedrich-Universität Bamberg
Bamberg, Germany

ISSN 2512-0778   ISSN 2512-0786 (electronic)
Edition ZfE
ISBN 978-3-658-23161-3   ISBN 978-3-658-23162-0 (eBook)
https://doi.org/10.1007/978-3-658-23162-0

Library of Congress Control Number: 2018959100

Springer VS
© Springer Fachmedien Wiesbaden GmbH, ein Teil von Springer Nature 2011, 2019
This work is subject to copyright. All rights are reserved by the Publisher, whether the whole or part of the material is concerned, specifically the rights of translation, reprinting, reuse of illustrations, recitation, broadcasting, reproduction on microfilms or in any other physical way, and transmission or information storage and retrieval, electronic adaptation, computer software, or by similar or dissimilar methodology now known or hereafter developed.
The use of general descriptive names, registered names, trademarks, service marks, etc. in this publication does not imply, even in the absence of a specific statement, that such names are exempt from the relevant protective laws and regulations and therefore free for general use.
The publisher, the authors and the editors are safe to assume that the advice and information in this book are believed to be true and accurate at the date of publication. Neither the publisher nor the authors or the editors give a warranty, express or implied, with respect to the material contained herein or for any errors or omissions that may have been made. The publisher remains neutral with regard to jurisdictional claims in published maps and institutional affiliations.

Responsible for production: Stefanie Laux

This Springer VS imprint is published by the registered company Springer Fachmedien Wiesbaden GmbH part of Springer Nature
The registered company address is: Abraham-Lincoln-Str. 46, 65189 Wiesbaden, Germany

Editorial

Like other modern industrialized societies, Germany has evolved into a knowledge-based economy in which the roles of education and educational institutions have become key factors in all phases of the life course. More than ever before, education has become a lifelong process in which individuals continue to learn throughout their lives in formal, nonformal, and informal environments. As a result, their educational careers and competencies and how these unfold in relation to family, educational institutions, workplaces, and private life activities are a topic of major national interest. Although understanding what is happening over the life course requires longitudinal data, most empirical evidence in German educational research is still cross-sectional and therefore only a kind of snapshot of different individuals at particular points in their educational careers. Successive snapshots from different individuals in a series of cross-sectional surveys certainly highlight the changes in the structure as a whole. Yet, they do not show the changing (and sometimes) unchanging experiences of individuals as their educational careers progress. Panel data, with information on many individuals measured on several occasions spread over time, can be used to describe these patterns of change over the life course. They are especially able to trace the magnitude and regularity of change across groups defined by different characteristics or by exposure to different individual life-course experiences.

Thus, there is an increasing demand for high-quality longitudinal educational research in Germany. In particular, there is a clear need to work on improving the analytical and methodological tools needed to understand educational pathways through the life course and how they lead to different outcomes. The National Educational Panel Study (NEPS) for Germany has been designed to meet these challenges. It is collecting longitudinal data on educational processes and individual competence development across the entire life span from early childhood to late adulthood. Preparing the NEPS proposal was a long-term and time-consuming process extending over many years. The resulting NEPS dataset is the outcome of a close collaboration between scientists and research institutions in a network of excellence all over Germany. Members of this consortium come from major research institutions and are experts in various disciplines (psychology, educational science, sociology, economics, demography, migration studies, statistics, survey methods, etc.). They have been collaborating in order to pool the expertise, experience, and efforts needed to deliver the best longitudinal data on educational processes in Germany. In 2007 and 2008, the first NEPS proposals were evaluated scientifically by two panels of leading international experts in the field of education organized by the *Deutsche Forschungsgemeinschaft* (German Research Foundation, DFG). Thanks to the enthusiastic recommendations of these international reviewers, the *Bundesministerium für Bildung und Forschung* (Federal Ministry of Education and Research, BMBF) decided to finance the NEPS with an exceptionally large grant. We would like to thank the BMBF for its initiative in launching the NEPS and the financial support it granted us throughout the initial years. At the beginning, the NEPS was hosted by the *Institut für bildungswissenschaftliche Längsschnittforschung (Institute for Longitudinal Educational Research*, INBIL) at the University of Bamberg.

In 2014, after yet another favorable evaluation, the *Leibniz-Institut für Bildungsverläufe e. V.* (Leibniz Institute for Educational Trajectories, LIfBi) was founded in Bamberg. The LIfBi took over the leading role of hosting, conducting, and disseminating NEPS. We would like to thank the German Federal Government and the German Federal States for their financial support of the LIfBi. As a member of the Leibniz Association, the LIfBi is an independent research institution set up specifically to provide a research infrastructure facility of supraregional importance and national scientific interest.

This volume begins in Chaps. 1 and 2 with a more general description of NEPS and the role of education as a lifelong process. NEPS is based on six key theoretical dimensions. The first three of these dimensions are based on the observation that individuals' educational trajectories over the life course are the result of a dynamic interplay of (1) educational decision making, (2) learning processes within different educational contexts, and (3) individual competence development. The central assumptions of NEPS are therefore that (1) decisions (by parents, students, adults, teachers, etc.) determine whether and to what extent individuals participate in specific educationally relevant social and institutional contexts; (2) these contexts promote or impede learning processes; and (3) these contexts impact on individual's competence development – and this, in turn, establishes the conditions for educational decision making in the next step of the life course. By focusing on these three key theoretical dimensions and their time-dependent interaction mechanisms, which generate change and development in education over the life course, NEPS has established a powerful foundation for theoretically grounded explanations and evidence-based research in the educational sciences. A fourth theoretical dimension has been added during the last years that is focusing on the role of motivation and personality as regulative forces across the life course.

In addition, there are many indications that the educational outcomes of migrants' children differ substantially from those of their peers from native families. These differences are likely to persist across the whole life course and follow very specific theoretical mechanisms. Therefore, a fifth theoretical dimension of NEPS is addressing the specifics of the educational careers of migrants and their descendants. It is focusing on the two largest groups of migrants in Germany at the beginning of the 2010s: Turks and ethnic Germans from the former Soviet Union (*Spätaussiedler*).

Finally, a sixth important theoretical dimension of NEPS concerns returns to education. NEPS is focusing on not only economic but also noneconomic returns to educational qualifications such as income, job opportunities, job careers, health, reduced crime, increased political participation, family formation, fertility behavior, and homogamy. Alongside these "objective" kinds of returns, it is also assessing individuals' subjective well-being.

These six theoretical dimensions are also labeled "pillars" in NEPS, because they integrate the multicohort sequence design of NEPS in terms of content, theory, and methods. These theoretical dimensions or pillars are described in Chaps. 4–9.

When starting a panel study, its methodological design is a major issue. To deliver relevant information on major educational stages and the transitions between these stages as quickly as possible, NEPS is implementing a multicohort sequence design based on eight crucial educational stages in the life course: Stage 1: From Birth to Early Child Education and Care; Stage 2: From Kindergarten to Elementary School; Stage 3: From Elementary School to Lower Secondary School; Stage 4: From Lower to Upper Secondary School; Stage 5: From Upper Secondary School to Higher Education, Vocational Training, or the Labor Market; Stage 6: From Vocational Training to the Labor Market; Stage 7: From Higher Education to the Labor Market; and Stage 8: Adult Education and Lifelong Learning. Panel sweeps of the cohorts included in the NEPS are being conducted at least once a year. The surveys include competence tests and interviews with target persons and – at least for the younger cohorts – also interviews with parents and educators. These educational stages and their consequences for NEPS are discussed in detail in Chaps. 11–17.

The multicohort sequence design is following up six starting cohorts over time. The first is the "adult" cohort in which fieldwork already started in 2009. Four further cohorts (Kindergarten, 5th-grade students, 9th-grade students, college students) started in fall 2010. Fieldwork on the sixth "infant" cohort, which traces early child development, early entry into child care facilities (nursery, Kindergarten, etc.), and entrance into the school system, started in 2012. This later start was due to the extended time needed to prepare the specific instruments for this cohort (video studies, etc.).

The specific methodological problems of NEPS are addressed by a group of methodologists and statisticians. Sampling issues and methodological challenges are described in Chaps. 3. Because different instruments have to be linked across several stages, there is a special need to disentangle setting and mode effects. This is described in Chaps. 10.

The aim of the NEPS project is to deliver the best data on educational trajectories and competence development to the scientific community, and to do this as quickly as possible. Before dissemination, NEPS data is documented in a user-friendly way and subjected to strict quality controls. In addition, the project has to make sure that datasets comply with Germany's strict personal data privacy requirements. Data from each wave are made available within 18 months of the completion of fieldwork. They are released through the Research Data Center of the LIfBi (accredited by the *Rat für Sozial- und*

Wirtschaftsdaten, German Data Forum, RatSWD) in three modes: (1) Scientific Use Files that can be downloaded from the NEPS website, (2) modern remote access technology (RemoteNEPS), and (3) on-site access at the LIfBi. The Research Data Center of the LIfBi provides support for users of longitudinal data. In particular, it is running regular training courses on how to use the NEPS database and conduct longitudinal analyses with NEPS data. There is also a NEPS help desk for data users. Data protection issues and the Research Data Center are described in Chaps. 18 and 19.

This volume is a revised and updated version of the Special Issue on "Education as a Lifelong Process" in the *Zeitschrift für Erziehungswissenschaft*. It informs data users on significant changes since the first edition in 2011. The updated volume does not contain any planning for NEPS activities in the coming years.

In the name of the entire NEPS consortium, we would like to take this opportunity to thank the BMBF for its marvelous support in initiating and developing the NEPS and for making such an exceptional investment in the infrastructure of the social sciences. We also thank all those partners taking part in the transition from the NEPS as a project at the University of Bamberg to an independent institute within the Leibniz Association. By name, we shall mention only the BMBF and the *Bayerisches Staatsministerium für Wissenschaft und Kunst* (Bavarian State Ministry of Science and the Arts), but we emphasize that this in no way denies the important contributions of other partners. We are also grateful for the strong support of the *Kultusministerkonferenz* (Standing Conference of the Ministers of Education and Cultural Affairs of the Federal States in Germany, KMK) and the 16 *Bundesländer* (Federal States) in gaining access to schools and institutes of higher education. We thank the members of the Scientific Board as well as the Board of Trustees of the LIfBi for their advice and expert support. We also wish to express our great appreciation to the DFG for organizing the proposal review processes in a way that ensured the highest academic standards, to the international experts and proposal reviewers for their evaluation and advice, and to the *Wissenschaftsrat* (German Council of Science and Humanities, WR) for conducting the evaluation that led to the establishment of the LIfBi. We would also like thank the DFG for funding the Priority Programme "Education as a Lifelong Process" that allowed researchers from many different disciplines to start utilizing NEPS data immediately. Finally, we would like to thank Jutta von Maurice, who served as the third editor in the first edition. Due to time constraints, she unfortunately has not been able to work on this new revised volume. Last but not least, we would like to thank Petra Ries and Martina Alsfasser for their coordination of the revisions to the chapters in the new edition of the book, Jonathan Harrow for his rigorous proofreading and language editing of the manuscripts, and Joachim M. Seemüller for the final formatting of the typescript.

Hans-Peter Blossfeld
(First principal investigator of the NEPS)

Hans-Günther Roßbach
(Second principal investigator of the NEPS
and founding director of the LIfBi)

Contents

1. **The National Educational Panel Study: Need, Main Features, and Research Potential** 1
   Hans-Peter Blossfeld, Jutta von Maurice and Thorsten Schneider

2. **Education as a Lifelong Process** 17
   Hans-Peter Blossfeld and Jutta von Maurice

3. **Sampling Designs of the National Educational Panel Study: Setup and Panel Development** 35
   Christian Aßmann, Hans-Walter Steinhauer, Ariane Würbach, Sabine Zinn, Angelina Hammon, Hans Kiesl, Götz Rohwer, Susanne Rässler and Hans-Peter Blossfeld

4. **Development of Competencies Across the Life Course** 57
   Sabine Weinert, Cordula Artelt, Manfred Prenzel, Martin Senkbeil, Timo Ehmke, Claus H. Carstensen and Kathrin Lockl

5. **Education Processes in Life-Course-Specific Learning Environments** 83
   Thomas Bäumer, Eckhard Klieme, Susanne Kuger, Kai Maaz, Hans-Günther Roßbach, Ludwig Stecher and Olaf Struck

6. **Social Inequality and Educational Decisions in the Life Course** 101
   Volker Stocké, Hans-Peter Blossfeld, Kerstin Hoenig and Michaela Sixt

7. **The Education of Migrants and Their Children Across the Life Course** 119
   Cornelia Kristen, Aileen Edele, Frank Kalter, Irena Kogan, Benjamin Schulz, Petra Stanat and Gisela Will

8. **Educational Returns Over the Life Course** 137
   Christiane Gross, Anika Bela, Monika Jungbauer-Gans, Andreas Jobst and Johannes Schwarze

9 **Measuring Motivational Concepts and Personality Aspects in the National Educational Panel Study** 155
Florian Wohlkinger, A. Raphaela Blumenfelder, Michael Bayer, Jutta von Maurice, Hartmut Ditton and Hans-Peter Blossfeld

10 **Disentangling Setting and Mode Effects for Online Competence Assessment** 171
Ulf Kroehne, Timo Gnambs and Frank Goldhammer

11 **From Birth to Early Child Care: The Newborn Cohort Study of the National Educational Panel Study** 195
Claudia Hachul (née Schlesiger), Manja Attig, Jennifer Lorenz, Sabine Weinert, Thorsten Schneider and Hans-Günther Roßbach

12 **Kindergarten and Elementary School: Starting Cohort 2 of the National Educational Panel Study** 215
Karin Berendes, Tobias Linberg, Doreen Müller, Sebastian E. Wenz, Hans-Günther Roßbach, Thorsten Schneider and Sabine Weinert

13 **Transition and Development from Lower Secondary to Upper Secondary School** 231
Paul Fabian, Martin Goy, Stephan Jarsinski, Kerstin Naujokat, Anna Prosch, Rolf Strietholt, Inge Blatt and Wilfried Bos

14 **Upper Secondary Education in Academic School Tracks and the Transition from School to Postsecondary Education and the Job Market** 253
Wolfgang Wagner, Michaela Kropf, Jochen Kramer, Julia Schilling, Karin Berendes, Ricarda Albrecht, Nicolas Hübner, Sven Rieger, Anna Bachsleitner, Josefine Lühe, Gabriel Nagy, Oliver Lüdtke, Kathrin Jonkmann, Sonja Gruner, Kai Maaz and Ulrich Trautwein

15 **Vocational Education and Training and Transitions into the Labor Market** 277
Wolfgang Ludwig-Mayerhofer, Reinhard Pollak, Heike Solga, Laura Menze, Kathrin Leuze, Rosine Edelstein, Ralf Künster, Ellen Ebralidze, Gritt Fehring and Susanne Kühn

16 **Higher Education and the Transition to Work**..................... 297
Julia-Carolin Brachem, Florian Aschinger, Gritt Fehring, Michael Grotheer, Sonja Herrmann, Marie Kühn, Uta Liebeskind, Andreas Ortenburger and Hildegard Schaeper

Contents

17 Adult Education and Lifelong Learning 325
Jutta Allmendinger, Corinna Kleinert, Reinhard Pollak, Basha Vicari,
Oliver Wölfel, Agnieszka Althaber, Manfred Antoni, Bernhard Christoph,
Katrin Drasch, Florian Janik, Ralf Künster, Marie-Christine Laible,
Kathrin Leuze, Britta Matthes, Michael Ruland,
Benjamin Schulz and Annette Trahms

18 Data Protection Issues in the National Educational Panel Study 347
Antonia Schier, Meike Bender, Tobias Koberg, Brigitte Bogensperger,
Sonja Gruner, David Schiller, Jutta von Maurice and
Henriette Engelhardt-Wölfler

**19 The Research Data Center: Making National Educational
Panel Study Data Available for Research** 361
Daniel Fuß and Knut Wenzig

Glossary of Institutions in the German Education System 379

References 383

The National Educational Panel Study: Need, Main Features, and Research Potential

Hans-Peter Blossfeld, Jutta von Maurice and Thorsten Schneider

Abstract

The German National Educational Panel Study (NEPS) was set up to study the acquisition of education, to assess the consequences of education for life courses, and to describe central education processes and trajectories across the entire life span. It is organized as a network of excellence linking together researchers from different disciplines with the life-course perspective serving as its preeminent theoretical characteristic. Although focusing on eight stages ranging over the entire life span, it ensures longitudinal integration through its theoretical orientation toward six major dimensions ("pillars"): competence development, learning environments, social inequalities and educational decisions, educational processes of migrants, returns to education, as well as motivation and personality. Methodologically, NEPS follows a multicohort sequence design starting with a total number of more than 60,000 target persons from six cohorts (early childhood, Kindergarten children, 5th graders, 9th graders,

---

This is an updated and shortened version of Blossfeld et al. (2011) as well as Blossfeld and Schneider (2011).

H.-P. Blossfeld (✉)
University of Bamberg, Bamberg, Germany
E-Mail: hans-peter.blossfeld@uni-bamberg.de

J. von Maurice
Leibniz Institute for Educational Trajectories, Bamberg, Germany
E-Mail: jutta.von-maurice@lifbi.de

T. Schneider
University of Leipzig, Leipzig, Germany
E-Mail: thorsten.schneider@uni-leipzig.de

first-year college students, and adults who, in most cases, had already left the educational system). Different instruments including questionnaires and competence tests are being administered in all six cohorts. Each new wave of the panel study is being made available to the scientific community as quickly as possible.

Keywords

Education · Panel study · Interdisciplinary research · Life-course perspective Multicohort sequence design

1.1 Project Overview

In modern knowledge societies, education has not just become the key factor for economic growth and prosperity. It has also become decisive for coping with the challenges of a rapidly changing globalized world. Moreover, education is an important precondition for active participation as responsible citizens in a democratic society. However, the Programme for International Student Assessment (PISA), initiated by the Organization for Economic Co-operation and Development (OECD), has shown that major proportions of Germany's students are insufficiently prepared to meet these challenges at the end of their compulsory school attendance. Furthermore, analyses of PISA data have also repeatedly confirmed a strong correlation between social origins and competencies in Germany (most recently in the sixth round of the PISA assessments 2015 with a focus on science, OECD 2016). Despite all educational reforms, equal opportunity still seems to be a distant goal, even though the importance of education has tended to increase rather than to decline in recent decades—not only for positioning on the labor market but also for chances in individual and social life such as obtaining a partner on the marriage market.

Educational institutions deal with young people's acquisition of knowledge, skills, and competencies. Other important issues are attitudes, values, and norms. However, the educational system also assesses student performance, documenting it in grades, certificates, and degrees. These assessments may well determine potential access to specific education tracks such as the transition to a Gymnasium (upper secondary school offering university entrance qualification) or admission to a university, and they are also very important for job placement in many sectors of the labor market. In this way, schools and training institutes contribute to increasing or decreasing an individual's chances in later life.

Research and policy have stressed the need to broaden the view beyond school, vocational education and training, and university. First, we need to take a closer look at the time before compulsory education, at the first years of life. Several findings indicate that promoting children from less privileged families in preschool institutions has long lasting positive consequences that can still be found even at the age of 40 (Heckman and Masterov 2007). The other issue concerns lifelong learning. For members of modern information and service economies, learning does not end by obtaining a final qualification in the general or vocational education system. They are obliged to acquire new knowledge and new competencies continuously throughout their lives. This is why the Programme for the International Assessment of Adult Competencies (PIAAC) focuses on the qualifications of the working-age population (OECD 2004).

The technological and organizational transformation of the economy is not just increasingly reducing the need for routine work. It is also leading to a rapid growth in jobs in the service sector and in highly qualified positions requiring complex social and communicative competencies. This upgrading of the job structure raises the demand for highly qualified people and enhances the value of education and training both on the labor market and in society. In addition, globalization is leading to a strong acceleration of social and economic change in modern societies, and this increasingly requires more flexibility and adaptability both at work and in society. The ability to acquire new knowledge and to take on new tasks has become an important precondition for both finding new jobs and acting as responsible citizens. This makes it necessary to ask how education and training processes in childhood and adolescence relate to such an ability and willingness to acquire new competencies over the life course. How do learning processes need to be designed so that they will encourage and enable children, adolescents, and adults to carry on educating themselves throughout their lives?

Germany is also going through fundamental demographic changes. These changes include a declining birth rate, a drop in the number of students, an aging population due to higher life expectancy, and a growing proportion of people with a migration background. Such demographic changes create new challenges for the educational system and the organization of education across the life span.

To gain new insights into the process of educational acquisition and its returns, we need high-quality data collected with theory-driven test and survey instruments. Cross-national achievement assessments such as PISA, the Third International Mathematics and Science Study (TIMSS), or the international Progress in Reading Literacy Study (PIRLS) have delivered very important findings on the distribution of competencies among students in elementary and secondary schools. However, one single survey—just like one single snapshot with a camera—delivers only a detailed picture of the situation at one specific point in time. Even though successive snapshots obtained from a series of cross-sectional surveys highlight changes in the structure as a whole, they do not show the changing (and sometimes) unchanging experiences of individual students as their educational careers progress.

There is widespread consensus that panel data and the methodological advantages it provides are essential for a rigorous approach to the types of questions that drive and are central to life-course-oriented educational research (Halaby 2004). In particular, panel data improves the possibilities of describing trajectories of growth and development over the life course and of studying the patterns of causal relationships over longer time spans. The strengths of panel data become particularly evident when compared with the commonly collected cross-sectional data (see Chap. 2, this volume). In contrast to cross-national student assessments, we stick to a longitudinal view, tracing individuals over longer spans of time.

1.2 Review of Existing Longitudinal Studies on Education

Before starting a new large panel study, we needed to intensively review the available longitudinal studies conducted in Germany and abroad (for details see Blossfeld and Schneider 2011). In Germany, there are two genuine nationwide panel studies with education-relevant data: the Socio-economic Panel Study (SOEP) and the Panel Analysis of Intimate Relationships and Family Dynamics (pairfam). These studies do not include detailed data on educational contexts outside the family or on the development of domain-specific competencies, even though some measures of cognitive competencies and personality traits have been included in the SOEP in recent years, and pairfam will focus on parenting and child achievement.

Some German longitudinal studies address educational issues, including repeated measurements of competencies. But only limited conclusions can be drawn from these. They either confine themselves to a certain region or concentrate primarily on either one stage of education or a specific transition within the educational career (for details see Blossfeld and Schneider 2011). With short-term studies, it is impossible to understand how the competencies of individuals develop over the life course; how these competencies interact with educational decisions at various critical transitions in the individuals' careers; and how these competencies are influenced by the family and by the way teaching and learning processes are arranged in Kindergarten, school, professional education, and university. Furthermore, these studies do not cast light on how competencies relate to the achievement of educational qualifications, and which competencies are responsible for being successful on the labor market and in private and social life. Thus, there is a strong demand for high-quality longitudinal educational research in Germany. In particular, there is a great need for both analytical and methodological progress that will enable us to understand educational pathways throughout the life course and how they lead to different outcomes. In sum, a large National Educational Panel Study covering the whole life course is what was needed.

1.3 Organization and Funding

NEPS was set up 2009 in order to study the acquisition of education in Germany, to assess the consequences of education for life courses, and to describe central educational processes and trajectories across the entire life span. The guiding principles of NEPS are to ask how competencies unfold over the life course; if and how they influence—together with so-called noncognitive variables such as motivation and personality—educational careers at various critical transitions; and how and to what extent competencies are influenced in turn by learning opportunities—not only those within the family and the peer group but also those resulting from the way teaching and learning processes are shaped in Kindergarten, school, higher education, vocational education and training, and adult education. NEPS should also help to understand which competencies are decisive for gaining educational qualifications, for lifelong learning, and for a successful personal and social life.

To achieve this aim, NEPS was established and organized as an interdisciplinary endeavor. It integrates theories and findings from disciplines such as educational science, educational psychology, developmental psychology, the sociology of education, the economics of education, labor market and vocational research, poverty research, research on childhood and adolescence, family studies, gender studies, migration studies, demography, cultural studies, survey research, and research on diagnostics and test theory. To implement this integration, an interdisciplinary consortium of research institutes, groups of researchers, and renowned researchers was set up that links the available experiences and competencies in longitudinal research to be found at various locations in Germany and forms an effective network of excellence.

Although the NEPS network has been quite stable over the intervening years, some changes have occurred. Currently, in January 2018, the following institutes are involved particularly strongly because of their highly relevant expertise: the Federal Institute for Vocational Education and Training (*Bundesinstitut für Berufsbildung*, BIBB) in Bonn; the German Institute for International Educational Research (*Deutsches Institut für Internationale Pädagogische Forschung*, DIPF) in Frankfurt; the German Youth Institute (*Deutsches Jugendinstitut*, DJI) in Munich; the German Centre for Higher Education Research and Science Studies (*Deutsches Zentrum für Hochschul- und Wissenschaftsforschung*, DZHW) in Hanover; the European Forum for Migration Studies (*Europäisches Forum für Migrationsstudien*, efms) in Bamberg; the Institute for Employment Research (In*stitut für Arbeitsmarkt- und Berufsforschung*, IAB) in Nuremberg; the State Institute for Family Research (*Staatsinstitut für Familienforschung*, ifb) in Bamberg; the Institute for Economic Research (*Institut für Wirtschaftsforschung*, ifo) in Munich; the State Institute of Early Childhood Research (*Staatsinstitut für Frühpädagogik*, IFP) in Munich; the Institute for School Development Research (*Institut für Schulentwicklungsforschung*, IFS) at the TU Dortmund; the Leibniz Institute for Science and Mathematics Education (*Leibniz-Institut für die Pädagogik der Naturwissenschaften und Mathematik*, IPN) in Kiel; the Institute for Educational Quality Improvement (*Institut zur Qualitätsentwicklung im Bildungswesen*, IQB) in Berlin; the Max Planck Institute for Human Development (*Max-Planck-Institut für Bildungsforschung*, MPIB) in Berlin; the Social Science Research Center Berlin (*Wissenschaftszentrum Berlin für Sozialforschung*, WZB) in Berlin; and the Center for European Economic Research (*Zentrum für Europäische Wirtschaftsforschung*, ZEW) in Mannheim. In addition, the consortium also includes renowned colleagues holding chairs at universities in Bamberg, Berlin (Freie Universität and Humboldt Universität), Bochum (Ruhr-Universität), Erlangen-Nuremberg, Gießen, Leipzig, Mannheim, Munich (Ludwig-Maximilians-Universität and Technische Universität), Siegen, and Tübingen. Figure 1.1 presents the geographical distribution of the participating institutes and universities in Germany.

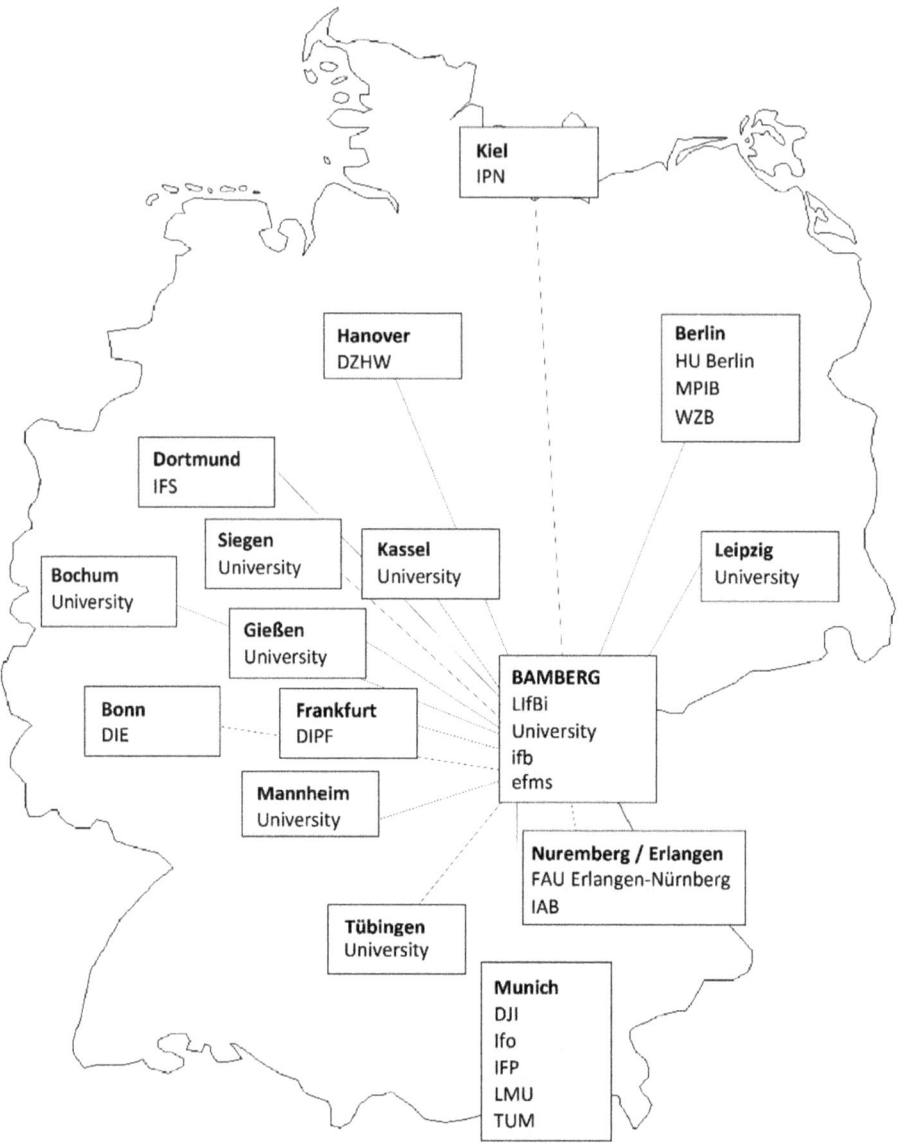

Fig. 1.1 Geographical distribution of institutes and universities participating in NEPS (November 2018). *Source* Own image

The history of NEPS is marked by several organizational milestones. After preparatory work, the NEPS consortium applied for funding through the Federal Ministry of Education and Research (*Bundesministerium für Bildung und Forschung*, BMBF). The BMBF commissioned the German Research Foundation (DFG) in 2007 and 2008 to organize review processes for the proposal to establish NEPS. The international experts strongly recommended financing this project. The first funding period lasted from 2009 till 2013 with NEPS being housed in the Institute for Longitudinal Educational Research (*Institut für bildungswissenschaftliche Längsschnittforschung Bamberg,* INBIL) at the University of Bamberg. Because education and science are considered to be the most important resources in today's society, NEPS was integrated into the Framework Programme for the Promotion of Empirical Education Research (BMBF 2008).

In 2012, the DFG started an 8-year Priority Program "Education as a Lifelong Process" focusing on substantive analyses utilizing the NEPS database, on research linking and analyzing NEPS data together with other national and/or international datasets in order to conduct theory-driven (comparative) analyses, and on projects addressing methodological issues relevant to NEPS.

After successful work during the first years, both state and federal government supported the process of changing organizational structures: Instead of a third-party project within the University of Bamberg, NEPS was integrated into the Leibniz Institute for Educational Trajectories (LIfBi)—an independent research-based infrastructure facility under the umbrella of the Leibniz Association. Within this structure, NEPS will receive sustained BMBF and federal government funding as long as regular scientific evaluations confirm its value to science and society.

1.4 Dimensions and Stages: The Framing Concept

An instrument designed to capture educational processes must be not only methodologically sound but also based on a strong theoretical paradigm focusing on the following six dimensions: competence development in different domains, the importance of various learning environments in a diachronic and synchronic perspective, social inequality and educational decisions over the life course, the specific situation of migrants and their descendants, returns to education across different life domains, and the role of motivational aspects and personality variables.

The life-course perspective is crucial within NEPS. This orientation has prompted a decisive shift in how educational researchers approach issues of schooling, skills, competence, and attainment. In particular, it redirects attention toward the process of educational and competence development, and it links changing social structure to the unfolding of human lives. It also serves as a bridge between psychological and sociological perspectives and between individual development and social structure. Thus, the life course provides an excellent framework for studying education at the nexus of social pathways, developmental trajectories, and social change (Baltes et al. 1999; Diewald and Mayer 2009; Elder and Giele 2009; Elder et al. 2003; see also Chap. 2, this volume).

At the same time, the longitudinal integration of the educational stages of NEPS is ensured by the six following theoretical dimensions called "pillars":

- Competence Development Across the Life Course
  The role of the competence dimension is to formulate developmental models to trace competencies across the different educational stages and over the entire life course. The following competencies are being assessed within NEPS: (a) domain-general cognitive functions; (b) domain-specific cognitive competencies with a special focus on German-language competencies, mathematical literacy, and scientific literacy; (c) metacompetencies and social competencies, including information and communication technologies literacy (ICT), metacognition, self-regulation, and social competencies; and finally, (d) stage-specific (curriculum- or job related) competencies and outcome measures. One central task has been to develop test instruments for the longitudinal measurement of these competencies (see Chap. 4, this volume).
- Education Processes in Life-Course-Specific Learning Environments
  The emphasis on educational processes and competence development over the life course requires a perspective that does not just take the processes occurring within a learning environment into account but also examines the transitions between successive and temporally parallel learning environments in the educational biography. This requires the analysis of different conditions within the relevant learning environments along with how these conditions impact on competence development and educational processes. Learning environments can be formal (e.g., school, apprenticeship, university) or nonformal/informal (e.g., training on the job, courses offered by sport associations, music schools, and the child and youth services, as well as learning from peers and the media). There is also a particularly strong focus on the family as an important learning environment (see Chap. 5, this volume).
- Social Inequality and Educational Decisions in the Life Course
  This dimension is examining how far and why educational decisions such as school enrollment, the choice of a secondary school track, choice of a profession, choice of a study course, continuing education, or participation in further training vary across socioeconomic groups and gender. These differences in educational decisions can even be found when levels of competence are comparable. This makes it necessary to explain the importance of class-specific educational aspirations, motivations, expectations of success, and assessments of costs (vocational training, choice of study course; see Chap. 6, this volume).
- Educational Acquisition With Migration Background in the Life Course
  Ethnic or national origins, migration biographies, and their contextualization (relations to the country of origin, integration in ethnic communities and networks) have an impact on competence development and educational decisions that goes beyond the mechanisms of social inequality. As a result, they are being assessed separately. There is a particular focus on two groups: migrants with a Turkish background and ethnic German immigrants from the former Soviet Union. The migration dimension is also addressing the methodological issue of designing appropriate survey instruments to study migrants who are unable to participate in German-language surveys (see Chap. 7, this volume).

- Returns to Education in the Life Course
  In a narrow sense, the concept of (economic) returns to education addresses income, employment, as well as labor market and career opportunities. However, NEPS also includes returns to education in a broader sense covering such topics as political participation, social commitment, physical and mental health, opportunities for seeking a partner, fertility behavior, and subjective well-being (see Chap. 8, this volume).
- Motivational Concepts and Personality Aspects Across the Life Course
  This dimension focuses on so-called noncognitive variables and their effect on competence development and educational trajectories across the life course. Variables include, for example, achievement motivation, general and topic-related interests, the self-concept, the Big Five, and social behavior (see Chap. 9, this volume).

In line with the structure of the German education system, NEPS divides educational careers into the following eight stages:

- Stage 1: From Birth to Early Child Care (see Chap. 11, this volume)
- Stage 2: From Kindergarten to Elementary School (see Chap. 12, this volume)
- Stage 3: From Elementary School to Lower Secondary School (see Chap. 12, this volume)
- Stage 4: From Lower to Upper Secondary School (see Chap. 13, this volume)
- Stage 5: From Upper Secondary School to Higher Education, Vocational Training, and the Labor Market (see Chaps. 14 and 15, this volume)
- Stage 6: From Vocational Training to the Labor Market (see Chap. 15, this volume)
- Stage 7: From Higher Education to the Labor Market (see Chap. 16, this volume)
- Stage 8: Adult Education and Lifelong Learning (see Chap. 17, this volume)

The six theoretical dimensions ("pillars") can be combined with these stages and transitions in the educational system to form a two-dimensional matrix.

As mentioned above, the dimensions ensure the theoretical and methodological integration of the various stages in the life course. The advantage of this model is that it enables all studies of single stages and transitions in the educational system such as school entry or the transition to the labor market to be carried out within a unified mold. The general framing concept of the six central dimensions ("pillars") links all stages together longitudinally.

1.5 Main Research Questions

Based on the theoretical priorities set by the six central dimensions ("pillars"), NEPS is designed to contribute to finding mid- and long-term answers to numerous questions. These include, for example:

- What are the decisive determinants for the acquisition of competencies and educational decisions in the single educational stages?
- What role do educational institutions as well as nonformal/informal learning environments (e.g., family, peers, youth services, cultural provisions, or new media) play in the acquisition of competencies and in educational decisions?
- How does competence acquisition relate to social and economic conditions (e.g., socioeconomic living conditions, regional contexts, migration background, gender-specific characteristics, and cultural traditions)? What is the role of primary and secondary effects within different educational decisions?
- Are there "metacompetencies" such as learning strategies and self-regulation that are particularly important for a successful career in the educational system and on the labor market? Which role do so-called noncognitive variables such as motivation and personality play in competence development and educational processes?
- How can ethnic inequalities in education be explained? Which resources can foster educational advancement within different groups of migrants?
- Which competencies are particularly crucial for success in vocational education and training, in higher education, and on the labor market? Are the reading, mathematical, and problem-solving competencies assessed in international academic achievement studies really those competencies that determine success in vocational education and training, higher education, and work careers? Once competencies have been acquired, how far and how quickly do they become lost again after general school education has been left behind?
- How do acquired knowledge, trained skills, and competencies relate to the educational certificates acquired?
- What are the economic, social, and health-related returns to acquired competencies and to certificates?
- How far do adults take part in education? What are the opportunities and barriers to adult education and learning processes in later life?

1.6 Multicohort Sequence Design

The previously mentioned overview of longitudinal studies based on different designs, especially the overview on designs used for educational studies outside of Germany, made several things clear. Birth cohort studies take too much time to acquire a "complete" picture of the educational career. Indeed, it would take nearly 20 years to study children's development and transitions until the end of secondary school level. Another important point is that any generalization of findings based on a single cohort can be limited. A lot of research based on the German Life History Study has shown how the educational, professional, and family careers of different birth cohorts can differ according to historical and economic circumstances. Also in the case of the school-to-work transition, which is a sensitive phase in educational careers, it can be observed that

1 The National Educational Panel Study ...

panels in England and Wales, the United States, and Australia repeatedly draw new starting cohorts (for details, see Blossfeld and Schneider 2011).

It is more efficient to concentrate on important sequences in the educational career. Samples must be drawn for every relevant sequence. Such a multicohort sequence design quickly provides relevant information. However, this has to be followed by drawing new starting cohorts and carrying out refreshments. This enables us to observe historical changes and evaluate not only major educational reforms at different transition points such as school, university, or the labor market, but also differences within competence development at comparable education stages. Such a design is comparable to that of the US National Center for Education Statistics. In contrast, however, we have to pay additional attention to lower secondary school and adults and ensure that we follow up persons for as long as possible.

Because of this, NEPS followed a multicohort sequence design right from the beginning (see Fig. 1.2). To obtain relevant data as quickly as possible, we started off with six

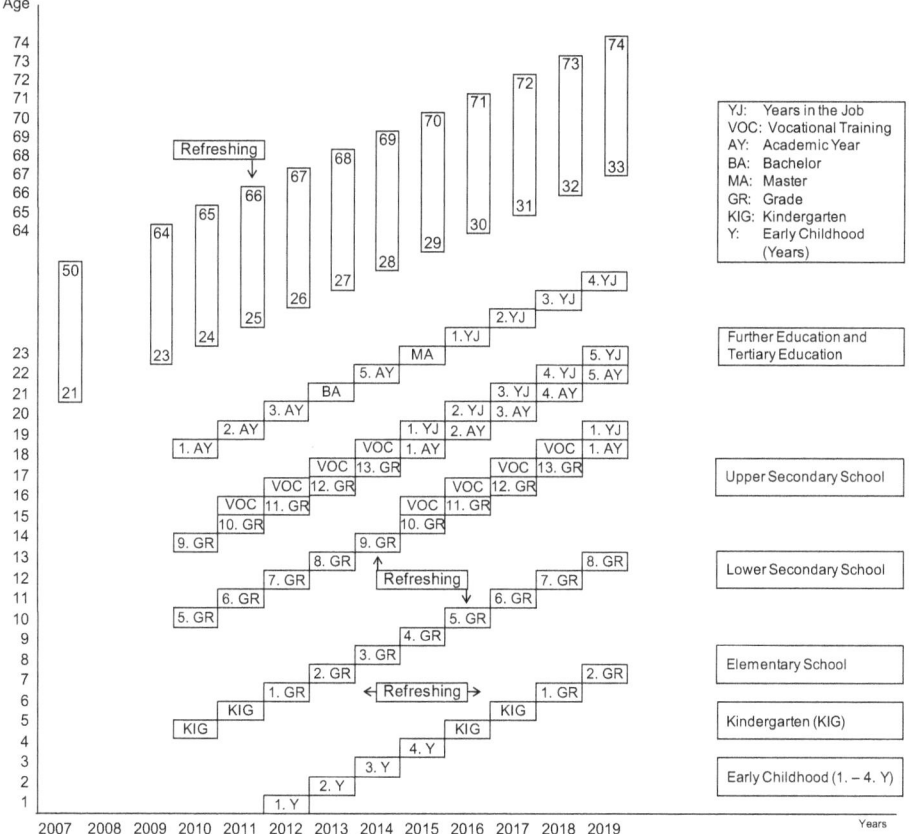

Fig. 1.2 The NEPS multicohort sequence design. *Source* Own image

separate cohorts. The first kind of cohort is defined by a specific point in the educational system. This reflects the major transitions into, within, and out of the general education and vocational training system. The second kind of cohort is age-based; members range from newborns to adults. Whereas all newborns enter formal care settings and educational institutions, some adults might take part sooner or later in some type of (further) education, whereas others might not. Members of all starting cohorts are being surveyed and tested over longer spans of time.

Four cohorts were recruited in fall/winter 2010. The first one started with 4-year-old children attending Kindergarten almost 2 years before entering elementary school. The Kindergarten sample was expanded 2 years later in Grade 1 of elementary school to include the cohort children's classmates as well as further schools and students. The second cohort targeted 5th graders immediately after entering the tracked secondary school system in most German federal states; this cohort was expanded in Grade 7. The third cohort included 9th graders who were almost at the end of compulsory education when being sampled. They split into one group heading toward vocational education and training, which is often offered in a firm-based way in Germany, and another group continuing general education in upper secondary schools. A fourth group consisted of new entrants to higher education. Finally, there were two other cohorts that were recruited at different starting points. The fifth cohort was a representative sample of 23- to 64-year-olds, irrespective of their current participation in education or the labor market. Because NEPS was able to integrate the large-scale ALWA study (*Arbeiten und Lernen im Wandel*) conducted by the Institute for Employment Research (IAB) of the German Federal Employment Agency in 2007 (Kleinert et al. 2008), data collection for the adult cohort already started in 2009. Both data from 2007 and the members of the ALWA sample were integrated into NEPS. A refreshment of the sample was implemented in Wave 3 in 2011. The sixth cohort is documenting and analyzing early childhood development and the entry to institutions for early childhood care (day nursery, Kindergarten, etc.) and started in 2012.

The NEPS design enabled us to quickly obtain findings on all central transitions in the education trajectory. At the same time, NEPS is also able to assess competence trajectories and educational careers across longer phases in people's lives. Therefore, the six subsamples are also being followed up beyond the first critical transitions.

To document and analyze historical changes in the way people pass through these stages (e.g., enlargement of early education and care, reforms in the school system, changes in further education), new starting cohorts are also being recruited in later years (creating a succession of cohorts).

1.7 Sampling and Data Collection

Sampling procedures frequently distinguish between individual and cluster sampling. In an individual sample, each individual has the same probability of being recruited. In cluster sampling, a unit on a higher lever (e.g., school class, firm) is drawn, and then either all or some members of the selected units are tested or surveyed. This sampling strategy not only permits the assessment of institutional and compositional context features but also reduces the costs of carrying out competence tests and surveys. We drew cluster samples in Kindergartens, schools, and (applied or theoretically oriented) institutes of higher education. This means, for example, that as many students of one class as possible were recruited for NEPS (for more detailed information, see Chap. 3, this volume).

In subsequent years, all participants have been followed up even if they are no longer in the same group or class, studying the same subject, or attending different universities. This makes it possible to extend documentation to cover the educational pathways of students who have to repeat a school year, change the type of school they attend or their study course, or even drop out of school or higher education. It permits, for example, analyses of the educational careers of at-risk students. In addition, all students heading toward vocational education and training are being followed up individually after leaving general education. Because they disperse across so many alternative institutions, assessments in institutions would simply require too much time and effort.

It is not possible to start with institution-based samples in the newborn and adult cohorts. In these subsamples, there is either no common context or, regarding the adults, the situation is at least as complex as that for students in the vocational education and training systems. As a result, individual samples were recruited. When possible, context features have been added to the individual data from secondary data sources.

The six starting cohorts contained a total number of more than 60,000 participants. All participants are being surveyed regularly over an extended period of time. Their competencies are also being assessed at set intervals.

Table 1.1 shows the sample sizes of the starting cohorts at the first measurement wave (see also Chap. 3, this volume). Extensions of the sample by design were made at several points (e.g., in the year of elementary school admission, to include the classmates of children who had been observed longitudinally plus an additional sample of 1st graders). Surveys in the field of early childhood, Kindergarten, and school also assess persons from the children's and students' immediate surroundings. To obtain detailed reports on, for example, the family environment, one parent is interviewed regularly. Furthermore, Kindergarten staff and principals as well as class teachers, selected subject teachers, and school directors are asked to complete written surveys at regular intervals.

Since 2009, data collection has been organized by the Data Processing and Research Center of the International Association for the Evaluation of Educational Achievement (IEA-DPC) and by the Institute for Applied Social Sciences (infas). Close cooperation between these institutes and the NEPS consortium ensures the implementation of high-quality data collection procedures.

Table 1.1 NEPS sample sizes

Starting cohorts	Sampling	Sample size	Participants
Early childhood	Individual sample	3,431	Child, mother, educator, childminder
Kindergarten	Institutional sample	3,007 +refreshment 6,342 in 1st grade	Child, parents, educator, principal
5th Grade	Institutional sample	6,112 +refreshment 2,205 in 7th grade	Students, parents, teacher, principal
9th Grade	Institutional sample	16,425	Students, parents, teacher, principal
College	Institutional sample	17,910	College students
Adult education and lifelong learning	Individual sample	13,576 +refreshment 5,208 in 2011	Adults

1.8 Data Access and Expectations

The NEPS database is an infrastructural facility for science, and all data are made available to the scientific community as promptly as possible after data collection sweeps. The data collected for NEPS are subjected to immediate and strict quality controls before being processed and documented in a user-friendly way (for data dissemination, see Chap. 19, this volume). While complying strictly with personal data privacy requirements (see Chap. 18, this volume), this grants researchers in Germany and other countries the opportunity to analyze the data as exhaustively as possible and thereby contributes to the greatest possible progress in education research. NEPS also offers trainings on the use of the database. The aim is to prepare data from all starting cohorts so quickly that they become available in an anonymous form for both national and international scientists 18 months after the end of fieldwork.

NEPS delivers the first nationally representative database with a multilevel structure that provides longitudinal information on individual education careers and competence development while simultaneously documenting information on the family, peers, the education institutes attended, the training centers and workplaces, and general living conditions. With its rich potential for analyses in various disciplines (demography, economics, education science, psychology, sociology, etc.), the data makes it possible not only to test discipline-specific theories more effectively but also to formulate integrative approaches toward interdisciplinary theories in educational science. In particular, the data generate new knowledge about competence development in the life course; the role of education institutions, families, and peers in the acquisition of education; the causes of socially unequal education decisions; the acquisition of education in migrants; as well as the consequences of competencies, certificates, and educational paths for (later) private and occupational paths through life.

NEPS not only delivers innovative impulses for basic research but also provides a major information source for policymakers. In particular, it is an important additional source of data for national education reporting, and it strengthens our knowledge of education over the life course and in developmental processes and trajectories. Especially by implementing cohort successions, it also becomes possible to study political reforms and their effects on, for example, the acquisition of competencies or equal opportunity in the educational system. In sum, we expect that NEPS will constantly improve analysis conditions for empirical education research in Germany, make a major contribution to promoting the careers of young scientists, and lead to a notable improvement in the international standing of German education research.

References

Baltes, P. B., Staudinger, U. M., & Lindenberger, U. (1999). Lifespan psychology: Theory and application to intellectual functioning. *Annual Review of Psychology, 50*, 471–507.

Blossfeld, H. -P., & Schneider, T. (2011). Data on educational processes: National and international comparisons. In H.-P. Blossfeld, H.-G. Roßbach, & J. von Maurice (Eds.), *Education as a lifelong process - The German National Educational Panel Study (NEPS)*. (Zeitschrift für Erziehungswissenschaft; Special Issue 14) (pp. 35–50). Wiesbaden, Germany: VS Verlag für Sozialwissenschaften.

Blossfeld, H. -P., von Maurice, J., & Schneider, T. (2011). The National Educational Panel Study: Need, main features, and research potential. In H.-P. Blossfeld, H.-G. Roßbach, & J. von Maurice (Eds.), *Education as a lifelong process - The German National Educational Panel Study (NEPS)*. (Zeitschrift für Erziehungswissenschaft; Special Issue 14) (pp. 5–17). Wiesbaden, Germany: VS Verlag für Sozialwissenschaften.

Bundesministerium für Bildung und Forschung (BMBF) (2008). *Rahmenprogramm zur Förderung der empirischen Bildungsforschung/Framework Programme for the Promotion of Empirical Education Research*. Schriftenreihe Bildungsforschung, Bd. 22. Bonn, Berlin, Germany: Bundesministerium für Bildung und Forschung.

Diewald, M. & Mayer, K. U. (2009). The sociology of the life course and life span psychology: Integrated paradigm or complementing pathways? *Advances in Life Course Research, 14*, 5–14.

Elder, G. H. Jr., & Giele, J. Z. (Eds.). (2009). *The craft of life course research*. New York, NY: The Guilford Press.

Elder, G. H. Jr., Kirkpatrick, J. M., & Crosnoe, R. (2003). The emergence and development of life course theory. In J. T. Mortimer & M. J. Shanahan (Eds.), *Handbook of the life course* (pp. 3–19). New York, NY: Kluwer Academic/Plenum Publishers.

Halaby, C. N. (2004). Panel models for the analysis of change and growth in life course studies. In J. T. Mortimer & M. J. Shanahan (Eds.), *Handbook of the life course* (pp. 503–528). New York, NY: Kluwer Academic/Plenum Publishers.

Heckman, J. J., & Masterov, D. V. (2007). The productivity argument for investing in young children. *Review of Agricultural Economics, 29*, 446–493.

Kleinert, C., Matthes, B., & Jacob, M. (2008). *Die Befragung „Arbeiten und Lernen im Wandel". Theoretischer Hintergrund und Konzeption.* IAB-Forschungsbericht 5/2008. Retrieved June 16, 2018, from http://doku.iab.de/forschungsbericht/2008/fb0508.pdf.

OECD (2004). *Programme for the International Assessment of Adult Competencies (PIAAC). Draft strategy paper. Policy objectives, strategic options and cost implications.* Stockholm. Retrieved June 16, 2018, from http://www.oecd.org/dataoecd/3/3/34463133.pdf.

OECD (2016). *PISA 2015 Results (Volume I): Excellence and equity in education, PISA.* Paris: OECD Publishing. Retrieved June 16, 2018, from http://www.oecd.org/education/pisa-2015-results-volume-i-9789264266490-en.htm.

Education as a Lifelong Process

Hans-Peter Blossfeld and Jutta von Maurice

Abstract

In modern societies, education has become a lifelong process. This has made the principles of life-course research of utmost significance in empirical education research. As stated by Glen H. Elder, these can be described as: (1) focusing on long-term educational processes over the individual lifespan; (2) considering individual educational pathways within their institutional and social embeddedness (e.g., within not only formal educational institutions but also nonformal/informal contexts such as the family, peer groups, and other social networks); (3) analyzing decision-making processes in education linked to the idea of agency and the idea of plan-making, creative, and self-determining actors; (4) investigating the time structure and timing of educational events and transitions and the consequences they have for the subsequent educational pathways and educational chances; and (5) conceptually differentiating age, cohort, and period effects. This chapter discusses the importance of these five principles for the conception, design, and possibilities for analysis of the German National Educational Panel Study (NEPS). In the context of these principles, we formulate methodological advantages of longitudinal data on educational processes that can be attained within the idea of NEPS. In particular, panel data improve the opportunities to describe trajectories of growth and development over the life course and to study the patterns of causal relationships over longer time spans.

H.-P. Blossfeld (✉)
University of Bamberg, Bamberg, Germany
E-Mail: hans-peter.blossfeld@uni-bamberg.de

J. von Maurice
Leibniz Institute for Educational Trajectories, Bamberg, Germany
E-Mail: jutta.von-maurice@lifbi.de

Keywords

Education · Panel study · Life-course perspective
Empirical education research · Longitudinal data

2.1 Education as a Lifelong Process: Five Theoretical Principles

The preeminent theoretical orientation of the National Educational Panel Study (NEPS) takes a life-course perspective. This has prompted a decisive shift away from how educational researchers have traditionally approached issues of schooling, skills, competence, and attainment. In particular, it redirects attention toward the *processes* of education and competence *development* and links the *changing* social structure to the *unfolding* of human lives. It also serves as a bridge between psychological and sociological perspectives and between individual development and social structure. Thus, the life course provides an excellent framework for studying education at the nexus of social pathways, developmental trajectories, and social change. (Elder et al. 2004) have summarized the following *five general principles of life-course research* (see also Elder and Giele 2009; see, for the perspective of lifespan developmental psychology, Baltes 1990; Baltes et al. 1980).

2.1.1 The Principle of Lifespan Development

The first principle emphasizes the importance of focusing on long-term individual development over the lifespan. Developmental psychologists often work with the notions of *stages, progressions, growth, and evolution* (Dannefer 1984; Lewontin 2000). The resulting emphasis is on *systematic pathways of development (change) over time*. With regard to competence development, there are two major relevant issues that, nonetheless, possess different regularities and mechanisms (OECD 1999): (a) the question *how competencies develop (cumulatively) over the life course*; and (b) the question *how stable are differences among individuals over time* once they have passed the formative phase of early experiences.

Sociological life-course approaches, while incorporating these individual differences and notions of law-like development such as aging, emphasize variability and exogenous influences on the course of development over time that cannot be predicted by focusing solely on enduring individual traits or ontogenetic past experiences. As a result, important aspects of educational careers are time-varying educational contexts that foster or hinder learning and educational progress. The sociological life-course perspective therefore focuses on the emergent properties over the life course based on structural experiences (Sampson and Laub 2004).

For sociologists, education as a *lifelong process* is to a large extent *age-differentiated*, because age and time often formally influence movement through *educational institutions* during childhood, adolescence, and early adulthood (Settersten 2004). In Germany, elementary and lower secondary educational institutions are strictly age-graded. Educational curricula require the completion of a specific number of hours; courses must be tackled in a specific sequence; and time limits are set for obtaining certificates. However, Germany does have a more *informal age structuring* after the end of compulsory schooling in vocational, tertiary, and further education in which the degree of formal time structuring is not as exacting. Therefore, it is important to examine how individuals regulate their development in the face of "nonnormative" demands of formal institutions after compulsory school, because *individuals must then adopt a more active role* to compensate for the lack of structure.

The movement of individuals through the educational system is a central object of NEPS, both as a phenomenon to be explained and as a determinant of subsequent economic and noneconomic outcomes throughout the life course. The concept of the *career* can be used to refer to an individual's sequence of roles. Kerckhoff et al. (1996) have proposed treating the concept of *educational career* as being synonymous with *educational trajectory*. The conceptual tool of trajectory encompasses both *sequences of different qualitative states* and *continuous increases or decreases in quantitative characteristics* such as competence development or skill trajectory. Careers can be distinguished from *career lines*, a sequence of educational positions common to the experience of many individuals (Spenner et al. 1982). Educational career lines often depend strongly on *structural features of the educational systems*, and thus draw attention to the ways in which opportunity structures shape the educational careers of individuals (Spilerman 1977). Educational career lines can be viewed as a *flow chart* in which previous decisions and experiences can influence subsequent decisions and experiences, and various pathways can have different consequences in terms of competence development. The term *pathway* is defined here as being identical to career line. There is also a need to *detect single and multiple risks* associated with these pathways.

The educational systems of modern societies intentionally sort students into differing positions whether within schools, between schools, or both. Natriello (1994) discusses *tracking*, *ability grouping*, *age grouping*, and *interest grouping* as the most common within-school stratification mechanisms in modern societies. These mechanisms structure educational career lines by opening up some doors and closing others. NEPS promises a rich account of educational trajectories, largely because students' positions are measured at multiple points over time. NEPS thereby traces trajectories of individuals from early childhood to Kindergarten, to elementary school, to lower and upper secondary school, to postsecondary schooling (which includes vocational education and training, university education, further education, and on-the-job training), to entry into the labor market, to later job careers, and into new activities after retirement.

Life-course research shows that the *events* and *states* of earlier educational stages often have consequences for later educational processes and outcomes (Mayer and Tuma 1990). Dannefer (1987) introduced the so-called *Matthew effect* into the literature on the life course. The Matthew effect means that initial educational inequalities become magnified over the lifespan. Thus, there seems to be a logic in educational careers that the "already educated get even more education" and the "poorly educated get poorer." The Matthew effect is sometimes also referred to as the *cumulative disadvantage/ advantage hypothesis* (O'Rand and Henretta 1999). It offers a cumulative explanation of how intracohort inequality is engendered in the life course. This effect seems to be particularly important in the case of further education. The literature also reveals the hypotheses of *"status maintenance"* and *"status leveling."* The first hypothesis contends that initial educational inequalities are carried along as individuals move through the life course (Pallas 2002). The second one points to the possibility of a narrowing of the inequality gap (O'Rand and Henretta 1999). Educational research has paid relatively little attention to the challenges of describing and explaining long-term educational trajectories, because longitudinal data have rarely been available over longer time spans.

Finally, the life-course perspective implies that *educational careers should not be studied in isolation from events in other domains of life at the level of the individual*, because most life domains are interdependent in complex ways (Mayer and Tuma 1990). For example, young people often combine their participation in schooling with other activities such as working; others, in contrast, leave and reenter the school system multiple times.

2.1.2 The Principle of Linked Lives

The second principle of life-course research concerns the *interdependence of lives over time*, especially in the family where individuals are linked across generations by bonds of kinship and processes of intergenerational transmission (Moen and Hernandez 2009). NEPS examines long-term relationships between parents and children and how these relationships influence the educational careers of children, adolescents, and adults over the life course. NEPS also covers the role of social networks such as peers, because an individual's beliefs and decisions are molded in interactions with others. Finally, NEPS can analyze the role of an adult's own family change (single, living in consensual or marital unions, the birth of a child, etc.) on her or his participation in further education over the life course.

In contrast to an age-based perspective emphasizing aging and educational careers, a *kin-based perspective on the life course* focuses on families and the ways societies reproduce themselves across generations. Modern educational research merges these two models. For example, Mare (1980) has conceptualized educational attainment as movement through an *ordered sequence of educational transitions*. He argues that educational attainment can be modeled as a set of ordered school continuation probabilities depicting the probability of attaining a given level of schooling as being conditional on having completed the level immediately preceding it. These conditional probabilities are then modeled as a function of individuals' *social backgrounds* and birth cohort membership. Mare's logistic regression estimates reveal that within cohorts, social background is very important at the beginning of the educational career, but its effects on educational transitions decline from earlier to later transitions. Shavit and Blossfeld (1993) used Mare's model in their comparative study, and found similar declining effects of family background on successive educational transitions over the life course for a broad selection of modern societies.

Cameron and Heckman (1998) have criticized Mare's model on at least two grounds: First, they demonstrated that the empirical pattern of declining social background effects across successive educational transitions depends on arbitrary assumptions about the nature of the selection bias stemming from unobserved heterogeneity in the data. NEPS can add empirical evidence to this discussion, because it *measures variables such as domain-general and domain-specific cognitive competencies*. Cameron and Heckman (1998) have also suggested that individuals do not just concentrate on the next respective educational transition in their *educational decision making*, but choose the ultimate level of schooling that maximizes their net returns to schooling, and that all of the successive transitions are governed by this more *long-term view*. Finally, Breen and Jonsson (2000) have raised the criticism that Mare's (1980) binary sequence decision model fails to represent the more differentiated pathways of European educational systems. NEPS is able to address these issues and provide better empirical evidence with which to decide between these competing models.

The life-course perspective of "linked lives" also refers to *important relationships outside the family*. These include the interactional influences of institutions such as Kindergarten and school, neighborhoods, and peers. *Kindergarten and school* are the first educational organizations that children experience, and they constitute a large part of most children's lives. They are the school setting in which knowledge and competencies are constantly tested, evaluated, and *compared with other students*, and in which children develop a sense of their intellectual efficacy. Research has demonstrated that conceptions of *self-efficacy formed early in life* tend to become self-fulfilling prophecies by either encouraging or discouraging students from taking risks and undertaking new and challenging tasks (Marsh et al. 2006). Schools also provide favorable circumstances for the *emergence of peer groups*. Bandura (1997) observed that, because of similarities in age and experiences, peers provide the most relevant reference group in late childhood and adolescence. Interacting with these peers has a wide range of consequences for children's self-concept and self-efficacy.

2.1.3 The Principle of Agency

The third principle guiding NEPS concerns *agency in human development* and the idea that *planfulness and intention* can affect life-course processes and outcomes. From a psychologist's perspective, the self is at the core of human agency. Bandura's (1982) sociocognitive theory of self-efficacy views individuals not simply as reactive creatures shaped by external events, but as being *agentic, self-regulating, creative, and proactive*.

Self-efficacy refers to the perception of oneself as a causal agent in one's environment. Such beliefs are a major basis of action and interaction over the life course. *Individuals* are active agents in the construction of their lives and *make choices* within the constraints of institutional and sociohistorical structures.

In sociology, the idea of agency is closely related to the so-called *theories of methodological individualism and rational action theory*—that is, theories that the macrolevel aggregates of educational inequality have to be reconstructed via the educational and occupational choices that individuals make under certain constraints in the life course. This is a point that Breen and Goldthorpe (1997) as well as Erikson and Jonsson (1996) have addressed very clearly. These authors try to understand why class differentials in educational participation rates persist even in the face of educational expansion. Drawing on *rational action theory*, they have developed models of educational decisions. These *micro–macro models* provide important conceptual tools for understanding how individuals might incorporate the risk of failure along with beliefs about what kind of choices are possible when performing a rational calculation of costs and benefits.

2.1.4 The Principle of Timing of Events and Transitions

The fourth principle of the life-course perspective emphasizes that developmental consequences of life transitions, events, and behavioral patterns vary according to their timing in a person's life. It recognizes that the impact of life events is contingent on when they occur in an individual's life. There is a need to detect single and multiple risks associated with these pathways. For example, Blossfeld (1990) has shown that the institutions of the educational system in Germany produce "vulnerable" and "less vulnerable" phases in the educational career. These phases result from the educational system's use of age as an organizing principle, and the fact that the educational system consists of different types of institutions. Educational transition decisions are hard to revise once they have been made in Germany. The most "vulnerable" phases in an educational career in Germany are (a) timing of entry into the school system; (b) the period of transition to secondary school (the *Hauptschule*, the *Realschule*, or the *Gymnasium*); (c) the period of transition from secondary school to vocational education and training, university, or the employment system; and (d) the periods of transition within the different types of vocational education and training.

2.1.5 The Principle of Time and Place

The fifth principle of time and place states that the educational careers of individuals are embedded and shaped by the very specific historical times and places they experience in their life courses. During the last decades, life-course research has demonstrated the necessity of *nesting individual lives in social and historical contexts*. Life-course researchers often refer to a set of mechanisms such as the age–period–cohort model of social change. The *age effect* in this model means that individuals change as they get older due to some combination of biological, psychological, or social mechanisms. The *period effect* means that—independent of their specific phases in the life course—all individuals are influenced by the same contemporary historical conditions in similar ways. Finally, the *cohort effect* refers to a persisting change across successive (birth) cohorts as specific groups of individuals experience different historical conditions at certain critical periods or transitions in the life course (e.g., changing transition rules that create increasing/decreasing opportunities at crucial educational transitions, or changing labor market conditions at the time of entry into the vocational education and training system). The *cohort sequential design* of NEPS, which follows repeated cohorts over longer time spans of their lives, delivers an appropriate way to identify age, period, and cohort effects (Schaie 1996). In addition, modern *multilevel modeling techniques* allow researchers to specify the complexities of time and environments more accurately for educational processes.

2.2 Methodological Advantages of Longitudinal Data on Educational Processes

Nowadays, there is widespread consensus that if researchers want to rigorously address the types of questions that drive and are central to life-course-oriented educational research, it is essential to use panel data with the methodological advantages they provide (Halaby 2004). In particular, panel data increase the opportunities for describing trajectories of growth and development over the life course and studying the patterns of causal relationships over longer time spans. The strengths of panel data are particularly evident when compared with the commonly collected cross-sectional data (Blossfeld 2009).

2.2.1 Charting Trajectories of Change and Development on the Individual Level

In Germany, most empirical evidence in educational research is still *cross-sectional* (e.g., the Programme for International Student Assessment, PISA) and therefore only a *snapshot* of different students at a particular point in their educational careers. Successive snapshots in a series of cross-sectional surveys highlight the changes in the structure as a whole. However, they do not show the changing (and sometimes unchanging) experiences of *individual* students as their educational careers progress. Coleman (1981) has stressed that one must be very cautious when using single cross-sectional observations, because the data often suggest that the process under study is characterized by stability. However, when we study educational careers, *change and development seem to be the rule rather than the exception.* For example, an educational career consists of the sequence and timing of participation in certain age-graded and institutionally structured educational processes. Panel data, with information on many individuals measured on several occasions spread over time, can be used to describe these *patterns of change* over the life course. They are especially able to trace the *magnitude and regularity of change* across groups defined by different characteristics or by exposure to different life-course experiences. Even if there should be stability in some measures on the individual level, only temporal data can be used to demonstrate whether this stability actually does exist (Tuma and Hannan 1984).

The notions of development and educational career also suggest a focus on the dependencies among the successive states occupied by an individual over time. Educational careers and developmental processes are often *cumulative in nature* (Mayer and Müller 1986; O'Rand 2009). One example is the Matthew effect discussed above that describes *cumulative disadvantage/advantage processes*. There are also *complex layers of selectivity in educational careers* (Cameron and Heckman 1998), which means that there is a strong likelihood that only quite specific individuals will enter specific schools or parts of the educational system over time. Thus, educational research has to take into account the *details of educational histories* as an indispensable factor in *understanding the present time*. In general, cross-sectional data are not very suitable for achieving this goal, because most such datasets provide only sparse retrospective information. In addition, if performance is assessed only at one single point in time, as is the case in the PISA study, it is not clear whether and to what extent these observed competencies are indeed *relevant for the individual's future success* in the educational system or on the labor market. A *prospective panel study* such as the NEPS that follows up individuals over longer periods of time can help to answer this kind of question.

Educational careers in Germany are often structured by *transitions* linked in *career lines*. Every transition implies that one needs at least two observations—one on the original state (at time t) and the other on the destination state (at time $t+1$)—to describe the flows of individuals at various branching points of the educational system. Educational transitions therefore cannot be studied with cross-sectional data. Panel data offer an excellent opportunity to analyze these transition processes in educational careers over the life course.

In sum, NEPS facilitates the description of the *long-term development of education as a lifetime process* on three dimensions: competence development, educational environments, and educational decision making. NEPS also makes it possible to study *differences between various target groups* such as natives and individuals with a migration background. In particular, NEPS is oversampling *Turkish migrants* and *ethnic Germans from the former Soviet Union (Spätaussiedler)*. Finally, it considers important forms of *economic* (i.e., job career, employment, income) and *noneconomic returns to education* (health, family formation, reduced crime, political and social participation, and subjective well-being) and links them to the various educational pathways.

2.2.2 Studying Causal Processes

The goal of seeking scientifically based evidence for causal relationships in educational research raises methodological design questions such as which inference model is appropriate to specify the relationship between cause and effect and which data and statistical procedures can be used to determine the strength of that relationship (Schneider et al. 2007). Over the last three decades, two different models of causal inference have dominated the work of practitioners in educational research: (a) *causation as robust dependence* and (b) *causation as consequential manipulation*. Recently, Cox (1990, 1992) has proposed a third understanding of *causation as generative process*, and this seems to be particularly relevant for a more systematic and theoretically grounded life-course perspective.

The "*causation as robust dependence*" approach—which, in multiple regression, is known as the "control-variable" approach (Blalock 1970)—is often applied in cross-sectional studies. The advocates of this approach call X a "genuine" cause of Y insofar as the dependence of Y on X cannot be eliminated by introducing additional variables into the statistical analysis. Thus, in this approach, causation is established essentially through the elimination of spurious (or noncausal) influences. Although this approach has dominated the social sciences for several decades, nowadays, it is clearly considered to be too limited. In particular, when cross-sectional data are used, a major problem is that these data cannot *establish the time order of cause and effect variables*. Therefore, the researcher has to make strong assumptions about the direction of causality. Second, because *scientists rarely know all the causes of observed effects* or how they relate to one another, it is impossible to be sure that all other important variables actually have been controlled (Shadish et al. 2002). Based on this model, a variable X can therefore never be regarded as having causal significance for Y in anything more than a provisional sense (Goldthorpe 2001).

The second understanding of *causation as consequential manipulation* seems to have emerged as a reaction to the limitations of *causation as robust dependence*. Instead of "establishing the causes of effects," Holland (1986, 1988) and Rubin (1974, 1978, 1980) are concerned with "establishing the effects of causes." They make clear that it is more to the point to take causes simply as given, and to concentrate on the question of how their effects can be measured securely. According to this approach, causes can be only those factors that could serve as *treatments or interventions in well-designed controlled experiments or quasi-experiments*.

However, in the educational sciences, the situation in which causal inferences have to be drawn is often complex and complicated. In many situations, randomization is practically or ethically unacceptable. In addition, strict experimental controls are often hard to apply. Thus, well-designed randomized controlled experiments or quasi-experiments can be applied only rarely by life-course researchers, and most causal inference must be based on nonexperimental observations of social processes.

2.2.3 NEPS Can Take Advantage of "Natural Experiments"

Of course, a panel design such as NEPS can take advantage of *"natural experiments"* in the educational system. In Germany, responsibility for general and vocational schools and universities lies in the hands of the various federal state (*Bundesländer*) governments. Thus, policy implementations of reforms in the educational system often vary between *Bundesländer*. For example, if the opportunity for parents to decide about their children's type of school at the end of elementary school has been abolished in some *Bundesländer*, one can observe whether the relationship between parents' socioeconomic position and school choice varies between before versus after this reform and between reforming versus nonreforming states (difference-in-difference analysis). Therefore, the impact of educational reforms can be studied as a kind of *"natural treatment effect,"* and evidence from different timepoints can serve to improve the evaluation or planning of policies that intervene in the process in order to promote beneficial outcomes or prevent adverse ones.

2.2.4 Techniques to Approximate Randomized Controlled Experiments Using Observational Data

Because observational data are often highly selective, Rubin (1980) and Holland (1986, 1988) have recommended that social scientists should make the process of unit assignment itself a prime concern of inquiry in their empirical work. A whole battery of statistical techniques has been developed to help to approximate randomized controlled experiments with observational data (Schneider et al. 2007). These methods include *fixed-effects models* (i.e., the adjustment for fixed, unobserved individual characteristics), *instrumental variables* (i.e., a method to correct for omitted variables bias due to unobserved characteristics), *propensity score matching* (an approach in which individuals are matched on the basis of their observed aggregate characteristics), and *regression discontinuity designs* (in which samples and comparisons between groups are restricted to individuals who fall just above or just below a specific cutoff point and, at the same time, are likely to be similar on a set of unobserved variables).

The panel design of NEPS is particularly strong in dealing with the threats of unit heterogeneity and temporal instability (Allison 1994; Halaby 2004; Hsiao 1986; Maddala 1987). *Unit heterogeneity* means that the units compared are different and, hence, heterogeneous with respect to *stable unobserved properties* that may confound the attribution of effect to the causal variable. Because, in panel studies, the same units are observed at different times, many *unobserved properties* remain *stable* and, hence, can be ruled out as explanations of change in the response variable by so-called *"fixed-effects"* or *"difference-in-difference"* estimators. *Temporal instability* means that over time, *changes in unobserved exogenous variables* offer alternative explanations for researchers interested in assessing how *changes* in explanatory variables bring about *changes* in a response variable. *Temporal stability that comes with observing different units at the same time* can be exploited to deal with temporal instability in unobserved influences that threaten inferences from longitudinal data. In addition to these unobserved heterogeneity models, the effects of time-varying and time-invariant explanatory variables on the time trajectory of a response variable can be estimated in *growth models* (McArdle and Epstein 1987; Willet and Sayer 1994). A major attraction of *multilevel* (Goldstein 1995) and *hierarchical models* (see Snijders and Bosker 1999) is the very flexible estimation of growth trajectories that life-course researchers might well find useful.

2.2.5 Causation as Generative Process

A serious issue for the social scientist arises from the insistence of the exponents of the *causation-as-consequential-manipulation* approach that causes must be manipulable (by an experimenter or intervener—at least in principle) (e.g., Holland 1986). The idea is that once the treatment or intervention is introduced, it will quasi-automatically lead to an outcome. The units of analysis in the social sciences—the individuals—are therefore assumed to be passive subjects whose behavior is explained only by causal factors, and their "objectives, knowledge, reasoning and decisions have no further relevance" (Goldthorpe 2001, p. 8). This understanding of causation clearly reduces the testability of relevant theories and models in the social sciences. In particular, it does not seem to be compatible with the microfoundation of modern sociological theory in which actors are considered to have agency, individuals have objectives and knowledge, and, when faced with a choice between different courses of action, they make decisions. Thus, the *causation-as-consequential-manipulation* approach has a limited bearing for social scientists who have moved on conceptually from so-called factor-based to so-called actor-based models (Macy 1991; Macy and Willer 2002).

These issues lead us to the third understanding of *causation as generative process*. According to Cox (1990, 1992), one crucial precondition for claiming a causal link is for there to be an elaboration of an underlying generative process that exists in time and space. A causal association between X and Y must be considered as being produced by a process and being created by some (substantive) mechanism. A major shortcoming of the approaches of *causation as robust dependence* and *causation as consequential manipulation* is that no explicit notion of an underlying generative process is present in these models. Thus, *causation as generative process* seems to be a necessary expansion of these two understandings of causation.

According to *causation as generative process*, it is important to realize that the role of time in causal explanations does not just lie in specifying a temporal order in which the effect follows the cause in time. It additionally implies that there is a *temporal interval between the causal event and the effect event*. That is, it takes some finite amount of time for the cause to produce a detectable effect. For example, when a student enters a new school, it will take some time before any effect at all can be observed on her or his competence level. This time interval may be very short or very long, but can never be zero or infinite (Kelly and McGrath 1988). In some causal relationships, effects occur almost instantaneously. In other cases, effects imply lengthy *time lags* between the causal event and the appearance of an effect that must be specified and modeled in an appropriate causal analysis. In current cross-sectional analyses in educational research, this interval between causal and effect events is simply left unconsidered and unspecified. Only temporal data allows the researcher to address and model such temporal lags.

In addition to the question regarding the length of the lag between the timing of the cause and the beginning of the unfolding of the effect, there might also be *different patterns by which the causal effect develops over time*. It is rarely the case that the effect is time-constant. For example, the development of students' competencies in a new school environment is likely to increase nonlinearly over time. However, if the causal effect increases or decreases monotonically or linearly over time, oscillates in cycles, or shows any other complicated time-related pattern, then the strength of the observed (cross-sectional) effect is dependent on the timing of the observation. That is, if only a cross-sectional observation is used, there is a great danger of misspecification. Only time-related data allow the identification of time-related effect patterns in educational careers and their association with other important life-course conditions (family background, income, institutional structure of the educational system, school environment, peer groups, regional context, health, marital status, etc.).

2.2.6 Studying Educational Processes Within Contexts

Contemporary educational theories in sociology, economics, or psychology emphasize individual change and its institutional and historical contexts. *Context effects* exist at different aggregation levels and refer to situations in which changes in the group context themselves influence the dependent variable. Understanding change in educational pathways therefore requires not only time-related data at the individual level but also time-related context information. This information tells us about the growth and decline of personal components under different environmental conditions. Temporal data are much better suited than cross-sectional data to identify such influences at different aggregation levels.

Contexts as causal forces are best studied with longitudinal data. Educational research has to specify in detail the causal mechanisms that link educational contexts (family, peers, community, workplaces, schools, and universities) with educational outcomes over the life course (an early example is the classic study by Coleman et al. 1966). In Bronfenbrenner's ecology of human development, it is the individual's day-to-day routines and activities, "the objectives to which he responds or the people with whom he interacts on the face-to-face basis" (Bronfenbrenner 1979, p. 7) that have a direct influence on her or his development. Few studies have sought to *disentangle the simultaneous effects of contextual and individual factors with longitudinal data*. However, developmental outcomes are likely to be a result of the interaction between individuals and their environment (Magnusson and Törestad 1992). One can suppose that the impact of the context is stronger at the point in time when a particular developing characteristic undergoes its most rapid development (e.g., Earls and Carlson 1995). As a result of increasing agency through childhood and adolescence, it is further likely that individuals become generally more active and selective in relation to their learning environments, and therefore gradually enhance their potential to influence their own course of educational development. The strengths of the *impact of context* on the individual educational career may therefore be *dependent on the phase of the life course*. More recent developments in *multilevel statistical methods* allow the inclusion of more systematic social observations of contexts as well as individual histories of contexts.

Based on cross-sectional analysis, it is sometimes believed that the effects of context on educational outcomes are weak in terms of the proportion of variance "explained." However, from a longitudinal point of view, there are several reasons why this inference based on cross-sectional evidence could be false (Wikström and Sampson 2003): First, *cross-sectional variance components are only descriptive statistics* that reflect observed distributions at a certain point in time rather than a causal effect. Second, what appears as an *individual characteristic* (e.g., competence level) at one point in time may, at least partly, be an *outcome of earlier context influences (e.g., school type) on the development of the particular characteristic*. One can argue that the context in which the individual grows up is more or less likely to have influenced the development of all individual characteristics relevant for educational outcomes. It is therefore important to *trace not only the individual characteristics over time but also the changes in educational contexts*. Third, in comparison with measures of individual characteristics, context measures are generally crude and less well developed. NEPS contributes to improving this situation.

2.2.7 Studying the Effects of Age Versus Stage

Finally, longitudinal studies are able to show whether competence development is related more to *age or to the respective stage in the educational system*; that is, to ask whether the competence level of a student is explained by the fact that she or he has a certain age (say age 15) or is attending a certain grade (say 9th grade) in school. The relationship between age and the stages in the educational system may also change over the educational career and over historical time. However, cohort effects can be detected in NEPS only if successive cohorts are observed over a longer period. For example, *cohort effects* could be derived from the size of a birth cohort of students competing for a place at the *Gymnasium* or in the vocational education and training system, or they may be caused by specific educational reforms (the amalgamation of *Hauptschule* and *Realschule*). Some effects can also impact on all students over a certain period of time. This would be the case if the publication of the results of a large-scale student assessment study leads (temporarily) to greater efforts on behalf of students and teachers at all stages of education.

In summary, given the rising importance of education as a lifelong process embracing all life domains, there is a huge demand for panel data and high-quality longitudinal educational research in Germany. In particular, there is a clear need for both analytical and methodological progress in order to *understand educational decisions, the role of educational contexts connected to various pathways and competence development through the life course, and how these work together to produce different outcomes*. Educational participation and processes are embedded in various *life-course-specific formal, and nonformal/informal* learning environments, and they are influenced by specific historical times. Available multipurpose panel studies such as, for example, the German Socio-Economic Panel Study (SOEP) and the German Family Panel have severe limitations for the study of education as an on-going process. In particular, they provide only small numbers of observations for specific groups of individuals at various educational branching points, they do not measure competence development over the life course, they lack information covering the educational decision process, and they provide only a partial cover of various educational environments. NEPS as a *nationally representative theme-specific research instrument* makes a big step forward in this direction, because it places education over the life course at the center of the panel. It creates a sound *scientific evidence base* with which a broad range of basic and applied questions can be addressed in the field of education that also allow us to inform policymaking. In particular, NEPS can significantly improve the database for the biennial National Educational Report commissioned jointly by the Standing Conference of the Ministers of Education and Cultural Affairs of the Bundesländer in the Federal Republic of Germany (KMK) and the Federal Ministry of Education and Research (BMBF).

Finally, key variables are defined and measured in a way that *makes it easy to link NEPS to other relevant datasets*. Examples of such datasets include the educational databases of the Official Statistical Office, process-produced employment data of the Federal Employment Agency, the Socio-Economic Panel Study (SOEP), or the various national and international assessment studies such as the Third International Mathematics and Science Study (TIMSS), the Progress in International Literacy Study (PIRLS), the Programme for International Student Assessment (PISA), the Programme for the International Assessment of Adult Competencies (PIAAC), or the Adult Literacy and Lifeskills Survey (ALL). Harmonization of measurements is also sought with regard to the models of student competencies as specified in the national educational standards developed by the Institute for Development of Quality in the Training System (IQB) in Berlin.

2.3 Conclusion

NEPS takes a life-course perspective and refers to the five principles formulated by Glen H. Elder et al. (2004). With its specially developed longitudinal design (see Chap. 1, this volume), NEPS is able to describe individual growth and development from birth to retirement on a very detailed level, thereby providing a huge research potential for scientists working in the different disciplines with an interest in education as a lifelong process. We have now come a long way from the traditional approach, and we are beginning to see that NEPS is able to make its own considerable contribution to the methodological and theoretical debate about educational processes and competence development over the life course.

References

Allison, P. D. (1994). Using panel data to estimate the effects of events. *Sociological Methods & Research, 23*, 174–199.

Baltes, P. B. (1990). Entwicklungspsychologie der Lebensspanne. Theoretische Leitsätze. *Psychologische Rundschau, 41*, 1–24.

Baltes, P. B., Reese, H. W., & Lipsitt, L. P. (1980). Life-span developmental psychology. *Annual Review of Psychology, 31*, 65–110.

Bandura, A. (1982). Self-efficacy mechanism in human agency. *American Psychologist, 37*, 122–147.

Bandura, A. (1997). *Self-efficacy: The exercise of control*. New York, NY: Freeman.

Blalock, H. M. (Ed.). (1970). *Causal models in the social sciences*, Chicago, IL: Aldine.

Blossfeld, H.-P. (1990). Changes in educational careers in the Federal Republic of Germany. *Sociology of Education, 63*(3), 165–177.

Blossfeld, H.-P. (2009). Comparative life course research: A cross-national and longitudinal perspective. In G. H. Elder, Jr. & J. Z. Giele (Eds.), *The craft of life course research* (pp. 280–306). New York, NY: The Guilford Press.

Breen, R., & Goldthorpe, J. H. (1997). Explaining educational differentials. Towards a formal rational action theory. *Rationality and Society, 9*, 275–305.

Breen, R., & Jonsson, J. O. (2000). Analyzing educational careers: A multinomial transition model. *American Sociological Review, 65*, 754–772.

Bronfenbrenner, U. (1979). *The ecology of human development. Experiments by nature and design*. Cambridge, MA: Harvard University Press.

Cameron, S. V., & Heckman, J. J. (1998). Life cycle schooling and dynamic selection bias: Models and evidence for five cohorts of American males. *Journal of Political Economy, 106*, 262–333.

Coleman, J. S. (1981). *Longitudinal data analysis*. New York, NY: Basic Books.

Coleman, J. S., Campbell, E. Q., Hobson, C. J., McPartland, J., Mood, A. M., Weinfeld F. D., & York, R. L. (1966). *Equality of educational opportunity*. Washington, DC: U. S. Government Printing Office.

Cox, D. R. (1990). Role of models in statistical analysis. *Statistical Science, 5*, 169–174.

Cox, D. R. (1992). Causality: Some statistical aspects. *Journal of the Royal Statistical Society Series A, 155*, 291–301.

Dannefer, D. (1984). Adult development and social theory: A paradigmatic reappraisal. *American Sociological Review, 49*, 100–116.

Dannefer, D. (1987). Aging as intercohort differentiation: Accentuation, the Matthew Effect, and the life course. *Sociological Forum, 2*, 211–236.

Earls, E., & Carlson, M. (1995). Promoting human capability as an alternative to early crime prevention. In P.-O. Wikström, R.V. Clarke, & J. McCord (Eds.), *Integrating crime prevention strategies: Propensity and opportunity* (pp. 141–168). Stockholm, Sweden: National Council for Crime Prevention.

Elder, G. H. Jr., & Giele, J. Z. (2009). Life course studies: An evolving field. In G. H. Elder, Jr. & J. Z. Giele (Eds.), *The craft of life course research* (pp. 1–24). New York, NY: Guilford Press.

Elder, G. H. Jr., Johnson, M. K., & Crosnoe, R. (2004). The emergence and development of life course theory. In J. T. Mortimer & M. J. Shanahan (Eds.), *Handbook of the life course* (pp. 3–19). New York, NY: Springer.

Erikson, R., & Jonsson, J. O. (1996). Explaining class inequality in education: The Swedish case. In R. Erikson & J. O. Jonsson (Eds.), *Can education be equalized? The Swedish case in comparative perspective* (pp. 1–63). Oxford, England: Westview Press.

Goldstein, H. (1995). *Multilevel statistical models*. London, England: Edward Arnold.

Goldthorpe, J. H. (2001). Causation, statistics, and sociology. *European Sociological Review, 17*, 1–20.

Halaby, C. N. (2004). Panel models for the analysis of change and growth in life course studies. In J. T. Mortimer & M. J. Shanahan (Eds.), *Handbook of the life course* (pp. 503–528), New York, NY: Springer.

Holland, P. W. (1986). Statistics and causal inference. *Journal of the American Statistical Association, 81*, 945–960.

Holland, P. W. (1988). Causal inference, path analysis, and recursive structural equations models. *Sociological Methodology, 18*, 449–484.

Hsiao, C. (1986). *Analysis of panel data*. Cambridge, England: Cambridge University Press.

Kelly, J. R., & McGrath, J. E. (1988). *On time and method*. Newbury Park, CA: Sage.

Kerckhoff, A. C., Fogelman, K., Crook, D., & Reeder, D. (1996). *Going comprehensive in England and Wales: A study of uneven change*. London, England: Woburn Press.

Lewontin, R. (2000). *The triple helix: Gene, organism, and environment*. Cambridge, MA: Harvard University Press.

Macy, M. W. (1991). Chains of cooperation: Threshold effects in collective action. *American Sociological Review, 56*, 730–747.

Macy, M. W., & Willer, R. (2002). From factors to actors: Computational sociology and agent-based modeling. *Annual Review of Sociology, 28*, 143–166.

Maddala, G. S. (1987). Limited dependent variable models using panel data. *Journal of Human Resources, 22*, 307–338.

Magnusson, D., & Törestad, B. (1992). The individual as an interactive agent in the environment. In W. B. Walsh, K. H. Craik, & R. H. Price (Eds.), *Person-environment psychology: Models and perspectives* (pp. 89–126). Hillsdale, NJ: Erlbaum.

Mare, R. D. (1980). Social background and school continuation decisions. *Journal of the American Statistical* Association, *75*, 295–305.

Marsh, H. W., Hau, K.-T., Artelt, C., Baumert, J., & Peschar, J. L. (2006). OECD's brief self-report measure of educational psychology's most useful affective constructs: Cross-cultural, psychometric comparisons across 25 countries. *International Journal of Testing, 6*, 311–360.

Mayer, K. U., & Müller, W. (1986). The state and the structure of the life course. In A. B. Sørensen, F. E. Weinert, & L. R. Sherrod (Eds.), *Human development and the life course. Multidisciplinary perspectives (*pp. 217–245). Hillsdale, NJ: Lawrence Erlbaum Associates.

Mayer, K. U. & Tuma, N. B. (Eds.). (1990). *Event history analysis in life course research*. Madison, WI: University of Wisconsin Press.

McArdle, J. J., & Epstein, D. (1987). Latent growth curves with developmental structural equation models. *Child Development, 58,* 110–133.

Moen, P., & Herandez, E. (2009). Social convoys: Studying linked lives in time, context, and motion. In G. H. Elder, Jr. & J. Z. Giele (Eds.), *The craft of life course research* (pp. 258–279). New York, NY: Guilford Press.

Natriello, G. (1994). Coming together and breaking apart: Unifying and differentiating processes in schools and classrooms. *Research in Sociology of Education and Socialisation, 10,* 111–145.

OECD (1999). Measuring student knowledge and skills. A new framework for assessment. Paris, France: OECD.

O'Rand, A. M. (2009). Cumulative processes in the life course. In G. H. Elder, Jr. & J. Z. Giele (Eds.), *The craft of life course research* (pp. 121–140). New York, NY: Guilford Press.

O'Rand, A. M., & Henretta, J. C. (1999). *Age and inequality: Diverse pathways through later life.* Boulder, CO: Westview Press.

Pallas, A. M. (2002). Educational participation across the life course: Do the rich get richer? In R. A. Settersten, Jr. & T. J. Owens (Eds.), *Advances in life course research. New frontiers in socialisation* (pp. 327–354). Oxford, England: Elsevier.

Rubin, D. B. (1974). Estimating causal effects of treatments in randomized and nonrandomized studies. *Journal of Educational Psychology, 66,* 688–701.

Rubin, D. B. (1978). Bayesian inference for causal effects: The role of randomization. *Annals of Statistics, 6,* 34–58.

Rubin, D. B. (1980). Randomization analysis of experimental data: The Fisher Randomization Test comment. *Journal of the American Statistical Association, 75,* 591–593.

Sampson, R. J., & Laub, J. H. (2004). Desistance from crime over the life course. In J. T. Mortimer & M. J. Shanahan (Eds.), *Handbook of the life course* (pp. 295–310). New York, NY: Springer.

Schaie, K. W. (1996). *Intellectual development in adulthood: The Seattle longitudinal study.* Cambridge, England: Cambridge University Press.

Schneider, B., Carnoy, M., Kilpatrick, J., Schmidt, W. H., & Shavelson R. J. (2007). *Estimating causal effects: Using experimental and observational designs.* Washington DC: American Educational Research Association.

Settersten, R. A. Jr. (2004). Age structuring and the rhythm of the life course. In J. T. Mortimer & M. J. Shanahan (Eds.), *Handbook of the life course* (pp. 81–102). New York, NY: Springer.

Shadish, W. R., Cook, T. D., & Campbell, D. T. (2002). *Experimental and quasi-experimental designs for generalized causal inference.* Boston, MA: Houghton Mifflin.

Shavit, Y., & Blossfeld, H.-P. (1993). *Persistent inequality: Changing educational attainment in thirteen countries.* Social inequality series. Boulder, CO: Westview Press.

Snijders, T., & Bosker, R. (1999). *Multilevel analysis: An introduction to basic and advanced multilevel modeling.* London, England: Sage.

Spenner, K. I., Otto, L. B,. & Call, V. R. (1982). *Career lines and careers.* Lexington, MA: Lexington Heath.

Spilerman, S. (1977). Careers, labor market structure, and socioeconomic achievement. *American Journal of Sociology, 83,* 551–593.

Tuma, N. B., & Hannan, M. T. (1984). *Social dynamics: Models and methods.* Orlando, FL: Academic Press.

Wikström, P.-O. H., & Sampson, R. J. (2003). Social mechanisms of community influences on crime and pathways in criminality. In B. B. Lahey, T. E. Moffitt, & A. Caspi (Eds.), *Causes of conduct. Disorder and juvenile delinquency* (pp. 118–148). New York, NY: Guilford Press.

Willet, J. B., & Sayer, A. G. (1994). Using covariance structure analysis to detect correlates and predictors of individual change over time. *Psychological Bulletin, 116,* 363–381.

Sampling Designs of the National Educational Panel Study: Setup and Panel Development

Christian Aßmann, Hans Walter Steinhauer, Ariane Würbach, Sabine Zinn, Angelina Hammon, Hans Kiesl, Götz Rohwer, Susanne Rässler and Hans-Peter Blossfeld

Abstract

The German National Educational Panel Study (NEPS) was set up to provide an empirical basis for longitudinal analyses of individuals' educational careers and competencies and how they unfold over the life course in relation to family, formal educational institutions, and private life. Educational developments and decisions over the life span are being tracked in six starting cohorts as a foundation for characterizing and analyzing educational processes. These six starting cohorts include newborns, Kindergarten children, secondary school children (5th and 9th grade), first-year undergraduate students, and adults. Because access to the target population in several

---

When finalizing the manuscript we were struck by the sudden and unexpected death of Susanne Rässler. We mourn for a highly reputed scientist, colleague, mentor, and a most generous human being. With her engagement and her international scientific reputation she led the NEPS working unit "Sampling, weighting, and imputation" and thereby ensured the long-term visibility of this essential part of the NEPS.

Strategien der Stichprobenziehung im Rahmen des Nationalen Bildungspanels: Design und Panelverlauf.

C. Aßmann (✉) · S. Rässler · H.-P. Blossfeld
University of Bamberg, Bamberg, Germany
E-Mail: christian.assmann@uni-bamberg.de

H.-P. Blossfeld
E-Mail: hans-peter.blossfeld@uni-bamberg.de

starting cohorts was gained via educational institutions such as Kindergartens and schools, multistage sampling approaches were implemented that reflect the clustered structure of the target populations. Samples in individual contexts, such as those in the adult and newborn cohorts, were established via register-based stratified cluster approaches. This chapter briefly reviews the designs of the implemented sampling strategies for each established starting cohort and provides information on the levels of attrition in the panel development.

Keywords

Panel study · Multistage sampling · Explicit and implicit stratification · Nonresponse

3.1   Introduction

To provide an empirical basis for the paradigms and theories discussed in a multidisciplinary context within educational and life-course research, the National Educational Panel Study (NEPS) established six starting cohorts of newborns, Kindergarten children, secondary school children (5th and 9th grade), students, and adults to implement the multicohort sequence design (see Chap. 1, this volume). Whereas the starting cohorts of children in Kindergartens, children in secondary schools, and students at universities cover important episodes in the German educational system, the sample of newborns allows us to analyze educational developments before entering formal educational institutions. The implementation of the multicohort sequence approach designed to span all important episodes in educational life was then completed with a sample of adults who had already left the formal educational institutions. These six cohort samples were designed to ensure that every individual in the corresponding target population had a chance to be part of

---

H. W. Steinhauer · A. Würbach · S. Zinn · A. Hammon
Leibniz Institute for Educational Trajectories, Bamberg, Germany
E-Mail: hans-walter.steinhauer@lifbi.de

A. Würbach
E-Mail: ariane.wuerbach@lifbi.de

S. Zinn
E-Mail: sabine.zinn@lifbi.de

A. Hammon
E-Mail: angelina.hammon@lifbi.de

H. Kiesl
Regensburg University of Applied Sciences, Regensburg, Germany
E-Mail: Hans.Kiesl@hs-regensburg.de

G. Rohwer
University of Bochum, Bochum, Germany
E-Mail: Goetz.Rohwer@rub.de

the study. The surveying of the six cohorts started in periods allowing for investigation and recording of important educational transitions and decisions from the very beginning of the panel study. In detail, these educational decisions and transitions were as follows: entering Kindergarten, enrollment in elementary school, transition to secondary schools and vocational tracks, and transition to higher tertiary education. Because individual competence tests conducted in all studies are costly and time-consuming, samples were based as far as possible on clusters of individuals. It is easier and more cost-efficient to conduct competence tests in larger organizational units such as Kindergarten groups or school classes. In addition, such clusters also allow for multilevel analyses of educational processes. Thus, whenever possible, an institutionally based random sample using clusters of Kindergartens, schools, or fields of study at universities was preferred. Hence, the cohorts starting in the institutional context of Kindergartens, schools, and universities were based on a multistage sampling approach using as primary sampling units the Kindergarten, the school, or the field of study. Since the initial survey, all respondents have been followed up as far as possible in their institutional contexts. Participants leaving the institutional contexts prevailing at the beginning of the panel study are being followed up individually or in their new institutional contexts. Examples are children entering elementary school earlier or later than average school enrollment, students repeating a grade, or students changing their school type during the lower secondary level. Whereas all participants are being surveyed on a yearly basis, testing is conducted typically at larger intervals only. However, from a sampling and longitudinal weighting perspective, individuals remain related to their starting cohorts and samples. To trace the later educational experiences and careers of persons who have either not yet entered or already left the educational system, sampling of individuals is register-based. Since the start of the NEPS, the six panel cohort samples have developed and educational transitions have occurred. The corresponding development of the starting cohorts will be discussed and highlighted here by analyzing panel attrition with discrete time event history models.

The chapter proceeds as follows: Sect. 3.2 provides detailed definitions of the populations and intended sample sizes underlying the samples. Section 3.3 presents some methodological background on the sampling strategies applied including their theoretical properties. Detailed information on the implemented schemes for the main and the additional samples is discussed in Sect. 3.4. Information on the development of panel cohorts is provided in Sect. 3.5 and conclusions are given in Sect. 3.6.

3.2 Definitions of Target Populations and the Actual Initial Sample Sizes

3.2.1 NEPS Starting Cohort 1 (Newborns)

The target population of NEPS Starting Cohort 1 covers all children born in Germany between January and June 2012. Panel participants are being tested individually and interviews are conducted with their mothers. Within the first wave, 3,481 six- to eight-month-old children and their mothers participated, of whom 3,431 provided consent to carry on participating in the panel.

3.2.2 NEPS Starting Cohort 2 (Kindergarten and Elementary School Children)

Target persons are children at about the age of 4 years attending German Kindergartens in the 2010/2011 school year who were expected to begin schooling in the 2012/2013 school year. Because the time period covered by school years varies across federal states with the beginning of the school year ranging from August to September, the age of the surveyed children differed across federal states. Furthermore, Kindergartens are defined as institutions in which children are taken care of for the whole day or a part of it. In these institutions, children are being cared for and educated on a regular basis by full- or part-time working staff with an operating license according to §45, Volume VIII of the German Social Code Book or an equivalent license. Special needs day care centers are not considered. Kindergartens are funded by public, nongovernmental, or private bodies. Note that children receiving day care as regularized by §43, Volume VIII of the German Social Code Book (*Tagesmütter*) are excluded. Overall, panel consent was provided by 3,007 children and their parents before the first survey. The elementary school children population was defined as all children attending 1st grade in state-approved or officially recognized elementary schools in Germany in the 2012/2013 school year. Panel consent was provided by 6,342 children and their parents.

3.2.3 NEPS Starting Cohorts 3 and 4 (Secondary School Children—5th and 9th Grade)

Target persons for these starting cohorts are all children in Germany attending secondary school in 5th or 9th grade in the 2010/2011 school year. Access to these populations was gained via the corresponding institutions. The set of secondary schools included all officially recognized and state-approved educational institutions in Germany providing schooling for 5th or 9th grade students. Overall, 6,112 children provided panel consent in Starting Cohort 3 and 5,778 participated in the first survey wave. A total of 16,425 children provided panel consent in Starting Cohort 4 and 16,106 participated in the first survey wave. The number of 9th-grade students was higher to make it sufficiently large to follow up students switching to a vocational track after 9th grade with large enough sample sizes to allow precise empirical analyses. The survey of children is being complemented by parental interviews and information provided by teachers and principals. Within these two starting cohorts, an oversampling of special needs children was also incorporated (for details, see Aßmann et al. 2011).

3.2.4 NEPS Starting Cohort 5 (First-Year Undergraduate Students)

The population of first-year students is all students (German and non-German) enrolled for the first time in officially recognized and state-approved institutions of higher education in Germany aiming toward a bachelor's degree, a state examination (Staatsexamen) in medicine, law studies, pharmacy and teaching, or a diploma or master's degree in Catholic or Evangelical theology in the 2010/2011 academic year. A special focus was on students with a nontraditional admission certificate (see for more details, Chap. 16, this volume). Students attending universities, universities of technology, or universities of applied sciences run by federal ministries or federal states for members of their public services were excluded. Within the first survey wave, 17,910 students participated in the first telephone interview that established the panel cohort.

3.2.5 NEPS Starting Cohort 6 (Adults)

The target population consists of all people living in private households in Germany belonging to the birth cohorts from 1944 to 1986. Access to this target population was gained via three channels. The first channel was the sample of the survey "*Arbeiten und Lernen im Wandel*" (ALWA) conducted by the Institute for Employment Research (IAB) in 2009 (see Antoni et al. 2010). This survey covers the birth cohorts ranging from 1955 to 1986. In the first NEPS survey wave of the adult cohort, this core sample was refreshed and an additional (augmentation) sample was drawn for the early births cohorts of 1944 to 1954. In summary, 11,649 adults were surveyed in first NEPS survey. Starting Cohort 6 was augmented by a refreshment sample in 2013/14 providing a further 5,208 participants.

3.3 Methodological Background

3.3.1 Stratified Multistage Sampling Based on Explicit and Implicit Stratification

Probability sampling is an essential prerequisite for conducting educational surveys. A sampling design with sample size n is called simple random sampling if every combination of n units from the population is equally likely to be chosen. In most cases, it is neither possible nor desirable to draw a simple random sample. Because the main goal of any survey is to gain estimates that are as precise as possible, sampling designs that differ from simple random sampling might increase their precision. On the other hand, simple random sampling might be infeasible when no sampling frame including all population units is available. In the context of sampling school children, simple random sampling is unfeasible, because no listing of all school children is available, and it is also undesirable, because other designs (e.g., stratified sampling) are more efficient.

Stratified sampling means that the target population is partitioned into subpopulations (called strata), and then samples are drawn independently from each stratum. There are several possible strategies for allocating the total sample size to the different strata. If the sample sizes are proportional to the population sizes within each stratum, this is called proportional allocation and results in equal sampling rates across strata (and usually in more precise estimates for characteristics of the whole population). Because the precision of estimates for subpopulations depends mainly on the sample size within these subpopulations, varying sampling rates across strata might be a reasonable way to increase the precision of estimates for special groups (using higher sampling rates among certain strata is called oversampling). Thus, stratified sampling has two main advantages: It generally leads to more precise estimates of the whole population, and it allows the use of different sampling rates in different strata to control the precision of subgroup estimates.

In cluster sampling, a sample (possibly stratified) is drawn in such a way that clusters of units are selected at once. In one-stage cluster sampling, every unit in each selected cluster is surveyed. Usually, however, only a sample of units within each selected cluster will be drawn; this is called two-stage sampling or (if subclusters are drawn within the first-stage clusters) multistage sampling. Cluster sampling is likely to reduce the precision of estimates compared to simple random sampling (with equal sample size), because units within clusters tend to be more similar than units in different clusters. This is often outweighed, however, by the advantages of cluster sampling: First, in some applications, lists of clusters are the only available sampling frame (for surveys of school children, lists of schools are available, but complete lists of all children are not). Second, cluster sampling is usually much cheaper than individual-based sampling (e.g., testing children within the same school can be done more quickly and more cheaply than testing the same number of children in different schools). Third, cluster sampling is appropriate to measure context effects. For all three reasons, NEPS uses multistage cluster sampling when applicable.

Stratification and cluster sampling may be combined, resulting in stratified multistage cluster samples. Within each stratum, units or clusters might be sampled with designs that differ from simple random sampling. Often, the sampling frame is ordered by some variables, and then a systematic sample is drawn. The precision of the resulting estimates is similar to the results of stratification with proportional allocation, and therefore this procedure is called implicit stratification in contrast to explicit stratification as described above (implicit stratification is usually done within explicit strata).

Unbiased estimation of population characteristics based on a sample is possible only if every unit in the target population has a nonzero probability of being part of the sample (these probabilities are called inclusion probabilities). The inclusion probabilities depend on the way the sample is selected. In simple random sampling and also in systematic sampling, every unit in the sample has the same inclusion probability; the same is true for stratified simple random sampling with proportional allocation of sample size. Differential sampling rates among strata result in unequal inclusion probabilities. In multistage cluster sampling, first-stage clusters are often selected with inclusion probabilities that are proportional to some measure of cluster size; this is called pps ("probability proportional to size") sampling. For a thorough treatment of the theory and the pros and cons of different sampling designs, see, for example, Cochran (1977), Lohr (2009), or Särndal et al. (2003).

The use of stratified multistage approaches with pps sampling is common for educational surveys given the nested and hierarchical structure of educational systems. For example, within the Trends in International Mathematics and Science Study (TIMSS), schools were drawn with a probability proportional to student enrollment at the first stage. At the second stage, classes (as clusters of students) were then selected with equal probability (see Joncas 2008). For the Programme of International Student Assessment (PISA), schools were drawn by pps sampling with the measure of size being related to the number of target students in each school (OECD 2009). The National Educational Longitudinal Survey of 1988 (NELS:88) applied a two-stage design with schools at the first stage and students within schools at the second stage. The inclusion probabilities for the first stage units were proportional to their estimated 8th-grade enrollment, and students were selected with equal probabilities in the second stage (Thurgood et al. 2003). A further example is the IQB-Bildungstrend analyzing competencies of 4th graders (see Rjosk et al. 2017). Based on an explicit stratification according to school type and federal state, schools were sampled with probabilities proportional to competence variation at the stratum level observed in former surveys. Typically, all of these studies use explicit stratification; the TIMSS and PISA studies also adopted implicit stratification.

Regardless of the chosen sampling design (given positive inclusion probabilities for every population unit), the Horvitz–Thompson estimator calculates an unbiased estimate for the population total t_Y of any variable Y, using the sample values $y_1, \ldots, y_n$:

$$\hat{t}_{Y,HT} = \sum_{i=1}^{n} \frac{y_i}{\pi_i} \sum_{i=1}^{n} w_i y_i;$$

π_i is the inclusion probability of sample unit i (in multistage samples, π_i is the product of the (conditional) inclusion probabilities at each stage); the inverse of π_i is called the sampling or design weight w_i of unit i (the intuition behind this is that sample unit i "represents" w_i elements of the population). Thus, the estimate for the population total is the sum of the sample values weighted by the sampling weights. Using the sampling weights, estimates for other population characteristics (e.g., means, quantiles, correlations) may be constructed as well. There are also more advanced estimators taking nonresponse into account or incorporating auxiliary information (see, e.g., Särndal et al. 2003). It is also important to note that the variance of the Horvitz–Thompson estimator (and thus the precision of the estimates) depends not only on π_i but also on the specific sampling design.

3.3.2 Indirect Sampling

In general, sampling designs as described in the previous section are based on a complete list (sampling frame) of all units (or clusters of units) representing the target population. For different reasons, it may be the case that a sampling frame is not available, thus hindering a direct application of established sampling strategies. In this situation, Lavallée (2007) suggests using a different approach called indirect sampling. In NEPS, indirect sampling was used when constructing the Kindergarten sample.

Suppose there exists a population U_A with an available sampling frame, and this population is somehow "linked" to the target population U_B. A natural idea is then to draw a sample s_A from population U_A and subsequently choose all elements from U_B that are linked to elements in s_A and define them as the sample s_B from U_B. Although the calculation of inclusion probabilities for units in s_B is usually difficult or unfeasible under this setting, it is nevertheless possible to construct an unbiased estimator for population totals of U_B.

To formally describe the connection between the two populations, let $\theta_{ab} \geq 0$ represent the link between $a \in A$ and $b \in B$ (if $\theta_{ab} = 0$, no link exists between a and b). In our application, U_B is the population of Kindergartens, U_A is the population of elementary schools, and θ_{ab} may be defined as the number of children moving from Kindergarten b to elementary school a in some reference year. In general, how best to define the links θ_{ab} depends on the application at hand.

For every $b \in B$, let $\theta_{+b} := \sum_{a \in U_A} \theta_{ab}$ be the sum of all links from U_A to b. We assume that $\theta_{+b} > 0$ for all $b \in B$, that is, there exists a link to every $b \in B$; otherwise unbiased estimation for U_B is impossible.

The key observation is that the total of any variable Y in population U_B might be written as follows:

$$t_y = \sum_{b \in U_B} y_b = \sum_{b \in B} \left(y_b \cdot \underbrace{\sum_{a \in U_A} \frac{\theta_{ab}}{\theta_{+b}}}_{=1} \right) = \sum_{a \in U_A} \sum_{b \in U_B} \frac{\theta_{ab}}{\theta_{+b}} y_b = \sum_{a \in U_A} \tilde{y}_a = t_{\tilde{Y}},$$

with $\tilde{y}_a := \sum_{b \in U_B} \frac{\theta_{ab}}{\theta_{+b}} y_b$.

Thus, the total of some variable Y in population U_B can be written as the total of the corresponding variable $\tilde{Y}$ in population U_A. Because inclusion probabilities for s_A are known, the Horvitz–Thompson estimator may be used for an unbiased estimation $t_{\tilde{Y}}$ and thus also t_Y. The (unbiased) indirect sampling estimator for the total of Y in U_B is defined as

$$\hat{t}_{Y;IS} := \hat{t}_{\tilde{Y};HT} = \sum_{a \in s_A} \frac{\tilde{y}_a}{\pi_a} = \sum_{a \in s_A} \sum_{b \in U_B} \frac{\theta_{ab}}{\theta_{+b}} \frac{y_b}{\pi_a} = \sum_{b \in s_B} w_{b_s} y_b$$

with weights $w_{b_s} = \sum_{a \in s_A} \frac{\theta_{ab}}{\pi_a \cdot \theta_{+b}}$ for $b \in S_B$ These weights are sample-dependent, and, in general, they differ from the inverse inclusion probabilities (although they are equal in expectation).

If the elements of U_B are actually clusters of individuals, all units within cluster b get the same sampling weight w_{bs}. In this case, it is also possible to add another subsampling stage within the clusters in s_b and then change the sampling weights accordingly (two-stage indirect sampling; see Lavallée 2007 for details). Indirect sampling has been applied in different surveys such as the Survey of Labour and Income Dynamics (SLID) and the Project to Improve Provincial Economic Statistic (PIPES)—both conducted by Statistics Canada. However, NEPS is the first application of indirect sampling techniques in the context of educational surveys (for further details, see Kiesl 2010; Steinhauer et al. 2015).

3.4 Sampling Strategies

3.4.1 Starting Cohort 1: Newborns

The sampling of newborns was conducted as a stratified cluster sampling. Clusters were defined as municipalities in which sampling was stratified according to regional classification criteria such as federal states and counties. Sampled municipalities were then asked to provide the register-based address information on the defined target population.

3.4.2 Starting Cohort 2: Kindergarten and Elementary School Children

The sampling of Kindergarten and elementary school children was designed to provide random samples for each of the two underlying populations. Surveying of elementary school children started in 2012 when most of the sampled Kindergarten children moved to elementary schools. The design of the two samples was therefore coordinated in such a way that parts of the Kindergarten sample would show up in the elementary school sample. The idea behind such an overlap yielding institutional context information for school children already surveyed in Kindergartens was to extend the range of research questions that can be addressed in longitudinal analyses.

Because Kindergartens and elementary schools are connected in that children transfer from one to the other, an indirect sampling approach using this link information was defined when establishing both samples. The first stage for establishing a sample of Kindergarten children simultaneously also provided a sample of schools allowing access to elementary school children. Given that the survey of Kindergarten children started 2 years earlier, the elementary school children sample increased the total number of available cases of the then approximately 6-year-old Kindergarten children. The measure of size for pps sampling of elementary schools was defined as the number of children attending 1st grade based on the available frame information referring to the 2008/2009 school year. Furthermore, sampling was based on an implicit stratification of schools according to federal states, regional classification, and organizing institution. All children attending 1st grade in the sampled schools were surveyed. Because schools facilitate to gain access to Kindergartens via indirect sampling, the defined measure of size increased the probability that each school would be linked to at least one Kindergarten, thus providing access to the population of Kindergarten children.

Based on the sample of elementary schools as the first sampling stage of the implemented indirect sampling approach for surveying Kindergarten children, the second stage was administered as follows: Sampled schools were asked to list all Kindergarten institutions from which children had entered these schools in the 2009/2010 school year. From these lists of Kindergartens, Kindergarten sampling was performed proportional to the number of transferring children. Based on a small-scale simulation study using data on Bavarian Kindergartens, proportional sampling was chosen in order to enlarge the rate of children surveyed in the context of Kindergartens and schools, thereby extending the range of possibilities for longitudinal analyses. Note that this procedure provides access only to the population of Kindergarten children in institutions already established in 2009/2010. Given the selection probabilities for schools at the first stage and Kindergartens at the second stage, the resulting indirect sampling weights were then additionally based on the number of children transferring from Kindergartens to elementary schools and the total number of children per Kindergarten entering schools in the 2009/2010 school year. Overall, the sampling approach provided an overlap of 557 children.

3.4.3 Starting Cohorts 3 and 4: 5th- and 9th-Grade Secondary School Children

Sampling children within an institutional context provides important information on the institutional background, thereby increasing the range of questions that can be analyzed with the survey. Furthermore, as an important aspect for a longitudinal survey, tracking of children is easier and also reduces administrative survey costs.

The large variety of federal-state-specific school systems is a challenge for sampling 5th- and 9th-grade children. Because educational policy is the responsibility of each single federal state, many different school types engaging in different transitions between elementary and secondary schooling institutions make up the set of institutions providing access to the target population. For the purpose of sampling, the population of schools was therefore stratified by school type. Based on the available frame information on the 2009/2010 school year, a total of six school type strata were defined. The first stratum comprised all *Gymnasia*; the second stratum, all *Hauptschulen*; the third stratum, all *Realschulen*; the fourth, all *Gesamtschulen*; and the fifth, included all schools offering all tracks of secondary education except the academic track *(Schulen mit mehreren*

Bildungsgängen). Finally, the sixth explicit stratum comprised all schools providing schooling to 5th-grade but not to 9th-grade students. In addition to explicit stratification according to school types, an implicit stratification based on the same variables as for sampling elementary schools (i.e., federal states, regional classification, and organizing institution) was adapted for sampling secondary schools. The definition of these six explicit strata made it possible to cover two important aspects: The first related to establishing the sample of 9th-grade children as the starting point for a longitudinal survey of young adults entering vocational tracks within the next years. To ensure sufficient sample sizes for statistical analyses within this heterogeneous population stemming to a large extent from *Hauptschulen* and *Gesamtschulen*, an oversampling of children attending these school types was incorporated. The second aspect covered by the explicit stratification was the possibility of reaching the 5th- and 9th-grade population via the same set of schools, thereby reducing administrative survey costs for schools by establishing the access point to the longitudinal study of the population of 5th-grade children, but also representing all children attending 5th-grade classes in Germany. Given the first-stage sample of schools, at the second stage, two school classes within each school were sampled when at least three classes were present; otherwise, all classes were surveyed.

A measure of size for sampling schools was defined that yields a variation in design weights within strata that was as low as possible. Given the sampling of two classes within schools, a reasonable measure of size for sampling schools is proportional to $\frac{N_{classes,i}}{\min(N_{classes,i};2)}$, resulting, in combination with a simple random sampling of (at most) two classes within schools, in roughly equal design weights within each stratum. Unfortunately, some variance of the weights cannot be avoided completely. Because sampling of schools is based on a frame provided by the statistical offices of the federal states based on information available in the 2008/2009 school year, the current situation in schools was not mirrored to a full extent in the available school information. Hence, for some selected schools, the number of classes listed for the 7th grade differed from the number of 9th-grade classes actually surveyed in the 2010/2011 school year due to fluctuations in student enrollment. Using available frame information within a simulation study on the development of the number of classes referring to a particular schooling cohort, a measure of size proportional to the number of classes in the 7th grade in the 2008/2009 school year showed substantially less variation in design weights than alternative measures of size based on other characteristics such as average class size. Moreover, currently implemented school reforms that often cause a change in the school type are not fully reflected within the available school frame. Given a change of school type occurs for a sampled school, but classes in 5th or 9th grade are still available, participation of the school in the survey is continued.

A further issue was how to handle institutional refusals to participate within the survey. Schools might have refused to participate in order to avoid a further workload arising from participating in other studies. Because the resulting sample size reduction on the level of students should be compensated in order to ensure sample sizes large enough to analyze subpopulation differences, replacement schools were defined in advance according to a matching rule. The matching rule defined replacement schools as schools from the same explicit and similar implicit stratum as the original school. Although the use of replacement schools did not eliminate the risk of bias due to nonresponse, employing implicit and explicit stratification increased the chances that any school's replacement would have similar characteristics.

3.4.4 Starting Cohort 5: First-Year Undergraduate Students

Sampling first-year undergraduate students with ordinary admission certificates is achieved via a stratified cluster sampling approach. Note that as well as surveying these students, the intention was also to use postal recruitment to survey all first-year students with a nontraditional admission certificate (for details, see Chap. 16, this volume). For sampling purposes, a cluster was defined as a field of study to be attended at a higher educational institution. Within each cluster, all students were to be surveyed. To achieve high response rates, all sampled students were approached using two different contact modes: first, they were all contacted by mail. Second, field workers attended central first-year courses to ask for participation. In a pilot study, this twofold recruitment process yielded both higher participation rates and a higher panel attendance. The student cohort was set up to incorporate an oversampling of students attending teaching tracks and students attending private higher educational institutions (i.e., private universities and private universities of applied sciences). This objective was addressed by setting up a first stratification level that grouped clusters according to their educational institutions. This first stratification level defined four strata: Stratum h_1 comprised the clusters linked to teaching tracks; Stratum h_2, all fields of study to be attended via public universities; stratum h_3 all fields of study offered via public universities of applied sciences; and stratum h_3, all study tracks offered by private universities or private universities of applied sciences. This level of stratification allowed an oversampling of students in teaching tracks and attending private higher educational institutions using different sampling rates of clusters in the various strata.

However, given the heterogeneous distribution of students across the officially listed fields of study, sampling within the defined strata would have resulted in a large variation in the range of fields of study within the sample. Hence, a further level of stratification was introduced that defined strata by groups of related fields of study. This stratification was accompanied by an exclusion of clusters with less than 30 enrolled students in 2008/2009. In summary, the 60 officially listed fields of study were grouped into several study groups per first-stage stratum. Hence, Strata s_1 to s_3 grouped fields of study in Stratum h_1; Strata s_4 to s_{19}, in first-stage Stratum h_2; Strata $s_{20}, \ldots, s_{26}$, in Stratum h_3; and s_{27} to s_{29}, in Stratum h_4. To reproduce the distribution of students across the fields of study and ensure homogeneous inclusion probabilities within Strata h_1 to h_4, an appropriate allocation of the number of clusters to be drawn within each stratum was specified.

This allocation was also necessary to incorporate the planned oversampling. In particular the number of clusters c_{h_i} sampled within Stratum h_i was calculated according to

$$c_{h_i} = \frac{P_{h_i}}{\frac{1}{K_{h_i}} \sum_{k=1}^{K_{h_j}} N_k}$$

by dividing planned sample P_{h_i} Stratum h_i by average cluster size measured in terms of the number of first-year students N_k in 2008/2009 for each cluster. This resulted in 54 clusters to be sampled for Stratum h_1 and 73 clusters for Stratum h_4. For Strata h_2 and h_3, in which no oversampling was adopted, a total of $n_{23} = 348$ clusters to be sampled were found to be sufficient to generate the planned gross sample sizes with clusters being allocated proportionally to the number of overall clusters in both strata resulting in 203 clusters to be sampled in Stratum h_2 and 145 clusters in Stratum h_3. For each of the substrata, the number of clusters to be sampled from strata $h_i, i = 1, \ldots, 4$ was allocated according to

$$c_{S_j} = c_{h_j} \frac{K_{S_j}}{K_{h_j}},$$

in which K_{S_j} denotes the number of clusters in Stratum s_j and K_{h_j} the number of clusters in first-stage Stratum h_j.

The following strategy was defined to handle institutional nonparticipation. Because the refusal of a university to participate would lead to the loss of the fields of study sampled at that specific university, only institutions were eligible for replacement that would make it possible to maintain the original sample composition with regard to the sampled departments and fields of study. For every combination of sampled fields of study at a particular higher educational institution, all institutions offering the same combination of fields of study within the frame were listed irrespective of whether the institutions had already been sampled or not. Institutions not sampled were given preferential consideration in the choice of replacement colleges. Given that multiple possible replacement institutions offer the combination of fields of study to be replaced, the replacement institution was defined as the one with the smallest difference in numbers of enrolled students compared to the nonparticipating institution.

3.4.5 Starting Cohort 6: Adults

Given the three channels (ALWA, refreshment, augmentation) providing access to the defined target population, a stratified two-stage cluster sampling approach was implemented for each sample connected to a particular channel. The 12,429 German municipalities existing in 2008 were defined as primary sampling units. Stratification according to federal states and a classification of urbanization (BIK scale) were incorporated.

Sampling of primary sampling units was achieved via sampling of artificial units called sample points. Sample points were defined as regional entities in which the same number of target persons were gathered, with one or more sample points being assigned to each municipality depending on its size. This made it possible to draw multiples of these sampling points from single municipalities. This procedure clusters multiple sample points at the level of municipalities. The number of sample points as artificial primary sampling units to be sampled within each explicit stratum was allocated proportional to the number of target persons. Sampling of persons as secondary sampling units was performed via systematic sampling.

3.5 Panel Development

The development of the six NEPS starting cohorts is detailed in Zinn et al. (2018). This part of the chapter summarizes the progress in the six panel cohorts by reporting the number of participants per wave. Furthermore, it briefly presents findings on panel attrition. Details on the initial nonresponse processes occurring when the panel cohorts in the institutional contexts were set up can be found in Steinhauer et al. (2015). With regard to the individual contexts, more details on initial nonresponse can be found in Würbach (2017) and Würbach et al. (2016) for Starting Cohort 1; Zinn et al. (2017) for Starting Cohort 5; and Hammon et al. (2016) for Starting Cohort 6. Further details on wave-specific analyses are documented in the corresponding technical reports accompanying the Scientific Use Files (SUFs) (see www.neps-data.de and Chap. 19, this volume).

3.5.1 Starting Cohort 1: Newborns

The initial number of panel participants in NEPS Starting Cohort 1 (SC1) dropped from 3,431 to 3,281 at the beginning of Wave 3; and to 3,143 at the beginning of Wave 4. However, the participation rate has been consistently high with 2,862 valid interviews (83.4%) in Wave 2, 2,609 valid interviews (79.5%) in Wave 3, and 2,478 valid interviews (78.8%) in Wave 4. The number of temporary dropouts has remained reasonably stable across panel waves. The number of final dropouts rose steeply between Waves 4 and 5. Due to continuous nonparticipation over a period of 2 years, 143 of the 541 temporary dropouts in Wave 4 were regarded as attrition from the panel survey. For a more detailed presentation of the panel progress, see Zinn et al. (2018).

Table 9 in Zinn et al. (2018) reports the results from analyzing panel attrition in SC1. Figures are for all targets that are still part of the panel in relation to the panel sample at the start for all waves on which data have been published so far in SUFs (Waves 1 to 4). As can be seen, the propensity to drop out from the panel sample is influenced by the characteristics of the participating parent. These characteristics are: educational attainment, employment status, migration background, and marital status. Unemployed parents as well as parents with a migration background exhibit a significantly increased propensity to drop out from the panel compared to those who are employed or have no migration background. However, parents with a higher educational level have a remarkably lower propensity to become a final dropout. It must be noted, however, that missing information on marital status is also strongly associated with attrition. Wave-specific analyses can be found in Würbach et al. (2016) and the technical reports complementing the corresponding SUF (e.g., for the current SUF, Würbach 2017).

3.5.2 Starting Cohort 2: Kindergarten and Elementary School Children

At the beginning of Wave 2, NEPS Starting Cohort 2 (SC2) had 2,996 panel participants left (from 3,007 at the start). However, due to the augmentation sample of 1st-grade students, the panel cohort increased to 9,337 before Wave 3. Attrition from the panel was quite small up to Wave 6, with 9,331 Kindergarten children still in the panel in Wave 4; 9,282, in Wave 5; and 9,044, in Wave 6. The attrition rate peaked clearly after Wave 6. This could be attributed partially to the summation of parent withdrawals in previous studies. Until Wave 6, the affected target persons could be surveyed and tested despite any parental withdrawal. However, in Wave 7, all school children transitioned to the individual field, and surveying had to continue in the family home, which was inconceivable for children with parent withdrawal. For this reason, 526 target persons had to be dropped from the panel sample. In SC2, the participation rate is also quite high although decreasing slightly: 98.1% in Waves 1 and 2, 97.3% in Wave 3, 96.1% in Wave 4, 94.1% in Wave 5, and 81.8% in Wave 6 (corresponding to 2,949, 2,727, 6,733, 6,340, 5,799, and 6,943 valid interviews respectively). The peaks in temporary and final dropouts within Wave 6 apply to a large extent to the subsample of Kindergarten children who were not surveyed and tested again until Wave 6 because they had transitioned to an elementary school that was not being tracked institutionally. These students are now part of the individual field. Zinn et al. (2018) provides a more detailed presentation of the panel progress.

The figures in Table 10 in Zinn et al. (2018) on panel attrition in SC2 refer to the panel sample at the start across all six waves observed so far, but separately for each of the three subsamples—that is, Waves 3 to 6 for the augmentation subsample of 1st-grade students. The educational attainment of the responding parent significantly influences the propensity for further participation in the panel. Children whose responding parent has a higher level of education showed a remarkably lower propensity to be a final dropout. This holds for all three subsamples. In the panel sample of the augmentation subsample in Grade 1, respondents from Western Germany have a significantly higher propensity to drop out from the panel compared to those from Eastern Germany including Berlin. Positive effects on panel willingness can be observed for children from public schools as well as for school children with parents having no migration background. In the subsample of Kindergarten children being surveyed in the institutional context, the propensity to drop out from the panel sample decreased significantly for targets living in semiurban areas opposed to those living in rural areas. Wave-specific analyses can be found in Steinhauer et al. (2016a) and the technical reports complementing the corresponding SUF (e.g., for the current SUF, see Würbach 2018).

3.5.3 Starting Cohort 3: 5th Grade Secondary School Children

Starting Cohort 3 (SC3) commenced in the 2010/2011 school year with 6,112 students providing panel consent. In Wave 2, there were still 6,099 students in the panel with only 13 refusing further cooperation. In the 2012/2013 school year, when students were surveyed in 7th grade, an additional sample of 2,205 students augmented the SC3 panel so that it contained 8,295 students in Wave 3. After that, the size of the panel cohort dropped to 8,256 students in Wave 4, 7,643 in Wave 5, and 7,403 in Wave 7. Up to now, seven waves have been conducted on the SC3 panel and the cohort for the next wave, Wave 8, consists of 7,254 students. The majority of students who dropped out of the panel are students from special educational needs school, who were not surveyed after grade 8 (wave 4). In the first wave, 5,778 students participated, yielding a participation rate of almost 95%. Over the seven panel waves conducted so far, the participation rate has decreased from 90.8% (5,537) in Wave 2 to 88.2% (7,277) in Wave 3, 81.4% (6,718) in Wave 4, 75.6% (5,778) in Wave 5, and 75.5% (5,586) in Wave 6. It then slightly increased again to 77.6% (5,491) in Wave 7. For a more detailed presentation of panel progress, see Zinn et al. (2018).

Looking at panel attrition, students from the original sample with good and medium mathematical competencies had a lower propensity to drop out of the panel, compared to those with poor mathematical competencies. Further, students in the original sample from western Germany had a higher propensity to drop out of the sample than those from the eastern part of Germany. Finally, students from the original sample, who had left elementary schools or school-type-independent orientation stages after 6th grade were more likely to drop out of the panel compared to students who did not leave their schools.

Students from the augmentation sample in 7th grade were more likely to drop out of the panel when living in western compared to eastern Germany. Like students in the original sample, good or medium competencies in mathematics led to a lower propensity to drop out of the sample than poor competencies in mathematics. Finally, students, whose parents have a higher educational background had a lower probability to drop out of the panel compared to students whose parents have a lower educational background. The wave-specific analyses can be found in Steinhauer and Zinn (2016a) and in the technical reports accompanying the corresponding SUF.

3.5.4 Starting Cohort 4: 9th Grade Secondary School Children

Starting Cohort 4 (SC4) commenced in the 2010/2011 school year with 16,425 students providing panel consent. Over the course of the panel, the size of the cohort dropped to 16,356 students in Wave 3, 16,253 in Wave 4, 16,241 in Wave 5, 15,754 in Wave 6, 15,692 in Wave 7, 15,099 in Wave 8, and finally to 13,038 in Wave 9. In the first wave, 16,106 students participated, resulting in a participation rate of 98%.[1] As the panel proceeded, participation rates decreased to 92.6% (15,215) in Wave 2, 85.7% (14,011) in Wave 3, 74.5% (1,351) in Wave 4,[2] 80.6% (12,982) in Wave 5, 88.1% (5,392) in Wave 6, 76.3% (11,830) in Wave 7, 71.6% (9,871) in Wave 8, and 69.4% (9,044) in Wave 9. From 10th grade onward, students had to decide whether to enter the academic track or leave secondary school and start, for example, vocational training. In Wave 9, all students had left their schools. A large proportion of students dropping out of the panel were dismissed, because they had not participated in survey for a period of more than 2 years. For a more detailed presentation of the panel progress, see Zinn et al. (2018).

Looking at panel attrition in more detail, we found that students in the vocational track had a higher propensity to drop out of the panel compared to students on the academic track. This was most likely because students on the academic track were still being surveyed in their regular school, whereas participants in the vocational track were being surveyed individually in their homes, were more mobile, and were thus harder to track. Further, the school type at which students were sampled initially had a strong effect on panel attrition. Here, students educated in schools offering secondary education until only 9th or 10th grade were more likely to drop out of the panel compared to students in Gymnasium or other school types offering higher secondary education who can continue to attend their schools until 12th or 13th grade. Moreover male students and older students were more likely to leave the panel cohort compared to their female and younger counterparts. For students with a medium or a higher mathematical competence, we found a lower probability of dropping out of the sample compared to students with lower mathematical competence. Finally, students whose parents have a upper secondary school qualification or higher were more likely to remain in the panel sample, compared to students whose parents have no more than a completed vocational training. The wave-specific analyses can be found in Steinhauer et al. (2016b), Steinhauer and Zinn (2016b), and the technical reports accompanying the corresponding SUF.

---

[1] The participation rate is calculated based on the number of students who were assigned to be surveyed in the corresponding wave.

[2] In Wave 4 and Wave 6, the entire cohort was not assigned to be surveyed. Here, only students who had left their regular schools and had participated in the previous wave were surveyed.

3.5.5 Starting Cohort 5: First-Year Undergraduate Students

All students participating in the Wave 1 survey constitute the initial panel cohort of SC5 comprising 17,910 students. Telephone interviews took place in Waves 1, 3, 5, 7, 9, 10, and 12. Online surveys were conducted in the remaining waves. In Waves 1, 5, 7, and 12, students were additionally administered competence tests. Over the course of the panel, proportionally more students took part in the telephone interviews (between 73.5 and 66.5%) than in the online surveys (between 68.6 and 58.1%) or the testing (between 50.6 and 33.2%). There were 12,273 students participating in Wave 2; 13,113, in Wave 3; 11,202, in Wave 4; 12,694, in Wave 5; 10,183, in Wave 6, 9,611, in Wave 7; 8,629, in Wave 8; 10,096, in Wave 9; 9,090, in Wave 10; 7,020, in Wave 11; and 8,552, in Wave 12. However, the proportion of students who could be reached for an interview or test declined significantly over time, mainly because of missing contact data, conversion of long-term nonparticipants into final dropouts, and withdrawals of panel consent. Withdrawals of panel consent and final dropouts occurred more often in telephone interviews than in online interviews. Overall, 19 final dropouts occurred in Wave 1; 40, in and after Wave 2; 211, in and after Wave 3; 33, in and after Wave 4; 296, in and after Wave 5; 66, in and after Wave 6; 29; 2,551, in and after Wave 7; 12, in and after Wave 8; 1,154, in and after Wave 9; 1,425, in and after Wave 10; 18, in and after Wave 11; and 463, in Wave 12. The high numbers in Waves 7, 9, and 10 were caused by the conversion of long-term nonparticipants into final dropouts after the respective waves. More details on the progression of the SC5 panel cohort including information on the distribution along the sample strata are given in Zinn et al. (2018). This also reports a study of the selectivity of the sample. For this purpose, relevant design variables and student characteristics such as the type of university at which students started their careers, their degrees while allowing for university admission, birth year, competence scores, and so forth were regressed on a student's remaining in the SC5 panel cohort. Among others, we found that younger students and students studying in the Eastern part of Germany were less likely to leave the panel sample than their counterparts. The same applied to students performing well in the mathematical competence test at Wave 1 and university students. Finally, students with missing information on their competence level and on their university admission certificate showed a strong propensity to leave the panel. For detailed information on this analysis, see Zinn et al. (2018). Wave-specific nonresponse analyses are provided along with the data documentation of NEPS in Zinn et al. (2017), Zinn (2017a, b).

3.5.6 Starting Cohort 6: Adults

Starting Cohort 6 (SC6) commenced in 2009 with 11,649 adults participants who were living in Germany and had been born between 1944 and 1986. There were 283 individuals from the ALWA subsample who participated only in NEPS Wave 2. These cases and participants in NEPS Wave 1 defined the first panel cohort of SC6 (ALWA/NEPS1). In NEPS Wave 3, the initial sample was expanded by a refreshment sample from which 5208 individuals (i.e., 30.4% of the drawn gross sample) finally participated in the study. This sample constituted the second panel cohort of SC6 (NEPS3). Over the course of the panel, 9,323 individuals participated in NEPS Wave 2; 14,112, in Wave 3 (including the 5,208 members of the refreshment sample); 11,696, in Wave 4; 10,639, in Wave 5; 9,770, in Wave 6; and 9,326, in Wave 7. Through the waves, it could be observed that units from the ALWA subsample were more likely to participate in the surveys than individuals from the newly drawn NEPS samples. In particular, the refreshment sample of NEPS Wave 3 exhibited a strong drop in participation rates, with only 77.5% of the administered persons agreeing to participate in the latest available Wave 7 compared to 85.1% of the ALWA subgroup. In addition, temporary dropouts decreased considerably over time in all subsamples. More details on the panel progress can be found in Zinn et al. (2018).

Examining panel attrition over study time and the associated selectivity of the current sample in more detail revealed that in the ALWA/NEPS1 subsample, people from the oldest birth cohort as well as individuals living in Western Germany showed a higher probability of leaving the panel. Furthermore, single and married respondents were more likely to drop out from the study over time, whereas individuals living in cities with more than 500,000 inhabitants had a lower dropout rate than those living in towns with less than 50,000 inhabitants. With increasing educational level, the likelihood of leaving the panel study declined. In addition, children in the household led to higher panel affinity; and three or more persons living in the household resulted in a higher dropout probability. For the NEPS3 subsample, we also observed a higher dropout rate for individuals in the oldest birth cohort and for those living in multiperson households. However, in this group, educational level and living in Western or Eastern Germany had no significant effects on panel dropout. Nonetheless, members with a migration background were more likely to leave the panel study. For more information on the performed selectivity analysis for Starting Cohort 6, see Zinn et al. (2018). In addition, the wave-specific analyses can be found in Hammon et al. (2016).

3.6 Conclusion

To recruit random samples of all mentioned populations in which access was gained via educational institutions, we applied multistage and indirect sampling techniques, as well as stratified cluster sampling techniques. These sampling techniques are especially suited to incorporate the institutional settings into the sampling process. As long as individuals are participating in formal educational institutions such as Kindergartens, schools, or institutions of higher education, well-defined clusters exist—and they are being used. Multistage sampling procedures can also be tailored to cope with the different focuses of the six starting cohorts. The six starting cohorts were established to implement the multicohort sequence design and facilitate educational life-course analyses within the defined underlying target populations. Stratified cluster sampling strategies were employed to establish a sample of first-year students at tertiary level institutions and a sample for the individual-based survey of adults. This sampling strategy made it possible to deal with the heterogeneous landscape of different fields of study not present at all tertiary educational institutions. Next to sampling strategies, information on panel development and attrition was provided. With the progress of the panel cohort samples, participation typically depends on factors influencing reachability and also on the educational background of participants. Hence, these are crucial factors for data analysis.

References

Antoni, M., Drasch, K., Kleinert, C., Matthes, B., Ruland, M., & Trahms, A. (2010). Arbeiten und Lernen im Wandel, Teil I: Überblick über die Studie (FDZ-Methodenreport 5/2010). Nürnberg, Germany: Forschungsdatenzentrum (FDZ) der Bundesagentur für Arbeit im Institut für Arbeitsmarkt- und Berufsforschung.

Aßmann, C., Steinhauer, H. W., Kiesl, H., Koch, S., Schönberger, B., Müller-Kuller, A., Rohwer, G., Rässler, S., & Blossfeld, H.-P. (2011). Sampling designs of the National Educational Panel Study: Challenges and solutions. In H.-P. Blossfeld, H.G. Roßbach, & J. von Maurice (Eds.), Education as a lifelong process: The German National Educational Panel Study (NEPS) (ZfE Sonderheft, 14, pp. 51–65). Wiesbaden, Germany: VS Verlag für Sozialwissenschaften.

Cochran, W. G. (1977). Sampling techniques (3rd ed.). Hoboken, NJ: Wiley.

Hammon, A., Zinn, S., Aßmann, C., & Würbach, A. (2016). Samples, weights, and nonresponse: The adult cohort of the National Educational Panel Study (Wave 2 to 6) (NEPS Survey Paper No. 7). Bamberg, Germany: Leibniz Institute for Educational Trajectories, National Educational Panel Study.

Joncas, M. (2008). TIMSS 2007 sample design. In J. F. Olson, M. O. Martin, & I. V. Mullis (Eds.), TIMSS 2007 Technical Report (pp. 77–92). Chestnut Hill, MA: TIMSS and PIRLS International Study Center.

Kiesl, H. (2010). Selecting kindergarten children by three stage indirect sampling. In American Statistical Association (Ed.), Proceedings of the Survey Research Methods Section (pp. 2730–2738). Alexandria: VA: American Statistical Association.

Lavallée, P. (2007). Indirect sampling. New York, NY: Springer.

Lohr, S. (2009). Sampling: Design and analysis (2nd ed.). Boston, MA: Brooks/Cole.

OECD (2009). PISA 2006 technical report. Paris, France: OECD.

Rjosk, C., Engelbert, M., Schipolowski, S., & Kohrt, P. (2017). Anlage, Durchführung und Auswertung des IQB-Bildungstrends 2016. In P. Stanat, S. Schipolowski, C. Rjosk, S. Weireich, & N. Haag (Eds.), IQB-Bildungstrend 2016. Kompetenzen in den Fächern Deutsch und Mathematik am Ende der 4. Jahrgangsstufe in zweiten Ländervergleich (pp. 83–105). Münster, Germany: Waxmann.

Särndal, C.-E., Swensson, B., & Wretman, J. (2003). Model assisted survey sampling. New York, NY: Springer.

Steinhauer, H. W., Aßmann, C., Zinn, S., Goßmann, S., & Rässler, S. (2015). Sampling and weighting cohort samples in institutional contexts. AStA Wirtschafts- und Sozialstatistisches Archiv, 9(2), 131–157. https://doi.org/10.1007/s11943-015-0162-0.

Steinhauer, H. W., & Zinn, S. (2016a). NEPS technical report for weighting: Weighting the sample of Starting Cohort 3 of the National Educational Panel Study (Waves 1 to 3) (NEPS Working Paper No. 63). Bamberg, Germany: Leibniz Institute for Educational Trajectories, National Educational Panel Study.

Steinhauer, H. W., & Zinn, S. (2016b). NEPS technical report for weighting: Weighting the sample of Starting Cohort 4 of the National Educational Panel Study (Wave 1 to 6) (NEPS Survey Paper No. 2). Bamberg, Germany: Leibniz Institute for Educational Trajectories, National Educational Panel Study.

Steinhauer, H. W., Zinn, S., & Aßmann, C. (2016). Weighting panel cohorts in institutional contexts. In H.-P. Blossfeld, J. von Maurice, M. Bayer, & J. Skopek (Eds.), Methodological issues of longitudinal surveys (pp. 39–62). Wiesbaden, Germany: Springer. https://doi.org/10.1007/978-3-658-11994-2_3.

Steinhauer, H. W., Zinn, S., Gaasch, C., & Goßmann, S. (2016). NEPS Technical Report for Weighting: Weighting the sample of Kindergarten children and Grade 1 students of the National Educational Panel Study (Wave 1 to 3) (NEPS Working Paper No. 66). Bamberg, Germany: Leibniz Institute for Educational Trajectories, National Educational Panel Study.

Thurgood, L., Walter, E., Carter, G., Henn, S., Huang, G., Nooter, D., Smith, W., Cash, R. W., & Salvucci, S. (2003). National Education Longitudinal Study of 1988 (NELS:88). In M. Seastrom, T. Phan, & M. Cohen (Eds.), NCES handbook of survey methods (pp. 53–66). Washington, DC: U.S. Department of Education, National Center for Education Statistics.

Würbach, A. (2017). Samples, weights, and nonresponse: The early childhood cohort of the National Educational Panel Study (Wave 4) (NEPS Technical Report). Bamberg, Germany: Leibniz Institute for Educational Trajectories, National Educational Panel Study.

Würbach, A. (2018). Samples, weights, and nonresponse: The Kindergarten cohort of the National Educational Panel Study (Waves 1 to 6) (NEPS Technical Report). Bamberg, Germany: Leibniz Institute for Educational Trajectories, National Educational Panel Study.

Würbach, A., Zinn, S., & Aßmann, C. (2016). Samples, weights, and nonresponse: The early childhood cohort of the National Educational Panel Study (Wave 1 to 3) (NEPS Survey Paper No. 8). Bamberg, Germany: Leibniz Institute for Educational Trajectories, National Educational Panel Study.

Zinn, S. (2017a). Samples, weights, and nonresponse: Wave 9 of the student sample of the National Educational Panel Study (Supplement to NEPS:SC5:9.0.0). Bamberg, Germany: Leibniz Institute for Educational Trajectories, National Educational Panel Study.

Zinn, S. (2017b). Samples, weights, and nonresponse: Wave 10 of the student sample of the National Educational Panel Study (Supplement to NEPS:SC5:10.0.0). Bamberg, Germany: Leibniz Institute for Educational Trajectories, National Educational Panel Study.

Zinn, S., Steinhauer, H. W., & Aßmann, C. (2017). Samples, weights, and nonresponse: The student sample of the National Educational Panel Study (Wave 1 to 8) (NEPS Survey Paper No. 18). Bamberg, Germany: Leibniz Institute for Educational Trajectories, National Educational Panel Study.

Zinn, S., Würbach, A., Steinhauer, H. W., & Hammon, A. (2018). Attrition and selectivity of the NEPS starting cohorts: An overview of the past 8 years (NEPS Survey Paper No. 34). Bamberg, Germany: Leibniz Institute for Educational Trajectories, National Educational Panel Study.

Development of Competencies Across the Life Course

Sabine Weinert, Cordula Artelt, Manfred Prenzel, Martin Senkbeil, Timo Ehmke, Claus H. Carstensen and Kathrin Lockl

---

Besides the authors, expert teams at the LIfBi in Bamberg, the IPN in Kiel, and the DIPF in Frankfurt have been working on the development of the test instruments described in this chapter; these teams are coordinated by Cordula Artelt and Claus Carstensen (Bamberg), Olaf Köller and Aiso Heinze (Kiel), and Frank Goldhammer in Frankfurt.

This article is an updated version of Weinert et al. (2011).

S. Weinert (✉) · C. H. Carstensen
University of Bamberg, Bamberg, Germany
E-Mail: sabine.weinert@uni-bamberg.de

C. H. Carstensen
E-Mail: claus.carstensen@uni-bamberg.de

C. Artelt · K. Lockl
Leibniz Institute for Educational Trajectories, Bamberg, Germany
E-Mail: cordula.artelt@lifbi.de

K. Lockl
E-Mail: kathrin.lockl@lifbi.de

M. Prenzel
University of Vienna, Vienna, Austria
E-Mail: manfred.prenzel@univie.ac.at

M. Senkbeil
IPN-Leibniz-Institute Kiel, Kiel, Germany
E-Mail: senkbeil@ipn.uni-kiel.de

T. Ehmke
Leuphana University of Lüneburg, Lüneburg, Germany
E-Mail: tehmke@leuphana.de

Abstract

The selection and measurement of competencies, reflecting educational effects in a lifelong learning perspective, represents a major challenge for the German National Educational Panel Study (NEPS). Data on the development of competencies serves as a central point of reference for all other parts of the study. These competencies have to be relevant not only for a successful and responsible individual life but also for a well-functioning modern democratic society. Hence, the aim is not just to describe the development of such competencies, but also to analyze relevant prerequisites, conditions, and courses of competence acquisition. The lifelong learning perspective will shed light on how different competencies are acquired over the life span, how they interact over time and across educational stages, and in which way they may contribute to individual and group-specific life-course outcomes. This chapter gives an overview on the selection, rationale, and conceptualization of competencies within NEPS.

Keywords

Competencies · Life-span development · Panel study

4.1 General Remarks on the Concept of Competence and on the Dynamic of Competence Development

Educationally relevant competencies are often referred to as functional, context-bound, domain- and demand-specific (cognitive) achievement dispositions that are subject to educational influence and interventions (e.g., reading competence, mathematical competence) (see Rychen and Salganik 2001, 2003; Weinert 2001). These domain- and demand-specific competencies are distinguished from both (a) (primary) domain-general and rather context-free cognitive capacities (e.g., fluid intelligence or working memory capacity) and (b) specialized content-specific knowledge structures and procedural skills. Furthermore, educationally relevant competencies are often conceptualized as either curricular (i.e., subject-bound) or cross-curricular (i.e., cross-subject).

From an empirical point of view, there has been much research on the development of various competencies in school (e.g., reading and mathematics; see Denissen et al. 2007; Kwiatkowska-White et al. 2016; Pfost et al. 2014; Prenzel et al. 2006; Spengler et al. 2016; Weinert and Helmke 1997), and social disparities have been documented extensively (e.g., Lühe et al. 2017; Neumann et al. 2014; Sammons 1995). Nonetheless, there is comparatively little research on these competencies in adulthood; in addition, little is known about the cumulative development of competencies across educational stages. Thus, important empirical questions in the National Educational Panel Study (NEPS) relate to the development and relevance of these competencies from both early on and beyond school, their importance for future job careers, and their impact on general life satisfaction. Which are the early roots of competence development? How do they develop further in different educational contexts? In which way do they contribute to the acquisition of competencies specific to tertiary education or working life (e.g., the mathematical competencies acquired in school may differ from those necessary for and acquired through tertiary education at university level and from those necessary for post-tertiary work in this area)? How does the cross-stage acquisition of competencies vary across subgroups depending on socioeconomic status and migration and/or language background?

Thus, central topics in NEPS refer to the questions: "In which way do domain-specific functional competencies emerge on the basis of individual prerequisites for learning and formal as well as nonformal/informal education during different educational stages (crib level, preschool level, elementary and secondary school level, university level, vocational training, and on-the-job training)?" and "What is the significance of specific competencies throughout the life span?" These questions address:

1. The interrelation between competence development and the themes of the other so called NEPS "pillars"—that is, family education, education in and outside of institutions (focus of Pillar 2; see Chap. 5, this volume), educational decisions and their distal and proximal determinants (focus of Pillar 3; see Chap. 6, this volume), issues of migration (focus of Pillar 4; see Chap. 7, this volume), educational returns (focus of Pillar 5; see Chap. 8, this volume), and motivational and personality aspects (see Chap. 9, this volume).
2. The analysis of developmental relationships between (a) the acquisition of basic domain- and demand-specific functional competencies (e.g., reading competence, mathematical competence), (b) the acquisition of domain-general individual abilities/capacities, and (c) the construction of content-related knowledge and procedural skills as indicated by stage-specific outcome measures.

From a life-span perspective, it should be noted that the development of basic competencies is subject to a stage-specific dynamic that may change across educational stages: Competencies (e.g., reading, mathematical, and scientific literacy), which are subject to domain-specific development during the school age period in which they form a subject-specific focus, become kinds of cross-curricular basic competencies during later stages (job training and tertiary education). In the same vein, when entering elementary school, most children have already acquired a host of language-based as well as cognitive competencies (Damon and Lerner 2006). Although these competencies were acquired in a highly domain-specific way during their first years of life (Weinert 2000), they can be conceptualized in school as cross-subject basic competencies for school learning.

In addition, developmental psychology as well as research into the acquisition of expertise support the view that the interrelations between domain-general psychological capacities (e.g., fluid intelligence, working memory) and the acquisition of domain-specific competencies may vary systematically by age, educational stage, and expert status—in much the same way as interrelationships between different competencies may change over time (Ericsson et al. 2006; Weinert 2000, 2007a). NEPS is contributing considerably to our knowledge about the developmental interrelations between (a) domain- and demand-specific competence acquisition within and across educational stages; (b) previously acquired as well as not yet developed, more general cross-domain abilities and psychological capacities; and (c) the evolving content-specific knowledge base including procedural skills.

4.2 Which Competencies Are Included in the NEPS: An Overview

From a lifelong learning perspective, looking at "outcomes" of educational processes cannot be the only objective of NEPS. The "outcomes" at a certain age function as conditions for development in the ensuing stage. One of the major challenges is to describe and explain the processes of competence development within and across educational stages while also analyzing their relevance for future prospects. This implies both a sufficient coverage of important competencies and a (pragmatically and theoretically thoughtful and justifiable) concentration on certain relevant competence domains to be assessed over the life span. With regard to the NEPS pillars, it seems necessary to select competence domains that promise insights into the stability and plasticity of competence development, the (long-term) effects and consequences of institutional efforts to influence these developments, their relevance for educational decision making, their relevance for educational returns across the life span, and their interrelation with motivational and personality factors, while also additionally focusing on competence acquisition in certain social groups such as migrants.

Recent discussions on the relevance of competencies across the life span place special emphasis on cognitive competencies as well as on various social skills, motivational dispositions, attitudes, and expectations (see e.g., OECD 2018). Obviously, cognitive and the so-called noncognitive components interact in everyday applications. Nevertheless, it seems reasonable to distinguish systematically between cognitive and noncognitive components from both an analytical point of view and the perspective of a longitudinal reconstruction of the development of educationally relevant competencies. A distinct assessment of constructs allows the analysis of both the interplay and the developmental dynamics of these components (Weinert 2001).

For NEPS, we concentrate on both cognitive and noncognitive (social and motivational) competencies. Whereas some competencies are reconstructed in their lifelong internal dynamics of developmental change, the assessment of others depends on and varies according to the affordances of certain educational stages (see below). Thus, with respect to measurement, we differentiate competencies that are measured in a coherent way across the life span, aiming at a comprehensive reconstruction of their internal dynamics of emergence and developmental change over the life course, from competencies that are assessed with more stage-specific instruments.

Central research questions regarding the development of basic domain-specific functional competencies are the following: (a) How and to what extent do domain-general and content-free cognitive capacities shape the effects of schooling and the development of these basic functional competencies? (b) What are the relationships between (selected) school-curriculum-specific skills and the development of these basic functional competencies? These two research questions are not only interesting from a theoretical/analytical point of view, but are also directly relevant to the field of applied education. Implications for the assessment agenda are as follows: The assessment of basic (subject-) domain- and demand-specific competencies that are sensitive to learning and institutional efforts (i.e., that are the result of individual prerequisites and learning processes, along with family-based and institutional as well as nonformal/informal learning opportunities) needs to be complemented by analytically oriented measures of domain-general and more culture-fair capacities of the individual (i.e., indicators of abstract and logical reasoning, and indicators of processing speed) that enable the acquisition of domain-specific competencies through interactions with environmental stimuli and learning opportunities. In addition, these rather content-free areas are complemented by more specific content-related variables and stage-specific outcome measures. The major focus thus lies on analyzing the developmental trajectories and interactions of the corresponding competencies, capacities, and skills as well as assessing their relevance for future educational and occupational careers and also life satisfaction.

This conceptualization can also be applied to developmental phases beyond school. Again, basic functional competencies that have now become cross-curricular (e.g., mathematical, reading, foreign-language, and scientific literacy) are complemented with subject-specific knowledge, attainment, and skills in tertiary education as well as job-related proficiency outside university. This approach permits an analysis of the relevance of basic domain-specific functional competencies as well as their further development (stagnation or decline) beyond formal schooling and the interplay of these competencies with job-specific attainment, competencies, and skills or with competencies specific to selected fields of tertiary education. Of course, from a pragmatic point of view, it is obviously necessary to concentrate on a carefully selected number of types of jobs and fields of tertiary education.

In addition, from the perspective of lifelong learning as well as from the perspective of the NEPS pillars, we suggest broadening the perspective systematically by including additional competence areas and specifically metacompetencies (see below).

To summarize: Four areas of individual abilities and competencies are differentiated and assessed in NEPS: (A) domain-general cognitive abilities/capacities; (B) domain-specific cognitive competencies; (C) metacompetencies and social competencies; and (D) stage-specific (curriculum- or job related) attainments, skills, and outcome measures. These areas will be described in more detail below.

4.2.1 Area A: Domain-General Cognitive Abilities and Capacities

From a developmental perspective, it is necessary to point out that it is not just acquired domain-specific competencies that are subject to typical age- or development-related changes over the life span. The same also applies to domain-general abilities that are characterized as being relatively context-free and culture-fair. These basic individual abilities and capacities have been described and extensively explored within the framework of intelligence theories, and they form an important basis of intelligent thinking and action (see Baltes et al. 2006). As rather general individual abilities/capacities, they have been conceptualized as "fluid intelligence" (Cattell 1971) or "cognitive mechanics" (Baltes et al. 2006). Whereas the mechanics (fluid intelligence, basic capacities) refer to performance differences in the speed of elementary cognitive processes, in the capacity of working memory, or in the ability to apply deductive or analogous thinking in new situations, the intellectual pragmatics (Baltes et al. 2006) or crystallized intelligence (Cattell 1971) refer particularly to the declarative and procedural knowledge and skills that a person acquires during the life course. Education-relevant competencies in the way they are emphasized by NEPS (see Area B) tend to belong more to intellectual pragmatics. From a developmental and educational point of view, both components of cognitive architecture—that is, intellectual pragmatics and intellectual mechanics—are subject to typical age-related changes across the life span. Nonetheless, they (a) reveal different characteristics of change over their course and (b) are influenced to a varying degree by different determinants (see Baltes et al. 2006).

Considering cognitive performance, it is important to note that the contrast between cognitive mechanics and cognitive pragmatics does not imply that they are independent of each other. This is one reason why the domain-specific measurements of competencies in NEPS require a supplementary assessment of at least some brief indicators of intellectual mechanics. Thus, although NEPS focuses specifically on the acquisition of education-dependent, domain-specific competencies, these assessments have to be supplemented by additional indicators of cognitive mechanics that can be taken to be more "culture-fair" and language-free. From not only a theoretical but also an empirical and pragmatic perspective, we proposed that cognitive mechanics should be assessed through two indicators within NEPS, in particular, through:

- Tasks assessing figural reasoning. To avoid partial overlaps with the specific competence domains assessed in NEPS, no verbal or numerical reasoning tasks were proposed that are more likely to tap language and mathematical skills. In NEPS, a matrices test is implemented that requires respondents to deduce the logical rules on which the pattern of the geometrical elements is based.
- Tasks assessing perceptual speed. These are preferred to other speed measures, because they tend to be more language-independent and more culture-fair than, for example, rapid naming tasks. The NEPS test assessing perceptual speed requires

figures or numbers to be matched with graphical symbols (see Brunner et al. 2014; Lang et al. 2014).

4.2.2 Area B: Domain-Specific Cognitive Competencies

With respect to the cognitive domains, discussions about the relevance of competencies for future prospects are influenced strongly by international large-scale assessments of students' and adults' performance (e.g., the *Programme for International Student Assessment* (PISA), the *Third International Mathematics and Science Study* (TIMSS), the *Adult Literacy and Life Skills* (ALL) Study, and the *Programme for the International Assessment of Adult Competencies* (PIAAC); see also Chap. 2, this volume). The frameworks of these assessments place special emphasis on basic school-related and demand-specific cognitive competencies. There is overall consensus on the relevance of the following competencies: (German-)language competencies (particularly reading competence), mathematical competence, scientific literacy, and foreign-language competencies (see, e.g., Bynner 2004; Forum Bildung 2002; OECD 2006, 2016; Rychen and Salganik 2001, 2003; Tenorth 2004).

Especially the OECD's Programme for International Student Assessment (PISA) raised the claim that competencies such as reading, mathematical, and scientific literacy are not only school-related competencies in a narrow sense but also highly relevant for success in later life. Literacy is understood as a predictor of successful participation in society (OECD 2006, 2016). Within the conceptualization of domain-specific competencies, the notion of participation is considered as functional literacy. This leads to an assessment in such tests that relies heavily on everyday problems that are more or less distant to school curricula. There are many reasons why competencies in the sense of functional literacy should be included in NEPS—one being the assumed relevance largely agreed upon in educational policies, educational sciences, as well as the general public. Another reason is the importance of linking NEPS to international large-scale assessments. Additionally, NEPS offers unique opportunities for longitudinal analyses of the assumed relevance of these basic functional competencies for future prospects, the early roots and courses of developmental change in these basic competencies, and their interrelations with other competence domains and variables assessed in NEPS.

Thus, in NEPS, we are measuring the following competence domains:

- German-language competencies (reading competence and listening comprehension)
- Mathematical competencies (mathematical literacy)
- Natural science competencies (scientific literacy)

In addition, we are assessing indicators of foreign-language competencies.

In particular, reading competence, mathematical literacy, and scientific literacy are assessed consistently and coherently across the life span so that their genesis and cumulative development can be reconstructed across educational stages. The acquisition of foreign-language competencies in the sense of learning one (or several) language(s) beyond the acquisition of the specific first language(s) is not assessed until later school age. Here we focus on English language competencies (see Chap. 14, this volume). In addition, indicators of first-language competencies are assessed when these do not refer to German. Here we focus on Russian and Turkish language competencies. This is the responsibility of the expert team in Pillar 4 (Migration, see Chap. 7, this volume).

Challenges of Modeling Domain-Specific Cognitive Competencies
Modeling domain-specific competence development over the life span is confronted with at least two major challenges: (a) the stipulation of benchmarks for the judgment of competence development over the life span (which also means for different requirements and standards across the life span) and (b) a coherent modeling of competence development over different educational stages allowing the description of cumulative developmental progress over time (scale anchoring). These challenges will be illustrated in the following paragraph.

(a) Although the labels (reading, mathematics, science) remain the same, the corresponding competence domains change during the life span. The school-subject domain obviously offers a different point of reference to that of the scientific discipline. A fixation on a school-related competence model implies that further competence development after formal schooling would not be covered appropriately in NEPS, even though analyzing the extent to which school-related competencies (e.g., mathematical) are instrumental for further studies, different jobs, or everyday problem solving would be an interesting task. From this perspective, it seems necessary to consider multiple reference points. These can be organized around life coherences (with corresponding domain-specific demands). One approach would be to use institutional learning environments (school, vocational training, tertiary education, on-the-job training) or everyday life experiences (e.g., political and cultural participation, health behavior). Different reference points can be accounted for by applying structural models of domain-specific competencies that disengage from school-subject-related and academic structuring and aim to identify (declarative/conceptual and procedural/process-related) core components of competence. A concrete example can be found in the PISA approach (OECD 2003) of modeling mathematical competencies around "overarching ideas" (space and shape, change and relationships, quantity, uncertainty). These overarching ideas can be applied not only to mathematics as an academic discipline but also to everyday life as a tool. When describing and analyzing competence development across the life span around these ideas, it seems likely that the use and relevance of mathematical competencies in different life circumstances can be assessed adequately, and that possible future trends can be described. In a similar vein, modeling of "processes/procedures" for other domains seems possible as well. In the domain of science, these are "big ideas" or basic components of scientific thinking and working (e.g., identifying scientific issues, explaining phenomena scientifically, using scientific evidence). With respect to reading competence, the requirement of retrieving information, interpreting texts, and of reflection and evaluation can be subsumed under central reading processes and demands.

(b) The above-mentioned example for modeling mathematical competencies around overarching ideas can be seen as an example for coherent competence models that are necessary for describing and analyzing cumulative development. Using the concept of overarching ideas allows us to study whether and to what degree traditional computing demands in everyday life (shopping, calculating the costs of a cell phone, or making leasing contracts) are instrumental for the stabilization of competencies in the field of quantity; and to ask whether further developmental progress in the field of space and shape or the field of change and relationships is linked rather closely to the domain of advanced studies or to the specifics of a job. In the field of scientific competence, the thematic context of "health" can be used as a coherent reference point for a lifelong perspective, making it possible to study changes and development in scientific competence in relation to aspects of health. Again, these examples show that content-related and theoretically based developmental trajectories should be formulated for domain-specific competencies. If it is possible to master these challenges in the process of modeling competence development, NEPS will contribute significantly to our understanding of fundamental developmental processes in educational contexts across the life span. These considerations result in the steps specified in the next paragraph that apply to each of the domain-specific cognitive competencies to be assessed in NEPS.

Framework for Each Competence Domain and Scaling Issues

For each domain, a competence model has been developed that describes a consistent structure of that competence domain across ages and cohorts. These theoretical assumptions as well as their operational characterizations are to be specified in the competence framework. A short overview of these frameworks for each competence domain under study is presented below. Based on these models, test instruments were developed for the various age groups. Item pools were pretested in qualitative and quantitative pilot studies and then analyzed and selected using item response theory. Combined with additional linking studies or specific anchor item designs, the instruments developed should allow for a coherent assessment of competence development over the life span.

4.2.2.1 Assessment of German-Language Competencies (Reading Competence and Listening Comprehension) Across the Life Course

Being competent in the lingua franca used by the majority of society is indisputably one of the central, education-relevant cognitive competencies. It is exceptionally significant for taking advantage of education opportunities and participating in a society's political and cultural life. In fact, language is not only an important means of communication in everyday life and work but also the object, learning environment, and medium of a variety of formal and nonformal/informal learning contexts. At the same time, language forms an important coding and (self-) control system with a lasting influence on not only cognitive but also social and sociocognitive development (see, for a summary, e.g., Weinert 2006, 2017).

Language acquisition is viewed, on the one hand, as a primary, genetically anchored basic human ability (Geary 1995). On the other hand, both international studies and research in German-speaking countries have shown that even early language acquisition is influenced in a lasting way by social and education-related family background variables (e.g., Ebert et al. 2013; Weinert et al. 2010). The social disparities that have become apparent in later school age through international comparisons of academic achievement—particularly in Germany (e.g., Baumert et al. 2001)—are attributed in part to differences in verbal competencies (Esser 2006; Stanat 2006; Weinert 2017). Language is *the* central medium for the acquisition of content- and problem-solving-related knowledge including important self-regulated learning abilities. In schools as well as in tertiary education, verbal activities such as "formulating and solving tasks," "listening to teachers' lectures and answering teachers' questions" (which are used as an illocutionary tactic relative to everyday questions), "explanation or reformulation," as well as "justifying, explaining, arguing, and estimating," and, not least, "processing written texts" are a central means of knowledge acquisition and knowledge transfer to the next generation. Language and verbal communication also play an important role in social interaction and both social and sociocognitive development, as already demonstrated by the Soviet cultural historical school of Vygotsky (see Wertsch 1996; Weinert 2007b, 2017).

Despite different conceptualizations of the construct "verbal competence," there is broad consensus that language and verbal competencies can be viewed from both a structural and a communicative-functional perspective. This analytic distinction does not imply, as sometimes assumed mistakenly, a corresponding separation when concrete communication and acquisition situations are to be considered. The function and structure of language are inseparable here; both aspects are mutually dependent and combine to form language. Thus, on the one hand, component models of language (differentiating between grammar, lexicon, pragmatics, etc.) have proved their worth from both a developmental as well as from a clinical and educational perspective, and they have been well received in language diagnosis. On the other hand, from an education-related perspective, the integrative functional verbal abilities have been emphasized, with distinctions generally being made between productive and receptive as well as between auditory and written verbal competencies in the sense of reading competence, listening comprehension, writing, and communicative or interactive speech (see also Jude and Klieme 2007). When deciding how verbal competencies should be conceptualized and measured within NEPS, it was necessary to consider not only theoretical aspects but also the practical demands within the framework of a large-scale study such as NEPS. The aspects assessed have to retain their meaningfulness across a broad range of ages and age cohorts in terms of both their relevance for and their dependence on education processes.

Against this background, NEPS is concentrating on the assessment of *reading competence* and *listening comprehension* (see Berendes et al. 2013).

The framework depicted in Table 4.1 is used to design test instruments to assess reading competence across the life span (see Gehrer et al. 2013).

For each of the five text types/text functions, a number of age-adequate items have been constructed covering each of the main cognitive requirements (see Gehrer et al. 2013). In addition to the comprehensive indicator on reading competence, a supplementary indicator of reading speed is assessed at least once for every starting cohort. The reading speed indicators primarily capture basic reading processes such as decoding and, thus, focus on automatized reading processes.

With respect to the listening comprehension framework, we differentiate between word, sentence, and discourse level. Specifically, we assess receptive vocabulary,

Table 4.1 Conceptual differentiations of the reading competence framework

Comprehension requirement[a]	*I. Finding information in the text:* Identifying a statement in a text when the wording is identical in both the task and the text Identifying a statement in a text when the wording in the task and the text deviate from each other *II. Drawing text-related conclusions:* Integrating statements from successive sentences Integrating statements from several sentences or sentences located far apart Comprehension of important ideas in the text, which requires the ability to comprehend relevant text passages that are larger or more complex *III. Reflecting and assessing:* Understanding the main statement of a text, the main content, the main event Recognizing the purpose and intention of a text and being able to judge its credibility Drawing further inferences on the basis of a text, which requires the integration of background knowledge
Functions of texts/or text types	Information function, e.g., factual texts, reports, articles Commenting function, e.g., comments, glossaries, essays Literary-aesthetic function. Exclusively prose texts, e.g., short stories, passages from novels Instruction, functional text, e.g., assembly instructions and user instructions, package inserts for taking medicines Appeals, advertising, e.g., job vacancies, vacation travel ads
Age level	Adaptation with respect to text difficulty as well as the selection of topics

[a]Note that these eight (I. to III.) types of demands for the reading items are neither meant as distinct dimensions nor as a statement on the hierarchy of information processing

because it has proved to be one of the best indicators of both crystallized intelligence and language competencies (see, for a short summary, Weinert et al. 2007). In young children, we add measures of sentence comprehension to assess receptive grammar (see Berendes et al. 2013; Lorenz et al. 2017). As an additional indicator of listening comprehension in secondary school children, we assess functional listening comprehension on text or discourse level. The conceptualization of functional listening comprehension is comparable to reading competence in some aspects (e.g., comprehension requirements) but different in others (e.g., discourses with more than one speaker). Memory and especially reading requirements are reduced as far as possible and the texts/discourses are quasi-authentic and presented by sound carrier (for more detailed information see Hecker et al. 2015).

4.2.2.2 Assessment of Mathematical Literacy Across the Life Course

Mathematical literacy is considered to be an important key competence in today's knowledge society, and increasing importance is being assigned to the requirement to understand and apply mathematical data and methods in manifold situations (NCTM 2003). For instance, mathematical literacy is necessary in many professional fields in which calculations must be drawn up, mathematical or abstract problems must be solved, logical argumentation is called for, or different representations of numbers and relations in newspapers must be understood. In the private sphere, mathematical literacy is also called for if one, for example, wants to compare and evaluate different finance or insurance models.

The importance of mathematics in our present society can also be seen from the fact that the OECD regularly conducts international comparisons of education systems by surveying the mathematical literacy of young people in, for example, PISA. Mathematical literacy is thereby understood as "an individual's capacity to identify and understand the role that mathematics plays in the world, to make well-founded judgments and to use and engage with mathematics in ways that meet the needs of that individual's life as a constructive, concerned and reflective citizen" (OECD 2003, p. 24). It thereby describes the extent to which students and also adults can flexibly apply the mathematics they have learned in school to problematic situations mostly outside the field of mathematics.

Although the importance of mathematical literacy for successful participation in society is uncontested, up until now, little empirically founded knowledge has been gained on how it develops over the life span from early childhood to late adulthood. How do numerical competencies at preschool age influence mathematical literacy in elementary school? How do mathematical skills develop over the course of schooling? Which role does mathematical literacy play when progressing to the next level in education? How does mathematical literacy differ in adulthood?

In order to survey mathematical literacy over the life course, we developed a theoretical framework that defines the structure of mathematical competence for all age groups. The starting point for this was the comprehensive competence structure for four age groups described in the National Council of Teachers of Mathematics framework conception (NCTM 2003) and the framework for mathematical literacy of 15-year-old students in the OECD's PISA (2003; see OECD 2003). The framework for the assessment of mathematical competence in NEPS differentiates between mathematical content areas and between mathematical and cognitive processes required for solving the test items (Table 4.2). This framework has been used for the development of test instruments for all age groups (see Ehmke et al. 2009; Neumann et al. 2013; Knopp et al. 2014).

Table 4.2 Conceptual differentiations of the mathematical competence framework

Content areas	*I. Quantity:* Understanding numeric phenomena as well as quantitative relationships and patterns Using numbers to represent quantities and quantifiable attributes of real-world objects (counts and measures) Understanding the meaning of operations, mental arithmetic, and estimating *II. Change and relationship:* Understanding mathematical manifestations of change, functional relationships, and dependency among variables Expressing mathematical relationships given in equations or inequalities Understanding mathematical relationships given in a variety of different representations *III. Space and shape:* Understanding spatial and geometric phenomena and relationships Analyzing the components of shapes and recognizing shapes in different representations Understanding the properties of objects and their relative positions *IV. Data and chance:* Understanding probabilistic and statistical phenomena and relationships Organizing data and using graphical representation forms Analyzing collected data and drawing conclusions from it
Mathematical and cognitive processes	These include: Mathematical communication Mathematical argumentation Modeling Using representational forms Mathematical problem solving Technical abilities and skills
Age level	Adaptation with respect to task difficulty as well as the selection of mathematical concepts

Linking and validation studies showed that the NEPS mathematics framework is very similar to the frameworks of the mathematics assessments in TIMSS 2011, PISA 2012, and the IQB's National Assessment Study 2012 (Nissen 2017; van den Ham et al. 2014) and that the measurement scales of these assessments can be linked together (Nissen et al. 2015; van den Ham et al. 2017).

4.2.2.3 Assessment of Scientific Literacy Across the Life Course

Scientific literacy enables an individual to participate in a society in which science and technology play a significant role. A large proportion of the problems and issues that individuals encounter in their daily lives require some understanding of science and technology before they can be fully understood and addressed. Current debates about the desired outcomes of science education thus emphasize the importance of a science education for all people (Osborne and Dillon 2008). Such an education would provide a basis for lifelong learning that would also impact on career perspectives. This is particularly true when scientific literacy is conceptualized as consisting of the knowledge, the competencies, and the attitudes needed to solve everyday problems. These problems require a flexible application of acquired knowledge that is appropriate to the particular situation. A corresponding conception was used in the PISA study. It was elaborated in detail for the framework conception of PISA 2006 and later PISA 2016 with its focus on science (see OECD 2006, 2016; Prenzel et al. 2007; Schiepe-Tiska et al. 2016). Rather than focusing on the reproduction of memorized knowledge, PISA aims to assess the ability to apply one's existing scientific knowledge in different everyday contexts and situations. This broad idea of literacy recognizes the importance and relevance of the competencies, knowledge, methods, and values that define the scientific disciplines and that are considered to be of great importance for an actively participating citizen. Our rapidly changing and developing society increasingly demands scientific literacy in order to understand and make use of technological innovations, to adequately face environmental challenges (such as climate change), and to reflect on one's own actions as a responsible citizen (see, e.g., AAAS 1993; Bybee 1997). Alongside a more content-oriented basic understanding of scientific concepts and facts (knowledge of science), PISA also emphasizes the importance of a more process-oriented basic understanding of scientific thinking and reasoning as well as of scientific methods (knowledge about science). The latter enables people to use an evidence-based approach when facing new or contradictory information in their everyday lives. Scientific methodology is an expression of an analytical, rational, and reflective approach toward an understanding of our world. As a result, scientific literacy is becoming more and more important in a world that, in turn, is continually becoming more and more complex.

NEPS aims to assess the development of scientific literacy over the life span. Thus, a theoretical framework was developed that defines the structure and content of scientific literacy for all age groups. The PISA 2006 framework of scientific literacy was chosen as a starting point, because it explicitly outlines what 15-year-old students should know, value, and be able to do in situations involving science and technology (OECD 2006). Like PISA, the NEPS framework conceptualizes scientific literacy in everyday situations; namely, within the three contexts health, environment, and technology. These contexts were chosen because of their importance and relevance with respect to everyday life and lifelong learning processes. Similar to PISA, the NEPS framework also differentiates between *knowledge of science (KOS)* and *knowledge about science (KAS)*. *Knowledge of science* is assessed within the four concept areas substances, systems, development, and interactions. *Knowledge about science* is concerned with the two concepts scientific inquiry and scientific reasoning. These concepts are widely regarded as representing central and important aspects of scientific literacy (AAAS 1993). The NEPS framework of scientific literacy is presented in Table 4.3 (see Hahn et al. 2013; Wagner et al. 2014).

4.2.3 Area C: Metacompetencies and Social Competencies

Over and above the assessment of cognitive competencies, we have suggested broadening the perspective systematically and including additional competence areas—specifically metacompetencies and "noncognitive" competence domains.

When selecting competence domains for a national panel study, a major challenge was to appropriately cover concepts and areas relevant to certain age groups (such as infants and the middle aged and aged) that have been widely neglected by earlier model building and research designs in education. Which are the early roots of cognitive, metacognitive, and socioemotional competencies? Do competencies acquired early on in institutional settings remain as relevant in adulthood as they were before? Which indicators adequately cover life satisfaction or the tendency to act in a reflected and responsible way? Which of the competencies that can be covered in a large-scale panel study and mapped with the NEPS pillars play a significant role for the aged? Learning processes subsequent to compulsory education need to be regulated by individuals rather than educational institutions. Learning becomes more and more dependent on the initiative of individual people (or families, unions, employers). The farther away from formal education, the stronger the need to initiate and regulate one's own learning as well as to form decisions about the contents of learning. To cover these metacompetencies, we decided to broaden the set of indicators and include indicators of metacognition and self-regulation.

Furthermore, aspects of social behavior and cooperation as reflected in interpersonal skills may be of high impact (i.e., cooperation with others, working together in a team, perspective taking). Compared to the competencies mentioned in Area B above, which are described in terms of their developmental trajectories in NEPS, the measurement and status of social behavior and personality indicators is slightly different. A reconstruction of the internal developmental dynamic of their emergence and development across the life span is hardly the main focus of NEPS; instead, they are analyzed primarily with respect to their role (i.e., as predictors, moderators, possibly compensators) for competence development within educational stages and as predictors between stages.

Table 4.3 Conceptual differentiations of the scientific literacy framework

Concepts	***Content related components (knowledge of science, KOS)*** *Substances*: Relation between substances and particles Relation between structure and properties of matter Chemical changes of matter *Systems*: Different systems but also elements of one specific system are interacting with each other. Systems are characterized by specific properties (e.g., regulation and control, conversion of matter or energy) Stable conditions are systems in equilibrium *Development*: Living systems change with time and are characterized by development. Individual development is caused by genetic heritance and environmental influences. Humans directly and indirectly change the environment. *Interactions*: The interaction of different bodies can lead to deformation or changes in the state of motion Energy can interact with matter. During this process, both energy and matter can change their properties
	Process-related components (knowledge about science, KAS) *Scientific inquiry and scientific reasoning*: Identifying scientific issues in different contexts Deducing information in a context-related way Observing and explaining phenomena Postulating, testing, and evaluating hypotheses and theories Evaluating and using scientific evidence Measurement and measurement errors
Contexts	The concepts form the basis for the scientific literacy required in the following selected *contexts*: *Health*: Nutrition; maintenance of health; diseases; control of diseases, infection, and epidemics *Environment*: Pollution, waste disposal, sustainability, quality of life, and nature *Technology*: Materials, devices, processes, transportation, sources of energy, and genetic modifications

This means that these indicators are chosen with specific reference to the educational stage under study and thus may vary slightly from those chosen in yet another stage—both in terms of content and in terms of their relative weight/importance for a specific stage.

NEPS includes direct and/or indirect measures of:

- Metacognition and self-regulation
- Information and communication technologies (ICT) literacy
- Social competencies

Finally (see Chap. 9), we include a brief indicator of rather stable dimensions of personality (for a very economic instrument for measuring the Big Five, see Asendorpf 2007) as well as indicators of achievement motivation, personal goals, general and topic-related interests, as well as of general and domain-specific self-concept. These latter aspects as well as social competencies are assessed by questionnaires and thus will not be detailed in this article (see Chap. 9, this volume).

Metacognition. Metacognition concerns knowledge about and control over one's own cognitive system. Drawing on the work of Flavell (1979) and Brown (1987), NEPS distinguishes between declarative and procedural aspects of metacognition. Declarative metacognition refers to the knowledge about memory, comprehension, and learning processes that an individual can verbalize. This includes knowledge about the strengths and weakness of one's own memory and one's own learning as well as knowledge about ways and means (e.g., general and domain-specific strategies) of attaining cognitive learning and achievement goals. In NEPS, declarative metacognition is being assessed with a scenario-based metacognitive knowledge test (see Händel et al. 2013; Lockl et al. 2016). Procedural metacognition, in contrast, focuses on how the learning process is regulated through planning, monitoring, and control activities. In NEPS, it is being measured along with the domain-specific competence tests in which participants have to estimate their own achievement score in the respective test (see Händel et al. 2013).

ICT literacy. In our modern knowledge and information society, the ability to search for information and to handle information and communication technologies (ICT) competently is indispensable for coping with a host of demands in various life domains (e.g., ETS 2002; NRC 1999; Wirth and Klieme 2002). The ability to comprehend, use, and communicate information conveyed by the electronic media is not just important for coping with professional tasks in many work fields. The growing encroachment of ICT into all walks of life (ETS 2002) is also granting these abilities a major status in the everyday world. Therefore, mastery of ICT can be viewed as a general cultural technique whose acquisition is an essential precondition for successful participation in society and for the fulfillment of personal and career goals (e.g., Katz and Macklin 2007; Konsortium Bildungsberichterstattung 2006). Current conceptions of ICT literacy emphasize the importance of a goal-directed and problem-oriented approach to contents and information conveyed by electronic media (NRC 1999). Therefore, ICT literacy refers particularly to information-related competencies (e.g., location and access of information) for which technology-related competencies (declarative and procedural knowledge about computer and Internet applications) are also a prerequisite (e.g., Eisenberg 2008; Katz 2007) (see Table 4.4).

Social competencies and self-regulation. For these areas, special expert reports have been commissioned to compare the measurement instruments available for different stages and evaluate their coherence (Arnold et al. 2009; Stamov-Roßnagel et al. 2009). These areas are being assessed predominantly by questionnaires and more stage-specific instruments and are therefore not treated in any more depth within this chapter (see Chap. 9, this volume).

4.2.4 Area D: Stage-Specific (Curriculum- or Job-Related) Attainments, Skills, and Outcome Measures

In addition, a selection of stage-specific abilities, attainments, and skills are also assessed. For schools, for example, this means that the assessment of the competencies described under Area B is supplemented by collecting data on selected close-to-curriculum abilities and skills. For instance, orthography competence has been measured as a stage-specific supplement in secondary school from Grades 5 to 9 and in elementary school in Grade 4 (Blatt et al. 2011). As another example, indicators of phonological awareness, which have been shown to be important prerequisites of reading competencies, are assessed in Kindergarten children (Berendes et al. 2013; Berendes and Weinert 2016). For tertiary education and vocational training, some study-subject- and job-related attainments and

Table 4.4 Conceptual differentiations of the ICT literacy framework (see Senkbeil et al. 2013a, b)

Competencies	Information literacy: ability to recognize when information is needed and have the ability to locate, evaluate, and use the needed information effectively Technological literacy: underlying knowledge of hardware, software applications, networks, and elements of digital technology
Process components	Define: using ICT tools to identify an information need Access: basic knowledge and basic operations (e.g., opening, saving, and printing files) Manage: using ICT tools to locate information Create: using ICT tools to adapt, apply, design or invent information Integrate: using ICT tools to summarize, compare, and contrast information from multiple sources Evaluate: judging the degree to which information satisfies the needs of the task in ICT environments, including determining authority, bias, and timeliness of materials Communicate: communicating information properly in its context (audience, media) in ICT environments
Software application	Word processing Spreadsheet Presentation software E-mail/communication tools Search engines/Internet

skills are also assessed for selected subjects (e.g., business administration in university students) and professions. This permits an estimation of the stage-specific significance of the competence domains described under Area B while simultaneously providing—in combination with grades and certificates—a stage-specific educational outcome measure. The major responsibility for conceptualizing these measurements belongs to the expert groups focusing on specific educational stages (see Chaps. 11–17, this volume). In addition, predictive outcome measures of early educational stages (e.g., language abilities acquired from early on as indicated by receptive vocabulary and grammar as well as by measures of phonological awareness) can be analyzed with respect to their relative significance to and interrelation with the domain-specific functional competencies assessed (see Area B). For Area D, but also for special adaptations in Area C, it is particularly the expert groups focusing on specific educational stages who are responsible for this.

4.3   Assessment Design and Outlook

The assessment frequencies of individual competence domains have been arranged to allow for systematic intra- and interindividual comparisons across ages and cohorts. At each measurement point, a set of competencies is tested in rather fixed combinations. Taken together, the realized design plan is guided by two principles: (a) enabling systematic comparisons of participants of the same age but in different educational stages or tracks, and (b) implementing rather fixed intervals between assessment waves, especially for those domains that will be modeled coherently over the life span. These intervals are shorter during lower stages in which greater changes are expected, whereas they become longer in older cohorts.

An important issue refers to the ways of linking competence scores across time in order to be able to analyze developmental change over the life course. Different linking strategies are employed in the assessment design (see Fischer et al. 2016): The tests for mathematical literacy are connected through common items, whereas tests for reading competence and scientific literacy have no common items in consequent assessment waves and are, therefore, linked via separate linking studies in which test instruments from two adjacent waves are administered to an additional sample.

Whereas at the beginning of NEPS, testing was paper-based and usually only one instrument was prepared to measure domain-specific competencies for every participant in an age group (regardless of their previous performance), the focus is now on branched or difficulty-tiered testing that allows us to examine competencies of low and high-performing test takers more precisely. Also, emphasis is placed on the methodological and technological advancement of computer-based competence tests that not only allow for difficulty-tiered and adaptive testing but also open up the possibility to use complex tasks (e.g., simulation tasks) and to analyze incidentally generated log- and process data as indicators of competence assessment.

All in all, the measurement of competencies over the life span is one of the major challenges facing NEPS. As well as selecting a broad, but nevertheless limited number of competencies to be included in NEPS, it is important to operationalize these competencies within a coherent framework and to convert them adequately into assessment instruments for all age groups and cohorts. It is essential for these tests to be sensitive to individual change between measurement cycles if we are to obtain a solid database for monitoring, describing, and analyzing educational processes that will deliver an in-depth understanding of developmental trajectories, their conditions, and their significance for (different) life courses.

References

American Association for the Advancement of Science (AAAS) (1993). *Benchmarks for science literacy. Project 2061*. New York, NY: Oxford University Press.

Arnold, K.-H., Lindner-Müller, C., & Riemann, R. (2009). *Erfassung sozialer Kompetenz bei Kindern und Erwachsenen. Eine Expertise für das Nationale Bildungspanel (NEPS)*. Bamberg, Germany: Leibniz-Institut für Bildungsverläufe, Nationales Bildungspanel.

Asendorpf, J. B. (2007). Persönlichkeitsmerkmale: Big Five. In S. Weinert (Koordination), *Expertise zur Erfassung von psychologischen Personmerkmalen bei Kindern im Alter von fünf Jahren im Rahmen des SOEP* (Data Documentation 20, pp. 30–35), Berlin, Germany: Deutsches Institut für Wirtschaftsforschung (DIW).

Baltes, P. B., Lindenberger, U., & Staudinger, U. M. (2006). Life-span theory in developmental psychology. In W. Damon & R. M. Lerner (Eds.), *Handbook of child psychology* (Vol. 1, pp. 569–664). New York, NY: Wiley.

Baumert, J., Klieme, E., Neubrand, M., Prenzel, M., Schiefele, U., Schneider, W., Stanat, P., Tillmann, K.-J., & Weiß, M. (Eds.). (2001). *PISA 2000: Basiskompetenzen von Schülerinnen und Schülern im internationalen Vergleich*. Opladen, Germany: Leske + Budrich.

Berendes, K., & Weinert, S. (2016). Selecting appropriate phonological awareness indicators for the kindergarten cohort of the National Educational Panel Study: A theoretical and empirical approach. In H.-P. Blossfeld, J. von Maurice, M. Bayer, & J. Skopek (Eds.), *Methodological issues of longitudinal surveys: The example of the National Educational Panel Study* (pp. 401–426). Wiesbaden, Germany: VS Verlag für Sozialwissenschaften.

Berendes, K., Weinert, S., Zimmermann, S., & Artelt, C. (2013). Assessing language indicators across the lifespan within the German National Educational Panel Study (NEPS). *Journal for Educational Research Online, 5*(2), 15–49.

Blatt, I., Voss, A., Kowalski, K., & Jarsinski, S. (2011). Messung von Rechtschreibleistung und empirische Kompetenzmodellierung. In U. Bredel (Ed.), *Weiterführender Orthographieunterricht* (pp. 226–256). Baltmannsweiler, Germany: Schneider Verlag Hohengehren.

Brown, A. L. (1987). Metacognition, executive control, self-regulation, and other more mysterious mechanisms. In F. E. Weinert & R. H. Kluwe (Eds.), *Metacognition, motivation, and understanding* (pp. 65–116). Hillsdale, NJ: Lawrence Erlbaum Associates.

Brunner, M., Lang, F. R., & Lüdtke, O. (2014). Erfassung der fluiden kognitiven Leistungsfähigkeit über die Lebensspanne im Rahmen der National Educational Panel Study: Expertise (NEPS Working Paper No. 42). Bamberg, Germany: Leibniz-Institut für Bildungsverläufe, Nationales Bildungspanel.

Bybee, R. W. (1997). Towards an understanding of literacy. In W. Gräber & C. Bolte (Eds.), *Scientific literacy – An international symposium* (pp. 37–68). Kiel, Germany: Institut für die Pädagogik der Naturwissenschaften (IPN).

Bynner, J. (2004). *Participation and progression: Use of British Cohort Study data in illuminating the role of basic skills and other factors* (Nuffield Review of 14–19 Education and Training Working Paper 9). Adelaide, Australia: National Centre for Vocational Education Research.

Cattell, R. B. (1971). *Abilities: Their structure, growth, and action.* Boston, MA: Houghton Mifflin.

Damon, W., & Lerner, R. M. (2006). *Handbook of child psychology* (Vol. 2). Hoboken, NJ: Wiley.

Denissen, J. J. A., Zarett, N. R., & Eccles, J. S. (2007). I like to do it, I'm able, and I know I am: Longitudinal couplings between domain-specific achievement, self-concept, and interest. *Child Development, 78*(2), 430–447. https://doi.org/10.1111/j.1467-8624.2007.01007.x.

Ebert, S., Lockl, K., Weinert, S., Anders, Y., Kluczniok, K., & Roßbach, G. (2013). Internal and external influences on vocabulary development in preschool age. *School Effectiveness and School Improvement, 24*, 138–154.

Educational Testing Service (ETS) (2002). *Digital transformation. A framework for ICT literacy.* Princeton, NJ: ETS.

Ehmke, T., Duchhardt, C., Geiser, H., Grüßing, M., Heinze, A., & Marschick, F. (2009). Kompetenzentwicklung über die Lebensspanne – Erhebung von mathematischer Kompetenz im Nationalen Bildungspanel. In A. Heinze & M. Grüßing (Eds.), *Mathematiklernen vom Kindergarten bis zum Studium. Kontinuität und Kohärenz als Herausforderung für den Mathematikunterricht* (pp. 313–327). Münster, Germany: Waxmann.

Eisenberg, M. B. (2008). Information literacy: Essential skills for the information age. *Journal of Library & Information Technology, 28*(2), 39–47.

Ericsson, K. A., Charness, N., Hoffman, R. R., & Feltovich, P.J. (2006). *The Cambridge handbook of expertise and expert performance.* Cambridge, MA: Cambridge University Press.

Esser, H. (2006). *Migration, Sprache und Integration. AKI-Forschungsbilanz* (Vol. 4). Berlin, Germany: Arbeitsstelle Interkulturelle Konflikte und gesellschaftliche Integration, Wissenschaftszentrum Berlin für Sozialforschung (WZB).

Fischer, L., Rohm, T., Gnambs, T., & Carstensen, C. H. (2016). *Linking the data of the competence tests* (NEPS Survey Paper No. 1). Bamberg, Germany: Leibniz Institute for Educational Trajectories.

Flavell, J. H. (1979). Metacognition and cognitive monitoring: A new area of cognitive-developmental inquiry. *American Psychologist, 34*, 906–911.

Forum Bildung. (2002). *Expertenberichte des Forum Bildung. Ergebnisse des Forum Bildung III.* Bonn, Germany: Forum Bildung.

Geary, D. C. (1995). Reflections of evolution and culture in children's cognition: Implications for mathematical development and instruction. *American Psychologist, 50*, 24–37.

Gehrer, K., Zimmermann, S. Artelt, C., & Weinert, S. (2013). NEPS framework for assessing reading competence and results from an adult pilot study. *Journal for Educational Research Online, 5*(2), 50–79.

Händel, M., Artelt, C., & Weinert, S. (2013). Assessing metacognitive knowledge: Development and evaluation of a test instrument. *Journal of Educational Research Online, 5*(2), 162–188.

Hahn, I., Schöps, K., Rönnebeck, S., Martensen, M., Hansen, S., Saß, S., Dalehefte, I. M., & Prenzel, M. (2013). Assessing scientific literacy over the lifespan – A description of the NEPS science framework and the test development. *Journal for Educational Research Online, 5*(2), 110–138.

Hecker, K., Südkamp, A., Leser, C., & Weinert, S. (2015). *Entwicklung eines Tests zur Erfassung von Hörverstehen auf Textebene bei Schülerinnen und Schülern der Klassenstufe 9* (NEPS

Working Paper No. 53). Bamberg, Germany: Leibniz-Institut für Bildungsverläufe, Nationales Bildungspanel.

Jude, N., & Klieme, E. (2007). Definitionen sprachlicher Kompetenz – ein Differenzierungsansatz. In B. Beck & E. Klieme (Eds.), *Sprachliche Kompetenzen. Konzepte und Messung. DESI-Studie* (pp. 9–22). Weinheim, Germany: Beltz.

Katz, I. R. (2007). Testing information literacy in digital environments: ETS's iSkills assessment. *Information Technology and Libraries, 26*, 3–12.

Katz, I. R., & Macklin, A. S. (2007). Information and communication technology (ICT) literacy: Integration and assessment in higher education. *Journal of Systemics, Cybernetics and Informatics, 5*, 50–55.

Knopp, E., Duchhardt, C., Ehmke, T., Grüßing, M., Heinze, A., & Neumann, I. (2014). Von Mengen, Zahlen und Operationen bis hin zu Daten und Zufall - Erprobung eines Itempools zum Erfassen der mathematischen Kompetenz von Kindergartenkindern. *Zeitschrift für Grundschulforschung, 7*(1), 20–34.

Konsortium Bildungsberichterstattung (2006). *Bildung in Deutschland. Ein indikatorengestützter Bericht mit einer Analyse zu Bildung und Migration.* Bielefeld, Germany: Bertelsmann.

Kwiatkowska-White, B., Kirby, J. R., & Lee, E. A. (2016). A longitudinal study of reading comprehension achievement from grades 3 to 10: Investigating models of stability, cumulative growth, and compensation. *Journal of Psychoeducational Assessment, 34*(2), 153–165. https://doi.org/10.1177/0734282915593188.

Lang, F. R., Kamin, S., Rohr, M., Stünkel, C., & Williger, B. (2014). Erfassung der fluiden kognitiven Leistungsfähigkeit über die Lebensspanne im Rahmen des Nationalen Bildungspanels: Abschlussbericht zu einer NEPS-Ergänzungsstudie (NEPS Working Paper No. 43). Bamberg, Germany: Leibniz-Institut für Bildungsverläufe, Nationales Bildungspanel.

Lockl, K., Händel, M., Haberkorn, K., & Weinert, S. (2016). Metacognitive knowledge in young children: Development of a new test procedure for first graders. In H.-P. Blossfeld, J. von Maurice, M. Bayer, & J. Skopek (Eds.), *Methodological issues of longitudinal surveys: The example of the National Educational Panel Study* (pp. 465–484). Wiesbaden, Germany: VS Verlag für Sozialwissenschaften.

Lorenz, C., Berendes, K., & Weinert, S. (2017). *Measuring receptive grammar in kindergarten and elementary school children in the National Educational Panel Study* (NEPS Survey Paper No. 24). Bamberg, Germany: Leibniz Institute for Educational Trajectories, National Educational Panel Study.

Lühe, J., Becker, M., Neumann, M., & Maaz, K. (2017). Geschlechtsspezifische Leistungsunterschiede in Abhängigkeit der sozialen Herkunft. Eine Untersuchung zur Interaktion zweier sozialer Kategorien. *Zeitschrift für Erziehungswissenschaft, 20,* 499–519.

National Council of Teachers of Mathematics (NCTM) (2003). *Principles and standards for school mathematics.* Reston, VA: Author.

National Research Council (NRC) (1999). *Being fluent with information technology.* Washington, DC: National Academy Press.

Neumann, M., Becker, M., & Maaz, K. (2014). Soziale Ungleichheiten in der Kompetenzentwicklung in der Grundschule und der Sekundarstufe I. *Zeitschrift für Erziehungswissenschaft, 17(2),* 167–203. https://doi.org/10.1007/s11618-013-0468-z.

Neumann, I., Duchhardt, C., Grüßing, M., Heinze, A., Knopp, E., & Ehmke, T. (2013). Modeling and assessing mathematical competence over the lifespan. *Journal for Educational Research Online, 5*(2), 80–109.

Nissen, A. (2017): Assessments verknüpfen – neue Aussagen ermöglichen. Verlinkung der mathematischen Kompetenzmessungen im Primarbereich des Nationalen Bildungspanels mit

TIMSS und dem Ländervergleich. Leuphana Universität Lüneburg: Lüneburg, Germany. URL: http://opus.uni-lueneburg.de/opus/volltexte/2018/14486/pdf/Annika_Nissen_Dissertation.pdf.

Nissen, A., Ehmke, T., Köller, O., & Duchhardt, C. (2015). Comparing apples with oranges? An approach to link TIMSS and the National Educational Panel Study in Germany via equipercentile and IRT methods. *Studies in Educational Evaluation, 47,* 58–67. https://doi.org/10.1016/j.stueduc.2015.07.003.

Organisation for Economic Co-operation and Development (OECD) (2003). The PISA 2003 assessment framework. Mathematics, reading, science and problem solving knowledge and skills. Paris, France: OECD.

Organisation for Economic Co-operation and Development (OECD) (2006). *Assessing scientific, reading and mathematical literacy. A framework for PISA 2006.* Paris, France: OECD.

Organisation for Economic Co-operation and Development (OECD) (2016). PISA 2015 assessment and analytical framework: Science, reading, mathematic and financial literacy. Paris, France: OECD.

Organisation for Economic Co-operation and Development (OECD) (2018). *The future of education and skills. The OECD learning framework 2030.* Paris, France: OECD (http://www.oecd.org/education/2030/learning-framework-2030.htm).

Osborne, J. F., & Dillon, J. (2008). *Science education in Europe: Critical reflections.* A report to the Nuffield Foundation. Retrieved December 10, 2010 from http://www.pollen-europa.net/pollen_dev/Images_Editor/Nuffield%20report.pdf.

Pfost, M., Hattie, J., Dörfler, T., & Artelt, C. (2014). Individual differences in reading development: Reviewing 25 years of empirical research on Matthew effects in reading. *Review of Educational Research, 84*(2), 203–244. https://doi.org/10.3102/0034654313509492.

Prenzel, M., Baumert, J., Blum, W., Lehmann, R., Leutner, D., Neubrand, M., Pekrun, R., Rost, J., & Schiefele, U. (2006). *PISA 2003. Untersuchungen zur Kompetenzentwicklung im Verlauf eines Schuljahres.* Münster, Germany: Waxmann.

Prenzel, M., Schöps, K., Rönnebeck, S., Senkbeil, M., Walter, O., Carstensen, C. H., & Hammann, M. (2007). Naturwissenschaftliche Kompetenz im internationalen Vergleich. In M. Prenzel, C. Artelt, J. Baumert, W. Blum, M. Hammann, E. Klieme, & R. Pekrun (PISA Konsortium Deutschland), *PISA 2006. Die Ergebnisse der dritten internationalen Vergleichsstudie* (pp. 63–106). Münster, Germany: Waxmann.

Rychen, D. S., & Salganik, L. H. (2001). *Defining and selecting key competences.* Göttingen, Germany: Hogrefe and Huber Publishers.

Rychen, D. S. M., & Salganik, L. H. (2003). *Key competences for a successful life and a well-functioning society.* Göttingen, Germany: Hogrefe and Huber Publishers.

Sammons, P. (1995). Gender, ethnic and socio-economic differences in attainment and progress: A longitudinal analysis of student achievement over 9 years. *British Educational Research Journal, 21,* 465–485.

Schiepe-Tiska, A., Rönnebeck, S., Schöps, K., Neumann, K., Schmidtner, S., Parchmann, I., & Prenzel, M. (2016). Naturwissenschaftliche Kompetenz bei PISA 2015 – Ergebnisse des internationalen Vergleichs mit einem modifizierten Testansatz. In K. Reiss, Ch. Sälzer, A. Schiepe-Tiska, E. Klieme, & O. Köller (Eds.), *PISA 2015. Eine Studie zwischen Kontinuität und Innovation* (pp. 45–98). Münster, Germany: Waxmann.

Senkbeil, M., Ihme, J. M., & Wittwer, J. (2013a). The Test of Technological and Information Literacy (TILT) in the National Educational Panel Study: Development, empirical testing, and evidence for validity. *Journal for Educational Research Online, 5*(2), 139–161.

Senkbeil, M., Ihme, J. M., & Wittwer, J. (2013b). Entwicklung und erste Validierung eines Tests zur Erfassung technologischer und informationsbezogener Literacy (TILT) für Jugendliche am Ende der Sekundarstufe I. *Zeitschrift für Erziehungswissenschaft, 16,* 671–691.

Spengler, M., Brunner, M., Martin, R., & Lüdtke, O. (2016). The role of personality in predicting (change in) students' academic success across four years of secondary school. *European Journal of Psychological Assessment, 32*, 95–103.

Stamov-Rossnagel, C., Bittner, J. V., & Staudinger, U. M. (2009). *Self-regulation across the lifespan: Its conceptualization and assessment in the National Educational Panel Study (NEPS)* (Expert report for NEPS). Bamberg, Germany: Leibniz Institute for Educational Trajectories, National Educational Panel Study.

Stanat, P. (2006). Schulleistungen von Jugendlichen mit Migrationshintergrund: Die Rolle der Zusammensetzung der Schülerschaft. In J. Baumert, P. Stanat, & R. Watermann (Eds.), *Herkunftsbedingte Disparitäten im Bildungswesen: Differenzielle Bildungsprozesse und Probleme der Verteilungsgerechtigkeit* (pp. 189–219). Wiesbaden, Germany: VS Verlag für Sozialwissenschaften.

Tenorth, H.-E. (2004). Stichwort: Grundbildung und Basiskompetenzen – Herkunft, Bedeutung und Probleme im Kontext allgemeiner Bildung. *Zeitschrift für Erziehungswissenschaft, 7*, 169–182.

van den Ham, A.-K., Ehmke, T., Nissen, A., & Roppelt, A. (2017). Assessments verbinden, Interpretationen erweitern? Lassen sich die mathematischen Kompetenzskalen im Nationalen Bildungspanel und im IQB-Ländervergleich 2012 verbinden? *Zeitschrift für Erziehungswissenschaft, 20*(1), 89–111. https://doi.org/10.1007/s11618-016-0686-2.

van den Ham, A.-K., Nissen, A., Ehmke, T., Sälzer, C., & Roppelt, A. (2014). Mathematische Kompetenz in PISA, IQB-Ländervergleich und NEPS - Drei Studien, gleiches Konstrukt? *Unterrichtswissenschaft, 42*(4), 321–341. doi:09201404321.

Wagner, H., Schöps, K., Hahn, I., Pietsch, M., & Köller, O. (2014). Konzeptionelle Äquivalenz von Kompetenzmessungen in den Naturwissenschaften zwischen NEPS, IQB-Ländervergleich und PISA. *Unterrichtswissenschaft, 42*(4), 301–320.

Weinert, S. (2000). Beziehungen zwischen Sprach- und Denkentwicklung. In H. Grimm (Ed.), *Sprachentwicklung* (Enzyklopädie der Psychologie C/III/3) (pp. 311–361). Göttingen, Germany: Hogrefe.

Weinert, F. E. (2001). Concept of competence: A conceptual clarification. In D. S. Rychen & L. H. Salganik (Eds.), *Defining and selecting key competencies* (pp. 45–65). Göttingen, Germany: Hogrefe and Huber Publishers.

Weinert, S. (2006). Sprachentwicklung. In W. Schneider & B. Sodian (Eds.), *Kognitive Entwicklung* (Enzyklopädie der Psychologie C/V/2) (pp. 609–719). Göttingen, Germany: Hogrefe.

Weinert, S. (2007a). Kompetenzentwicklung und Kompetenzstruktur im Vorschulalter. In M. Prenzel, I. Gogolin, & H.-H. Krüger (Eds.), *Kompetenzdiagnostik. Zeitschrift für Erziehungswissenschaft, Sonderheft 8* (pp. 89–106). Wiesbaden, Germany: VS Verlag für Sozialwissenschaften.

Weinert, S. (2007b). Wie Sprache das Wissen und Denken beeinflusst. In A. Bucher, A. M. Kalcher, & K. Lauermann (Eds.), *Sprache leben. Kommunizieren & Verstehen* (pp. 23–49). Wien, Austria: G & G Verlagsgesellschaft.

Weinert, S. (2017). Sprachliche Bildung – Sprache in der Bildung. In A. Krause, G. Lehmann, W. Thielmann, & C. Trautmann (Eds.), *Form und Funktion. Festschrift für Angelika Redder zum 65. Geburtstag* (pp. 595–608). Tübingen, Germany: Stauffenburg.

Weinert, S., Artelt, C., Prenzel, M., Senkbeil, M., Ehmke, T., & Carstensen, C. H. (2011). Development of competencies across the life span. In H.-P. Blossfeld, H.-G. Roßbach & J. von Maurice (Eds.), *Zeitschrift für Erziehungswissenschaft [Special Issue 14]. Education as a lifelong process: The German National Educational Panel Study (NEPS)* (pp. 67–86). Wiesbaden: VS Verlag für Sozialwissenschaften.

Weinert, S., Asendorpf, J. B., Beelmann, A., Doil, H., Frevert, S., Hasselhorn, M., & Lohaus, A. (2007). *Expertise zur Erfassung von psychologischen Personmerkmalen bei Kindern im Alter von fünf Jahren im Rahmen des SOEP* (Data Documentation 20). Berlin, Germany: Deutsches Institut für Wirtschaftsforschung (DIW).

Weinert, S., Ebert, S., & Dubowy, M. (2010). Kompetenzen und soziale Disparitäten im Vorschulalter. *Zeitschrift für Grundschulforschung, 1,* 32–45.

Weinert, F. E., & Helmke, A. (1997). *Entwicklung im Grundschulalter.* Weinheim, Germany: Beltz.

Wertsch, J. (1996). *Die gesellschaftliche Bildung des Bewußtseins.* Marburg, Germany: BdWi-Verlag.

Wirth, J., & Klieme, E. (2002). Computer literacy im Vergleich zwischen Nationen, Schulformen und Geschlechtern. *Unterrichtswissenschaft, 30,* 136–157.

Education Processes in Life-Course-Specific Learning Environments

5

Thomas Bäumer, Eckhard Klieme, Susanne Kuger, Kai Maaz, Hans-Günther Roßbach, Ludwig Stecher and Olaf Struck

Abstract

Pillar 2 of the German National Educational Panel Study (NEPS) conceptualizes and operationalizes the learning opportunities individuals experience throughout their lives. These learning opportunities can occur in different formal, nonformal, informal, and familial learning environments. NEPS is tapping them both quantitatively and

---

T. Bäumer (✉)
Leibniz Institute for Educational Trajectories, Bamberg, Germany
E-Mail: thomas.baeumer@lifbi.de

E. Klieme
German Institute of International Educational Research (DIPF), Frankfurt, Germany
E-Mail: klieme@dipf.de

S. Kuger
German Youth Institute (DJI), Munich, Germany
E-Mail: kuger@dji.de

K. Maaz
German Institute of International Educational Research (DIPF), Berlin, Germany
E-Mail: maaz@dipf.de

H.-G. Roßbach · O. Struck
University of Bamberg, Bamberg, Germany
E-Mail: hans-guenther.rossbach@uni-bamberg.de

O. Struck
E-Mail: olaf.struck@uni-bamberg.de

L. Stecher
University of Giessen, Gießen, Germany
E-Mail: Ludwig.Stecher@erziehung.uni-giessen.de

© Springer Fachmedien Wiesbaden GmbH, ein Teil von Springer Nature 2019
H.-P. Blossfeld and H.-G. Roßbach (eds.), *Education as a Lifelong Process*,
Edition ZfE 3, https://doi.org/10.1007/978-3-658-23162-0_5

qualitatively. The quality of learning opportunities is framed within an opportunity-use model to bring together a social-environmental and an individual perspective. The information provided covers what learning opportunities an individual uses, their duration and intensity and—whenever possible—an estimation of their quality. Also, relations and transitions between different learning environments are covered at some critical intersections (e.g., school entry). Whereas NEPS focuses on the individual perspective, it also asks different actors beside the target person to contribute to the assessment of learning environments in specific cohorts and at specific stages. This leads to a comprehensive view of the cumulation of learning experiences and their effects on competence development, educational biographies, and educational decisions.

Keywords

Education · Panel study · Learning Environments · Learning opportunities Educational quality

5.1 Introduction

During the life course, individuals experience educational processes in a variety of (synchronic or diachronic) formal, nonformal, informal, and familial learning environments. Chronologically, these can be conceived as a succession of different formal learning environments that structure and partly standardize the life course. This is especially true for the formal educational system in which individuals experience at least two compulsory learning environments (elementary school and secondary school). Different educational settings are experienced before and after formal schooling, and transitions between these consecutive learning environments also have to be taken into account. In Germany, many children attend Kindergarten or day care. After general school, individuals may attend vocational education and training, colleges and universities, and also engage in adult learning courses. During adulthood and the course of working life, additional learning environments are experienced that comprise or foster educational processes (e.g., training on the job, private studies, or mass media). Alongside the chronologically consecutive settings, it is also necessary to take synchronic, coexisting learning environments into account. Educational processes take place within a multitude of settings of a nonformal or informal nature such as the nonformal provisions in the youth welfare system or informal learning in youth clubs, from peers, or from the (mass) media. During childhood and early adolescence, participation in out-of-school activities offered by, for example, sports clubs or music schools are also relevant. Moreover, the family has to be considered, not only as a rather general condition and context for educational decisions but also as a learning environment itself. Thus, the surroundings of an individual that need to be considered in the National Educational Panel Study (NEPS) are composed of a complex interwoven network of different synchronic and chronological settings with different interconnections and transitions between them. In a life-course perspective, the cumulation of experiences in this complex web of learning environments leads to educational outcomes rather than experiences in a single setting. The main research questions NEPS is addressing are: What kind of learning opportunities are experienced by an individual during the life course? What do experiences in different learning environments look like? How are different learning environments related to each other? What kind of cumulative experiences across different learning environments exist? How do specific learning environments and the cumulation of educational experiences across learning environments relate to individual development and educational decisions? How are learning environments influencing educational returns? But conversely, it also asks what does the use of a learning environment depend on?

Pillar 2 tries to introduce two quite unique aspects to NEPS: First, we address a great variety of learning opportunities a person experiences throughout her or his life. These learning opportunities take place in different formal, nonformal, and informal learning environments. Formal settings, in particular, also comprise educational stages that a person passes through during her or his education. Therefore, Pillar 2 works in close cooperation with the NEPS stages. Due to the diversity and multiplicity of learning opportunities, our first task is to capture as much of these experiences as possible. Besides their mere occurrence, we are also surveying the duration and intensity of learning opportunities. To the best of our knowledge, this is the first time in education research that the analysis of learning opportunities tries to incorporate all learning environments and their interrelationships into one comprehensive approach. Our second task is to supplement, wherever possible, these quantitative aspects with an investigation of the quality of these learning opportunities. An innovative approach applies an overall framework model for all kinds of learning environments and learning opportunities.

5.2 Conceptual Perspectives

When considering education processes, one has to account for the interplay of different actors: at a minimum, someone who educates and someone who is educated. Therefore, teaching or instruction and learning are just two sides of the same coin (e.g., Vermunt and Verloop 1999). Nevertheless, until recently, teaching theories and learning theories have been developed relatively unrelated to each other. Approaches to learning used today—such as social cognitive theory (Bandura 1986) or social constructivist approaches based on Vygotsky's sociocultural theory (e.g., Reusser 2006)—point out that learning is a socially mediated process. The same is true for theories of teaching and instruction. Here, there has been a shift from teaching as the transmission of knowledge to teaching as the (co-)construction of knowledge (e.g., Wellenreuther 2004). Teaching then takes the form of supplying learning opportunities to the student, who, in turn, has to make use of these experiences. The basic notion of the interplay between learning opportunities and their use has been proposed by Helmut Fend (2006) as a model that captures the interaction between the learning environment and the individual. The model is nondeterministic and thus aligns with modern, constructivist views on learning. It is also consistent with recent theoretical developments in the psychology of motivation and interests that stress the role of the environment in offering support for autonomy, competence, and social relatedness (Ryan and Deci 2000). Support, however, needs to be perceived and taken up by the learner. From a systems theory point of view, the interplay of opportunities and their use can be understood as describing the exchange between the social-interactive and personal systems that constitute the basic operations of the educational system (Luhmann 2002). Thus, the concept of learning environments or, even more, that of learning opportunities points to the notion that education is always a relation between an actor and her or his (social) environment.

The terms formal, nonformal, and informal are often used to characterize learning, but unfortunately in a rather diffuse way (e.g., Overwien 2005). This is especially true in the case of formal learning, because the organizational issue of certifying an educational outcome is confounded with an individual process of achieving this outcome. It is not learning itself that is formal, nonformal, or informal, but the context in which it takes place. A more appropriate and well-established conceptualization of learning makes use of another distinction: that between intentional and incidental learning (e.g., Reber 1989; Sun et al. 2005). The term informal learning often connotes both forms of learning. Therefore, we propose that the terms formal, nonformal, and informal should not be applied to the learning process itself but to the contexts or environments in which learning takes place (e.g., Rauschenbach 2007). Both intentional and incidental learning can occur in all these different environments.

5.2.1 Diversity of Learning Environments

Education is associated most prominently with formal learning environments, notably schools. As a result, it is not surprising that education research is, for the most part, school research. NEPS Pillar 2 also draws from this research for its conceptualization—as will be seen later. *Formal learning environments* are always bound to a specific form of organization with characteristics such as hierarchical stratification, division of labor, goal directedness, and societal function. In addition, one of their major and distinguishing tasks is the certification of educational outcomes. Therefore, educational careers are governed to a great extent by this eligibility function. Personnel in formal learning environments act in an educationally intentional manner, and learning is also intentional but not self-directed (e.g., Fend 2001). In fact, at least in certain age groups (age 6 to 15 years, or for 9 school years), formal education is compulsory in Germany. Educational processes are highly structured in terms of content, timing, and order of subject matter. This strict analysis of formal learning environments holds especially for schools. However, in university, for example, at least the decision on what to study and, to some extent, also the course of instruction are self-determined. In the interest of stringency, we sacrifice certification as a constituting element and also denominate learning environments occurring before or after school and university as formal: namely, Kindergarten and firms or other enterprises in which vocational education and training and other forms of adult learning take place. This allows for a conceptualization of educational careers as trajectories through a more or less ordered educational system, starting in Kindergarten and going through elementary, lower, and upper secondary school or vocational education and training up to tertiary and further education. Not incidentally, this succession also comprises the sequence of stages within NEPS (see Chap. 1, this volume). In addition, comprehensive descriptions of the German educational system also take this broader view, accounting for Kindergartens at one end and employers and other providers of lifelong learning at the other (e.g., Cortina et al. 2008).

Nonformal and informal learning environments always accompany formal learning environments but differ markedly in that they are not compulsory but self-imposed. Nonformal learning environments are similar to formal learning environments due to the other-directed organization of learning, whereas learning in informal learning environments is essentially self-directed. Nonformal learning environments are also designated as being there for intentional learning, because their use is based on freedom of choice (Rauschenbach et al. 2004). As said before, it is not always easy to separate intentional and incidental learning processes in informal learning environments (e.g., Dohmen 2001). Nevertheless, to qualify as learning experiences, the individual has to perceive them, at least afterwards, as a learning opportunity. In contrast to formal and nonformal learning environments, the informal learning environment does not necessarily offer these learning opportunities intentionally. But, on the other hand, learning in informal learning environments is always self-directed (e.g., Boekaerts and Minnaert 1999). Also—again in contrast to formal and nonformal learning environments—the roles of teachers and students are not defined in a clear-cut way. Often, individuals learn all by themselves—as is the case for media use. But also in other informal learning environments such as peer groups, the roles of teachers and students are not defined at all or change constantly.

Another informal learning environment is of special interest in NEPS: the family. We treat the *familial learning environment* as a special unit of research, because it has a profound significance for education at least for children and adolescents (e.g., Melhuish et al. 2008). It is also the first and a very long-lasting learning environment that precedes, accompanies, and even outlasts most other learning environments. Certainly, families have long-lasting effects not only on educational outcomes and success but in every realm of life (e.g., Schneewind 2008). NEPS Pillar 2 pays special attention to the family of origin as a learning environment and looks at the efforts parents undertake to foster their children's advancement. Later in life, we also examine the individual's own family as a supportive environment for learning. However, Pillar 3 is responsible for families as a more general context for development and as a decision-making unit for educational choices (see Chap. 6, this volume).

5.2.2 Cumulation of Learning Opportunities

Educational processes take place in many different settings. They are influenced by the conditions of specific learning environments and the cumulation of experiences across different learning environments in the life course. All the aforementioned learning environments have to be considered, because education is more than learning and instruction in formal institutions. The family is usually the first environment in which learning opportunities are offered to a child. From birth onward, children interact with their parents, and there is strong evidence that the home learning environment exerts a profound influence on cognitive and social development (e.g., Bradley et al. 2001). Most children then experience a second learning environment: Kindergarten. From age 3 to 6, they spend a great amount of their time in this setting. Even at this young age, children experience additional learning opportunities of a nonformal or informal kind. This continues through the course of formal schooling, which is certainly the main though not the sole source of learning opportunities in childhood and adolescence. Over the course of life, the individual is confronted with an increasing quantity of learning opportunities. From a biographical perspective, single learning environments then lose relevance for the individual. In our opinion, especially for schools and teachers, this should not be treated as a threat to their effectiveness but as a relief from liability. Formal, nonformal, informal, and familial learning environments thus form a complex web of synchronic as well as chronological learning opportunities. Little is known about their cumulative effects as well as their potential reciprocal, oppositional, or diminishing effects. As well as registering all the learning opportunities experienced, it is also necessary to account for the relations between different learning environments. Again, this holds for both a chronological and a synchronic perspective. In a chronological perspective, it is particularly necessary to consider the transitions between successive formal learning environments. NEPS Pillar 2 is predominantly interested in what these transitions imply for the individual, and what measures the learning environments offer to facilitate the transition. A synchronic perspective has to include the relations of formal learning environments to nonformal and informal learning environments (e.g., use of subsidiary offers) as well as the relation of the family to formal learning environments (e.g., parental involvement).

To map the complex web of learning opportunities, some additional points should be considered: Only some learning opportunities can be surveyed retrospectively. Schooling history is one example. But even in such cases, it is only the mere episodes that can be examined. If one wants to gain a comprehensive picture of other learning opportunities and of some other features of these as well, one can examine only a limited time period. In NEPS, we decided to limit this time period to approximately one year back. Therefore, richer information on learning opportunities is possible only from one year before a single panel wave. This makes it necessary to take a longitudinal perspective and observe different cohorts. A second point is that the quantification of learning opportunities should not stop at documenting their mere occurrence. Whenever possible, we therefore also assess duration and intensity of the single learning opportunities. Last, as said before, formal learning environments correspond in most cases to the stages of NEPS. Therefore, Pillar 2 focuses on nonformal, informal, and familial learning environments and works on formal learning environments in close cooperation with the stages of the NEPS.

Whereas there are a lot of findings on the effects of the occurrence of learning opportunities, especially in economic research (e.g., Heckman et al. 2010), an additional feature has to be considered: Not only quantitative effects but also the influence of the quality of learning opportunities is of strong significance.

5.2.3 Quality of Learning Opportunities

Over the last few years, educational research has gained a basic understanding of the core factors of learning opportunities (e.g., Hugener et al. 2009; Klieme et al. 2009; Klieme and Rakoczy 2008; Kuger and Klieme 2016; Meyer 2005; Scheerens 2008; Seidel and Shavelson 2007). There is even a lot of shared understanding of these factors across school-based research and research on nonformal and informal, for example, out-of-school activities (e.g., Mahoney et al. 2005; Miller 2003) as well as on all-day provision at school (e.g., Radisch et al. 2008; Stecher et al. 2009). The core factors of learning opportunities apply first of all to the interaction between the teaching and the learning person. Therefore, they are often designated as process quality. Four basic factors (more precisely, three plus one, as will be shown below), which hold in a rather general sense, can be distinguished: *Structure*, as a basic factor of learning opportunities, relates to the arrangement of the educational processes taking place in the learning environment, thus providing, for example, safeness, stability, or clarity of rules to the learner. *Support* is reflected in positive emotional relations to peers and adults in the learning environment, understanding, feedback, support for autonomy and competence, and social embedding. *Challenge* relates to tasks that are not too demanding but also not too simple to be solved by the learner, thus leading her or him to a "zone of proximal development." Such tasks will also be cognitively activating. *Orientation* can be seen in, for example, shared values and norms, coherence among members of the group/organization, and clear expectations. Whereas the first three factors describe the educational processes directly and can therefore be observed straightforwardly, orientation impacts more indirectly by influencing the behavior of the actors in the educational process. In the following, we refer to these four basic dimensions as "SSCO." Although conceptualized originally in relation to (classroom) instruction, there have been several efforts to describe other learning environments with SSCO as well. Moreover, other conceptualizations have been proposed that we can easily link to the SSCO model. Table 5.1 recapitulates some of these concepts. Because orientation is not always present in other conceptualizations and can be seen as an overarching principle that is related to structure, support, and challenge, please note that it is not included in the table.

Table 5.1 Concepts of educational quality

Learning environment	Structure	Support	Challenge	Reference
Formal: School	Classroom management, clarity and structure	Supportive climate	Cognitive activation and deep content	Klieme et al. (2009)
Formal: School	Classroom instruction and management	Student–teacher social interactions	Student–teacher academic interactions	Wang et al. (1993)
Formal: School	Efficient classroom management	Personal learning support	Cognitively activating elements	Kunter and Baumert (2006)
Formal: Elementary school	Classroom organization	Emotional supports	Instructional supports	Pianta and Hamre (2009)
Nonformal/Informal: After-school program	Structure/Organization	Social climate	Focus on skill building and mastery	Mahoney et al. (2007)
General/Formal: Teaching	Regulation function of teaching	Affective function of teaching	Processing function of teaching	Vermunt and Verloop (1999)
General/Formal: Learning	Metacognitive regulation activities	Affective learning strategies	Cognitive processing activities	Vermunt and Verloop (1999)
General: Environments	System maintenance	Relationship	Personal development	Insel and Moos (1974)

Alongside these four basic factors that are proximal to the learning opportunity under consideration, it is also necessary to allow for more distal factors in which the basic factors of process quality are embedded and take the multilayered structure of learning environments into account. For a formal learning environment, SSCO relates basically and especially to the instruction in specific subjects. However, it can also be differentiated on a school level, especially when orientation is considered (e.g., school regulations, social and cognitive climate, achievement expectations). We use Fend's (2006) opportunity–use model of educational quality as refined by Helmke (2007) and Klieme (2006) as a kind of overarching theoretical framework. This depicts not only SSCO but also structural characteristics of the learning environment (e.g., in a classroom setting, the class size, class schedule, or class composition as well as school size or school composition on a broader level). This proximal learning environment itself is embedded within a broader context with, for example, specific socioeconomic compositions. The same conceptualization holds true for the family. The learning opportunities in the familial learning environments—such as in a homework situation—can also be described in terms of the structure, support, and challenge given by parents. These interactions are assumed to be influenced by the parents' educational orientations and further characteristics (e.g., their general educational level) and the home environment with its structural characteristics (e.g., available books, family income). The family, again, is itself embedded in a regional-local environment and its social networks. The same is true for nonformal and informal learning environments. The interactions between the person receiving learning opportunities (target person) and the person(s) offering them (e.g., music teacher, sports trainer, peers) take place under circumstances that can be described using more structural as well as more contextual features.

In relation to the design of NEPS, we address these differentiated levels of learning opportunities within learning environments. Thus, for each educational setting of focal interest, we consider characteristics contained in the following three dimensions:

- *SSCO*: (a) Structure: safeness, stability, clarity of rules, monitoring, and scaffolding; (b) Support: positive emotional relations to peers and adults, understanding, feedback, support for autonomy, competence, and social embedding; (c) Challenge: demanding tasks, cognitive activation, and adequate pacing; and (d) Orientation: shared values and norms of the actors, coherence among actors, general attitudes and orientations related to educational processes and attitudes toward attributions of academic achievements. These characteristics are proposed to be valid in every educational setting, regardless of its formal versus nonformal or informal set up. Nevertheless, the specific features establishing the basic factors of structure, support, challenge, and orientation will differ between various learning environments. It has to be kept in mind that SSCO is also valid on more aggregated levels such as the study program or the school as a whole.
- *Structural characteristics*: Comparatively persistent general conditions for educational processes in the different learning environments. For example, with regard to the learning environment school, the conditions of the class in the general education system: class size and class composition, number of lessons in different subjects according to the class schedule, equipment of the class, education and experience of teachers, and so forth; with regard to the school level: size and structure of the whole school. This scheme can be related easily to nonformal and informal settings such as sports groups. For familial learning environments, similar features can be proposed such as family size, family composition, or time and material resources.
- *Contextual characteristics*: Framing conditions of the learning environment under consideration. For example, with regard to the learning environment school: regional-local characteristics such as urban/rural, unemployment, migration structure, and so forth. For the family, contextual characteristics are treated in more detail in NEPS Pillar 3 (see Chap. 6, this volume).

As proposed in the opportunity–use model, the multilayered characteristics of learning opportunities do not unfold their relevance by themselves, but have to be perceived and used by the individual (as the target person whose educational biography stands at the center of NEPS). Especially for the *perception* of SSCO, we expect the frame of reference to become broader with age. In preschool age, for example, the Kindergarten group seems to be the appropriate learning environment to be explored, whereas in higher education, the study program should be analyzed. The *use* made of learning opportunities may be characterized by constructs such as learning activities or study time. Here, one should bear in mind that outcomes of earlier learning opportunities may also function in the use of later ones. That is to say that competencies and motivation will also influence the use of learning opportunities (see Chaps. 4 and 9, this volume). In addition, these characteristics will become more and more prominent with age. Therefore, the characteristics of the target person in the use of learning opportunities are not at the center of NEPS Pillar 2, but will be treated in some stage-specific survey topics.

The just-mentioned characteristics have been conceptualized mainly within school and teacher effectiveness research. Especially for secondary schooling in general and for math instruction in particular, some major research results are available (e.g., Kunter et al. 2005; Lipowsky et al. 2009) and there are also some for German language instruction (e.g., Klieme et al. 2010). In sum, research shows that challenge is related mainly to competence development and achievement outcomes, whereas support is related to motivation and interest development. Finally, structure as well as orientation seem to serve as a necessary, but not sufficient condition for the quality of education. There is also evidence from research that proximal characteristics influence educational outcomes to a greater extent than more distal ones. Nevertheless, this does not mean that these features are not relevant, especially when taking educational, sociological, and economic perspectives into account. For example, the monitoring of returns to educational inputs and guiding policy in the design of the educational system requires information on the more distal characteristics (see Chap. 8, this volume).

Going back to the succession of formal learning environments in the educational system, research on elementary schools is sparse compared with research on secondary schooling. But results show that the relevant features are much the same as the aforementioned ones (e.g., Helmke and Weinert 1997). Concerning Kindergarten, research conducted so far has relied mainly on global dimensions of educational quality. However, by differentiating structural, orientational, and process quality, the conception strongly resembles the framework of Pillar 2 (e.g., Tietze et al. 2005).

This holds even more when we follow the educational career after compulsory schooling. Whereas there is some information on formal learning environments in higher education and vocational education and training, findings on further education are sparse – maybe due to the fact that occupational settings are seldom treated as formal learning environments. Nevertheless, we conceive these educational settings as offering structure, support, and challenge to the individual and shared educational orientations just like the other formal settings that have been conceptualized more frequently from this perspective.

As noted above, there are hints that our concept of educational quality also holds for nonformal and informal settings (e.g., Mahoney et al. 2007; Miller 2003). This is true for the family as well (e.g., Melhuish et al. 2008; Wild and Gerber 2007).

5.3 Perspectives of Analysis

The basic perspectives of analysis within NEPS Pillar 2 are twofold: They can be conducted on an environmental/institutional level or an individual level.

On the level of learning environments, interest focuses on the quality of single learning opportunities. One can ask how many persons attend different learning environments (e.g., private lessons, music lessons, sport clubs) and how do they rate the quality of education within these learning environments. One can ask how learning environments of the same kind (e.g., secondary schools, Kindergartens) differ, and how do their differences relate to individual development. A wealth of information is being provided on level of the learning environment. This includes structural and contextual characteristics and especially also features of the basic factor "orientation" on the level of the school or Kindergarten. Therefore, through its longitudinal design, the NEPS is also addressing questions concerning the long-term effectiveness of the learning environment and even changes and developments of effectiveness over time (e.g., Klieme and Steinert 2008).

On the level of the individual, we ask about the extent of use and the consequences of different learning opportunities and their cumulation over the life course. Questions are: What learning opportunities are used to what extent, permanence, and intensity? What are the individual and social determinants on which this usage depends? What is the role of the family as a special learning environment? Are there out-of-school educational biographies? Is the perception and evaluation of different learning environments related? Does the use of learning opportunities depend on experiences of their quality or the quality of antecedent learning opportunities? How do amount and quality of learning opportunities relate to competence development? What influence on professional development can be attributed to the learning environment? One unique feature of NEPS is that we can take a look at all the relevant learning environments in the educational biography of the individual in a longitudinal perspective. This is delivering a rich source of data to the scientific community interested in educational research.

5.4 Surveying Learning Environments

After depicting the conceptual frame of NEPS Pillar 2, we now want to show some operationalizations of the aforementioned constructs that are already being implemented. It should be noted that in relation to the living conditions of the actors in particular stages, the focus is on different learning opportunities such as homework or private lessons in the context of students' familial learning environments; work experiences as learning opportunities at the end of schooling or during university studies; or advanced training courses in further education in adulthood.

Depending on the specific cohort and stage under observation, information on learning opportunities is captured from different actors. Whereas in adult samples, we examine only the target person's view, in samples of children and adolescents, data is provided by parents as well as educational and administrative staff. The latter give information mainly on contextual, structural, and compositional characteristics of the factual learning environment and also on their educational orientations. Information from parents relates especially to the home and out-of-home learning environments they offer to their children.

A note has to be made on the assessment of SSCO. The process quality of learning opportunities is not easy to grasp. Different perspectives have to be taken into account that all have advantages and disadvantages depending on the dimension under consideration. For process quality of classroom instruction, Clausen (2002) has argued that a comprehensive view necessitates the triangulation of the perspectives of teachers, students, and external observers. In NEPS, an external observation is not feasible—due not only to assessment costs but also to issues of data privacy in scientific use files. Moreover, in some cohorts and for some learning environments (e.g., nonformal and informal learning opportunities) in general, only target persons (i.e., students) are surveyed. On the one hand, students are reliable sources, because they have much more experience with a specific setting than an external observer. On the other hand, however, their evaluations are prone to subjective bias. For example, it is hard to assess challenge independently from one's own competence level. Students also tend to evaluate instruction from a global perspective (e.g., Gruehn 2000). Nevertheless, student achievement correlates more strongly with student self-reports than reports from the teacher's or external observer's perspective. In Kindergarten, children are too young to be surveyed on process quality. Here we have to rely solely on the perspective of their educators.

Another issue is the limited amount of interview time or item numbers within NEPS. We decided primarily to gain a comprehensive picture of the learning opportunities an individual perceives by quantifying their use and complementing this picture whenever possible with some quality aspects. Overall, assessment of quality has to remain quite global. Nevertheless, we have succeeded in capturing quality features for most learning environments under consideration. We shall close with some examples of the corresponding efforts made so far.

A study was conducted to relate process quality in Kindergarten as assessed by trained observers to variables collected in the educator's questionnaire of the NEPS Kindergarten sample (Bäumer and Roßbach 2016). It can be shown that on a global level, Kindergarten quality can be reproduced quite well by the use of questionnaire data. But it has to be stressed that one should not expect to find one single indicator of Kindergarten quality, and any conclusions, especially causal ones, have to be drawn with caution.

In collaboration with NEPS Stage 7 (Higher Education and the Transition to Work; see Chap. 16, this volume), an online survey was conducted targeting the process quality of study programs from the perspective of students. This resulted in the following measurement model of the core factors: Structure is represented by the factors "coordination of courses offered" and "structuredness of lectures and classes." Support comprises "rapport with lecturer," "rapport with fellow students," and "motivation." Challenge is illustrated by "pressure to perform," "meaning orientation," "reproduction orientation," "knowledge construction" and "knowledge transmission." Finally, orientation is captured with respect to "research," "practice," and "interdisciplinarity" (Schaeper and Weiß 2016).

As a last example, we discuss assessment of the quality of nonformal learning opportunities—for example, practical courses for adolescents during their time at school and courses of further education in adulthood. Here, the battery of questions has to be very short, usually 9 to 10 single items to cover at least three dimensions (structure, support, challenge). Whereas an exploratory analysis resulting in one single principal component showed a tendency toward an overall evaluation, in confirmatory analyses, a multidimensional solution in line with the core factors is usually superior to a single solution.

In the following, we shall give a short overview of the constructs measured and published so far. Because data is provided separately for each of the six NEPS Starting Cohorts (SC) and every SC has a focus on different learning environments, we describe the measurements for the SC individually. Detailed information is available on the NEPS website (www.neps-data.de). Corresponding construct papers are not yet available. They will be published by the end of 2019.

The main focus of *SC 1 Newborns* (see Chap. 11, this volume) with respect to learning opportunities is on parent–child activities. These have been surveyed in all four waves (2012–2015; age of children 0.5 to 3 years) that are available as Scientific Use Files (SUF). There are age-specific versions of the items, with at least one "anchor item" (reading to the child). As a special case, parent–child activities were also assessed by video observation in Waves 1 to 3 (Sommer and Mann 2015), giving additional information on, for example, parental sensitivity and responsivity. Beginning with Wave 2, pedagogical staff in early childhood education and care (ECEC) settings were also surveyed with drop-off questionnaires. Because these instruments are based largely on instruments developed for SC 2, we shall discuss them in the next section.

SC 2 Kindergarten (see Chap. 12, this volume) is an institution-based sample. Therefore, questionnaires for educators and heads of the ECEC facilities are a main focus of Pillar 2. These questionnaires were administered in Waves 1 and 2. In Wave 3, the main sample of target children were enrolled in elementary school. Instruments for teachers and school principals again draw on instruments from SC 3 and will be discussed later. SUF are available from Wave 1 to Wave 6, targeting Grade 4 students (last year of elementary school in Germany). The educators' and head teachers' questionnaires contain a wealth of information on structural and compositional characteristics of the ECEC settings and groups of the target children (e.g., group size, opening hours, average age, and age variability of children). Staff characteristics (e.g., years of education, further training) are also included. Process quality is captured in terms of materials and activities offered to the children. The focus of the parent interview is again on parent–child activities and, later, on parental monitoring. Parents are also asked about the out-of-home activities of their children. From Wave 3 onward, school-related variables are also assessed.

Variables related to school are the main focus of *SC 3 Grade 5* (see Chap. 13, this volume). Data for Wave 1 to Wave 7 have been published so far, covering Grade 5 to Grade

10. Parents as well as target students give information on private tuition, parental support of school work, and satisfaction with school. Students also give information on instruction, extracurricular activities at school, and school involvement. However, students also report out-of-school activities such as sports or courses at music or art schools. Questionnaires for teachers cover aspects of instructional quality but also such aspects as teacher attitudes, teamwork, or further education. School principals give information mainly on structural (e.g., school size, facilities) and compositional (teaching staff and students body) characteristics of the school. Every second year (Grade 6, Grade 8, Grade 10), they provide data on all-day school programs at their schools.

The same information is available for *SC 4 Grade 9* (see Chaps. 14 and 15, this volume), as long as target students stay in school. Students leaving school are followed up individually. Information from context persons is no longer available. The SUF for SC 4 comprises nine waves so far. At the first interview, students were asked about support in the transition out of school (into work). In later waves, they were surveyed on the quality of vocational training when they were in last year of training.

As said before, the main focus of Pillar 2 regarding *SC 5 First-Year Students* (see Chap. 16, this volume) is on the process quality of study programs. The corresponding online questionnaires have been conducted in Wave 2 (2011) and Wave 6 (2013/2014). Other online questionnaires provide information on learning groups, university activities, and voluntary activities (Wave 4 and Wave 8). SUFs for Wave 1 to Wave 10 are already available.

The adult sample *SC 6 Adults* (see Chap. 17, this volume) is concerned mainly with further education courses. Besides quantifying these courses, target persons also evaluate their quality. They also give information on more informal learning opportunities. Data on these issues is provided in each of the eight waves published as SUF so far. In addition, information on work tasks (variety of requirements, range of activity) is available for Wave 4 and Wave 8. These not only demand knowledge but also influence informal learning. Data on volunteer activities are available for Wave 6.

To conclude, despite the challenges associated with assessing the core factors of Pillar 2, results have shown that they can be surveyed quite successfully. Moreover, data on the structural and contextual characteristics of the learning environment, which also capture the multitude of learning opportunities itself, provide a rich resource for different analyses by the different academic disciplines conducting education research.

5.5 Outlook

During their educational careers, individuals pass through a variety of formal, nonformal, and informal learning environments. It can be said that the succession of these settings as well as their synchronic structuring mold—at least in part—an individual's educational career. The major advantage, challenge, and innovative potential of NEPS is that it brings together diverse and, in some cases, perhaps conflicting learning environments within a general framework. The framework we propose describes educational environments as offering learning opportunities that the individual can make use of, and this leads to a cumulation of learning experiences across time and settings. By focusing on the educational quality of the learning opportunities, it becomes possible to examine the educational system and its effects on the individual's educational career as a whole, thereby relating diverse findings to each other and combining them to gain a deeper understanding of the educational processes taking place in Germany.

References

Bandura, A. (1986). *Social foundations of thought and action: A social cognitive theory.* Englewood Cliffs, NJ: Prentice-Hall.

Bäumer, T., & Roßbach, H.-G. (2016). Measurement of preschool quality within the National Educational Panel Study – Results from a methodological study. In H.-P. Blossfeld, J. von Maurice, M. Bayer, & J. Skopek (Eds.), *Methodological issues of longitudinal surveys. The example of the National Educational Panel Study* (pp. 543–560). Wiesbaden, Germany: Springer VS.

Boekaerts, M., & Minnaert, A. (1999). Self-regulation with respect to informal learning. *International Journal of Educational Research, 31,* 533–544.

Bradley, R. H., Corwyn, R. F., Burchinal, M., McAdoo, H. P., & Coll, C. G. (2001). The home environments of children in the United States Part II: Relations with behavior development through age thirteen. *Child Development, 72,* 1868–1886.

Clausen, M. (2002). *Qualität von Unterricht – Eine Frage der Perspektive?* Münster, Germany: Waxmann.

Cortina, K. S., Baumert, J., Leschinsky, A., Mayer, K. U., & Trommer, L. (Eds.). (2008). *Das Bildungswesen in der Bundesrepublik Deutschland: Strukturen und Entwicklungen im Überblick* (2nd ed.). Reinbek bei Hamburg, Germany: Rowohlt.

Dohmen, G. (2001). *Das informelle Lernen. Die internationale Erschließung einer bisher vernachlässigten Grundform menschlichen Lernens für das lebenslange Lernen aller.* Bonn, Germany: BMBF.

Fend, H. (2001). *Qualität im Bildungswesen: Schulforschung zu Systembedingungen, Schulprofilen und Lehrerleistung* (2nd ed.). Weinheim, Germany: Juventa.

Fend, H. (2006). *Neue Theorie der Schule. Einführung in das Verstehen von Bildungssystemen.* Wiesbaden, Germany: VS Verlag für Sozialwissenschaften.

Gruehn, S. (2000). *Unterricht und schulisches Lernen: Schüler als Quellen der Unterrichtsbeschreibung* (Pädagogische Psychologie und Entwicklungspsychologie: Bd. 12). Münster, Germany: Waxmann.

Heckman, J. J., Moon, S. H., Pinto, R., Savelyev, P. A., & Yavitz, A. (2010). The rate of return to the HighScope Perry Preschool Program. *Journal of Public Economics, 94,* 114–128.

Helmke, A. (2007). *Unterrichtsqualität – erfassen, bewerten, verbessern* (5th ed.). Seelze, Germany: Klett.

Helmke, A. & Weinert, F. E. (1997). Unterrichtsqualität und Leistungsentwicklung: Ergebnisse aus dem SCHOLASTIK-Projekt. In F. E. Weinert & A. Helmke (Eds.), *Entwicklung im Grundschulalter* (pp. 241–251). Weinheim, Germany: Psychologie Verlags Union.

Hugener, I., Pauli, C., Reusser, K., Lipowsky, F., Rakoczy, K., & Klieme, E. (2009). Teaching patterns and learning quality in Swiss and German mathematics lessons. *Learning and Instruction, 19,* 66–78.

Insel, P. M., & Moos, R. H. (1974). Psychological environments. Expanding the scope of human ecology. *American Psychologist, 29*, 179–188.

Klieme, E. (2006). Empirische Unterrichtsforschung: Aktuelle Entwicklungen, theoretische Grundlagen und fachspezifische Befunde. *Zeitschrift für Pädagogik, 52*, 765–773.

Klieme, E., Pauli, C., & Reusser, K. (2009). The Pythagoras Study – Investigating effects of teaching and learning in Swiss and German mathematics classrooms. In T. Janik & T. Seidel (Eds.), *The power of video studies in investigating teaching and learning in the classroom* (pp. 137–160). Münster, Germany: Waxmann.

Klieme, E., & Rakoczy, K. (2008). Empirische Unterrichtsforschung und Fachdidaktik. Outcome-orientierte Messung und Prozessqualität des Unterrichts. *Zeitschrift für Pädagogik, 54*, 222–237.

Klieme, E., & Steinert, B. (2008). Schulentwicklung im Längsschnitt. Ein Forschungsprogramm und erste explorative Analysen. In M. Prenzel & J. Baumert (Eds.), *Vertiefende Analysen zu PISA 2006* (Zeitschrift für Erziehungswissenschaft: Sonderheft 10, pp. 221–238). Wiesbaden, Germany: VS Verlag für Sozialwissenschaften.

Klieme, E., Steinert, B., & Hochweber, J. (2010). Zur Bedeutung von Schulqualität für Unterricht und Lernergebnisse. In W. Bos, E. Klieme, & O. Köller (Eds.). *Schulische Lerngelegenheiten und Kompetenzentwicklung* (pp. 227–251). Münster, Germany: Waxmann.

Kuger, S., & Klieme, E. (2016). Dimensions in context assessment. In S. Kuger, E. Klieme, N. Jude, & D. Kaplan (Eds.), *Assessing contexts of learning. An international perspective* (pp. 3–38). Cham, Switzerland: Springer.

Kunter, M., & Baumert, J. (2006). Who is the expert? Construct and criteria validity of student and teacher ratings of instruction. *Learning Environments Research, 9*, 231–251.

Kunter, M., Brunner, M., Baumert, J., Klusmann, U., Krauss, S., Blum, W., Jordan, A., & Neubrand, M. (2005). Der Mathematikunterricht der PISA-Schülerinnen und -Schüler: Schulformunterschiede in der Unterrichtsqualität. *Zeitschrift für Erziehungswissenschaft, 8*, 502–520.

Lipowsky, F., Rakoczy, K., Pauli, C., Drollinger-Vetter, B., Klieme, E., & Reusser, K. (2009). Quality of geometry instruction and its short-term impact on students' understanding of the Pythagorean theorem. *Learning and Instruction, 19*, 527–537.

Luhmann, N. (2002). *Das Erziehungssystem der Gesellschaft*. Darmstadt, Germany: Wissenschaftliche Buchgesellschaft.

Mahoney, J. L., Larson, R. W., & Eccles, J. S. (Eds.). (2005). *Organized activities as contexts of development: Extracurricular activities, after-school and community programs*. Mahwah, NJ: Erlbaum.

Mahoney, J. L., Parente, M. E., & Lord, H. (2007). After-school program engagement: Links to child competence and program quality and content. *Elementary School Journal, 107*, 385–404.

Melhuish, E. C., Phan, M. B., Sylva, K., Sammons, P., Siraj-Blatchford, I., & Taggart, B. (2008). Effects of the home learning environment and preschool center experience upon literacy and numeracy development in early primary school. *Journal of Social Issues, 64*, 95–114.

Meyer, H. (Ed.). (2005). *Was ist guter Unterricht?* (3rd ed.). Berlin, Germany: Cornelsen.

Miller, B. M. (2003). *Critical hours: Afterschool programs and educational success*. Quincy, MA: Nellie Mae Education Foundation. Retrieved September 14, 2010, from http://www.nmefdn.org/uploads/Critical_Hours.pdf

Overwien, B. (2005). Stichwort: Informelles Lernen. *Zeitschrift für Erziehungswissenschaft, 8*, 339–355.

Pianta, R. C., & Hamre, B. K. (2009). Conceptualization, measurement, and improvement of classroom process: Standardized observation can leverage capacity. *Educational Researcher, 38*, 109–119.

Radisch, F., Fischer, N., Stecher, L., & Klieme, E. (2008). Qualität von unterrichtsnahen Angeboten an Ganztagsschulen. In T. Coelen & H. U. Otto (Eds.), *Grundbegriffe Ganztagsbildung. Das Handbuch* (pp. 910–917). Wiesbaden, Germany: VS Verlag für Sozialwissenschaften.

Rauschenbach, T. (2007). Im Schatten der formalen Bildung: Alltagsbildung als Schlüsselfrage der Zukunft. *Diskurs Kindheits- und Jugendforschung, 2,* 439–453.

Rauschenbach, T., Leu, H. R., Lingenauber, S., Mack, W., Schilling, M., Schneider, K., & Züchner, I. (2004). *Non-formale und informelle Bildung im Kindes- und Jugendalter. Konzeptuelle Grundlagen für einen Nationalen Bildungsbericht* (Bildungsreform Bd. 6). Berlin, Germany: BMBF.

Reber, A. S. (1989). Implicit learning and tacit knowledge. *Journal of Experimental Psychology: General, 118,* 219–235.

Reusser, K. (2006). Konstruktivismus – vom epistemologischen Leitbegriff zur Erneuerung der didaktischen Kultur. In M. Baer, M. Fuchs, P. Füglister, K. Reusser, & H. Wyss (Eds.), *Didaktik auf psychologischer Grundlage. Von Hans Aeblis kognitionspsychologischer Didaktik zur modernen Lehr- und Lernforschung* (pp. 151–168). Bern, Switzerland: h.e.p.

Ryan, R. M., & Deci, E. L. (2000). Self-determination theory and the facilitation of intrinsic motivation, social development, and well-being. *American Psychologist, 55,* 68–78.

Schaeper, H., & Weiß, T. (2016). The conceptualization, development, and validation of an instrument for measuring the formal learning environment in higher education. In H.-P. Blossfeld, J. von Maurice, M. Bayer, & J. Skopek (Eds.), *Methodological issues of longitudinal surveys. The example of the National Educational Panel Study* (pp. 267–290). Wiesbaden, Germany: Springer VS.

Scheerens, J. (2008). *Review of research on school and instructional effectiveness.* Enschede, Netherlands: University of Twente. Retrieved September 14, 2010, from http://www.reva-education.eu/download.php?file_url=IMG/pdf/scheerens_report.pdf

Schneewind, K. A. (2008). Sozialisation und Erziehung im Kontext der Familie. In R. Oerter & L. Montada (Eds.), *Entwicklungspsychologie* (6th ed., pp. 117–145). Weinheim, Germany: Beltz.

Seidel, T., & Shavelson, R. J. (2007). Teaching effectiveness research in the past decade: The role of theory and research design in disentangling meta-analysis results. *Review of Educational Research, 77,* 454–499.

Sommer, A., & Mann, D. (2015). *Qualität elterlichen Interaktionsverhaltens. Erfassung von Interaktionen mithilfe der Eltern-Kind-Interaktions Einschätzskala im Nationalen Bildungspanel* (NEPS Working Paper No. 56). Bamberg, Germany: Leibniz-Institut für Bildungsverläufe, Nationales Bildungspanel.

Stecher, L., Klieme, E., Radisch, F., & Fischer, N. (2009). Unterrichts- und Angebotsentwicklung—Kernstücke der Ganztagsschulentwicklung. In F. Prüß, S. Kortas, & M. Schöpa (Eds.), *Die Ganztagsschule: von der Theorie zur Praxis* (pp. 185–201). Weinheim, Germany: Juventa.

Sun, R., Slusarz, P., & Terry, C. (2005). The interaction of the explicit and the implicit in skill learning: A dual-process approach. *Psychological Review, 112,* 159–192.

Tietze, W., Roßbach, H. G., & Grenner, K. (2005). *Kinder von 4 bis 8 Jahren: Zur Qualität der Erziehung und Bildung in Kindergarten, Grundschule und Familie.* Weinheim, Germany: Beltz.

Vermunt, J. D., & Verloop, N. (1999). Congruence and friction between learning and teaching. *Learning and Instruction, 9,* 257–280.

Wang, M. C., Haertel, G. D., & Walberg, H. J. (1993). Toward a knowledge base for school learning. *Review of Educational Research, 63,* 249–294.

Wellenreuther, M. (2004). *Lehren und Lernen – aber wie? Empirisch-experimentelle Forschungen zum Lehren und Lernen im Unterricht* (Grundlagen der Schulpädagogik Bd. 50). Hohengehren, Germany: Schneider.

Wild, E., & Gerber, J. (2007). Charakteristika und Determinanten der Hausaufgabenpraxis in Deutschland von der vierten bis zur siebten Klassenstufe. *Zeitschrift für Erziehungswissenschaft, 10,* 356–380.

Social Inequality and Educational Decisions in the Life Course

Volker Stocké, Hans-Peter Blossfeld, Kerstin Hoenig and Michaela Sixt

Abstract

Research has shown consistently that social origin has exceptionally strong effects on educational outcomes in Germany. Alongside the primary effects of social origin, it is the secondary effects that are especially strong. The reasons for these differences in educational decisions, which persist even when academic abilities are held constant, are not clear. Several theoretical approaches claim to explain the association between social origin and educational decisions. These include rational choice theory and different versions of bounded rationality; theories based on the relevance of values, social norms, and reference groups; social capital theory; and cultural capital theory. However, simultaneously judging the relative merits of these approaches requires the appropriate data. Up to now, there has been a particular lack of consistent measures

---

We regret the sudden and untimely death of Volker Stocké, who died on August 22, 2017.

V. Stocké
University of Kassel, Kassel, Germany

H.-P. Blossfeld (✉)
University of Bamberg, Bamberg, Germany
E-Mail: hans-peter.blossfeld@uni-bamberg.de

K. Hoenig · M. Sixt
Leibniz Institute for Educational Trajectories, Bamberg, Germany
E-Mail: kerstin.hoenig@lifbi.de

M. Sixt
E-Mail: michaela.sixt@lifbi.de

across all relevant educational stages over the life course. Longitudinal data offer great advantages for determining the causal effect of the factors under consideration. Previous data has been restricted to a single educational decision and has been either cross-sectional or restricted to locally defined samples. Pillar 3 of the German National Educational Panel Study (NEPS) aims to measure the relevant factors for explaining educational decisions and inequality in educational opportunity in all relevant stages over the life course.

Keywords
Education · Social inequality · Rational choice · Social capital · Cultural capital

6.1 Introduction

Pillar 3 of the National Educational Panel Study (NEPS) focuses on educational decisions and inequality in educational opportunity (IEO) over the life course. There is a rich tradition of theoretical work in this field. Some of these theoretical approaches aim to use social origin to explain all relevant educational decisions over the life course as well as the inequality in these decisions (see, for explanations of ethnic inequality, Chap. 7, this volume). The four most important theories are (a) rational choice theory and bounded rationality; (b) values, social norms, and reference groups; (c) social capital theory; and (d) cultural capital theory.[1] This section provides an overview of the core theories forming the basis of Pillar 3 and how these theories are being operationalized to explain different transitions and decisions over the life course.

From birth to retirement, individuals face a vast number of important educational decisions. Some of these—such as the choice of school type after elementary school—have received extensive scientific attention, whereas others have been mostly neglected up to now. Shortly after a child's birth, parents have the option of choosing different child care arrangements, followed by the decision on whether to attend Kindergarten (and for how long), when to start elementary school, and which type of secondary school to attend. Then, there is the decision about leaving school instead of continuing education, the choice between academic and vocational studies, and the question whether to attend vocational education and training or a tertiary track. After leaving the educational system, there is the decision to participate in various forms of lifelong learning. Furthermore, actors can decide to modify or correct most of these choices at a later point in time by, for example, switching school types, dropping out of university, or obtaining a second degree.

Two important factors have to be taken into account when explaining educational decisions. First, the relative weight of different actors changes over the life course. Whereas in early stages, decisions are made mainly by a child's parents, with growing

---

[1]Other theoretical constructs pertaining to the decision formation, namely motivational concepts are discussed in Chap. 9, this volume.

age, the importance of the child increases. As a result, data collection in different educational stages has to concentrate on the appropriate decision agents. Second, educational decisions lead to different learning environments (e.g., school types), and these, in turn, influence future learning opportunities and outcomes. Thus, the interdependence between competence development (see Chap. 4, this volume), learning environments (see Chap. 5, this volume), and educational decisions has to be taken into account.

Many studies have shown considerable inequality in the above-mentioned educational decisions. For instance, children with less favorable social backgrounds spend less time at Kindergarten (Becker and Lauterbach 2008), select less ambitious secondary school tracks (Ditton 2007), and are less likely to continue school after a first school leaving certificate (Tieben 2011). Furthermore, lower social origins lead to less participation in higher (Reimer and Pollak 2010) and adult education (Schömann and Becker 1995). The extent of educational attainment has serious consequences for peoples' life chances. More education leads to higher income (Boockmann and Steiner 2006) and a lower unemployment risk (Kettunen 1997). There are important non-labor-market returns as well: Education is associated with better health (Sander 1998), lower risk of becoming criminal (Lochner and Moretti 2004), more life satisfaction (Hartog and Oosterbeck 1998), and better political representation (Milligan et al. 2004) (see, for all dimensions of returns, Chap. 8, this volume).

According to Boudon (1974), the reasons for inequality in educational opportunity (IEO) can be divided into primary and secondary effects of social class. Whereas primary effects operate through class differences in educationally relevant competencies, secondary effects lead to class inequality in educational choices at the same level of academic competence. Results for early educational stages prove that secondary effects are relatively strong in Germany (Becker 2009). Findings on the transition to secondary school in the state of Rhineland-Palatinate reveal that 53% of the effect of parental class and 71% of educational origin are due to secondary effects (Stocké 2007a). Similarly, secondary effects account for 40% of class inequality and 43% of effects of educational background in the states of Bavaria and Hesse (Relikowski et al. 2009). According to nationwide data, 59% of the effect of families' educational status is attributable to secondary effects (Neugebauer 2010). In the case of the transition to tertiary education, secondary effects have even been found to be as high as 53% and 79% (Neugebauer et al. 2013). Because secondary effects are of such pivotal significance for IEO, the third pillar deals with educational decisions.

For younger birth cohorts, the gender gap in secondary school degrees has changed considerably. Today, female students even receive higher educational degrees in Germany (Diefenbach and Klein 2002) and are less susceptible to grade retention (Krohne and Meier 2004). At the same time, men and women still choose gender-specific school subjects, fields of study, vocational education and training programs, and apprenticeships (e.g., Ayalon 1995). Some researchers explain these gender-related choices as the result of rational decisions (Jonsson 1999); others point to the relevance of biased beliefs about one's own abilities, gender differences in field-related self-concepts, or gender roles. In addition to improving the documentation of the most recent trends in gender differences in the transition properties at the important branching points in educational careers, NEPS seeks to examine the explanatory potential of these competing theoretical explanations.

6.2 Theoretical Models and Empirical Evidence

This section gives an overview on the above-mentioned four most important theories for explaining educational inequality.

6.2.1 Rational Choice Theory and Bounded Rationality

There are three different versions of the theory of rational educational decisions: human capital theory (Becker 1964), the theory of planned behavior (Ajzen 1991), and sociological rational choice theory (Breen and Goldthorpe 1997; Erikson and Jonsson 1996; Esser 1999). Rational choice theory (RCT) can be regarded as a sound compromise between the extremes of human capital theory and the theory of planned behavior. Furthermore, this version of the theory has stimulated empirical research on selection between secondary school tracks and the decision to enter higher education (see, for a comparison of the different theories and the available empirical evidence, Stocké 2010). Thus, RCT is utilized as a theoretical basis of Pillar 3.

Sociological RCT assumes that the summary evaluation of an educational option O_i can be represented as the subjective expected utility SEU (O_i) (Breen and Goldthorpe 1997; Erikson and Jonsson 1996; Esser 1999). This SEU value is based on different educational returns that are evaluated on the basis of the actors' objectives j and result in the utility values U_{ij}. Relevant objectives are labor market returns such as income, job security, and job prestige (Stocké 2007b). An especially important non-labor-market outcome is to avoid intergenerational status demotion. Another important determinant of SEU is the subjective probability p_i of successfully completing an educational option O_i, so that the benefits U_{ij} can be realized. This expectation of success is the outcome of all the individual and structural factors that facilitate or hinder educational success. The last determinant of the expected utility SEU (O_i) is the direct and opportunity costs C_{ik} for completing educational option O_i. Direct costs include financial expenditures for textbooks, teaching materials, or tuition fees, whereas opportunity costs are all those forgone benefits that could have been realized instead of participating in educational training. The theory also includes nonfinancial burdens, for example, having to commute, time pressure, or alienation from friends and family. The theory assumes that the overall evaluation of each educational option can be expressed by the following formula: SEU $(O_i) = p_i \cdot U_{ij} - C_{ik}$. Actors then choose the option with the highest expected utility.

Three factors explain IEO: First, because of different endowments with time and resources, the burden of educational participation differs according to origin. Second, own abilities combined with the support that can be mobilized from others make actors differ in how far they trust in their abilities to succeed in their respective educational careers. Third, the expected utility of educational returns may differ, for instance, because of anticipated discrimination on the labor market or because higher certificates are unnecessary for status maintenance.

Theoretical approaches and empirical evidence suggest that decision mechanisms are often much less than perfectly instrumentally rational. Instead, they are assumed to reflect satisficing (Simon 1993), be affected by frame selection (Esser 2001), and result from utilizing heuristics (Gigerenzer and Todd 1999) and attitudes. Furthermore, mode-choice models assume a variable kind of rationality (Heiner 1983). Another important determinant not taken into account by conventional RCT is the actor's time preference. It is assumed that people downscale and discount results of behavior that are expected to occur further on in the future (Fishburn and Rubinstein 1982). Thus, actors with higher discount rates can be expected to invest less in education, because costs are incurred in the present whereas advantages will come only later.

6.2.2 Values, Social Norms, and Reference Groups

Sociological approaches to explaining IEO have stressed the role of class-specific beliefs and values about educational success and differences in educational preferences conceptualized as achievement attitudes, norms, and values (e.g., Hyman 1966). Within the widely acclaimed Wisconsin Model, these subcultural differences in beliefs and values are assumed to result from social influence processes (Sewell et al. 1970). In particular, the learners' educational and occupational aspirations are expected to be shaped by reference groups and significant others. The resulting aspiration level is predicted to explain differences in educational outcomes. The theory assumes socially shaped aspirations to be the crucial mediating factor between social origin and educational behavior, and that this factor establishes motivational differences between status groups.

An often neglected but important differentiation is that between realistic and idealistic aspirations. Realistic aspirations represent forecasts of educational careers that take all factors facilitating or constraining educational attainment into account. In contrast, idealistic aspirations entail either self-commitment or a normative expectation to reach a certain educational level (see, for this differentiation, Haller 1968; Stocké 2005a). Whereas in many cases, it is unclear whether realistic expectations or idealistic wishes are being measured (e.g., Laanan 2003), idealistic aspirations are tapped more clearly by other measures (e.g., Dandy and Nettelbeck 2002). Although idealistic wishes may be the primary source of motivational effects on educational behavior, realistic expectations will be measured as well.

Interpersonal influences depend on the quality of the relationship and, in particular, on the strength of ties (Granovetter 1973). Influential others have been found to represent strong ties in terms of the frequency of interpersonal contact and communication

(Friedkin 1993), the duration of the relationships (Ganter 2003), and their length and intimacy (Hoffman et al. 1992). In order to take the relative effect of reference persons into account, proxy information about the strength of ties has to be measured.

Whereas the aforementioned influences establish normative reference group effects that are relevant for the formation of aspirations and values, reference groups also serve as a standard of comparison (Singer 1981). In order to realistically evaluate their own academic performance and their prospects of success in the future, actors utilize the performance of their social context as a standard for comparison. As a consequence, a well-performing reference group may have negative effects on learners' self-esteem and self-efficacy beliefs and consequently deteriorating effects on their achievement motivation (Bandura et al. 1996). Hence, normative and comparative reference group effects may exert contradictory effects on the learner's achievement motivation.

6.2.3 Social Capital Theory

Learners and families with large amounts of social capital can be expected to have privileged chances of reaching favorable educational outcomes. However, "social capital" can be regarded as an umbrella concept covering a range of different kinds of mechanisms. First, social capital refers to the existence of relations of trust and effective social norms that facilitate the provision of collective goods. According to Coleman (1988), functional communities around schools work together in order to enforce ambitious achievement norms and create positive attitudes toward learning (see, for normative reference group effects, paragraph 6.2.2, above). Many studies have confirmed the positive effect of social closure on educational success (e.g., Thorlindsson et al. 2007; for negative evidence, see Morgan and Todd 2009). Second, social capital encompasses differences in the quality and quantity of resources in a broader sense that a person can access and mobilize through social relations (Lin 1999). Three kinds of such resources can be differentiated. These are (a) information, for example, social networks provide access to adequate and cheap information about educational options (Granovetter 1973); (b) support, for example, well-educated parents can offer their children more qualified help in school-related issues (Teachman et al. 1997); and (c) obligations, for example, social credit built up in the past may help the actor to find a well-paid job (Bourdieu 1986). Many studies have shown that information (e.g., knowledge about job vacancies and inside information about job requirements) and support (e.g., referrals) also exert positive effects on labor market outcomes. As well as being directly beneficial for educational success, social capital also increases achievement motivation through different educational returns. Lower status families, being less well endowed with all kinds of social capital, have lower educational success and furthermore achieve lower returns to education on the labor market.

6.2.4 Cultural Capital Theory

Following social reproduction theory by Pierre Bourdieu and Jean-Claude Passeron, cultural capital has been hypothesized to be a major resource in the reproduction of educational inequalities and the existing class structure (Bourdieu 1986; Bourdieu and Passeron 1971). Basically, the authors assume that the class structure is reproduced across generations through the transmission of cultural capital within the family and through the way the cultural capital of the higher classes is rewarded within schools. In other words, the authors suppose that there is an intergenerational continuity of social positions backed by an only seemingly meritocratic educational system. Cultural capital comprises familiarity with and participation in the dominant culture in a society. Bourdieu (1986) distinguishes three different forms of cultural capital: (a) objectified cultural capital (resources such as pictures, musical instruments, books, and computers), (b) embodied cultural capital (such as cultural knowledge and linguistic competencies), and (c) institutionalized cultural capital (educational certificates and degrees).

Applications of the theory of cultural reproduction follow two different views on cultural capital: public cultural participation that serves to communicate status distinctions versus private forms of activities—such as reading—that help to develop specific skills (Crook 1997; see also de Graaf et al. 2000). Studies adopting the first perspective find a sizeable effect on educational success whatever specific educational outcome variable is chosen (school grades, years of schooling, or various transitions in the educational system; see DiMaggio 1982; Rössel and Beckert-Ziegelschmidt 2002). However, studies that additionally take into account activities directly supporting the development of skills find that participation in highbrow culture loses much of its explanatory power (de Graaf et al. 2000; Sullivan 2001). According to these studies, it is reading and watching certain valuable television programs that particularly foster students' educational attainment. Another important issue is whether cultural capital is surveyed in the parents (de Graaf et al. 2000), the students (DiMaggio 1982), or both (Aschaffenburg and Maas 1997; Rössel and Beckert-Ziegelschmidt 2002). If indicators of cultural capital are assessed only in students or parents, the hypothesis on the transmission of cultural capital from parents to children remains untested (see, for an exception, Sullivan 2001).

In the field of cultural capital, there are several open questions: First, applications of the theory are restricted to school students and their educational success. Is cultural capital relevant for educational success in later stages in the educational biography as well? Second, which kind of cultural capital has the strongest effect on educational success? Third, does the educational system positively sanction distinctive highbrow cultural capital, independent from competencies?

6.3 NEPS Measures for the Constructs in the Educational Stages

Given the various different educational decisions actors face over the life course, the main challenge for Pillar 3 is to develop a consistent concept of measurement for each construct over the eight educational stages. When doing so, adequate consideration must also be given to the specific situation within each stage. Therefore, the result has to be a balance between stage-specific and comparable measurements over the life course. As well as operationalizing the four theories for explaining educational decisions, the measurement of sociodemographics and social origin is central for Pillar 3. Here, rigorously standardized measurements are essential not only to retain comparability over the educational stages within NEPS but also to link up with existing (international) research.

Because there is a large overlap between reference group theories and social capital approaches such as that of Coleman (1988)—both dealing with normative climates and interpersonal influence—these constructs are generally measured at the same time points and treated together in Sect. 6.3.3. The target person's own aspirations and attitudes toward education are included in the section on bounded rationality.

6.3.1 Principles of Measuring Social Origin and Sociodemographics

Measuring social origin and sociodemographics is of central importance to NEPS. First, sociodemographic characteristics are essential for describing the composition of the sample, calculating weights, and performing imputation. Second, sociodemographic characteristics serve as proxy measures for several theoretically relevant constructs. And third, they are partly used as indicators for inequality in educational opportunity. The latter is of particular interest for Pillar 3, because we focus on social inequality and educational decisions.

Consequently, we attach great importance to an internationally comparable measurement of social origin and sociodemographic characteristics, and especially to the measurement of educational degrees and the structure of social inequality connected to status positions in the labor market. General and vocational degrees are measured so that they can be coded in line with the International Standard Classification of Educational Degrees (ISCED; OECD 1999) and the educational classification of the Comparative Analysis of Social Mobility in Industrial Nations (CASMIN; König et al. 1988) project. To measure the structure of social inequality, we collect detailed data about occupational positions. We are able to recode our data in line with, for example, the International Standard Classification of Occupations (ISCO; ILO 1990) as well as the International Socio-Economic Index of Occupational Status (ISEI; Ganzeboom et al. 1992) and the Erikson–Goldthorpe–Portocarero class scheme (EGP, Erikson et al. 1979; see also Erikson and Goldthorpe 1992).

In general, sociodemographic characteristics need to be ascertained for (a) the target person (i.e., for the child, adolescent, and adult who is the learner and decision maker); (b) the family of origin (both parents of the target person as well as siblings); and (c) the target person's own family (partner and children). Whenever possible, information is collected through self-reports by the individuals to whom the information is referring. Consequently, one reason to conduct a parental interview in Stages 1–5 is to obtain valid information about the social origin of the target persons and the sociodemographics of both target persons and parents. Depending on the educational stage under study, characteristics are being measured for different persons and in varying detail (see Table 6.1).

In addition, information on the target person's migration characteristics (see Chap. 7, this volume) as well as on her or his educational and employment history is collected for all cohorts. The basic instruments for measuring this history retrospectively are taken and adapted from the ALWA study ("*Arbeiten und Leben im Wandel*") of the Institute for Employment Research (Kleinert and Jacob 2006; see Chap. 17, this volume). Furthermore, in all educational stages, information is being collected on general and vocational educational level, employment, occupation, and migration history of mother and father in the family of origin and in the current partner. We are also collecting some information on the educational degrees and occupational status of siblings. Moreover, information on household income (see Chap. 8, this volume), household composition, and local residence is being measured in each stage. Adolescent or adult target persons in Stages 6–8

Table 6.1 Overview: measurement of sociodemographic characteristics

	Target persons		Family of origin		Own family	
	Stage 1–5	Stage 6–8	Parents	Siblings	Partners	Children
Basic sociodemographics	x	x	x	x	x	x
Migration characteristics (for details, see Pillar 4)	x	x	x		x	
Educational history	x	x				
Employment history		x				
General and vocational educational qualifications	x	x	x	x	x	x
Current employment status		x	x	x	x	
Current (or last) occupation and occupational status		x	x		x	
Household income and individual income (for details, see Pillar 5)	x	x	x			
Partnership status		x	x			
Household composition	x	x				
Regional information	x	x				

are additionally being asked for information on their personal income (see Chap. 8, this volume) and partnership status. Sociodemographic characteristics were measured in the first panel wave and are being updated each wave when status changes occur.

6.3.2 Measuring Rational Choice and Bounded Rationality

Finding a framework for operationalizing rational choice theory (RCT) and bounded rationality in NEPS poses the dilemma that instruments must be not only comparable across stages but also tailored to the decisions specific to each stage. A further problem is that there are substantial differences in the amount of previous research and operationalizations for the different educational decisions. Whereas several panel studies such as the projects "Educational Processes, Competence Development and Selection Decisions in Pre- and Primary School Age" (BiKS), "*Kompetenzaufbau und Laufbahnen im Schulsystem* [competence development and education careers in the school system]" (KOALA-S), and the "Mannheim Educational Panel Study" (MEPS), include rational choice constructs for the transition from elementary to secondary school, there are little to no explicit operationalizations for other stages. Furthermore, the existing concepts were developed with only one decision in mind, and it is not easy to transfer them to other contexts. Therefore, most of the constructs discussed in this section were developed specifically for NEPS.

To ensure comparability across stages, question format (including sentence structure, word choice, and response options) is being kept as constant as possible, whereas content varies according to the respective decision. All our operationalizations of RCT are strictly prospective, and we always focus on the most important upcoming decision. These are:

- Decisions about early child care arrangements (Stage 1)
- When to enter Kindergarten (Stage 1)
- When to enter elementary school (Stage 2)
- Choice of secondary school (Stage 3)
- Change of school type and choice of secondary degree (Stage 4)
- Choice of vocational education and training or university options (Stage 4, Stage 5)
- Discontinuation or change of vocational education and training/field of study (Stage 6, Stage 7)
- Choice of obtaining a master's degree/doctorate (Stage 7)
- Choice of reentering formal education (Stage 8)
- Participation in lifelong learning (Stage 8).

6.3.2.1 Expected Probability of Success, Costs, and Benefits

For each of these decisions, we operationalize the expected probability of success and the most relevant cost and benefit dimensions for each decision alternative. Depending on the stage, relevant cost dimensions include all or several of the following: financial costs (both direct and indirect, e.g., missed income), social costs (e.g., losing friends who go to a different school/being sanctioned for not meeting social expectations), time costs, and effort costs. Benefits can include prospects for future jobs, access to other education options, and personal enjoyment of the chosen option. Which of these dimensions are used to explain a given decision depends on whether there is variation on a particular dimension for the different alternatives, whether previous research leads us to expect the dimension to be relevant, and whether the respondent is able to form an opinion about this dimension. For instance, it is the parents and not the school children themselves who are usually able to assess the financial implications of attending different school tracks.

6.3.2.2 Motive of Status Maintenance

NEPS includes an extensive operationalization of the motive of status maintenance, including maintenance of both educational and occupational status of the target person's mother and father. In Stages 1–5, we survey the parents' motive that their child should maintain their status. Stages 4–8 include the target person's motive of status maintenance. Thus, we can compare parents' and target persons' attitudes for the duration of secondary school.

For both educational and occupational status, we assess the subjective importance for the target person of maintaining the status of each parent. Consequently, the data provide evidence for testing the assumption that low status groups are less motivated to maintain their parents' status. For occupational status, we additionally ask respondents how likely they think it is that the mother's and father's status can be maintained when each of the possible educational options is chosen, thereby providing researchers with the opportunity to model an interaction of likelihood and importance, that is, subjective expected probability and utility.

6.3.2.3 Information and Time Horizon

The RCT assumes that actors are reasonably well informed about their options, and that their time horizon stretches far enough to consider the future implications of their actions. Therefore, we ask participants how well informed they feel about the institutional setting and the regulations relevant to the upcoming educational decision. Time horizon is operationalized by asking how often the respondent already thinks about a future decision. In addition, Pillars 3 and 4 have developed an instrument to measure actual information about the value of different educational degrees as well as certain institutional features of the education system in the form of a short quiz.

6.3.2.4 Aspirations and Value Orientations

Unlike most previous studies, NEPS distinguishes clearly between realistic and idealistic aspirations. In Stages 1–3 (birth to elementary school), we focus on parents' aspirations for their child's secondary school track. In Stage 4 (secondary school, Grades 5–10), we are surveying parents' and children's aspirations for the child's secondary degree every year. Additionally, we inquire about the child's expected and desired occupation and their realistic and idealistic plans after graduation. Occupational aspirations are also measured in Stages 5–8. Additionally, we measure plans for after graduation (with a special focus on tertiary education) in Stage 5 (upper secondary school), vocational education and training aspirations in Stage 6 (vocational education and training), and aspirations for tertiary degrees in Stage 7 (university).

We assess value orientations in the form of a generalized attitude toward education, using a reduced version of the scale developed by Stocké (2005b). This scale is supplemented by stage-specific items in Stages 7 and 8.

6.3.3 Measuring Social Capital and Reference Group Effects

Operationalizations for the various dimensions of social capital and reference group effects are being developed in cooperation with Pillar 4. For an overview of social capital in regard to migration, see Chap. 7 in this volume.

6.3.3.1 Networks of Information, Support, and Obligation

We rely on a combination of established and newly developed instruments. Using a similar strategy as for RCT, our general approach is to rely on a common question format in all stages—thereby maintaining comparability—but to vary question content according to the decision of interest.

In all stages, we use a short version of the position generator (Lin et al. 2001) developed for the project "Immigrant children and youths in the German and Israeli educational systems" to determine network status composition (Schulz et al. 2017). Until the end of secondary school (Stages 1–5), the position generator is administered to the target person's parents. We also measure the composition of the respondent's network of close friends in terms of gender, migration background, and education.

We operationalize access to resources in a format similar to the resource generator proposed by van der Gaag and Snijders (2004, 2005). This instrument presents a list of resources and asks (a) whether the respondent knows somebody who has access to this resource and (b) whether this person is a family member, friend, or acquaintance, as a proxy for tie strength. However, instead of presenting a long list of general resources, we focus on a small number of carefully selected resources that are relevant to the decision at hand. For instance, we ask those about to graduate from lower secondary school and to enter vocational education and training whether they think that it is likely that somebody they know could give them information on where to apply. If this is the case, we ask (a) what their relationship to these persons is; (b) how many persons they know; and (c) gender, education, and migration background composition of the group of possible resource providers. Thus, we do not just know whether there is access to this resource, but also have a rough indication of quantity and quality.

In addition to this prospective measure of resource availability, we operationalize actual use of those resources retrospectively after the particular decision (such as change of occupation, the start of vocational education and training, or enrollment in university) has taken place. Again, we measure the type of relationship; the number of people who provide the resource; and gender, education, and migration background composition.

6.3.3.2 Normative Climate and Reference Groups

The importance of different reference groups changes over the life course. The first and most important reference group is arguably the family, especially parents. In all stages, we therefore inquire about the educational outcomes parents expect from their children. The second reference group includes friends whose influence can be expected to increase over the life course. We ask our subjects about the expectations their friends have for their educational achievement, as well as proxy information about their friends' own educational values and aspirations. While children are still in school, we also ask parents about their own network of friends. A third reference group is composed of those with whom the target persons interact regularly in institutional settings: classmates (Stages 3–5), fellow university students (Stage 7), and coworkers (Stages 6 and 8). For each of these stages, we ask about the predominant attitudes toward education among these groups.

In Stages 2–5 (Kindergarten to upper secondary school), intergenerational closure is operationalized by asking parents how many of the parents of their child's friends and classmates they know personally. We also survey how often and in what form parents have contacts with the school or Kindergarten. To operationalize family climate, we use a short item battery previously developed within the BiKS project.

6.3.4 Dimensions of Cultural Capital

As already described, Bourdieu (1986) distinguishes three different forms of cultural capital: (a) objectified cultural capital, (b) institutionalized cultural capital, and (c) embodied cultural capital. All three forms are measured in NEPS.

6.3.4.1 Objectified Cultural Capital

To measure objectified cultural capital, NEPS has adopted a scale from the student questionnaire of the Programme for International Student Attainment (PISA) 2003 (Ramm et al. 2006). This scale contains questions on cultural possessions ("Are there any books in your home on classical literature [e.g., Goethe], books on poetry, and pieces of art [e.g., paintings]?"), home educational resources ("Which of the following is available in your home: a desk for learning, a room of your own, software for learning, books you can use for homework, a dictionary?"), and the number of books in the household. Whereas the cultural possessions scale assesses an element of the symbolic power path, the other two indicators assess aspects of a stimulating learning environment at home. As studies show, these PISA indicators are associated strongly with children's educational competencies (Jungbauer-Gans 2006).

6.3.4.2 Institutionalized Cultural Capital

Institutionalized cultural capital is conceptualized in the context of measuring social origin as described above: NEPS is surveying the educational history of all target persons and asking about the general and vocational educational qualifications of the mother and father of the family of origin.

6.3.4.3 Embodied Cultural Capital

The plan is to measure embodied cultural capital by developing an objective knowledge test following Sullivan (2001) for later waves. Embodied cultural capital is also being measured in the classical way (adopted from the ALWA study, see Matthes and Trahms 2010) by the frequency of participation in highbrow cultural activities such as going to the theater, museums or exhibitions, classic concerts, and opera. Furthermore, there are questions on the frequency of playing a musical instrument and listening to classical music that are similar to the questions in MEPS and BiKS. Finally, there is a scale measuring cultural involvement that contains the frequency of discussing political and social questions, books, as well as works of art and culture in general. This scale is adopted from PISA 2000 (Kunter et al. 2002).

6.3.4.4 Reading Culture

Besides measuring highbrow cultural activities, Pillar 3 is interested in measuring reading culture, because it has been shown to foster students' educational attainment (Crook 1997; see also de Graaf et al. 2000). Consequently, questions about the time spent on reading are asked in each NEPS cohort. Because of the emphasis on "Reading Engagement" in Stage 4, students are additionally asked how frequently they read literature of various genres as well as journals and magazines together with their attitude toward reading in general (see Chap. 13, this volume).

A further important issue in Stages 4 and 5 is to survey cultural capital in the parental interviews as well as in the students' questionnaires in order to test hypotheses on the transmission of cultural capital from parents to children. Therefore, the parents' questionnaire contains a shortened version of the questions about cultural capital.

All in all, the measurement of cultural capital has a high level of comparability over all stages; only slight adjustments are being made to respective instruments. The different dimensions of cultural capital are surveyed in the first wave of NEPS in all stages, except for Stage 1 and 7, in which rational choice is asked in the first wave, and Stage 8 in which social capital is a key aspect. Because it is assumed that cultural capital is relatively stable, measures are repeated less frequently than other core constructs.

References

Ajzen, I. (1991). The theory of planned behavior. *Organizational Behavior and Human Decision Processes, 50*, 179–211.

Aschaffenburg, K., & Maas, I. (1997). Cultural and educational careers: The dynamics of social reproduction. *American Sociological Review, 62*, 573–587.

Ayalon, H. (1995). Math as a gatekeeper: Ethnic and gender inequality in course taking of the sciences in Israel. *American Journal of Education, 104*, 34–56.

Bandura, A., Barbaranelli, C., Caprara, G., & Pastorelli, C. (1996). Multifaceted impact of self-efficacy beliefs on academic functioning. *Child Development, 67*, 1206–1222.

Becker, G. (1964). *Human capital*. New York, NY: Columbia University Press.

Becker, R. (2009). Wie können ‚bildungsferne' Gruppen für ein Hochschulstudium gewonnen werden? Eine empirische Simulation mit Implikationen für die Steuerung des Bildungswesens. *Kölner Zeitschrift für Soziologie und Sozialpsychologie, 61*, 563–593.

Becker, R., & Lauterbach, W. (2008). Vom Nutzen vorschulischer Erziehung und Elementarbildung – Bessere Bildungschancen für Arbeiterkinder? In R. Becker & W. Lauterbach (Eds.), *Bildung als Privileg – Erklärungen und Befunde zu den Ursachen der Bildungsungleichheit* (pp. 129–160). Wiesbaden, Germany: VS Verlag für Sozialwissenschaften.

Boockmann, B., & Steiner, V. (2006). Cohort effects and the returns to education in West Germany. *Applied Economics, 38*, 1135–1152.

Boudon, R. (1974). *Education, opportunity, and social inequality: Changing prospects in Western society*. New York, NY: Wiley.

Bourdieu, P. (1986). The forms of capital. In J. G. Richardson (Ed.), *Handbook of theory and research for the sociology of education* (pp. 241–258). New York, NY: Greenwood Press.

Bourdieu, P., & Passeron, J.-C. (1971). *Die Illusion der Chancengleichheit: Untersuchungen zur Soziologie des Bildungswesens am Beispiel Frankreichs*. Stuttgart, Germany: Klett.

Breen, R., & Goldthorpe, J. H. (1997). Explaining educational differentials: Towards a formal rational action theory. *Rationality and Society, 9*, 275–305.

Coleman, J. S. (1988). Social capital in the creation of human capital. *The American Journal of Sociology, 94*, 95–120.

Crook, C. J. (1997). The dimensionality of stratification-related cultural practices in Australia. *Journal of Sociology, 33*, 226–238.

Dandy, J., & Nettelbeck, T. (2002). Research note: A cross-cultural study of parent's academic standards and educational aspirations for their children. *Educational Psychology, 22*, 621–627.

de Graaf, N., de Graaf, P., & Kraaykamp, G. (2000). Parental cultural capital and educational attainment in the Netherlands: A refinement of the cultural capital perspective. *Sociology of Education, 73*, 92–111.

Diefenbach, H., & Klein, M. (2002). „Bringing Boys Back In": Soziale Ungleichheit zwischen den Geschlechtern im Bildungssystem zuungunsten von Jungen am Beispiel der Sekundarschulabschlüsse. *Zeitschrift für Pädagogik, 48*, 938–958.

DiMaggio, P. (1982). Cultural capital and school success: The impact of status culture participation on the grades of U.S. high school students. *American Sociological Review, 47*, 189–201.

Ditton, H. (2007). *Kompetenzaufbau und Laufbahnen im Schulsystem*. Münster, Germany: Waxmann.

Erikson, R., & Goldthorpe, J. (1992). *The constant flux: A study of class mobility in industrial societies*. Oxford, England: Clarendon Press.

Erikson, R., Goldthorpe, J., & Portocarero, L. (1979). Intergenerational class mobility in three Western European societies: England, France and Sweden. *British Journal of Sociology, 30*, 415–441.

Erikson, R., & Jonsson, J. O. (1996). Explaining class inequality in education: The Swedish case. In R. Erikson & J. O. Jonsson (Eds.), *Can education be equalized? The Swedish case in comparative perspective* (pp. 1–63). Oxford, England: Westview Press.

Esser, H. (1999). *Situationslogik und Handeln. Soziologie: Spezielle Grundlagen*. Frankfurt a.M., Germany: Campus.

Esser, H. (2001). *Sinn und Kultur. Soziologie: Spezielle Grundlagen.* Frankfurt a.M., Germany: Campus.

Fishburn, P. C., & Rubinstein, A. (1982). Time preference. *International Economic Review, 23,* 677–694.

Friedkin, N. E. (1993). Structural bases of interpersonal influence in groups: A longitudinal case study. *American Sociological Review, 58,* 861–872.

Ganter, S. (2003). Soziale Netzwerke und interethnische Distanz. Theoretische und empirische Analysen zum Verhältnis von Deutschen und Ausländern. Wiesbaden, Germany: Westdeutscher Verlag.

Ganzeboom, H., de Graaf, P., & Treiman, D. (1992). A standard international socio-economic index of occupational status. *Social Science Research, 21,* 1–56.

Gigerenzer, G., & Todd, P. M. (1999). Fast and frugal heuristics: The adaptive toolbox. In G. Gigerenzer, P. M. Todd, & The ABC Research Group (Eds.), *Simple heuristics that make us smart* (pp. 3–35). New York, NY: Oxford University Press.

Granovetter, M. (1973). The strength of weak ties. *The American Journal of Sociology, 78,* 1360–1380.

Haller, A. O. (1968). On the concept of aspiration. *Rural Sociology, 33,* 484–487.

Hartog, J., & Oosterbeek, H. (1998). Health, wealth and happiness: Why pursue a higher education? *Economics of Education Review, 17,* 245–256.

Heiner, R. A. (1983). The origin of predictable behavior. *American Economic Review, 73,* 560–595.

Hoffman, J. J., Hofacker, C., & Goldsmith, E. B. (1992). How closeness affects parental influence on business college students' career choices. *Journal of Career Development, 19,* 65–73.

Hyman, H. H. (1966). The value systems of different classes: A social psychological contribution to the analysis of stratification. In R. Bendix & S. M. Lipset (Eds.), *Class, status, and power: Social stratification in comparative perspective* (pp. 488–499). New York, NY: The Free Press.

ILO (1990). ISCO-88/International Standard Classification of Occupation. Geneva: International Labour Office.

Jonsson, J. O. (1999). Explaining sex differences in educational choice: An empirical assessment of a rational choice model. *European Sociological Review, 15,* 391–404.

Jungbauer-Gans, M. (2006). Kulturelles Kapital und Mathematikleistungen – eine Analyse der PISA 2003-Daten für Deutschland. In W. Georg (Eds.), *Soziale Ungleichheit im Bildungssystem. Eine empirisch-theoretische Bestandsaufnahme* (pp. 175–198). Konstanz, Germany: UVK Verlagsgesellschaft mbH.

Kettunen, J. (1997). Education and unemployment duration. *Economics of Education Review, 16,* 163–170.

Kleinert, C., & Jacob, M. (2006). *Qualifications, competencies and working life* (project description). Nuremberg, Germany: Institut für Arbeitsmarkt- und Berufsforschung.

König, W., Lüttinger, P., & Müller, W. (1988). A comparative analysis of the development and structure of educational systems: Methodological foundations and the construction of a comparative educational scale (CASMIN Working Paper 12). Mannheim, Germany: University of Mannheim.

Krohne, J. A., & Meier, U. (2004). Sitzenbleiben, Geschlecht und Migration. In G. Schümer, K.-J. Tillmann, & M. Weiß (Eds.), Die Institution Schule und die Lebenswelt der Schüler. Vertiefende Analysen der PISA-2000-Daten zum Kontext von Schülerleistungen (pp. 117–148). Wiesbaden, Germany: VS Verlag für Sozialwissenschaften.

Kunter, M., Schümer, G., Artelt, C., Baumert, J., Klieme, E., Neubrand, M., Prenzel, M., Schiefele, U., Schneider, W., Stanat, P., Tillmann K.-J., & Weiß, M. (2002). *PISA 2000: Dokumentation der Erhebungsinstrumente* (Materialien aus der Bildungsforschung 72). Berlin, Germany: Max-Planck-Institut für Bildungsforschung.

Laanan, F. S. (2003). Degree aspirations of two-year college students. *Community College Journal of Research and Practice, 27,* 495–518.

Lin, N. (1999). Social networks and status attainment. *Annual Review of Sociology, 25,* 467–487.

Lin, N., Fu, Y., & Hsung, R. (2001). The position generator: Measurement techniques for investigations of social capital. In N. Lin, K. Cook, & R. S. Burt (Eds.), *Social capital: Theory and research* (pp. 57–81). New York, NY: Aldine de Gruyter.

Lochner, L., & Moretti, E. (2004). The effect of education on crime: Evidence from prison inmates, arrests, and self-reports. *The American Economic Review, 94,* 155–189.

Matthes, B., & Trahms, A. (2010). *Arbeiten und Lernen im Wandel Teil II – Codebuch* (FDZ-Datenreport 02/2010). Nuremberg, Germany: Institut für Arbeitsmarkt- und Berufsforschung.

Milligan, K., Moretti, E., & Oreopoulos, P. (2004). Does education improve citizenship? Evidence from the United States and the United Kingdom. *Journal of Public Economics, 88,* 1667–1695.

Morgan, S. L., & Todd, J. J. (2009). Intergenerational closure and academic achievement in high school: A new evaluation of Coleman's conjecture. *Sociology of Education, 82,* 267–287.

Neugebauer, M. (2010). Bildungsungleichheit und Grundschulempfehlung beim Übergang auf das Gymnasium: Eine Dekomposition primärer und sekundärer Herkunftseffekte. *Zeitschrift für Soziologie, 39,* 202–214.

Neugebauer, M., Reimer, D., Schindler, S., & Stocké, V. (2013). Primary and secondary effects at the transitions to secondary school and tertiary education in Germany. In M. Jackson (Ed.), *Determined to succeed? Determined to succeed? Performance versus choice in educational attainment* (pp. 56–88). Stanford, CA: Stanford University Press.

OECD (1999). *Classifying educational programmes: Manual for ISCED-97 implementation in OECD countries.* Paris, France: Organization for Economic Co-operation and Development.

Ramm, G., Prenzel, M., & Baumert, J. (2006). *PISA 2003: Dokumentation der Erhebungsinstrumente.* Münster, Germany: Waxmann-Verlag.

Reimer, D., & Pollak, R. (2010). Educational expansion and its consequences for vertical and horizontal inequalities in access to higher education in West Germany. *European Sociological Review, 26,* 415–430.

Relikowski, I., Schneider, T., & Blossfeld, H.-P. (2009). Primary and secondary effects of social origin in migrant and native families at the transition to the tracked German school system. In M. Cherkaoui & P. Hamilton (Eds.), *Raymond Boudon: A life in sociology. Essays in honour of Raymond Boudon* (Vol. 3, pp. 149–170). Oxford, England: Bardwell Press.

Rössel, J., & Beckert-Zieglschmid, C. (2002). Die Reproduktion kulturellen Kapitals. *Zeitschrift für Soziologie, 31,* 497–513.

Sander, W. (1998). The effects of schooling and cognitive ability on smoking and marijuana use by young adults. *Economics of Education Review, 17,* 317–324.

Schömann, K., & Becker, R. (1995). Participation in further education over the life course: A longitudinal study of three birth cohorts in the Federal Republic of Germany. *European Sociological Review, 11,* 187–208.

Schulz, B., Horr, A., & Hoenig, K. (2017). *The Position Generator in the NEPS* (NEPS Survey Paper No. 23). Bamberg, Germany: Leibniz Institute for Educational Trajectories.

Sewell, W. H., Haller, A. O., & Ohlendorf, G. W. (1970). The educational and early occupational status attainment process: Replication and revision. *American Sociological Review, 35,* 1014–1027.

Simon, H. A. (1993). *Homo rationalis: Die Vernunft im menschlichen Leben.* Frankfurt a.M., Germany: Campus.

Singer, E. (1981). Reference groups and social evaluations. In M. Rosenberg & R. H. Turner (Eds.), *Sociological perspectives* (pp. 66–93). New York, NY: Basic Books.

Stocké, V. (2005a). Idealistische Bildungsaspirationen. In A. Glöckner-Rist (Eds.), *ZUMA-Informationssystem: Elektronisches Handbuch sozialwissenschaftlicher Erhebungsinstrumente. Version 9.00.* Mannheim, Germany: Zentrum für Umfragen, Methoden und Analysen.

Stocké, V. (2005b). Einstellung zu Bildung. In A. Glöckner-Rist (Eds.), *ZUMA-Informationssystem: Elektronisches Handbuch sozialwissenschaftlicher Erhebungsinstrumente: Version 9.00*. Mannheim, Germany: Zentrum für Umfragen, Methoden und Analysen.

Stocké, V. (2007a). *Strength, sources, and temporal development of primary effects of families' social status on secondary school choice* (SFB 504 Discussion Paper 07-60). Mannheim, Germany: Sonderforschungsbereich 504, University of Mannheim.

Stocké, V. (2007b). Explaining educational decision and effects of families' social class position: An empirical test of the Breen–Goldthorpe model of educational attainment. *European Sociological Review, 23*, 505–519.

Stocké, V. (2010). Der Beitrag der Theorie rationaler Entscheidungen zu Erklärung von Bildungsungleichheit. In G. Quenzel & K. Hurrelmann (Eds.), *Bildungsverlierer. Neue Ungleichheiten* (pp. 73–94). Wiesbaden, Germany: VS Verlag für Sozialwissenschaften.

Sullivan, A. (2001). Cultural capital and educational attainment. *Sociology, 35*, 893–912.

Teachman, J. D., Paasch, K., & Carver, K. (1997). Social capital and the generation of human capital. *Social Forces, 75*, 1343–1359.

Thorlindsson, T., Bjarnason, T., & Sigfusdottir, I. D. (2007). Individual and community processes of social closure: A study of adolescent academic achievement and alcohol use. *Acta Sociologica, 50*, 161–178.

Tieben, N. (2011). Parental resources and relative risk aversion in intra-secondary transitions: A trend analysis of non-standard educational decision situations in the Netherlands. *European Sociological Review, 27*(1), 31–42.

Van Der Gaag, M., & Snijders, T. (2004). Proposals for the measurement of individual social capital. In H. Flap & B. Völker (Eds.), *Creation and returns of social capital: A new research program* (pp. 199–218). London, England: Routledge.

Van Der Gaag, M., & Snijders, T. (2005). The resource generator: Social capital quantification with concrete items. *Social Networks, 27*, 1–29.

7. The Education of Migrants and Their Children Across the Life Course

Cornelia Kristen, Aileen Edele, Frank Kalter, Irena Kogan, Benjamin Schulz, Petra Stanat and Gisela Will

Abstract

Pillar 4 of the German National Education Panel Study addresses migrants' and their descendants' acquisition of education across the life course. Apart from documenting the evolution of ethnic educational inequalities throughout the educational career by focusing on different origin groups and distinct indicators of educational success, we

C. Kristen (✉)
University of Bamberg, Bamberg, Germany
E-Mail: cornelia.kristen@uni-bamberg.de

A. Edele · P. Stanat
Humboldt-University Berlin, Berlin, Germany
E-Mail: aileen.edele@iqb.hu-berlin.de

P. Stanat
E-Mail: iqboffice@iqb.hu-berlin.de

F. Kalter
University of Mannheim, Mannheim, Germany
E-Mail: kalter@uni-mannheim.de

I. Kogan
Societal Comparisons, University of Mannheim, Mannheim, Germany
E-Mail: irena.kogan@uni-mannheim.de

B. Schulz
WZB Social Science Center, Berlin, Germany
E-Mail: benjamin.schulz@wzb.eu

G. Will
Leibniz Institute for Educational Trajectories, Bamberg, Germany
E-Mail: gisela.will@lifbi.de

seek to uncover the origins of these disparities. Beyond the mechanisms associated with social inequalities, Pillar 4 aims to disentangle those processes that impact particularly on immigrants and their children and to assess their empirical relevance. We apply the prominent distinction between primary and secondary effects to students of immigrant origin and then link this distinction to a general resources framework that we further adapt for migrants. This leads to the crucial debate within integration research on whether the resources and opportunities available within the migrant group foster educational success. One stream within this debate refers to the contested question whether proficiency in the language of the country of origin influences competence development in the country of residence. Another important stream concerns the role of ethnic networks and social capital for educational success. We discuss the mechanisms predicting either beneficial, neutral, or harmful effects and present available empirical evidence. Based on this account, we highlight the analysis potential of the data gathered in Pillar 4.

Keywords
Migrants · Education · Language skills · Social capital · Panel study

7.1 Introduction

Over the past decades, the number of immigrant students has grown substantially. In 2006, according to the school achievement studies PIRLS (Progress in International Reading Literacy Study) and PISA (Programme for International Student Assessment), 26% of 4th-grade students and 19% of 15-year-olds had at least one parent who was born outside Germany (Schwippert et al. 2007; Walter and Taskinen 2007). These students have lower chances of attaining favorable educational and vocational qualifications. They are at a disadvantage with respect to the acquisition of knowledge and skills as well as with respect to their educational participation. In fact, the performance gap between migrant students and students from native-born families tends to be larger in Germany than in other OECD countries (Stanat and Christensen 2006). Given the increasing proportions of individuals of immigrant origin on the one hand and the central role of education for the integration of these students on the other, ethnic disparities in education are a major concern for researchers, policymakers, and the general public.

Ethnic educational inequalities can be found throughout the school career. Children from migrant families already lag behind on qualifications when they start school (Becker and Biedinger 2006). They attend the highest, college-bound secondary track, the Gymnasium less often, and concentrate instead in the Hauptschule, the lowest track (Autorengruppe Bildungsberichterstattung 2010). They also encounter difficulties in landing an apprenticeship in Germany's dual system of vocational training, and they differ from the majority population in the degrees eventually completed (Autorengruppe Bildungsberichterstattung 2010). At the same time, there is substantive variation in these gaps across immigrant groups with some, such as students of Turkish origin, facing pronounced disadvantages; but others, such as those from the former Soviet Union, doing relatively better (Segeritz et al. 2010). Additional variation arises within groups when considering different indicators of school success. For example, students of Turkish origin encounter considerable difficulties in terms of test scores in elementary and secondary school (e.g., Kristen 2008; Müller and Stanat 2006), but given similar test results or grades, they outperform the majority at certain educational transitions (Kristen and Dollmann 2010; Kristen et al. 2008).

Even though the description of these patterns has improved substantially over the past decade, we do not yet have a comprehensive picture of the educational careers of children of immigrants that not only captures different stages in the school system but also goes beyond the prominent immigrant–majority distinction. The National Educational Panel Study (NEPS) Pillar 4 with its focus on "Education Acquisition with Migration Background in the Life Course" does not just seek to complement the description of ethnic educational inequalities across the educational career by focusing on different origin groups and distinct indicators of educational success such as competencies, transitions, participation, and eventual outcomes. Most importantly, it seeks to uncover the origins of these inequalities.

A crucial finding of previous research in this field is that the difficulties immigrants and their children face in the school system are largely the result of differences in educational and social background (Alba et al. 1994; Heath et al. 2008; Kristen and Granato 2007; Müller and Stanat 2006; Segeritz et al. 2010). They are a matter of social rather than of specific ethnic inequalities (Kalter 2005). Therefore, an account of the emergence of these disparities has to refer to the social inequality mechanisms addressed in other NEPS pillars (e.g., Pillars 1 and 3; see Chaps. 4 and 6, this volume).

The specific focus of the migration Pillar 4 is then on those educational differences that persist after controlling for social origin. Accordingly, NEPS Pillar 4 aims to disentangle the mechanisms that apply particularly to immigrants and their children and to assess their empirical relevance across the life course.

In this chapter, we present the central considerations underlying NEPS Pillar 4 and, based on this account, highlight the pillar's analysis potential. In order to explain ethnic inequalities in education, we start with the prominent distinction between primary and secondary effects (Boudon 1974) and apply this to students of immigrant origin (Sect. 7.2). We link this distinction with a general resources framework and adapt it for immigrants and their descendants. This leads to one of the most important debates within current integration research: that centering on the question whether the resources and opportunities available within the migrant group foster educational success. We discuss the underlying arguments and illustrate them with two crucial streams within this debate. The first refers to the contested question whether proficiency in the language of the country of origin benefits, hinders, or is irrelevant for competence development in the country of residence (Sect. 7.3). The second concerns the role of ethnic networks and social capital for educational success (Sect. 7.4). In both sections, we discuss the mechanisms predicting either beneficial, neutral, or harmful effects and present available empirical evidence. Against this background, we then turn to the analysis potential of NEPS Pillar 4 (Sect. 7.5).

7.2 "Ethnic Resources" and the Education of Immigrants and Their Offspring

In order to detect the mechanisms explaining the emergence and persistence of ethnic educational inequality, it is helpful to follow the common distinction between primary and secondary effects (Boudon 1974). In stratification research, this refers to the impact of social origin on competencies and on educational decisions (see Chap. 6, this volume). When applied to migrants and ethnic minorities, it corresponds to the independent influence of ethnicity on competencies and decisions (e.g., Heath and Brinbaum 2007; Heath et al. 2008; Kristen and Dollmann 2010). The primary and secondary effects of ethnic origin thus capture those immigration-specific influences that persist after controlling for the effects of social origin.

This distinction can be linked to a general resources framework according to which differences in the distribution of relevant resources or characteristics translate into a differential development of competencies as well as into distinct educational decisions. Depending on the resources available in the environment, the conditions for school success vary systematically. For example, financial, cultural, and social resources influence parental support and childhood conditions. Especially parental education is a crucial prerequisite for school success. Better educated parents are not just able to provide more qualified help that improves learning processes (i.e., primary effects of social origin). They also have experience with the more demanding educational pathways, and this strategic knowledge places them in an advantageous position at important educational transitions (i.e., secondary effects of social origin; e.g., Erikson and Jonsson 1996).

This reasoning applies to all students alike. For immigrants and their children, however, it is necessary to consider an additional aspect of the resources argument, namely, that the resources required to develop school-relevant skills as well as to make favorable educational transitions are, to some extent, specific to the educational setting. Therefore, immigrant parents who grew up and attended school in their country of origin have not acquired these resources through their own school careers. At the same time, the resources they bring with them may be of a different relevance in the country of residence (Chiswick 1978).

Restricted transferability of origin-specific resources can affect the education of students from migrant families both in terms of primary and secondary effects of ethnic origin. A prime example for a primary ethnic effect is proficiency in the language of the country of residence. Competencies in the language of instruction are crucial for learning in school and an obvious source of disadvantage among migrant students (e.g., Esser 2006; Müller and Stanat 2006). Knowledge about the functioning of the school system can serve as an example for a secondary ethnic effect. If parents attended school in the country of origin, it is more difficult to navigate the country of residence's educational system. Information resources may matter most at important branching points in the school career when knowledge about relevant regulations and appropriate behaviors can be crucial for making advantageous choices (Kristen 2008).

Note, however, that the primary and secondary effects of ethnic origin can also work in favor of students from immigrant families. For example, one important current debate addresses the contested assumption that good skills in the language of origin improve cognitive learning processes, the acquisition of the language of instruction, and consequently school success (Cummins 1979). Arguments stressing the benefits of "ethnic resources" have also been brought forward with regard to secondary ethnic effects. For example, it has been reasoned that migrants "tend to be 'positively selected' for their ambition and drive" (Heath and Brinbaum 2007, p. 291), and that the relatively high educational aspirations prevalent in coethnic social networks may put them in a favorable position at educational transitions (e.g., Jonsson and Rudolphi 2010; Kristen and Dollmann 2010).

These examples point to one of the most pressing issues in current integration research, namely, whether the resources and opportunities available within the immigrant or ethnic minority group provide favorable conditions for educational and labor market success (Kalter 2008). In this regard, some scholars, most prominently the proponents of the so-called theory of segmented assimilation, argue that being embedded in one's origin group in terms of relationships, networks, orientations, identities, or language use permits the mobilization of other resources that compensate for ethnic disadvantages and foster educational success (Portes 1995, 2003; Portes and Rumbaut 2001; Zhou 1997). Others, however, argue that the focus on one's own ethnic group might prove to constrain immigrants' advancement in the receiving society, because ethnic networks generally do not provide the same amount of helpful resources as networks consisting mostly of majority group members (Kalter 2006). In other words, to succeed in the country of residence, it is necessary to acquire those resources that are relevant within this context (Esser 2004, 2006). This kind of reasoning is often subsumed under new assimilation theory (e.g., Alba and Nee 1997, 2003; Esser 2004; Kalter 2008; Perlmann and Waldinger 1997; Waters and Jiménez 2005).

Although available empirical studies seem to support both types of arguments, they often rely on only weak data. One reason why, for example, the role of proficiency in the language of origin is so controversial is the almost complete lack of studies that have been carried out with sufficient empirical rigor (Esser 2006; Limbird and Stanat 2006; Söhn 2005). Moreover, evidence for the helpful role of ethnic communities is often derived from the fact that ethnic group membership still shows a positive effect after controlling for many relevant determinants of school success (e.g., Portes and Hao 2004; Portes and MacLeod 1996). However, since there could be many alternative explanations, there is an obvious need for more direct empirical tests of the assumed mechanisms (Kroneberg 2008). Furthermore, most studies deal with the situation in the United States. Apart from small-scale studies, little is known about the relative importance of both types of arguments in Germany.

NEPS Pillar 4 aims to close this gap. It is delivering comprehensive empirical contributions on the situation in Germany in general along with unique empirical tests, because many of the mechanisms underlying the conflicting theoretical views are well-captured by the general structure and many of the central concepts measured in NEPS.

To illustrate the migration pillar's contribution in the following, we shall focus on the role of "ethnic resources" and discuss two controversial streams of the debate: the effects of proficiency in the language of origin for educational advancement and those of ethnic networks and social capital.

7.3 Proficiency in L1[1]: Beneficial, Hindering, or Irrelevant for Educational Success?

Mastery of L2 is seen as an important indicator of and prerequisite for migrants' social integration (e.g., Esser 2006), and it is often considered to be one of the most crucial primary ethnic effects. Its impact for immigrants' educational success is largely undisputed. In contrast, the effects of proficiency in L1 on immigrants' educational success are highly controversial. On the one hand, some arguments and findings suggest that L1 proficiency has positive effects on L2 acquisition and educational success (e.g., Cummins 1979). On the other hand, detrimental or zero effects of L1 proficiency are also postulated (e.g., Esser 2006).

The role of L1 proficiency for educational success is related to the question whether educational systems should make provisions for the promotion of L1, by, for example, offering so-called *heritage language instruction* or bilingual programs. Proponents of such programs typically assume that they will improve not only students' skills in L1 but also their learning more generally. Yet the empirical evidence on this issue is inconclusive as well (Limbird and Stanat 2006; Söhn 2005). Therefore, NEPS is providing a database that allows researchers to explore the interrelationships among proficiency in L1, proficiency in L2, and indicators of educational success over time. In this way, it is also contributing to settling a crucial issue within the debate about the relevance of "ethnic resources."

7.3.1 L1 as a Beneficial Resource

The strongest theoretical argument in favor of beneficial effects of L1 is the so-called *linguistic interdependence hypothesis,* also labeled the *transfer hypothesis* (Cummins 1979). This states that the acquisition of a second language depends on the acquisition of

---

[1] The term L1 (first language) is used here interchangeably with the language of the country of origin, whereas L2 (second language) refers to the language of the country of residence, regardless of whether these languages are indeed acquired successively, as the labeling L1 and L2 suggests, or simultaneously.

the first language. According to Cummins (1980, p. 175), "proficiencies in both L1 and L2 are manifestations of the same underlying dimension." Based on this *common underlying proficiency,* proficiency in the first language is expected to transfer to the second language and vice versa while also exerting beneficial effects on cognitive development in general. Thus, a causal relationship between first and second language proficiency is assumed. Presumably, however, this transfer will occur only if a certain threshold proficiency is reached in the first language *(threshold hypothesis)*. Methodologically appropriate research on the role of L1 proficiency and bilingualism for L2 proficiency and educational success is scarce, and findings are mixed. Evidence in support of positive effects of L1 proficiency stems from analyses exploring the role of L1 proficiency for L2 acquisition, for third language learning, and for cognitive functioning more generally.

Analyses within the Children of Immigrants Longitudinal Study (CILS) have revealed a positive relationship between self-reported proficiency in L1 and L2 (Esser 2006). Yet, this relationship emerged only after controlling for confounding variables such as socioeconomic status and age at migration. This underlines the importance of including relevant background variables in analyses of language interdependence. Although the CILS accounted for many of these aspects, it did not control for general cognitive ability as a plausible underlying mechanism. Moreover, these findings are based on self-reports of L1 and L2 proficiency, and these may well be biased.

Longitudinal studies with children that did not rely on self-reports but actually tested L1 and L2 proficiency also found some evidence for a beneficial role of L1 proficiency on L2 acquisition. For instance, a recent longitudinal study tracked preschoolers from immigrant families who predominantly used L1 at home over a 3-year period and compared them to preschoolers without a migration background (Lesemann et al. 2009). A small positive transfer effect of L1 proficiency on some aspects of L2 proficiency occurred even after controlling for general cognitive ability and other possible confounds, but no transfer was identified for other aspects of L2 (see also Verhoeven 1994).

In addition, there is evidence that bilingualism is beneficial for third language learning. For instance, a recent study in Germany examined the outcomes of another language than L2 spoken at home on the acquisition of English as a third language (DESI-Konsortium 2008). After controlling for possible confounds, students who had acquired L1 and L2 either simultaneously or consecutively outperformed monolingual German-speaking students in English skills (Hesse et al. 2008). Thus, the presence of L1 as a first language seems to relate positively to third language acquisition.

Because many children of immigrants acquire L2 and L1 simultaneously, research exploring the outcomes of simultaneous bilingualism is also informative in the present context. Research on this issue consistently reveals positive effects of bilingualism on various aspects of cognitive functioning such as metacognitive and metalinguistic awareness (Adesope et al. 2010; Bialystok 1988)—especially when it involves attention processes; the resolution of cognitive conflicts, for example, rule switching (Carlson and Meltzoff 2008); or working memory tasks that demand high levels of executive control (Bialystok 2009). Thus, bilingualism seems to be beneficial for executive functioning.

Executive functioning encompasses a set of cognitive functions including attention and inhibition processes responsible for controlling and managing other cognitive functions. Bialystok (2009) proposes that these advantages are due to bilinguals constantly having to manage conflict resolution demands. More specifically, because both languages are activated jointly in bilinguals, they continuously need to select the right language and to inhibit the other. This, in turn, seems to enhance their executive control system.

7.3.2 L1 as a Hindrance or Irrelevant Skill

There are also positions and findings suggesting that L1 may impede or be irrelevant for educational success. One major argument construing L1 as a hindrance is the *time-on-task hypothesis*. This suggests that L1 may have detrimental effects if time that otherwise could be dedicated to the acquisition of L2 or other school subjects is spent on L1 (e.g., Hopf 2005). This argument draws upon Carroll's (1963) model of school learning. The model emphasizes the time component in learning by defining the degree of learning as a function of the time spent on learning divided by the time needed to learn a specific content. Following this approach, it can be argued that as long as immigrant students' L2 proficiency lags behind that of nonimmigrant students, the available time should be dedicated exclusively to the further acquisition of L2. In fact, some evidence suggests that bilingualism may be associated with negative effects on specific aspects of L2 proficiency, that is vocabulary, and that L1 proficiency and bilingualism are unrelated to educational success.

Research on bilingualism consistently shows that bilingual children possess a smaller vocabulary in each language than their monolingual peers (e.g., Oller and Eilers 2002) and that bilingual adults have greater difficulties in verbal retrieval (e.g., Kaushanskaya and Marian 2007). Bialystok (2009) argues that the mechanisms underlying bilinguals' advantages in executive control are also responsible for the negative outcomes of bilingualism on vocabulary and verbal access. She proposes that the joint activation of both languages creates a conflict between the two, which, in turn, impedes vocabulary access. Of course, bilinguals' combined vocabulary in both languages often exceeds the vocabulary size of monolinguals (e.g., Oller et al. 2007), which can also be interpreted as a positive outcome of bilingualism. However, with regard to educational success, the size of the vocabulary in the language of instruction is likely to be crucial. Therefore, the reduced vocabulary in L2 may have negative effects on learning development.

The relationship between proficiency in L1 and educational success has also been explored with panel data. The results of these studies are mixed as well. Analyses of the National Educational Longitudinal Study (NELS) yielded zero effects of immigrant students' bilingualism on grades, but negative outcomes on mathematics skills (Mouw and Xie 1999). Analyses of CILS data resulted in either positive or zero effects depending on the methodological approach taken. Regression analyses simultaneously including self-reported L1 and L2 proficiency as predictors showed a positive effect of L1 beyond the effect of L2 on mathematics skills, but not on reading (Esser 2006). However, these models did not address the effect of bilingualism that, by definition, consists of a combination of L1 and L2 competencies. When immigrants were divided into groups according to their proficiency in L1 and L2 (high vs. low), migrants with a high proficiency in both L1 and L2 ("competent bilingualism") did not perform better in either reading or in mathematical skills compared to immigrants with a high command of L2 but low L1 proficiency ("assimilation") (Esser 2006).

Another study comparing the group of competent bilinguals to the group of immigrants with high proficiency in L2 alone also challenges the view that competent bilingualism is beneficial for educational outcomes beyond the effects of L2 proficiency. In a sample of elementary school students, Dollmann and Kristen (2010) could not identify any advantages of competent bilinguals in terms of cognitive, mathematical, or reading skills as well as mathematics grades compared to immigrant students with high proficiency in L2 but not in L1. Unlike the panel studies cited above, the data in this study included objective measures of L1 proficiency rather than self-reports. Nevertheless, the study was restricted to a specific context (a large city in Germany), a specific migrant group (Turkish descent), and a specific age group (3rd to 4th grade), thereby casting doubt on the generalizability of its findings. Taken together, the empirical evidence for effects of L1 proficiency and bilingualism on educational success is ambiguous, and the empirical foundation far from satisfactory.

7.4 Ethnic Networks as Promoters of Educational Success?

Another important stream in the debate on "ethnic resources" concerns the role of ethnic networks and communities for educational success in terms of both competence development (i.e., primary ethnic effects) and transitions (i.e., secondary ethnic effects).

The general lines of argument parallel those on the role of L1 very closely. Proponents of segmented assimilation theory reason that ties to coethnics can compensate for disadvantages (e.g., Portes 1995, 2003; Portes and Rumbaut 2001; Zhou 1997), whereas proponents of new assimilation theory argue that these ties might prove to constrain the advancement of students of immigrant origin (e.g., Alba and Nee 1997, 2003; Esser 2004; Kalter 2008; Perlmann and Waldinger 1997; Waters and Jiménez 2005). Theoretically, Pillar 4 aims to overcome these seemingly conflicting standpoints by integrating them into a more comprehensive model of intergenerational integration (Esser 2008) in which each type of argument constitutes a special case, and positive or negative effects of ethnic communities are seen as being conditional on a set of further conditions such as opportunity structures and specific characteristics of the coethnics (Kroneberg 2008).

7.4.1 Ethnic Networks as a Beneficial Resource

Ethnic networks are assumed to be helpful for succeeding in the educational system of a receiving society via several, often connected, ways. Most importantly, it has been argued that ethnic communities might provide a kind of protection against the danger of "downward assimilation," that is, adopting the lifestyles and attitudes of the disadvantaged segments in the country of residence such as the Black urban underclass in the United States (Portes and Zhou 1993; Portes and Rumbaut 2001). Immigrant families and communities that possess strong educational aspirations and emphasize the importance of education can foster the advancement of their offspring by means of social control and direct support. This, according to the argument, works especially well if ethnic networks are dense and rather closed. In these instances, immigrants are obliged to meet educational goals, and deviant behaviors can be sanctioned effectively (Portes and Zhou 1993). For example, family members, friends, or neighbors can encourage students to do their homework and spend time on school-related tasks, or simply prevent them from fooling around. This could result in positive primary effects of ethnic origin.

A further mechanism assumes indirect beneficial effects of ethnic networks: If faced with discrimination, exclusion policies, or exclusive regulations, ethnic networks—along with strong ethnic identity and/or ethnic solidarity—can protect immigrants and their descendants from experiencing these confrontations, stereotypes, and possible threats in their everyday lives (Portes and Rumbaut 2001). This increases the probability that these students will maintain their efforts to perform well at school or on the job—even within a (possibly hostile) receiving context. Ethnic networks are seen to be especially important for recently arrived immigrants. They face the well-known problem of capital devaluation, meaning that many aspects of their skills and knowledge are no longer useful in the receiving society (Friedberg 2000)—most importantly, their language (see Sect. 7.3). Here ethnic communities provide an alternative "mode of production" and promise instant help: They can offer information relevant for succeeding in the receiving society even without supplementary skills. Whereas these arguments are often made in the context of labor market integration (Aguilera and Massey 2003), they can be transferred easily to the education system. Even without knowing one single word of German herself, a just-arrived mother who can draw on the knowledge available within her network will have a better chance of accessing information on how the German school system functions, which schools are good, that it might be worth considering Kindergarten, and so forth. This would point to a positive secondary ethnic effect.

Altogether, these segmented assimilation arguments suggesting that ethnic networks facilitate social and economic mobility for immigrants and their offspring (Portes and Zhou 1993) explicitly challenge the assumptions of classical or new assimilation theory that social assimilation is the more promising track and that ethnic networks are less useful for upward mobility.

7.4.2 Ethnic Networks as a Hindrance

The general shortcomings of arguments favoring the beneficial effects of ethnic networks on educational success can be understood very well by referring more explicitly to the concept of social capital. Social capital encompasses resources possessed by individuals on the basis of their relationships to others; that is, it is seen as a result of the embedding of individuals into a collective system (Bourdieu 1983; Coleman 1988; Esser 2000; Lin 2003). Roughly speaking, the basic argument behind seeing ethnic networks as a hindrance for educational advancement is that there can be a trade-off between ethnic ties and ties to the receiving society, and that there is reason to assume that, in most cases, the latter will deliver more helpful resources in the end. For example, one could relate directly to the discussion on language proficiency above, and stress the negative impact of ethnic networks on L2 acquisition: A high level of incorporation into ethnic networks is associated with more frequent use and exposure to L1—and less use and exposure to L2. This, in turn, would affect competence development (i.e., a primary ethnic effect).

In general, ethnic communities, by definition, provide fewer opportunities for interethnic contacts. This increases social distance and reduces the availability of information specific to the receiving context (Farwick 2009). Hence, strong ethnic networks are often seen as a mobility trap (Wiley 1970) and are perceived as either irrelevant or harmful to educational and social mobility (Esser 2009). Social networks provide access to others' resources, and one crucial resource is information, for example, that on the functioning of the school system. This information may encompass knowledge about important transitions, the requirements that need to be met to enter a certain pathway, the set of schools available, and so forth (i.e., secondary ethnic effects). Obviously, a timely communication of this kind of knowledge along with a thorough understanding of the steps one has to take to navigate the system successfully are also essential at later stages in the educational career. For adolescents and young adults, for instance, it is important to know how to write a proper application for an apprenticeship or to be familiar with which (cultural) codes to follow during a job interview.

Apart from providing relevant information, the effect of social capital and ethnic networks on educational and labor market success is just as much about references and recommendations. They can be vital for placement in a certain position (Granovetter 1973; Montgomery 1991).

How much information and support are accessible and how helpful these are depends on network characteristics such as homogeneity and relationship quality (Granovetter 1973). Weak ties to other networks can provide nonredundant information. To conceptualize this more appropriately, Granovetter (1974) introduced the term social bridges for those key ties that build up singular connections between (otherwise) separate networks. New, nonredundant information can come only via these social bridges. The closer one is located to a bridge builder and the stronger one's relation to her or him, the more likely it is that one will be able to mobilize social capital accessible through this bridge (Lin 2003). Therefore, what matters is the quality of relations in terms of closeness, contact frequency, degree of kinship, or duration. In this regard again, strong ethnic networks can result in disadvantages for immigrants and their descendants: Among their weak, but especially among their strong ties, they find relatively few majority group members and many coethnics who may be less able to provide the information and support that is relevant for educational advancement in the country of residence (Haug and Pointner 2007; Gestring 2007).

Interestingly, even the proponents of segmented assimilation theory see a possible "downside" of ethnic capital when the resources included in it are contraproductive. The basic mechanisms of social control and enforceable trust can also work in a negative direction: Ambitious immigrants can be slowed down or deterred from investing particularly in education by an ethnic network that does not share these ambitions and therefore sanctions such escapees (Portes and Rumbaut 2001). Portes and MacLeod (1999) found a strong increase in the probability of lower educational success if a "fatal combination" of strong integration into ethnic communities offering only poor social capital is accompanied by low human capital and strong ethnic identities.

7.5 Analytical Potential of NEPS

Empirical tests of the arguments outlined above require an appropriate research design and the careful selection of constructs. Against the background of this chapter, we highlight the pillar's analysis potential starting with some general remarks on the distinction between generations and migrant groups and then focusing on a selection of important constructs covered by Pillar 4. In line with the preceding sections, we pay special attention to language proficiency and social networks.

Complementing the description of ethnic educational inequalities across the life course and disentangling their origins requires the identification of different generations and distinct immigrant groups, because the extent to which the above-mentioned arguments apply differs substantially. Pillar 4 implements a broad definition of generation status based on the country of birth of the target person, the parents, and the grandparents (e.g., Rumbaut 2004). This makes it possible to identify not only the first and second generation, but, in contrast to most other large-scale data sources, also the third generation. In addition, users of NEPS data can differentiate between more fine-grained combinations, for example, between individuals born to two foreign-born parents (i.e., the second generation), and those with only one parent born in Germany and the other born abroad (i.e., the so-called 2.5 generation).

As illustrated in Sect. 7.3, an adequate assessment of language skills is crucial to Pillar 4. Because most studies addressing bilingualism had methodological limitations, evidence is still inconclusive, and it has not yet been possible to settle the controversy. In order to overcome the various methodological problems of previous studies, L1 proficiency in Russian and Turkish is being tested at three measurement points: in Grade 2 in order to assess L1 proficiency at an early stage of the educational career; in Grade 7 after the whole sample has transited into secondary school; and in Grade 9 shortly before the transition from school to work will take place for many students in the lower tracks of the school system.

The tests focus on listening comprehension. We chose this focus because migrant students typically learn L1 in the family context and are not necessarily able to read or write in this language. The test developed for secondary school consists of several short recordings of clearly spoken texts including dialogues as well as expository and narrative content presented by native speakers of Turkish or Russian respectively. In order to avoid effects of previous knowledge on the test results, the content of the units was chosen so that either all students should be familiar with the subject matter (e.g., a classroom situation) or no students (e.g., the living conditions of a rare mammal). Listening comprehension is tested with several multiple-choice questions per unit. In order to broaden the empirical basis for questions related to L1 proficiency, other aspects of L1 proficiency that are not tested (reading, writing, and speaking) are assessed as self-reports in all immigrant students and also at other stages of the educational process.

NEPS is the first study in Germany to provide objective indicators of L1 proficiency for a representative sample of immigrant students. Moreover, the data are being generated in a sample whose educational trajectories are followed up longitudinally, and for which a multitude of other competence measures as well as background variables is available. Some of the language-related research questions that can be explored with NEPS data include the effects of L1 proficiency on school achievement and competence development in different domains; its relation to other indicators of immigrants' integration such as aspects of identity or psychological adaptation; and its influence on the transition to vocational training. In addition, the conditions of L1 acquisition and bilingualism in the family and in educational institutions can be examined more closely. NEPS will not be able to resolve all of the issues concerning the outcomes of L1 proficiency. Yet, it offers a unique analytical potential for researchers interested in the conditions and outcomes of the L1 proficiency of immigrants in Germany.

To examine the impact of ethnic networks and social capital on educational success, Pillar 4 includes information on network characteristics such as diversity, ethnic composition, heterogeneity, and positioning. The basic social capital measurements are covered by Pillar 3 (see Chap. 6, this volume). Pillar 4 adds the immigrant-specific constructs.

For each educational stage, social capital measurements include a resource generator that covers sources of information and support including the source's ethnic origin. For example, individuals are being asked whether they know someone who could help them to write an application or to gather information on job vacancies. In addition, a position generator is applied to examine the network's social and ethnic composition. For each accessible (social) position, we ask for the person's ethnic origin. Whereas for the early stages in the educational career, the focus is on parents' networks, attention shifts to the target persons' networks as they grow older. We also measure the proportion of individuals in the immediate environment who come from the same country of origin. Social capital is being measured prospectively and retrospectively. Measurements also include the actual use of social capital after important educational decisions. In combination with the repeated-measurements panel design, this allows us to address major theoretical and methodological criticisms. For instance, only this design makes it possible to address the question whether people who possess more social capital are actually more likely to use it. Otherwise, one could argue that social capital effects are a mere artifact of unobserved heterogeneity (Kalter 2010) or a result of the homophilious formation of friendship networks (Mouw 2006).

Apart from focusing on social networks and language proficiency, Pillar 4 implements instruments covering further important resources and characteristics. For example, identification orientations and their behavioral manifestations indicate the context toward which individuals direct their educational investments. Therefore, we capture identifications with one's own group, the country of origin, and its culture as well as those with the majority population, the country of residence, and its culture. These constructs will be measured for parents within the Kindergarten and school stages and for target persons beginning in Grade 3. We also consider behaviors that reflect these orientations, such as visits to the country of origin, contacts to family members and friends in the country of origin, and remittances. Other important behavioral manifestations include mating behavior and cultural habits—for example, the celebration of country-specific holidays or cooking habits. These measures always cover the orientation toward both the country of origin and the country of residence. Regarding cultural capital, we complement the instruments of Pillar 3 (see Chap. 6, this volume) with immigrant-specific aspects. For instance, when measuring reading habits, we add the language of media consumption.

NEPS Pillar 4 is providing unique information on the education of immigrants and their offspring in Germany. The database allows analyses of general processes leading to ethnic inequalities in education, and it offers manifold opportunities for substantial contributions to current debates, in particular on the role of "ethnic resources" for educational success.

References

Adesope, O. O., Lavin, T., Thompson, T., & Ungerleider, C. (2010). A systematic review and meta-analysis of the cognitive correlates of bilingualism. *Review of Educational Research, 80*(2), 207–249.

Aguilera, M. B., & Massey, D. (2003). Social capital and the wages of Mexican migrants: New hypotheses and tests. *Social Forces, 82*(2), 671–701.

Alba, R. D., Handl, J., & Müller, W. (1994). Ethnische Ungleichheiten im deutschen Bildungssystem. *Kölner Zeitschrift für Soziologie und Sozialpsychologie, 46*(2), 209–237.

Alba, R., & Nee, V. (1997). Rethinking assimilation for a new era of immigration. *International Migration Review, 31*(4), 826–874.

Alba, R., & Nee, V. (2003). *Remaking the American mainstream.* Cambridge, MA: Harvard University Press.

Autorengruppe Bildungsberichterstattung (2010). *Bildung in Deutschland 2010: Ein indikatorengestützter Bericht mit einer Analyse zu Perspektivendes Bildungswesens im demografischen Wandel.* Bielefeld, Germany: Bertelsmann.

Becker, B., & Biedinger, N. (2006). Ethnische Bildungsungleichheit zu Schulbeginn. *Kölner Zeitschrift für Soziologie und Sozialpsychologie, 58*(4), 660–684.

Boudon, R. (1974). *Education, opportunity, und social inequality. Changing prospects in western society.* New York, NY: Wiley.

Bourdieu, P. (1983). Ökonomisches Kapital, Kulturelles Kapital, Soziales Kapital. In R. Kreckel (Ed.), *Soziale Ungleichheiten* (Soziale Welt: Sonderband. 2, pp. 183–198). Göttingen, Germany: Schwartz.

Bialystok, E. (1988). Levels of bilingualism and levels of linguistic awareness. *Developmental Psychology, 24*, 560–567.

Bialystok, E. (2009). Effects of bilingualism on cognitive and linguistic performance across the lifespan. In I. Gogolin & U. Neumann (Eds.), *Streitfall Zweisprachigkeit – The Bilingualism Controversy* (pp. 31–52). Wiesbaden, Germany: VS Verlag für Sozialwissenschaften.

Carlson, S. M., & Meltzoff, A. N. (2008). Bilingual experience and executive functioning in young children. *Developmental Science, 11*, 282–298.

Carroll, J. B. (1963). A model of school learning. *Teachers College Record, 64*(8), 723–733.

Chiswick, B. R. (1978). The effect of Americanization on the earnings of foreign-born men. *Journal of Political Economy, 86*, 897–922.

Coleman, J. S. (1988). Social capital in the creation of human capital. *American Journal of Sociology, 94*(Suppl. 95), 95–120.

Cummins, J. (1979). Linguistic interdependence and the educational development of bilingual children. *Review of Educational Research, 49*(2), 222–251.

Cummins, J. (1980). The cross-lingual dimensions of language proficiency: Implications for bilingual education and the optimal age issue. *TESOL Quarterly, 14*(2), 175–187.

DESI-Konsortium (Eds.). (2008). *Unterricht und Kompetenzerwerb in Deutsch und Englisch. Ergebnisse der DESI-Studie*. Weinheim, Germany: Beltz Verlag.

Dollmann, J., & Kristen, C. (2010). Herkunftssprache als Ressource für den Schulerfolg? – Das Beispiel türkischer Grundschulkinder. In C. Allemann-Ghionda, P. Stanat, K. Göbel, & C. Röhner (Eds.), *Migration, Identität Sprache und Bildungserfolg*. (Zeitschrift für Pädagogik, Beiheft 55., pp. 123–146). Weinheim, Germany: Beltz Verlag.

Erikson, R., & Jonsson, J. O. (1996). Explaining class inequality in education: The Swedish case. In R. Erikson & J. O. Jonsson (Eds.), *Can education be equalized? The Swedish case in comparative perspective* (pp. 1–63). Oxford, England: Westview Press.

Esser, H. (2000). *Soziologie. Spezielle Grundlagen, Bd. 2: Die Konstruktion der Gesellschaft*. Frankfurt a. M., Germany: Campus.

Esser, H. (2004). Does the "new" immigration require a "new" theory of intergenerational integration? *International Migration Review, 38*, 1126–1159.

Esser, H. (2006). *Sprache und Integration: Die sozialen Bedingungen und Folgen des Spracherwerbs von Migranten*. Frankfurt a. M., Germany: Campus Verlag.

Esser, H. (2008). Assimilation, ethnische Schichtung oder selektive Akkulturation? Neuere Theorien der Eingliederung von Migranten und das Modell der intergenerationalen Integration. In F. Kalter (Ed.), *Migration und Integration* (Kölner Zeitschrift für Soziologie und Sozialpsychologie: Sonderband 48, pp. 81–107). Wiesbaden, Germany: VS Verlag für Sozialwissenschaften.

Esser, H. (2009). Der Streit um die Zweisprachigkeit: Was bringt Bilingualität? In I. Gogolin & U. Neumann (Eds.), *Streitfall Zweisprachigkeit – The Bilingualism Controversy* (pp. 69–90). Wiesbaden, Germany: VS Verlag für Sozialwissenschaften.

Farwick, A. (2009). *Segregation und Eingliederung. Zum Einfluss der räumlichen Konzentration von Zuwanderern auf den Eingliederungsprozess*. Wiesbaden, Germany: VS Verlag für Sozialwissenschaften.

Friedberg, R. M. (2000). You can't take it with you? Immigrant assimilation and the portability of human capital. *Journal of Labor Economics, 18*, 221–251.

Gestring, N. (2007). Ethnische Segregation, Quartierstypen und soziale Netzwerke. In F. Meyer (Ed.), *Wohnen – Arbeit – Zuwanderung: Stand und Perspektiven der Segregationsforschung* (pp. 135–145). Berlin, Germany: LIT.

Granovetter, M. S. (1973). The strength of weak ties. *American Journal of Sociology, 78*, 1360–1380.

Granovetter, M. S. (1974). *Getting a job: A study of contacts and careers.* Cambridge, MA: Harvard University Press.

Haug, S., & Pointner, S. (2007). Soziale Netzwerke, Migration und Integration. In A. Franzen (Ed.), *Sozialkapital: Grundlagen und Anwendungen* (Kölner Zeitschrift für Soziologie und Sozialpsychologie: Sonderheft 47, pp. 367–396). Wiesbaden, Germany: VS Verlag für Sozialwissenschaften.

Heath, A., & Brinbaum, Y. (2007). Explaining ethnic inequalities in educational attainment. *Ethnicities, 7*(3), 291–305.

Heath, A., Rothon, C., & Kilpi, E. (2008). The second generation in Western Europe: Education, unemployment and occupational attainment. *Annual Review of Sociology, 34,* 211–235.

Hesse, H.-G., Göbel, K., & Hartig, J. (2008). Sprachliche Kompetenzen von mehrsprachigen Jugendlichen und Jugendlichen nicht-deutscher Erstsprache. In DESI-Konsortium (Ed.), *Unterricht und Kompetenzerwerb in Deutsch und Englisch: Ergebnisse der DESI-Studie* (pp. 208–230). Weinheim, Germany: Beltz Verlag.

Hopf, D. (2005). Zweisprachigkeit und Schulleistung bei Migrantenkindern. *Zeitschrift für Pädagogik, 51*(2), 236–251.

Jonsson, J. O., & Rudolphi, F. (2010). Weak performance — strong determination: School achievement and educational choice among children of immigrants in Sweden. *European Sociological Review.* https://doi.org/10.1093/esr/jcq021.

Kalter, F. (2005). Ethnische Ungleichheit auf dem Arbeitsmarkt. In M. Abraham & T. Hinz (Eds.), *Arbeitsmarktsoziologie: Probleme, Theorien, empirische Befunde* (pp. 303–332). Wiesbaden, Germany: VS Verlag für Sozialwissenschaften.

Kalter, F. (2006). Auf der Suche nach einer Erklärung für die spezifischen Arbeitsmarktnachteile von Jugendlichen türkischer Herkunft. *Zeitschrift für Soziologie, 35*(2), 144–160.

Kalter, F. (2008). Stand, Herausforderungen und Perspektiven der empirischen Migrationsforschung. In F. Kalter (Ed.), *Migration und Integration* (Kölner Zeitschrift für Soziologie und Sozialpsychologie: Sonderband. 48, pp. 11–36). Wiesbaden, Germany: VS Verlag für Sozialwissenschaften.

Kalter, F. (2010). Social capital and the dynamics of temporary labour migration from Poland to Germany. *European Sociological Review 7*(5), 555–569. https://doi.org/10.1093/esr/jcq025.

Kaushanskaya, M., & Marian, V. (2007). Bilingual language processing and interference in bilinguals: Evidence from eye tracking and picture naming. *Language Learning, 57,* 119–163.

Kristen, C. (2008). Primary school choice and ethnic school segregation in German elementary schools. *European Sociological Review, 24,* 495–510.

Kristen, C., & Dollman, J. (2010). Sekundäre Effekte der ethnischen Herkunft: Kinder aus türkischen Familien am ersten Bildungsübergang. In B. Becker & D. Reimer (Eds.), *Vom Kindergarten bis zur Hochschule* (pp. 117–144). Wiesbaden, Germany: VS Verlag für Sozialwissenschaften.

Kristen, C., & Granato, N. (2007). The educational attainment of the second generation in Germany. Social origins and ethnic inequality. *Ethnicities, 7*(3), 343–366.

Kristen, C., Reimer, D., & Kogan, I. (2008). Higher education entry of Turkish immigrant youth in Germany. *International Journal of Comparative Sociology, 49,* 127–151.

Kroneberg, C. (2008). Ethnic communities and school performance among the new second generation. Testing the theory of segmented assimilation. *The Annals of the American Academy of Political and Social Science, 620,* 138–160.

Lesemann, P. P. M., Scheele, A. F., Mayo, A. Y., & Messer, M. H. (2009). Bilingual development in early childhood and the language used at home: Competition for scarce resources? In I. Gogolin & U. Neumann (Eds.), *Streitfall Zweisprachigkeit – The Bilingualism Controversy* (pp. 317–331). Wiesbaden, Germany: VS Verlag für Sozialwissenschaften.

Limbird, C., & Stanat, P. (2006). Prädiktoren von Leseverständnis bei Kindern deutscher und türkischer Herkunftssprache: Ergebnisse einer Längsschnittstudie. In A. Ittel & H. Merkens (Eds.), *Veränderungsmessung und Längsschnittstudien in der Erziehungswissenschaft* (pp. 93–123). Wiesbaden, Germany: VS Verlag für Sozialwissenschaften.

Lin, N. (2003). *Social capital: A theory of social structure and action.* Cambridge, England: Cambridge University Press.

Montgomery, J. D. (1991). Social networks and labor-market outcomes: Toward an economic analysis. *The American Economic Review, 81,* 1408–1418.

Mouw, T. (2006). Estimating the causal effect of social capital: A review of recent research. *Annual Review of Sociology, 32,* 79–102.

Mouw, T., & Xie, Y. (1999). Bilingualism and the academic achievement of first and second generation Asian Americans: Accommodation with or without assimilation? *American Sociological Review, 64,* 232–252.

Müller, A. G., & Stanat, P. (2006). Schulischer Erfolg von Schülerinnen und Schülern mit Migrationshintergrund: Analysen zur Situation von Jugendlichen aus der ehemaligen Sowjetunion und der Türkei. In J. Baumert, P. Stanat, & R. Watermann (Eds.), *Herkunftsbedingte Disparitäten im Bildungswesen: Differenzielle Bildungsprozesse und Probleme der Verteilungsgerechtigkeit* (pp. 221–256). Wiesbaden, Germany: VS Verlag für Sozialwissenschaften.

Oller, D. K., & Eilers, R. E. (Eds.). (2002). *Language and literacy in bilingual children.* Clevedon, England: Multilingual mattters ltd.

Oller, D. K., Pearson, B. Z., & Cobo-Lewis, A. B. (2007). Profile effects in early bilingual language and literacy. *Applied Pschololinguistics, 28*(2), 191–230.

Perlmann, J., & Waldinger, R. (1997). Second generation decline? Children of immigrants, past and present—A reconsideration. *International Migration Review, 31*(4), 893–922.

Portes, A. (1995). Children of immigrants: Segmented assimilation and its determinants. In A. Portes (Ed.), *The economic sociology of immigration: Essays on networks, ethnicity, and entrepreneurship* (pp. 248–280). New York, NY: Russell Sage Foundation.

Portes, A. (2003). Ethnicities: Children of migrants in America. *Development, 46*(3), 42–52.

Portes, A., & Hao, L. (2004). The schooling of children of immigrants: Contextual effects on the educational attainment of the second generation. *Proceeding of National Academy of Science, 101*(33), 11920–11927.

Portes, A., & MacLeod, D. (1996). Educational progress of children of immigrants: The roles of class, ethnicity, and school context. *Sociology of Education, 69*(4), 255–275.

Portes, A., & MacLeod, D. (1999). Educating the second-generation: Determinants of academic achievement among children of immigrants in the United States. *Journal of Ethnic and Migration Studies, 25*(3), 373–396.

Portes, A., & Rumbaut, R. G. (2001). Not everyone is chosen: Segmented assimilation and its determinants. In A. Portes & R. G. Rumbaut (Eds.), *Legacies. The story of the immigrant second generation* (pp. 44–69). Berkeley, CA: University of California Press.

Portes, A., & Zhou, M. (1993). The new second generation: Segmented assimilation and its variants among post-1965 immigrant youth. *Annals of the American Academy of Political and Social Science, 530,* 74–98.

Rumbaut, R. (2004). Ages, life stages, and generational cohorts: Decomposing the immigrant first and second generation in the United States. *International Migration Review, 38*(3), 1160–1205.

Schwippert, K., Hornberg, S., Freiberg, M., & Stubbe, T. (2007). Lesekompetenzen von Kindern mit Migrationshintergrund im internationalen Vergleich. In W. Bos, S. Hornberg, K.-H. Arnold, G. Faust, L. Fried, E.-M. Lankes, K. Schwippert, & R. Valtin (Eds.), *IGLU 2006: Lesekompetenz von Grundschulkindern in Deutschland im internationalen Vergleich* (pp. 249–269). Münster, Germany: Waxmann.

Segeritz, M., Walter, O., & Stanat, P. (2010). Muster des schulischen Erfolgs von jugendlichen Migranten in Deutschland: Evidenz für segmentierte Assimilation? *Kölner Zeitschrift für Soziologie und Sozialpsychologie, 62,* 113–138.

Söhn, J. (2005). *Zweisprachiger Schulunterricht für Migrantenkinder. Ergebnisse der Evaluationsforschung zu seinen Auswirkungen auf Zweitspracherwerb und Schulerfolg.* Berlin, Germany: Wissenschaftszentrum Berlin für Sozialforschung (WZB).

Stanat, P., & Christensen, G. (2006). *Where immigrant students succeed – A comparative review of performance and engagement in PISA 2003.* Paris: OECD.

Verhoeven, L. (1994). Transfer in bilingual development: The linguistic interdependence hypothesis revisited. *Language Learning, 44,* 381–415.

Walter, O., & Taskinen, P. (2007). Kompetenzen und bildungsrelevante Einstellungen von Jugendlichen mit Migrationshintergrund in Deutschland: Ein Vergleich mit ausgewählten OECD-Staaten. In PISA-Konsortium Deutschland (Eds.), *PISA 2006: Die Ergebnisse der dritten internationalen Vergleichsstudie* (pp. 337–366). Münster, Germany: Waxmann.

Waters, M. C., & Jiménez, T. R. (2005). Assessing immigrant assimilation: New empirical and theoretical challenges. *Annual Revue of Sociology, 31,* 105–125.

Wiley, N. F. (1970). The ethnic mobility trap and stratification theory. In P. I. Rose (Ed.), *The study of society. An integrated anthology* (pp. 397–408). New York, NY: Random House.

Zhou, M. (1997). Segmented assimilation: Issues, controversies, and recent research in the new second generation. *International Migration Review, 31*(4), 975–1008.

Educational Returns Over the Life Course

Christiane Gross, Anika Bela, Monika Jungbauer-Gans, Andreas Jobst and Johannes Schwarze

Abstract

Pillar 5 of the German National Educational Panel Study (NEPS) focuses on various returns to education over the life course. The longitudinal design allows us to study the complex and dynamic interaction processes when qualifications, competencies, and educational certificates are turned into economic and noneconomic returns. In this chapter, we outline the central theoretical concepts for analyzing returns to education and describe how they are implemented within NEPS. We discuss economic returns such as income and other labor market-related outcomes with an emphasis on expected income as an innovative concept. Noneconomic returns may come in the

---

J. Schwarze—We regret the sudden and untimely death of Johannes Schwarze on September 12, 2010.

C. Gross (✉)
University of Wurzburg, Würzburg, Germany
E-Mail: christiane.gross@uni-wuerzburg.de

A. Bela
Leibniz Institute for Educational Trajectories, Bamberg, Germany
E-Mail: anika.bela@lifbi.de

M. Jungbauer-Gans
Leibniz University of Hanover, Hannover, Germany
E-Mail: jungbauer@dzhw.eu

J. Schwarze
University of Bamberg, Bamberg, Germany

© Springer Fachmedien Wiesbaden GmbH, ein Teil von Springer Nature 2019
H.-P. Blossfeld and H.-G. Roßbach (eds.), *Education as a Lifelong Process*,
Edition ZfE 3, https://doi.org/10.1007/978-3-658-23162-0_8

form of better health, increased subjective well-being, increased social and political participation, and changing processes of family formation. Over the life cycle, returns related to health and subjective well-being will tend to accrue from early childhood through adulthood, whereas returns related to political participation will tend to set in during late adolescence. In order to identify causal relationships, it is necessary to avoid considerable bias in the estimation of returns to education. One crucial source of biased estimators is the omission of the financial restrictions faced by the parents' household. Thus, Pillar 5 implements several measures to control for the economic situation of the household such as household income and wealth.

Keywords
Education · Panel study · Returns · Income · Health

8.1 Theoretical Concepts[1]

The National Educational Panel Study (NEPS) is providing the first ever opportunity to gauge causal returns to different measures of education in terms of different outcomes. The pillar "Returns to Education Across the Life Course" focuses not only on economic but also on important noneconomic returns (Schuller et al. 2004) such as health, political and social participation, subjective well-being, and family formation. The importance of these different indicators of educational returns varies over the life course. Whereas monetary returns do not occur before labor market entry and further labor market mobility, returns in terms of health and subjective well-being arise already during childhood. Social and political participation tend to accrue during adolescence.

The selection of variables to be controlled when analyzing returns to education is guided by several labor market theories. Human capital theory regards education as an investment that enhances an individual's productivity and therefore future earnings. Whereas higher returns amortize direct and opportunity costs, individuals maximize lifetime earnings by choosing the optimal level of education (Becker 1964; Mincer 1974). Within the theoretical framework of filtering and signaling (see Arrow 1973; Spence 1973), information about a person's productivity is assumed to be imperfect, and educational certificates serve as a signal for a worker's productivity. Whereas costs of educational attainment depend on cognitive and noncognitive skills, individuals try to attain credentials according to expected returns.

Moreover, structural aspects have to be considered. According to job competition and vacancy chain models, positions in the labor market are not freely available to anyone with the same personal resources (Sørensen 1977). Therefore, it is not changes in individual competencies but the creation of vacancies that is the central mechanism of job mobility and income gains. When the transition from school to work is considered, differences between birth cohorts are analyzed in terms of feedback effects of educational

---

[1] We thank Laura Mayer for research assistance.

expansion and in terms of a destandardization of the transition process and the pathways taken (Raffe 2007). How institutional arrangements influence the different pathways and educational trajectories is an important issue. Theories of segmented labor markets are another group of structural theories that deal with mechanisms of job placement, wage differences, and wage growth.

Sociological class reproduction theory argues that educational credentials reflect advantages from family background such as economic, cultural, and social capital as well as status group memberships that are used as a mechanism of intergenerational advantage transfer. The economic argument that capital markets are incomplete, and that family background is therefore important for financing and investing in children's capital is in line with social reproduction theory (Bourdieu and Boltanski 1981). Another aspect is the influence of domain-general cognitive functions such as intelligence on both educational attainment and labor market outcomes. This indicates that the observed returns on educational measures alone do not reflect the whole picture, and that it is necessary to control for former competencies (Card 1999; Harmon et al. 2003). Consideration of the personal and social background variables will yield a better understanding of the way education produces its beneficial outcomes.

Additionally, a comprehensive investigation of the causal relationships is necessary to avoid considerable bias in estimating the benefits of education. For example, the endogeneity bias represents a serious obstacle for estimating returns to education with respect to health outcomes: The question is whether persons are healthier due to a higher level of education, or whether more healthy persons have better access to educational resources. Nonmarket returns to education are more important for earlier stages in the educational career. A further question is how far early acquired competencies facilitate additional learning. Panel data on test scores permit a causal estimation of returns to skills and competencies as well as different educational inputs such as class size, teacher education, or spending per student while including fixed effects for students and schools (Wößmann and West 2006). Well-educated individuals are expected to be inclined toward more health-conscious behavior. NEPS data will show how far cognitive competencies and knowledge about health and medicine mediate between education and health behavior.

Education impacts on behavior in further areas such as family formation because of rising opportunity costs due to educational attainment. Looking at family formation and marriage, we expect a negative relationship between women's increasing level of education and rates of entry into marriage and motherhood, thus explaining low levels of nuptiality and fertility and increasing female labor force participation. Another outcome of increasing educational participation is the higher likelihood of educational homogamy across cohorts (Blossfeld and Timm 2003). Moreover, political and social participation increases with more education, because specific competencies and skills are a necessary precondition for participation in social life (Dee 2004). Finally, education might impact on preferences such as patience and risk aversion (Oreopoulos and Salvanes 2011; Perez-Arce 2017) that are expected to influence educational decisions and participation in turn.

At the same time, individual preferences have been identified as important determinants of life outcomes such as labor market outcomes or health (Becker et al. 2012).

A final indicator of nonmarket returns considered in NEPS is subjective well-being. Studies have shown that life satisfaction is a valid measure of individual well-being (Frey and Stutzer 2002). The central question here is whether education has a genuine impact on well-being. Again, the panel data can be used to shed some light on the issue of whether education is a cause or consequence of well-being.

8.2 Labor Market Success as a Key Return to Education

As discussed above, classic outcomes of education are economic outcomes, particularly labor market earnings (see Sect. 8.2.1). Because these returns accrue principally when individuals have left the educational system and started to work in the labor market, economists are also interested in expected returns by individuals who are still in the educational system. Though income expectations are crucial in economic theory, knowledge about this is sparse, and this is why assumptions are restrictive (see Sect. 8.2.2). Whatever the case, social capital is an outstanding determinant of educational achievement (see Chap. 6, this volume). In light of incomplete capital markets, financial restrictions can be decisive for educational decision making. In order to picture families' potential to fund further education, Pillar 5 captures information on household income, wealth, and student grants (see Sect. 8.2.3 Funding of Education).

8.2.1 Earnings

The central labor market outcome of educational investment is income, more specifically, labor market earnings and income from self-employment. Thus, Pillar 5 gathers income data from employed adolescents and adults. The appropriate income definition for Germany is monthly gross and net income from employment. Other important labor market outcomes such as labor market performance, job stability, occupational career, working time, working conditions, and limitation of the working contract are dealt with in Stage 8 (see Chap. 17, this volume) and Pillar 3 (see Chap. 6, this volume). Through its longitudinal approach, NEPS extends the scope of analyses of economic returns to education. NEPS data may help us to reconsider the determinants of education in classic estimates of returns to years of education, and it promotes research on returns to school quality and acquired cognitive and noncognitive competencies.

NEPS data on educational attainment go far beyond the classic measure of mere years of education. By recording the educational career and measuring competencies and skills over the whole life course, they enable an unbiased investigation of returns to education. One exemplary question with a serious political background is whether gender-specific wage differentials are created within the educational system, or whether they are caused by anticipatory behavior of women in light of job discontinuities due to childbearing and maternity leave. NEPS data is providing new insights into the causes of the gender wage gap.

The quality of educational institutions may have a strong impact on educational achievements and thus on labor market opportunities, and this is something that varies considerably (Hanushek 2005). By linking labor market outcomes to institutional features such as school quality and competition within the educational system, NEPS data are able to provide evidence on different measures of education that are more policy relevant than mere years of education. An important extension of knowledge on economic returns to education is gained from the linkage of educational measures surveyed in the childhood and adolescent years to subsequent individual labor market outcomes. Thus, a valuable feature of the NEPS dataset lies in the long run when economic returns can be assessed in terms of cognitive competencies rather than years of education. There is evidence that returns to education vary by ability (Brand and Xie 2010; Heckman et al. 2016): Economic returns to cognitive competencies are higher than returns to mere quantitative measures of years of education (see Hanushek and Wößmann 2007) or educational credentials. Data from the United States show that with regard to labor market outcomes, the importance of cognitive competencies has risen over time (see Murnane et al. 1995). Even among school dropouts, there are returns to cognitive competencies (Tyler et al. 2000), and higher test scores have also been shown to be associated with higher labor force participation and lower unemployment rates (McIntosh and Vignoles 2001).

8.2.2 Income Expectations

Basic economic theory assumes individuals to be more or less informed about future earning streams (conditional on different educational trajectories) when making educational decisions. Though expectations on future earnings are central to an economic analysis of schooling decisions, research on expectations itself is rare. Experimental designs have shown the effect of expectations about educational returns on schooling decisions (Jensen 2010). If students' expectations of returns to education are not observed, however, inferences about the decision process can be misleading, because observed choice data may be consistent with expectations and many alternative specifications of preferences or decision rules (Manski 2004). If students with higher expected gains from schooling demand more education, and expected returns correlate with actual realized returns, we are confronted with a selection problem. That is, the observed returns of schooled people would differ from the hypothetical returns of unschooled people if they were to have enjoyed the same education (see Griliches 1977). As long as we do not know the underlying process of school choice, we cannot infer unbiased returns to education. Subjective data on income expectations may solve these problems and help to disentangle returns to education (cf. Manski 2004).

Dominitz and Manski (1996) calculated subjective income distributions with a computer-assisted self-administered interview. By analyzing the distribution of expected income, they were able to make inferences on uncertainty, risk behavior, and perceived income inequality. Only a few other studies have elicited income expectations in the same way (e.g., Wolter 2000). Due to limitations to the design of questionnaires, point estimates of expected income are most prevalent. For example, Betts (1996) asked undergraduates about their beliefs regarding the current starting and average salaries of workers in different professions conditional on achieved educational credentials. Other studies have elicited income expectations on the individual level. Most of these combined questions on the general knowledge of the income distribution with students' personal income expectations are conditional on varying scenarios regarding age and educational achievement (see Brunello et al. 2004; Webbink and Hartog 2004), whereas others collected this information unconditionally (see Blau and Ferber 1991). Another issue is whether there are differences by gender and age of children in the way income expectations and perceived risks of students and parents determine schooling decisions (Attanasio and Kaufmann 2012).

By comparing expected wages in several occupations with the national average income in these jobs, Betts (1996) found that knowledge about current income distribution was far from complete. However, expectations become more realistic in the final episode of education. Wolter and Zbinden (2002) have explained differences between current actual wages and expected incomes in terms of students' own job prospects, the perception of their own academic performance, and—as in Betts (1996)—duration of college attendance. Whereas students tend to slightly overestimate their expected starting salaries, they clearly overstate income growth after some years of work. According to Blau and Ferber (1991) and Wolter and Zbinden (2002), it is especially men who are prone to overestimate own future earnings. Supplementary to this, Brunello et al. (2004) found a tradeoff between the expected level of starting salaries and expected income growth. Findings concerning uncertainty as measured by expected wage dispersion are ambiguous. Compared to actual wage dispersion in Switzerland, a country in which it is relatively low, Wolter (2000) detected an even lower degree of expected wage dispersion among students. In contrast, although actual wage inequality is relatively high in the United States, Dominitz and Manski (1996) found that students additionally overestimated actual wage dispersion.

In order to gather knowledge about the formation of income expectations and its role in educational decision making, NEPS focuses on students from 9th grade up to university graduation in this research area. According to their ability to state income expectations, students are being asked about their expectations regarding their own income and the prevailing income distribution.

8.2.3 Funding of Education: Family Background and Financing Strategies

A strong impact on educational achievement is ascribed to family background. On the one hand, parents' educational attainment is a crucial determinant for children's own achievements (see Chap. 6, this volume); on the other hand, financial restrictions—which are determined most often within the family or rather within the household context—influence educational decisions. Whereas educational decisions are made under uncertainty regarding future outcomes, people's risk perceptions are determined by restrictions on the capital market.

Because most parents fund children's education for many years, the economic situation of the household is crucial for decision making. NEPS is capturing the economic situation of a household by its disposable monthly income and basic information on its wealth assets. Disposable monthly household income describes continuous income streams predominantly used for daily expenditures. Wealth serves as an income generator, and is a crucial attribute regarding access to the capital market. Besides funding aspects, the economic situation of the household correlates with determinants of educational performance such as access to learning opportunities (e.g., private music lessons or club membership) and learning conditions (e.g., own room for homework and additional teaching material) (Bradley et al. 2001). Consequently, parents are asked about their disposable monthly household income, and, as long as they are being surveyed, a screener for aggregated wealth information on the household level is being applied on at least one occasion.

Apart from family resources, there are also other financial sources individuals can rely on—especially during tertiary education. The majority of students in Germany cover their living costs mainly with money from three sources: their family, student jobs, and/or publicly funded grants and loans (Middendorff et al. 2013). Hence, students within the NEPS studies are asked to report on their available funds from different sources, whether they applied for the German grant program (BAföG), and whether they receive such public financial aid. This makes it possible to investigate the role of financing strategies for study performance and thus for economic and noneconomic outcomes.

8.3 Nonmarket Returns to Education

Apart from monetary economic returns and returns in terms of later education, there are additional nonmonetary returns to education in several areas. Most notably, nonmarket returns may come in the form of better health (Sect. 8.3.1), greater subjective well-being (Sect. 8.3.2), increased social and political participation (Sect. 8.3.3), and modified family formation (Sect. 8.3.4).

8.3.1 Health and Health Behavior

The relationship between people's educational background and their health has been a much neglected issue in the standard analysis of returns to education. Physical as well as mental health may be determined to a great extent by one's education. Well-educated people are expected to be inclined toward health-conscious behavior (cf. Grossman 2006). They live on higher quality nutrition, smoke less, are less likely to consume drugs, and are physically more active (e.g., Jungbauer-Gans and Gross 2009). Moreover, overweight and obesity in youth has considerable impact on health status in later life, and chronic diseases such as diabetes and hypertension constitute an increasing share of health expenditure.

The measurement of returns to education with respect to health outcomes is likely to produce a considerable bias if it disregards the endogeneity of the causal effect. One of the central findings in the sociology of health is that education (in addition to socioeconomic status and income, which themselves depend to a great degree on education) correlates highly with morbidity and mortality. Lundborg (2013) used a sample of monozygotic twins to show the positive association between schooling (completing high school) and several health outcomes. However, additional years of schooling after the high school degree do not lead to additional health benefits. Furthermore, it has been shown that the so-called social gradient in health has even increased over time (Mackenbach 2006). In recent years, the focus of research efforts has shifted to models explaining the correlation between education and health. Recent studies also model the interplay of education and job conditions on one side and health and work ability on the other side by showing the social mechanisms that moderate causal and selection effects (Gross et al. 2017; Schoger and Gross 2018).

Working and living conditions include specific resources (material and psychosocial environment), psychological stress, and environmental stress. We focus on the interplay of behaviors, cognitions, and emotions addressed by the theoretical approach of effort–reward imbalance (Siegrist 1996). This approach relies on the notion of social reciprocity. Mutual cooperative investments are based on the norm of return expectancy in which efforts are equalized by respective awards. Violations of this norm cause strong negative emotions, whereas appropriate social rewards promote well-being and health. It is mainly the imbalance between a high level of effort invested in working life and a low reward structure that is causal for chronic distress. Chronic distress itself is seen as one of the most influential dimensions affecting poor health outcomes such as higher morbidity and higher mortality (Rugulies and Siegrist 2002).

Health habits and risk behavior such as smoking, drinking alcohol, substance abuse, sport, and nutrition have been shown to not only correlate with education but also influence physical and mental health (e.g., Jungbauer-Gans and Gross 2009). The theoretical discussion on determinants of health suggests that some indicators of health behavior should be included especially when surveying children and young adults. During late childhood and adolescence, risk behavior such as smoking or drinking alcohol is initiated, and health habits are developed that influence health in later life (Langness et al. 2005). Smoking as one part of this dimension is related more strongly to education than to income (Gross and Groß 2008). Formal education has been shown to have a causal effect on reducing weight (Atella and Kopinska 2014). Nutrition has an impact on body weight that is important with respect to cardiovascular diseases or arthropathy. Because nutrition and also to some extent physical activities cannot be measured in an economic way, we use the Body Mass Index (BMI) as proxy. The BMI is the customary index of weight calculated using body weight and height. In addition, physical activities, especially performed in groups or sport clubs, are also seen as a learning environment, and therefore belong to Pillar 2 (see Chap. 5, this volume).

The use of medical care depends on education, income, and socioeconomic status even in countries in which health insurance covers most expenses for almost all people. Several important indicators of health in early childhood correlate with the social status of parents. This is especially important in early childhood when medical care is a substantial need, especially for newborns, and health shortcomings can have a major impact on early child development. Moreover, serious complications at birth (e.g., prematurity) may cause long lasting delays in child development that are detrimental to learning processes. Indicators are body weight and height at the time of birth, complications at birth (prematurity, serious problems during the first four weeks of life), and use of medical care.

Furthermore, selection processes could take place when educational outcomes, labor market participation, or (downward) social mobility are influenced by health status. This may lead to an endogeneity bias when the returns of education on health are estimated. Thus, there are reasons to consider both causal paths: The first path treats health as one dimension of nonmonetary returns to education, and the reversed causal path argues that educational outcomes themselves are influenced by the health status (e.g., disabilities or mental health) during school (see, e.g., Jungbauer-Gans and Gross 2009). The use of panel data could shed some light on whether one of these paths is more important than the other.

Whenever we survey children and adolescents, we also have to control for their socioeconomic status, the education of their parents, and their migration background (Wadsworth and Bartley 2006). Empirical evidence shows that the social status of parents correlates with the competence and educational attainment of children (e.g., Fuchs and Wößmann 2007). The social status of parents may also influence health status and health behavior of children. A migration background and potentially related language barriers can lead to poor understanding in dialogue with physicians. This may trigger disadvantages even when the physician's time is distributed equally between all patients (Balsa and McGuire 2001).

Another important issue is how far cognitive competencies as well as knowledge about health and medicine mediate between education and health status or health behavior. Therefore, the application of scientific knowledge on issues of health evaluated in Pillar 1 (see Chap. 4, this volume) can be used to assess the meaning of knowledge for health outcomes in a straightforward manner. In the economics of health, Grossman (1972) argues that better educated persons are able to produce health more efficiently due to their knowledge about risky or health-promoting behavior (Becker 1964). Agüero and Bharadwaj (2014) have been able to show a positive causal effect of education on health literacy that lead to more preventive behavior regarding HIV infections. Conti et al. (2010) have detected a causal effect of early cognitive abilities on a broad range of health outcomes. However, they warn against focusing on cognitive abilities alone by showing a causal effect of personality traits on health and healthy behaviors in later life.

Health in general is a multidimensional construct that includes physical, emotional, mental, social, and behavior-related dimensions of well-being and productivity (Schumacher et al. 2003). Measurements of health without using laboratory data and medical records have been shown to have high predictive validity even when mortality is considered (Idler and Benyamini 1997; Schwarze et al. 2000). A fundamental indicator is self-rated health measured on a Likert scale. Chronic illnesses and disabilities are included together with a statement asking whether and how far these illnesses and disabilities impair school attendance, learning processes, and school-related activities. Finally, days absent from school due to illness seems to be a simple indicator of health status.

8.3.2 Subjective Well-Being and Education

Monetary and nonmonetary outcomes of education can be brought together within the broad concept of individual subjective well-being, thus providing an integrated picture of the welfare effects of education. Economic theory assumes that utility is a function of income, leisure, and probably of health. Education enters this function only indirectly as a productivity- and health-enhancing factor. However, an interesting question in this context is whether education has a genuine direct impact on well-being. A direct test of such a hypothesis would require an econometric model in which life satisfaction is regressed on education and earnings, health, leisure, and other control variables. Nowadays, there is a broad consensus that responses to questions about life satisfaction or specific domains are valid measures of individual well-being or utility (Frey and Stutzer 2002). Although the economic literature on life satisfaction is publishing a growing number of regressions containing education as a control variable, evidence is still puzzling and ambiguous: For the most part, studies show a slightly positive impact of education on well-being; however, a negative effect of education on satisfaction can also be observed (Argyle 2003; Blanchflower and Oswald 2004; Schwarze and Härpfer 2007). The direction of causality between education and satisfaction is still unclear. Heckman (1976), for example, enters the human capital stock into the utility function multiplicatively in connection with leisure, assuming that education leads to a more efficient use of leisure. Thus, education is expected to have a positive impact on life satisfaction. However, if satisfaction measures something like optimism, and if optimistic people tend to be more successful, they will also tend to have a higher education (Argyle 2003). Moreover, better education might increase expectations about earnings and other employment-related outcomes. If expectations are not realized in later life, well-educated people might be less satisfied with their lives. In addition, overeducation may also cause dissatisfaction. Because these losses of utility cannot be compensated by a reasonable wage increase at the start of the first employment, overeducation is mostly involuntary and enhances productivity costs. However, negative consequences of overeducation diminish with professional experience (Verhaest and Omey 2009).

In summary, empirical analyses of the satisfaction–education nexus have to be carried out cautiously due to problems of endogeneity, selection bias, and omitted variables. This shows that data quality and econometric modeling are important issues. Most of these problems can be tackled by studying the process of education and development of individual well-being (satisfaction) simultaneously from the early stages onward across the whole life course. Pillar 5 offers a coherent design for answering questions on satisfaction over the whole life course and focuses on life satisfaction as well as satisfaction with health, standard of living, family, friends, and the currently predominant activity (school, vocational education and training, studies, or work). All these concepts of subjective well-being capture topics that are supposed to correlate with educational success. Additionally, each domain is applicable over the whole life course from the early school years onward (see Cummins 2006, Cummins and Lau 2005).

8.3.3 Political and Social Participation

Education has a substantial impact on how far individuals partake in the community. Having specific competencies and skills is a necessary precondition for participation in social life and becoming a respected member of society through civic participation, civic knowledge, and attitudes. Rich information about social background factors, attitudes, personal traits, values, and motivations gathered by NEPS allow researchers to analyze the causal link between a person's education and her or his propensity to community participation. This can significantly improve our understanding of the determinants of, for example, volunteering (for evidence in the United States and United Kingdom, see Dee 2004; for Germany, Erlinghagen et al. 1999). The new insights can be incorporated into the calculation of private and social rates of return to education. Although a broad body of literature supports the strong association between educational attainment and political participation, a causal link is questionable in the light of current research (Berinsky and Lenz 2011; Mayer 2011).

The indicators for social and political participation may be assigned to two major dimensions: attitudes and behavior. Although attitudes may originate in knowledge based on education, they may also lead to a selective information-seeking process. However, political and social participation can obviously be seen as a consequence of educational background (Hadjar and Becker 2006, 2007). The correlation between attitudes and behavior has also been discussed broadly (e.g., Fishbein and Ajzen 1975). Political action as a whole (including illegal demonstrations as well as voter participation), but also membership of and activities in political organizations can be regarded as behavioral indicators of political participation. In contrast, interest in and personal distance to politics can be assigned to the attitudinal dimension of political participation. Social participation involves the frequently used measurements of social trust toward fellow citizens and the anomia items known from the German ALLBUS. Furthermore, behavioral aspects are represented by active membership in organizations, voluntary work, and participation in school and cultural activities. The behavioral dimension of social and political participation is seen in the light of learning environments (Pillar 2). Therefore, it is discussed in Chap. 5 of this volume.

8.3.4 Family Formation and Educational Homogamy

In line with educational expansion, the share of women participating in higher education has increased dramatically in recent decades (Erikson and Jonsson 1996). For the educational system as a marriage market, this means that the likelihood of finding a partner of the opposite sex with a homogeneous educational level has also enlarged across cohorts (Blossfeld and Timm 2003). Several studies have shown a strong inverse relationship between fertility and education for women in postindustrial societies. Better educated women and men are older at the time of the birth of their first child than less educated women and men. But, whereas better educated women more often remain childless, the opposite is true for men (e.g., Kravdal and Rindfuss 2008). Bauer and Jacob (2010) pinpoint the constellation of both partners' educational level to explain parenthood: Traditional couples with men who are more highly educated than women are most likely to have children followed by couples with equally educated partners who are more likely to have children than couples with better educated women. In the United States, the relationship between education and family formation has also been shown to vary by ethnic background (Glick et al. 2006).

Additionally, unemployment leads to a postponement of the first child's birth. Whereas in Western Germany, the unemployment of the male partner leads to this shift, in Eastern Germany, it is female unemployment in couples that leads to a deferment of starting a family. Kreyenfeld (2010) found that the relationship between job uncertainty and postponement of parenthood varies with the woman's educational level. Whereas highly educated women react to employment uncertainty by postponing their first child's birth, women with low educational background respond by starting a family.

NEPS provides very detailed data on the respondents' educational enrollment, competencies, and employment combined with some relevant data on their partners or spouses. This provides optimal conditions for exploring the dynamics and interdependencies of educational enrollment and family aspirations.

8.4 Conclusion

We conclude with the words of Hout (2012, p. 379): "Education correlates strongly with most important social and economic outcomes such as economic success, health, family stability, and social connections. [...] Investments in education pay off for individuals in many ways. The size of the direct effect of education varies among individuals and demographic groups."

Pillar 5 dealing with monetary and nonmonetary returns to education responds to the fact that education plays a crucial role in many areas of life in (post-)modern societies. A long-term panel study such as NEPS is well advised to focus on aspects going beyond competencies and knowledge. Several other aspects besides education might be important for income, health, well-being, or social and political participation, and these aspects need to be covered by appropriate theoretical frameworks. Pillar 5 provides items adjusted to the requirements of the different stages and target persons included in NEPS while continuing to ensure coherence. The longitudinal quality of the data and natural experiments allow us to address issues of causality, thereby rendering the data of interest to economists as well as sociologists.

References

Agüero, J. M., & Bharadwaj, P. (2014). Do the more educated know more about health? Evidence from schooling and HIV knowledge in Zimbabwe. *Economic Development and Cultural Change, 62*(3), 489–517.

Argyle, M. (2003). 18 causes and correlates of happiness. In D. Kahneman, E. Diener, & N. Schwarz (Eds.), *Well-being—The foundations of hedonic psychology* (pp. 353–373). New York, NY: Sage.

Arrow, K. J. (1973). Higher education as a filter. *Journal of Public Economics, 2*(3), 193–216.

Atella, V., & Kopinska, J. (2014). Body weight, eating patterns, and physical activity: The role of education. *Demography, 51*(4), 1225–1249.

Attanasio, O., & Kaufmann, K. (2012). Education choices and returns to schooling: Intrahousehold decision making, gender and subjective expectations. *Working Paper, Bocconi University, Milan.*

Balsa, A. I., & McGuire, T. G. (2001). Statistical discrimination in health care. *Journal of Health Economics, 20*, 881–907.

Bauer, G., & Jacob, M. (2010). Fertilitätsentscheidungen im Partnerkontext. Eine Analyse der Bildungskonstellation von Paaren für die Familiengründung anhand des Mikrozensus 1996–2004. *Kölner Zeitschrift für Soziologie und Sozialpsychologie, 62*, 31–60.

Becker, G. S. (1964). *Human capital.* New York, NY: National Bureau of Economic Research.

Becker, A., Deckers, T., Dohmen, T., Falk, A., & Kosse, F. (2012). The relationship between economic preferences and psychological personality measures. *Annual Review of Economics 4*(1), 453–478.

Berinsky, A. J., & Lenz, G. S. (2011). Education and political participation: Exploring the causal link. *Political Behavior, 33*(3), 357–373.

Betts, J. R. (1996). What do students know about wages? *The Journal of Human Resources, 31*(1), 27–56.

Blanchflower, D., & Oswald, A. (2004). Wellbeing over time in Britain and the USA. *Journal of Public Economics, 88*(7–8), 1359–1386.

Blau, F. D., & Ferber, M. A. (1991). Career plans and expectations of young women and men. *The Journal of Human Resources, 26*(4), 581–607.

Blossfeld, H.-P., & Timm, A. (2003). Who marries whom? Educational systems as marriage markets in modern societies. Dordrecht, Netherlands: Kluwer.

Bourdieu, P., & Boltanski, L. (1981). The educational system and the economy: Titles and jobs. In C. C. Lemert (Ed.), *French sociology: Rupture and renewal since 1968* (pp. 141–151). New York, NY: Columbia University Press.

Bradley, R. H., Corwyn, R. F., McAdoo, H. P., & Coll, C. G. (2001). The home environments of children in the United States. Part I: Variations by age, ethnicity, and poverty status. *Child Development 72*(6), 1844–1867.

Brand, J. E., & Xie, Y. (2010). Who benefits most from college? Evidence for negative selection in heterogeneous economic returns to higher education. *American Sociological Review, 75*(2), 273–302.

Brunello, G., Lucifora, C., & Winter-Ebmer, R. (2004). The wage expectations of European business and economics students. *The Journal of Human Resources, 39*(4), 1116–1142.

Card, D. (1999). The causal effect of education on earnings. In O. Ashenfelter & D. Card (Eds.), *Handbook of Labor Economics* (3. ed., pp. 1801–1863). Amsterdam, Netherlands: North-Holland.

Conti, G., Heckman, J., & Urzua, S. (2010). The education-health gradient. *American Economic Review, 100(2)*, 234–38.

Cummins, R. A. (2006). *Personal Wellbeing Index—Adult (PWI-A) manual*. Melbourne, Australia: The Australian Centre on Quality of Life, Deakin University.

Cummins, R. A., & Lau, A. L. D. (2005). *Personal Wellbeing Index—School Children (PWI-SC) manual*. Melbourne, Australia: School of Psychology, Deakin University.

Dee, T. S. (2004). Are there civic returns to education? *Journal of Public Economics, 88*(9), 1697–1720.

Dominitz, J., & Manski, C. F. (1996). Eliciting student expectations of the returns to schooling. *The Journal of Human Resources, 31*(1), 1–26.

Erikson, R., & Jonsson, J. O. (1996). Explaining class inequality in education: The Swedish case. In R. Erikson & J. O. Jonsson (Eds.), *Can education be equalized? The Swedish case in comparative perspective* (pp. 1–63). Oxford, England: Westview Press.

Erlinghagen, M., Rinne, K., & Schwarze, J. (1999). Ehrenamt statt Arbeitsamt? Soziöokonomische Determinanten ehrenamtlichen Engagements in Deutschland. *WSI Mitteilungen, 52*(4), 246–255.

Fishbein, M., & Ajzen, I. (1975). Believe, attitude, intention, and behavior: an introduction to theory and research. Reading, MA: Addison-Wesley.

Frey, B. S., & Stutzer, A. (2002). What can economists learn from happiness research? *Journal of Economic Literature, 40*, 402–435.

Fuchs, T., & Wößmann, L. (2007). What accounts for international differences in student performance? A re-examination using PISA data. *Empirical Economics, 32*, 433–464.

Glick, J. E., Ruf, S. D., White, M. J., & Goldscheider, F. (2006). Educational engagement and early family formation: Differences by ethnicity and generation. *Social Forces, 84*(3), 1391–1415.

Griliches, Z. (1977). Estimating the returns to schooling: Some econometric problems. *Economet-rica, 45*(1), 1–22.

Griliches, Z. (1977). Estimating the returns to schooling: Some econometric problems. *Economet-rica, 45*(1), 1–22.

Gross, C., & Groß, J. (2008). Rational-Choice-Erklärungen zum Rauchverhalten und ihre empirische Relevanz. *Soziale Welt, 59*(3), 247–268.

Gross, C., Hofmann, S., Mühlenweg, A., Pikos, A. K., Rigotti, T., & Schoger, L. (2017). Theoretische und empirische Perspektiven auf Bildung, Gesundheit und Arbeitsfähigkeit – ein interdisziplinärer Überblick. *Sozialer Fortschritt, 66*(1), 3–30.

Grossman, M. (1972). *The demand for health: a theoretical and empirical investigation*. New York, NY: National Bureau of Economic Research.

Grossman, M. (2006). Education and nonmarket outcomes. In E. A. Hanushek & F. Welch (Eds.), *Handbook of the economics of education* (pp. 577–634). Amsterdam, Netherlands: North-Holland.

Hadjar, A., & Becker, R. (2006). Politisches Interesse und politische Partizipation. In A. Hadjar & R. Becker (Eds.), *Die Bildungsexpansion: erwartete und unerwartete Folgen* (pp. 179–204). Wiesbaden, Germany: VS Verlag für Sozialwissenschaften.

Hadjar, A., & Becker, R. (2007). Unkonventionelle politische Partizipation im Zeitverlauf. Hat die Bildungsexpansion zu einer politischen Mobilisierung beigetragen? *Kölner Zeitschrift für Soziologie und Sozialpsychologie, 59,* 410–439.

Hanushek, E. A. (2005). The economics of school quality. *German Economic Review, 6*(3), 269–286.

Hanushek, E. A., & Wößmann, L. (2007). *The role of school improvement in economic development. NBER Working Paper 12832*. Cambridge, MA: National Bureau of Economic Research.

Harmon, C., Oosterbeek, H., & Walker, I. (2003). The returns to education: Microeconomics. *Journal of Economic Surveys, 17*(2), 115–155.

Heckman, J. J. (1976). A life-cycle model of earnings, learning, and consumption. *Journal of Political Economy, 84,* 11–44.

Heckman, J. J., Humphries, J. E., & Veramendi, G. (2016). *Returns to education: The causal effects of education on earnings, health and smoking*. (IZA Discussion Papers, No. 9957). Bonn, Germany: Institute for the Study of Labor (IZA).

Hout, M. (2012). Social and economic returns to college education in the United States. *Annual Review of Sociology, 38,* 379–400.

Idler, E. L., & Benyamini, Y. (1997). Self-rated health and mortality: A review of twenty-seven community studies. *Journal of Health and Social Behaviour, 38,* 21–37.

Jensen, R. (2010). The (perceived) returns to education and the demand for schooling. *The Quarterly Journal of Economics, 125*(2), 515–548.

Jungbauer-Gans, M., & Gross, C. (2009). Erklärungsansätze sozial differenzierter Gesundheitschancen. In M. Richter & K. Hurrelmann (Eds.), *Soziologie gesundheitlicher Ungleichheit. Theorien, Konzepte und Methoden* (2. ed., pp. 77–98). Wiesbaden, Germany: VS Verlag für Sozialwissenschaften.

Kravdal, Ø., & Rindfuss, R. R. (2008). Changing relationships between education and fertility: A study of women and men born 1940 to 1964. *American Sociological Review, 73,* 854–873.

Kreyenfeld, M. (2010). Uncertainties in female employment careers and the postponement of par- enthood in Germany. *European Sociological Review, 26*(3), 351–366.

Langness, A., Richter, M., & Hurrelmann, K. (2005). Gesundheitsverhalten im Jugendalter: Ergebnisse der internationalen "Health Behaviour in School-aged Children"-Studie. *Das Gesundheitswesen, 67,* 422–431.

Lundborg, P. (2013). The health returns to schooling—what can we learn from twins? *Journal of Population Economics, 26*(2), 673–701.

Mackenbach, J. P. (2006). *Health inequalities: Europe in profile. An independent expert report commissioned by the UK presidency of the EU*. London, England: Department of Health.

Manski, C. F. (2004). Measuring expectations. *Econometrica, 72*(5), 1329–1376.

Mayer, A. K. (2011). Does education increase political participation?. *The Journal of Politics, 73*(3), 633–645.

McIntosh, S., & Vignoles, A. (2001). Measuring and assessing the impact of basic skills on labour market outcomes. *Oxford Economic Papers, 53*(3), 453–481.

Middendorff, E., Apolinarski, B., Poskowsky, J., Kandulla, M., & Netz, N. (2013). Die wirtschaftliche und soziale Lage der Studierenden in Deutschland 2012. 20. Sozialerhebung des Deutschen Studentenwerks durchgeführt durch das HIS-Institut für Hochschulforschung. Bonn, Berlin: Bundesministerium für Bildung und Forschung (BMBF).

Mincer, J. (1974). *Schooling, experience and earnings*. New York, NY: Columbia University Press.

Murnane, R. J., Willett, J. B., & Levy, F. (1995). The growing importance of cognitive skills in wage determinantion. *Review of Economics and Statistics, 77*(2), 251–266.

Oreopoulos, P., & Salvanes, K.G. (2011). Priceless. The nonpecuniary benefits of schooling. *Journal of Economic Perspectives 25*(1), 159–184.

Perez-Arce, F. (2017). The effect of education on time preferences. *Economics of Education Review 56*, 52–64.

Raffe, D. (2007). Vocational upper-secondary education and the transition from school. *European Sociological Review, 23*, 49–63.

Rugulies, R., & Siegrist, J. (2002). Soziologische Aspekte der Entstehung und des Verlaufs der kor- onaren Herzkrankheit. Soziale Ungleichverteilung der Erkrankung und chronische Distress- Erfahrungen im Erwerbsleben. Frankfurt a. M., Germany: VAS.

Schoger, L., & Gross, C. (2018). Modell zur Erklärung von beruflichen Fehlzeiten. *Sozialer Fortschritt, 67*, 303–325.

Schuller, T., Preston, J., Hammond, C., Brassett-Grundy, A., & Bynner, J. (Eds.). (2004). *The benefits of learning. The impact of education on health, family life and social capital*. London, England: Routledge.

Schumacher, J., Klaiberg, A., & Brähler, E. (2003). Diagnostik von Lebensqualität und Wohlbefinden. Eine Einführung. In J. Schumacher, A. Klaiberg, & E. Brähler (Eds.), *Diagnostische Verfahren zu Lebensqualität und Wohlbefinden* (pp. 1–18). Göttingen, Germany: Hogrefe.

Schwarze, J., Andersen, H. H., & Anger, S. (2000). *Self-rated health and changes in self-rated health as predictors of mortality—First evidence from German panel data* (DIW Discussion Paper No. 203). Berlin, Germany: Deutsches Institut für Wirtschaftsforschung.

Schwarze, J., & Härpfer, M. (2007). Are people inequality averse, and do they prefer redistribution by the state? Evidence from German longitudinal data on life satisfaction. *Journal of Socio-Economics, 36*(2), 233–249.

Siegrist, J. (1996). Adverse health effects of high effort—low reward conditions at work. *Journal of Occupational Health Psychology, 1*, 27–43.

Sørensen, A. B. (1977). The structure of inequality and the process of attainment. *American Sociological Review, 42*(6), 965–978.

Spence, A. M. (1973). Job market signaling. *The Quarterly Journal of Economics, 87*(3), 355–374.

Tyler, J. H., Murnane, R. J., & Willett, J. B. (2000). Do the cognitive skills of school dropouts matter in the labor market? *Journal of Human Resources, 35*(4), 748–754.

Verhaest, D., & Omey, E. (2009). Objective over-education and worker well-being: A shadow price approach. *Journal of Economic Psychology, 30*(3), 469–481.

Wadsworth, M., & Bartley, M. (2006). Social inequality, family structure and health in the life course. In C. Wendt & C. Wolf (Eds.), *Soziologie der Gesundheit.* (Kölner Zeitschrift für Soziologie und Sozialpsychologie: Sonderheft 46, pp. 125–143). Wiesbaden, Germany: VS Verlag für Sozialwissenschaften.

Webbink, D., & Hartog, J. (2004). Can students predict starting salaries? Yes! *Economics of Education Review, 23*(2), 103–113.

Wolter, S. C. (2000). Wage expectations: A comparison of Swiss and US students. *Kyklos, 53*(1), 51–69.

Wolter, S. C., & Zbinden, A. (2002). Labour market expectations of Swiss university students. *International Journal of Manpower, 23*(5), 458–470.

Wößmann, L., & West, M. R. (2006). Class-size effects in school systems around the world: Evidence from between-grade variation in TIMSS. *European Economic Review, 50*(3), 695–736.

Measuring Motivational Concepts and Personality Aspects in the National Educational Panel Study

Florian Wohlkinger, A. Raphaela Blumenfelder, Michael Bayer, Jutta von Maurice, Hartmut Ditton and Hans-Peter Blossfeld

Abstract

This chapter outlines the use and measurement of motivational concepts and personality aspects in the German National Educational Panel Study (NEPS). The selection of concepts combines elements that prevalent motivation and personality theories have in common, thereby promoting research from different theoretical perspectives. The constructs measured are learning motivation and effort, personal goals and goal pursuit, general interest orientations, topic-related interests, self-concept (both general and domain-specific), personality aspects, and selected social skills and parenting behavior dimensions. These theoretical constructs and their corresponding measurements presented in this chapter were chosen on the basis of their applicability across

---

F. Wohlkinger (✉) · H. Ditton
LMU Munich, Munich, Germany
E-Mail: florian.wohlkinger@edu.lmu.de

H. Ditton
E-Mail: ditton@lmu.de

A. R. Blumenfelder · M. Bayer · J. von Maurice
Leibniz Institute for Educational Trajectories, Bamberg, Germany
E-Mail: raphaela.blumenfelder@lifbi.de

M. Bayer
E-Mail: michael.bayer@lifbi.de

J. von Maurice
E-Mail: jutta.von-maurice@lifbi.de

H.-P. Blossfeld
University of Bamberg, Bamberg, Germany
E-Mail: hans-peter.blossfeld@uni-bamberg.de

© Springer Fachmedien Wiesbaden GmbH, ein Teil von Springer Nature 2019
H.-P. Blossfeld and H.-G. Roßbach (eds.), *Education as a Lifelong Process*,
Edition ZfE 3, https://doi.org/10.1007/978-3-658-23162-0_9

the complete life course. Within NEPS, this integrated compilation of motivational concepts and personality aspects improves our understanding of educational processes and competence development from infancy to late adulthood.

Keywords
Education · Panel study · Motivation · Personality

9.1 Introduction

Educational processes and competence development across the life course depend heavily on motivational concepts and personality aspects. The National Educational Panel Study (NEPS) raises some challenges connected with these concepts. The concepts to be included in the design (see Chap. 1, this volume) have to be selected carefully. Different facets of motivational concepts (in the broadest sense) and personality can be considered when investigating educational processes and the development of competencies. A well-founded selection is needed, because of the extensive number of items usually found within the available instruments and the broad variety of concepts in this field of research. Moreover, measuring these concepts is a particular challenge because they not only form an interdisciplinary research field but also have to be measured from childhood to adulthood.

A number of motivational and personality factors can be disentangled within the framework of educational processes and competence development. Some of these are quite stable; others are more variable and situation-adaptive. When selecting concepts to be included in NEPS, we integrated the different research traditions and interests of psychologists, educational scientists, sociologists, and economists. Although motivational concepts and personality aspects relate substantially to each of the other five central NEPS dimensions (see Chaps. 4–8, this volume), this topic constitutes its own research field within NEPS.

Many different framework conceptions deal with how motivational concepts and personality aspects relate to educational performance and processes of life-long learning: the expectancy-value theory of achievement motivation (Wigfield and Eccles 2000), the motivational theory of life-span development (Heckhausen et al. 2010), self-determination theory (Deci and Ryan 1985), or self-efficacy theory (Bandura 1997)—to name but a few. Due to the quantity of work in this area, there is a plurality of concepts that all use related terms and similar instruments (see, for a detailed overview, Eccles and Wigfield 2002). For NEPS, we selected some common main components of multiple theoretical perspectives in order to guarantee a wide variety of possible uses of these concepts in different disciplines. This also makes it possible to compare different theories and untangle how they relate to each other.

Among both psychologists and educational scientists, one of the currently most popular motivational theories is expectancy-value theory from Wigfield and Eccles (2000).

This theory posits that decisions are based on a set of influences: on the one hand, ability beliefs defined as "the individual's perception of his or her current competence at a given activity"; on the other hand, expectancies for success defined as persons' "beliefs about how well they will do on upcoming tasks" (Wigfield and Eccles 2000, p. 70). These two basic components are then combined with different task-value components (see Wigfield and Eccles 2000): attainment value (how important succeeding in this activity is to the individual), intrinsic value (how much joy the individual gets from performing the task or how much interest the individual has in it), utility value (how well a task corresponds to short- and long-term goals), and cost (the negative aspects that emerge when performing an activity). Other models (e.g., Bandura 1997; Hidi et al. 2004) include different contributory factors such as ability or academic self-concepts, interests, and achievement goals.

For the purposes of NEPS, following the central ideas of Eccles and Wigfield's (2002) framework offers the chance to include various common features from different theoretical perspectives. Integrating this cross section of characteristics from varying approaches into our study allows us to choose various applications from several theoretical orientations and to combine elements of different models. The following sections will describe the motivational and personality components measured in NEPS.

9.2 Motivation

9.2.1 Learning Motivation and Effort

According to Deci and Ryan (1985), motivation can be divided generally into two components: intrinsic motivation defined as a "motivation to engage in an activity for its own sake," and extrinsic motivation defined as "motivation to engage in an activity as a means to an end" (Pintrich and Schunk 2002, p. 245). Depending on the theoretical framework, extrinsic motivation can be broken down into further facets. For example, Schiefele et al. (2002) distinguish performance-related, competition-related, and job-related extrinsic motivation. Selecting an adequate instrument to measure learning motivation within NEPS is a challenging task for several reasons such as the limited measurement time or the task of measuring motivation across the life course. Schiefele et al.'s (2002) scale met all our needs for students in university, but had to be adjusted slightly to measure learning motivation in school and during the apprenticeship phase. During the stage of adulthood, we intended to implement a measure on learning motivation in the context of further education and advanced training.

In addition to learning motivation, students' effort is being assessed in Starting Cohorts 3 and 4, because part of the shock caused by PISA was a lack (or at least insufficient amount) of students' effort besides other factors such as school quality. The items implemented in NEPS were developed on basis of an instrument from the Pythagoras study (Rakoczy et al. 2005). Three dimensions of effort are available in the data: effort in school in general, subject-specific effort in mathematics, and subject-specific effort in German.

9.2.2 Personal Goals and Goal Pursuit

Starting in Grade 8, the assessment of motivation is being supplemented by the measurement of *personal goals*. Because a large proportion of students leave the school system after Grade 9 or 10 in order to start vocational education and training, work aspirations are of outstanding relevance. Therefore, the measurement of the *meaning of work* adds an important aspect to the bundle of motivational concepts. Suitable scales are, on the one hand, an adaptation of the *work aspirations* instrument used in the TOSCA study (Transformations of the Secondary School System and Academic Careers; cf. Köller 2004) and, on the other hand, the *desired work conditions* instrument from the MOW International Research Team (1987). Both measures cover slightly different subdimensions such as extrinsic orientation (cf. Trautwein et al. 2006) or economic aspects (cf. Borchert and Landherr 2007).

Another facet of personal goals is the field of work-related and private goals. Over the life course, individuals have to struggle with different challenges such as important transitions (e.g., from school to work or to further education) or life events (e.g., family formation or unemployment). These are often combined with certain time windows for the achievement of such personal goals. According to the motivational theory of life-span development, different motivational and self-regulatory strategies are needed to deal with these challenges (Heckhausen et al. 2010). Therefore, NEPS provides—in cooperation with Jutta Heckhausen—two 12-item scales for these strategies (differentiable in goal disengagement and goals disengagement strategies) in the key domains of work life and the private sphere. In Starting Cohorts 4, 5, and 6, the individual work-related and private goals are assessed in an open question format. In the data, there are coded formats as well as the open answers available for both key domains, thereby providing manifold options for answering research questions and performing data analyses.

Another important component in motivation research is *goal pursuit*. During school life, every student has to deal with positive and negative consequences for her or his learning behavior in the form of school grades. Even more influential are students' experiences after major educational decisions such as the choice of school type. According to Brandtstädter and Renner (1990), coping with results of changes can follow two alternative strategies: adjusting personal goals to given situations ("accommodative coping") versus adjusting the environmental circumstances to the individual preferences ("assimilative coping"). Life-course researchers have recognized a shift from assimilative activities in early life stages to accommodative behavior in later life (see Brandtstädter and Rothermund 2002). NEPS provides an outstanding framework for monitoring this shift over the complete life span. Moreover, it offers the opportunity to start observation at very early ages and thus deepen our understanding of the underlying processes. Conversely, the measurement of these strategies contributes to the motivational concepts in terms of allowing for a different account of the above-mentioned motivational theories. Therefore, we integrate two short versions of scales developed to measure the two coping strategies: the *Tenacious Goal Pursuit* and the *Flexible Goal Adjustment* scales (Brandtstädter and Renner 1990).

9.3 Interests

The development and stabilization of individual *interests* both inside and outside of school is a topic of major importance for educational scientists (see, e.g., Daniels 2008; Krapp 1992; Todt 1978). Interests are closely connected to intrinsic motivation and always aim at a specific content (see Krapp 1999).

9.3.1 General Interest Orientations

An internationally recognized model conceptualizing *general interest orientations* is Holland's (1997) hexagonal model. This is based on the differentiation of six interest and commensurate environment types (see Bergmann and Eder 2005):

- Realistic type (R): prefers activities that include the explicit and systematic manipulation of objects, tools, machines, or animals.
- Investigative type (I): favors activities that can be characterized by an observing, symbolic, systematic, and creative investigation of physical, biological, or cultural phenomena.
- Artistic type (A): prefers ambiguous, open, and unsystematic activities that imply the manipulation of physical, verbal, or human materials to create artistic forms and products.
- Social type (S): prefers activities to inform, train, educate, cure, or advise other people.
- Enterprising type (E): favors activities that include the manipulation of other people to achieve organizational goals or to gain economic returns.
- Conventional type (C): prefers activities characterized by the explicit and systematic manipulation of data to gain organizational or economic returns.

Those six ideal types can be arranged in a preference order to form an individual interest profile. A total of 720 interest patterns can be differentiated by combining these six types. According to their intercorrelations, the six types are arrayed in a circumplex or hexagon (Holland and Gottfredson 1992). These relations are reflected by the acronym RIASEC, which is therefore often used as a synonym for Holland's (1997) interest model. A central concept within the model is congruence. People especially select environments that are congruent to their interests and they change (or leave) incongruent environments.

In order to measure RIASEC interests, NEPS has developed a new instrument (IILS; Interest Inventory Life Span, with a child and an adult version). It is based on the following inventories: (a) a German (30-item) version of the Inventory of Children's Activities–Revised (ICA-R) from Tracey and Ward (1998), German version ICA-D from von Maurice (2006) that has been developed and tested for elementary school age (von Maurice and Bäumer 2014); (b) the (60-item) Allgemeiner Interessen-Struktur-Test in its revised edition (AIST-R; Bergmann and Eder 2005) that can be used from 14 years of age onward. To measure general interest orientations over the life course, these instruments have been shortened and combined in NEPS: In the child version of the IILS (from Grade 4 to Grade 8), we chose two items from the ICA-D and one item from the AIST-R per scale; in the adult version of the IILS (from Grade 9 to adulthood), we used one item from the ICA-D and two items from the AIST-R per scale. Item selection was based on empirical analyses and plausibility checks. Consequently, a very short 18-item instrument for measuring the six Holland-scales R, I, A, S, E and C is available in both versions.

Although the RIASEC model allows us to conceptualize general interest orientations over the life course, it is best suited for the domain of work. The integration of Holland's model in NEPS offers a great potential for many educational researchers because of its cross-cultural relevance.

9.3.2 Topic-Related Interests

In school studies, the measurement of interests is often oriented toward measuring interest in the respective school subject. This approach is insufficient for NEPS, because it is following individual development over the entire life span. After students have left school, subject-specific measurement seems rewarding only when another school-similar context follows that is also arranged in subjects (e.g., university). Hence, it is advisable to avoid gathering this information in a school-subject-oriented way (subject-related interest; German term '*Fachinteresse*'), but to use a different approach and ask for more general interest fields independently from school subjects (see Daniels 2008). Focusing on *topic-related interests* (German term '*Sachinteresse*') enables us to use the same instrument across school stages as well as after finishing school. This makes it possible to analyze topic-related interests over different stages (see Chap. 1, this volume). Similarly, NEPS Pillar 1 covers competence domains not in close relation to a curriculum but in a more general, naturalistic way (see Chap. 4, this volume).

Throughout the whole of NEPS, one particular focus is on the subjects German and mathematics. Accordingly, subject teachers are being interviewed during the school stages in addition to the target persons (see Chap. 13 this volume). In analogy to this characteristic, the measuring of interest should include at least the two domains German and mathematics in order to allow research on the interdependence of interests, other motivational components, and school achievement. For this reason, we capture topic-related interests in the two domains German and mathematics. Using items taken from a study by Baumert et al. (2003), we are able to implement the same instrument across the whole life course.

The life-span perspective implemented in NEPS provides an important opportunity to study individuals' development of interests. Because interests are known to have profound consequences for human (choice) behavior (see Nagy et al. 2006), knowing whether interests do or do not "crystallize" across the life span is an important step in understanding the development of individuals' behavioral plasticity.

9.4 Self-Concept

Self-concept is a major indicator for achievement and is of central importance in current educational research (see Bong and Clark 1999; Helmke and van Aken 1995; Kaufmann 2008; Shavelson and Bolus 1982; Wohlkinger et al. 2016). It can be defined as a person's perception of her- or himself and her or his abilities (see Marsh and Shavelson 1985; Shavelson et al. 1976; Watermann et al. 2010).

Theoretically, the structure of NEPS suggests a quite differentiated recording of self-concept: On the one hand, there are the school stages and their obvious close connection to school subjects. On the other hand, there are university students with an environment that is not structured by subjects as in school, but shaped by topic-oriented courses. And finally, there is the domain of working people, whose environment is no longer arranged in an explicit structure with regard to contents (though it should be noted that occupational environments can be described in terms of the RIASEC model, especially in comparison to general interest orientations, thus allowing us to examine, e.g., vocational decisions or person–environment fit). Therefore, it seems a challenging task to measure the self-concept across all stages in an identical way. However, because the self-concept is characterized by a hierarchical structure (see, e.g., Lichtlein 2000; Marsh 1987; Marsh and Shavelson 1985; Shavelson et al. 1976), it is possible to realize a consistent capture as well as a differentiating measure of the theoretical construct—as the following section will show.

9.4.1 General Self-Concept

The hierarchy of the self-concept provides a particularly convenient possibility of differentiating measurement throughout NEPS: Across the life course, the general self-concept—a dimension that is explicitly not connected to any domain such as school, university, or work—can be measured in exactly the same way at all stages. This provides the advantage of being able to compare different age groups to each other and monitor the development and stability of the general dimension of self-concept throughout the life course.

Among the conceivable measures, the Rosenberg Self-Esteem Scale (Rosenberg 1965) seems to fulfill the requirements, because self-esteem forms the main element of self-concept (see Ferring and Filipp 1996). Concretely, our choice from among the available German instruments was the revised *Self-Esteem Scale* from von Collani and Herzberg (2003a). As in the original version by Rosenberg (1965), this scale includes positive as well as negative facets and offers good psychometric properties in terms of reliability and validity (von Collani and Herzberg 2003a, b). These results were affirmed in two NEPS developmental studies for Grade 5 students and for university students in whom the self-esteem scale was also tested. Furthermore, the scale is very economical with only 10 items, thus meeting the needs of a large-scale survey study such as NEPS.

9.4.2 Domain-Specific Self-Concept

At the school stages, measurement of the *domain-specific self-concept* is geared to the PISA 2000 study that had gathered three subdimensions: overall academic self-concept, verbal self-concept, and mathematical self-concept (see Kunter et al. 2002). This entirely matches the specific structure of the school stages as well as the typical hierarchy in school. Furthermore, every subdimension consists of only three items. Therefore, the instrument perfectly suits the needs of NEPS and is being applied in the school stages. In addition to self-concept, we measure *helplessness*. The notion of helplessness goes back to Abramson et al. (1978) and was adapted in a study by Ditton (2007). In analogy to its use there, we integrated the measure of helplessness separately into NEPS for both German and mathematics, thereby complementing the measurement of domain-specific self-concept.

Of course, neither the PISA instrument nor helplessness as covered by Ditton (2007) would be adequate for the cohort of university students. Here, the measurement follows the idea of Dickhäuser et al. (2002) by using their absolute academic self-concept scale, whereas helplessness is geared to Jerusalem and Schwarzer's (2006) study-specific helplessness.

9.5 Personality

Alongside the dimensions of motivation, personal goals, interests, and self-concept, another element is of major importance: an individual's *personality*. By measuring personality characteristics starting at a very young age and continuing up to adulthood, it should be possible to identify not only developmental risks but also protective factors against just these risks (Weinert et al. 2007). In psychological research, a widespread model with a very long tradition is the five factor model (FFM) of personality that can be recovered in most western cultures (e.g., Asendorpf and van Aken 2003; McCrae and Costa 1985, 1991; Weinert et al. 2007). Many instruments are available for collecting information on personality. The so-called 'Big Five' factors are Openness, Conscientiousness, Extraversion, Agreeableness, and Neuroticism. Because most instruments such as the well-known NEO-FFI (Borkenau and Ostendorf 1993) use extensive item batteries with about 50–100 items (see Rammstedt 2007) to access the Big Five, their use for

NEPS is very limited. A well-established very short version is the BFI-10 by Rammstedt and John (2007). It has been developed explicitly for contexts in which there is limited time for questioning, and it provides valuable psychometric characteristics with only two items per dimension. Merely for the agreeableness dimension, Rammstedt and John (2007) recommend adding a third item. Because this factor might be crucial for profound analyses on specific research questions, this item has also been included.

For younger cohorts, no self-reported measure of personality is available. Here parents and educators can provide valuable information about a child's personality. According to recent research, the parents' judgment is a useful and quite stable indicator even for 4-year-old children (see Müller et al. 2016; Weinert et al. 2007).

For younger children, parents' and caregivers' evaluation of the child's *temperament* can lead to a better understanding of personality development and its relation to educational processes, because personality emerges out of early temperament in conjunction with the learning environment (Bayer et al. 2015; Putnam and Rothbart 2006). Therefore, NEPS utilizes a multiactor perspective and thus provides information about the personality from very early ages up to the adult life. In this manner, we are able to monitor the development of personality traits over the complete life course, and, in the long term, collect and link data about personality, competence development, educational success, and occupational prospects.

9.6 Social Skills and Parenting Behavior

Another important domain in educational processes and competence is social behavior. Socially competent behavior is of central importance for denoting risks of negative behavior development (see Beelmann et al. 2006; Weinert et al. 2007). Capturing social skills in general is a challenging task, because many different instruments are available. Extensive scales focusing on as many distinct facets as possible are not suitable within the framework of a panel study. Therefore, a slightly narrowed perspective seemed appropriate. Here, we concentrate on some subdomains of social behavior and thereby focus on behavioral attributes. A popular instrument for measuring such social skills is Goodman's (1997, 1999) Strengths and Difficulties Questionnaire (SDQ). The SDQ "provides balanced coverage of children and young people's behaviours, emotions, and relationships" (Goodman 1997, p. 581), and consists of five dimensions, namely Emotional Symptoms, Conduct Problems, Hyperactivity, Peer Problems, and Prosocial Behavior. A major advantage of the SDQ is the availability of versions for teachers and parents. Thus, we are again able to overcome the problematic lack of self-reported measures for younger children by taking the multiactor perspective. For economic reasons, we applied psychometric and content criteria to select items for NEPS (see Bettge et al. 2002; Hagquist 2007).

Furthermore, in the Kindergarten stage, educators and parents give additional information on aggressive and disruptive behavior. Here we ask them questions taken from the Teacher Assessment of Social Behaviour (TASB; see Cassidy and Asher 1992). Hence, we gain a quite differentiated picture of social behavior from a very young age onward, and it is based on data from the different perspectives taken by multiple informants.

Beginning at the age of 18, another social skill facet is added by measuring negative assertion and conflict management. These two concepts are part of the German version of the Interpersonal Competence Questionnaire (see Riemann and Allgöwer 1993). Both facets were adapted to the challenges of telephone interviewing, so that the NEPS version cannot be compared on the level of items with the original version from Riemann and Allgöwer (see Bayer et al. 2012).

9.7 Measurement Schedule

All six NEPS starting cohorts contain an individual selection of the motivational concepts and personality aspects presented above. Table 9.1 displays the measurement points for all currently available instruments. Because there are some cases in which only subgroups were surveyed, there may occur some deviations within single waves (e.g., students in school vs. apprentices in vocational training). Further information can be found on the NEPS website.

9.8 Conclusion

The aim of this article has been to give an outline of the use and measurement of motivational concepts as well as personality aspects within NEPS. When selecting instruments, we focused particularly on their applicability across the complete life course. As questioning time is a scarce good, the economy of the instrument in terms of item count is also crucial—extensive scales with large item batteries could not be incorporated into our study. Further important decision criteria were, of course, to select concepts that are used in several distinct motivational theories, and ones that are relevant for educational sciences and competence development research. The constructs measured are achievement motivation, personal goals, general interest orientations, topic-related interests, self-concept facets, self-regulation, personality aspects such as the Big Five, and selected social behavior dimensions. The integration of motivational concepts and personality aspects into NEPS allows researchers from different disciplines to analyze both educational processes and competence development on a sophisticated level.

Table 9.1 Overview: measurement of motivational concepts and personality aspects

	SC1—Early childhood	SC2—Kindergarten	SC3—Grade 5	SC4—Grade 9	SC5—First-year students	SC6—Adults
Motivation						
Intrinsic motivation		W7	W4, W8	W5, W8	W5	
Extrinsic motivation			W4, W8	W5, W8	W5	
Effort			W8	W5		
Personal goals and goal pursuit						
Tenacious goal pursuit and flexible goal adjustment			W7	W3	W4	
Locus of control						W6
Meaning of work			W4	W3, W9	W3	
Optimization strategies			W7	W9		
Interests						
General interest orientations		W6	W2, W6	W2, W7, W8, W9	W1, W9	W4, W7
Topic-related interests			W2, W6	W2	W1	W4
Self-concept						
General self-concept			W1, W5	W1, W7, W8	W3, W10	W6
Domain-specific self-concept			W1, W5	W1, W7, W8	W2, W6	
Helplessness			W3, W6	W2	W2, W6	
Personality						
Big Five self-rating	W5°		W3, W5	W1, W9	W3, W10	W5, W8
Big Five informant rating		W2, W4	W3, W6			
Temperament	W1, W2, W3, W4, W5					
Social skills and parenting behavior						
Parenting styles and goals	W2, W5					
SDQ subscales—self-rating			W2, W6	W2		
SDQ subscales—informant rating	W4		W1, W5	W2, W6	W1	
Disturbing behavior (TASB)		W1, W4				
Self-rating of Interpersonal Competence Questionnaire				W7, W8	W8	W6

W: wave
°self-rating parent

References

Abramson, L. Y., Seligman, M. E., & Teasdale, J. D. (1978). Learned helplessness in humans: Critique and reformulation. *Journal of Abnormal Psychology, 87,* 49–74.

Asendorpf, J. B., & van Aken, M. A. G. (2003). Validity of Big Five personality judgments in childhood: A 9 year longitudinal study. *European Journal of Personality, 17,* 1–17.

Bandura, A. (1997). *Self-efficacy: the exercise of control.* New York, NY: Freeman.

Baumert, J., Gruehn, S., Heyn, S., Köller, O., & Schnabel, K. (2003). *Bildungsverläufe und psychosoziale Entwicklung im Jugendalter (BIJU). Dokumentation: Bd. 1 Skalen Längsschnitt 1. Wellen 1–4.* Unpublished documentation at the Max Planck Institute for Human Development, Berlin, Germany.

Bayer, M., Ditton, H., & Wohlkinger, F. (2012). *Konzeption und Messung sozialer Kompetenz im Nationalen Bildungspanel* (NEPS Working Paper No. 8). Bamberg, Germany: Otto-Friedrich-Universität, Nationales Bildungspanel.

Bayer, M., Wohlkinger, F., Freund, J.-D., Ditton, H., & Weinert, S. (2015). Temperament bei Kleinkindern – Theoretischer Hintergrund, Operationalisierung im Nationalen Bildungspanel (NEPS) und empirische Befunde aus dem Forschungsprojekt ViVA (NEPS Working Paper No. 58). Bamberg, Germany: Leibniz-Institut für Bildungsverläufe, Nationales Bildungspanel.

Beelmann, A., Lösel, F., Stemmler, M., & Jaursch, S. (2006). Beurteilung von sozialen Verhaltensproblemen und Erziehungsschwierigkeiten im Vorschulalter. *Diagnostica, 52,* 189–198.

Bergmann, C., & Eder, F. (2005). *Allgemeiner Interessen-Struktur-Test mit Umwelt-Struktur-Test (UST-R) – Revision* (3rd ed.). Weinheim, Germany: Beltz-Test.

Bettge, S., Ravens-Sieberer, U., Wietzker, A., & Hölling, H. (2002). Ein Methodenvergleich der Child-Behavior Checklist und des Strengths and Difficulties Questionnaire. In B.-M. Kurth (Ed.), *Kinder- und Jugendgesundheitssurvey* (Das Gesundheitswesen: Sonderband. 1, pp. 119–124). New York, NY: Georg Thieme Verlag.

Bong, M., & Clark, R. E. (1999). Comparison between self-concept and self-efficacy in academic motivation research. *Educational Psychologist, 34,* 139–153.

Borchert, M., & Landherr, G. (2007). *Meaning Of Work* (Arbeitsbericht). Duisburg, Germany: Universität Essen-Duisburg.

Borkenau, P., & Ostendorf, F. (1993). NEO-Fünf-Faktoren-Inventar (NEO-FFI) nach Costa und McCrae. Handanweisung. Göttingen, Germany: Hogrefe.

Brandtstädter, J., & Renner, G. (1990). Tenacious goal pursuit and flexible goal adjustment: Explication and age-related analysis of assimilative and accommodative strategies of coping. *Psychology and Aging, 5,* 58–67.

Brandtstädter, J., & Rothermund, K. (2002). The life-course dynamics of goal pursuit and goal adjustment: A two-process framework. *Developmental Review, 22,* 117–150.

Cassidy, J., & Asher, S. R. (1992). Loneliness and peer relations in young children. *Child Development, 63,* 350–365.

Daniels, Z. (2008). *Entwicklung schulischer Interessen im Jugendalter.* Münster, Germany: Waxmann.

Deci, E. L., & Ryan, R. M. (1985). *Intrinsic motivation and self-determination in human behavior.* New York, NY: Plenum Publishing Co.

Dickhäuser, O., Schöne, C., Spinath, B., & Stiensmeier-Pelster, J. (2002). Die Skalen zum akademischen Selbstkonzept. Konstruktion und Überprüfung eines neuen Instrumentes. *Zeitschrift für Differentielle und Diagnostische Psychologie, 23,* 393–405.

Ditton, H. (2007). *Kompetenzaufbau und Laufbahnen im Schulsystem. Ergebnisse einer Längsschnittuntersuchung an Grundschulen.* Münster, Germany: Waxmann.

Eccles, J. S., & Wigfield, A. (2002). Motivational beliefs, values, and goals. *Annual Review of Psychology, 53*, 109–132.

Ferring, D., & Filipp, S.-H. (1996). Messung des Selbstwertgefühls: Befunde zu Reliabilität, Validität und Stabilität der Rosenberg-Skala. *Diagnostica, 42*, 284–292.

Goodman, R. (1997). The Strengths and Difficulties Questionnaire: A research note. *Journal of Child Psychology and Psychiatry and Allied Disciplines, 38*, 581–586.

Goodman, R. (1999). The extended version of the Strengths and Difficulties Questionnaire as a guide to child psychiatric caseness and consequent burden. *Journal of Child Psychology and Psychiatry and Allied Disciplines, 40*, 791–799.

Hagquist, C. (2007). The psychometric properties of the self-reported SDQ – An analysis of Swedish data based on the Rasch model. *Personality and Individual Differences, 43*, 1289–1301.

Heckhausen, J., Wrosch, C., & Schulz, R. (2010). A motivational theory of life-span development. *Psychological Review, 117*(1), 32–60.

Helmke, A., & van Aken, M. A. G. (1995). The causal ordering of academic achievement and self-concept of ability during elementary school: A longitudinal study. *Journal of Educational Psychology, 87*, 624–637.

Hidi, S., Renninger, A. K., & Krapp, A. (2004). Interest, a motivational variable that combines affective and cognitive functioning. In D. Y. Dai & R. J. Sternberg (Eds.), *Motivation, emotion, and cognition: Integrative perspectives on intellectual functioning and development* (pp. 89–115). Mahwah, NJ: Erlbaum.

Holland, J. L. (1997). *Making vocational choices. A theory of vocational personalities and work environments* (3rd ed.). Odessa, FL: Psychological Assessment Resources Inc.

Holland, J. L., & Gottfredson, G. D. (1992). Studies of the hexagonal model: An evaluation (or, the perils of stalking the perfect hexagon). *Journal of Vocational Behavior, 40*, 158–170.

Jerusalem, M., & Schwarzer, R. (2006). Dimensionen der Hilflosigkeit. In A. Glöckner-Rist (Hrsg.), *ZUMA-Informationssystem. Elektronisches Handbuch sozialwissenschaftlicher Erhebungsinstrumente. ZIS Version 10.00*. Mannheim, Germany: Zentrum für Umfragen, Methoden und Analysen.

Kaufmann, A. (2008). *Die Rolle motivationaler Schülermerkmale bei der Entstehung sozialer Disparitäten des Schulerfolgs. Eine Längsschnittuntersuchung an Grundschulen in Bayern und Sachsen*. Berlin, Germany: Mensch-und-Buch-Verlag.

Köller, O. (2004). *Wege zur Hochschulreife in Baden-Württemberg. TOSCA – eine Untersuchung an allgemein bildenden und beruflichen Gymnasien*. Opladen, Germany: Leske + Budrich.

Krapp, A. (1992). *Interesse, Lernen, Leistung. Neuere Ansätze der pädagogisch-psychologischen Interessenforschung*. Münster, Germany: Aschendorff.

Krapp, A. (1999). Intrinsische Lernmotivation und Interesse. Forschungsansätze und konzeptuelle Überlegungen. *Zeitschrift für Pädagogik, 45*, 387–406.

Kunter, M., Schümer, G., Artelt, C., Baumert, J., Klieme, E., Neubrand, M., Prenzel, M., Schiefele, U., Schneider, W., Stanat, P., Tillmann, K.-J., & Weiß, M. (2002). *PISA 2000: Dokumentation der Erhebungsinstrumente* (Vol. 72). Berlin, Germany: Max-Planck-Institut für Bildungsforschung.

Lichtlein, M. (2000). *Selbstkonzeptentwicklung in der beruflichen Erstausbildung unter besonderer Berücksichtigung motivationaler Aspekte*. München, Germany: Utz, Wiss.

Marsh, H. W. (1987). The hierarchical structure of self-concept and the application of hierarchical confirmatory factor analysis. *Journal of Educational Measurement, 24*, 17–39.

Marsh, H. W., & Shavelson, R. (1985). Self-concept: Its multifaceted, hierarchical structure. *Educational Psychologist, 20*, 107–123.

McCrae, R. R., & Costa, P. T. (1985). Comparison of EPI and psychoticism scales with measures of the five-factor model of personality. *Personality and Individual Differences, 6*, 587–597.

McCrae, R. R., & Costa, P. T., Jr (1991). The NEO Personality Inventory: Using the Five-Factor Model in counseling. *Journal of Counseling and Development, 69*, 367–372.

MOW – The MOW International Research Team. (1987). *The meaning of working.* London, England: Academic Press.

Müller, D., Linberg, T., Bayer, M., Schneider, T., & Wohlkinger, F. (2016). Measuring personality traits of young children: Results from a NEPS pilot study. In H.-P. Blossfeld, J. von Maurice, M. Bayer, & J. Skopek (Eds.), *Methodological issues of longitudinal surveys. The example of the National Educational Panel Study* (pp. 169–180). Wiesbaden, Germany: VS Verlag für Sozialwissenschaften.

Nagy, G., Trautwein, U., Köller, O., Baumert, J., & Garrett, J. (2006). Gender and course selection in upper secondary education: Effects of academic self-concept and intrinsic value. *Educational Research and Evaluation, 12*, 323–345.

Pintrich, P. R., & Schunk, D. H. (2002). *Motivation in education. Theory, research, and applications* (2nd ed.). Upper Saddle River, NJ: Merrill, Prentice Hall.

Putnam, S. P., & Rothbart, M. K. (2006). Development of short and very short forms of the Children's Behavior Questionnaire. *Journal of Personality Assessment, 87*(1), 103–113.

Rakoczy, K., Buff, A., & Lipowsky, F. (2005): Dokumentation der Erhebungs- und Auswertungsinstrumente zur schweizerisch-deutschen Videostudie 'Unterrichtsqualität, Lernverhalten und mathematisches Verständnis', Teil 1: Befragungsinstrumente (Materialien zur Bildungsforschung, 13). Frankfurt am Main, Germany: GFPF.

Rammstedt, B. (2007). The 10-item Big Five Inventory – Norm values and investigation of sociodemographic effects based on a German population representative sample. *European Journal of Psychological Assessment, 23*, 193–201.

Rammstedt, B., & John, O. P. (2007). Measuring personality in one minute or less: A 10-item short version of the Big Five Inventory in English and German. *Journal of Research in Personality, 41*, 203–212.

Riemann, R., & Allgöwer, A. (1993). Eine deutschsprachige Fassung des ‚Interpersonal Competence Questionnaire' (ICQ). *Zeitschrift für Differentielle und Diagnostische Psychologie, 14*(3), 153–163.

Rosenberg, M. (1965). *Society and the adolescent self-image.* Princeton, NJ: Princeton University Press.

Schiefele, U., Moschner, B., & Husstegge, R. (2002). *Skalenhandbuch SMILE-Projekt.* Unpublished manuscript, Department of Psychology, Bielefeld University, Bielefeld, Germany.

Shavelson, R. J., & Bolus, R. (1982). Self-concept: The interplay of theory and methods. *Journal of Educational Psychology, 74*, 3–17.

Shavelson, R. J., Hubner, J. J., & Stanton, G. C. (1976). Self-concept: Validation of construct interpretations. *Review of Educational Research, 46*, 407–441.

Todt, E. (1978). *Das Interesse: Empirische Untersuchungen zu einem Motivationskonzept.* Bern, Switzerland: Huber.

Tracey, T. J. G., & Ward, C. C. (1998). The structure of children's interests and competence perceptions. *Journal of Counseling Psychology, 45*, 290–303.

Trautwein, U., Jonkmann, K., Gresch, C., Lüdtke, O., Neumann, M., Klusmann, U., Husemann, N., Maaz, K., Nagy, G., Becker, M., & Baumert, J. (2006). *Transformation des Sekundarschulsystems und Akademische Karrieren (TOSCA). Dokumentation der eingesetzten Items und Skalen. Welle 3.* Berlin, Germany: Max-Planck-Institut für Bildungsforschung.

von Collani, G., & Herzberg, P. Y. (2003a). Eine revidierte Fassung der deutschsprachigen Skala zum Selbstwertgefühl von Rosenberg. *Zeitschrift für Differentielle und Diagnostische Psychologie, 24*, 3–7.

von Collani, G., & Herzberg, P. Y. (2003b). Zur internen Struktur des globalen Selbstwertgefühls nach Rosenberg. *Zeitschrift für Differentielle und Diagnostische Psychologie, 24*, 9–22.

von Maurice, J. (2006). ICA-D. *Deutschsprachige Version des Inventory of Children's Activities – Revised (ICA-R, Tracey & Ward, 1998)*. Unpublished manuscript, Otto-Friedrich-Universität Bamberg, Bamberg, Germany.

von Maurice, J., & Bäumer, T. (2014). Entwicklung allgemeiner Interessenorientierungen beim Übergang von der Grundschule in den Sekundarbereich. In C. Tarnai & F. G. Hartmann (Eds.), *Berufliche Interessen: Beiträge zur Theorie von J. L. Holland* (pp. 63–85). Münster, Germany: Waxmann Verlag GmbH.

Watermann, R., Klingebiel, F., & Kurtz, T. (2010). Die motivationale Bewältigung des bevorstehenden Grundschulübergangs aus Schüler- und Elternsicht. In K. Maaz, J. Baumert, C. Gresch, & N. McElvany (Eds.), *Der Übergang von der Grundschule in die Sekundarstufe* (pp. 355–383). Berlin, Germany: Bundesministerium für Bildung und Forschung.

Weinert, S., Asendorpf, J. B., Beelmann, A., Doil, H., Frevert, S., Hasselhorn, M., & Lohaus, A. (2007). *Expertise zur Erfassung von psychologischen Personmerkmalen bei Kindern im Alter von fünf Jahren im Rahmen des SOEP* (DIW: Data Documentation 20). Berlin, Germany: Deutsches Institut für Wirtschaftsforschung.

Wigfield, A., & Eccles, J. S. (2000). Expectancy-value theory of achievement motivation. *Contemporary Educational Psychology, 25*, 68–81.

Wohlkinger, F., Bayer, M., & Ditton, H. (2016). Measuring self-concept in the NEPS. In H.-P. Blossfeld, J. von Maurice, M. Bayer, & J. Skopek (Eds.), *Methodological issues of longitudinal surveys. The example of the National Educational Panel Study* (pp. 181–193). Wiesbaden, Germany: VS Verlag für Sozialwissenschaften.

Disentangling Setting and Mode Effects for Online Competence Assessment

10

Ulf Kroehne, Timo Gnambs and Frank Goldhammer

Abstract

Many large-scale competence assessments such as the National Educational Panel Study (NEPS) have introduced novel test designs to improve response rates and measurement precision. In particular, unstandardized online assessments (UOA) offer an economic approach to reach heterogeneous populations that otherwise would not participate in face-to-face assessments. Acknowledging the difference between delivery, mode, and test setting, this chapter extends the theoretical background for dealing with mode effects in NEPS competence assessments (Kroehne and Martens in Zeitschrift für Erziehungswissenschaft 14:169–186, 2011 2011) and discusses two specific facets of UOA: (a) the confounding of selection and setting effects and (b) the role of test-taking behavior as mediator variable. We present a strategy that allows the integration of results from UOA into the results from proctored computerized assessments and generalizes the idea of motivational filtering, known for the treatment of rapid guessing behavior in low-stakes assessment. We particularly emphasize the relationship between paradata and the investigation of test-taking behavior, and illustrate how a reference sample formed by competence assessments under standardized and supervised conditions can be used

---

U. Kroehne (✉) · F. Goldhammer
German Institute for International Educational Research (DIPF), Frankfurt am Main, Germany
E-Mail: kroehne@dipf.de

F. Goldhammer
E-Mail: goldhammer@dipf.de

T. Gnambs
Leibniz Institute for Educational Trajectories; Johannes Kepler University Linz, Bamberg, Germany
E-Mail: timo.gnambs@lifbi.de

to increase the comparability of UOA in mixed-mode designs. The closing discussion reflects on the trade-off between data quality and the benefits of UOA.

Keywords

Education · Panel study · Online testing · Computer-based competence test
Mode effects · Paradata · Test-taking behavior

10.1 Introduction

The National Educational Panel Study (NEPS) started with paper-based assessments but now uses different variants of technology-based assessment to measure the development of competencies across the life course (see Chap. 4). The challenge of mode effects (see Kroehne and Martens 2011) in standardized testing conditions (e.g., paper-based vs. computer-based competence assessment embedded in computer-assisted interviews, CAPI) is met with cross-mode studies making use of random assignment of test takers to different modes. Experimental mode effect studies are designed to create valid comparisons regarding the mode while keeping other factors such as the testing conditions constant. This permits the investigation of mode differences regarding measurement invariance based on the assumption of random equivalent groups (see, e.g., Buerger et al. 2016), or invariant items (e.g., Heine et al. 2016).

This chapter extends the theoretical framework for the treatment of mode effects in NEPS competence tests administered under standardized and supervised conditions (Kroehne and Martens 2011) to also cover online testing. Thus, we present a proposal on how to integrate data collected in *online assessments* (i.e., educational tests embedded in computer-assisted web interviews, CAWI). Online assessments of educational tests can be characterized by many *U* words:[1] *u*nstandardized (concerning the test setting) and *u*nsupervised (concerning the absence of an interviewer or a test administrator). These two main characteristics emphasize that online assessments are typically answered using *u*ndefined hardware (e.g., any web-enabled device with any screen size and input method) and with *u*ser-selected software (e.g., the test takers' favorite browser can be used), accompanied by *u*nknown test-taking behavior and *u*nobserved selection and dropout processes. Moreover, these assessments are not only *u*nsupervised in the sense that no supervisor is present who offers at least limited support during the assessment, but also *u*nproctored, meaning that there is no monitoring of test security. Accordingly, online assessments of competencies represent unstandardized and unsupervised computer-based test scenarios that, hereafter, will be referred to as *unstandardized online assessments* (UOAs). Whereas NEPS routinely uses online surveys in mixed-mode designs, the applicability of this approach to the delivery of competence assessments, which are already administered in computer-based form in many waves and starting cohorts, is not yet well

---

[1] The similarity to *big data*, characterized with *V*'s (see, for instance, Kitchin and McArdle 2016) has been chosen carefully.

understood. Consequently, the first UOA was introduced to NEPS in 2013 as part of an experimental mixed-mode design.

UOA can reach a large number of test takers as a delivery in which the operational effort don't rise proportionally to the number of administered tests. Beyond reaching more test takers, UOA also allows participation of panel members who are hard to assess with other test deliveries (and vice versa). For instance, students undertaking a semester abroad can be reached only in personal interviews or group testing sessions at their home universities with (a relatively) immense effort. Mixed-mode designs with UOA seem particularly attractive regarding the costs for competence tests that were already implemented as computer-based assessment using "web technologies" (e.g., HTML). However, in mixed-mode designs, the coherent construct measurement across different assessment conditions is frequently questionable.

From survey research it is known that the trade-off between benefits and costs accompanying mixed-mode designs requires comparability studies and studies that investigate hypotheses about the potential causes of differences between assessment conditions (e.g., Jäckle et al. 2010). Accordingly, up to now, the UOA of competences in NEPS has been incorporated into experimental designs with random samples as control groups that were tested under standardized and supervised conditions (e.g., embedded in CAPIs as mentioned above or administered in supervised group testing conditions in educational institutions such as schools or universities).

This chapter introduces a general strategy for dealing with mixed-mode competence assessments in panel studies. We describe requirements to achieve comparability in mixed-mode designs from a psychometric point of view (in terms of potential mode and delivery effects) and with respect to the validity of the assessment (in terms of threats to the validity of interpretations of the score obtained from tests administered in different settings). The goal of this discussion is to outline how to achieve competence scores that are comparable across different assessments in mixed-mode designs, particularly when measuring change over time.

Therefore, we start with a detailed description of the empirical phenomenon of UOA in comparison to other methods used for the administration of competence tests in NEPS (10.2), followed by a discussion on the role of test-taking behavior when comparing UOA to other standardized test administrations (Sect. 10.3). Subsequently, in Sect. 10.4, we describe the general framework in which paradata (e.g., Kreuter 2013) are used to incorporate differences in response processes between assessments, including a brief review of the existing literature on selected criteria for evaluating test-taking behavior. In the closing Sect. 10.5, we summarize limitations of the current framework as well as possible generalizations that could also include mobile assessments.

The chapter goes beyond existing literature on mixed-mode measurements by focusing explicitly on educational tests (instead of surveys or questionnaires) and by describing a framework that uses standardized as well as supervised assessments as a reference to achieve comparability of UOA. This allows us to distinguish delivery and mode effects that can be corrected using bridge studies (or other linking approaches) from differences in test-taking behavior that cannot be corrected without making strong assumptions regarding the fit of the underlying measurement models of the educational tests (e.g., Wise and DeMars 2006).

10.1.1 Preliminary Remarks

By describing the theoretical background and a strategy for dealing with test-taking behavior in UOA, this chapter does not aim to favor or suggest a specific test delivery method for future assessments in NEPS. For sure, it also cannot replace survey papers and accompanying psychometric analyses of competence data in the various scientific use files. Moreover, the strategy described in this chapter, and, in particular, the criteria mentioned for filtering cases with conspicuous test-taking behavior in UOAs, are not necessarily suitable for the UOAs in NEPS. This requires further research to reasonably weigh the pros and cons. Nonetheless, this chapter does aim to provide a framework as a starting point that can—if used—deal potentially and to some degree with the lack of standardization of UOA.

In light of ongoing research on mixed-mode assessments of competencies, we hope that this framework can serve as a starting point for a fruitful discussion on UOA and how to achieve comparable measurements across different testing conditions. In time, these suggestions might be developed into a standard for the treatment of unstandardized and unsupervised assessment.

10.2 Investigating Online Assessment

10.2.1 Defining Unstandardized Online Competence Tests

This section deals specifically with UOAs used to administer competence tests in NEPS. As Table 10.1 reveals, competence tests in NEPS are administered in different modes (paper-based, PBA, and computer-based, CBA), embedded in different test settings (personal interviews, group testing, or unknown). Standardized competence assessments so

Table 10.1 Summary of test administrations used for competence tests in NEPS

Mode	Test setting	Interviewer	Test place	Delivery	Standardized
PBA	Personal interview	Yes	Household	Interviewer	Yes
PBA	Group testing	Yes	Institution	Test administrator	Yes
CBA	Personal interview	Yes	Household	Interviewer	Yes
CBA	Group testing	Yes	Institution	Test administrator	Yes
CBA	Online	No	Unknown	Web-based	No

far have been conducted while an interviewer (personal interview) or a test administrator (group testing) was present, either in the household or in different institutions such as schools or universities, with the interviewer or test administrator delivering the competence tests to the test takers.

The crucial features of *online assessment* are neither the web-based *delivery* nor the computer-based testing per se.[2] Instead, the central defining characteristic of UOA is the *test setting* at unknown locations that differ from standardized assessments conducted in groups or embedded in individual interviews. This results in a potential *setting effect* (see Frein 2011).

Standardization is a central part of the definition of competence assessment (e.g., Kraus et al. 2010). The lack of (experimental) control over the test place and the absence of an interviewer or test administrator in UOA can introduce additional construct-irrelevant variability compared to standardized conditions. Whereas this setting effect can be seen as part of the ecological validity in the context of psychological experiments (Reips 2000), it might threaten the validity of competence assessments (e.g., Barry and Finney 2009).

UOA also differs from traditional paper-and-pencil tests in terms of the *mode* (CBA vs. PBA). The mode is understood as a combination of multiple properties of an assessment, such as the medium, the input device, the format (portrait vs. landscape), possible feedback on the number of missing items, and other properties (see Kroehne and Martens 2011). However, additional factors beyond the *mode* can affect the comparability of assessments and contribute to the necessity of treating UOA cautiously.

In the remaining part of this subsection, we elaborate on these additional factors in detail, starting with apparent differences between competence assessments under standardized and supervised conditions and UOA. This will be followed by emphasizing possible differences in setting-specific (self-)selection processes that result in either complete participation or dropping off from an UOA. Subsequently, we close this section by pointing out the theoretical relationship between selection and setting effects.

10.2.2 Delivery Mode Differences

UOA as defined above is understood as administering test items in a browser-based environment, using identical items and identical implementations as used for supervised computer-based testing.[3] However, UOA differs regarding the following five apparent features from computer-based assessments under standardized conditions.

---

[2]Computer-based assessments are used routinely in NEPS in standardized settings, and online delivered tests can also be administered in standardized settings (e.g., Csapó et al. 2014).

[3]Apparent differences between modes—such as different layouts, question and task designs, and so forth in the sense of Dillman (2000)—were avoided (*unified design*) as far as technically possible.

First, the identity of test takers is typically either completely unknown, meaning there is no identity security (called *open mode*, Bartram 2005), or the test is made available to known test takers only (called *controlled mode*). Human supervision can be achieved to some extent in so-called *online proctored testing* (Rios and Liu 2017). In open mode and controlled mode, there is no guarantee that only the designated test taker answers the test. A third person, such as a more capable conspirator, can influence the answers gathered in UOA. Moreover, test takers might use additional materials that are either unauthorized or at least not available under standardized testing conditions (e.g., Bloemers et al. 2016). Note, although for low-stakes assessments, no apparent reason exists to fake results beside impression management, many tests takers will do so anyway, given the opportunity (Steger et al. in press). The apparent difference is that standardized, and in particular, supervised assessments are conducted in the so-called *managed mode* (Bartram 2005) in which human supervision has control over the test-taking environment.

Second, tests administered in UOA can be answered at different locations, including the private home, the test taker's workplace, and any public site such as trains, cafés, or all other areas that either provide Internet access or allow the use of private devices to access web pages. The place chosen by the test taker to answer questions or items in an online assessment represents a proxy for different properties that change along with the location. Noise, distraction, the presence of colleagues, family members, strangers, and other characteristics of the specific setting vary with the situation chosen mainly by the test taker.

Third, both hardware (e.g., tablet, notebook with touchpad, or desktop computer with mouse and keyboard) and software (e.g., web browser) used to access the test material in UOA are chosen by the test takers in UOA, resulting in an additional source of heterogeneity that is neither construct-related nor of interest because it does not represent any interindividual differences regarding the measured construct. A possible approach to reduce this heterogeneity is the formulation of restrictive inclusion criteria (i.e., requirements concerning the devices allowed or the browsers supported for a particular study). Consequently, online assessments might require prerequisites (such as a desktop computer with minimal display size and Internet access) that might either exclude some test takers from participation (International Test Commission 2006) or, at least, impose an additional burden on them.

Fourth, UOAs can be answered at self-selected time points. Whereas supervised tests administered in groups at, for instance, schools or universities are often scheduled in advance requiring a strict timing, assessments embedded in individual interviews (e.g., CAPI) in respondents' private homes are typically less restrictive, but still typically require arrangements between the test taker and the interviewer. The self-selection of testing time in UOAs (i.e., the time of day chosen to start the assessment) might lead to data that are gathered at times convenient for the test takers. The apparent difference is that UOA can result in test administrations at times of day that are not observed in standardized assessment in managed mode. Because the individually chosen time of testing might reflect individual differences in unobserved traits, testing time might also relate indirectly to the measured ability (e.g., Könen et al. 2015). Thus, the time of assessment might affect the comparability of standardized and supervised computer-based assessment and UOA. However, it is not necessarily the case that UOA is unrestricted concerning the time of day for participation. If announced properly, online test administration could easily be restricted to an eligible time window (e.g., between 6 a.m. and 10 p.m.), that would be more comparable to standardized testing.

Fifth, the social situation during test taking differs between the different test administrations summarized in Table 10.1. Effects of the social situation are known for interview-administered surveys and questionnaires in which the answering process differs from self-administered instruments (e.g., Klausch et al. 2013a). Moreover, as shown, for instance, in a meta-analysis by Gnambs and Kaspar (2015), a mode effect exists for items and issues that are conventionally perceived as sensitive topics. Beyond other factors, this effect might also be influenced by the presence of other test takers, as is the case in group-based test sessions. Moreover, differences in how test takers are recruited (e.g., an invitation via e-Mail or in a telephone interview) and differences in the level of human supervision of the test sessions (Bartram 2005) are considered to create different levels of commitment contributing to the social situation during testing. As discussed by Maddox (2017) for the computer-based assessment embedded in the interviews conducted for the Programme for International Assessment of Adult Competencies (PIAAC), the household creates a specific testing situation that is influenced by many factors. Although we are typically not able to quantify the impact of the social situation on the assessment results, UOA and assessment in the presence of an interviewer are expected to show systematic differences on this dimension of the test setting.

10.2.3 Setting-Specific (Self-)Selection

It is known that UOA versus supervised and standardized computer-based testing (either in individual or group settings) could result in mode-specific *response rates*. Indeed, the assumption that different people reply in different modes underlies the general idea of mixed-mode surveys (Klausch et al. 2013b). Everything else equal,[4] different response

---

[4]To achieve a meaningful comparison of response rates between deliveries (UOA vs. CAPI), the assumption that *everything else is equal* is crucial when taking into account the complete process of recruitment and invitation to an assessment. Depending on the design of a particular wave, different assessment modes might be combined. A combination used in one particular wave in NEPS is the mixture of CAPI for one random subsample of the cohort and a combination of CATI and UOA for the remaining subsample. The mixture of CATI and UOA incorporates two selection processes: participating in the CATI first followed by the decision to participate in the UOA. Taking both together, the sample composition for the assessment part of interest (i.e., the competence test administered in the CAPI and UOA delivery) is the result of two different selection processes that might best be described as one measurement point (CAPI) versus two measurement points (CATI and UOA). For the resulting samples, the assumption of random equivalent groups seems hardly justifiable without additional verifications and, if necessary, subsequent adjustments.

Table 10.2 Examples for decision processes related to UOA in the three stages "starting," "ending," and "taking"

Stage	Examples
Starting	Coverage/proportion of the cohort that can participate Cost of participation/effort required for participation Perceived attractiveness of the assessment/expectancy and value …
Ending	Self-paced answering and the resulting number of not-reached items Short interruptions and the tendency to abandon the setting Test abortion/dropout (and costs regarding social desirability) …
Taking	Tendency to answer items or to omit responses (missing propensity) Compliance with instruction and directions given for the assessment Test-taking effort and motivation (tendency to show rapid guessing) …

rates are considered to be an outcome of features of test deliveries and test setting that lead to different hurdles for participating in the assessment that, in turn, represent the consequences of underlying and unobserved decision processes. The resulting net effects regarding response rates might turn out to be higher for online assessments when factors that increase the probability of responding (such as the freedom to choose location and time point) dominate over factors that decrease this probability (such as the prerequisites for participation, e.g., the availability of a specific hardware).

It should be emphasized again that the test *setting* for UOA differs from standardized and supervised assessments in multiple ways. Hence, the specific phenomenon of the test setting incorporates not only multiple decision processes that might result in dissimilar selection biases for starting the assessment but also in setting-specific processes for ending the assessment and differences while taking the assessment.

As shown in Table 10.2, the decision processes in an UOA can be structured into three stages: (a) processes that result in the decision to participate in an assessment (*starting*), (b) processes that determine how and when the assessment is completed (*ending*), and (c) processes that influence the way in which the assessment is answered (*taking*).

Note that Table 10.2 is not exhaustive: Depending on the design of a study, the first stage (starting) might require the consideration of refusal rates and general participation rates concerning nonresponse errors. For simplification, we restrict the discussion of the online-specific aspect of non-response-related processes to the assessment of panel members by assuming that the online competence assessment is not the first contact with panel members who have already participated in a previous wave. Hence, the three stages are considered as part of a panel design for a particular cohort.

The selectivity of participation in an online administered test is a phenomenon that requires incorporating *time* in two ways: a longitudinal perspective of participation in different waves[5] and a short-term perspective of decisions to persevere in test *taking* instead of *ending* the assessment after it has started.

Starting an online delivered test is associated with lower costs than agreeing to be visited by an interviewer or arranging for participation in a group testing session. However, once a test taker overcomes the initial threshold for a standardized test setting, the social pressure to complete the test, at least on the surface, is much higher compared to unsupervised online delivery. UOAs provide more information about the decision process by giving access to incomplete data resulting from test takers who would probably not have overcome the threshold to participate in other assessment deliveries. Hence, even if more test takers drop out in UOAs, the data quality is not necessarily worse, because either more or different test takers participate. However, test takers might not only drop out more often but also answer questions differently. In other words, the question answering process might differ in UOA (e.g., de Leeuw et al. 2011). As we shall describe in the following, this represents a confounding of selection and setting effects.

10.2.4 Confounding of Selection Effects and Setting Effects

The delivery and the mode can be *randomly assigned* to test takers, for instance, by inviting panel members to participate either in a standardized and supervised CBA embedded in an interviewer delivered CAPI or an UOA including a competence test. Random assignment and careful experimental designs allow, for instance, an unbiased interpretation of the effect of the assigned delivery on comparable outcome measures (e.g., Jäckle et al. 2010). This line of reasoning could be used to compare the number of started test administrations according to some liberal criterion (i.e., test takers who at least start to read the instructions for a computer-based administered competence test, either UOA or integrated into a standardized and supervised setting). However, concerning the comparison of the measured competencies, the interpretation is limited by the fact that, for instance, the dropout behavior cannot be randomly assigned. Consequently, *selection effects* and *setting effects* are confounded (Klausch et al. 2013a).[6] This confounding was described by, for instance, Vannieuwenhuyze et al. (2011) for mixed-mode designs in which different types of respondents choose different modes (i.e., self-selection of

---

[5]Response rates, given a sample member has responded in a previous wave, correspond to attrition rates (if the unit nonresponse is a final dropout) or temporary dropouts. In waves with competence assessments, temporary dropout is equivalent to test refusal).

[6]Note that this is true if the random assignment of respondents to the delivery mode cannot be conducted after the recruitment (Jäckle et al. 2010) that serves as the decision to participate in a particular wave in a panel study.

modes, labeled by the authors as *measurement effect*). This confounding is supported by empirical examples. For instance, Preckel and Thiemann (2003) found items of an online-administered high potential intelligence test to be easier compared to a paper-and-pencil version. These differences could be explained by self-selection, motivation, and dropout rates. However, the different delivery-specific response and completion rates result in a similar confounding even under randomization. Differences (or similarities) between the outcomes can be caused by either differences between the sample compositions (due to selectivity) or differences in the way the instrument works (due to the setting).

10.3 Test-Taking Behavior

Dropout from a started assessment is an example of a setting-specific test-taking behavior that might create incomparable assessments if not acknowledged appropriately. As mentioned above, other examples range from using material or tools not available under standardized and supervised conditions (e.g., calculator or dictionary), searching the internet for solution-relevant information, or getting help from others. All of these have been discussed for unstandardized online assessment in the context of *cheating* (e.g., Lievens and Burke 2011; Bloemers et al. 2016; for meta-analytic evidence, see also Steger et al., in press).

For the experimental comparison of UOA and CBA under standardized and supervised conditions, test-taking behavior becomes a *mediator*. The notion of *mediator variables* (from research on causal inference) emphasizes the limitations of random assignment of test takers to specific test-taking behavior(s). What can be assigned is the test delivery (e.g., web-based as for UOA), and this delivery is associated with a particular test setting. However, the resulting test-taking behavior, such as the dropout tendency, is neither defined deterministically by the random assignment nor under experimental control once the delivery is assigned. Instead, test-taking behavior is the result of usually unobserved processes that are facilitated differently in different settings.[7]

---

[7]Test-taking behavior can be studied experimentally by, for instance, using different instructional sets, as often done to determine the limits on fakability of personality scales (see for a meta-analysis, Viswesvaran and Ones 1999). Similarly, mediator variables can become treatment variables. However, when the test setting (and not the test-taking behavior) is randomly assigned, the values of the mediator are only observed variables.

10.3.1 Setting-Specific Behavior as Mediator

Bosnjak and Tuten (2001) classify response behavior on the two dimensions "Number of Displayed Questions" and "Number of Questions Answered" into seven different segments in web-based surveys.[8] For instance, test takers showing a response pattern with a high number of displayed questions and a low number of answered questions were labeled as *lurkers*, referring to a phenomenon generally observed in online communication (see, e.g., Sun et al. 2014). Similarly, one might take the number of not reached items[9] into account as a measure of test-taking behavior that is related to speed and ability (e.g., Goldhammer 2015). If there is a higher tendency to take tests with a higher speed level in UOA, the number of not reached items should be lower and, thus, reflect a setting effect.

Response times also allows defining dropout at the item level as the number of not answered items after the last answered item when the time limit for a domain has not been reached. Dropout behavior in online assessments might reflect lower levels of commitment to the test (e.g., Reips 2000). Accordingly, if the proportion of test takers with a lower commitment is higher in UOA, dropout is expected to occur more often as a setting-specific response behavior.

Response times can also be used to describe test-taking behavior for completed tests. In particular, fast responses are used to identify rapid-guessing behavior (Schnipke and Scrams 1997) that is related to test-taking engagement (Wise and Kong 2005). Although Rios and Liu (2017) found no difference between proctored and unproctored online assessment, the presence of test administrators was found to affect test-taking engagement (Lau et al. 2009). Hence, rapid guessing is expected to differ between UOA and standardized, and, in particular, supervised testing.

The dropout tendency and rapid guessing behavior are examples for test-taking behaviors for which it could be hypothesized that they transmit the effects of the independent variable (test setting) to the outcome variables (item responses). After conceptualizing setting-specific behavior as a mediator that is triggered only by the setting, it becomes essential to formulate theoretical expectations regarding the appraisal of test-taking behavior. For instance, available theoretical considerations, such as the assumption about the existence of lurkers in online assessments (Bosnjak and Tuten 2001) or the link between response time and test-taking effort (Wise and Kong 2005), can be used to derive indicators of specific test-taking behaviors.

---

[8] Complete Responders, Unit Nonresponders, Answering Dropouts, Lurkers, Lurking Drop-Outs, Item Nonresponders, and Item Nonresponding Dropouts.

[9] Competence tests are administered with time limits for each domain. Due to the time limits, it is possible to distinguish between omitted responses (i.e., unanswered items that are followed by answered questions) and not reached items (i.e., unanswered items that are not followed by an answered question in a test part due to the time constraint).

10.3.2 Criteria for Comparable Behavior

The methodology to evaluate *measurement invariance* across mode effects (e.g., PBA vs. CBA, administered under identical conditions) and setting effects (CBA vs. UOA) can be applied to noncognitive measures with multiitem scales (e.g., Hox et al. 2015; Pajkossy et al. 2015) and cognitive measures such as competence tests (e.g., Buerger et al. 2016). The investigation of measurement invariance requires either items that are not affected by mode and setting of the test administration or the assumption of (random) equivalent groups.

Comparability concerning test-taking behavior, as a prerequisite for both approaches, can be achieved by generalizing approaches developed for the treatment of rapid guessing behavior. *Motivation filtering*, used by Wise et al. (2004), might make it possible to increase the validity of test score interpretations (see also Wise et al. 2006). Such *filtering* on rapid guessing as test-taking behavior was found to be superior to filtering on self-reported effort (Rios et al. 2014). The simple idea is to use only those cases from UOA that show a comparable test-taking behavior to the standardized and supervised condition. Test takers with unusual behavior that is not observed in the standardized and supervised condition could be filtered. Remaining selection effects can be adjusted in a second step. Phrasing this in causal inference terminology, filtering could be applied to establish *common support* regarding the values of the mediator between the different test settings. As soon as test-taking behaviors overlap between test settings, different techniques, such as matching or conditioning can be used to adjust for the remaining differences in observed variables.

By imposing the requirement that only cases from UOA are used that show a test-taking behavior comparable to standardized and supervised assessments, we create a trade-off between the benefits of online assessment (more liberal filtering) and the interpretability of competence assessment in terms of standardization (stricter filtering). Furthermore, this conceptualization assumes that the test-taking behavior observed in a standardized and supervised assessment represents the valid standard. This might not necessarily be the case, if, for instance, rapid guessing occurs in standardized and supervised assessments. Then, motivation filtering should be applied to both the standardized and the unstandardized assessment, because it is known from previous research that rapid guessing threatens the validity of assessment results (e.g., Wise and DeMars 2005). Hence, if possible, thresholds for acceptable behavior should be derived like those obtained with different methods for rapid-guessing behavior (e.g., Kong et al. 2007). If this is not possible, the standardized test administration can be used as reference sample in the context of mixed-mode assessments (Fricker 2005; Vannieuwenhuyze et al. 2011). This justifies the idea of filtering (instead of weighting), because it makes it possible to exclude particularly test-taking behavior that was not found at all under standardized conditions. Note that choosing standardized and supervised settings as the reference might, in fact, manifest the bias. However, the choice of standardized and supervised settings seems justifiable because NEPS uses this kind of setting for the majority of competence assessments (see for a similar perspective, e.g., Russell and Hubley 2017).

The filtered UOA sample and the sample from standardized and supervised testing could either be used directly for further analyses, or remaining differences in additional variables (beyond indicators for test-taking behavior) could be adjusted using weighting, matching, or regression-based approaches.

10.3.3 The Importance of Paradata

The theoretical perspective described above requires the integration of two phenomena for investigating setting effects and establishing comparability of competence assessments between UOA and computer-based testing in standardized and supervised conditions: First, UOA attracts different test takers (i.e., the initial selection) with heterogeneous devices, varying internet connectivity, test taking at different times of day, and so forth. Second, test-taking behavior can vary between settings resulting in both: (a) more dropout in UOA and (b) different response processes in UOA that reflect, for example, differences in motivation, distraction, and honesty.

Paradata defined in a broader sense (e.g., McClain et al. 2018) can provide valuable information to account for both sources of differences between standardized and unstandardized testing. Indeed, paradata can be a *"way of identifying behaviours that might be relevant to response processes related to the construct and validity"* (Russell and Hubley 2017, p. 243).

Access-related paradata, in the form of device information (e.g., information provided in the "user agent string," see Callegaro 2010) can provide insights into, for instance, the relationship between the device type and higher probabilities of ending an online administered competence test ahead of time before reaching the last item. Access-related paradata such as connection speed, screen size, and the time required for scrolling can also explain interindividual time differences in UOA (e.g., Couper and Peterson 2017).

Response-related paradata such as timestamps collected for each answer change, can help to identify rapid-guessing behavior by flagging unmotivated responses that are presented faster than *solution behavior* would require. Similarly, an overall measure of test speededness, such as the number of not-reached items or the total testing time can be derived from response-related paradata that might help to identify speed-related differences between test settings.

Finally, *process-related paradata*, which incorporate all gathered raw log events of an assessment platform (e.g., Kroehne et al. 2016), can be used to derive indicators from paradata for specific test-taking behavior, such as *short-term interruptions* (see Sect. 10.4.3).

Robling et al. (2010, p. 10) suggested, that *"as global descriptions of data collection method can obscure underlying mode features, comparative studies should describe these features more fully."* Similarly, the collection of paradata should be implemented as completely as possible without negatively impacting on the collection of substantive data, because until now, no standard for the collection of paradata exists.

10.4 Framework for Integrating UOA

In this section, we present a possible framework for integrating UOA into standardized and supervised comptence assessments.

10.4.1 Reference Sample

In NEPS, test administrations under standardized and supervised conditions present the current standard. Therefore standardized and supervised computer-based define the reference against which UOAs are compared. Up to now, NEPS has used UOA only in combination with standardized and supervised test settings. The implemented designs combined random assignment of respondents to different test administrations, but allowed respondents to switch from the standardized and supervised assessment to UOA if they chose to (self-selection). Accordingly, data from randomly assigned respondents can be used as the empirical reference sample. These data are not affected by individual mode preferences, but still reflect mode-specific response rates (see Sect. 10.2.2).

The randomly selected test takers from the empirical reference sample (tested under standardized and supervised conditions) could be used to derive cutoff values for indicators that represent typical test-taking behavior under the current NEPS standard.[10] Respondents in UOA who fall outside these cut-offs are suspected of employing setting-specific test-taking behavior. In particular, a reference sample would be crucial for criteria that were not investigated previously, such as the interruption of test-taking.

10.4.2 Potential Criteria

Two approaches can be adopted to identify appropriate criteria to compare test-taking behavior between UOA and the computer-based standardized and supervised testing. The *top-down* approach follows theoretical reasoning on, for example, motivation and engagement, speededness and time spent in the assessment, nonresponse and dropout, cheating and aberrant responses, as well as test takers' attention, and uses this reasoning to derive indicators for test-taking behavior. The top-down perspective emphasizes the

---

[10]Using the empirical reference sample allows us to apply the approach even if no normative threshold exists or the appropriateness of thresholds is in doubt (e.g., outdated, derived for a different target population or different domain, etc.).

need for theoretical justifications of the criteria used to benchmark test-taking behavior. Moreover, the selection of criteria allows the targeting of specific concerns of domain experts regarding the validity of online assessments.

The *bottom-up* approach focuses on the available paradata for a given competence assessment and aims to find observable indicators that allow a comparison of test-taking behavior between individual test takers. This bottom-up approach is conducted specifically for each UOA, because the gathered paradata are highly specific for the platform used to implement the computer-based assessment instrument (e.g., the CBA ItemBuilder, Rölke 2012). This bottom-up perspective permits adjustment of the procedure to unexpected behavior such as cases showing hints of technical abnormalities.

In the following, we present an overview of potential indicators that might be used to filter online cases from UOA with test-taking behavior that would not occur under standardized supervised conditions.

Short interruptions: In NEPS competence assessments, test takers are instructed to work on the assessment without interruption for 60 min.[11] Although it is possible that respondents take unexpected breaks (e.g., using the bathroom), in line with the instructions given to test takers, we have no substantive reason to assume that periods of inactivity should occur more often in UOA as compared to standardized assessment (using the identical software platform). Therefore, aberrant test-taking behavior in UOA can be expected to result in more and longer periods without any logged interaction (Sendelbah et al. 2016). From the log data, time intervals without any activity can be identified for each test taker that allow the creation of a filter to exclude these cases. However, filtering requires an appropriate threshold to consider the interruptions for a given test taker unusual (e.g., the threshold should be substantively longer than the expected maximum reading time, and test takers who are slow but motivated must not be excluded). A similar approach has already been presented for online surveys (Beckers et al. 2011; Stieger and Reips 2010). However, the thresholds of 5 and 4 min used by the authors to exclude cases seem arbitrary. More recently, Sendelbah et al. (2016) used standardized time measures to derive cutoffs by incorporating the distribution of the indicator into the definition of thresholds. As the aim is to filter test takers from the online sample who show interruptions that do not occur under the standardized condition, we prefer deriving the cutoff value from the distribution of the indicator in the reference sample (i.e., by taking the reference sample as the norm and deriving the thresholds empirically). The sensitivity of the filtering approach to different cutoff values needs to be investigated empirically.

---

[11]"Für die ersten zwei Teile haben Sie jeweils 30 Minuten Zeit. Es ist nicht möglich, die Bearbeitung der Aufgaben zu unterbrechen und später fortzusetzen. Nehmen Sie sich deshalb bitte eineinhalb Stunden am Stück Zeit." [For each of the first two parts, you have 30 min. It is not possible for you stop answering the tasks to take a break and continue later. So please reserve 1.5 h time for the test.]

Focus detection: Leaving the current page in the web browser, as indicated by a focus detection (Diedenhofen and Musch 2017) could be interpreted as an additional hint of aberrant test-taking behavior or respondent multitasking, or at least an interruption of the test session. Relative to a threshold, the number of interruptions (i.e., the number of defocusing events; Diedenhofen and Musch 2017) could be used to filter test takers with conspicuous behavior.

Technical issues: In case of technical issues, such as interrupted internet connectivity, paradata might be generated. One specific consequence of UOA administered in controlled mode is the registration of *re-logins*. Moreover, long-term interruptions during online testing might also indicate technical issues on the server side (Sinharay et al. 2014, 2015). If a substantial amount of cases is affected by technical issues, filtering could be considered to improve the validity of the competence assessment.

Test speededness: The number of not reached items is expected to be identical between settings if self-paced test-taking is comparable concerning the speed–ability compromise (Goldhammer 2015). However, the duration (time spent on the test) was found to be higher for an online assessment (compared to paper-and-pencil testing; Bayazit and Askar 2012). Even though time is typically not included in mode effect comparisons due to the lack of timestamps from paper-based assessment (see, for an exception, Dirk et al. 2017), there is some evidence that test speededness differs within standardized and supervised settings between CBA and PBA (Bodmann and Robinson 2004; Kroehne et al. 2018). If this result is replicated for UOA even after filtering for rapid guessing behavior, speededness could be considered as a potential mediator of setting effects.

Missing propensity: Beyond the number of not reached items, also the number of omitted responses (and the propensity to omit items, e.g., Köhler et al. 2014) should be comparable between UOA as well as standardized and supervised conditions. *Lurkers*, for instance, defined as test takers with an unexpectedly high amount of omitted responses (i.e., a striking test-taking behavior characterized by viewing but not answering most items), could be considered for filtering to achieve comparability.

The possibility of using these indicators is strengthened by the availability of a reference sample (see 10.4.1), because currently *"the links between observed behaviours or patterns and underlying processes are speculative, and have not been explored directly"* (Russell and Hubley 2017, p. 234).

Rapid guessing: For some selected indicators, such as solution behavior in relationship to test-taking engagement, robust theories (e.g., Wise and Kong 2005; Wise 2015; Guo et al. 2016) and sound evidence from previous research (e.g., Lee and Jia 2014; Finn 2015; Goldhammer et al. 2016; Liu et al. 2015; Rios et al. 2017) are available allowing the derivation of thresholds that can be used without the need for a reference sample. Thus, taking into account the mode- and setting-specific response time distribution and the proportion of correct responses conditional on response time to create item-level thresholds (e.g., Wise and Ma 2012) would make it possible to apply motivational filtering to both the UOA sample and the reference sample.

10.4.3 Creating Comparable Ability Estimates

Ability estimates can be derived using data gathered under standardized assessment conditions as well as data from UOA. Within each setting, specific characteristics of the test-taking behavior are possible, and one test setting is not necessarily superior to another. Accordingly, unfiltered data could be used independently for the subsamples created by the randomly assigned or self-selected test delivery (standardized vs. online). However, as soon as ability estimates are to be used interchangeably, effects of the mode and setting should be taken into account.

Within each setting, for instance, within group testing sessions at universities, random assignment of test takers to modes can justify the assumption of random equivalent groups (Buerger et al. 2016). As discussed in this chapter, the treatment of mode effects cannot be adapted directly to adjust for setting effects when test-taking behavior mediates the setting effect. In particular, when a test-taking behavior (such as short interruptions) is observed only in one setting, strong assumptions would be required (extrapolation).

In this chapter, we generalize the idea of motivation filtering (Wise et al. 2004) as a first step before a potential treatment of mode effects. Filtering in this first step is expected to be most effective if implemented as liberally as possible. After controlling for differences in test-taking behavior, remaining differences in the sample composition can be corrected if necessary, for instance, by using weighting or matching techniques.

Filtering regarding test-taking behavior and possibly the additional adjustment for the sample composition result in groups that can be assumed to be equal concerning their competence. Subsequently, measurement invariance can be investigated, and at least construct equivalence should be established.

Finally, remaining dissimilarities in the test-taking behavior within test settings, for instance, interindividual differences in the number of not reached items as a measure of test speededness, could be included in the background model when estimating person parameters—an approach recently implemented in PISA (see, e.g., Heine et al. 2016).

10.5 Discussion and Outlook

In this chapter, we discussed treating test-taking behavior as a mediator for the effect of test settings on the results of assessments. The idea of generalizing the filtering approach, known for motivation filtering in low-stakes assessments, was a response to two main challenges: concerns about the validity of online assessments (lurking, rapid guessing, inattentive responding, use of additional material) and the need for an argument for creating random equivalent groups as the prerequisite for dealing with psychometric differences between settings.

Altogether, the framework introduces a trade-off between the benefits of online assessment (that might result in more data, including more incomplete test administrations and test takers who are harder to reach with standardized assessments) and the restriction to cases with test-taking behavior that is also observed under standardized testing conditions.

As illustrated with selected examples, hints for different test-taking behaviors can be found in additional data about the processes by which the survey and test data were collected (paradata). Accordingly, as soon as paradata are used to exclude cases (i.e., filtering), procedures for cleaning and validating paradata would be required to ensure data quality. Moreover, to foster the reproducibility of analyses and results, strategies for disseminating the information used from paradata should be developed that balance between the effort to create scientific use files (e.g., including indicators derived from paradata) and the research potential (e.g., the possibility of investigating new indicators). Disseminating indicators requires established measures (such as time and sequence of questions) that are of general use for investigating test taker behavior. This applies not only for cognitive measures, but also for survey data, because it would allow, for instance, an investigation of rapid guessing for noncognitive measures (e.g., Johnston 2016) or straightlining as response behavior in questionnaires (e.g., Kim et al. 2018). Providing raw log data rests not only on the availability of resources to anonymize and document them, but also on the tools that can be used by substantive researchers to analyze these kinds of data (such as the PIAAC Log- Data Analyzer, Goldhammer et al. 2017). Given both prerequisites, providing access to raw log data might be desirable because it would particularly make it possible to investigate methodological research questions such as the effect of technical problems and re-logins (e.g., Sinharay et al. 2014) on online assessments.

Previous work on the treatment of mode effects for competence tests (see Kroehne and Martens 2011) has been extended here to incorporate online assessments that are conducted under different, unstandardized test settings. This extension was necessary even for studies that use identical computerizations of items used in CAPI and UOA. Further research will be necessary as soon as ability estimates from different computerizations of instruments are compared (see, e.g., Bennett 2003), for instance, across cohorts. The extension described in this chapter provides a framework for dealing with low-stakes UOA. This includes studies conducted for instrument development. As Barry and Finney (2009) showed by comparing UOA and different standardizations of classroom testing, standardized test conditions are superior even for test development.

A major limitation of the described strategy to deal with UOA is that it focuses only on the psychometric modeling of mode effects after treating the potential confounding due to setting-specific test-taking behavior with filtering. A valuable extension in further research might particularly be to address the measurement of setting-specific attitudes, privacy concerns, and the perceived level of supervision in standardized conditions.

Incorporating differences in test-taking behavior as they occur between assessments conducted in different settings is also relevant for assessments obtained on mobile devices (Huff 2015; Illingworth et al. 2015; King et al. 2015). This is another area of future research. However, when screen sizes and display sizes are small, identical layouts, as assumed for the comparison between online assessment and computer-based testing are no longer possible.

An additional area for future research relates to the choice of the reference condition. The core idea of considering test-taking behavior as a mediator for the comparison of assessments between settings can be applied with different choices of a reference condition. The suggestion to exclude cases with unexpected test-taking behavior by using cutoff values derived from a reference administration should be understood as a pragmatic approach that is justifiable, particularly when the sample size of the online administered tests is much larger compared to the sample size gathered under standardized conditions. Further research is needed to develop more sophisticated techniques that will also overcome the arbitrary selection of one of the possible test settings used as the reference to derive cutoff values. Because the reference test setting might be the result of setting-specific selection behaviors as well, measures of representativeness, such as r indicators (Schouten et al. 2009, Shlomo et al. 2012), could be used to balance selection effects concerning the derivation of cutoff values.

Finally, further research might study the person fit across modes, bridging the gap between the measurement model used to scale competence tests and the answering behavior of test takers (Glas and Meijer 2003; Goegebeur et al. 2010; Sinharay 2015).

References

Barry, C. L., & Finney, S. J. (2009). Does it matter how data are collected? A comparison of testing conditions and the implications for validity. *Research & Practice in Assessment, 3*, 1–15.
Bartram, D. (2005). Testing on the internet: Issues, challenges and opportunities in the field of occupational assessment. In D. Bartram & R. K. Hambleton, (Eds.), *Computer-based testing and the internet* (pp. 13–37). Chichester, England: John Wiley & Sons.
Bayazit, A., & Aşkar, P. (2012). Performance and duration differences between online and paper–pencil tests. *Asia Pacific Education Review, 13*, 219–226.
Beckers, T., Siegers, P., & Kuntz, A. (2011, March). *Speeders in online value research*. Paper presented at the GOR 11, Düsseldorf, Germany.
Bennett, R. E. (2003). *Online assessment and the comparability of score meaning* (ETS-RM-03-05). Princeton, NJ: Educational Testing Service.
Bloemers, W., Oud, A., & van Dam, K. (2016). Cheating on unproctored internet intelligence tests: Strategies and effects. *Personnel Assessment and Decisions, 2*, 21–29.
Bodmann, S. M., & Robinson, D. H. (2004). Speed and performance differences among computer-based and paper-pencil tests. *Journal of Educational Computing Research, 31*, 51–60.
Bosnjak, M., & Tuten, T. L. (2001). Classifying response behaviors in web-based surveys. *Journal of Computer-Mediated Communication, 6*(3).
Buerger, S., Kroehne, U., & Goldhammer, F. (2016). The transition to computer-based testing in large-scale assessments: Investigating (partial) measurement invariance between modes. *Psychological Test and Assessment Modeling, 58*, 597–616.

Callegaro, M. (2010). Do you know which device your respondent has used to take your online survey? *Survey Practice, 3*, 1–12.

Couper, M. P., & Peterson, G. J. (2017). Why do web surveys take longer on smartphones? *Social Science Computer Review, 35*, 357–377.

Csapó, B., Molnár, G., & Nagy, J. (2014). Computer-based assessment of school readiness and early reasoning. *Journal of Educational Psychology, 106*, 639–650.

de Leeuw, E., Hox, J., & Scherpenzeel, A. (2011). Mode effect or question wording? Measurement error in mixed mode surveys. *Proceedings of the Survey Research Methods Section, American Statistical Association* (pp. 5959–5967). Alexandria, VA: American Statistical Association.

Diedenhofen, B., & Musch, J. (2017). PageFocus: Using paradata to detect and prevent cheating on online achievement tests. *Behavior Research Methods, 49*, 1444–1459.

Dillman, D. A. (2000). *Mail and internet surveys: The total design method*. New York, NY: Wiley.

Dirk, J., Kratzsch, G. K., Prindle, J. P., Kroehne, U., Goldhammer, F., & Schmiedek, F. (2017). Paper-based assessment of the effects of aging on response time: A diffusion model analysis. *Journal of Intelligence, 5*, 12.

Finn, B. (2015). *Measuring motivation in low-stakes assessments*. Research Report No. RR-15-19. Princeton, NJ: Educational Testing Service.

Frein, S. T. (2011). Comparing in-class and out-of-class computer-based tests to traditional paper-and-pencil tests in introductory psychology courses. *Teaching of Psychology, 38*, 282–287.

Fricker, S. (2005). An experimental comparison of web and telephone surveys. *Public Opinion Quarterly, 69*, 370–392.

Glas, C. A., & Meijer, R. R. (2003). A Bayesian approach to person fit analysis in item response theory models. *Applied Psychological Measurement, 27*, 217–233.

Gnambs, T., & Kaspar, K. (2015). Disclosure of sensitive behaviors across self-administered survey modes: A meta-analysis. *Behavior Research Methods, 47*, 1237–1259.

Goegebeur, Y., De Boeck, P., & Molenberghs, G. (2010). Person fit for test speededness: Normal curvatures, likelihood ratio tests and empirical Bayes estimates. *Methodology, 6*, 3–16.

Goldhammer, F. (2015). Measuring ability, speed, or both? Challenges, psychometric solutions, and what can be gained from experimental control. *Measurement: Interdisciplinary Research and Perspectives, 13*, 133–164.

Goldhammer, F., Lüdtke, O., Martens, T., & Christoph, G. (2016). *Test-taking engagement in PIAAC*. OECD Education Working Papers 133. Paris, France: OECD Publishing.

Goldhammer, F., Naumann, J., Rölke, H., Stelter, A., & Tóth, K. (2017). Relating product data to process data from computer-based competency assessment. In D. Leutner, J. Fleischer, J. Grünkorn, & E. Klieme (Eds.), *Competence assessment in education: Research, models and instruments* (pp. 407–425). Cham, Switzerland: Springer.

Guo, H., Rios, J. A., Haberman, S., Liu, O. L., Wang, J., & Paek, I. (2016). A new procedure for detection of students' rapid guessing responses using response time. *Applied Measurement in Education, 29*, 173–183.

Heine, J.-H., Mang, J., Borchert, L., Gomolka, J., Kroehne, U., Goldhammer, F., & Sälzer, C. (2016). Kompetenzmessung in PISA 2015. In K. Reiss, C. Sälzer, A. Schiepe-Tiska, E. Klieme, & O. Köller (Eds.), *PISA 2015 Eine Studie zwischen Kontinuität und Innovation*, (pp. 383–540). Münster, Germany: Waxmann.

Hox, J. J., De Leeuw, E. D., & Zijlmans, E. A. O. (2015). Measurement equivalence in mixed mode surveys. *Frontiers in Psychology, 6*, 1–11.

Huff, K. C. (2015). The comparison of mobile devices to computers for web-based assessments. *Computers in Human Behavior, 49*, 208–212.

Illingworth, A. J., Morelli, N. A., Scott, J. C., & Boyd, S. L. (2015). Internet-based, unproctored assessments on mobile and non-mobile devices: Usage, measurement equivalence, and outcomes. *Journal of Business and Psychology, 30*, 325–343.

International Test Commission (2006). International guidelines on computer-based and internet-delivered testing. *International Journal of Testing, 6*, 143–171.

Jäckle, A., Roberts, C., & Lynn, P. (2010). Assessing the effect of data collection mode on measurement. *International Statistical Review, 78*, 3–20.

Johnston, M. M. (2016). Applying solution behavior thresholds to a noncognitive measure to identify rapid responders: An empirical investigation. PhD Thesis, James Madison University, Harrisonburg, VA.

Kim, Y., Dykema, J., Stevenson, J., Black, P., & Moberg, D. P. (2018). Straightlining: Overview of measurement, comparison of indicators, and effects in mail–web mixed-mode surveys. *Social Science Computer Review, 29*, 208–220.

King, D. D., Ryan, A. M., Kantrowitz, T., Grelle, D., & Dainis, A. (2015). Mobile internet testing: An analysis of equivalence, individual differences, and reactions. *International Journal of Selection and Assessment, 23*, 382–394.

Kitchin, R., & McArdle, G. (2016). What makes big data, big data? Exploring the ontological characteristics of 26 datasets. *Big Data & Society, 3*, 1–10.

Klausch, T., Hox, J. J., & Schouten, B. (2013a). Measurement effects of survey mode on the equivalence of attitudinal rating scale questions. *Sociological Methods & Research, 42*, 227–263.

Klausch, T., Hox, J. J., & Schouten, B. (2013b). Assessing the mode-dependency of sample selectivity across the survey response process. *Discussion Paper 2013-03*. The Hague, Netherlands: Statistics Netherlands (Available from https://www.cbs.nl/-/media/imported/documents/2013/12/2013-03-x10-pub.pdf).

Köhler, C., Pohl, S., & Carstensen, C. H. (2014). Taking the missing propensity into account when estimating competence scores: Evaluation of item response theory models for nonignorable omissions. *Educational and Psychological Measurement, 75*, 1–25.

Könen, T., Dirk, J., & Schmiedek, F. (2015). Cognitive benefits of last night's sleep: Daily variations in children's sleep behavior are related to working memory fluctuations. *Journal of Child Psychology and Psychiatry, 56*, 171–182.

Kong, X. J., Wise, S. L., & Bhola, D. S. (2007). Setting the response time threshold parameter to differentiate solution behavior from rapid-guessing behavior. *Educational and Psychological Measurement, 67*, 606–619.

Kraus, R., Stricker, G., & Speyer, C. (Eds., 2010). Online counseling: A handbook for mental health professionals. Practical resources for the mental health professional. Boston, MA: Academic Press.

Kreuter, F. (Ed., 2013). Improving surveys with paradata: Analytic uses of process information. Hoboken, NJ: Wiley & Sons.

Kroehne, U., Hahnel, C., & Goldhammer, F. (2018, April). *Invariance of the response process between modes and gender in reading assessment*. Paper presented at the annual meeting of the National Council on Measurement in Education, New York.

Kroehne, U. & Martens, T. (2011). Computer-based competence tests in the national educational panel study: The challenge of mode effects. *Zeitschrift für Erziehungswissenschaft, 14*, 169–186.

Kroehne, U., Roelke, H., Kuger, S., Goldhammer, F., & Klieme, E. (2016, April). *Theoretical framework for log-data in technology-based assessments with empirical applications from PISA*. Paper presented at the annual meeting of the National Council on Measurement in Education, Washington, DC.

Lau, A. R., Swerdzewski, P. J., Jones, A. T., Anderson, R. D., & Markle, R. E. (2009). Proctors matter: Strategies for increasing examinee effort on general education program assessments. *The Journal of General Education, 58,* 196–217.

Lee, Y.-H. & Jia, Y. (2014). Using response time to investigate students' test-taking behaviors in a NAEP computer-based study. *Large-scale Assessments in Education, 2,* 8.

Lievens, F., & Burke, E. (2011). Dealing with the threats inherent in unproctored Internet testing of cognitive ability: Results from a large-scale operational test program: Unproctored internet testing. *Journal of Occupational and Organizational Psychology, 84,* 817–824.

Liu, O. L., Rios, J. A., & Borden, V. (2015). The effects of motivational instruction on college students' performance on low-stakes assessment. *Educational Assessment, 20,* 79–94.

Maddox, B. (2017). Talk and gesture as process data. *Measurement: Interdisciplinary Research and Perspectives, 15,* 113–127.

McClain, C. A., Couper, M. P., Hupp, A. L., Keusch, F., Peterson, G., Piskorowski, A. D., & West, B. T. (2018). A typology of web survey paradata for assessing total survey error. *Social Science Computer Review,* Online First.

Pajkossy, P., Simor, P., Szendi, I., & Racsmány, M. (2015). Hungarian validation of the Penn State Worry Questionnaire (PSWQ): Method effects and comparison of paper-pencil versus online administration. *European Journal of Psychological Assessment, 31,* 159–165.

Preckel, F., & Thiemann, H. (2003). Online-versus paper-pencil version of a high potential intelligence test. *Swiss Journal of Psychology, 62,* 131–138.

Reips, U.-D. (2000). The Web experiment method: Advantages, disadvantages, and solutions. In M. H. Birnbaum (Ed.), *Psychological experiments on the Internet* (pp. 89–118). San Diego, CA: Academic Press.

Rios, J. A., Guo, H., Mao, L., & Liu, O. L. (2017). Evaluating the impact of careless responding on aggregated-scores: To filter unmotivated examinees or not? *International Journal of Testing, 17,* 74–104.

Rios, J. A., & Liu, O. L. (2017). Online proctored versus unproctored low-stakes internet test administration: Is there differential test-taking behavior and performance? *American Journal of Distance Education, 31,* 226–241.

Rios, J. A., Liu, O. L., & Bridgeman, B. (2014). Identifying low-effort examinees on student learning outcomes assessment: A comparison of two approaches. *New Directions for Institutional Research, 161,* 69–82.

Robling, M. R., Ingledew, D. K., Greene, G., Sayers, A., Shaw, C., Sander, L., Russell, I. T., Williams, J. G., & Hood, K. (2010). Applying an extended theoretical framework for data collection mode to health services research. *BMC Health Services Research, 10,* 180.

Rölke, H. (2012). The ItemBuilder: A graphical authoring system for complex item development. In T. Bastiaens & G. Marks (Eds.), *Proceedings of World Conference on E-Learning in Corporate, Government, Healthcare, and Higher Education* (pp. 344–353). Chesapeake, VA: AACE. Retrieved from http://www.editlib.org/p/41614.

Russell, L. B., & Hubley, A. M. (2017). Some thoughts on gathering response processes validity evidence in the context of online measurement and the digital revolution. In B. D. Zumbo & A. M. Hubley, (Eds.), *Understanding and investigating response processes in validation research* (pp. 229–249). Cham, Switzerland: Springer.

Schnipke, D. L., & Scrams, D. J. (1997). Modeling item response times with a two-state mixture model: A new method of measuring speededness. *Journal of Educational Measurement, 34,* 213–232.

Schouten, B., Cobben, F., & Bethlehem, J. (2009). Indicators for the representativeness of survey response. *Survey Methodology, 35,* 101–113.

Sendelbah, A., Vehovar, V., Slavec, A., & Petrovčič, A. (2016). Investigating respondent multi-tasking in web surveys using paradata. *Computers in Human Behavior, 55*, 777–787.

Shlomo, N., Skinner, C., & Schouten, B. (2012). Estimation of an indicator of the representativeness of survey response. *Journal of Statistical Planning and Inference, 142*, 201–211.

Sinharay, S. (2015). Assessment of person fit for mixed-format tests. *Journal of Educational and Behavioral Statistics, 40*, 343–365.

Sinharay, S., Wan, P., Choi, S. W., & Kim, D.-I. (2015). Assessing individual-level impact of interruptions during online testing. *Journal of Educational Measurement, 52*, 80–105.

Sinharay, S., Wan, P., Whitaker, M., Kim, D.-I., Zhang, L., & Choi, S. W. (2014). Determining the overall impact of interruptions during online testing. *Journal of Educational Measurement, 51*, 419–440.

Steger, D., Schroeders, U., & Gnambs, T. (in press). A meta-analysis of test scores in proctored and unproctored ability assessments. *European Journal of Psychological Assessment*. Manuscript accepted for publication.

Stieger, S., & Reips, U.-D. (2010). What are participants doing while filling in an online questionnaire: A paradata collection tool and an empirical study. *Computers in Human Behavior, 26*, 1488–1495.

Sun, N., Rau, P. P.-L., & Ma, L. (2014). Understanding lurkers in online communities: A literature review. *Computers in Human Behavior, 38*, 110–117.

Vannieuwenhuyze, J., Loosveldt, G., & Molenberghs, G. (2011). A method for evaluating mode effects in mixed-mode surveys. *Public Opinion Quarterly, 74*, 1027–1045.

Viswesvaran, C., & Ones, D. S. (1999). Meta-analyses of fakability estimates: Implications for personality measurement. *Educational and Psychological Measurement, 59*, 197–210.

Wise, S. L. (2015). Effort analysis: Individual score validation of achievement test data. *Applied Measurement in Education, 28*, 237–252.

Wise, S. L., & DeMars, C. E. (2005). Low examinee effort in low-stakes assessment: Problems and potential solutions. *Educational Assessment, 10*, 1–17.

Wise, S. L., & DeMars, C. E. (2006). An application of item response time: The effort-moderated IRT model. *Journal of Educational Measurement, 43*(1), 19–38.

Wise, S. L., Kingsbury, G. G., Thomason, J., & Kong, X. (2004, April). *An investigation of motivation filtering in a statewide achievement testing program*. Paper presented at the annual meeting of the National Council on Measurement in Education, San Diego, California.

Wise, S. L. and Kong, X. (2005). Response time effort: A new measure of examinee motivation in computer-based tests. *Applied Measurement in Education, 18*(2), 163–183.

Wise, S. L., & Ma, L. (2012, May). *Setting response time thresholds for a CAT item pool: The normative threshold method*. Paper presented at the annual meeting of the National Council on Measurement in Education, Vancouver.

Wise, V., Wise, S., & Bhola, D. (2006). The generalizability of motivation filtering in improving test score validity. *Educational Assessment, 11*, 65–83.

From Birth to Early Child Care: The Newborn Cohort Study of the National Educational Panel Study

11

Claudia Hachul (née Schlesiger), Manja Attig, Jennifer Lorenz, Sabine Weinert, Thorsten Schneider and Hans-Günther Roßbach

Abstract

The newborn cohort study in the German National Educational Panel Study (NEPS) takes up the challenge of measuring education-relevant conditions and processes together with the development of competencies in the first years of a child's life. The rationale for beginning "from the crib on" can be found in results of infant and early childhood research. We review the design and main features of existing birth

---

This article is an updated version of Schlesiger et al. (2011).

C. Hachul (née Schlesiger)
DLR Project Management Agency, Bonn, Germany
E-Mail: claudia.hachul@dlr.de

M. Attig (✉)
Leibniz Institute for Educational Trajectories, Bamberg, Germany
E-Mail: manja.attig@lifbi.de

J. Lorenz
AWO Family center, Bamberg, Germany
E-Mail: familienstuetzpunkt@awo-bamberg.de

S. Weinert · H.-G. Roßbach
University of Bamberg, Bamberg, Germany
E-Mail: sabine.weinert@uni-bamberg.de

H.-G. Roßbach
E-Mail: hans-guenther.rossbach@uni-bamberg.de

T. Schneider
University of Leipzig, Leipzig, Germany
E-Mail: thorsten.schneider@uni-leipzig.de

© Springer Fachmedien Wiesbaden GmbH, ein Teil von Springer Nature 2019
H.-P. Blossfeld and H.-G. Roßbach (eds.), *Education as a Lifelong Process*,
Edition ZfE 3, https://doi.org/10.1007/978-3-658-23162-0_11

cohort studies in the field of education conducted in developed countries. Most studies begin when infants are between 6 and 11 months old with subsequent waves annually or every second year. The most common instruments are computer-assisted parent interviews sometimes accompanied by additional self-completion modules or completely self-administered questionnaires. We discuss early childhood developmental indicators and instruments that can be applied in large-scale assessments carried out in private homes. We favor measurements with predictive validity for subsequent development. The newborn cohort study (NEPS Starting Cohort 1; NEPS-SC1) started in 2012 with a representative sample of almost 3,500 children born that year in Germany.

Keywords
Birth cohort study · Early childhood · Education · Panel study

11.1 The Competent Infant

Fifty or more years ago, newborns and infants were seen as mostly sleeping, drinking, or crying bundles who could not yet think, speak, behave socially, or interact with their environment. Nowadays, infant and childhood research tells us a different story. The widely known book *"The scientist in the crib"* by Gopnik et al. (2000) summarizes this shift in infant and childhood research as follows: "For the last thirty years scientists like us have been looking in cribs—and in playpens and nurseries and preschools. There have been hundreds of rigorous scientific studies that tell us how babies and young children think and learn" (Gopnik et al. 2000, p. vii).

Infants are no longer seen as showing merely reflexes. Instead, the so-called "competent infant" (Stone et al. 1973) is able to perceive the surrounding environment according to her or his own needs, to structure even very early experiences in the first months of life, to memorize and to compare known to new experiences, and to integrate this into further perceptions and actions. The infant is endowed with not only general early learning abilities and social-emotional skills such as imitating, reacting to special parental behaviors, and turn-taking in early interaction (Papoušek and Bornstein 1992), but also domain-specific competencies such as preverbal language processing (Hennon et al. 2000; Weinert 2006, 2011) and intuitive attentiveness to object characteristics such as number or categorical similarities (Pauen 2003). Up to their third birthday, toddlers extend these early abilities while interacting with their caregivers and exploring the environment (see, for an overview, Fthenakis et al. 2007). The 12th German Report on Children and Youth (Bundesministerium für Familie, Senioren, Frauen und Jugend 2005) defines education as an active and co-constructional process, and emphasizes the family as the first learning environment and one of the most important factors in explaining educational inequalities. Results of the US-American Early Childhood Longitudinal Study—Birth Cohort (ECLS–B) have shown that cognitive and social skills already vary in infants and toddlers according to family background: "… as early as 9 months of age, statistically significant developmental disparities are identified for children based on … demographic characteristics …. Furthermore, disparities between children … become more prominent by 24 months of age" (Halle et al. 2009, p. 17). These findings are comparable to results of the Millennium Cohort Study (MCS) revealing that social influences on developmental disparities became more prominent in 3-year-olds than in 9-months-olds (Hansen and Joshi 2007).

Not only structural aspects of family background but also quality of maternal caregiving in the first 3 years of life are a strong predictor of children's later achievements (Belsky et al. 2007; NICHD Early Child Care Research Network 2002). Additionally, the quality of nonfamilial learning environments influences children's educational outcome, especially if family background (e.g., migration background) is taken into account (see Roßbach 2005).

These examples underline the need to study educational processes as early as possible in the familial and nonfamilial setting. Therefore, a panel study on newborns was established in the National Educational Panel Study (NEPS). The NEPS framework divides the educational biography into different stages (see Chap. 1, this volume). This chapter focuses on Stage 1 covering the first 4 years. The subsequent stages are described from Chap. 12 onward in this volume.

In the next section, we review the design features and instruments in existing birth cohort studies that have been conducted mainly in countries other than Germany. Then, we discuss important findings from early childhood research on the predictive validity of developmental indicators. This discussion leads to the presentation of some instruments that we use in the NEPS newborn cohort study with a special focus on early competencies and the home learning environment. The methodological requirements for the selection of our measures are large-scale practicability and reliability in familial settings, that is, private homes. We give an overview of our sample design and conclude with an outlook (see, for a more detailed description, Weinert et al. 2016).

11.2 Cross-National Overview of Longitudinal Large-Scale Infant Cohort Studies Focusing on Education

The Centre of Longitudinal Studies, based at the Institute of Education, University of London, provides a list of the most important large-scale panel studies.[1] In addition, Roßbach and Weinert (2008) have summarized longitudinal studies covering preschool education. The following cross-national overview on infant cohorts is based on both of these sources while adding two smaller longitudinal studies on children with special needs: the Finish Jyväskylä Longitudinal Study of Dyslexia (Lyytinen et al. 2015)

---

[1] For details see http://www.cls.ioe.ac.uk/.

Table 11.1 Overview of infant cohort studies with a focus on education

Study title	Country/region/starting year	Initial sample size
NCDS National Child Development Study	UK 1958	17,500
BCS 70 British Cohort Study	UK 1970	17,198
Mannheim Study of Children at Risk	Germany 1986	384
NICHD Study of Early Child Care	USA 1991	1,364
JLD Jyväskylä Longitudinal Study of Dyslexia	Finland 1993	200
DALSC Danish Longitudinal Survey of Children	Denmark 1995	7,200
QLSCD Québec Longitudinal Study of Child Development	Canada 1998	2,817
ECLS-B Early Childhood Longitudinal Study	USA 2001	10,700
MCS Millennium Cohort Study	UK 2001	18,818
LASC Longitudinal Study of Australian Children	Australia 2004	5,107
GUS Growing Up in Scotland	Scotland 2005	5,000
GUI Growing Up in Ireland	Ireland 2008	11,000
ELFE French Longitudinal Study of Children	France 2011	18,000
Growing Up in New Zealand	New Zealand 2009	7,000
PSKC Panel Study on Korean Children	Korea 2008	2,150

and the German Mannheim Study of Children at Risk (MARS; Blomeyer et al. 2013). Table 11.1 gives an overview of infant cohort studies. For our purpose, we focus on those panel studies with a first wave conducted in the first year after the birth of the target person, that is, the child.² Because this chapter focuses on infants and toddlers, the following overview of infant cohort studies takes into account only the early waves of data collection.

One of the first infant cohort studies, the National Child Development Study (NCDS), started in the United Kingdom in 1958 and is still continuing. Whereas the NCDS focused initially on health issues directly after birth, the following waves with older children and adults also tap educational issues.

The subsequent infant cohort study in the United Kingdom, the British Cohort Study (BCS 70), accounts increasingly for aspects of infants' and toddlers' development and early education. The BCS 70 recruited mothers of newborns born during one week in April 1970. Areas of interest are pre-, peri-, and postnatal health of infants and their mothers as well as day care and family background.³

The Study of Early Child Care and Youth Development (SECCYD) was conducted by the National Institute of Child Health and Human Development (NICHD). The non-representative sample excluded families who were not fluent in English, had preterm children or children with birth complications, intended to move, or in which the parents themselves were minors. The NICHD study focuses mainly on the effects of early child care and sociodemographic background on children's language and cognitive development. Multiple methods such as questionnaires, interviews, observations (in the family home and in child care), and testing (in a laboratory) were used to assess children's development and learning environment. The first measurement points were at the ages of 1, 6, 15, 24, and 36 months.⁴ Some of the best known rating scales and tests used in the NICHD study are the Bayley Scales of Infant Development (Bayley 1993), the Child Behavior Checklist (Achenbach 1992), the Home Observation for Measurement of the Environment (Caldwell and Bradley 1984), the MacArthur Communicative Development Inventories (Fenson et al. 1991), the NEO Five Factor Inventory (Costa and McCrae 1989), the Parenting Stress Index (Abidin 1983), and the Peabody Picture Vocabulary Test—Revised (Dunn and Dunn 1981).

The Danish Longitudinal Survey of Children (DALSC) started in 1995 with a sample of 6,011 children born in 1995 to mothers with Danish citizenship together with two smaller samples consisting of children with a migration background and children recruited in care environments such as residential institutions or foster families. Main research questions of the DALSC are the influences of socioeconomic situation, ethnicity, home learning environment, and education on children's and adolescent's development and

---

²Not mentioned in Table 11.1 is the German Socio-Economic Panel Study (SOEP) that has expanded its survey program and is gathering additional education-relevant information with questionnaires on newborns since 2003, on 2- to 3-year olds since 2005, on 5- to 6-year olds since 2008, and so forth (see also https://www.diw.de/en/diw_02.c.238114.en/questionnaires_fieldwork_documents.html).

³For details see http://www.cls.ioe.ac.uk/.

⁴A complete list of all study instruments and their rationale can be found on the website of the NICHD, see https://www.nichd.nih.gov/research/supported/seccyd.

participation in society. The first two waves considered children at the ages of 6 months and 3 years. Mothers as the primary respondents were interviewed and the remaining questionnaires used in the DALSC were for self-completion on paper or computerized.

The Québec Longitudinal Study of Child Development (QLSCD) is situated in the francophone Canadian Province of Québec. Families were visited in the first waves when infants were 5, 17, 29, and 41 months old. Both parents completed computer-assisted personal interviews and questionnaires about their child's temperament, social and motor development, home learning environment, daily routines, parent–child attachment, social capital, and leisure activities. Observers additionally administered the Home Observation for Measurement of the Environment (Caldwell and Bradley 1984). Infants' motor and social skills were tested with subscales of the Bayley Scales of Infant Development (Bayley 1993), and their sensorimotor development was assessed with a specially developed task. At the age of 41 months, the Peabody Picture Vocabulary Test—Revised (Dunn and Dunn 1981) was administered as well.

The infant cohort of the Early Childhood Longitudinal Study (ECLS-B) started with a representative sample of 9-month-old infants who were reassessed at the age of 24 months. The ECLS-B provides detailed information on children's development and learning experiences in the family and in day care. Children's cognitive development was assessed using a short-form research edition of the Bayley Scales of Infant Development (Bayley 1993). Trained observers coded videotaped parent-child interactions using the Nursing Child Assessment Teaching Scale (Summer and Spietz 1995). At the age of 24 months, the Infant/Toddler Environment Rating Scale (Harms et al. 2003) and the Family Day Care Rating Scale (Harms and Clifford 1989) were used.

Children in the Millennium Cohort Study (MCS) were born between 2000 and 2002, and the first wave took place when most of the infants were 9 months old. Both parents were asked about their infant's general development, temperament, language, and motor abilities in a computer-assisted personal interview. Items were chosen from rating scales that are traditionally used to screen early development such as the MacArthur Communicative Development Inventories (Fenson et al. 1991) and the Carey Temperament Scales (Carey and McDevitt 2007) for the infants and the Strength and Difficulties Questionnaire (Goodman 1999) for the 3-year-olds. At the age of 3, a test was also administered to directly assess basic mathematical and natural science knowledge about colors, letters, numbers, and shapes. Apart from that, the parent interviews covered topics such as child care, family structure, social capital, and health. The MCS also integrated self-completion modules concerning private questions about social relationships, attitudes, and values. Subgroups such as disadvantaged families or families with an ethnic minority background were oversampled.

In Australia the infant cohort study of the Longitudinal Study of Australian Children (LASC) started when most infants were in their first year of life. Parents were interviewed at home and filled out self-completion questionnaires including a so-called time use diary displaying the hours their child spent on activities such as eating, sleeping, or playing with toys on a typical day. The main research questions in the LASC were about the home learning environment, amount and quality of day care, social capital of families, and health. Children's language competencies and their social-emotional development were also assessed indirectly via two rating scales, the Communication and Symbolic Behavior Scales (Wetherby and Prizant 1993) and the Brief Infant-Toddler Social Emotional Assessment (Briggs-Gowan and Carter 2002).

The infant cohort of the Growing up in Scotland Study (GUS) performs an annual follow up of infants born between 2004 and 2005 who were 11 months old when their parents were interviewed for the first time. Computer-assisted personal interviews with integrated self-completion modules are being administered every year, and focus particularly topics such as child's competencies, health, nonfamilial learning environment, and social capital.

Growing Up in Ireland (GUI) interviewed families with 9-month-old infants between September 2008 and April 2009. They were reassessed when the children were 3 and 5 years of age. Parents filled out questionnaires about their infant's development, daily routines, child care arrangements, and their own lifestyle and parental experiences. In cases in which infants were cared for by other persons for more than 8 h per week, a questionnaire was also sent to these caregivers. A subgroup of 120 families was additionally interviewed in a conversation format to record their views and experiences of family life, interests, and aspirations in their own words. The results of this qualitative study will be linked to the main study.

The French Longitudinal Study of Children (ELFE) started in 2011 and collects data from about 18,000 families at maternity hospitals shortly after birth and at 2 months, 1 year, and 2 years after birth. It was then continued when the child was about 3 and 5 years old. Mothers and fathers are interviewed (face-to-face/telephone interview). Key questions in the ELFE address health, social inequalities, and other aspects such as the social environment that influence physical, psychological, social, and professional development.

Growing Up in New Zealand started in 2009 with the recruitment of around 7,000 children and their families. Starting antenatally, both mother and father were interviewed. During the first 2 years, mothers were interviewed (in person or by telephone) six times. When the children were 2 years of age, child measurements and observations were applied. Growing Up in New Zealand collected information on health and well-being, psychosocial and cognitive development, education, family, culture, identity, societal context, and the neighborhood environment.

The Panel Study on Korean Children (PSKC) started in 2008. Around 2,150 families were confirmed as study sample. The goal of the study was to examine the child and the effects of the environment such as characteristics of each child's development and developmental requirements, the characteristics of parental psychology, the childrearing conditions, the functions of child care support services, and their impact on child care. In the first 5 years, mothers were interviewed every year. Fathers were involved over questionnaires via mail. Aspects of the development of the child (e.g., gross and fine motor skills; problem solving, communication) were collected in the first 3 years, language abilities and observation of the home environment (EC-HOME) were administered in the fourth year.

Apart from these infant cohort studies, which recruited representative samples (except the NICHD study), there are also infant cohort studies tracking special populations, such as the already mentioned Finish Jyväskyla Longitudinal Study of Dyslexia and the German Mannheim Study of Children at Risk. Both are performing in-depth assessments of children's cognitive and language abilities, temperament, and home learning environment at least every 6 months from birth onward through experimental tasks, observations, parent questionnaires, and directly administered tests.

To summarize, the need to study developmental and educational processes already in infancy has been perceived especially in the United Kingdom and the United States. These countries have already conducted two or more longitudinal studies including infants and toddlers. The most common instruments are parent interviews, either computer-assisted, sometimes accompanied by additional self-completion modules, or completely self-administered questionnaires. Parents are always asked about their sociodemographic background, own health, and the health of their child. Most studies include items related to families' daily routines, the home environment, child care arrangements, and social capital. The most common instrument for rating the home learning environment is the Home Observation of the Environment (Caldwell and Bradley 1984), which is based on a parent interview and observations by the interviewer. Some studies also code videotaped parent–child interactions by using more objective and detailed coding schemes. Cognitive or motor abilities are commonly assessed directly with the Bayley Scales of Infant Development (Bayley 1993). Most large-scale longitudinal studies do not directly test children's cognitive, language, and motor abilities before the age of 3, but prefer to use parent interviews as a source of data on the development of infants' and toddlers' competencies. In the next chapter, we shall discuss quality criteria of early childhood measures and present the instruments for measuring early competencies and the home learning environment that we used in the NEPS newborn cohort study.

11.3 Early Childhood Developmental Indicators in the NEPS Newborn Cohort Study

In NEPS, educational conditions and processes are measured over the life course in terms of six major dimensions (or "pillars") (see Chap. 1, this volume): Competence Development across the Life Course (Dimension 1), Education Processes in Life-Course-Specific Learning Environments (Dimension 2), Social Inequality and Educational Decisions in the Life Course (Dimension 3), Educational Acquisition with Migration Background in the Life Course (Dimension 4), Returns to Education in the Life Course (Dimension 5), and Motivational Concepts and Personality Aspects across the Life Course (Dimension 6).

Most of the theoretical constructs in Dimensions 2 to 6 can be surveyed by interviewing parents. These include structural aspects of the learning environments and parents' or educators' and childminders' attitudes and orientations (Dimension 2); the socioeconomic status of the family, the decision for or against the use of different care settings, and mother's return to labor market (Dimension 3); parents' migration background, languages used in their own childhood, and those used currently (Dimension 4); parents' income situation, information on pregnancy and birth complications, as well as child's health status from birth onward (Dimension 5), and, for example, child's temperament, early self-regulatory capacities, pro-social and problem behavior (Dimension 6).

The main challenges facing Stage 1 are to develop, select, and administer instruments to measure different aspects of infants' and toddlers' competencies. A further goal is to assess the quality of learning environments beyond parents' self-reports. The prerequisite for generating good quality indicators is instruments that are objective, reliable, and valid. An adequate theoretical background and predictive validity are of particular importance to measure stability and change over time and to assure the alignment of data over the lifespan. Other more methodological requirements for instruments in a panel such as NEPS are large-scale practicability in terms of administration time, coding restrictions, and logistic demands. Moreover, the burden of every assessment should be kept low to avoid high rates of panel attrition.

The following sections describe how we identified, selected, and developed items and instruments to measure early competencies and learning environments.

11.3.1 Indicators of Competence Development in Infants and Toddlers

This chapter began with the "competent infant" in order to emphasize the relevance of early development for educational research. Educational competencies can be seen as functional, context-sensitive, domain-specific, and capable of being influenced by education (Weinert 2007). Measuring competencies in the first year of life requires sophisticated methods. Competencies measured in school-age and adulthood cannot simply be transferred to early childhood, because competencies develop dynamically over the lifespan (see Weinert 2007). However, it is important to detect the essential prerequisites for the development of auditory language comprehension, reading competence, math competence, natural science competence, metacognition and self-regulation, the ability to handle information technologies, as well as socio-emotional and basic nonverbal cognitive abilities and skills. As a result, the newborn cohort in NEPS has to conceptualize and operationalize

- Basic cognitive capacities
- Preverbal communication and early language
- Early numeracy
- Building of categories

The internationally most common instrument for assessing young children's sensorimotor and basic cognitive abilities, skills, and developmental status is the mental scale of the Bayley Scales of Infant Development (Bayley 1993). The ECLS-B administered a short-form research edition of this test instrument when children were 9 months old and at the age of 2 years; the NICHD study, when children were 15 months old and also at the age of 2 years. The most recent version is the cognitive scale of the Bayley Scales of Infant and Toddler Development—Third Edition (Bayley 2006). This is described in the following while accentuating important modifications in comparison to the prior version. The cognitive scale assesses sensorimotor development, exploration, manipulation, habituation, and other aspects of cognitive processing. Items in the second edition of the Bayley Scales of Infant Development (Bayley 1993) with demands on language or motor skills have been removed from the cognitive scale and added to the language or motor scale in the third edition. A standardized set of objects and toys is provided for the procedure such as a rattle, blocks, balls, squeeze toys, books, cups, spoons, a doll, and—for toddlers—also puzzle boards. The examiner performs a specific task with the object or toy and observes whether the child shows an expected reaction or not. In addition, a spontaneous action or reaction by the child can be scored. Table 11.2 gives an example of an item for a 7-month-old child.

Up to now, empirical evidence on the quality criteria of the third edition is still rare and a standardized test administration is challenging (Weinert et al. 2016). Although Domsch et al. (2009)—using the second edition—showed significant correlations between individual differences at 6 and 24 months of age and later childhood intelligence in a German sample, empirical findings are contradictory (see also, e.g., Hack et al. 2005). Reviews from Bjorklund (2000), Fagan and Singer (1983), and Harris (1983) show that the predictive validity of sensorimotor tests of development is rather poor compared to the predictive validity of the so-called habituation paradigm, which is described below. Though the third edition of the Bayley Scales of Infant and Toddler Development (Bayley 2006) is expected to be more predictive (Lennon et al. 2008), this has not yet—as mentioned above—been validated empirically. In particular, the German version of the third edition was published in 2014—hence too late for the first measurement points in the newborn cohort study of NEPS and the transferability of items regarding translation, application procedure, and play toys cannot just be taken for granted. Thus, we adopted a second measure for early cognitive capacities: the habituation paradigm.

Two longitudinal studies, the already mentioned Mannheim Study for Children at Risk (MARS, see Table 11.1) and the Avon Longitudinal Study of Parents and Children

Table 11.2 Example of an item from the Bayley Scales of Infant and Toddler Development (Bayley 2006, p. 54)

Persistent reach
Place the object on the table in front of the child, and just beyond his or her reach. Observe the child's efforts to obtain it
1 point: Child persistently reaches for the object, even if he or she fails to obtain it 0 points: Child does not reach for the object. Child only initially reaches for the object

(ALSPAC)—a panel focusing on health issues started in the United Kingdom in 1991 (Golding 1990)—have applied the habituation paradigm (see, for details, Bornstein et al. 2006; Laucht et al. 2000).

Habituation is defined as the reduction of attention to a repeatedly presented stimulus (e.g., pictures) that is not based simply on fatigue of the sensory receptors. The speed of habituation is measured mostly by the number of trials presented in which the child fixes the stimulus visually before fixation time drops to less than 50% of the initial fixation time at the first presentations of the stimulus. However, the proportional reduction of attention during the phase of familiarization and the reaction to a new stimulus after familiarization, the so-called dishabituation (or preference of novelty), have also been used as predictive measures in different studies. Briefly, visual habituation is viewed as a manifestation of encoding speed, whereas dishabituation is taken to be the ability to differentiate the habituation stimulus from a new stimulus. These mental functions are interpreted as forms of information processing—that is, the speed, exactness, and completeness of the encoding along with the memorization, recognition, and comparison to a new and different stimulus (Bornstein and Sigman 1986; Fagan et al. 2007; Fagan and McGrath 1981; Kavšek 2004; McCall and Carriger 1993). As shown in several reviews and meta-analyses, these abilities are closely tied to the results of intelligence tests later in childhood (Bornstein and Sigman 1986; Kavšek 2004). Bornstein and Sigman (1986) found correlations of up to $r=0.47$ between habituation measures in the first 7 months of life and children's intelligence from 2 to 8 years. Fagan et al. (2007) showed that infants' habituation correlates up to $r=0.34$ with measurements of intelligence at 21 years and up to $r=0.32$ with the achieved academic degree. All these studies support the notion that there is continuity between infants' information processing abilities and later measurements of intelligence.

Moreover, if stimuli are chosen that represent a certain amount of objects or members of a specific category, it may even be possible to gain insight into possibly domain-specific early number processing or categorization processes. Some studies have shown that early habituation correlates not only with later intelligence but also with domain-specific competencies such as later language development (Colombo et al. 2009).

One advantage of the habituation paradigm is its cultural fairness if presented with nonverbal and neutral stimulus material. This feature is very important for testing basic cognitive capacities in children with diverse family backgrounds. The challenge of the newborn cohort study in NEPS is to transfer this experimental paradigm to the home setting, because all children are visited and observed at home (see Sect. 11.4 for the procedure). To face these challenges, extensive feasibility studies were conducted to develop a habituation paradigm that can be applied in a large-scale study in a home setting. After this pilot phase the habituation paradigm was applied in the first two waves of the NEPS newborn cohort study when the children were 7 and 17 months, respectively (Weinert et al. 2016).

Apart from testing and observing early cognitive skills directly, it is also possible to ask parents about their impression of their child's behavior. There is some evidence from an American study that direct and indirect measures of early cognition correlate with each other (Gollenberg and Lynch 2009).

Besides general cognitive abilities, language is a key competence for educational outcome. In the preverbal phase, important precursor skills for language development are turn-taking skills and the reception and production of typical prosodic shapes (Hennon et al. 2000; Mampe et al. 2009). From 9 months onward, infants build up joint attention and receptive vocabulary. The amount of joint attention episodes in the communication between infant and parents correlates with later language development (Bornstein et al. 1999). Possible methods for assessing these preverbal competencies are the observation of turn-taking and joint attention in (semistructured) parent–child interactions. Later on, during the two-word phase, vocabulary and early grammar are important predictors for later language competencies (Fenson et al. 1994) and can be assessed by parent questionnaires and developmental tests. The size of vocabulary measured in the second year of life is the best predictor for grammar development in the third year of life (Fenson et al. 1994). In bilingual children, the size of vocabulary around the second birthday correlates more strongly with subsequent language development than measures of general development or the amount of contact to a special language (Conboy and Thal 2006; Marchman et al. 2004). Of special interest are children who fail to build up a vocabulary of 50 spoken words up to their second birthday. These so-called late talkers are at risk for specific language impairment (Grimm 1999; Weinert 2005, 2006) and have significantly lower skills in academic language than control peers up to adulthood (Rescorla 2009). The most widely used questionnaire to assess vocabulary in toddlers is the MacArthur–Bates Communicative Inventory (Fenson et al. 2007) that is also being used in the MCS and NICHD study. Versions of this questionnaire are now available in other languages including German, Turkish, and Russian.

Other areas that are important indicators of young children's development are gross- and fine-motor skills (Michaelis 2003). Easily observable motor skills can be measured with parent questionnaires. In addition, child characteristics can be observed and coded based on semistandardized parent–child interactions as described in the following paragraph.

11.3.2 Indicators of Quality of Early Learning Environments

A widely accepted instrument for the home learning environment of young children is the Home Observation for Measurement of the Environment (Caldwell and Bradley 1984). It has been used in the NICHD study, the QLSCD, and the Mannheim Study for Children at Risk, and it can also be applied in Turkish families (Otyakmaz 2007). Early social skills can be observed in the dyadic and, later on, triadic interaction of the infant with her or his environment. It is important not only to analyze parent's behavior (see below) but also to reveal the children's part in the interactive process. For example, the Nursing Child Assessment Teaching Scale (Summer and Spietz 1995) offers the opportunity to score child and parent separately according to the child's responsiveness and the parent's responsiveness and teaching behavior. The interaction has to be videotaped and interpreted afterwards. Whereas the ECLS-B used the Nursing Child Assessment Teaching Scale (Summer and Spietz 1995), the NICHD study developed its own scoring procedures for videotaped interaction to operationalize the quality of children's learning environment in the first 3 years of life (NICHD Early Child Care Research Network 1999; see also Lohaus et al. 2004). Here, maternal sensitivity or responsiveness is an important predictor for later social development and has been shown to have a positive association to both language development and overall cognitive ability (Bornstein and Tamis-LeMonda 1989; Page et al. 2010). Responsiveness is defined as mothers' prompt, contingent, and appropriate (not simply contiguous) behaviors (Bornstein and Tamis-LeMonda 1989). Two forms of responsiveness can be measured: either toward nondistress activities such as smiling, or toward infants' distress such as crying. Analyses can be carried out macroanalytically, for example, by scoring whether a special behavior occurs; or microanalytically, for example, by scoring the amount of a special behavior in a set time interval. Drawing on the procedures and codings of the NICHD study, in the NEPS newborn cohort study, semi-standardized mother–child interactions were videotaped at the first three assessment waves and coded according to five child characteristics and eight interactional characteristics of the mother (Sommer and Mann 2015; Weinert et al. 2016).

The model applied in NEPS for analyzing the process quality of the learning environment is structure, support, challenge, and orientation, also called the SSCO model (see Chap. 5, this volume). The intuitive didactic processes (Papoušek and Bornstein 1992) that allow mothers to react promptly, contingently, and appropriately to their infants and later on to scaffold their toddlers' abilities can be subsumed under structure and support. The challenge aspect occurs whenever parents provide activating stimulation, play tasks, toys, or activities to their children. The attitudes and values concerning childrearing, caring, and educating are the orientation that influences the familial and also nonfamilial environment. The macroanalytic procedure for coding the videotaped parent–child interaction considers these facets.

Regarding nonfamilial day care, the available instruments for measuring quality of early child care are the Krippen-Skala (KRIPS-R, Tietze et al. 2005a), which is the German version of the Infant/Toddler Environment Rating Scale (ITERS-R, Harms et al. 2003), and the Tagespflege-Skala (TAS, Tietze et al. 2005b), which is the German version of the Family Day Care Rating Scale (FCDRS, Harms and Clifford 1989). A questionnaire on early nonfamilial day care (child care provisions and childminders) was applied, because of the (ongoing) expansion of day care places for children under the age of 3 in Germany. The questionnaire covers structural (e.g., group size, group composition) and process characteristics (e.g., joint activities, language use) of early nonfamilial day care.

Another important variable that influences child's well-being and learning especially in the early years is attachment (Grossmann and Grossmann 2003; Korntheuer et al. 2007). Because temperament contributes directly to social-emotional development and interacts with parenting and other environmental variables (Rothbart and Gartstein 2008), it should be integrated as a moderator variable when measuring learning environments.

Altogether, the quality of familial and nonfamilial learning environments can be measured only if the interdependency of the quality of structural aspects (e.g., the familial or institutional background), the quality of processes (e.g., intuitive or, later on, explicit didactics and interactions), and the orientations behind the structures and processes are taken into account when collecting and analyzing the data (see Roßbach 2005).

11.4 Sample Design and Procedure of the Newborn Cohort Study

A two-stage sampling procedure was used to ensure a nationally representative sample of children born in 2012 in Germany (see Chap. 3 in this volume for more information on the sampling strategy or Aßmann et al. 2015). For the newborn cohort, addresses were sampled in two birth tranches. The first tranche covered children born between February and April 2012, the second tranche involved children born between May and July.[5] After the first wave, the panel sample consisted of 3,431 families.

Field phases of the main study lasted around 6 months for two reasons: because individual sampling requires every child to be visited at home, and because the exact age of infants is very important at this age due to rapid developmental changes during infancy. During the first 2 years, three waves were carried out. Except for Wave 2, all waves were conducted in the home of the families as computer-assisted personal interviews (CAPI). In Wave 2, all families were surveyed by computer-assisted telephone interviews (CATI) and—for half of the sample—video-taped observational measures at the child's home. In Wave 1, infants were around 7 months old; in Wave 2, they were about 14 months when the telephone interviews were conducted and 17 months when the observational measures were taken; in Wave 3, children were 27 months old. From then onward, assessments took place every year (see Table 11.3).

During the visit to the family, an approximately 30-min long computer-assisted personal interview is administered with one parent (normally the mother) and approximately another 30 min is needed to observe the child's competencies and the home learning environment.

---

[5]Due to the unexpected high response rate, families with children born in July were not contacted by the survey institute. Consequently, all children in SC1 were born between February and June 2012.

Table 11.3 Child's age, sample size and survey mode of the first six waves of the newborn cohort study of the NEPS

	Wave 1	Wave 2	Wave 3	Wave 4	Wave 5	Wave 6
Year of assessment	2012–2013	2013	2014	2015	2016	2017
Child's age (survey mode)	7 months (CAPI + video)	12–15 months (CATI) 16–17 months (CAPI + video)	25–27 months (CAPI + video)	37–39 months (CAPI, CBA)	4 years (CAPI, CBA)	5 years (CAPI, CBA)
Sample size						
Families	3,481	2,849 (CATI) 1,510 (CAPI)	2,609	2,478	2,381	2,209
Child care (PAPI)						
Educator		171	449	625	628	683
Childminder		73	110			
Institution manager				571	521	543
Year SUF released	2015	2015	2016	2017	2018	2019

Note CAPI: computer-assisted personal interview. CATI: computer-assisted telephone interview. CBA: computer based assessment. PAPI: paper and pencil interview. SUF: scientific use file

11.5 Prospect

Studying education as a lifelong process makes it necessary to start at the beginning, that is, from birth onward. The challenge is to identify early indicators at this age that are relevant for educational processes. The measurement of early developmental indicators requires indirect methods such as parent interviews and parent questionnaires, and—for an in-depth assessment of infants' and toddlers' competencies and learning environments—also direct methods such as observational situations, experimental tasks, and tests (for toddlers and older children). The prerequisite for this is an interdisciplinary perspective on child development and education that integrates psychological, educational, and sociological issues. As Roßbach and Blossfeld (2008) have noted, the desiderata of research in early education especially concern the impact of early learning environments on child development and the educational career and vice versa—including the problem of the social disparities that are already evident in infancy and toddlerhood. Because of the paucity of research on educational processes in this age group, extensive feasibility and validation studies were, and still are, necessary to manage all the challenges of a newborn cohort study carried out in the family households. Thus, the newborn cohort started later than the other cohorts in 2012.

References

Abidin, R. R. (1983). Parenting Stress Index Manual. Charlottesville, VA: Pediatric Psychology Press.

Achenbach, T. M. (1992). Manual for the Child Behavior Checklist/2-3 and 1992 Profile. Burlington, VT: University of Vermont Department of Psychiatry.

Aßmann, C., Zinn, S., & Würbach, A. (2015). Sampling and weighting the sample of the early childhood cohort of the National Educational Panel Study (Technical Report of SUF SC1 Version 2.0.0). Retrieved from https://www.neps-data.de/Portals/0/Survey%20Papers/SP_VIII.pdf.

Bayley, N. (1993). Bayley Scales of Infant Development (2nd ed.). San Antonio, TX: Harcourt Assessment.

Bayley, N. (2006). Bayley Scales of Infant and Toddler Development (3rd ed.). San Antonio, TX: Harcourt Assessment.

Belsky, J., Burchinal, M., McCartney, K., Lowe Vandell, D., Clarke-Stewart, K., & Tresch Owen, M. (2007). Are there long-term effects of early child care? Child Development, 78, 681–701.

Bjorklund, D. F. (2000). Children's thinking: Development function and individual differences (3rd ed.). Belmont, TN: Wadsworth, Thomson Learning.

Blomeyer, D., Laucht, M., Coneus, K., & Pfeiffer, F. (2013). Early life adversity and children's competence development: Evidence from the Mannheim Study of Children at Risk. Jahrbücher für Nationalökonomie und Statistik 233, 467–485. http://www.jbnst.de/download/2013-top/Blomeyer_et_al_2013.pdf.

Bornstein, M. H., Hahn, C., Bell, C., Haynes, O. M., Slater, A., Golding, J., Wolke, D., & the ALSPAC Study Team. (2006). Stability in cognition across early childhood: A developmental cascade. Psychological Science, 17, 151–158.

Bornstein, M. H., & Sigman, M. D. (1986). Continuity in mental development from infancy. Child Development, 57, 251–274.

Bornstein, M. H., & Tamis-LeMonda, C. S. (1989). Maternal responsiveness and cognitive development in children. In M. H. Bornstein (Ed.), Maternal responsiveness: Characteristics and consequences (pp. 49–62). San Francisco, CA: Jossey-Bass.

Bornstein, M. H., Tamis-LeMonda, C. S., & Haynes, O. M. (1999). First words in the second year: Continuity, stability, and models of concurrent and predictive correspondence in vocabulary and verbal responsiveness across age and context. Infant Behavior and Development, 22, 65–85.

Briggs-Gowan, M. J., & Carter, A. S. (2002). Brief Infant-Toddler Social and Emotional Assessment (BITSEA) Manual, Version 2.0. New Haven, CT: Yale University.

Bundesministerium für Familie, Senioren, Frauen und Jugend (2005). Zwölfter Kinder- und Jugendbericht. Bericht über die Lebenssituation junger Menschen und Leistungen der Kinder- und Jugendhilfe in Deutschland. http://dip21.bundestag.de/dip21/btd/15/060/1506014.pdf. Accessed 9 Sept 2010.

Caldwell, B. M., & Bradley, R. H. (1984). Home observation for measurement of the environment. Little Rock, AR: University of Arkansas at Little Rock.

Carey, W. B., & McDevitt, S. C. (2007). Carey Temperament Scales (CTS). San Antonio, TX: Pearson Assessment.

Colombo, J., Shaddy D. J., Blaga, O. M., Anderson, C. J., Kannass, K. N., & Richman, W. A. (2009). Early attentional predictors of vocabulary in childhood. In J. Colombo, P. McCardle, & L. Freund (Eds.), Infant pathways to language: Methods, models, and research directions (pp. 143–168). New York, NY: Erlbaum.

Conboy, B. T., & Thal, D. J. (2006). Ties between the lexicon and grammar: Cross-sectional and longitudinal studies of bilingual toddlers. Child Development, 77, 712–735.

Costa, P., & McCrae, R. (1989). NEO Five-Factor Inventory (NEO-FFI). Odessa FL: Psychological Assessment Resources.

Domsch, H., Lohaus, A., & Hoben, T. (2009). Prediction of childhood cognitive abilities from a set of early indicators of information processing capabilities. Infant Behavior and Development, 32(1), 91–102.

Dunn, L. M., & Dunn, L. M. (1981). *Peabody Picture Vocabulary Test - revised*. Circle Pines, MI: American Guidance Service.

Fagan, J. F., Holland, C. R., & Wheeler, K. (2007): The prediction, from infancy, of adult IQ and achievement. *Intelligence, 35,* 225–231.

Fagan, J. F., & McGrath, S. K. (1981). Infant recognition memory and later intelligence. *Intelligence, 5,* 121–130.

Fagan, J. F., & Singer, L. T. (1983). Infant recognition memory as a measure of intelligence. In L. P. Lipsitt (Ed.), *Advances in infancy research* (pp. 31–78). Norwood, MA: Ablex.

Fenson, L., Dale, P. S., Reznick, J. S., Bates, E., Thal, D. J., & Pethik S. J. (1994). Variability in early communicative development. *Monographs of the Society for Research in Child Development, 59*(5), 1–185.

Fenson, L., Dale, P. S., Reznick, J. S., Thal, D., & Reilly, J. S. (1991). *Technical manual for MacArthur Communicative Development Inventories*. San Diego, CA: San Diego State University.

Fenson, L., Marchmann, V. A., Thal, D. J., Dale, P. S., Reznick, J. S., & Bates, E. (2007). *MacArthur- Bates Communicative Development Inventories. User's guide and technical manual* (2nd ed.). Baltimore, MD: Paul H. Brookes.

Fthenakis, W. E., Gisbert, K., Griebel, W., Kunze, H.-R., Niesel, R., & Wustmann, C. (2007). *Auf den Anfang kommt es an: Perspektiven für eine Neuorientierung frühkindlicher Bildung*. Bonn, Germany: BMBF.

Golding, J. (1990). Children of the nineties: A longitudinal study of pregnancy and childhood based on the population of Avon (ALSPAC). *West of England Medical Journal, 105,* 80–82.

Gollenberg, A. L., & Lynch, C. D. (2009). Concurrent validity of the parent-completed Ages and Stages Questionnaires, 2nd ed. with the Bayley Scales of Infant Development II in a low-risk sample. *Child: Care, Health and Development, 36,* 485–490.

Goodman, R. (1999). The extended version of the Strengths and Difficulties Questionnaire as a guide to caseness and consequent burden. *Journal of Child Psychology and Psychiatry, 40,* 791–799.

Gopnik, A., Meltzoff, A. N., & Kuhl, P. K. (2000). The scientist in the crib: What early learning tells us about the mind. New York: HarperCollins.

Grimm, H. (1999). Störungen der Sprachentwicklung. Grundlagen – Ursachen – Diagnose – Intervention – Prävention. Göttingen, Germany: Hogrefe.

Grossmann, K. E., & Grossmann, K. (2003). (Eds.). Bindung und menschliche Entwicklung. John Bowlby, Mary Ainsworth und die Grundlagen der Bindungstheorie. Stuttgart, Germany: Klett-Cotta.

Hack, M., Taylor, G., Drotar, D., & Schluchter, M. (2005). Poor predictive validity of the Bayley Scales of Infant Development for cognitive function of extremely low birth weight children at school age. *Pediatrics, 116,* 333–341.

Halle, T., Forry, N., Hair, E., Perper, K., Wandner, L., Wessel, J., & Vick, J. (2009). Disparities in early learning and development: Lessons from the Early Childhood Longitudinal Study – Birth Cohort (ECLS-B). Washington, DC: Child Trends.

Hansen, K., & Joshi, H. (2007). *Millennium Cohort Study. Second survey. A user's guide to initial findings.* London, England: Institute of Education, Centre for Longitudinal Studies.

Harms, T., & Clifford, R. M. (1989). *Family Day Care Rating Scale.* New York, NY: Teachers College Press.

Harms, T., Cryer, D., & Clifford, R. M. (2003). *Infant/Toddler Environment Rating Scale* (revised ed.). New York, NY: Teachers College Press.

Harris, P. L. (1983). Infant cognition. In M. M. Haith & J. J. Campos (Eds.), *Handbook of child psychology: Vol. 2. Infancy and developmental psychobiology.* (4th ed., pp. 689–782). New York, NY: Wiley.

Hennon, E., Hirsh-Pasek, K., & Golinkoff, R. M. (2000). Die besondere Reise vom Fötus zum spracherwerbenden Kind. In H. Grimm (Ed.), *Sprachentwicklung. Enzyklopädie der Psychologie, C/III/3* (pp. 41–103). Göttingen, Germany: Hogrefe.

Kavšek, M. (2004). Predicting later IQ from infant visual habituation and dishabituation: A meta-analysis. *Journal of Applied Developmental Psychology, 25,* 369–393.

Korntheuer, P., Lissmann, I., & Lohaus, A. (2007). Bindungssicherheit und die Entwicklung von Sprache und Kognition. *Kindheit und Entwicklung, 16,* 180–189.

Laucht, M., Esser, G., & Schmidt, M. H. (2000). Längsschnittforschung zur Entwicklungsepidemiologie psychischer Störungen: Zielsetzung, Konzeption und zentrale Befunde der Mannheimer Risikokinderstudie. *Zeitschrift für Klinische Psychologie und Psychotherapie, 29,* 246–262.

Lennon, E. M., Gardner, J. M., Karmel, B. Z., & Flory, M. J. (2008). Bayley Scales of Infant Development. In M. M. Haith & J. B. Benson (Eds.), *Encyclopedia of infant and early childhood development* (pp. 145–156). Oxford, England: Elsevier.

Lohaus, A., Keller, H., Ball, J., Voelker, S., & Elben, C. (2004). Maternal sensitivity in interactions with three- and 12-month-old infants: Stability, structural composition, and developmental consequences. *Infant and Child Development, 13,* 235–252.

Lyytinen, H., Erskine, J., Hämäläinen, J., Torppa, M., & Ronimus, M. (2015). Dyslexia: Early identification and prevention: Highlights from the Jyväskylä Longitudinal Study of Dyslexia. *Current Developmental Disorders Reports,* 2(4), 330–338. https://doi.org/10.1007/s40474-015-0067-1; https://jyx.jyu.fi/dspace/handle/123456789/50671.

Mampe, B., Friederici, A. D., Christophe, A., & Wermke, K. (2009). Newborns' cry melody is shaped by their native language. *Current Biology, 19,* 1–4.

Marchman, V. A., Martinez-Sussmann, C., & Dale, P. S. (2004). The language specific nature of grammatical development: Evidence from bilingual learners. *Developmental Science, 7,* 212–224.

McCall, R. B., & Carriger, M. S. (1993). A meta-analysis of infant habituation and recognition memory performance as a predictor of later IQ. *Child Development, 64,* 57–79.

Michaelis, R. (2003). Motorische Entwicklung. In H. Keller (Ed.), *Handbuch der Kleinkindforschung* (3rd ed., pp. 815–860). Bern, Switzerland: Huber.

NICHD Early Child Care Research Network (1999). Child care and mother–child interaction in the first 3 years of life. *Developmental Psychology, 35,* 1399–1413.

NICHD Early Child Care Research Network (2002). Child-care structure – process – outcome: Direct and indirect effects of child-care quality on young children's development. *Psychological Science, 13,* 199–206.

Otyakmaz, B. O. (2007). Familiale Entwicklungskontexte im Kulturvergleich. Cross-cultural comparison of familial context. Lengrich, Germany: Pabst.

Page, M., Wilhelm, M. S., Gamble, W. C., & Card, N. A. (2010). A comparison of maternal sensitivity and verbal stimulation as unique predictors of infant social-emotional and cognitive development. *Infant Behavior and Development, 33,* 101–110.

Papoušek, H., & Bornstein, M. H. (1992). Didactic interactions: Intuitive parental support of vocal and verbal development in human infants. In H. Papoušek, U. Jürgens, & M. Papoušek (Eds.), *Nonverbal vocal communication: Comparative and developmental approaches* (pp. 209–229). Cambridge, England: Cambridge University Press.

Pauen, S. (2003). Säuglingsforschung aus kognitiver Sicht. In H. Keller (Ed.), *Handbuch der Kleinkindforschung* (3rd ed., pp. 283–318). Bern, Switzerland: Huber.

Rescorla, L. (2009). Age 17 language and reading outcomes in late-talking toddlers: Support for a dimensional perspective on language delay. *Journal of Speech, Language, and Hearing Research, 52,* 16–30.

Roßbach, H.-G. (2005). Effekte qualitativ guter Betreuung, Bildung und Erziehung im frühen Kindesalter auf Kinder und ihre Familien. In Sachverständigenkommission Zwölfter Kinder- und Jugendbericht (Ed.), *Bildung, Betreuung und Erziehung von Kindern unter sechs Jahren. Materialien zum 12. Kinder- und Jugendbericht* (Vol. 1, pp. 55–174). Munich, Germany: Verlag Deutsches Jugendinstitut.

Roßbach, H.-G., & Blossfeld, H.-P. (Eds.). (2008). *Frühpädagogische Förderung in Institutionen* (Zeitschrift für Erziehungswissenschaft: Sonderheft 11). Wiesbaden, Germany: VS Verlag für Sozialwissenschaften.

Roßbach, H.-G., & Weinert, S. (2008). *Kindliche Kompetenzen im Elementarbereich: Förderbarkeit, Bedeutung und Messung* (Bildungsforschung Band 24). Bonn, Germany: BMBF.

Rothbart, M. K., & Gartstein, M. A. (2008). Temperament. In M. M. Haith & J. B. Benson (Eds.), *Encyclopedia of infant and early childhood development* (pp. 318–333). Oxford, England: Elsevier.

Schlesiger, C., Lorenz, J., Weinert, S, Schneider, T. & Roßbach, H.-G. (2011): From birth to early child care. In H.-P. Blossfeld, H.-G. Roßbach, & J. von Maurice (Eds.), *Education as a Lifelong Process. The German Educational Panel Study (NEPS)* (Zeitschrift für Erziehungswissenschaft: Sonderheft 14, pp. 187–202). Wiesbaden, Germany: VS-Verlag für Sozialwissenschaften.

Sommer, A. & Mann, D. (2015). Qualität elterlichen Interaktionsverhaltens. Erfassung von Interaktionen mithilfe der Eltern-Kind-Interaktions Einschätzskala im Nationalen Bildungspanel (NEPS Working Paper No. 56). Bamberg, Germany: Leibniz-Institut für Bildungsverläufe, Nationales Bildungspanel. https://www.neps-data.de/Portals/0/Working%20Papers/WP_LVI.pdf.

Stone, J., Smith, H., & Murphy, L. (1973). *The competent infant.* New York, NY: Basic Books.

Summer, G., & Spietz, A. L. (1995). *NCAST Caregiver/Parent–Child Interaction Teaching Manual* (2nd ed.). Seattle, WA: NCAST Publications, University of Washington.

Tietze, W., Bolz, M., Grenner, K., Schlecht, D., & Wellner, B. (2005a). Krippen-Skala. Revidierte Fassung (KRIPS-R). Feststellung und Unterstützung pädagogischer Qualität in Krippen. Deutsche Fassung der Infant/Toddler Environment Rating Scale – Revised Edition von Thelma Harms, Debby Cryer, Richard M. Clifford. Weinheim, Germany: Beltz.

Tietze, W., Knobeloch, J., & Gerszonowicz, E. (2005b). Tagespflege-Skala (TAS). Feststellung und Unterstützung pädagogischer Qualität in der Kindertagespflege. Deutsche Fassung der Family Day Care Rating Scale von Thelma Harms und Richard M. Clifford. Weinheim, Germany: Beltz.

Weinert, S. (2005). Umschriebene Entwicklungsstörungen der Sprache. In P. F. Schlottke, R. K. Silbereisen, S. Schneider, & G. W. Lauth (Eds.), *Störungen im Kindes- und Jugendalter – Grundlagen und Störungen im Entwicklungsverlauf, Enzyklopädie der Psychologie D/II/5* (pp. 483–543). Göttingen, Germany: Hogrefe.

Weinert, S. (2006). Sprachentwicklung. In W. Schneider & B. Sodian (Eds.), Kognitive *Entwicklung. Enzyklopädie der Psychologie C/V/2* (pp. 609–719). Göttingen, Germany: Hogrefe.

Weinert, S. (2007). Kompetenzentwicklung und Kompetenzstruktur im Vorschulalter. In M. Prenzel, I. Gogolin, & H.-H. Krüger (Eds.), *Kompetenzdiagnostik* (Zeitschrift für Erziehungswissenschaft: Sonderheft 8, pp. 89–106). Wiesbaden, Germany: VS Verlag für Sozialwissenschaften.

Weinert, S. (2011). Die Anfänge der Sprache: Sprachentwicklung im Kleinkindalter. In H. Keller (Ed.), *Handbuch der Kleinkindforschung* (pp. 610–642). Bern, Switzerland: Huber.

Weinert, S., Linberg, A., Attig, M., Freund, J.-D., & Linberg, T. (2016). Analyzing early child development, influential conditions, and future impacts: Prospects of a German newborn cohort study. *International Journal of Child Care and Education Policy, 10,* 1–20. https://doi.org/10.1186/s40723-016-0022-6.

Wetherby, A. M., & Prizant, B. M. (1993). *Communication and Symbolic Behavior Scales – Normed Edition.* Baltimore, MD: Paul H. Brookes.

# Kindergarten and Elementary School: Starting Cohort 2 of the National Educational Panel Study

Karin Berendes, Tobias Linberg, Doreen Müller, Sebastian E. Wenz, Hans-Günther Roßbach, Thorsten Schneider and Sabine Weinert

---

Slightly updated version of Berendes et al. (2011).

K. Berendes
University of Tübingen, Tübingen, Germany
E-Mail: karin.berendes@uni-tuebingen.de

T. Linberg
State Institute for School Quality and Education Research, München, Germany
E-Mail: tobias.linberg@isb.bayern.de

D. Müller
Leibniz Institute for Educational Trajectories, Bamberg, Germany
E-Mail: doreen.mueller@lifbi.de

S. E. Wenz
GESIS – Leibniz Institute for the Social Sciences, Köln, Germany
E-Mail: sebastian.wenz@gesis.org

H.-G. Roßbach · S. Weinert (✉)
University of Bamberg, Bamberg, Germany
E-Mail: hans-guenther.rossbach@uni-bamberg.de

S. Weinert
E-Mail: sabine.weinert@uni-bamberg.de

T. Schneider
University of Leipzig, Leipzig, Germany
E-Mail: thorsten.schneider@uni-leipzig.de

Abstract

The German National Educational Panel Study (NEPS) covers educational processes during Kindergarten and elementary school age in two stages: "Kindergarten and transition to elementary school" and "elementary school and transition to lower secondary school." One cohort covers both of these two stages. It started in winter 2010/2011 with a cluster sample of 3,000 target children aged 4 to 5 years attending Kindergarten. When most of these children entered school, the cohort more than doubled by integrating their classmates and a further subsample of 1st-grade students into the survey. In addition to direct assessment of children's competencies, their parents are interviewed and teachers and principals fill out self-administered questionnaires. In these stages, assessments focus on early scientific and mathematical literacy as well as on language competencies (e.g., vocabulary, grammar, phonological awareness). We also survey the structure and aspects of the quality of Kindergarten and elementary school, families, and nonformal learning environments. Information on parents' socioeconomic status and their evaluation of decision-relevant aspects allows us to model school choice and disentangle primary and secondary effects. Theoretically relevant aspects of migrants' situation are also surveyed. Further aspects are children's health, social competencies, and the different care settings.

Keywords

Kindergarten · Elementary school · Education · Panel study · Early childhood

12.1 Importance of Early Education and Elementary School

Early childhood is a period of extensive development in various cognitive and noncognitive domains—as emphasized by different research traditions in education science, psychology, and biology. Despite ongoing debates on the relative importance of either nature or nurture, there is abundant evidence for the influence of not only individual characteristics and preconditions but also environmental features on children's developmental progress and outcomes (e.g., Brooks-Gunn and Markman 2005; Silbereisen and Noak 2006). Ecological theories of development point out how development is influenced by the different environments children live and participate in (e.g., Bronfenbrenner and Ceci 1994; Marjoribanks 2002). A related major issue in educational research and current politics concerns the effect of the quantity and quality of early nonparental care and education on the development of children and the reconciliation between family life and parental participation in the labor market (e.g., Roßbach 2005; Roßbach et al. 2008a, b). Public expectations are high: Nonfamilial early child care and education settings should raise the level of educational attainment for all children. Another issue concerns early disparities and their long-term consequences. Early disparities in skills, competencies, and educational pathways are observable ahead of school enrollment and during elementary school and—again—there are strong expectations that nonfamilial care and education settings will make a special contribution to compensating for early disparities (e.g., Roßbach 2004). However, to gain more insight into the mechanisms generating differences in achievement, it is necessary to take a longitudinal perspective. Theoretical explanations and empirical data on the development of competencies are needed to allow for subgroup-specific analyses of students in preschool institutions and elementary school. It is beyond question that—in addition to child characteristics—both family and institutions such as Kindergarten and school influence the development of competencies. Current questions are addressing the relative importance of these environments and the mediating mechanisms that carry these effects. Answering these and similar questions could tell us, for instance, whether and to what extent early educational institutions serve as "great equalizers"—an issue that has important policy implications.

The effects of the family on the acquisition of competencies and, hence, on achievement differences are also known as primary effects of social stratification (Boudon 1974). In addition, decisions are of great importance for educational success in the German education system. The first decisions are made mainly by parents. Beside school enrollment, the transition to the explicitly tracked school system is of great importance. Parents are forced to make very early decisions about their child's future educational track—in most cases, this transition takes place after the 4th grade and thus around the age of 10. Theories that explicitly model educational choices may help us to understand what happens at the transitions and shed light on the mechanisms leading to group differences in educational choices—even conditional on competencies (Breen and Goldthorpe 1997; Erikson and Jonsson 1996; Esser 1999). It is also through these so-called secondary effects of stratification that parents influence the educational outcomes of their offspring (Boudon 1974).

Therefore, Stages 2 and 3 of the National Educational Panel Study (NEPS) focus on the transitions from Kindergarten to elementary school, the later transition to the tracked school system, the development of competencies, and the different learning environments during this time. To provide appropriate data, a cohort was drawn starting with children attending Kindergarten 2 years before their transition to school. This cohort was surveyed year by year and expanded at school entry. Extensive, theory-guided tests and interviews are being carried out with the children (as target persons), their parents, Kindergarten and elementary school teachers, and principals.

The subsequent sections give a brief overview on previous findings and theoretical explanations regarding educational participation and educational processes in preschool age; on the transition from Kindergarten to elementary school; on educational processes in elementary school; and on the transition from elementary school to secondary school. Then, Sect. 12.3 presents the stage-specific measures of the major theoretical dimensions—in earlier publications, also referred to as pillars of NEPS. Section 12.4 gives information on respondents and instruments. We conclude in Sect. 12.5 with an outlook on the research potential of the data being collected within Stages 2 and 3 of NEPS.

12.2 Previous Findings and Theoretical Considerations

In this section, we refer to earlier findings and address theoretically relevant questions along the educational pathway. We start at age 4 to 5 in Kindergarten and end at the transition from elementary school to the tracked school system.

12.2.1 Educational Participation and Processes in Preschool Age

From birth onward, development is influenced by familial and—later on—institutional conditions (for more information on developmental issues concerning children below age 3, see Chap. 11, this volume). The family is a child's first environment for socialization and learning processes. Furthermore, most children in Germany experience institutional learning environments before entering school. In 2009, about 92% of all 3- to 6-year-olds in Germany were attending Kindergarten[1] (Statistisches Bundesamt 2010) providing child care and education (*Erziehung, Bildung und Betreuung*) in mainly age-mixed groups. For children younger than 3 years, the percentage was much lower at about 17%. Despite high rates for older preschool children and the legally guaranteed places for every child from a specific age onward, there are social and regional disparities in utilization (Büchner and Spieß 2007; Kreyenfeld and Krapf 2010). It also has to be borne in mind that even though Germany has a federal law governing nonfamilial care and education settings (including Kindergarten) that stipulates the same frame conditions, the 16 federal states are responsible for these settings, and they interpret federal law in different ways with their own laws. This leads to more or less significant differences in Kindergarten regulations between the states. In 2004, the Standing Conference of the Ministers of Education and Cultural Affairs and the Conference of the Youth and Family Ministers agreed on curricular principles ("education plans") for institutional preschool education and adopted a common framework. However, the federal states have different education plans specifying their basic concept of education, and there are also differences regarding how compulsory these curricula are for individual Kindergartens. Hence, although the German Kindergarten is oriented toward future educational processes and the acquisition of competencies, large differences are possible in the way legal guidelines are implemented.

The quality of the different familial and institutional learning environments is assumed to be crucial for the acquisition of competencies. Pertaining to the quality of learning environments—here understood in respect to their cognitive stimulation—three

---

[1] In this article, we shall use the German term Kindergarten as a generic term for the different forms of institutional child care from age 3 or 4 and above and until school entry. For an overview of regulations and the organization of preschool and elementary school education, see EURYDICE (n.d.).

dimensions are often distinguished (see Roßbach et al. 2008a): (a) The quality of proximal processes pertains to interactions, such as parent-child activities or, just as equally, teacher-child activities or peer activities in Kindergarten. (b) Orientations refer to parents' and teachers' action-guiding cognitions such as childrearing values, belief systems, expectations, and aspirations. (c) The quality of structure, in contrast, is related to distal and more stable conditions of learning environments (e.g., the socioeconomic status [SES] of the family, group sizes, or SES composition in Kindergartens).

Empirical research on the effects of the use of institutional child care on children's outcomes shows that the duration of use correlates with cognitive outcomes (Sammons et al. 2008), the timing of school entry (Kratzmann and Schneider 2009), and further educational pathways through the tracked school system (Büchner and Spieß 2007; Seyda 2009). However, these studies normally do not control for the selectivity in entering Kindergarten (Becker and Lauterbach 2010). Looking at measures of the quality of institutional care and education, high quality is associated with better outcomes in social and cognitive competencies. Several studies reveal that it is particularly the quality of processes that is associated with children's language competencies (Peisner-Feinberg et al. 2001; Roßbach 2005; Sammons et al. 2008; Tietze et al. 2005), and that is important for the further educational career (Weinert 2007; Weinert et al. 2008). Sometimes the effects of quality are long lasting; at other times, they fade and disappear within the first years at school. Moreover, more distal structures such as group size or teacher–child ratio seem to influence development as well. Findings on whether use and quality of institutional care and education can reduce social disparities in achievement and have compensatory effects are somewhat inconsistent. Nonetheless, all children seem to benefit from high quality. With regard to educational investments in disadvantaged young children, Heckman and Masterov (2007) have reported unexpectedly large returns for individuals as well as for society as a whole. However, German longitudinal research on aspects of quality or on (language) support programs is sparse.

Comparisons of the power of effects of home learning environments and institutional learning environments on children's developmental outcomes reveal that the characteristics of home learning environments are more powerful predictors (e.g., Melhuish et al. 2008; Sammons et al. 2008; Sylva et al. 2004; Tietze et al. 2005). Most studies show that taking processes of the home learning environment into account reduces the influence of distal family variables. Activities such as reading aloud with the child showed a significant long-term impact after controlling for other more distal influences such as SES. Especially with regard to discussions on educational lags and the emergence of social disparities in the development of preschool children, there is a need for a more thorough understanding of mediating features within and between children's preschool learning environments.

12.2.2 Transition from Kindergarten to Elementary School

Compulsory education in Germany starts with elementary school when children are about 6 years of age—depending on the federal state they live in. However, school enrollment is possible either ahead of this time or later. It may be delayed because of the parents' wish or because the child is classified as not yet ready for school. This classification is more frequent among children from lower social class families and with a migration background (Biedinger et al. 2008).

This first transition is the most regulated in Germany's education system: In most federal states, each child is assigned to the one school responsible for the neighborhood she or he lives in—an exception being North Rhine-Westphalia that allows free parental choice. Nonetheless, parents are able to circumvent these regulations by picking a private school, often denominational schools, or simply moving to another neighborhood and hence school district. There is evidence that German upper middle-class families exploit both paths, thereby increasing levels of segregation along socioeconomic and ethnic lines in elementary schools (Kristen 2008; Riedel et al. 2010). Sociological models of educational choice have been applied to this transition using geographically restricted data (Kristen 2008).

12.2.3 Educational Processes in Elementary School Age

As the first institution of compulsory schooling, elementary school in Germany aims to develop both cognitive and noncognitive competencies while providing a first solid base of general education (Einsiedler et al. 2008). As in other countries, there is an achievement gap along social and ethnic lines at school entry (Becker and Biedinger 2006).

International large-scale assessments, such as the Progress in Reading Literacy Study (PIRLS, in Germany called IGLU: Internationale Grundschul-Lese-Untersuchung) and the Third International Mathematics and Science Study (TIMSS) conducted at the end of 4th grade, which coincides with the end of elementary school in Germany, provide evidence that students in Germany perform just as well as their counterparts in countries with similar socioeconomic conditions. Whereas inequality measured as variation in test scores is rather low, the correlation between socioeconomic indicators such as number of books at home or migrant status of the parents is—albeit not significantly—higher than the international average (Bos et al. 2007, 2008). According to the Programme for International Student Assessment (PISA), both indicators are very pronounced at the end of compulsory schooling in Germany (PISA-Konsortium Deutschland 2007).

Evidence from longitudinal studies on how competencies in different domains develop over time during elementary school is somewhat contradictory and restricted to particular regions or states. Whereas some authors find a stabilization of interindividual differences (Kammermeyer and Martschinke 2004; Weinert and Helmke 1997), others report a closing gap over the first years of schooling (see, for reading literacy,

Schneider et al. 1997; for reading literacy and numeracy, Ditton and Krüsken 2010), whereas a third group find a widening gap between children performing below and those performing above average (Klicpera and Gasteiger-Klicpera 1993; see, for similar results from the Netherlands, Meijnen 1987; van der Slik et al. 2006). There is evidence from many international and some national studies that high teacher quality and high quality of instruction are capable of increasing the average performance in a class (Babu and Mendro 2003; Staub and Stern 2002; Weinert and Helmke 1997). Less clear is the evidence on whether it is possible to lessen the achievement gap at the same time (Weinert and Helmke 1997).

Interestingly, international and national evidence on the correlation between socio-economic background and competence development is more clear-cut: The gap between children from low-SES families and those from high-SES families is widening over time. Studies from the United States looking at the causal effect of schooling on the achievement gap along social and ethnic lines suggest that schools may nevertheless serve as "great equalizers" (Downey et al. 2004). During the school year, cognitive competencies from children with different social and ethnic backgrounds tend to develop in parallel. However, over the summer months, students from disadvantaged families fall behind in their development (Entwisle and Alexander 1992; Heyns 1978). In a replication using data covering 4th and 5th graders from Berlin, Becker et al. (2008) found even more pronounced effects than those reported in studies conducted in the United States and other countries (Lindahl 2001; Verachtert et al. 2009). These findings underline that the family is an important, if not the main source of educational inequality.

12.2.4 Transition from Elementary School to Secondary School

The second and probably most important transition in the German education system is the one from elementary to secondary school. The secondary school system features explicit between-school tracking in all federal states (see, for the stage covering the first years of secondary school, Chap. 13, this volume). Whereas there are many considerable differences between the 16 federal states' education systems, most track students after 4 years of elementary school. Some states have longer lasting elementary schools; others provide a phase of orientation in 5th and 6th grade before tracking (see, also, Chap. 13, this volume). Future policy changes may affect this transition with regard to timing and other regulations.

Evidence is inconclusive on whether this relatively early tracking contributes to the comparatively high level of educational inequality in Germany in terms of competencies, attended tracks, and attained certificates (Baumert et al. 2009; Hanushek and Wößmann 2006; Pfeffer 2008). However, it is well known that teachers contribute to this inequality. Teachers, who are legally constrained to recommend a particular track, show some bias in favor of students from families with an upper middle-class background. Whether they also discriminate against children from particular ethnic groups is not yet clear (Kristen 2006).

There is also no clear evidence on the causes and mechanisms leading to these—potentially biased—recommendations. It would seem worth considering different explanations for these biases (Aigner and Cain 1977; Becker 1971; Holzer and Ludwig 2003; Pohlmann 2009).

Even more strongly than teachers' recommendations however, parents' decisions are also biased along the lines of social class. Evidence for single states and for Germany as a whole suggests that secondary effects of stratification are responsible for a considerable part of the overall level of inequality of educational opportunity (Maaz and Nagy 2009). Theories that explicitly model education decisions by taking into account different actual and perceived factors have been applied to this first transition (Stocké 2007). Evidence is needed on how secondary effects vary by educational regulations and between natives and different groups of migrants.

12.3 Theoretical Perspectives and Measures in Stages 2 and 3

As in all the other stages as well, six major dimensions (see Chap. 1) are considered in Stages 2 and 3. In addition, stage-specific constructs are included. The respondents are children and their parents along with teachers and principals of Kindergartens and elementary schools.

The preschool and school years are a period of intense development of competencies (Dimension 1). Moreover, the educational impact in this period is major. Describing and explaining the competence development of children throughout their Kindergarten attendance and first school years as well as their promotion in family and Kindergarten/elementary school is a major task for NEPS. Therefore, NEPS includes a broad conception of indicators of (a) domain-general cognitive capacities (nonverbal reasoning, perceptual speed), (b) domain-specific competencies (mathematical and scientific literacy; see Schöps 2013), phonological awareness (see Berendes and Weinert 2016), receptive grammar (see Lorenz et al. 2017), vocabulary and reading literacy (Rohm et al. 2017), and (c) metacompetencies (e.g., metacognition, information and communication technologies [ICT] literacy, see Chap. 4, this volume).

NEPS takes formal, nonformal/informal, and familial learning environments as well as their interplay into consideration (Dimension 2). Central for Stages 2 and 3 are the learning environments at Kindergarten and elementary school. Aspects of Kindergarten quality are being captured with the questionnaires for educators (see Bäumer and Roßbach 2016). The connectivity of educational processes in Kindergarten and elementary school is particularly decisive (cf., Roßbach 2006). Patterns of cumulative experiences in this phase of education are being analyzed by measuring aspects of learning environments annually. In addition, the history of extrafamilial care and education up to age 4 is being assessed retrospectively through interviews with parents. Special attention can be given to the transitions—first, from Kindergarten to elementary school and second, from elementary school to lower secondary school. The home learning environment is being assessed through different nonformal/informal learning opportunities in children's everyday lives (e.g., musical and sports activities). Of special interest are home-learning activities, the educational orientations and aspirations of parents, their formation during the early stage of the educational career of their children, and their dependencies on family background (see Chap. 5, this volume).

To gain more information on the importance of primary and secondary effects in educational decisions and to test competing theories on the causes of social-class-specific educational decisions (Dimension 3) and careers, Stage 3 focuses on secondary school choice. Besides the child's competencies, school decisions might be influenced by social-class-specific values, and cost-benefit analyses along with parents' aspirations, knowledge about the education system, or educational orientations (see Chap. 6, this volume).

Children with a migration background (Dimension 4) are, on average, less successful in the German education system (see Bonsen et al. 2008). They enter Kindergarten at higher ages, more often show a delayed school entry, repeat classes more often in elementary school, and have lower transition rates to the more demanding school tracks. However, large variation exists between different ethnic groups (see Chap. 7, this volume). Therefore, children from migrant families are followed particularly closely. The data are useful for testing whether ethnic differences in educational processes are merely social-class-specific inequalities or whether there are migration-specific influences such as generation status, cultural consumption, and orientations. Of special interest is the role of parents' and child's non-German language skills for child's competence development in different domains. Beside parents' self-report on language skills, students with a non-German language background (restricted to Russian and Turkish) are tested for their competencies in this language. The longitudinal observation of these groups from an early starting point should lead to a better understanding of the causes of the noted educational disadvantages. Furthermore, potential compensatory effects of measures of Kindergarten and elementary school can be deduced.

It seems essential to capture returns to education (Dimension 5). Following a broader conception of returns by viewing health, educational level, and subjective well-being as outcomes, these returns to education can be monitored simultaneously as the children progress through Kindergarten and school. The data allow analyses of both the degree to which and the mechanisms by which Kindergartens, schools, parents, and peers influence the health status and health-related behaviors of children. At the same time, it is important to analyze the reciprocal impact.

Furthermore, a child's personality and behavior are taken into account (Dimension 6). Brief indicators of presumably rather stable dimensions of the child's personality along with indicators of motivation, self-concept, and interests as well as social behavior are being captured by questionnaires (see Chap. 9, this volume). Due to the age of the target persons, these assessments have to rely mostly on reports from parents or teaching staff.

Although the measures of these dimensions cover a wide range of educationally relevant factors, additional stage-specific measures are needed to capture the most important predictors of educational processes, learning, and early literacy. For example, some stage-specific tests are additionally employed in Kindergarten. Given that language is a key competence for an educational career and academic success (see Holler 2007), a special focus in Kindergarten is on language and phonological processing. Thus, additional indicators of grammar, phonological awareness, and working memory are assessed. Further information on language performance, language development, and language support of the target child are provided by parents and teachers in Kindergarten and elementary schools. Moreover, questions about language support programs and the qualification of the Kindergarten staff to deliver these programs are implemented in the questionnaire. Besides language, metacompetencies such as self-regulation are predictive for academic performance and achievement and have to be assessed in a stage-specific fashion. In Kindergarten and at the end of elementary school, we assess self-regulation via delay of gratification tasks.

12.4 Respondents and Instruments

As mentioned above, nearly all children in Germany attend Kindergarten. Thus, the second cohort of NEPS started with Kindergarten children aged about 5 years (Stage 2) who were followed into elementary school (Stage 3) and even further (Stage 4).

Cohort 2 started in winter 2010/11 throughout Germany. The target persons were children who would normally enroll in elementary school 2 years later. Because Germany has age-mixed Kindergarten groups, the number of eligible target children in a group was only a subset of the total group. The actual sample size for the first wave was almost 3,000 children with their parents from nearly 280 Kindergartens plus data from principals and their Kindergarten teachers. As the majority of respondents entered elementary school, the sample was expanded in Grade 1 in two ways: For some kindergarten children, all classmates, their parents, and their schools were asked to take part. In addition, a nationwide refreshment sample of 1st graders was recruited leading to a large sample boost with about 6,700 students tested in 1st grade. For more information on the sampling design and sampling model, see Chap. 3 in this volume or Aßmann et al. (2013).

Children were tested individually in Kindergarten; later on in elementary school, they were tested in groups. In higher elementary school grades, short student questionnaires were administered as well. At the same time, one parent was interviewed by telephone (computer assisted telephone interview, CATI). Kindergarten children entering a school not taking part in the NEPS study form a special group. They were tested again at the end of elementary school, whereas their parents were asked for an interview every year. Because NEPS is interested in institutional effects on education processes, teachers and principals in Kindergarten and school were asked to fill out self-administered questionnaires at the same time as the children were being tested in these institutions. In addition, there was a brief questionnaire asking teachers to give some crucial information on each participating child. One year before the current wave of the main cohort was surveyed, the procedures and instruments were tested in a pilot study with small case numbers. Parallel or prior to the pilot study, cognitive interviews with experts and qualitative as well as small quantitative pretests in the field were conducted to ensure the high quality of instruments.

12.5 Concluding Remarks and Outlook

The data collected in Stages 2 and 3 provide a solid base for conducting theory-driven education research. Because of the panel design, modern techniques of modeling longitudinal data can be used. Major topics are (a) the development of competencies and educational careers in Kindergarten and elementary school age; (b) Kindergarten, elementary school, and family as learning environments; (c) the transition from Kindergarten to elementary school and from elementary to secondary school and the accompanying decisions on education; (d) the extent and the significance of social and ethnic disparities in children's early competencies and achievements; and (e) early returns to education. In particular, NEPS data are delivering new findings on the net effects of family characteristics, Kindergarten, and elementary school on the development of competencies over time.

When it comes to learning environments, researchers have the opportunity to gain a detailed picture of what institutional and familial learning environments look like in Germany. It is possible to examine the impact of learning environments at home, in Kindergarten, and in elementary school on various educational outcomes, and how these relate to questions of inequality of educational opportunity (IEO). What characteristics of home environments and parents' activities are the most important mediators of early primary effects of stratification (Boudon 1974)? This also targets the question whether and to what extent different forms of cultural capital can be seen as causal factors influencing educational outcomes. Alongside social class differences, it is now possible to investigate the importance of characteristics of different learning environments for gender and ethnic differences in achievement.

Educational decisions, also known as secondary effects of stratification (Boudon 1974), are of great importance in the German education system (Maaz and Nagy 2009). One of the most important transitions in the German education systems takes place at the end of elementary school when children are normally 9 to 10 years old. By exploiting NEPS data, researchers are gaining a deeper understanding of why parents in Germany pick a particular secondary school and how this relates to social class or ethnic group.

Regarding ethnic inequality, the data are useful for describing and analyzing disparities during elementary school. The effect of educational participation, ethnic capital, and orientations on the development of competencies and on parents' school decisions can be analyzed. In addition, with respect to students with a non-German language background, it is possible to analyze the influence of students' competencies in this language (at least in Russian and Turkish) as well as of language use at home and special language programs on the competence acquisition of children with a migration background.

References

Aigner, D., & Cain, G. (1977). Statistical theories of discrimination in labor markets. *Industrial and Labor Relations Review, 30(2)*, 175–187.

Aßmann, C., Steinhauer, H. W., Zinn, S., & Goßmann, S. (2013). *Sampling and weighting the Kindergarten cohort sample of the National Educational Panel Study* (NEPS Working Paper No. 29). Bamberg, Germany: University of Bamberg, National Educational Panel Study.

Babu, S. & Mendro, R. (2003, April). *Teacher accountability: HLM-based teacher effectiveness indices in the investigation of teacher effects on student achievement in a state assessment program.* Paper presented at the American Education Research Association annual meeting, Chicago, IL.

Bäumer, T., & Roßbach, H.-G. (2016). Measurement of preschool quality within the National Educational Panel Study—Results of a methodological study. In H.-P. Blossfeld, J. von Maurice, M. Bayer, & J. Skopek (Eds.), *Methodological issues of longitudinal surveys* (pp. 543–560). Wiesbaden, Germany: Springer VS.

Baumert, J., Becker, M., Neumann, M.& Nikolova, R. (2009). Frühübergang in ein grundständiges Gymnasium—Übergang in ein privilegiertes Entwicklungsmileu? Ein Vergleich von Regressionsanalyse und Propensity Score Matching. *Zeitschrift für Erziehungswissenschaft, 12(2)*, 189–215.

Becker, B., & Biedinger, N. (2006). Ethnische Bildungsungleichheit zu Schulbeginn. *Kölner Zeitschrift für Soziologie und Sozialpsychologie, 58(4)*, 660–684.

Becker, G. (1971). *The economics of discrimination* (2nd ed.). Chicago, IL: University of Chicago Press.

Becker, M., Stanat, P., Baumert, J., & Lehmann, R. (2008). Lernen ohne Schule: Differentielle Entwicklung der Leseleistungen von Kindern mit und ohne Migrationshintergrund während der Sommerferien. In F. Kalter (Ed.), *Migration und Integration* (Kölner Zeitschrift für Soziologie und Sozialpsychologie: Sonderheft 48, pp. 252–276). Wiesbaden, Germany: VS-Verlag für Sozialwissenschaften.

Becker, R., & Lauterbach, W. (2010). Bildungseffekte vorschulischer Erziehung und Elementarbildung – Bessere Bildungschancen für Arbeiter- und Migrantenkinder? In R. Becker & W. Lauterbach (Eds.), *Bildung als Privileg? Erklärungen und Befunde zu den Ursachen der Bildungsungleichheit* (4th ed., pp. 129–160). Wiesbaden, Germany: VS Verlag für Sozialwissenschaften.

Berendes, K., Fey, D., Linberg, T., Wenz, S. E., Roßbach, H.-G., Schneider, T. & Weinert, S. (2011). Kindergarten and elementary school. In H.-P. Blossfeld, H.-G. Roßbach, & J. von Maurice (Eds.), *Education as a lifelong process. The German Educational Panel Study (NEPS)* (Zeitschrift für Erziehungswissenschaft: Sonderheft 14, pp. pp. 203–216). Wiesbaden, Germany: VS-Verlag für Sozialwissenschaften.

Berendes, K., & Weinert, S. (2016). Selecting appropriate phonological awareness indicators for the kindergarten cohort of the National Educational Panel Study: A theoretical and empirical approach. In H.-P. Blossfeld, J. von Maurice, M. Bayer, & J. Skopek (Eds.), *Methodological issues of longitudinal surveys. The example of the National Educational Panel Study* (pp. 401–425). Wiesbaden, Germany: Springer VS.

Biedinger, N., Becker, B., & Rohling, I. (2008). Early ethnic educational inequality: The influence of duration of preschool attendance and social composition. *European Sociological Review, 24*, 243–256.

Bonsen, M., Frey, K. A., & Bos, W. (2008). Soziale Herkunft. In W. Bos, M. Bonsen, J. Baumert, M. Prenzel, C. Selter, & G. Walther (Eds.), *Mathematische und naturwissenschaftliche Kompetenzen von Grundschulkindern in Deutschland im internationalen Vergleich* (pp. 141–156). Münster, Germany: Waxmann.

Bos, W., Bonsen, M., Baumert, J., Prenzel, M., Selter, C., & Walther, G. (Eds.). (2008). *Mathematische und Naturwissenschaftliche Kompetenzen von Grundschulkindern in Deutschland in internationalen vergleich*. Münster, Germany: Waxmann.

Bos, W., Hornberg, S., Arnold, K.-H., Faust, G., Fried, L., Lankes, E.-M., Schwippert, K., & Valtin, R. (Eds.). (2007). *IGLU 2006: Lesekompetenzen von Grundschulkindern in Deutschland im internationalen Vergleich*. Münster, Germany: Waxmann.

Boudon, R. (1974). *Education, opportunity, and social inequality: Changing prospects in western societies*. New York, NY: Wiley & Sons.

Breen, R., & Goldthorpe, J. (1997). Explaining educational differentials: Towards a formal rational action theory. *Rationality and Society, 9(3)*, 275–305.

Bronfenbrenner, U., & Ceci, S. J. (1994). Nature–nurture reconceptualized in developmental perspective: A bioecological model. *Psychological Review, 101*, 568–586.

Brooks-Gunn, J., & Markman, L. B. (2005). The contribution of parenting to ethnic and racial gaps in school readiness. *The Future of Children, 15*(1), 139–168.

Büchner, C., & Spieß, K. (2007). *Die Dauer vorschulischer Betreuungs- und Bildungserfahrungen. Ergebnisse auf Basis von Paneldaten* (DIW- Diskussionspapiere 687). Berlin, Germany: German Institute for Economic Research.

Ditton, H., & Krüsken, J. (2010). Denn wer hat, dem wird gegeben? Eine Längsschnittstudie zur Entwicklung schulischer Leistungen und den Effekten der sozialen Herkunft in der Grundschulzeit. *Journal for Educational Research Online, 1*(1), 33–61.

Downey, D. B., von Hippel, P. T., & Broh, B. A. (2004). Are schools the great equalizer? Cognitive inequality during the summer months and the school year. *American Sociological Review, 69*(5), 613–635.

Einsiedler, W., Martschinke, S., & Kammermeyer, G. (2008). Die Grundschule zwischen Heterogenität und gemeinsamer Bildung. In K. S. Cortina, J. Baumert, A. Leschinsky, K. U. Mayer, & L. Trommer (Eds.), *Das Bildungswesen in der Bundesrepublik Deutschland* (pp. 325–374). Reinbek, Germany: Rowohlt.

Entwisle, D. R., & Alexander, K. L. (1992). Summer setback: Race, poverty, school composition, and mathematics achievement in the first two years of school. *American Sociological Review, 57*, 72–84.

Erikson, R., & Jonsson, J. (1996). *Can education be equalized? The Swedish case in comparative perspective*. Boulder, CO: Westview Press.

Esser, H. (1999). *Situationslogik und Handeln. Soziologie: Spezielle Grundlagen*. Frankfurt a.M., Germany: Campus.

EURYDICE (n.d.). *Overview Germany*. Brussels.https://webgate.ec.europa.eu/fpfis/mwikis/eurydice/index.php/Germany:Overview. Accessed 20 Mar 2018.

Hanushek, E. A., & Wößmann, L. (2006). Does educational tracking affect performance and inequality? Differences-in-differences evidence across countries. *The Economic Journal, 116*, C63–C76.

Heckman, J. J., & Masterov, D. V. (2007). The productivity argument for investing in young children. *Review of Agricultural Economics, 29*, 446–493.

Heyns, B. (1978). *Summer learning and the effects of schooling*. New York, NY: Academic Press.

Holler, D. (2007). Bedeutung sprachlicher Fähigkeiten für Bildungserfolge. In K. Jampert, P. Best, A. Guadatiello, D. Holler, & A. Zehnbauer (Eds.), *Schlüsselkompetenz Sprache: Sprachliche Bildung und Förderung im Kindergarten. Konzepte, Projekte und Maßnahmen* (pp. 24–28). Weimar, Berlin, Germany: Verlag das Netz.

Holzer, H. & Ludwig, J. (2003). Measuring discrimination in education: Are methodologies from labor markets useful? *Teachers College Record, 105*(6), 1147–1178.

Kammermeyer, G., & Martschinke, S. (2004). KILIA – Selbstkonzept- und Leistungsentwicklung im Anfangsunterricht. In G. Faust, M. Götz, & H. Hacker (Eds.), *Anschlussfähige Bildungsprozesse im Elementar- und Primarbereich* (pp. 204–217). Bad Heilbrunn, Germany: Klinkhardt.

Klicpera, C., & Gasteiger-Klicpera, B. (1993). *Lesen und Schreiben – Entwicklung und Schwierigkeiten: Die Wiener Längsschnittuntersuchungen über die Entwicklung, den Verlauf und die Ursachen von Lese- und Schreibschwierigkeiten in der Pflichtschulzeit*. Bern, Switzerland: Huber.

Kratzmann, J., & Schneider, T. (2009). Soziale Ungleichheit beim Schulstart. Empirische Untersuchungen zur Bedeutung und des Kindergartenbesuchs auf den Zeitpunkt der Einschulung. *Kölner Zeitschrift für Soziologie und Sozialpsychologie, 61*, 1–24.

Kreyenfeld, M., & Krapf, S. (2010). Soziale Ungleichheit und Kinderbetreuung – Eine Analyse der sozialen und ökonomischen Determinanten der Nutzung von Kindertageseinrichtungen. In R. Becker & W. Lauterbach (Eds.), *Bildung als Privileg* (4th ed., pp. 107–128). Wiesbaden, Germany: VS Verlag für Sozialwissenschaften.

Kristen, C. (2006). Ethnische Diskriminierung in der Grundschule? Die Vergabe von Noten und Bildungsempfehlungen. *Kölner Zeitschrift für Soziologie und Sozialpsychologie, 58(1)*, 79–97.

Kristen, C. (2008). Primary school choice and ethnic school segregation in German elementary schools. *European Sociological Review, 24*(4), 495–510.

Lindahl, M. (2001). *Summer learning and the effect of schooling. Evidence from Sweden* (IZA Discussion Paper No. 262). Bonn, Germany: IZA.

Lorenz, C., Berendes, K., & Weinert, S. (2017). *Measuring receptive grammar in kindergarten and elementary school children in the National Educational Panel Study* (NEPS Survey Paper No. 24). Bamberg, Germany: Leibniz Institute for Educational Trajectories, National Educational Panel Study.

Maaz, K., & Nagy, G. (2009). Der Übergang von der Grundschule in die weiterführenden Schulen des Sekundarschulsystems: Definition, Spezifikation und Quantifizierung primärer und sekundärer Herkunftseffekte. In J. Baumert, K. Maaz, & U. Trautwein (Eds.), *Bildungsentscheidungen* (Zeitschrift für Erziehungswissenschaft: Sonderheft 12, pp. 153–182). Wiesbaden, Germany: VS-Verlag für Sozialwissenschaften.

Marjoribanks, K. (2002). *Family and school capital: Towards a context theory of students' outcomes*. Dordrecht, Netherlands: Kluwer Academic Publishers.

Meijnen, G. W. (1987). From six to twelve. Different school careers in primary education. *Zeitschrift für Sozialisationsforschung und Erziehungssoziologie, 7*, 209–225.

Melhuish, E. C., Sylva, K., Sammons, P., Siraj-Blatchford, I., Taggart, B., & Phan, M. (2008). Effects of home learning environment and preschool center experience upon literacy and numeracy in early primary school. *Journal of Social Issues, 64*, 95–114.

Peisner-Feinberg, E. S., Burchinal, M. R., Clifford, M., Culkin, M. L., Howes, C., Kagan, S. L. & Yazejian, N. (2001).The relation of preschool child-care quality to children's cognitive and social development trajectories through second grade. *Child Development, 72(5)*, 1534–1553.

Pfeffer, F. E. (2008). Persistent inequality in educational attainment and its institutional context. *European Sociological Review, 25*(5), 543–565.

PISA-Konsortium Deutschland (Ed.). (2007). *PISA 2006. Die Ergebnisse der dritten internationalen Vergleichsstudie*. Münster, Germany: Waxmann.

Pohlmann, S. (2009). *Der Übergang am Ende der Grundschulzeit. Zur Formation der Übergangsempfehlung aus der Sicht der Lehrkräfte*. Münster, Germany: Waxmann.

Riedel, A., Schneider, K., Schuchart, C., & Weishaupt, H. (2010). School choice in German primary schools: How binding are school districts? *Journal for Educational Research Online, 2*(1), 94–120.

Rohm, T., Krohmer, K., & Gnambs, T. (2017). *NEPS Technical report for reading: Scaling results of Starting Cohort 2 for Grade 4* (NEPS Survey Paper No. 30). Bamberg, Germany: Leibniz Institute for Educational Trajectories, National Educational Panel Study.

Roßbach, H.-G. (2004). Kognitiv anregende Lernumwelten im Kindergarten. In D. Lenzen, J. Baumert, R. Watermann, & U. Trautwein (Eds.), *PISA und die Konsequenzen für die erziehungswissenschaftliche Forschung* (Zeitschrift für Erziehungswissenschaft: Beiheft 3, pp. 9–24). Wiesbaden, Germany: VS Verlag für Sozialwissenschaften.

Roßbach, H.-G. (2005). Effekte qualitativ guter Betreuung, Bildung und Erziehung im frühen Kindesalter auf Kinder und ihre Familien. In Sachverständigenkommission Zwölfter Kinder- und Jugendbericht (Eds.), *Bildung, Betreuung und Erziehung von Kindern unter sechs Jahren* (pp. 55–174). München, Germany: Verlag Deutsches Jugendinstitut.

Roßbach, H.-G. (2006). Institutionelle Übergänge in der Frühpädagogik. In L. Fried & S. Roux (Eds.), *Pädagogik der Frühen Kindheit. Handbuch und Nachschlagewerk* (pp. 280–292). Weinheim, Germany: Beltz.

Roßbach, H.-G., Kluczniok, K., & Isenmann, D. (2008a). Erfahrungen aus internationalen Längsschnittuntersuchungen. In H.-G. Roßbach & S. Weinert (Eds.), *Kindliche Kompetenzen im Elementarbereich: Förderbarkeit, Bedeutung und Messung* (pp. 7–88). Berlin, Germany: BMBF.

Roßbach, H.-G., Kluczniok, K., & Kuger, S. (2008b). Auswirkungen eines Kindergartenbesuchs auf den kognitiv-leistungsbezogenen Entwicklungsstand von Kindern. In H.-G. Roßbach & H.-P. Blossfeld (Eds.), *Frühpädagogische Förderung in Institutionen* (Zeitschrift für Erziehungswissenschaft: Sonderheft 11, pp. 139–158). Wiesbaden, Germany: VS Verlag für Sozialwissenschaften.

Sammons, P., Sylva, K., Melhuish, E., Siraj-Blatchford, I., Taggart, B. Hunt, S., & Jelicic, H. (2008). *Effective Pre-School and Primary Education 3–11 Project (EPPE). Influences On children's cognitive and social development in Year 6*. London, England: Institute of Education, University of London.

Schneider, W., Stefanek, J., & Dotzler, H. (1997). Der Erwerb des Lesens und Rechtschreibens in der Grundschulzeit. In F. E. Weinert & A. Helmke (Eds.), *Entwicklung im Grundschulalter* (pp. 113–129). Weinheim, Germany: Psychologie Verlags Union.

Schöps, K. (2013). *NEPS technical report for science – Scaling results of Starting Cohort 2 in Kindergarten* (NEPS Working Paper No. 24). Bamberg, Germany: University of Bamberg, National Educational Panel Study.

Seyda, S. (2009). Kindergartenbesuch und späterer Bildungserfolg. Eine bildungsökonomische Analyse anhand des Sozio-ökonomischen Panels. *Zeitschrift für Erziehungswissenschaft, 12*(2), 233–251.

Silbereisen, R. K., & Noak, P. (2006). Kontexte und Entwicklung. In W. Schneider & F. Wilkenning (Eds.), *Theorien, Modelle und Methoden der Entwicklungspsychologie* (Enzyklopädie der Psychologie, Serie V: Entwicklungspsychologie, Vol. 1, pp. 311–368). Göttingen, Germany: Hogrefe.

Statistisches Bundesamt (2010). *Kindertagesbetreuung regional 2009*. Wiesbaden, Germany: Statistisches Bundesamt.

Staub, F. C., & Stern, E. (2002). The nature of teachers' pedagogical content beliefs matters for students' achievement gains: Quasi-experimental evidence from elementary mathematics. *Journal of Educational Psychology, 93*, 144–155.

Stocké, V. (2007). Explaining educational decision and effects of families' social class position: An empirical test of the Breen–Goldthorpe model of educational attainment. *European Sociological Review, 23,* 505–519.

Sylva, K., Melhuish, E., Sammons, P., & Taggart, B. (2004). *The Effective Provision of Pre-School Education (EPPE) Project: Final report. A longitudinal study funded by the DfES 1997–2004.* London, England: Institute of Education, University of London.

Tietze, W., Roßbach, H.-G., & Grenner, K. (2005). *Kinder von 4 bis 8 Jahren. Zur Qualität der Erziehung, Bildung in Kindergarten, Grundschule und Familie.* Weinheim, Germany: Beltz.

van der Slik, F. W. P., Driessen, G. W. J. M., & de Bot, K. L. J. (2006). Ethnic and socioeconomic class composition and language proficiency: A longitudinal multilevel examination in Dutch elementary schools. *European Sociological Review, 22*(3), 293–308.

Verachtert, P., van Damme, J., Onghena, P., & Ghesquière, P. (2009). A seasonal perspective on school effectiveness: Evidence from a Flemish longitudinal study in kindergarten and first grade. *School Effectiveness and School Improvement, 20*(2), 215–233.

Weinert, F. E., & Helmke, A. (Eds.). (1997). *Entwicklung im Grundschulalter.* Weinheim, Germany: Beltz.

Weinert, S. (2007). Kompetenzentwicklung und Kompetenzstruktur im Vorschulalter. In M. Prenzel, I. Gogolin, & H.-H. Krüger (Eds.), *Kompetenzdiagnostik* (Zeitschrift für Erziehungswissenschaft: Sonderheft 8, pp. 89–106). Wiesbaden, Germany: VS Verlag für Sozialwissenschaften.

Weinert, S., Doil, H., & Frevert, S. (2008). Kompetenzmessung im Vorschulalter: Eine Analyse vorliegender Verfahren. In H.-G. Roßbach & S. Weinert (Eds.), *Kindliche Kompetenzen im Elementarbereich: Förderbarkeit, Bedeutung und Messung* (pp. 89–209). Berlin, Germany: BMBF.

Transition and Development from Lower Secondary to Upper Secondary School

13

Paul Fabian, Martin Goy, Stephan Jarsinski, Kerstin Naujokat, Anna Prosch, Rolf Strietholt, Inge Blatt and Wilfried Bos

Abstract

This chapter introduces the scope and research program of Stage 4 of the German National Educational Panel Study (NEPS). Stage 4 follows the target persons through secondary education up to their transitions to higher secondary education, vocational education and training, or direct entry into the labor market. From a life-course perspective, this stage allows us to monitor individuals' educational trajectories in lower

---

P. Fabian (✉) · M. Goy · S. Jarsinski · K. Naujokat · R. Strietholt · W. Bos
Center for Research on Education and School Development, TU Dortmund University, Dortmund, Germany
E-Mail: paul.fabian@tu-dortmund.de

M. Goy
E-Mail: martin.goy@tu-dortmund.de

S. Jarsinski
E-Mail: s.jarsi@gmail.com

K. Naujokat
E-Mail: kerstin.naujokat@tu-dortmund.de

R. Strietholt
E-Mail: rolf.strietholt@tu-dortmund.de

W. Bos
E-Mail: officebos-ifs.fk12@tu-dortmund.de

A. Prosch · I. Blatt
Department of Education, University of Hamburg, Hamburg, Germany
E-Mail: for-anna@web.de

I. Blatt
E-Mail: inge.blatt@uni-hamburg.de

secondary education as results of a dynamic interdependence of educational decision-making, different learning environments, and competence development while also paying attention to the educational careers of migrants and returns to education. Following a general introduction, this chapter gives an overview of the general survey program of Stage 4 regarding the tests and questionnaires administered to students as well as the questionnaires and interviews administered to their teachers, principals, and parents. It then goes on to outline the specific research focus of Stage 4 on the interrelated development of reading and orthography as well as on the cognitions, attitudes, and behaviors related to these two competencies. With regard to orthography, stage-specific tests are applied to assess the students' competency trajectories in this crucial domain. With regard to reading, Stage 4 focuses on the development of students' reading engagement. A third key aspect of the stage-specific research introduced in this chapter is the quality of instruction.

Keywords

Panel study · Orthography · Quality of instruction · Reading engagement
Secondary education

13.1 Introduction: Design of Stage 4 with Starting Cohorts 3 (Grade 5) and 4 (Grade 9)

Theoretically, the National Educational Panel Study (NEPS) takes a life-course perspective (see Chap. 2, this volume). This orientation has prompted a decisive shift in how educational researchers usually approach matters of schooling, skills, competence, and attainment, because it redirects attention toward the process of education and competence development while linking the changing social structure to the unfolding of human lives (see also Blossfeld et al. 2009).

Stage 4 follows the target persons through the course of secondary school up to their transitions to higher secondary education, vocational education and training, or direct entry into the labor market. In most German federal states, students enter secondary education after Grade 4. They choose between different tracks or types of school, mainly between the school types of Hauptschule, Realschule, Schule mit mehreren Bildungsgängen, Gesamtschule, and Gymnasium. Throughout lower secondary education, students can move upward or downward between school tracks, mainly depending on their school performance. The "downward mobility" of students from the academically oriented school type to the lower or middle secondary school and the comprehensive school type is, however, much more frequent than the "upward mobility" (Baumert et al. 2003). Lower secondary education ends with Grade 9 or 10. Depending on their achievement, students may enter upper secondary school (gymnasiale Oberstufe), which is located essentially in two school types, namely Gymnasium and Gesamtschule. Alternatively, they enter the vocational track or the labor market. NEPS Stage 5 focuses on those who change into higher secondary school and NEPS Stage 6 is concerned with those who leave institutionalized schooling in the academic school system (see Chaps. 14 and 15, this volume). To cover these transitions in detail, NEPS contains not only a starting cohort in Grade 5, but also one in Grade 9. Generally, students in both cohorts are being surveyed annually. However, in Grade 9, they are surveyed twice (Fall and Spring) because students have to decide whether to stay in school or start a vocational education and training.

To ensure a consistent measurement of the development of competencies as well as a consistent survey program over the life course, NEPS has anchored a number of research perspectives within a general survey program represented by the five NEPS pillars (see Chap. 1, this volume, as well as—transferred to Stage 4—Sect. 13.2). For students in lower secondary education, this general survey program is aligned within the survey program of NEPS Stage 4. One research perspective, for instance, is school choice and how this relates to the competence development of students during the course of this stage of their educational careers. It is of great interest to study, for example, why and how students change school tracks in lower secondary education and what causes the downward mobility that is so characteristic for the German education system.

In addition to the life-course perspective of the five pillars, it is especially important to consider the special features of each educational stage. Therefore, the eight stages in NEPS ensure a stage-specific view on the research perspectives of the five pillars and add stage-specific research questions. In Stage 4, this is a test in orthography and the focus on the development of the students' reading engagement. A third key aspect of Stage 4 is the quality of instruction (see, in detail, Sect. 13.3.4).

The first point of measurement in NEPS Stage 4 was in late autumn of 2010 for both starting cohorts. The 5th-grade sample consists of about 6,800 students in Germany; the 9th-grade sample, 13,500 (see, for further information on the sampling strategy, Chap. 3, this volume). Each wave of the panel study was preceded by a pilot study conducted in the previous year in order to test the procedures and the instruments as a whole. Because in some states (Berlin and Brandenburg), elementary education lasts until after Grade 6 and the transition from elementary to secondary education takes place later than in every other state, a refreshment in Grade 7 was conducted in order to take better account of students from these states and counter attrition. Students from Berlin and Brandenburg left the schools sampled by NEPS. The paths of these students are being followed with individual retracking (Sixt et al. 2016). This also applies to students in general who left the school in which they were sampled.

Longitudinal research designs make it possible to address a large variety of questions and to draw causal inferences (Blossfeld et al. 2009; Bos and Gröhlich 2009; Goy et al. 2010). In Germany, however, large-scale longitudinal studies in lower secondary school are scarce. The recent regional longitudinal study KESS (*Kompetenzen und Einstellungen von Schülerinnen und Schülern*), for example, provides insights into the functioning of secondary schools in Hamburg (Bos et al. 2009, 2010a), and PARS (Panel Study at the Research School 'Education and Capabilities') sets out to provide evidence in North Rhine-Westphalia. Further regional studies have been conducted (e.g., BiKs—*Bildungsprozesse, Kompetenzentwicklung und Selektionsentscheidungen im Vorschul- und Schulalter*, BERLIN-study—*Bildungsentscheidungen und Bildungsverläufe vor dem Hintergrund struktureller Veränderungen im Berliner Sekundarschulwesen*), but NEPS was the first national longitudinal study of student achievement with more than two observations. In this respect, it provides a unique data source.

13.2 Main Questions and General Survey Program of Stage 4—Starting Cohorts 3 and 4

To allow for a global view on the context and conditions that influence the development of competencies and educational careers, information is collected from the students themselves, their parents, their teachers, and the principals of the schools they are attending. In each wave, students are tested in a number of domains and complete a paper-and-pencil questionnaire. Furthermore, computer-assisted telephone interviews (CATI) are conducted with one parent of each target person to gain more information on the home context of the students. Additionally, class teachers, German teachers, mathematics teachers, and school principals are asked to provide information on the classroom and school context of the students in paper-and-pencil questionnaires.

13.2.1 Test Domains and Contents of the Student Questionnaires

One focus of NEPS is the measurement of competencies over the life course. Pillar 1 assesses domain-general and domain-specific cognitive competencies (German language, mathematical, and natural science competencies), meta-competencies, and social competencies (see Chap. 4, this volume) in both starting cohorts of Stage 4. Especially in school, the measurement of the endowment and development of these competencies is central, because they correlate directly with productivity and educational outcomes in school. These domains are supplemented by stage-specific measurement of orthographic competence in Starting Cohort Grade 5 (see Sect. 13.3.2). In the student questionnaires, information is collected on the students themselves. Important pieces of information are background characteristics such as sociodemographic basics, social origin (see Chap. 6, this volume), and migration background. Pillar 4 inquires more deeply into the migration history and background with questions about the three past generations. Beyond that, students with a native language other than German are asked specific questions to find out how they assess their knowledge and competencies in their first and second language and which languages they use in different situations (see Chap. 7, this volume).

In Stage 4, NEPS Pillar 2 focuses on information about formal and nonformal/informal learning environments (see Chap. 5, this volume). Concerning the formal learning environment, the main focus is on schooling (see also Sects. 13.2.3 and 13.2.4). In contrast, the assessment of nonformal/informal learning environments includes the family and activities in the students' leisure time. Because nonformal/informal and formal learning environments depend very strongly on age, students in 5th grade are asked about, for example, additional courses in school; and students in 9th grade, about their participation in associations or their work experience. The information on home learning environments for students in Grade 5 includes, for example, homework support and the transfer from elementary to secondary education (except in federal states with 6 years of elementary school). The survey program also asks students about their perceptions of these changes.

NEPS Pillar 3 concentrates on the prospective measurement of factors explaining educational decisions and social inequality in lower secondary education (see Chap. 6, this volume). One focus is on the transmission of cultural capital from parents to students. Therefore, information on cultural activities as well as on reading behavior is collected (for students and parents, see Sect. 13.2.2). In addition to the background of social inequality, Pillar 3 is also interested in the students' social capital, for example, what their parents, friends, and others expect them to achieve educationally. Factors of special interest are those that lead to educational decisions in the tradition of rational choice theory. Hence, students are asked, for example, whether they think that they can attain different educational degrees and what kind of benefits and costs they associate with different educational degrees.

Above and beyond migration background and language use, Pillar 4 (see Chap. 7, this volume) is interested in the integration and assimilation of students with a migration background not only in school but also in social life. Questions include, for example, in cooperation with Pillar 3, the proportion of migrants in social networks and cultural habits. Furthermore, Pillar 4 asks migrant students about their traditions, norms, and identity.

Items about satisfaction, subjective well-being, and health behavior are collected as nonmonetary returns by Pillar 5 (see Chap. 8, this volume). Students are asked about their height and weight as basic information as well as information on, for instance, their eating habits. In Grade 9, when the students are slightly older, there are also questions on fertility and family formation as well as on social and political participation.

Further questions in Grades 5 and 9 address personality traits, including the Big Five, self-concept, and self-esteem, as well as general and topic-related interests. The former psychological concepts are becoming more and more important in analyzing competence development and educational attainment in school (see Chap. 9, this volume).

As already mentioned, in addition to the life-course perspective of the pillars, it is important to consider the stage-specific situations in the life course of the students in 5th and 9th grades. Hence, NEPS Stage 4 focuses on specific processes. In Grade 5, there is a stage-specific test in orthography and a focus on reading engagement and quality of instruction. In contrast, for 9th grade, it is the transition into higher secondary education, vocational education and training, or the labor market that is of special interest. To gain a better understanding of the circumstances of this transition, Stage 6 is asking students about their job-seeking strategies, career aspirations, and orientations.

13.2.2 Contents of the Interviews with Parents

The computer-assisted telephone interview (CATI) with one parent of the target person is a crucial way to gain more and valid information about the family context and include a multiinformant perspective in some aspects. In general, the interview is conducted with the parent responsible for school concerns.

The main aim is to collect basic information about the students' context in both cohorts: for instance, sociodemographics, household context, migration background, the language use and proficiency of both students and parents, as well as their social background (education and occupation of both parents; see Chaps. 6 and 7, this volume). In view of the life-course perspective of NEPS, the collection of data on the school history of the students is also particularly vital. Therefore, information is gathered about each stage of schooling the student attends, beginning with their first ever day at school.

Moreover, additional and also more valid information from a partly multiinformant perspective is collected on the basis of the research program of the pillars. Pillar 2 is again concerned with learning environments and their quality, for example, the amount and content of private tuition a student receives. Pillar 3 supplements the students' educational decisions by information on the parental considerations as well as their social and cultural capital. For this purpose, Pillar 3, in cooperation with Pillar 4, applies the "Position Generator" (Lin et al. 2001) to gain information on the network of the target person's family. NEPS pillar 4 surveys not only the assimilation and integration of the students themselves but also of their parents, for instance the frequency of visits to the country of origin. Furthermore, in addition to measuring the household's income and wealth, Pillar 5 concentrates on questions about the health of the students. Beyond that, there are also questions addressing concepts such as the assessment of social competencies of the students by their parents (see Chap. 9, this volume). Again, in order to focus on the specific situation in life, parents of 5th-grade students are asked more about schooling (Stage 4), whereas parents of 9th-grade students give more information about their support at this important transition point (Stage 6).

13.2.3 Contents of the Teacher Questionnaires

Four different types of questionnaire for teachers are used to obtain information in different areas and from different perspectives: (a) the general questionnaire for all teachers, (b) the class teacher questionnaire, (c) the German teacher questionnaire, and (d) the mathematics teacher questionnaire. If the class teachers are also the German or mathematics teachers, they are asked to complete both the general questionnaire and their specific questionnaire.

The general questionnaire for all teachers covers typically relevant information. It contains basic sociodemographic data (Pillar 3), data on the history of migration and native language (Pillar 4), as well as data on their professional biography (developed by Pillar 5). Furthermore, Pillar 2 inquires into completed and planned educational training and collects information on pedagogical ideals and concepts.

The questionnaires for the 5th- and 9th-grade class teachers are almost identical. However, because the upcoming transition in Grade 9 is such an important change, 9th-grade teachers are asked additional questions on how they prepare their students for the transition to the vocational track (developed by Stage 6). Moreover, both questionnaires collect information on classroom equipment as well as on the gender-specific (Pillar 2), social (Pillar 3), and ethnic composition of the class (Pillar 4).

The survey of German teachers is an important source of information for the specific research focus of Stage 4. Items tap the quality of teaching German—specifically with regard to teaching orthography and instruction to promote reading engagement.

13.2.4 Contents of the Questionnaires for Principals

Whereas class teachers are asked to provide information on the composition of the class and room equipment, principals are asked to provide such information on the entire school. Furthermore, information on the competition of the school with other schools in the regional context (Pillar 5) is requested. Support programs for students with a history of migration as well as for students facing career entry are surveyed by Pillar 4 and Stage 6.

13.3 Stage-Specific Research Questions: Theoretical Foundations and Modes of Assessment

13.3.1 Research Focus of Stage 4

The specific research focus of Stage 4 is on the interrelated development of reading and orthography competencies over the course of lower secondary education and the transition to upper secondary education. These competencies are vitally important at this stage of the educational career, because they are the foundation for learning and communicating in all school subjects. The general theoretical perspective from which we regard reading and writing and their development is the concept of literacy. This concept emphasizes the development and the functional-pragmatic contextualization of specific competence domains in terms of different environments in which they are acquired (e.g., UNESCO 2004). In line with this characterization, Stage 4 focuses on the development of literacy in reading and writing—competencies that enable individuals to understand and communicate ideas so that they can participate successfully in a literate society.

Reading competency is assessed within NEPS in the framework of Pillar 1 (see Chap. 4, this volume). Next to reading, competence in orthography also influences the students' educational careers decisively (Schneider et al. 2008). Linguistic findings on graphematics have changed the view on orthography and orthography instruction in recent years (Eisenberg 1995; Eisenberg and Fuhrhop 2007). These have shown that the aspect of norm fulfillment ceases to be of primary importance. In turn, the relation of orthography to other linguistic competencies is outlined. Learning orthography promotes linguistic awareness as well as reading competence and text competence (Blatt 2010; Hinney 1997; Schneider et al. 2008). In light of these studies, Stage 4 of NEPS is using graphematically based tests to perform longitudinal assessments of orthographic competence as a stage-specific domain.

In accordance with the concept of literacy applied in many large-scale assessments of educational achievement, we regard reading and writing literacy as including not only the students' competencies in terms of achievement, but also their domain-related strategy knowledge, self-perceptions, motivations, and behaviors (see Chap. 9, this volume). In addition, we assess the quality of instruction as an aspect of schooling—the central formal learning environment during this stage of the educational career—and its impact on the domains of reading and orthography (see Chap. 5, this volume).

As a theoretical framework to relate the competencies to domain-specific cognitive, affective, and behavioral attributes of the target persons, we refer to an extended expectancy-value model (Eccles 1983, 1994). This model can also be regarded as a point of reference for more specific analyses of students' reading engagement (Guthrie and Wigfield 2000) that focus on the interrelatedness of different aspects of reading distinguished by the extended expectancy-value model. With school being the formal learning environment of specific relevance for acquiring reading and writing literacy and engagement, we further look specifically at the quality of instruction as part of the formal learning environment (see Sect. 13.3.4).

From the perspective of studying the development of reading and orthography competencies, we regard a number of student-level variables that determine and mediate this development: domain-related strategies, self-concept, motivation, and behavior as well as social interactions with fellow students, family, and peers. Such constructs and other personal traits are also considered in the general assessment framework of NEPS (see for further information, Chap. 9, this volume). In Stage 4, these surveys are being expanded to investigate the more domain-specific variables in depth.

Numerous studies confirm that these variables correlate significantly with or are even predictors of achievement in both domains (see, for overviews on the domain of reading, Artelt et al. 2007; Möller and Schiefele 2004). Motivational predictors are of special relevance for educational research, because these constructs correlate substantially with reading achievement scores and are easier to promote through pedagogical intervention programs than, for example, the students' basic cognitive abilities or word decoding abilities (ibid.). One long-standing model for systematizing such predictors of achievement is provided by motivation theory. The expectancy-value model proposes that the individuals' choice of achievement tasks, their persistence on these tasks, their vigor in carrying them out, and their performance on them can be explained by their beliefs about how well they will do on the respective activity chosen, and the extent to which they value such activity (Atkinson 1957; Eccles 1983; Wigfield et al. 2009). Möller and Schiefele (2004) adapted Eccles' (1994) extended expectancy-value model to outline motivational determinants of reading achievement. As a theoretical framework, such an extended expectancy-value model offers an adequate foundation for analyzing achievement predictors in our target domains of reading and, similarly, orthography.

A model that allows us to combine the different student-level variables with the components of formal learning environments is the comprehensive model of educational effectiveness proposed by Creemers and Kyriakides (2008; see Fig. 13.1). The model does not capture the great diversity of formal and informal/nonformal learning environments described in Chap. 5 in this volume, but targets the most important formal learning environment of Stage 4, namely, instruction in schools. It distinguishes between student, classroom, and school levels and is finally output-oriented because the variables considered at the different levels are assumed to result in students' achievement. In order to combine the expectancy-value model with classroom and school variables, which are important for the development of students' literacy in lower secondary school, we apply this model to our assessments in Stage 4. As stated above, the expectancy-value model considers the learning process as a function of students' beliefs about how well they will perform on a specific task and how they value such an activity. Consequently, the model highlights the student level. Nonetheless, institutional settings also influence students' opportunities to learn and the amount of time spent learning, so that they also have an impact on the students' learning processes. Because NEPS focuses on following individual educational careers, the mechanisms between school and classroom variables are not the primary research interest. We focus on the impact of student and classroom variables on students' literacy (Fig. 13.1).

13.3.2 Test Instrument to Assess Orthographic Competence

Empirical results from cross-sectional studies at the end of elementary school show that 4th-grade students still have problems with German orthography (Böhme and Bremerich-Vos 2009; Löffler and Meyer-Schepers 2005; Stanat et al. 2017). A NEPS study gives insight into the competence structure of successful and less successful fourth graders (Blatt et al. 2016b).

According to the national assessment studies conducted by the Institute for Educational Quality Improvement (IQB) to monitor student achievement in the German Federal States in relation to the national educational standards, the mean orthographic competencies in Grade 4 were even lower in 2016 than in 2011 (Stanat et al. 2017). Orthographic problems

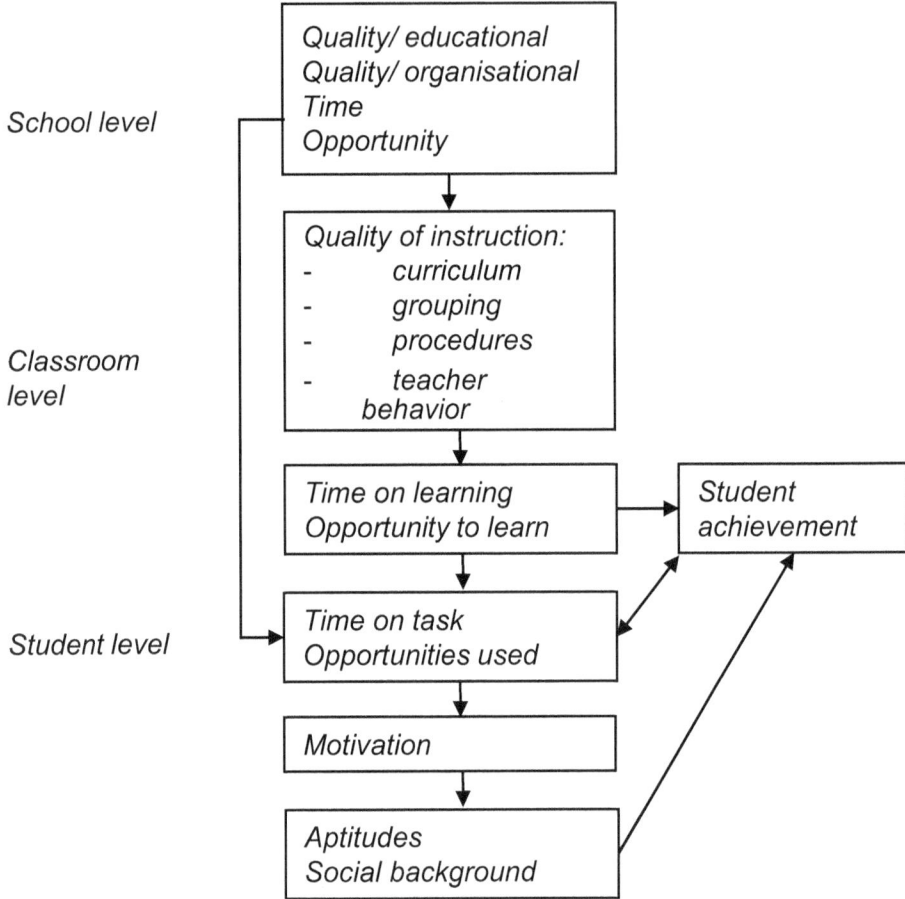

Fig. 13.1 The comprehensive model of educational effectiveness (cf. Creemers and Kyriakides 2008, p. 39)

seem to persist throughout secondary school and sometimes even intensify (summarized description: Prosch 2016, pp. 34–46). Results of orthographic studies in secondary school generally show only the mean values and therefore cannot reveal the orthographic problems of students specifically. There is a particular need for a theory-based framework of orthography as the basic concept for test construction.

Therefore, filling this gap in research is of vital importance, especially because in recent years, not only has there been a change in the educational view on orthography, but orthography has also become a focus of linguistic research. More recent linguistic results from the field of graphematics have pointed out that written language needs to be regarded as an autonomous system that has to be investigated independently before being related to spoken language (Eisenberg 1995; Eisenberg and Fuhrhop 2007). Previously, orthography was seen as dependent on spoken language and hence classified as unsystematic. In contrast, graphemic results stress the regularity of the core area of German orthography that determines 90% of native writing. Hinney (1997) emphasizes that the field of didactics needs to consider these findings and redefine orthographic concepts by focusing on regularities first before concentrating on irregular spellings. This will enable students to not only master but also gain an insight into the German orthographic system (Eisenberg 1995). Recent studies have shown that a teaching concept based on graphemic findings is successful for both fast and slow learners (Hein 2015). This clearly demonstrates how linguistic results have a strong impact on the fields of educational research and didactics. Therefore, the results can be used to develop a theory-based framework for test construction. Table 13.1 gives details on the five principles or dimensions according to the graphematics-based construct of orthography.

Construct validity has been investigated in several studies (Blatt et al. 2015, 2016a; Jarsinski 2014). Overall, dimensions correlate highly, although a multidimensional IRT model reveals a better model fit than a unidimensional model.

Statistical model comparisons show that the structure of competence changes during secondary school (Jarsinski 2014). Whereas in Grade 5, a five-dimensional model according to the five dimensions of the theoretical framework fits best, in Grades 7 and 9, the two principles of the core area merge to one dimension and the syntactic principle differentiates into two dimensions, a basic and an extended one. This is accompanied by learning progress and new contents.

After outlining the framework and the structure of orthography competence used for the NEPS orthography tests, we shall now present the tests in more detail. The tests were developed in developmental or pilot studies conducted in Grades 5, 6, 7, 8, and 9. The tests combine a cloze test and full sentences and have to be mastered in 25 min. Words are collected as whole words as well as being broken down into structural units according

Table 13.1 Overview of orthographic principles and respective skills

Principles of orthography	Skills
Phonographic and syllabic principle (core area)	Understanding the corresponding syllabic structure of written and spoken words
Morphological principle (core area)	Understanding the structure of words in inflected and derived forms (morphological stability) Understanding inflectional morphemes
Peripheral area	Identifying exceptions in spelling Knowing the correct spelling of foreign words
Word formation principle	Knowing parts of speech and derivational morphemes (i.e., for compounding)
Syntactic principle	Knowing and using syntactic structures for capitalization

Table 13.2 Content of the main study tests in Grades 5, 7, and 9 (Blatt and Prosch 2016, p. 66)

Study	Words (number of gaps and full sentences)	Orthographic principles (number of structural units)				
		Phonographic and syllabic principle	Morphological principle	Peripheral area	Word formation principle	Syntactic principle
Grade 5	61 (30 gaps/3 sentences)	53	49	23	71	39
Grade 7	103 (18 gaps/9 sentences)	61	73	40	103	87
Grade 9	95 (11 gaps/9 sentences)	54	72	44	105	85

to the five principles of the framework (see Table 13.1). Table 13.2 shows the contents of the main study tests in Grades 5, 7, and 9.

The test content changes in accordance with the guidelines of the federal states for school content. Therefore, the number of structural units also changes (Jarsinski 2014). Especially the regular core area of orthography decreases, whereas peripheral spellings and the syntactic principle are used more frequently by adding foreign words, punctuation, and capitalization. The longitudinal testing is based on an anchor item design (see Table 13.3).

In general, more difficult items (solution frequency of about 44% and below) were chosen as anchor items in order to meet the demands of the higher grades. Altogether, the test words had to provide sufficient information on all subskills to meet the conditions for an adequate analysis.

The statistic test criteria reliability was surveyed by default (Blatt et al. 2017, p. 13). For all grades, the reliability is between 0.94 and 0.96 on the whole-word level and

Table 13.3 Content of the main study tests in Grades 5, 7, and 9 (Prosch 2016, p. 66)

Anchor items						
Study	Number of structural units	Grade 5	Grade 6	Grade 7	Grade 8	Grade 9
Grade 5	234	100% (234)				
Grade 7	364	26.1% (95)	36.8% (134)	37.1% (135)		
Grade 9 (Main study)	360	18.6% (68)	23.1% (83)	22.2% (80)	19.7% (71)	16.1% (58)

between 0.93 and 0.94 on the structural unit level. With these high values, the tests can be assumed to be reliable. Validity was controlled by comparisons with the grade in German classes. For example, the correlation between the mean value of the whole word and the grade in German classes for the main study was $r = .58$ in Grade 5 (proof of own source). To assure objectivity during the survey, test instructions and test words and sentences were standardized by having them recorded by a professional speaker and played back during the survey. In addition, the surveys were conducted by trained administrators.

Experience has shown that a twofold correction is useful in order to account for all student mistakes (Blatt et al. 2011). The data were coded with a tool developed in cooperation with the Leibniz Institute for Educational Research and Educational Information (DIPF) (Frahm 2013). This software codes the structural units of a word as being wrong or right before allocating them to the related subskill. Coding with this tool is a lot less time consuming than a manual coding process, and it also proves to be more objective. Altogether, data analyses have different foci. They determine the orthographic competence of the students, examine quality criteria for the test, and analyze the relationship between competence and intervening variables such as quality of instruction or background variables.

A multidimensional one-parameter IRT model is used to estimate item difficulties and students' abilities. Qualitative analyses of the spelling variations also give further information on the students' insights into the regularities of the orthography system.

This longitudinal survey of orthographic competence in secondary school has already delivered new findings and conclusions, especially from doctoral research and further studies (Blatt and Prosch 2016; Blatt et al. 2016a, 2015; Frahm 2013; Jarsinski 2014; Prosch 2016). The Scientific Use files for Grades 5, 7, and 9 provide data for the scientific community engaging in research on orthography in secondary school (Blatt et al. 2017).

13.3.3 Reading Engagement

Student engagement in school and learning is a multidimensional construct that can be defined generally as participation in and commitment to a set of activities involving combinations of affective, cognitive, and behavioral processes (Fredricks et al. 2004; Reschly and Christenson 2012). In the domain of reading, engaged students are motivated to read, strategic in their approaches to reading, knowledgeable in their construction of meaning from text, and socially interactive in collaborative reading practices and exchanges on materials read (Guthrie et al. 2012).

The construct of reading engagement is highly relevant for educational research and practice as it is associated positively with reading achievement and the engagement dimensions are malleable by instructional practices (Guthrie et al. 2012; Wigfield et al. 2008, 2017). In addition, findings from large-scale assessments indicate that high levels of reading engagement may "compensate" for social background disadvantages. The National Assessment of Educational Progress in the United States has shown that highly engaged readers have higher achievement scores than the less engaged at each of the three ages surveyed (9, 13, and 17 years). The same national data indicate that highly engaged readers from low-SES families have higher achievement scores than less engaged readers from high-SES backgrounds (Campbell et al. 1997; Guthrie et al. 2001). A reanalysis of PISA 2000 data shows similar results internationally for the 15-year-old age group (Kirsch et al. 2002), and a reanalysis with PIRLS 2006 data reveals similar findings for 4th graders in Germany and Sweden (Goy et al. 2009). In view of the German education system, these findings are of considerable relevance, because international comparisons reveal a non-neglectable relation between students' socioeconomic status and their reading achievement, both at the end of elementary education (e.g., Hußmann et al. 2017) and in 15-year-old students (e.g., Ehmke and Jude 2010).

While the complex composition of the engagement construct is considered crucial for its power to explain educational success, the developmental and reciprocal dynamics of the engagement dimensions and their relations to classroom practices and student achievement as well as background variables pose research challenges (Eccles and Wang 2012). This emphasizes the need for multifaceted, multilevel, and longitudinal studies (ibid; see also Russell et al. 2005).

In Stage 4 of NEPS, we followed the definition of reading engagement proposed by Lutz et al. (2006) that distinguishes between four dimensions and adds a social component next to the affective, cognitive, and behavioral ones. The authors do this in line with earlier work on reading engagement (Guthrie and Wigfield 2000), to emphasize that exchange on reading experiences with relevant others in a "community of literacy" is an important part of student engagement in reading. Based on this definition, we included a selection of variables on intrinsic reading motivation (distinguishing between reading for interest and reading for enjoyment) as well as on the reading self-concept in the student questionnaires. Items were adapted from Möller and Bonerad's (2007) Habitual Reading Motivation Questionnaire. These items were complemented with variables on the students' reading strategies (adapted from the Berlin Reading Strategy Inventory; McElvany and Richter 2009), on their reading behaviors in terms of time spent reading and diversity of materials read (developed jointly by Stage 4 and Pillar 3), as well as on their social reading interactions in terms of communicating about materials read (adapted from PIRLS; Bos et al. 2010b).

13.3.4 Quality of Instruction

The diversity and quality of learning opportunities over the life course is part of the survey program of Pillar 2 (see Chap. 5, this volume). The most important formal learning environment in Stage 4 is the instruction students receive in schools. At first glance, syntheses and meta-analyses of studies on instruction might lead to the conclusion that instruction is well researched (Fraser et al. 1987; Scheerens and Bosker 1997; Seidel and Shavelson 2007; Wang et al. 1993). However, the findings from such reviews often do not agree, and the question which teaching variables can be attributed to students' literacy has yet to be answered satisfactorily in light of the great complexity of instruction. In their recent meta-analysis, Seidel and Shavelson (2007) reviewed studies carried out during the past decade. Only about 15 German studies were suitable for their analysis (i.e., they did not focus on students with learning disabilities and made at least some adjustment for students' preconditions). Consequently, there is a need to investigate instruction and its effect on students' literacy in depth (Fig. 13.2).

Although the limitations of cross-sectional designs for drawing causal inferences are well known, most studies in the above-mentioned meta-analyses were cross-sectional. Particularly with respect to instruction, Rowan et al. (2002) have shown that it is important to be aware of this issue. Otherwise it is likely that the explanatory power of teaching variables remains underestimated or undiscovered (ibid.). In recent theories on formal learning, different school settings and teacher behavior in classrooms are related to student learning by asking how schools and teachers succeed in fostering students to become self-regulated learners (e.g., Boekaerts 1997). Therefore, we employ Bolhuis' (2003) model on the components of lifelong learning to operationalize instruction. Seidel and Shavelson (2007) adopted this model and developed it further for their meta-analysis (see Seidel and Shavelson 2007, p. 461).

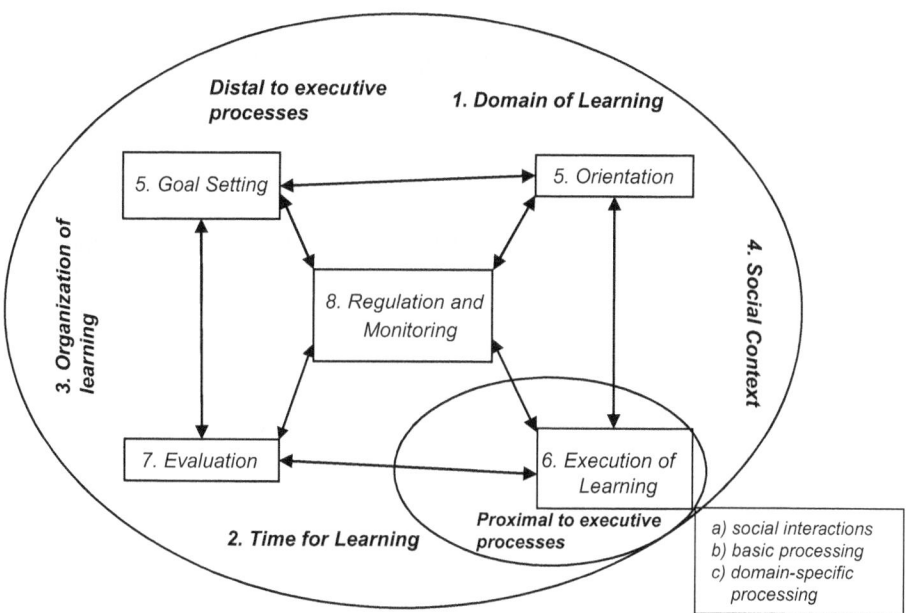

Fig. 13.2 Model of teaching and learning components (see Seidel and Shavelson 2007, p. 461)

In contrast to the theoretical models from Scheerens and Bosker's (1997) previous meta-analysis, Bolhuis' model proves to be more applicable and useful for the analysis. It views learning as a self-regulated, lifelong, and multidimensional process. First, learning is considered to be domain-specific: Therefore, assessments focus on instruction in German-language classes and not on all the instruction students receive in different subjects. Furthermore, the model regards the time for learning: In the school context, this is the minutes per lesson and the number of lessons per week. The social context (i.e., among peers and with the teacher) and the organization of learning are further dimensions that frame the learning process. The learning process itself is characterized by goal setting/orientation, ongoing evaluation and permanent regulation. Teachers set goals, encourage their students to either make these goals their own or set their own goals. Making use of formative and summative assessments can help teachers to give specific feedback or support students. Finally, the actual learning process comprises specific methods of instruction, didactics, and the social setting (e.g., teacher-centered or student-centered instruction). Table 13.4 lists the items administered in Starting Cohorts 3 and 4. The different dimensions can also be considered as subdimensions from the SSCO model (see Chap. 5, this volume) and therefore correspond with the general survey program from Pillar 2. Next to the basic dimensions of instruction described above, the questionnaires also include specific questions on teachers' attitudes and teaching behavior with respect to orthography and how they foster students' reading engagement.

To accommodate the great complexity of the metaconstruct of instruction, both students and teachers are being surveyed. Research on instruction has shown clearly that different perspectives on instruction do not necessarily agree (e.g., Clausen 2002; Kunter and Baumert 2006). Analyses revealed, for instance, specific conceptual structures, with teachers elaborating on the use of tasks and methods, and students focusing on their teacher's support in personal and learning matters. These research insights have been used to construct the NEPS questionnaires so that they make use of the specific validity given by different groups of raters.

Another crucial issue is the frequency of assessments. Instruction changes, because teachers adapt their behavior to the particular class; or classes have different teachers from one year to another. Therefore, instruction is surveyed annually. Such a tracking of German classes makes it possible to analyze the cumulative effect of instruction on students' literacy.

13.4 Conclusion

One major aim of NEPS is to map individual educational trajectories. This certainly is a major challenge. On the one hand, both tests and questionnaires have to be comparable throughout the course of the study, whereas, on the other hand, they need to be adequate for each target population. This implies the need to establish competence tests in several domains as well as to carefully plan contents that are interesting for the target population

Table 13.4 Instruments on instructional quality in German language instruction

Constructs	Items	Questionnaire	Sources
Time for learning	2 (ed0001h_D, ed0001m_D)	German teacher	D'Agostino (2000)
Organization of learning	4 (td0032a-d)	Student	Ditton and Merz (2000), Wagner et al. (2009)
Goal setting and orientation	5 (td0033a-e)	Student	Ryan and Patrick (2001)
Social context—perceived teacher autonomy support	3 (td0034a-c)	Student	Hardre and Reeve (2003)
Social context—promoting interactions	3 (td0035a-c)	Student	Ryan and Patrick (2001)
Goal setting and orientation	3 (td0036a-c)	Student	Ditton and Merz (2000), Wagner et al. (2009)
Execution of learning—social interaction	10 (ed0004a-j)	German teacher	Bos et al. (2005), Wagner et al. (2009)
Execution of learning—basic processing—cognitive activation	11 (ed0005a-k)	German teacher	Applebee et al. (2003)
Execution of learning—basic processing—cognitively challenging tasks	4 (ed0006a-d)	German teacher	Kunter and Baumert (2006)
Evaluation—type	10 (ed0007a-j)	German teacher	Bos et al. (2005), Wagner et al. (2009)
Evaluation—purposes	40 (ed0108a-ed0408j)	German teacher	Bos et al. (2005), Wagner et al. (2009)
Regulation and monitoring	8 (ed0009a-g)	German teacher	Ditton and Merz (2000)

Note. All instruments listed in this table were administered consistently in Survey Waves 1 to 5 of Starting Cohort 3. Further items on instructional quality were administered occasionally, in other starting cohorts, or in other subjects

and their current personal situation as well as informative for researchers who want to obtain significant research findings. For Stage 4, only a few studies provided sufficient information on tests and constructs for the samples being assessed (see Sect. 13.1). In addition, the age and skills of the target population have to be taken into consideration, because students should not be overtested. For test development, this means, for example, that the tests must be oriented toward school-related content. For orthography, new content has to be considered for each school year. Therefore, the underlying framework for orthography indicated the need for continuous adjustments.

Furthermore, because the students are sampled in their institutional contexts (schools and classes, see Chap. 3 in this issue) and the German school system offers a variety of possibilities to drop out of this context (e.g., upward and downward mobility, grade retention, or grade skipping), students who leave their institutional context are rather difficult to track.

In terms of time management, useful focal points have to be determined each year in order to provide all the information needed on secondary school within a limited testing time. Therefore, Stage 4 needs to collect constructs and items from all NEPS pillars, check their suitability for the target population, and then provide a cohesive concept. All these steps need to be conducted while bearing in mind the comparability throughout all stages and the need for instruments that are attractive for the persons surveyed. Last but not least, statistical analyses need to be planned, and the longitudinal survey must be designed to gain a maximum insight into the life course of the target population.

All these considerations have to be addressed consistently over time, because the multicohort-sequence design (see Chap. 3) involves the transition of younger cohorts (e.g., Starting Cohort 2, see Chap. 12) into Stage 4.

In summary, the complex study design poses challenges but certainly also offers great opportunities for research as outlined in this chapter. With the multiperspective view on learning environments in schools as well as the information on nonformal and informal ecologies, the surveys conducted in Stage 4 offer an opportunity to gain insight into the effects of multiple possible influences on the development of competencies as well as on the decision processes of subgroups (e.g., students with a migration background, students with low SES) and on the monetary and nonmonetary gains linked to individual educational trajectories. The considerable scientific use of the data of Starting Cohorts 3 and 4 that is beginning to show can be taken as an indicator of the research opportunities gained: As of April 2018, there are 158 published documents (including survey papers and technical reports) based on the surveys conducted in Stage 4 and Stages 5 and 6 (see Chaps. 14 and 15).

References

Applebee, A. N., Langer, J. A., Nystrand, M., & Gamoran, A. (2003). Discussion-based approaches to developing understanding: Classroom instruction and student performance in middle and high school English. *American Educational Research Journal, 40*(3), 685–730.

Artelt, C., McElvany, N., Christmann, N., Richter, T., Groeben, N., Köster, J., Schneider, W., Stanat, P., Ostermeier, C., Schiefele, U., Valtin, R., & Ring, K. (2007). *Förderung von Lesekompetenz. Expertise* (Reprint). Bonn, Germany: Bundesministerium für Bildung und Forschung.

Atkinson, J. W. (1957). Motivational determinants of risk-taking behavior. *Psychological Review, 64*, 359–372.

Baumert, J., Trautwein, U., & Artelt, C. (2003). Schulumwelten – institutionelle Bedingungen des Lehrens und Lernens. In J. Baumert, C. Artelt, E. Klieme, J. Neubrand, M. Prenzel, U. Schiefele, W. Schneider, K.-J. Tillmann, & M. Weiß (Eds.), *PISA 2000: Ein differenzierter Blick auf die Länder der Bundesrepublik Deutschland* (pp. 261–331). Opladen, Germany: Leske + Budrich.

Blatt, I. (2010). Sprachsystematische Rechtschreibdidaktik: Konzept, Materialien, Tests. In U. Bredel, A. Müller, & G. Hinney (Eds.), Schriftkompetenz und Schriftsystem: linguistisch, empirisch, didaktisch (pp. 101–132). Berlin, Germany: de Gruyter.

Blatt, I., Frahm, S., Prosch, A., Jarsinski, S., & Voss, A. (2015). Kompetenzmodellierung im Kontext des Nationalen Bildungspanels (NEPS) am Beispiel der Rechtschreibkompetenz. In U. Riegel, S. Schubert, G. Siebert-Ott, & K. Macha (Eds.), *Kompetenzmodellierung und Kompetenzmessung in den Fachdidaktiken* (pp. 43–60). Münster, Germany: Waxmann.

Blatt, I., Jarsinski, S., & Prosch, A. (2017). *NEPS Technical Report for orthography: Scaling results of Starting Cohort 3 in Grades 5, 7, and 9* (NEPS Survey Papers No. 15). Bamberg, Germany: Leibniz-Institut für Bildungsverläufe, Nationales Bildungspanel.

Blatt, I., & Prosch, A. (2016). Rechtschreibkompetenz in der Sekundarstufe I: Ausgewählte Ergebnisse aus der Längsschnittstudie Nationales Bildungspanel (NEPS). In M. Krelle & W. Senn (Eds.), *Qualitäten von Deutschunterricht* (pp. 109–138). Stuttgart, Germany: Fillibach bei Klett.

Blatt, I., Prosch, A., & Frahm, S. (2016a). Erfassung der Rechtschreibkompetenz in der Längsschnittstudie „Nationales Bildungspanel": Studiendesign und -ergebnisse. In B. Mesch & C. Noack (Eds.), *System, Norm und Gebrauch – drei Seiten einer Medaille? Orthographische Kompetenz und Performanz im Spannungsfeld zwischen System, Norm und Empirie* (pp. 53–74). Baltmannsweiler, Germany: Schneider Verlag Hohengehren.

Blatt, I., Prosch, A., & Lorenz, C. (2016b). Erhebung der Rechtschreibkompetenz am Ende der Grundschulzeit: Ausgewählte Ergebnisse aus einer Großpilotstudie im Rahmen des Nationalen Bildungspanels. *Zeitschrift für Grundschulforschung, 9*(2), 125–138.

Blatt, I., Voss, A., Kowalski, K., & Jarsinski, S. (2011). Messung von Rechtschreibleistung und empirische Kompetenzmodellierung. In U. Bredel (Ed.), *Weiterführender Orthographieunterricht. DTP 5*. Baltmannsweiler, Germany: Schneider Verlag Hohengehren.

Blossfeld, H.-P., Schneider T., & Doll, J. (2009). Methodological advantages of panel studies: Designing the new National Educational Panel Study (NEPS) in Germany. *Journal for Educational Research Online, 1*(1), 10–32.

Boekaerts, M. (1997). Self-regulated learning: A new concept embraced by researchers, policymakers, educators, teachers, and students. *Learning and Instruction, 7*(2), 161–186.

Böhme, K. & Bremerich-Vos, A. (2009). Diagnostik der Rechtschreibkompetenz in der Grundschule – Konstruktprüfung mittels Fehler- und Dimensionsanalysen. In D. Granzer, O. Köller & A. Bremerich-Vos (Hrsg.), Bildungsstandards Deutsch und Mathematik: Leistungsmessung in der Grundschule (S. 330–356). Weinheim: Beltz.

Bolhuis, S. (2003). Towards process-oriented teaching for self-directed lifelong learning: A multi-dimensional perspective. *Learning and Instruction, 13*(3), 327–347.

Bos, W., Bonsen, M., & Gröhlich, C. (Eds.). (2009). *KESS 7—Kompetenzen und Einstellungen von Schülerinnen und Schülern an Hamburger Schulen zu Beginn der Jahrgangsstufe 7*. Münster, Germany: Waxmann.

Bos, W., & Gröhlich, C. (Eds.). (2009). Longitudinal assessments and panel studies in educational research [Special issue]. *Journal for Educational Research Online, 1*(1).

Bos, W., Gröhlich, C., Guill, K., Scharenberg, K., & Wendt, H. (2010). Ziele und Anlage der Studie KESS 8. In W. Bos, C. Gröhlich, K. Guill, S. Ivanov, P. May, R. Nikolova, L. Scharenberg, & H. Wendt (Eds.), *KESS 8. Kompetenzen und Einstellungen von Schülerinnen und Schülern – Jahrgangsstufe 8* (pp. 1–12). Hamburg, Germany: Behörde für Schule und Berufsbildung.

Bos, W., Lankes, E.-M., Prenzel, M., Schwippert, K., Valtin, R., Voss, A., & Walter, G. (Eds.). (2005). *IGLU. Skalenhandbuch zur Dokumentation der Erhebungsinstrumente*. Münster, Germany: Waxmann.

Bos, W., Strietholt, R., Goy, M., Stubbe, T. C., Tarelli, I., & Hornberg, S. (2010). *IGLU 2006. Dokumentation der Erhebungsinstrumente*. Münster, Germany: Waxmann.

Campbell, J. R., Voelkl, K. E., & Donahue, P. L. (1997). *NAEP 1996 trends in academic progress* (NCES Publication No. 97-985r). Washington, DC: U.S. Department of Education.

Clausen, M. (2002). *Unterrichtsqualität: Eine Frage der Perspektive? Empirische Analysen zur Übereinstimmung, Konstrukt- und Kriteriumsvalidität*. Münster, Germany: Waxmann.

Creemers, B. P. M., & Kyriakides, L. (2008). *The dynamics of educational effectiveness*. London, England: Routledge.

D'Agostino, J. V. (2000). Instructional and school effects on students' longitudinal reading and mathematics achievements. *School Effectiveness and School Improvement, 11*(2), 197–235.

Ditton, H., & Merz, D. (2000). *Qualität von Schule und Unterricht. Kurzbericht über erste Ergebnisse einer Untersuchung an bayerischen Schulen*. Mimeo.

Eccles J. S. (1983). Expectancies, values, and academic behaviors. In J. T. Spence (Ed.), *Achievement and achievement motives. Psychological and sociological approaches* (pp. 75–146). San Francisco, CA: Freeman.

Eccles, J. S. (1994). Understanding women's educational and occupational choices. Applying the Eccles et al. model of achievement-related choices. *Psychology of Women Quarterly, 18*, 585–609.

Eccles, J., & Wang, M.-T. (2012) So what is student engagement anyway? In S. L. Christenson, A. L. Reschly, & C. Wylie (Eds.), *Handbook of research on student engagement* (pp. 133–145). New York, NY: Springer.

Ehmke, T., & Jude, N. (2010). Soziale Herkunft und Kompetenzerwerb. In Klieme, E., Artelt, C., Hartig, J., Jude, N., Köller, O., Prenzel, M., Schneider, W., & Stanat, P. (Eds.), *PISA 2009. Bilanz nach einem Jahrzehnt* (pp. 231–254). Münster, Germany: Waxmann.

Eisenberg, P. (1995). Der Buchstabe und die Schriftstruktur des Wortes. In *Der große Duden. Band 4: Die Grammatik* (5th ed., pp. 56–84). Mannheim, Germany: Dudenverlag.

Eisenberg, P., & Fuhrhop, N. (2007). Schulgraphematik und Orthographie. *Zeitschrift für Sprachwissenschaft, 26*(Jubiläumsheft), 15–41.

Frahm, S. (2013). *Computerbasierte Testung der Rechtschreibleistung in Klasse fünf – eine empirische Studie zu Mode-Effekten im Kontext des Nationalen Bildungspanels*. Berlin, Germany: Logos.

Fraser, B. J., Walberg, H. J., Welch, W. W., & Hattie, J. A. (1987). Syntheses of educational productivity research. *International Journal of Educational Research, 11*(2), 147–252.

Fredricks, J. A., Blumenfeld, P. C., & Paris, A. H. (2004). School engagement: Potential of the concept, state of the evidence. *Review of Educational Research, 74*, 59–109.

Goy, M., Gröhlich, C., Strietholt, R., Stubbe, T. C., Kanders, M., & Bos, W. (2010). Panelstudien als Antworten auf Forschungsdesiderate in der Sekundarstufe I. In W. Bos, N. Berkemeyer, H.-G. Holtappels, N. McElvany, & R. Schulz-Zander (Eds.), *Jahrbuch der Schulentwicklung. Daten, Beispiele, Perspektiven* (Vol. 16, pp. 37–70). Weinheim, Germany: Juventa.

Goy, M., Strietholt, R., & Bos, W. (2009, September). Reading engagement of fourth-grade students. Results from PIRLS 2006 for students from different socio-economic backgrounds. In T. Plomp, P. Kupari, W. Bos, & M. Goy (Chair Persons), *Towards explaining achievement: Findings from international comparative achievement studies*. Symposium conducted at the European Conference on Educational Research (ECER 2009), University of Vienna, Austria.

Guthrie, J. T., Schafer, W. D., & Huang, C.-W. (2001). Benefits of opportunity to read and balanced instruction on the NAEP. *Journal of Educational Research, 94*(3), 145–162.

Guthrie, J. T., & Wigfield, A. (2000). Engagement and motivation in reading. In M. Kamil, P. Mosenthal, D. Pearson, & R. Barr (Eds.), *Handbook of reading research* (Vol. III, pp. 403–422). Mahwah, NJ: Lawrence Erlbaum Associates.

Guthrie, J. T., Wigfield, A. & You, W. (2012). Instructional contexts for engagement and achievement in reading. In S. L. Christenson, A. L. Reschly, & C. Wylie (Eds.), *Handbook of research on student engagement* (pp. 601–634). New York, NY: Springer.

Hardre, P. L., & Reeve, J. (2003). A motivational model of rural students' intentions to persist in, versus drop out of, high school. *Journal of Educational Psychology*, 95(2), 347–356.

Hein, C. (2015). *Untersuchung von Unterrichtsbedingungen zu Erwerb und Entwicklung der Schriftkompetenz. Ergebnisse einer Interventionsstudie mit Kontrollklassen an einer Hamburger Grundschule von Klasse 1 bis 3*. Berlin, Germany: Logos.

Hinney, G. (1997). *Neubestimmung von Lerninhalten für den Rechtschreibunterricht. Ein fachdidaktischer Beitrag zur Schriftaneignung als Problemlöseprozeß*. Frankfurt a. M., Germany: Lang.

Hußmann, A., Stubbe, T. C., & Kasper, D. (2017). Soziale Herkunft und Lesekompetenzen von Schülerinnen und Schülern. In A. Hußmann, H. Wendt, W. Bos, A. Bremerich-Vos, D. Kasper, E.-M. Lankes, N. McElvany, T. C. Stubbe, & R. Valtin (Eds.), *IGLU 2016. Lesekompetenzen von Grundschulkindern in Deutschland im internationalen Vergleich* (pp. 195–217). Münster, Germany: Waxmann.

Jarsinski, S. (2014). *Quantitative Datenanalyse zur längsschnittlichen Erfassung der Rechtschreibkompetenz in NEPS unter besonderer Berücksichtigung der Kompetenzstruktur und der Einflussfaktoren*. Dissertation. Technische Universität Dortmund, Dortmund, Germany.

Kirsch, I. S., de Jong, J., Lafontaine, D., McQueen, J., Mendelovits, J., & Monseur, C. (2002). *Reading for change. Performance and engagement across countries. Results from PISA 2000*. Paris, France: OECD.

Kunter, M., & Baumert, J. (2006). Who is the expert? Construct and criteria validity of student and teacher ratings of instruction. *Learning Environments Research*, 9(3), 231–251.

Lin, N., Fu, Y., & Hsung R. (2001). The position generator: Measurement techniques for investigations of social capital. In N. Lin, K. Cook, & R. Burt (Eds.), *Social capital: Theory and research* (pp. 57–84). New York, NY: de Gruyter.

Löffler, I., & Meyer-Schepers, U. (2005). Orthographische Kompetenzen: Ergebnisse qualitativer Fehleranalysen, insbesondere bei schwachen Rechtschreibern. In W. Bos, E.-M. Lankes, M. Prenzel, K. Schwippert, R. Valtin, & G. Walther (Eds.), *IGLU. Vertiefende Analysen zu Leseverständnis, Rahmenbedingungen und Zusatzstudien* (pp. 81–108). Münster, Germany: Waxmann.

Lutz, S. L., Guthrie, J. T., & Davis, M. H. (2006). Scaffolding for engagement in elementary school reading instruction. *Journal of Educational Research*, 100, 3–20.

McElvany, N., & Richter, T. (2009). *Das Berliner Lesestrategie-Inventar (BLSI): Konzeption und Überprüfung der Objektivität, Reliabilität und Validität*. Unpublished manuscript, Max-Planck-Institute for Human Development, Berlin, and University of Cologne, Germany.

Möller, J., & Bonerad, E.-M. (2007). Fragebogen zur habituellen Lesemotivation. *Psychologie in Erziehung und Unterricht*, 54, 259–267.

Möller, J., & Schiefele, U. (2004). Motivationale Grundlagen der Lesekompetenz. In U. Schiefele, C. Artelt, W. Schneider, & P. Stanat (Eds.), *Struktur, Entwicklung und Förderung von Lesekompetenz. Vertiefende Analysen im Rahmen von PISA 2000* (pp. 101–124). Wiesbaden, Germany: VS Verlag für Sozialwissenschaften.

Prosch, A. (2016). *Entwicklung von Rechtschreibkompetenz. Differentielle Analysen mit NEPS-Daten der Haupterhebungen in den Klassenstufen fünf und sieben sowie der Entwicklungsstudien in den Klassenstufen sechs und sieben*. Berlin, Germany: Logos.

Reschly, A. L., & Christenson, S. L. (2012) Jingle, jangle, and conceptual haziness: Evolution and future directions of the engagement construct. In S. L. Christenson, A. L. Reschly, & C. Wylie (Eds.), *Handbook of research on student engagement* (pp. 3–20). New York, NY: Springer.

Rowan, B., Correnti, R., & Miller, R. J. (2002). What large-scale survey research tells us about teacher effects on student achievement: Insights from the "Prospects" study of elementary schools. *Teachers College Record, 104*(8), 1525–1567.

Russell, V. J., Ainley, M., & Frydenberg, E. (2005). *Schooling issues digest. Student motivation and engagement.* Canberra, Australia: Australian Government, Department of Education, Service and Training.

Ryan, A. M., & Patrick, H. (2001). The classroom social environment and changes in adolescents' motivation and engagement during middle school. *American Educational Research Journal, 38*(2), 437–460.

Scheerens, J., & Bosker, R. J. (1997). *The foundations of educational effectiveness.* Oxford, England: Pergamon.

Schneider, W., Marx, H., & Hasselhorn, M. (Eds.). (2008). *Diagnostik von Rechtschreibleistungen und -kompetenz.* Göttingen, Germany: Hogrefe.

Seidel, T., & Shavelson, R. J. (2007). Teaching effectiveness research in the past decade: The role of theory and research design in disentangling meta-analysis results. *Review of Educational Research, 77*(4), 454–499.

Sixt, M., Goy, M., & Besuch, G. (2016). The concept of individual retracking in NEPS. Approach, practice, and first empirical evidence from Starting Cohorts 3 and 4. In H.-P. Blossfeld, J. von Maurice, M. Bayer & J. Skopek (Eds.), *Methodological issues of longitudinal surveys. The example of the National Educational Panel Study* (pp. 111–132). Wiesbaden, Germany: Springer VS.

Stanat, P., Schipolowski, S., Rjosk, C., Weirich, S., & Haag, N. (Eds.). (2017). *IQB-Bildungstrend 2016. Kompetenzen in den Fächern Deutsch und Mathematik am Ende der 4. Jahrgangsstufe im zweiten Ländervergleich.* Münster, Germany: Waxmann.

UNESCO (2004). *The plurality of literacy and its implications for policies and programmes.* Paris, France: UNESCO.

Wagner, W., Helmke, A., & Rösner, E. (2009). *Deutsch Englisch Schülerleistungen International. Dokumentation der Erhebungsinstrumente für Schülerinnen und Schüler, Eltern und Lehrkräfte.* Frankfurt am Main, Germany: GFPF/DIPF.

Wang, M. C., Haertel, G. D., & Walberg, H. J. (1993). Toward a knowledge base for school learning. *Review of Educational Research, 63*(3), 249–294.

Wigfield, A., Gladstone, J., & Turci, L. (2017). Development of children's ability beliefs and values and school-based interventions to improve them. In F. Guay, H. W. Marsh, D. M. McInerney, & R. Craven (Eds.), *SELF – Driving positive psychology and wellbeing* (pp. 283–308). Charlotte, NC: Information Age Publishing.

Wigfield, A., Guthrie, J. T., Perencevich, K. C., Taboada, A., Klauda, S. L., McRae, A., & Barbosa, P. (2008). The role of reading engagement in mediating effects of reading comprehension instruction on reading outcomes. *Psychology in the Schools, 45*, 432–445.

Wigfield, A., Tonks, S., & Klauda, S. L. (2009). Expectancy-value theory. In K. R. Wentzel & A. Wigfield (Eds.), *Handbook of motivation at school* (pp. 55–75). New York, NY: Routledge.

14 Upper Secondary Education in Academic School Tracks and the Transition from School to Postsecondary Education and the Job Market

Wolfgang Wagner, Michaela Kropf, Jochen Kramer, Julia Schilling, Karin Berendes, Ricarda Albrecht, Nicolas Hübner, Sven Rieger, Anna Bachsleitner, Josefine Lühe, Gabriel Nagy, Oliver Lüdtke, Kathrin Jonkmann, Sonja Gruner, Kai Maaz and Ulrich Trautwein

Abstract

In Stage 5 of the German National Educational Panel Study (NEPS), we are focusing on upper secondary education in academic school tracks and the subsequent transitions. We give an overview of prior empirical studies of the upper secondary level and describe a number of unresolved general research questions that are being focused on in Stage 5. These questions mainly address the comparison of traditional and non-traditional pathways to the *Abitur* (the general qualification for university entrance),

---

W. Wagner (✉) · K. Berendes · N. Hübner · S. Rieger · U. Trautwein
University of Tübingen, Tübingen, Germany
E-Mail: wolfgang.wagner@uni-tuebingen.de

K. Berendes
E-Mail: karin.berendes@uni-tuebingen.de

N. Hübner
E-Mail: nicolas.huebner@uni-tuebingen.de

S. Rieger
E-Mail: sven.rieger@uni-tuebingen.de

U. Trautwein
E-Mail: ulrich.trautwein@uni-tuebingen.de

M. Kropf · A. Bachsleitner · J. Lühe · K. Maaz
DIPF | Leibniz Institute for Research and Information in Education, Berlin, Germany
E-Mail: kropf@dipf.de

A. Bachsleitner
E-Mail: bachsleitner@dipf.de

J. Lühe
E-Mail: luehe@dipf.de

the academic achievement levels of *Abitur* students (in different school types), social disparities (in traditional and nontraditional *Gymnasium*), and how well achievement indicators (school grades, competencies, *Abitur* certificate) predict students' further development. Although the NEPS research instrument is very broad, these guiding questions are central for its development. In addition to the panel study, Stage 5 is implementing two supplementary studies to reflect changes due to reforms of the *Gymnasium* and their consequences for the interpretation of NEPS longitudinal data. One study focuses on the organizational reform in Thuringia; the other on the reduction in the number of years of schooling for the *Abitur* (G8 reform) in Baden-Wuerttemberg. Both studies are described in some detail. The chapter closes with a short summary of the valuable contributions of NEPS in Stage 5.

Keywords

Education · General qualification for university entrance · Panel study School reform · Upper secondary education

K. Maaz
E-Mail: maaz@dipf.de

J. Kramer
Türkische Gemeinde in Baden-Württemberg e.V., Berlin, Germany
E-Mail: jochen.kramer@tgbw.de

J. Schilling
Landratsamt Forchheim, Forchheim, Germany
E-Mail: julia.schilling@lra-fo.de

R. Albrecht
Humboldt-Universität zu Berlin, Berlin, Germany
E-Mail: ricarda.albrecht@hu-berlin.de

G. Nagy · O. Lüdtke
(IPN) Leibniz Institute for Science and Mathematics Education at Kiel University, Kiel, Germany
E-Mail: nagy@ipn.uni-kiel.de

O. Lüdtke
E-Mail: oluedtke@ipn.uni-kiel.de

K. Jonkmann
University of Hagen, Hagen, Germany
E-Mail: kathrin.jonkmann@fernuni-hagen.de

S. Gruner
Würzburg, Germany

14.1 Introduction

In Germany, students must acquire specific school-leaving certificates if they are to enter postsecondary education at the college/university level ("higher education"). This access to higher education has been broadened over the last decades, with several alternative routes leading to the necessary certificates. However, the highest and most attractive school-leaving certificate is still the *Abitur* that provides access to the greatest range of higher education. In fact, the *Abitur* occupies the central role, and 80% of freshmen in Germany possess this qualification (winter semester 2011/12; at universities, this is even 96%—Scheller et al. 2013). The majority of young adults acquire their *Abitur* at the upper secondary level of a *Gymnasium*. Consequently, the main focus of this chapter is on this institution.

The organization of the upper secondary academic track education, the curriculum to be implemented, and the characteristics of the upper secondary school-leaving certificate, the *Abitur*, have always played a major role in scientific, political, and public discussions about the school system. Because it opens up access to a highly attractive range of careers for a selected group of students, the upper secondary academic track education and the *Abitur* have been the subject of several long-standing political and scientific debates (Baumert et al. 2003; Huber 2004; Köller et al. 2004; Trautwein et al. 2007, 2010a; Trautwein and Neumann 2008). To name but three questions in these debates: What role does social background play in predicting who will acquire the *Abitur* and in *Abitur* students' decisions for or against attending university? Are the subject- and competency-related standards appropriate (in view of the quality of preuniversity education)? How predictive are achievement levels at the *Abitur* for later success at university and in the job market? Before the National Educational Panel Study (NEPS), there had been no systematic nationwide empirical monitoring and evaluation of the upper secondary level that would give scientifically sound answers to these and other questions.

The German *Gymnasium* recently underwent two important transformations (see Trautwein and Neumann 2008). First, many states have reformed the curriculum and organization of upper secondary schooling with the aim of increasing the common knowledge basis for all students. The reforms have brought a substantial reduction of choice options (e.g., advanced course choices) with the aim of homogenizing the curriculum experienced by all students. Second, in recent years, most German states have implemented an 8-year (G8) in place of the 9-year (G9) *Gymnasium* system. Therefore, students who do not repeat any years will graduate with *Abitur* after 12 rather than 13 years. Such reforms may cause cohort effects in outcomes and students' educational biographies and are thus highly relevant for NEPS. However, it should be mentioned that several states have now revoked or eased this reform (see Hübner et al. 2017).

In the present chapter, we give an overview of the work in so-called Stage 5 of NEPS and its linkage to the NEPS pillars and the adjacent stages (for the framing concept of NEPS see Chap. 1, this volume). We begin in Sect. 14.2 with an overview of empirical studies on the upper secondary level that were already available before NEPS started. This shows that there was a clear need for a project such as NEPS. In Sect. 14.3, we then describe a number of unresolved general research questions revolving around the upper secondary level. Although the research instruments developed for NEPS are very broad, these guiding questions translate into elements of their implementation. The major elements of the research instruments are described in some more detail in Sect. 14.4. Over the last couple of years, there have been major changes in academic track education in many German states, and Sect. 14.5 describes how these changes and their consequences for the interpretation of NEPS data are reflected in the NEPS data collections.

14.2 Systematic Empirical Studies of Upper Secondary Education

Before NEPS started, there had been several empirical studies focusing on or including upper secondary education in Germany over the last decades, some of which have been quite influential in terms of their scientific or policy impact. The description of the studies will highlight some of their accomplishments. However, all these studies suffer from at least one of three major shortcomings, highlighting the methodological strength of NEPS. First, some studies are cross-sectional only—they do not cover the path into upper secondary education and the transition to higher education or the job market. Second, some large-scale studies focus on only one German state or on a restricted number of states. Third, several studies do not include standardized achievement measures. In the following, we shall give a short description of some of the studies that have had some impact on the discourse about upper secondary education.

Designed as a household panel study, the German Socio-Economic Panel Study (SOEP) provides an important database for educational research (Lohmann et al. 2009; Lohmann and Witzke 2011; Schupp 2009). Starting in 1984 with a sample at the household level, each member of the household as well as their offspring should be followed for as long as possible (Wagner et al. 2007). For research on educational participation and transitions in educational biographies, for instance, such data are highly valuable. Unfortunately, the SOEP does not provide standardized achievement measures (since 2006, however, general cognitive ability is being assessed by standardized tests; see Schupp et al. 2008).

The German Life History Study[1] (GLHS; *Lebensverläufe und gesellschaftlicher Wandel*) conducted by Karl Ulrich Mayer, started in 1979 with funding from the German Research Foundation (DFG; *Deutsche Forschungsgemeinschaft*), and has been continued at the Max Planck Institute of Human Development and Education in Berlin and the

---

[1] Documentation of the different substudies is available under https://www.mpib-berlin.mpg.de/de/forschung/beendete-bereiche/bildung-arbeit-und-gesellschaftliche-entwicklung/publikationen [Retrieved April 3, 2018].

Center for Research on Inequalities and the Life Course (CIQLE) at Yale University. The following cohorts were assessed in western Germany (including West Berlin): 1919–1921, 1929–1931, 1939–1941, 1949–1951, 1954–1956, 1959–1961, 1964, and 1971. The eastern German cohorts include 1929–1931, 1939–1941, 1951–1953, 1959–1961, and 1971 (Hillmert et al. 2004; Solga 1996; Wagner 1996). The major focus of the GHLS is on investigating social conditions before, during, and after German reunification, and it provides retrospective life-course information on, for instance, the family of origin, residential history, education, and work life. Because there have been several changes in the German educational system since the last birth cohorts of this study left school, more recent data are needed. The study also lacks academic achievement measures, and few instruments permit examinations of psychological characteristics associated with different educational biographies.

With the international comparison based on data from a total of 24 participating countries, the large-scale, representative Third International Mathematics and Science Study, Population III (TIMSS/III; Baumert et al. 2000) has been very influential. Three different competence areas were assessed (although some countries did not participate in all areas): mathematics and science literacy (22 countries), advanced mathematics (17 countries), and physics (18 countries). The international comparison showed that German students attained only average results in mathematics and science literacy despite their rather high mean age (19.5 years) compared to final school year students from other countries. With regard to college-preparatory education—the academic track—German students' mathematics as well as physics achievement lay in the average range of international results. TIMSS can be seen as the starting point for increasing interest in the use of standardized achievement tests to monitor the effectiveness of a school system. Unfortunately, no longitudinal component was included in this study.

Two longitudinal studies have been conducted in Hamburg (LAU; *Aspekte der Lernausgangslage und der Lernentwicklung*; see Lehmann et al. 2006; Trautwein et al. 2007 and KESS; *Kompetenzen und Einstellungen von Schülerinnen und Schülern*; see Scharenberg 2012; Vieluf et al. 2014). These studies were unique in that they tracked students from the first year of lower secondary education up to their last year of upper secondary education. Using standardized achievement tests in several school subjects, they provided unprecedented insights into individual development and the trajectories of achievement in different school types. For instance, with regard to the upper secondary level, there were large differences between different school types: Students in *Gesamtschule*, *Aufbaugymnasium* (a special school type leading to Abitur for students from *Realschule*), and *Wirtschaftsgymnasium* (upper secondary vocational school of economics) scored considerably lower on the mathematical literacy and advanced mathematics tests compared to students in the traditional *Gymnasium* and the *Technisches Gymnasium* (*Gymnasium* with a technical focus). Further, a comparison of *Gymnasium* students from the LAU and KESS cohorts with G9 (LAU) and G8 (KESS) educational tracks showed statistically significant differences regarding competencies partly in favor of the G8 students, and partly in favor of the G9 students (Ivanov et al. 2016). It should be noted, however, that due to the time lag of 7 years between both cohorts (and other organizational reforms besides the G8 reform implemented within this time period), the background characteristics of *Gymnasium* students in both studies were quite different. Moreover, both studies collected only a limited set of variables shedding light on characteristics of the students and their families that might help to explain the variability in educational biographies. Furthermore, studies were restricted to Hamburg alone.

The longitudinal Learning Processes, Educational Careers, and Psychosocial Development in Adolescence and Young Adulthood Study (BIJU; *Bildungsverläufe und psychosoziale Entwicklung im Jugendalter*) traced students' development from Grade 7 up to the transition to either higher or vocational education. Data from students in two eastern German states, one western German state, and Berlin (East and West) were collected at the start of the unification of the East and West German school systems in which the East German school system was largely transformed into the existing West German system. BIJU yielded several important findings. For instance, it showed that the school achievement of students with identical school-leaving certificates differed greatly depending on the state they lived in and the school type attended. Furthermore, research based on the BIJU dataset documented how the composition of the learning environment has a lasting impact on psychosocial outcomes (e.g., Marsh et al. 2007), found a positive impact of attending the academic track on psychometric intelligence (Becker et al. 2012), showed the reciprocal association between achievement and self-related cognitions (e.g., Trautwein et al. 2006a), and documented that gender effects on course selections in upper secondary education (biology and mathematics in Grade 12) can be explained fully by differences in achievement, self-concept, and intrinsic value (see Nagy et al. 2006). However, a central limitation of BIJU is the restriction to only four German states.

The multicohort longitudinal Transformation of the Secondary School System and Academic Careers Study (TOSCA; Köller et al. 2004; Trautwein et al. 2007) is currently one of the largest research projects focusing on the transition to higher education and the job market. Several thousand Grade 10 and *Abitur* students in the state of Baden-Wuerttemberg participated in school achievement tests and answered a student questionnaire focusing on their school biography, their family background, various psychological characteristics, and their plans for the future. The central limitation of the TOSCA dataset is its restriction to Baden-Wuerttemberg, a state whose school system and higher education system differ in several respects from those of other states.

The *Studienberechtigte* study (*Hochschul-Informations-System*; HIS) started in 1976. In the 2004/2005 school year, it was supplemented for the first time by an additional assessment half a year *before* students reached their qualification for higher education (university of applied sciences, university) (Heine et al. 2005; Heine and Willich 2006). The second assessment following the usual practice in the *Studienberechtigte* study took place half a year *after* students left school. A central aim of the study is to validate the prognostic potential of students' intentions to enroll at a university or a university of applied sciences (for results based on the panel in 2015, see Mentges and Renneberg

2018). Results based on the panel starting in 2010 (Spangenberg and Quast 2016) showed that 70% of the students started or seriously intended to start higher education studies at a university or a university of applied sciences; 12% were unsure whether to study or not. In a third assessment 4.5 years after leaving school, the percentage of students who were enrolled in academic education increased to 80%. The limitations to this dataset include the omission of standardized achievement tests.

In summary, each of the existing studies suffers from at least one major limitation (cross-sectional nature, omission of standardized achievement tests, limited scope in terms of regional outreach). Because of the restricted data situation, many questions of major educational and political interest cannot be answered. Consequently, NEPS has the potential to provide a more comprehensive as well as a more detailed picture of educational careers in Germany than the studies mentioned above.

14.3 Key Research Areas

There are many unresolved general research questions revolving around the upper secondary level and its linkages to other NEPS stages. The empirical work with the NEPS dataset has generated many research questions and answers that did not cross the minds of those responsible for designing the study right from the outset. Nonetheless, the research instrument developed for NEPS is purposefully quite broad and designed to accommodate questions that were not evident when the design and the variables were determined. Despite this breadth, several key questions guided the development of the final instrument. We describe four of these guiding questions in more detail.

14.3.1 Traditional and Nontraditional Pathways to the *Abitur*

The majority of students still receive their *Abitur* certificate from traditional *Gymnasium* schools. In recent decades, however, many German states have introduced alternative institutional structures that lead to higher education including *Gesamtschulen* and vocational *Gymnasien*. These long-lasting developments have led to a rather dyadic secondary school system in most German states nowadays, and alternative school types have become established as important institutions in which many students can receive Abitur certificates (Maaz et al. 2013; Neumann et al. 2013; Neumann et al. 2017; Tillmann 2012, 2016). The data collected in NEPS (see the contributions of the pillars and Stage 4, Chaps. 4, 5, 6, 7, 8, 9 and 13, this volume) can help to improve our understanding of the interplay of different factors predicting these pathways.

With respect to achievement differences (see also Pillar 1, Chap. 4, this volume), the small body of existing data seems to imply differences in students' academic achievement between traditional and nontraditional *Gymnasium* (Trautwein et al. 2007). These differences seem to reflect the different school careers of the students on traditional and nontraditional pathways to *Abitur* before Secondary Level II (Köller et al. 1999).

In terms of social disparities (see also Pillar 3, Chap. 6, this volume), it is still unclear whether opening up new paths to higher education results in increased or decreased social disparities. Based on data from the TOSCA project, Watermann and Maaz (2006) found a considerably lower socioeconomic background for vocational versus traditional *Gymnasium* students. This may indicate a positive effect of the nontraditional pathways to higher education. In a comparative study with data from 13 countries (including Germany), Blossfeld and Shavit (1993) found the effect of social selectivity to be highest at the first transition from elementary school, and that it then declined for later transitions (except in Switzerland). This result was also confirmed by a (West) German longitudinal study (Education, Training, and Occupation: Life Courses of the 1964 and 1971 Birth Cohorts in West Germany; Hillmert et al. 2004) drawing on data from the 1964 birth cohort until age 40 (Hillmert and Jacob 2010). However, Hillmert and Jacob (2005, 2010) also found that the relative advantage of students with a higher educational background increased at each stage in their educational careers. Additionally, the study showed the importance of a longitudinal perspective on the process of educational attainment: Besides the ideal-typical sequence of academic track transitions (elementary school—[traditional] *Gymnasium*—*Abitur*—higher education—attainment of a university degree), there are also many alternative pathways (e.g., second chance education, later entry or reentry to university).

There is strong evidence showing that students with a migration background (see also Pillar 4, Chap. 7, this volume) are underrepresented in preuniversity tracks (e.g., Avenarius et al. 2003). However, this relative disadvantage seems to vary across different states (e.g., Trautwein et al. 2007). Moreover, there may be differences in the achievement levels of students with and without a migration background, and the decisions regarding further education (e.g., attending university vs. starting an apprenticeship) might be associated with migration status.

Gaining adequate answers to research questions concerning traditional and nontraditional pathways to the *Abitur* requires a complex study design. The major limitation of present studies is their lack of a "complete picture." NEPS is designed to reduce these limitations. Central research questions concerning the different pathways to the *Abitur* include:

- Are the levels of academic achievement comparable across different school types with academic tracks in the *gymnasiale Oberstufe*?
- Are the nontraditional pathways to *Abitur* attractive alternatives to the traditional *Gymnasium*—in particular, for students from less favorable social backgrounds or with migration backgrounds? Do they decrease social disparities or even increase them?

14.3.2 Which Competencies Do *Abitur* Students Possess?

The competencies of students at the end of their school careers have been a cause of concern for many years (e.g., Deidesheimer Kreis 1997; Heine et al. 2008; Heublein et al. 2003). Are they well-prepared for higher education? Do they possess the necessary cognitive and noncognitive competencies to enter an apprenticeship? How important are formal and nonformal/informal learning environments for the development of the different competencies?

In the context of NEPS, the conceptualization described in Pillar 1 (see Chap. 4, this volume) is being implemented at the upper secondary education level. Thus, a broad conceptualization of competencies is being used that is based mainly on four clusters (domain-general cognitive functions, domain-specific cognitive competencies, metacompetencies/personality, and stage-specific competencies). The systematic assessment of core competencies helps close evident research gaps and provide important data for an efficient monitoring of the German school system. Possible research questions include:

- How strong are differences in the achievement levels across different pathways to the *Abitur*?
- Have students acquired the skills and strategies they will need at university, the readiness to adopt a science-oriented approach in everyday life, and an understanding of the limits of human understanding (Huber 1997)?
- What is the personality profile of successful *Abitur* students?

14.3.3 Social Disparities at the Transition to Higher Education

Specific emphasis should be placed on the association between family background and the options taken up at the post-*Abitur* transition. There is consensus in educational and social structure research that social inequality in educational participation emerges primarily at points of transition in the education system (Breen and Goldthorpe 1997; Schnabel et al. 2002). These transitions reflect the cumulative effects of previous educational decisions: the earlier educational choices have to be made, the more sustained the effects of social disparities (Shavit and Blossfeld 1993); the later in the educational career these decisions are made, the weaker the effects of social disparities (Mayer et al. 2007). Social disparities in access to higher education can be expected to be smaller, but they may still be of meaningful size (Hillmert and Jacob 2010). Also, with the educational expansion in the last decades, the odds ratio for students of less privileged backgrounds to achieve the *Abitur* has improved, whereas the inequality at the transition to higher education has increased (Lörz and Schindler 2011).

The effect of secondary social disparities at university entrance has been studied by examining the university aspirations of students with Abitur as well as the transition to higher education. Based on BIJU data, Schnabel et al. (2002) showed that the intention to enter university increases 1.5-fold when one parent holds the *Abitur* rather than a lower school certificate. Similarly, analyses with the TIMSS data (Schnabel and Gruehn 2000) showed that parents' highest educational qualification had a positive effect on university intentions after controlling for students' school performance. However, the effect of the educational milieu at home clearly decreased after controlling for the perception of parents' university expectations. This shows that the university aspirations of young adults develop in the context of their parents' expectations, and that these differ according to the social status of the family. Using the TOSCA dataset, Maaz (2006) showed that social class had only a small effect on participation in higher education (see also Watermann and Maaz 2006). However, there were differences in the type of university selected by students from different family backgrounds. Students with *Abitur* from a privileged family background were more likely than their peers with less favorable backgrounds to select university (rather than a university of applied sciences, college of education, or vocational academy; Maaz 2006; Trautwein et al. 2006b; Watermann and Maaz 2004).

A number of studies have examined social disparities at the transition to higher education based on datasets of the *Studienberechtigte* study (*Hochschul-Informations-System;* HIS) (e.g., Lörz 2012, 2013; Neugebauer et al. 2013; Reimer and Pollak 2010; Schindler and Reimer 2010, 2011). Schindler and Reimer (2010) quantified the relative strength of primary and secondary effects at the transition to tertiary education. Based on an effect decomposition proposed by Erikson and colleagues (2005), they showed that more than 80% of the disparities in the transition rates between students from working class and service class can be traced back to secondary effects (see also Neugebauer et al. 2013; see, for an overview, Watermann et al. 2014).

Watermann and Maaz (2010) examined which mechanisms mediate the association between social background and the decision to enter higher education. As a decision model, they adapted Ajzen's theory of planned behavior to the transition to higher education. Based on this theory, (a) attitudes to higher education, (b) the perceived expectations of the social background with respect to higher education, and (c) perceived behavioral control in terms of students' confidence in their ability to enter and succeed in higher education can be considered to be the key determinants of intention to study. Drawing on data from a subsample of participants in the TOSCA study, a decision model was specified for the analysis of secondary background effects, and the transition to higher education was analyzed from a longitudinal perspective. Thereby, the effects of social background were found to be mediated by the indicators of the decision model.

Based on the rational choice framework of Erikson and Jonsson (1996), Schindler and Reimer (2010) modeled secondary effects of social background at the transition to higher education in terms of perceived costs, returns, and success probability. Using the nonlinear effect decomposition proposed by Fairlie (2005), they quantified the extent to which grade of *Abitur* (primary effect) and motives of postsecondary career path (secondary effect) can explain the transition gap between students from service classes and students with a working class background. The perceived costs, operationalized via the relevance of financial independence, proved to be the item with the most explanatory power.

Questions pertaining to social disparities in access to higher education have always been of interest in social research, and they gain additional relevance in the current context of reform in the tertiary sector. For instance, relevant research questions include:

- How large are social disparities in access to higher education?
- Do these disparities differ for the different types of higher education?

14.3.4 Achievement, School Grades, and Certificates: Predicting Further Development?

Of course, one highly relevant research field to which NEPS is adding knowledge is the issue of long-term returns to education (see Pillar 5, Chap. 8, this volume). In this chapter, we shall focus on only one small subaspect: the relative predictive power of various indicators of achievement.

Prior research has documented that school achievement collected via standardized achievement tests correlates only rather moderately with teacher-assigned school grades or cognitive ability (Baumert et al. 2003; Volodina and Nagy 2016). This –and the increasing role of the university in the admission of students to highly valued study subjects—opens up a multitude of important research questions. A good final school grade gives students access to highly valued fields of study in which slots are assigned—at least in part—on the basis of the *Abitur* grade. When predicting a successful transition to vocational training or university (see Stages 6 and 7, Chaps. 15 and 16, this volume), NEPS is able to examine the role of school type attended, type of school-leaving certificate acquired, basic cognitive abilities, school achievement in the standardized school achievement tests, and teacher-assigned school grades. Which indicator is of special importance for a successful transition to university or the labor market (Nagy 2006; Volodina and Nagy 2016)?

Modern educational systems rely on the assumption that competence levels predict future success in higher education and in the vocational field. However, it has also been argued (e.g., Solga 2005) that employers rely heavily on the type of school-leaving certificate as a "signal" (Spence 1973) when taking on apprentices or hiring employees. The same might be true for universities. There is some reason to believe that—due to their easy availability for employers and admission boards—school-leaving certificates and school grades will have a more pronounced effect on students' success in the application process, whereas, in contrast, competencies and abilities predict success during university, vocational training, or the occupational career. However, as plausible as this reasoning may be, there is a need for studies that empirically separate the confounding effects of certificates and competence levels in the short and long run. Moreover, there is a need to differentiate between various facets of cognitive abilities. Several studies from the United States seem to indicate that general ability plays a more important role for training success than basic competencies or specific abilities (e.g., Ree and Earles 1991).

However, more convincing empirical support for such a pattern of results is largely lacking in the German context. For example, Volodina et al. (2015) found that only general cognitive abilities had a small albeit significant effect on dropout intentions in a sample of apprentices in vocational educational and training.

Another exception is Nagy's (2006) analysis of the TOSCA database. He used a broad set of variables assessed at the end of secondary schooling to predict success at university 2 years later. His analyses showed that grade point average (GPA), cognitive abilities, and school achievement test scores were all related to achievement in university. In the total sample, only GPA and cognitive abilities exerted significant effects, whereas school achievement measures had no incremental predictive power. However, Nagy (2006) also found that math test scores had a stronger predictive power for students entering math-intensive fields of study (e.g., engineering). These findings indicate that an examination of individual factors such as competencies (basic cognitive abilities, achievement, study-related competencies), vocational interest, motivation, and long-term plans should be complemented by the investigation of contextual factors (e.g., specific university types and subjects and type of vocational training).

Hence, some relevant research questions that may be addressed using the NEPS dataset include:

- Which indicators are most important in predicting long-term outcomes?
- To what extent does this prediction model differ when looking at different study fields or jobs?

14.4 Instruments

In line with the longitudinal design of NEPS, the majority of instruments administered to students, parents, and principals are the upper secondary versions of the standard instruments used throughout the school career (for the constructs being used, see the contributions of the pillars and Stage 4, Chaps. 4, 5, 6, 7, 8, 9 and 13, this volume). However, some additions and refinements are necessary to cover specific aspects of upper secondary education in the preuniversity track.

Wissenschaftspropädeutik. A specific focus is on study skills and critical and scientific thinking. These are subsumed under the heading *Wissenschaftspropädeutik* in the German educational literature. Self-report measures (see Heine 2002; Trautwein and Lüdtke 2004) as well as "tests" of critical and scientific thinking (e.g., Krettenauer 2005) have been used, but much work is needed to improve and enrich these instruments. We used the pilot testing phase of the NEPS to develop a more comprehensive measure of scientific thinking as metascientific reflection (Oschatz et al. 2018; Rieger et al. in prep).

English as a Foreign Language. English is the lingua franca (see Tenorth 2001) of today's scientific world, and, due to ongoing globalization processes, essential in many relevant areas of career and everyday life (e.g., economy, modern communication in the "global village"). Therefore, an additional assessment of English-language skills was realized in Grade 10, Grade 12, and (former) university students.

Stage-specific questions about educational and vocational choices. A battery of questions was used that focus on courses taken in upper secondary school, examination subjects in *Abitur*, and the transition to university or vocational training. The instruments used in the TOSCA study (Köller et al. 2004) as well as instruments developed in cooperation with Stages 6 and 7 (see Chaps. 15 and 16, this volume) provide the main source for this questionnaire. Students who changed schools and no longer attend a NEPS school are being tracked individually and assessed via an online module (see Chap. 1).

14.5 Documenting the Effects of the Recent Abitur Reforms: Systematic Assessment of Core Competencies Under Changing Institutional Conditions

The focus of NEPS is on individual development in the context of institutionalized and noninstitutionalized learning environments. For this reason, NEPS examines how schooling influences the lives of children and adults and how differences in school experiences translate into various outcomes. At the same time, the longitudinal nature of the study is of utmost importance, and not all variations in learning environments can be observed in desirable depths. Importantly, the sample size is not large enough for many possibly interesting analyses. Given the focus on longitudinal analyses, the level of detail with regards to the learning environment has to be somewhat restricted. Clearly, NEPS cannot and will not attempt to replace other studies that yield information on, for instance, either the quality of the educational system, the competence levels of teachers, or document changes in the school system. However, there are a small number of extensions to the longitudinal data base of NEPS that considerably strengthen the longitudinal analyses, including pilot studies and method studies.

At the upper secondary level, the NEPS design includes two additional data collections addressing two major changes in the *Gymnasium* system so that it can gauge the consequences of these reforms for individual educational biographies. These reforms can be viewed as "natural experiments" that provide a fascinating opportunity to assess the effect of institutionalized learning environments on educational outcomes (Morgan and Winship 2007). These two additional studies focused on an organizational reform (in Thuringia) and a G8 reform (in Baden-Wuerttemberg).

14.5.1 Reform of the Curriculum and Organization of Upper Secondary Schooling

A major reform of the *Gymnasium* concerns the curriculum and organization of upper secondary schooling: Baden-Wuerttemberg, Brandenburg, Hesse, Saxony-Anhalt, Lower Saxony, Mecklenburg-Western Pomerania, Hamburg, Saarland, Saxony, Schleswig-Holstein, Bavaria, and Thuringia have already implemented such reforms. Although the exact nature of these reforms differs from state to state (see Trautwein and Neumann 2008; Trautwein et al. 2010a), much more emphasis has been placed on a common knowledge basis for all students in all states, with a lower level of differentiation and student choice in the last 2 years of school, and less choice in the final examination (*Abitur*). For instance, students in most states no longer have to decide whether to study math and German at an advanced (*Leistungskurs*) or a basic level (*Grundkurs*). This development was subject to criticism (Huber 2008) and stands in marked contrast to reforms in other countries such as Sweden and the Netherlands (Mitter 2003) in which the degree of individualization has been increased.

Very little is known about the consequences of the effects of organizational and curricular reforms in the various states. Trautwein et al. (2010b) have performed a comparably systematic analysis of the organizational and curricular reforms in Baden-Wuerttemberg. At the traditional *Gymnasium*, these reforms led to an improvement of one-sixth of a standard deviation for preuniversity mathematics achievement, whereas average English achievement remained unchanged.

The organizational reform in Thuringia, the subject of an additional NEPS study, aimed mainly toward a broader education instead of a high degree of specialization without making any alterations to the official curriculum. The reform for the traditional *Gymnasium* was implemented in 2009 (hence, the first cohort left school in 2011).

The main research questions in the context of the study in Thuringia are: Does the abolition of the advanced and basic courses lead to changes in the average level of student achievement accompanied by a lower variability? Which effects of the reform are expected from the viewpoint of students, parents, and teachers? Furthermore, how do students and their parents judge the requirements concerning achievement, teaching, and homework time both before and after the implementation of the reform? Are there reform effects on students' motivation and academic self-concept in different subjects or on their well-being? Does the reform increase students' aspirations for higher education—particularly in the domain of science? First results on some of these questions can be found in Hübner et al. (2018).

Sample The first assessment in Thuringia (last cohort before the reform) took place in January 2010; the second (first cohort after the reform) was conducted in January 2011. At the first assessment (participation rate: 74%), more than 1,300 students participated. Details on the sampling design and data on the additional study in Thuringia can be found in IEA DPC (2010, 2011a) and LIfBI (2015a).

In the Additional Study Thuringia, students were asked to participate in student competence tests and complete a student questionnaire. Furthermore, their parents and teachers were asked to fill out specific questionnaires.

Student Competence Tests. These assessed domain-general cognitive functions and domain-specific cognitive competencies (mathematics, English, biology, and physics achievement). In the first wave, 1,374 (participation rate: 74%) and in the second wave, overall 900 (participation rate: 64.7%) students worked on at least one of the four competence tests. Further information on the competence tests is provided on the NEPS homepage. The competence tests were analyzed using item response theory (IRT). The resulting weighted maximum likelihood estimates (WLE; Warm 1989) are provided in the Scientific Use File of the Additional Study (e.g., Rieger et al. 2018).

Student Questionnaire. Central aspects covered by the student questionnaire are the expected reform effects, *Wissenschaftspropädeutik*, perceived (academic and time) demands of school, learning environment, parental aspirations, self-concept, motivation, interest (academic and vocational), personality, leisure activities, health complaints, occupational aspirations, intention to study, social background, and migration status. Here, 1,372 (participation rate: 73.9%) students participated in the first and 899 (participation rate: 64.6%) students participated in the second assessment.

Parent Questionnaire. This questionnaire focused on parents' expected reform effects, parents' educational and vocational aspirations for their child, perceived (academic and time) demands of school for their child, and social and migration status. Overall, 1,857 parents were asked to answer the parent questionnaire in the first assessment and 575 of them participated (participation rate: 31%). In the second assessment, 30.1% of the gross sample of 1,392 parents completed the questionnaire ($N = 419$).

Teacher Questionnaire. The main focus of the teacher questionnaire was on teachers' satisfaction with the course, stress in teaching the course, perceived teaching effectiveness, expected reform effects, and appropriateness of the level of students' choice (organizational aspects of the *gymnasiale Oberstufe*). Overall, 417 (participation rate: 80.4%) of the gross sample of 519 teachers completed the questionnaire in the first assessment, whereas 80.3% (310) of the 426 teachers asked to participate in the second assessment completed the questionnaire.

14.5.2 From 9 to 8 Years: the Introduction of the G8 *Gymnasium*

By the time NEPS started, most German states had switched from a 9-year (G9) to an 8-year (G8) *Gymnasium* system, meaning that *Gymnasium* students who did not repeat any years would finish school after 12 rather than 13 years. This change was being implemented sequentially in the different states (first G8 cohorts:[2] 2007 in Saxony-Anhalt, 2008 in Mecklenburg-Western Pomerania; 2009 in Saarland; 2010 in Hamburg; 2011 in Bavaria and Lower Saxony; 2012 in Baden-Wuerttemberg, Berlin, Brandenburg, and Bremen; 2013 in North Rhine-Westphalia and Hesse; 2016 in Schleswig-Holstein). As noted above (Sect. 14.1), in recent years, many states have switched back from a G8 to a G9 system. Investigations on the effects of G8 reforms seem to imply decreasing mathematical achievement in Saxony-Anhalt (Büttner and Thomsen 2010), and less leisure time—stated to be not sufficient for recreation—in Bavaria (Milde-Busch et al. 2010).

An additional NEPS study is focusing on the G8 reform effects in Baden-Wuerttemberg. The following research questions are of major interest: Is the shortening of schooling by one year accompanied by decreased scholastic achievement and domain-general cognitive functions (Ceci, 1996)? Are there negative reform effects on students' well-being and leisure-time activities (e.g., due to having to spend more time doing homework)? Is there an increased need for private tutoring in the G8 *Gymnasium* system? Results regarding these questions using data from the additional NEPS study on Baden-Wuerttemberg can be found in, for instance, Hübner et al. (2017) and Quis (2018).

Similar to the design of the Additional Study Thuringia (see Sect. 14.5.1), students were asked to work on student competence tests in mathematics, English, physics, and biology and to complete a general student questionnaire. Additionally, school principals and subject heads in math, German, and English were asked to work on a questionnaire.

Sample. In Baden-Wuerttemberg, 50 schools were sampled and asked to participate in three subsequent assessments from 2011 to 2013. Of these 50 schools, 48 agreed to participate in the Additional Study Baden-Wuerttemberg. Overall, 1,284 students, 130 head of department teachers, and 40 school principals were assessed in 2011, whereas 2,427 students, 128 head of department teachers, and 44 school principals participated in the second assessment. In the last assessment, 1,214 students 117 head of department teachers, and 44 school principals participated. The number of students who were willing to participate in the survey ranged between 67.7% (gross sample: $N=1,909$) in the last assessment and 72.2% in the first assessment (gross sample: $N=1,858$). Details on the sampling design and data of the Additional Study Baden-Wuerttemberg can be found in IEA DPC (2011b, 2012, 2013) and LIfBI (2015b).

Student Competence Tests. These assessed domain-general cognitive functions and domain-specific cognitive competencies (mathematics, English, biology, and physics achievement). In the first assessment, participation rate was higher or equal to 94.1% of

---

[2]Saxony and Thuringia have always had an 8-year Gymnasium school system. Rhineland-Palatinate is the only state that has not switched to a G8 system in general, but is reducing the last G9 school year by approximately 3 months.

all administered tests ($N=1{,}341$), in the second assessment, participation rate in student competence tests was higher or equal to 88.1% ($N=2{,}698$), and in the third assessment it amounted to 91.6% ($N=1{,}292$). Further information on the competence tests are provided on the NEPS Homepage. The competence tests were analyzed using item response theory (IRT), and the resulting weighted maximum likelihood estimates (WLE; Warm, 1989) are provided in the Scientific Use File of the Additional Study Baden-Wuerttemberg. Information regarding the scaling procedure can be found in, for example, Hübner et al. (2016) and Duchhardt (2015).

Student Questionnaire. Central aspects covered by the student questionnaire are: the expected reform effects, perceived (academic and time) demands of school, learning environment, leisure activities, health complaints, occupational aspirations, intention to study, social background, and migration status. Here, 1,341 students (participation rate: 95.5%) participated in the first, 2,698 students (participation rate: 89.8%) participated in the second, and 1,292 students (participation rate: 93.7%) participated in the third assessment.

Head of Department Teacher Questionnaire. Heads of departments were asked about, for instance, the curriculum toward which they oriented their teaching, the expected effects of the educational reform in general and regarding their subject, and the working climate among teachers at the school. In the first assessment, overall 42 heads of departments participated in math (participation rate: 91.3%), 42 in German (participation rate: 91.3%), and 46 in English (participation rate: 100%). In the second assessment, 44 heads of departments participated in math (participation rate: 91.7%), 40 in German (participation rate: 83.3%), and 44 in English (participation rate: 91.7%). Finally, in the last assessment, 37 heads of departments participated in math (participation rate: 77.1%), 41 in German (participation rate: 85.4%), and 39 in English (participation rate: 81.3%).

Principal Questionnaire. Principals were asked about, for instance, the expected effects of the reform in general, the expected effects on teacher motivation and teacher effort, and the expected effects on students. In the first assessment, 40 principals participated (participation rate: 87.0%), in the second and third assessments, 44 principals participated (participation rate: 91.7%).

14.6 Conclusion

Because of the longitudinal design, the nationwide sample, and the inclusion of standardized achievement tests, NEPS is providing an excellent database for answering many questions of major scientific and political interest. With regard to upper secondary schooling in the academic track, such questions address, for instance, the comparison of traditional and nontraditional pathways to the *Abitur*, academic achievement levels of *Abitur* students, social disparities, and the predictive power of indicators of achievement (school grades, competencies, *Abitur* certificate) on students' further development. Furthermore, the additional NEPS studies on two German *Abitur* reforms are delivering valuable information on (not) intended effects of such implementations.

References

Avenarius, H., Ditton, H., Döbert, H., Klemm, K., Klieme, E., Rürup, M., Tenorth, H.-E., Weishaupt, H., & Weiß, M. (2003). *Bildungsbericht für Deutschland: Erste Befunde*. Opladen, Germany: Leske & Budrich.

Baumert, J., Bos, W., & Lehmann, R. H. (Eds.). (2000). TIMSS/III. Dritte Internationale Mathematik- und Naturwissenschaftsstudie. Mathematische und naturwissenschaftliche Bildung am Ende der Schullaufbahn (Vol. 2). Opladen, Germany: Leske & Budrich.

Baumert, J., Roeder, P. M., & Watermann, R. (2003). Das Gymnasium—Kontinuität im Wandel. In K. S. Cortina, J. Baumert, A. Leschinsky, K. U. Mayer, & L. Trommer (Eds.), *Das Bildungswesen in der Bundesrepublik Deutschland: Strukturen und Entwicklungen im Überblick* (pp. 487–524). Reinbek bei Hamburg, Germany: Rowohlt.

Becker, M., Lüdtke, O., Trautwein, U., Köller, O. & Baumert, J. (2012). The differential effects of school tracking on psychometric intelligence: Do academic-track schools make students smarter? *Journal of Educational Psychology, 104*, 682–699.

Blossfeld, H.-P., & Shavit, Y. (1993). Persisting barriers: Changes in educational opportunities in thirteen countries. In Y. Shavit & H.-P. Blossfeld (Eds.), *Persistent inequality: Changing educational attainment in thirteen countries* (pp. 1–25). Boulder, CO: Westview Press.

Breen, R., & Goldthorpe, J. H. (1997). Explaining educational differentials: Towards a formal rational action theory. *Rationality and Society, 9*, 275–305.

Büttner, B., & Thomsen, S. L. (2010). Are we spending too many years in school? Causal evidence of the impact of shortening secondary school duration. Retrieved from ftp://zew.de/pub/zew-docs/dp/dp10011.pdf.

Ceci, S. C. (1996). *On intelligence: A bioecological treatise on intellectual development* (2nd ed.). Cambridge, MA: Harvard University Press.

Deidesheimer Kreis. (1997). Hochschulzulassung und Studieneignungstests. Studienfeldbezogene Verfahren zur Feststellung der Eignung für Numerus-clausus- und andere Studiengänge. Göttingen, Germany: Vandenhoeck & Ruprecht.

Duchhardt, C. (2015). *NEPS Technical Report for mathematics: Scaling results for the additional study Baden-Wuerttemberg* (NEPS Working Paper No. 59). Bamberg, Germany: Leibniz Institute for Educational Trajectories, National Educational Panel Study.

Erikson, R., Goldthorpe, J. H., Jackson, M., Yaish, M., & Cox, D. R. (2005). On class differentials in educational attainment. *Proceedings of the National Academy of Sciences, 102*, 9730–9733.

Erikson, R., & Jonsson, J. O. (1996). Explaining class inequality in education: The Swedish test case. In R. Erikson & J. O. Jonsson (Eds.), *Can education be equalized? The Swedish case in comparative perspective* (pp. 1–63). Boulder, CO: Westview Press.

Fairlie, R. W. (2005). An extension of the Blinder–Oaxaca decomposition technique to logit and probit models. *Journal of Economic and Social Measurement, 30*, 305–316.

Heine, C. (2002). *HIS Ergebnisspiegel 2002*. Hannover, Germany: HIS Hochschul-Informations-System GmbH.

Heine, C., Scheller, P., & Willich, J. (2005). Studienberechtigte 2005—Studierbereitschaft, Berufsausbildung und Bedeutung der Hochschulreife. Ergebnisse der ersten Befragung der Studienberechtigten 2005 ein halbes Jahr vor Schulabgang—Pilotstudie (HIS-Kurzinformation A16/2005). Hannover, Germany: HIS Hochschul-Informations-System GmbH.

Heine, C., & Willich, J. (2006). *Studienberechtigte 2005—Übergang in Studium, Ausbildung und Beruf* (HIS: Forum Hochschule Nr. F6/2006). Hannover, Germany: HIS Hochschul-Informations-System GmbH.

Heine, C., Willich, J., Schneider, H., & Sommer, D. (2008). *Studienanfänger im Wintersemester 2007/08. Wege zum Studium, Studien- und Hochschulwahl, Situation bei Studienbeginn* (HIS: Forum Hochschule Nr. F16/2008). Hannover, Germany: HIS Hochschul-Informations-System GmbH.

Heublein, U., Spangenberg, H., & Sommer, D. (2003). Ursachen des Studienabbruchs. Analyse 2002. Hannover, Germany: HIS Hochschul-Informations-System GmbH.

Hillmert, S., & Jacob, M. (2005). Institutionelle Strukturierung und inter-individuelle Variation: zur Entwicklung herkunftsbezogener Ungleichheiten im Bildungsverlauf. *Kölner Zeitschrift für Soziologie und Sozialpsychologie, 57,* 414–442.

Hillmert, S., & Jacob, M. (2010). Selections and social selectivity on the academic track: A life course analysis of educational attainment in Germany. *Research in Social Stratification and Mobility, 28,* 59–76.

Hillmert, S., Künster, R., Spengemann, P., & Mayer, K. U. (2004). *Projekt "Ausbildungs- und Berufsverläufe der Geburtskohorten 1964 und 1971 in Westdeutschland". Dokumentation.* Berlin, Germany: Max Planck Institute for Human Development.

Huber, L. (1997). Fähigkeit zum Studieren—Bildung durch Wissenschaft. Zum Problem der Passung zwischen Gymnasialer Oberstufe und Hochschule. In E. Liebau, W. Mack, & C. T. Scheilke (Eds.), *Das Gymnasium: Alltag, Reform, Geschichte, Theorie* (pp. 333–351). Weinheim, Germany: Juventa.

Huber, L. (2004). Stoff, Raum und Zeit für individuelle Bildung! Thesen zur Rettung und Weiterentwicklung der gymnasialen Oberstufe nach PISA. *Die Deutsche Schule, 96,* 23–31.

Huber, L. (2008). Kanon oder Interesse? Eine Schlüsselfrage der Oberstufen-Reform. In J. Keuffer & M. Kublitz-Kramer (Eds.), *Was braucht die Oberstufe? Diagnose, Förderung und selbstständiges Lernen* (pp. 20–35). Weinheim, Germany: Beltz.

Hübner, N., Rieger, S., & Wagner, W. (2016). *NEPS Technical Report for English reading: Scaling results for the additional study Baden-Württemberg* (NEPS Survey Paper No. 10). Bamberg, Germany: Leibniz Institute for Educational Trajectories, National Educational Panel Study.

Hübner, N., Wagner, W., Kramer, J., Nagengast, B., & Trautwein, U. (2017). Die G8-Reform in Baden-Württemberg: Kompetenzen, Wohlbefinden und Freizeitverhalten vor und nach der Reform. *Zeitschrift für Erziehungswissenschaft, 20,* 748–771. https://doi.org/10.1007/s11618-017-0737-3.

Hübner, N., Wagner, W., Nagengast, B., & Trautwein, U. (2018). Putting all students in one basket does not produce equality: Gender-specific effects of curricular intensification in upper secondary school. *School Effectiveness and School Improvement.* Advance online publication. https://doi.org/10.1080/09243453.2018.1504801.

IEA DPC (2010). *Methodenbericht. NEPS Zusatzstudie Thüringen. Haupterhebung – 1. Welle (A70). Frühjahr 2010.* Retrieved from https://www.neps-data.de/Portals/0/NEPS/Datenzentrum/Forschungsdaten/TH/1-0-0/Methodenbericht_MZP_1.pdf.

IEA DPC (2011a). *Methodenbericht. Reform der gymnasialen Oberstufe in Thüringen. Haupterhebung - Frühjahr 2011. A71.* Retrieved from https://www.neps-data.de/Portals/0/NEPS/Datenzentrum/Forschungsdaten/TH/1-0-0/Methodenbericht_MZP2.pdf.

IEA DPC (2011b). *Methodenbericht. NEPS Zusatzstudie zur G8-Reform in Baden-Württemberg. Haupterhebung – Frühjahr 2011 (A72)*. Retrieved from https://www.neps-data.de/Portals/0/NEPS/Datenzentrum/Forschungsdaten/BW/Methodenbericht_A72.pdf.

IEA DPC (2012). *Methodenbericht. NEPS Zusatzstudie zur G8-Reform in Baden-Württemberg. Haupterhebung – Frühjahr 2012 (A73)*. Retrieved from https://www.neps-data.de/Portals/0/NEPS/Datenzentrum/Forschungsdaten/BW/2-0-0/Methodenbericht_A73.pdf.

IEA DPC (2013). *Methodenbericht. NEPS Zusatzstudie zur G8-Reform in Baden-Württemberg. Haupterhebung – Frühjahr 2013 (A74)*. Retrieved from https://www.neps-data.de/Portals/0/NEPS/Datenzentrum/Forschungsdaten/BW/3-0-0/Methodenbericht_A74.pdf.

Ivanov, S., Nikolova, R., & Vieluf, U. (2016). G8 vs. G9 im Kohortenvergleich. Lernkontexte und Lernstände zweier Hamburger Abiturjahrgänge. In J. Kramer, M. Neumann, & U. Trautwein (Eds.), *Abitur und Matura im Wandel. Historische Entwicklungslinien, aktuelle Reformen und ihre Effekte* (pp. 81–106). Wiesbaden, Germany: Springer VS.

Köller, O., Baumert, J., & Schnabel, K. U. (1999). Wege zur Hochschulreife: Offenheit des Systems und Sicherung vergleichbarer Standards. Analysen am Beispiel der Mathematikleistungen von Oberstufenschülern an Integrierten Gesamtschulen und Gymnasien in Nordrhein-Westfalen. *Zeitschrift für Erziehungswissenschaft, 2*, 385–422.

Köller, O., Watermann, R., Trautwein, U., & Lüdtke, O. (Eds.). (2004). Wege zur Hochschulreife in Baden-Württemberg. TOSCA—Eine Untersuchung an allgemein bildenden und beruflichen Gymnasien. Opladen, Germany: Leske & Budrich.

Krettenauer, T. (2005). Die Erfassung des Entwicklungsniveaus epistemologischer Überzeugungen und das Problem der Übertragbarkeit von Interviewverfahren in standardisierte Fragebogenmethoden. *Zeitschrift für Entwicklungspsychologie und Pädagogische Psychologie, 37*, 69–79.

Lehmann, R., Vieluf, U., Nikolova, R., & Ivanov, S. (2006). LAU 13. *Aspekte der Lernausgangslage und Lernentwicklung—Klassenstufe 13*. Hamburg, Germany: Behörde für Bildung und Sport, Amt für Bildung.

LIfBi (2015a). *Additional study Thuringia: Curricular reform study in Thuringia (TH). Study Overview*. Retrieved from https://www.neps-data.de/Portals/0/NEPS/Datenzentrum/Forschungsdaten/TH/2-0-0/TH_Overview.pdf.

LIfBi (2015b). *Additional Study Baden-Wuerttemberg (BW) Study Overview*. Retrieved from https://www.neps-data.de/Portals/0/NEPS/Datenzentrum/Forschungsdaten/BW/3-0-0/BW_Overview.pdf.

Lohmann, H., Spieß, C. K., Groh-Samberg, O., & Schupp, J. (2009). Analysepotenziale des Sozioökonomischen Panels (SOEP) für die empirische Bildungsforschung. *Zeitschrift für Erziehungswissenschaft, 12*, 252–280.

Lohmann, H., & Witzke, S. (2011). BIOEDU (beta-Version): *Biographical data on educational participation and transitions in the German Socio-Economic Panel Study (SOEP)*. (Data Documentation 58). Berlin, Germany: DIW. Retrieved from: https://www.econstor.eu/bitstream/10419/129267/1/diw_datadoc_2011-058.pdf.

Lörz, M. (2012). Mechanismen sozialer Ungleichheit beim Übergang ins Studium: Prozesse der Status- und Kulturreproduktion. In R. Becker & H. Solga (Eds.), *Soziologische Bildungsforschung* (Kölner Zeitschrift für Soziologie und Sozialpsychologie: Sonderband. 52, pp. 302–324). Wiesbaden, Germany: Springer.

Lörz, M. (2013). Differenzierung des Bildungssystems und soziale Ungleichheit: Haben sich mit dem Ausbau der beruflichen Bildungswege die Ungleichheitsmechanismen verändert? *Zeitschrift für Soziologie, 42*, 118–137.

Lörz, M., & Schindler, S. (2011). Bildungsexpansion und soziale Ungleichheit: Zunahme, Abnahme oder Persistenz ungleicher Chancenverhältnisse—eine Frage der Perspektive? Zeitschrift für Soziologie, 40, 458–477.

Maaz, K. (2006). Soziale Herkunft und Hochschulzugang. Effekte institutioneller Öffnung im Bildungssystem. Wiesbaden, Germany: VS Verlag für Sozialwissenschaften.

Maaz, K., Baumert, J., Neumann, M., Becker, M., Dumont, H. (Eds.). (2013). Die Berliner Schulstrukturreform. Bewertung durch die beteiligten Akteure und Konsequenzen des neuen Übergangsverfahrens von der Grundschule in die weiterführenden Schulen. Münster, Germany: Waxmann.

Marsh, H. W., Trautwein, U., Lüdtke, O., Baumert, J., & Köller, O. (2007). The big-fish–little-pond effect: Persistent negative effects of selective high schools on self-concept after graduation. *American Educational Research Journal, 44,* 631–669.

Mayer, K. U., Müller, W., & Pollak, R. (2007). Institutional change and inequalities of access in German higher education. In Y. Shavit, R. Arum, A. Gamoran, & G. Menahem (Eds.), *Stratification in higher education. A comparative study* (pp. 240–265). Stanford, CA: Stanford University Press.

Mentges, H., & Renneberg, A. (2018). Der nachschulische Werdegang von Studienberechtigten - Ergebnisse des DZHW-Studienberechtigtenpanels. In Bundesinstitut für Berufsbildung (Ed.), *Datenreport zum Berufsbildungsbericht 2018. Informationen und Analysen zur Entwicklung der beruflichen Bildung* (pp. 256–263). Leverkusen, Germany: Budrich.

Milde-Busch, A., Blaschek, A., Borggräfe, I., von Kries, R., Straube, A., & Heinen, F. (2010). Besteht ein Zusammenhang zwischen der verkürzten Gymnasialzeit und Kopfschmerzen und gesundheitlichen Belastungen bei Schülern im Jugendalter? *Klinische Pädiatrie, 222,* 255–260.

Mitter, W. (2003). Entwicklungen im Sekundarbereich II. Exemplarische Anregungen aus dem europäischen Ausland. *Die Deutsche Schule, 95,* 280–292.

Morgan, S. L., & Winship, C. (2007). *Counterfactuals and causal inference: Methods and principles for social research.* Cambridge, England: Cambridge University Press.

Nagy, G. (2006). Berufliche Interessen, kognitive und fachgebundene Kompetenzen: Ihre Bedeutung für die Studienfachwahl und die Bewährung im Studium (Doctoral dissertation). Freie Universität Berlin, Berlin, Germany. Retrieved from http://www.diss.fu-berlin.de/diss/receive/FUDISS_thesis_000000002714.

Nagy, G., Trautwein, U., Baumert, J., Köller, O., & Garrett, J. (2006). Gender and course selection in upper secondary education: Effects of academic self-concept and intrinsic value. *Educational Research and Evaluation, 12,* 323–345.

Neugebauer, M., Reimer, D., Schindler, S., & Stocké, V. (2013). Inequality in transitions to secondary school and tertiary education in Germany. In M. Jackson (Eds.), *Determined to succeed? Performance versus choice in educational attainment* (pp. 56–88). Stanford, CA: Stanford University Press.

Neumann, M., Becker, M., Baumert, J., Maaz, K., & Köller, O. (Eds.). (2017). *Zweigliedrigkeit im deutschen Schulsystem: Potenziale und Herausforderungen in Berlin.* Münster, Germany: Waxmann.

Neumann, M., Maaz, K., & Becker, M. (2013). Die Abkehr von der traditionellen Dreigliedrigkeit im Sekundarschulsystem: Auf unterschiedlichen Wegen zum gleichen Ziel? *Recht der Jugend und des Bildungswesens, 61,* 274–292.

Oschatz, K., Kramer, J. & Wagner, W. (2018). The assessment of scientific thinking as metascientific reflection. Bamberg, Germany: Leibniz Institute for Educational Trajectories, National Educational Panel Study.

Quis, J. S. (2018). Does compressing high school duration affect students' stress and mental health? Evidence from the National Educational Panel Study. *Journal of Economics and Statistics*. Advance online publication. https://doi.org/10.1515/jbnst-2018-0004.

Ree, M. J., & Earles, J. A. (1991). Predicting training success: Not much more than g. *Personnel Psychology, 44*, 321–332.

Reimer, D., & Pollak, R. (2010). Educational expansion and its consequences for vertical and horizontal inequalities in access to higher education in West Germany. *European Sociological Review, 26*, 1–16.

Rieger, S., Hübner, N., Oschatz, K., Kramer, J., & Wagner, W. (in prep.). *NEPS technical report for scientific thinking: Scaling results for the Starting Cohort 4 in 12th Grade* (NEPS Survey Paper). Bamberg, Germany: Leibniz-Institute for Educational Trajectories, National Educational Panel Study.

Rieger, S., Hübner, N., & Wagner, W. (2018). *NEPS technical report for English reading: Scaling results for the additional study Thuringia* (NEPS Survey Paper No. 39). Bamberg, Germany: Leibniz Institute for Educational Trajectories, National Educational Panel Study.

Scharenberg, K. (2012). Leistungsheterogenität und Kompetenzentwicklung. Zur Relevanz klassenbezogener Kompositionsmerkmale im Rahmen der KESS-Studie. Münster, Germany: Waxmann.

Scheller, P., Isleib, S., & Sommer, D. (2013). *Studienanfängerinnen und Studienanfänger im Wintersemester 2011/12* (Tabellenband). Hannover, Germany: HIS Hochschul-Informations-System GmbH.

Schindler, S., & Reimer, D. (2010). Primäre und sekundäre Effekte der sozialen Herkunft beim Übergang in die Hochschulbildung. *Kölner Zeitschrift für Soziologie und Sozialpsychologie, 62*, 623–653.

Schindler, S., & Reimer, D. (2011). Differentiation and social selectivity in German higher education. *Higher Education, 61*, 261–275.

Schnabel, K. U., Alfeld, C., Eccles, J. S., Köller, O., & Baumert, J. (2002). Parental influence on students' educational choices in the United States and Germany: Different ramifications—same effect? *Journal of Vocational Behavior, 60*, 178–198.

Schnabel, K. U., & Gruehn, S. (2000). Studienfachwünsche und Beruforientierungen in der gymnasialen Oberstufe. In J. Baumert, W. Bos, & R. H. Lehmann (Eds.), *TIMSS/III. Dritte Internationale Mathematik- und Naturwissenschaftsstudie. Mathematische und naturwissenschaftliche Bildung am Ende der Schullaufbahn*, (Vol. 2, pp. 405–444). Opladen, Germany: Leske & Budrich.

Schupp, J. (2009). 25 Jahre Sozio-oekonomisches Panel – Ein Infrastrukturprojekt der empirischen Sozial- und Wirtschaftsforschung in Deutschland. *Zeitschrift für Soziologie, 38*, 350–357.

Schupp, J., Herrmann, S., Jaensch, P., & Lang, F. (2008). Erfassung kognitiver Leistungspotentiale Erwachsener im Sozio-oekonomischen Panel (SOEP). Berlin, Germany: DIW.

Shavit, Y., & Blossfeld, H.-P. (Eds.). (1993). *Persistent inequality: Changing educational attainment in thirteen countries*. Boulder, CO: Westview Press.

Solga, H. (1996). Lebensverläufe und historischer Wandel in der ehemaligen DDR. *ZA-Informationen, 38*, 28–38.

Solga, H. (2005). Ohne Abschluss in die Bildungsgesellschaft: Die Erwerbschancen gering qualifizierter Personen aus soziologischer und ökonomischer Perspektive. Opladen, Germany: Barbara Budrich.

Spangenberg, H., & Quast, H. (2016). Bildungsentscheidungen und Umorientierungen im nachschulischen Verlauf Dritte Befragung der Studienberechtigten 2010 viereinhalb Jahre nach Schulabschluss (HIS: Forum Hochschule 5/2016). Hannover, Germany: DZHW.

Spence, M. A. (1973). Market signaling: Informational transfer in hiring and related screening processes. Cambridge, MA: Harvard University Press.

Tenorth, H.-E. (Ed.). (2001). Kerncurriculum Oberstufe. Mathematik—Deutsch—Englisch. Expertisen im Auftrag der Ständigen Konferenz der Kultusminister. Weinheim, Germany: Beltz.

Tillmann, K.-J. (2012). Das Sekundarschulsystem auf dem Weg in die Zweigliedrigkeit. Historische Linien und aktuelle Verwirrungen. *Pädagogik, 64,* 8–12.

Tillmann, K.-J. (2016). *Das Sekundarschulsystem auf dem Weg in die Zweigliedrigkeit. Historische Linien und aktuelle Verwirrungen.* Bonn, Germany: Bundeszentrale für Politische Bildung. Retrieved from http://www.bpb.de/gesellschaft/kultur/zukunft-bildung/215556/zweigliedrigkeit.

Trautwein, U., Köller, O., Lehmann, R., & Lüdtke, O. (Eds.). (2007). *Schulleistungen von Abiturienten: Regionale, schulformbezogene und soziale Disparitäten.* Münster, Germany: Waxmann.

Trautwein, U., & Lüdtke, O. (2004). Aspekte von Wissenschaftspropädeutik und Studierfähigkeit. In O. Köller, R. Watermann, U. Trautwein, & O. Lüdtke (Eds.), *Wege zur Hochschulreife in Baden-Württemberg. TOSCA—Eine Untersuchung an allgemein bildenden und beruflichen Gymnasien* (pp. 327–366). Opladen, Germany: Leske & Budrich.

Trautwein, U., Lüdtke, O., Köller, O., & Baumert, J. (2006a). Self-esteem, academic self-concept, and achievement: How the learning environment moderates the dynamics of self-concept. *Journal of Personality and Social Psychology, 90,* 334–349.

Trautwein, U., Maaz, K., Lüdtke, O., Nagy, G., Husemann, N., Watermann, R., & Köller, O. (2006b). Studieren an der Berufsakademie oder an der Universität, Fachhochschule oder Pädagogischen Hochschule? Ein Vergleich des Leistungsstands, familiären Hintergrunds, beruflicher Interessen und der Studienwahlmotive von (künftigen) Studierenden aus Baden- Württemberg. *Zeitschrift für Erziehungswissenschaft, 9,* 393–412.

Trautwein, U., & Neumann, M. (2008). Das Gymnasium. In K. S. Cortina, J. Baumert, A. Leschinsky, K. U. Mayer, & L. Trommer (Eds.), *Das Bildungswesen in der Bundesrepublik Deutschland: Strukturen und Entwicklungen im Überblick* (pp. 467–501). Reinbek bei Hamburg, Germany: Rowohlt.

Trautwein, U., Neumann, M., Nagy, G., Lüdtke, O., & Maaz, K. (2010a). Institutionelle Reform und individuelle Entwicklung: Hintergrund und Fragestellungen der Studie TOSCA-Repeat. In U. Trautwein, M. Neumann, G. Nagy, O. Lüdtke, & K. Maaz (Eds.), *Schulleistungen von Abiturienten: Die neu geordnete gymnasiale Oberstufe auf dem Prüfstand* (pp. 15–36). Wiesbaden, Germany: VS Verlag für Sozialwissenschaften.

Trautwein, U., Neumann, M., Nagy, G., Lüdtke, O., & Maaz, K. (Eds.). (2010b). *Schulleistungen von Abiturienten: Die neu geordnete gymnasiale Oberstufe auf dem Prüfstand.* Wiesbaden, Germany: VS Verlag für Sozialwissenschaften.

Vieluf, U., Ivanov, S., & Nikolova, R. (2014). *KESS 12/13 - Kompetenzen und Einstellungen von Schülerinnen und Schülern an Hamburger Schulen am Ende der gymnasialen Oberstufe.* Retrieved from: http://bildungsserver.hamburg.de/contentblob/4396048/6b49c68061321ae400aaa4f7250ebe9f/data/kess12-13.pdf.

Volodina, A., & Nagy, G. (2016). Vocational choices in adolescence: The role of gender, school achievement, self-concepts, and vocational interests. *Journal of Vocational Behavior, 95–96,* 58–73.

Volodina, A., Nagy, G., & Köller, O. (2015). Success in the first phase of the vocational career: The role of cognitive and scholastic abilities, personality factors, and vocational interests. *Journal of Vocational Behavior, 91,* 11–22.

Wagner, G. G., Frick, J. R., & Schupp, J. (2007). The German Socio-Economic Panel Study (SOEP)—Scope, evolution and enhancements. *Schmollers Jahrbuch, 127,* 139–169.

Wagner, M. (1996). Lebensverläufe und gesellschaftlicher Wandel: Die westdeutschen Teilstudien. *ZA-Informationen, 38,* 20–27.

Warm T. A. (1989). Weighted likelihood estimation of ability in item response theory. *Psychometrika, 54,* 427–450.

Watermann, R., Daniel, A., & Maaz, K. (2014). Primäre und sekundäre Disparitäten des Hochschulzugangs: Erklärungsmodelle, Datengrundlagen und Entwicklungen. *Zeitschrift für Erziehungswissenschaft, 17,* 233–261.

Watermann, R., & Maaz, K. (2004). Studierneigung bei Absolventen allgemein bildender und beruflicher Gymnasien. In O. Köller, R. Watermann, U. Trautwein, & O. Lüdtke (Eds.), *Wege zur Hochschulreife in Baden-Württemberg. TOSCA—Eine Untersuchung an allgemein bildenden und beruflichen Gymnasien* (pp. 403–450). Opladen, Germany: Leske & Budrich.

Watermann, R., & Maaz, K. (2006). Effekte der Öffnung von Wegen zur Hochschulreife auf die Studienintention am Ende der gymnasialen Oberstufe. *Zeitschrift für Erziehungswissenschaft, 9,* 219–239.

Watermann, R., & Maaz, K. (2010). Soziale Herkunft und Hochschulzugang—eine Überprüfung der Theorie des geplanten Verhaltens. In W. Bos, E. Klieme, & O. Köller (Eds.), *Schulische Lerngelegenheiten und Kompetenzentwicklung. Festschrift für Jürgen Baumert* (pp. 311–329). Münster, Germany: Waxmann.

Vocational Education and Training and Transitions into the Labor Market

15

Wolfgang Ludwig-Mayerhofer, Reinhard Pollak, Heike Solga, Laura Menze, Kathrin Leuze, Rosine Edelstein, Ralf Künster, Ellen Ebralidze, Gritt Fehring and Susanne Kühn

---

W. Ludwig-Mayerhofer (✉)
University of Siegen, Siegen, Germany
E-Mail: ludwig-mayerhofer@soziologie.uni-siegen.de

R. Pollak (✉) · H. Solga
WZB Berlin Social Science Center and Freie Universität Berlin, Berlin, Germany
E-Mail: reinhard.pollak@wzb.eu

H. Solga
E-Mail: heike.solga@wzb.eu

L. Menze · R. Künster
WZB Berlin Social Science Center, Berlin, Germany
E-Mail: laura.menze@wzb.eu

R. Künster
E-Mail: ralf.kuenster@wzb.eu

K. Leuze
Friedrich-Schiller-University Jena, Jena, Germany
E-Mail: kathrin.leuze@uni-jena.de

R. Edelstein
Berlin Senate Department for Integration, Labour and Social Affairs, Berlin, Germany

E. Ebralidze
Leibniz Institute for Educational Trajectories, Bamberg, Germany
E-Mail: ellen.ebralidze@lifbi.de

G. Fehring
(DZHW) German Centre for Higher Education Research and Social Studies, Hannover, Germany
E-Mail: fehring@dzhw.eu

S. Kühn
Bremen Senate Department for Child and Educational Affairs, Bremen, Germany

© Springer Fachmedien Wiesbaden GmbH, ein Teil von Springer Nature 2019
H.-P. Blossfeld and H.-G. Roßbach (eds.), *Education as a Lifelong Process*,
Edition ZfE 3, https://doi.org/10.1007/978-3-658-23162-0_15

Abstract

Stage 6 of the German National Educational Panel Study (NEPS) 6 is devoted to the transition of young people from school to work. Stage 6 focuses in particular on the transition from school to vocational education and training and then to work (for tertiary education, see Chap. 16). In all Western societies, vocational education and training (VET) systems face a number of challenges, including the need to adapt to increasing skill requirements across the economy and to handle the danger of producing an "underclass" of low-skilled youth. This chapter presents the life-course approach for investigating school-leavers' pathways from school into the labor market within NEPS. Several factors shape young people's school-to-work transitions: their motivation and competence endowment, their decisions to apply for specific educational programs, the constraints they face regarding the opportunities for VET programs and the gatekeepers' recruitment behavior, the information and support youths may or may not receive from social networks, and the learning environments they encounter in firms and schools. We outline the basic theories that guide our research concerning these influences and discuss how we take them into account within NEPS Stage 6. Thus, we provide an overview of the study's research potential in the area of VET. For now, it is mainly the Scientific Use Files of Starting Cohort 4 (SC4) that provide ample opportunities for innovative interdisciplinary analyses—including analyses of students from special education schools. As the starting cohorts age, Starting Cohort 3 (SC3) has now also entered NEPS Stage 6 and its data on VET transitions will soon be available as well.

Keywords

Vocational education and training (VET) · School-to-work transition
Life-course approach · Panel study · Germany

15.1 Introduction

A national economy's competitiveness and performance is linked inherently to the productivity of its workforce. Changes in labor markets and the world of work imply an increase in the average level of skill and competence requirements as well as fast turnovers in the nature of skills. As many studies have shown, schooling and initial vocational and professional training remain of primary importance for occupational careers and social integration (see Mayer and Solga 2008). The content, duration, and frequency of individuals' skills and competence acquisition phases, however, are under pressure to change in accordance with ongoing transformations of work. Nonetheless, initial training, educational participation, and decisions made in earlier life periods are particularly important, because they influence the resources and opportunities available in later periods of individuals' skills and competence acquisition and work life (Elder and Johnson 2003; Mayer 1991). Therefore, Stage 6 of the National Educational Panel Study (NEPS),

"Vocational Education and Training and Transitions into the Labor Market," is devoted to educational biographies in youth's transition from school into the German labor market. Although NEPS produces a German database, most of these research questions are of general relevance for research on school-to-work transitions from a theoretical point of view or a comparative perspective (by combining these detailed data with other national datasets available).

15.2 The German VET System

For a full understanding of the German VET system, it is essential to consider the German "educational schism" (Baethge et al. 2007), that is, the quite unique and enduring institutional division of academic general education versus practical vocational training. Concerning the latter, the so-called dual system of vocational training (apprenticeship in a firm plus partly general and partly occupation-specific theoretical education in vocational schools) has attracted much attention in international debates and research. The dual system has been seen as one of the skill formation systems capable of not only reconciling high wages with high productivity via high skills and high value-added production, but also of integrating less-educated youths into enhancing skill formation processes (Culpepper and Finegold 1999; Culpepper and Thelen 2008; Streeck 1989). However, the ability of the German dual system to adapt to new technological and market conditions is being called into question increasingly regarding, for example, its applicability to the knowledge and service society and its ability to provide general basic competencies or life-long learning (see Baethge et al. 2007).

The dual system has often been portrayed incorrectly as the only form of VET in Germany (e.g., Shackleton 1995). In fact, the German VET system features a number of different tracks or educational pathways. Besides the firm-based dual system, there are school-based VET programs; and both firm and school-based programs lead to nationally recognized occupation-specific VET certificates. The dual system trains youth for manufacturing and industry occupations and some of the white-collar occupations (such as commercial, retail, and administrative occupations), whereas full-time school-based VET programs prepare trainees for personal service occupations (such as nurses, midwives, medium-level care professionals, Kindergarten teachers, and social workers) and medium-level technical occupations (such as the German *Meister* [master craftsmen] or technicians). From these examples, it is clear that firm- and school-based VET programs are not alternative pathways leading to the same occupations, but pathways segmented by occupations. Moreover, this differentiation between firm- and school-based training tracks is gendered: Whereas the dual system trains mainly young men, school-based VET programs are attended primarily by young women (Krüger 2003).

The various VET programs are quite diverse in terms of the skill level to be achieved. They range from comparatively simple manual and retail occupations (e.g., bricklayer, painter, or shop assistant) to rather complex white-collar occupations in banking, insurance, and IT, or even personal service occupations (e.g., speech therapist or midwife). Training programs are further diversified by the trainees' different levels of prior education: Whereas the majority of trainees in the latter occupations hold a *Realschule* or even *Gymnasium* degree (the *Abitur* that also entitles them to enter university), many trainees in the former occupations hold only a *Hauptschule* degree (Protsch and Solga 2016).

For a long time, the public debate on VET in Germany was dominated by the shortage of available apprenticeship positions that manifested itself as early as in the 1980s, with the debate gaining in momentum in the mid-1990s. Since the early 2010s, however, the debate has changed toward concerns about growing regional and occupational mismatches between the demand for and the supply of apprenticeship places ("*Passungsprobleme*") (Bundesinstitut für Berufsbildung 2017; Milde and Matthes 2016). Increasingly, employers do not find trainees and they leave training places vacant, whereas at the same time, a substantive share of young people remains without a training place.

At the same time, skill requirements in regular VET programs have been upgraded significantly. As a result, those who dropped out of school or graduated with only a lower school certificate are left with fewer training opportunities (Protsch 2014; Solga 2004). Today, these school-leavers often do not manage to enter regular VET programs directly and instead enter the so-called transition system that provides prevocational programs usually lasting one year. These programs, however, neither lead to a regular occupational training credential nor guarantee a trainee's successful transition into fully qualifying (firm or school-based) VET programs (Solga and Menze 2013). The number of young people entering this sector of the VET system depends heavily on the availability of regular training places. The transition system was expanded rapidly in times of shortage of training places and then experienced a decrease until 2014. Since then, numbers are increasing again due to the recent wave of newly arriving refugees who often enter programs in this sector of the VET system (Bundesinstitut für Berufsbildung 2017). At the current stage of research, our knowledge about the efficacy of these prevocational programs and the factors that impact positively on participants' school-to-work transitions has been scarce and often limited to certain regions or types of programs (see Behrendt et al. 2017; Beicht 2009; Geier and Braun 2014; Plicht 2016; Weißeno et al. 2016).

In 2015, about 271,000 school-leavers entered such prevocational programs, compared to about 481,000 young people entering firm-based VET programs (dual system) and about 206,000 starting school-based VET programs (Autorengruppe Bildungsberichterstattung 2016). Taking the 20- to 24-year-old population of Germany, about 12% of them have not completed a regular VET degree—so the German educational system still faces the danger of producing an "underclass" of low-skilled, unqualified youth, even though this share has been declining recently (see Bundesinstitut für Berufsbildung 2017; Gesthuizen et al. 2010; Solga 2008).

The problems of the German VET system also emerge when considering the transitions into the labor market of those young people who have graduated successfully from fully qualifying VET programs. About one-fifth of them enter the labor market in occupations that do not match the ones they were trained for—a trend that has increased for men (mainly trained in the dual system) since the 1970s. This sort of occupational mobility is related to jobseekers' employment below their level of vocational training, and it is accompanied by periods of unemployment after completing VET (Konietzka 2002). Thus, even for eventually successful VET graduates, school-to-work transitions often take longer, become more uncertain, and involve higher risks in terms of participation in prevocational measures, unemployment, and lower economic returns to education.

The "educational schism" between VET on the one hand and academic training on the other hand is constitutive for the German educational system. However, there are educational programs at the upper secondary level (vocational *Gymnasium*) and postsecondary/tertiary level (combined higher educational and vocational courses) that dissipate the old schism. Likewise, there are increasingly more legal and actual opportunities for VET graduates to continue to tertiary education programs, overcoming the formerly dead-end track of VET. In NEPS Stage 6, we focus on VET and pre-VET programs, but we collect data on these hybrid and new forms of education as well, enabling the data users to study different pathways in and out of vocational and academic training.

15.3 Research Approaches and Potential of Stage 6

Investigating youth's school-to-work transitions requires a life-course approach. The transition period from school to work is a cumulative—though not always sequential—and highly sensitive phase in an individual's life course. It is shaped by the interplay of institutional regulations, social environments, and individual abilities, competencies, and resources—all of them facilitating or hindering success (see Mayer and Müller 1986). For these reasons, we are interested in educational decision-making processes in constrained situations that differ for various educational and social groups of young adults. Within the school-to-work transition, we need to distinguish, at least analytically, between different, but interrelated status passages. These status passages are: (a) educational decision-making at the end of general schooling (based on occupational preferences and goals formed while at school), (b) transitions from school into the VET system (or into higher education, see Chaps. 14 and 16), (c) pathways through the VET system and completion of VET programs, and (d) entry into the labor market. In all of these status passages, we are interested in the impact of learning environments, individuals' prior educational biographies, competence endowment, and social resources on the patterns, determinants, and outcomes of their transition pathways and skill and competence acquisition.

To gain a full theoretical and empirical understanding, we also have to take into account that school-to-work transitions are not single-agent decisions but socially embedded social interactions that include the outcomes, choices, preferences, values, and experiences of other persons. Furthermore, VET research frequently assumes a steady accumulation of competencies during the transition from school to work regardless of differences in young people's transition pathways. It also tends to overemphasize the aspect of "choice" (see Leggatt-Cock 2005). With the NEPS data, we are able to take a closer look at the constraining influence of demand-side factors and at the impact of supply-side factors on individuals' educational decision-making processes, access to VET programs, and competence acquisition in young adulthood.

For these status passages, we now specify the main theoretical concepts used in developing the NEPS data collection along with important research questions that can be addressed by analyzing the NEPS data. Both our theoretical concepts and our research questions fit into the general framework of NEPS. We focus on decision making and the shaping of decisions by opportunities and constraints, on competencies both as a precondition and a result of successful VET, and on the learning environments young people may encounter during VET, and we discuss the challenges that arise particularly for young migrants.

15.3.1 Educational Decision-Making at the End of General Schooling

At the end of compulsory education in Grade 9 or 10 (depending on the federal state/*Bundesland*), young people face two related decisions: whether or not to continue school (provided their academic performance entitles them to continue general schooling after reaching the end of compulsory education), and, if leaving school, which type of occupation and VET program to choose (see Dombrowski 2015; Schnitzler and Granato 2016). Decision theories are relevant for both types of decisions. At this point, such theories are much more developed for the decision whether or not to continue school; we know much less about the factors and mechanisms underlying occupational aspirations or decisions and their interplay with the "first" decision on continuing schooling. Moreover, most decision theories lead to competing rather than compensatory hypotheses regarding the crucial factors in individual decision-making behavior. What is more, due to a shortage of data to test these hypotheses simultaneously, we also lack knowledge about the relevance of different decision-making factors for different social groups (in terms of class, gender, ethnicity; see Tjaden and Hunkler 2017; Wicht et al. 2017) and for different decision issues. Within Stage 6, we therefore generate data for different decision theories and the two decision issues mentioned above (see also Chap. 6, this volume).

One of the relevant theories in this context is the rational choice approach (see Breen and Goldthorpe 1997). According to this theory, educational decisions depend on so-called secondary effects, that is, on the economic resources of parents (or other family members), the estimated probabilities of a child's success in completing higher levels of schooling or the VET programs at hand, and expectations of returns to education. The costs of training in different fields are assessed in terms of the effort required and the risk of failure. Status maintenance and risk aversion are the two factors that, taken together, explain class differences in decision making on educational alternatives—also while controlling for educational performance. NEPS measures educational performance through a variety of different indicators: individuals' school degrees and school grades at the end of schooling as well as their cognitive competencies and personality traits in 9th grade (i.e., at the end of compulsory education).

Social cognitive theory (Bandura 1986) provides a different explanation for youths' educational decisions at this stage in life (see also Chap. 9, this volume). Self-efficacy beliefs—subjective beliefs about what one is able to accomplish—are considered to be more important than "objective" indicators of abilities or competencies such as grades. Social cognitive theory also emphasizes internal rewards: Individuals may choose to continue school or to enter VET programs not only because of their expectation to succeed economically but also because they may find it inherently satisfying to perform certain tasks skillfully (Bandura 1986). Self-efficacy beliefs are not seen as the only determinant of youths' decisions, however. If labor market prospects are perceived as bad, young people may change their educational and occupational preferences in spite of having low self-efficacy beliefs regarding their ability to continue school successfully or high self-efficacy beliefs regarding their occupational (VET) choice. Personal interests are also seen as an important motivational base of educational and occupational choices. For vocational training and occupational choice, Holland (1997) differentiates six domains of interests or occupational orientations: realistic, investigative, artistic, social, enterprising, and conventional (RIASEC). Whether or not individuals may realize these interests is connected closely to their educational decision about continuing general schooling—given the connection of these interests to different occupations, different training institutions (firm/school-based VET programs or study programs at universities), and different requirements regarding prior education. Generally speaking, whereas expectations regarding the return to education play an important role, self-efficacy beliefs are assumed to have the strongest influence on youths' educational and occupational choices.

Decisions about continuing general education or entering the VET system at age 15 or 16 are among the first important decisions in youths' lives in which they have a substantial degree of autonomy from their parents. Yet their preferences are also influenced by their social background as well as by other social and institutional factors. Parents are important not only because they provide financial support or serve as network resources for the VET search (see below), but also because they shape young people's aspirations (Chesters and Smith 2015; Roth 2017). Furthermore, teachers can influence youths' further educational biographies both directly (by awarding grades that either permit or do not permit them to continue higher secondary school) and indirectly (through their opinions about young people's aptitudes for certain occupations and by providing occupation-related information). Finally, young peoples' educational and occupational aspirations are influenced by their peers as well as the broader school and neighborhood context in which they are embedded (Roth 2017; Wicht and Ludwig-Mayerhofer 2014). The rich NEPS data include these factors of youth's decision-making processes at the end of compulsory education. School leavers from upper secondary education (Grades 12/13) face similar challenges. However, their educational pathways and their choice sets are different (see Chap. 14; Risius et al. 2017).

15.3.2 Determinants of Youth's Placement Within the VET System

Youth's success or failure in accessing and being placed within the VET system is an outcome of, on the one hand, their decisions about investment in education and their related application behavior and activities; and, on the other hand, the available opportunities along with the recruitment behavior of VET gatekeepers.

Constraints on access to VET positions in terms of opportunities and recruitment behavior are explained predominantly by referring to microeconomic theories—such as human capital theory (Becker 1964), signaling theory (Spence 1974), and job competition/vacancy chains (Sørensen 1977; Thurow 1975). Educational attainment is used by employers as an indicator of future productivity and trainability: the lower an individual's educational degree, the lower her or his rank in the applicants' queue and the lower her or his chances of being recruited for a vacant regular VET position (or job). According to this view, an individual's opportunity is defined by the individual's investment in schooling, the supply of more highly educated persons, and the amount of vacant VET positions (typically in the local geographical region). As a result, school leavers' training opportunities are determined to a considerable degree by their relative (as opposed to their absolute) competence endowment and educational certificates (Solga 2005).

Second, gatekeepers in the VET system make recruitment decisions under uncertainty, because it is difficult to observe an individual's productivity and trainability directly. Recruitment tests would increase transaction costs and would run the risk of being considered illegitimate. Hence, employers use individual characteristics such as prior educational attainment, but also gender, ethnicity, age, or disability/overt health status—deemed to be related to learning behavior and competence endowment—as indicators of individual productivity. One common mechanism for doing this is "statistical discrimination," according to which judgments about an individual's potential productivity are based on their group membership in certain social categories and on a probabilistic belief regarding that group's trainability and productivity. Concerning ethnicity, results based on NEPS Starting Cohort 4 have shown that even when school performance is controlled for, young people without a migration background are more likely to enter regular VET programs than young people with a migration history. This lower participation in regular VET programs among migrant youth is caused by both their lower preferences for participation in these programs (self-selection, see below) and the recruitment practices of gatekeepers in the dual system (Beicht and Walden 2017; Tjaden and Hunkler 2017).

There has been a lively theoretical and policy-related debate about the relevance of school certificates, school grades, and cognitive and noncognitive competencies for gatekeepers' decisions, and how strongly formal certificates function as "signals" shaping gatekeepers' assessments of a candidate's competencies in VET recruitment processes (see Kohlrausch and Solga 2012; Protsch and Dieckhoff 2011). Using data from NEPS Starting Cohort 4, Holtmann et al. (2017) were able to show that for low-achieving school leavers, variation in cognitive and noncognitive competencies does not matter for gatekeepers' recruitment decisions over and above formal school certificates and school grades. Furthermore, the structure of the regional labor and apprenticeship market is important for individuals' chances of entering regular VET programs (Hillmert et al. 2017; Wicht and Nonnenmacher 2017). For example, the regional supply and demand for training places can influence the recruitment criteria of employers (Protsch et al. 2017). To further investigate the role of regional characteristics for placement in the VET system, NEPS data can be supplemented with regional information from other sources such as that on the supply and demand for apprenticeship positions (by occupations), the sectoral structure of regional labor markets, and structural data on training firms (such as firm size and composition of employees).

What factors may explain youths' behavior in seeking and applying for positions in the VET system? Network theorists (e.g., Burt 1997; Elliott and Smith 2004) have shown that an individual's job search is determined significantly by socially stratified recruitment and supply networks. Networks provide information on vacant job positions, give second-hand accounts of employment experiences, and explain job requirements. They may also increase an applicant's reputation, because having employed persons in one's network is valuable (in terms of borrowed social capital). Network resources have been shown to be gendered, and that they contribute to channel women more often into female and men more often into male occupations (Straits 1998). Hence, networks entail structural differences in available contacts, in the base of experiences, as well as in assistance or resistance from others that youth can count on in their VET search (see also Chap. 6, this volume).

However, the role of network resources for VET search behavior and access to VET programs is largely underinvestigated. According to Granovetter (1974), weak ties in particular should provide favorable resources for accessing jobs (or here, apprenticeships). However, as Boxman et al. (1991) and Wegener (1989) have shown, this weak-ties mechanism applies only to upward mobility, especially among highly qualified individuals. In contrast, resources provided by strong ties could be particularly relevant for low-educated individuals, because strong ties (such as parents, siblings, or best friends) provide more reliable information on applicants' competencies than weak ties. A survey among German firms has shown that small companies in particular rely on "recommendations by others (especially parents and neighbors)" when recruiting low-educated youths for apprenticeships (Seyfried 2006, p. 35). Yet, the study by Holtmann et al. (2017) found that for low-achieving school-leavers, better parental resources improve neither their VET search behavior nor their chance of gaining access to regular VET programs. NEPS offers the opportunity to further investigate the role that different kinds of network resources play with regard to the chances different social groups have of entering VET programs.

Moreover, motivational, cognitive, and personality factors may influence youths' VET search behavior (see also Chap. 9 this volume). Youths' VET search intensity and activities should also be influenced by their motivation to continue their education in VET programs or to withdraw from educational institutions because of a low identification with educational goals as a result of unfavorable "cooling-out" processes (Clark 1960) and the fear of possible humiliation and further negative reactions (Jones et al. 1984, p. 111). According to social-psychological research on stereotypes and intergroup relations (see Brewer and Brown 1998), prior experiences in school and/or in prevocational programs should therefore affect youths' motivation in their initial and further VET search. Holtmann et al. (2017) show that low-achieving school leavers often withdraw from the apprenticeship market altogether, whereas higher aspirations and better vocational orientation are related to a stronger likelihood among them to both apply and be selected for regular VET programs.

In the matching process, career guidance offices (a department of the Federal Employment Agency) play an important role, especially for students from special education schools or *Hauptschule*. Career guidance officers often channel low-educated applicants into prevocational programs. As a prerequisite for being entitled to enter such programs, the youths in question have to be declared as not yet "mature enough for VET" (*ausbildungsreif*), a procedure that exposes them to processes of (self-)stigmatization that may affect their self-efficacy beliefs and self-concepts. Low-achieving school graduates, therefore, may face a higher risk of withdrawal or self-exclusion from competition over (scarce) regular VET positions. However, this risk might differ in terms of individuals' cognitive and noncognitive competencies (even given equal school certificates). NEPS Stage 6 data offer a unique data source to analyze inter- and intraindividual variation in the VET search behavior of young adults with detailed information on individual competencies, networks, life courses, educational performances, and parental resources. This is especially true for low-achieving students: For the first time, the NEPS data offer a nationally representative sample of former special education students, due to an oversampling of this group sponsored by the Federal Employment Agency.

15.3.3 Successful Completion of VET Programs

School-to-work transitions are not always defined by a single entrance into one VET program, but are often sequences of multiple VET episodes—both completed and uncompleted. Whereas young people's search for and access to subsequent VET positions is structured by the mechanisms elaborated above (Sects. 15.3.1 and 15.3.2), their prior VET biography, their search experiences within the VET system, possible "adaptations" of occupational aspirations (often made involuntarily), and the competencies acquired during previous VET episodes should also affect gatekeepers' perception of their skills on the one hand and their own motivation, search strategies, and resources on the other hand. The finding that individuals "correct" their occupational plans because of success or failure in accessing VET positions indicates the plasticity of how people navigate into and through the VET system (Heinz 2002). We have little knowledge, however, about the determinants of this intraindividual plasticity of educational/occupational goals and of the interindividual differences in the pathways through the VET system and their outcomes. NEPS enables us to fill this knowledge gap.

Young people may leave the VET system with very different outcomes in terms of *certificates*: They may finish a VET episode (a) without a completed recognized certificate (because they enter a short-track program without recognized certificates or have dropped out of fully qualifying VET programs once or several times); (b) with a recognized certificate after having completed one VET program or reentered further programs (with different companies and/or in different occupations); (c) with a recognized certificate after having upgraded their school degree and then (re-)entered programs (e.g., a sizable number of youths reenter school in order to increase their comparative advantage in competition for VET positions); or (d) with multiple certificates for different occupations after having reentered and completed several programs. In prevocational training programs, students do not earn a vocational degree, but they may complete a lower secondary general degree.

We know comparatively little about the factors that influence both the successful acquisition of certificates and the development of competencies. According to constructivist learning theories (e.g., Lanahan et al. 2005), learning is rooted in the learners' activities through which they make use of the opportunities for learning provided by teachers/trainers (i.e., specific learning tasks, learning materials, etc.). NEPS data offer a large set of motivational factors and items on learning environments. For example, how do learning environments have to be designed to trigger trainees' curiosity and challenge their capabilities without discouraging them? Can teachers or trainers enhance learners' motivation (see Chap. 5, this volume)? Given the longitudinal design of NEPS, we are able to investigate the impact of cognitive and noncognitive competencies acquired during school on taking advantage of learning opportunities during the transition from school to work.

In addition, there is no systematic knowledge about how learning settings and their specific properties contribute to the development of cognitive and noncognitive competencies. The same holds true for the effects of prevocational programs. Many researchers argue that these programs improve neither young people's skill level nor their general competencies (Behrendt et al. 2017; Weißeno et al. 2016).

NEPS is keen to provide data to study these issues in more depth. Collecting comprehensive objective information on learning environments in very different VET programs attended by young persons (i.e., information obtained from their teachers and trainers) is not feasible within a large-scale longitudinal survey such as NEPS. We therefore provide subjective information, that is, standardized information from the trainees' perspective. This information includes type of training attended, profile of VET program activities, extent of actual involvement in work processes in the workplace, quality of learning environment, and class composition in vocational school. Given that the German VET system is more diverse than is often assumed, collecting information within NEPS about these basic features of youths' learning environments from a large and representative sample of participants in a wide array of VET programs marks an important step toward a deeper understanding of the impact of learning environments on individuals' success in the VET systems.

Furthermore, it is surprising how little is known about the influence of cognitive competencies and motivational factors on the odds of completing a VET program successfully. It is unknown to which degree social-class-biased assessments (known from school research) occur in VET programs, and what the consequences are in terms of youths' efforts during VET. Although competencies may be the most important determinants of completing a training program successfully (as measured by successful graduation or by the grades obtained in the final examinations), assessments biased by social class, ethnicity, gender, or other factors affecting motivation may also play an important role.

Cognitive competencies are understood and measured as domain-specific and domain-general competencies (see Chap. 4). In an add-on study, we also measured occupation-specific competencies for one specific VET program (commercial office workers) in one specific school year. While results have been encouraging, we shall not be able to introduce measures of occupation-specific competencies for other VET programs in the NEPS data, because the development and the administration of such measures would go beyond the scope of NEPS.

In order to gain some information about the actual content and performance of training programs, we introduced a measure of job tasks (cf. Autor et al. 2003) in VET programs. Using this measure, data users can analyze to which degree VET programs with different learning environments (e.g., small and large firms, more or less encouraging instructors) use youth's cognitive or noncognitive competencies and prepare them for more complex tasks. The "job" task measurement in VET corresponds to the measure of job tasks in later jobs, so the data allow us to assess the development of job tasks from VET to early and mid-life career stages.

Finally, we should emphasize that participation in VET programs is not just related to the acquisition of skills, competencies, or certificates relevant for success in the labor market and at the workplace. It also constitutes an important step toward adulthood. Youths' feelings of not being able to master these challenges can have negative outcomes, including delayed or no family formation, less life satisfaction, less social or political participation, and early unemployment that can cause long-lasting "scarring" effects on young people's behavior and attitudes (Barklamb 2001).

15.3.4 Pathways from the VET System into the Labor Market

Research has shown that firm-based and occupation-specific VET systems like that in Germany produce less turbulence in the school-to-work transition than systems that focus on general education such as those in the United Kingdom and the United States (Allmendinger 1989; Buchmann 2002). In times of recession, delayed entries occur more frequently in Germany as well because firms increasingly choose not to offer their trainees continued employment after their apprenticeship (Dietrich and Gerner 2007). Likewise, transitions to the labor market might include firm and even occupational changes, overeducation, and unemployment. NEPS data from Stage 6 mirror smooth transitions as well as rather rough labor market entry histories of young people (Konietzka 2002; Seibert and Wydra-Somaggio 2017). In addition, some research literature suggests that a strong work ethic, ICT competencies, and so-called soft skills or personal styles should play an accentuated role in recruitment in times of high job competition (see, for the role of psychological factors, e.g., Diewald 2006), technological progress, and a growing service sector industry (see also Buchmann 2002; Murnane and Levy 1996). NEPS provides outstanding opportunities to investigate this assumed accentuation and its underlying processes in much more detail than ever before by taking advantage of the large regional and occupational differences in labor market competition within Germany and the manifold sources of information on educational and VET performance, noncognitive characteristics, and young adults' social environment factors.

As with VET placement, initial job placement and post-VET unemployment risks should result from the interplay of supply- and demand-side factors; or, in other words, from individuals' application behavior, gatekeepers' recruitment decisions, and structural labor market conditions. VET certificates are of crucial importance for both employers' recruitment decisions and young adults' job search because of German *credentialism* and the strong link between the VET system and the labor market (Blossfeld 1989; Solga and Konietzka 1999). Accordingly, recent research has shown that the training occupation highly structures the transition from VET to the labor market (Buchs et al. 2015; Menze 2017). This is why in Germany, school certificates used to have less influence on job placements than VET certificates. However, at least in public debates, employers seem to be increasingly demanding multiskilled "knowledge workers" who possess good vocational skills *and* general competencies (such as mathematical literacy, reading literacy, ICT literacy, and language skills) supplemented with problem-solving competencies and interpersonal and teamwork skills (Murnane and Levy 1996). However, it is still unknown why and to what extent cognitive and noncognitive competencies and school and VET certificates determine initial labor market placement. Some studies show that the effects of one's abilities differ by job complexity: the higher the complexity of jobs, the higher the influence of general cognitive abilities (the so-called "g factor") on occupational success (Gottfredson 1986). On the other hand, research by Schoon and Parsons (2002) has revealed that the importance of educational credentials for occupational attainment varies by economic and labor market conditions. This suggests that the relative influence of individuals' abilities and their educational certificates might depend on individuals' labor market context. The (absolute and relative) effect of cognitive competencies (such as reading or mathematical literacy) on individuals' first job placement is still entirely unknown for the German labor market. For Switzerland, the TREE project provides mixed evidence on the impact of cognitive competencies on job placement over and above VET certificates (Buchs et al. 2015; Müller and Schweri 2015). With the NEPS data, we are able to investigate the influence and (inter)relationship of school and VET certificates, educational biographies, cognitive and noncognitive competencies, and structural factors on patterns and outcomes of youth's labor market placements (see Chap. 8, this volume).

Finally, it should be added that NEPS provides excellent opportunities to study migrant youths' transition pathways and their outcomes, especially those of Turks and ethnic German youth who have emigrated from Eastern Europe (see Chap. 7, this volume). Research has found that young migrants—especially male Turks—have poorer labor market opportunities after having successfully completed regular VET program(s) than native German apprentices (Damelang and Haas 2006; Seibert and Solga 2005). They face higher risks of unemployment after leaving VET and, if employed, of entering only unskilled jobs. The explanations given by different researchers to account for this inequality are controversial. Some stress employers' discrimination based on an ethnically biased signaling value of VET certificates (Seibert 2005; Seibert and Solga 2005). Others, such as Kalter (2006), emphasize poorer job search resources, poorer human capital, and Turks' limited "social assimilation." There are good reasons to believe that supply- as well as demand-side factors are at work in producing these ethnic differences. NEPS provides for the first time data that allow us to simultaneously investigate the influence of demand-side and supply-side factors.

15.4 Concluding Remarks

The chapter has outlined some important research potentials of the longitudinal NEPS data in the area of transitions from school to work and the German VET system. The opportunity to study the interplay of demand- and supply-side factors in explaining intraindividual plasticity in educational and occupational decisions as well as interindividual differences in successful and unsuccessful transitions is a particular strength of the NEPS data. This potential is further increased when considering the interrelations of NEPS Stage 6 with Stage 5 (on participation in the Gymnasium, see Chap. 14, this volume), Stage 7 (on university attendance, see Chap. 16, this volume), and Stage 8 (on further education and work histories, see Chap. 17, this volume). Due to space limitations, we can only sketch a few of the interesting research issues here.

In connection with Stage 5, we are able to investigate differences in competence acquisition and transition patterns among youth holding an upper secondary school degree awarded by a *Gymnasium* or other school type (such as vocational school or evening classes). Concerning Stage 7, the replacement of traditional German university programs and degrees (i.e., *Diplom* and *Magister*) with 3-year bachelor's and 2-year master's programs and certificates at universities and universities of applied sciences may well impact on the VET system in the near future. These two sectors may increasingly compete directly with one another—not only in terms of student recruitment but also in terms of graduates' labor market opportunities (e.g., in commercial or technical occupations). And we witness the establishment of hybrid educational models combining VET and tertiary education. We are able to analyze whether these changes in tertiary education influence young people's decisions to participate in either VET or tertiary education, if and how these decisions differ by social groups, and what this means in terms of educational and social inequality. The NEPS participants in Starting Cohorts 4 and 3 receive stage-specific questionnaires depending on their current educational status. These questionnaires are designed specifically to allow for cohort-wide analyses. Finally with regard to Stage 8, we provide manifold educational measurements for the school-to-work transition period, measurements that can be used in causal analyses of interindividual differences in participation in further adult education, occupational success in later life, and patterns of employment careers. Moreover, we are able to compare the relationships of different supply-side and demand-side factors and their group-specific impact on VET and later job placement processes. All of this could help us understand the underlying social mechanisms that produce different outcomes in terms of VET and labor-market placement—and eventually enable us to support policy interventions on an empirically sound base.

References

Allmendinger, J. (1989). Educational systems and labor market outcomes. *European Sociological Review, 5*(3), 231–250.

Autor, D., Levy, F., & Murnane, R. J. (2003). The skill content of recent technological change. *The Quarterly Journal of Economics, 118*(4), 1279–1333.

Autorengruppe Bildungsberichterstattung (2016). *Bildung in Deutschland 2016*. Bielefeld, Germany: W. Bertelsmann Verlag.

Baethge, M., Solga, H., & Wieck, M. (2007). *Berufsbildung im Umbruch*. Berlin, Germany: Friedrich-Ebert-Stiftung. Retrieved January 10, 2008, from http://library.fes.de/pdf-files/stabsabteilung/04258/index.html.

Bandura, A. (1986). *Social foundations of thought and action*. Englewood Cliffs, NJ: Prentice-Hall.

Barklamb, S. (2001). *Meeting the youth employment challenge*. Geneva, Switzerland: International Labor Office.

Becker, G. S. (1964). *Human capital*. New York, NY: National Bureau of Economic Research.

Beicht, U. (2009). Verbesserung der Ausbildungschancen oder sinnlose Wartschleife? Zur Bedeutung und Wirksamkeit von Bildungsgängen am Übergang Schule – Berufsausbildung. Bonn, Germany: BIBB.

Beicht, U., & Walden, G. (2017). Generationeneffekte beim Übergang von Schulabgängern mit Migrationshintergrund in betriebliche Ausbildung. *Zeitschrift für Berufs- und Wirtschaftspädagogik, 113*(3), 428–460.

Behrendt, S., Nickolaus, R., & Seeber, S. (2017). Entwicklung der Basiskompetenzen im Übergangssystem. *Unterrichtswissenschaften, 45*(1), 51–66.

Blossfeld, H.-P. (1989). *Kohortendifferenzierung und Karriereprozeß*. Frankfurt a.M., Germany: Campus.

Boxman, E. A. W., de Graaf, P. M., & Flap, H. D. (1991). The impact of social and human capital on the income attainment of Dutch managers. *Social Networks, 13*(1), 51–73.

Breen, R., & Goldthorpe, J. H. (1997). Explaining educational differentials. *Rationality and Society, 9*(3), 275–305.

Brewer, M. B., & Brown, R. J. (1998). Intergroup relations. In D. T. Gilbert, S. T. Fiske, & L. Gardner (Eds.), *Handbook of social psychology* (pp. 554–594). Boston, MA: McGraw-Hill.

Buchmann, M. (2002). Labor market entry and beyond: Some reflections on the changing structure of work. *Education + Training, 44*(4/5), 217–223.

Buchs, H, Müller, B., & Buchmann, M. (2015). Qualifikationsnachfrage und Arbeitsmarkteintritt in der Schweiz. Arbeit im erlernten Beruf, Berufswechsel oder Arbeitslosigkeit. *Kölner Zeitschrift für Soziologie und Sozialpsychologie, 67*(4), 709–736.

Bundesinstitut für Berufsbildung (2017). *Datenreport zum Berufsbildungsbericht 2017*. Bonn, Germany: BIBB.

Burt, R. S. (1997). The contingent value of social capital. *Administrative Science Quarterly, 42*(2), 339–365.

Chesters, J., & Smith, J. (2015). Social capital and aspirations for educational attainment: A cross-national comparison of Australia and Germany. *Journal of Youth Studies, 18*(7), 932–949.

Clark, B. R. (1960). The "cooling-out" function of higher education. *American Journal of Sociology, 65*(6), 569–576.

Culpepper, D. C., & Finegold, D. (1999). *The German skills machine*. New York, NY: Berghahn Books.

Culpepper, P. D., & Thelen, K. (2008). Institutions and collective actors in the provision of training: Historical and cross-national comparisons. In K. U. Mayer & H. Solga (Eds.), *Skill formation – Interdisciplinary and cross-national perspectives* (pp. 21–49). New York, NY: Cambridge University Press.

Damelang, A., & Haas, A. (2006). *Arbeitsmarkteinstieg nach dualer Berufsausbildung – Migranten und Deutsche im Vergleich* (IAB-Forschungsbericht 17/2006). Nürnberg, Germany: Institut für Arbeitsmarkt- und Berufsforschung.

Dietrich, H., & Gerner, H.-D. (2007). The determinants of apprenticeship training with particular reference to business expectations. *Zeitschrift für Arbeitsmarktforschung, 40*(2/3), 221–233.

Diewald, M. (2006). Spirals of success and failure? The interplay of control beliefs and working. In M. Diewald, A. Goedicke, & K. U. Mayer (Eds.), *After the fall of the wall. East German life courses in transition* (pp. 214–236). Stanford, CA: Stanford University Press.

Dombrowski, R. (2015). *Berufswünsche benachteiligter Jugendlicher. Die Konkretisierung der Berufsorientierung gegen Ende der Vollzeitschulpflicht*. Bielefeld, Germany: W. Bertelsmann Verlag.

Elder, G. H., & Johnson, M. K. (2003). The life course and aging. In R. A. Settersten (Ed.), *Invitation to the life course* (pp. 48–81). Amityville, NY: Baywood.

Elliott, J. R., & Smith, R. A. (2004). Race, gender, and workplace power. *American Sociological Review, 69*(3), 365–386.

Geier, B., & Braun, F. (2014): Hauptschulabsolventinnen und -absolventen im Übergangssystem: Ergebnisse aus einer Längsschnittstudie. *Zeitschrift für Berufs- und Wirtschaftspädagogik, 110*(2), 168–187.

Gesthuizen, M., Solga, H., & Künster, R. (2010). Context matters: Economic marginalisation of low-educated workers in cross-national perspective. *European Sociological Review* (advance publication: https://doi.org/10.1093/esr/jcq006).

Gottfredson, L. S. (Ed.). (1986). The g factor in employment. *Journal of Vocational Behavior 29*(3), 379–410.

Granovetter, M. (1974). *Getting a job: A study of contacts and careers*. Cambridge, MA: Harvard University Press.

Heinz, W. R. (2002). Transition discontinuities and the biographical shaping of early work careers. *Journal of Vocational Behavior, 60*(2), 220–240.

Hillmert, S., Hartung, A., & Weßling, K. (2017). A decomposition of local labour-market conditions and their relevance for inequalities in transitions to vocational training. *European Sociological Review, 33*(4), 534–550.

Holland, J. L. (1997). *Making vocational choices: A theory of vocational personalities and work environments*. Odessa, FL: Psychological Assessment Resources.

Holtmann, A. C., Menze, L., & Solga, H. (2017). Persistent disadvantages or new opportunities? The role of agency and structural constraints for low-achieving adolescents' school-to-work transitions. *Journal of Youth and Adolescence, 46*(10), 2091–2113.

Jones, E. E., Amerigo, F., Hastorf, A. H., Hazel, M., Miller, D. T., & Scott, R. A. (1984). *Social stigma*. New York, NY: Freeman.

Kalter, F. (2006). Auf der Suche nach einer Erklärung für die spezifischen Arbeitsmarktnachteile Jugendlicher türkischer Herkunft. *Zeitschrift für Soziologie, 35*(2), 144–160.

Kohlrausch, B., & Solga, H. (2012). Übergänge in Ausbildung: Welche Rolle spielt die Ausbildungsreife? *Zeitschrift für Erziehungswissenschaften, 15*(4), 753–773.

Konietzka, D. (2002). Die soziale Differenzierung der Übergangsmuster in den Beruf. *Kölner Zeitschrift für Soziologie und Sozialpsychologie, 54*(4), 645–673.

Krüger, H. (2003). Berufliche Bildung. Der deutsche Sonderweg und die Geschlechterfrage. *Berliner Journal für Soziologie, 13*(4), 497–510.

Lanahan, L., McGrath, D. J., McLaughlin, M., Burian-Fitzgerald, M., & Salganik, L. (2005). *Fundamental problems in the measurement of instructional processes*. Washington, DC: American Institutes for Research.

Leggatt-Cook, C. (2005). *Contemporary school to work transitions* (Research Report No. 4/2005). Auckland, New Zealand: Massey University, Labor Market Dynamics Research Program.

Mayer, K. U. (1991). Soziale Ungleichheit und die Differenzierung von Lebensverläufen. In W. Zapf (Ed.), *Die Modernisierung moderner Gesellschaften* (pp. 667–687). Frankfurt a.M., Germany: Campus.

Mayer, K. U., & Müller, W. (1986). The state and the structure of the life course. In A. B. Sørensen, F. E. Weinert, & L. R. Sherrod (Eds.), *Human development and the life course* (pp. 217–245). Hillsdale, NJ: Lawrence Erlbaum.

Mayer, K. U., & Solga, H. (2008). *Skill formation – Interdisciplinary and cross-national perspectives*. New York, NY: Cambridge University Press.

Menze, L. (2017). Horizontale und vertikale Adäquanz im Anschluss an die betriebliche Ausbildung. Zur Bedeutung von Merkmalen des Ausbildungsberufs. *Kölner Zeitschrift für Soziologie und Sozialpsychologie, 69*(1), 79–107.

Milde, B., & Matthes, S. (2016). Passungsprobleme am Ausbildungsmarkt – Entwicklungen im Jahr 2015. *Berufsbildung in Wissenschaft und Praxis, 4,* 11–15.

Müller, B., & Schweri, J. (2015). How specific is apprenticeship training? Evidence from interfirm and occupational mobility after graduation. *Oxford Economic Papers, 67*(4), 1057–1077.

Murnane, R., & Levy, F. (1996). *Teaching the new basic skills*. New York, NY: Free Press.

Plicht, H. (2016). Die ersten fünf Jahre nach einer berufsvorbereitenden Bildungsmaßnahme (BvB) – Befunde zum Übergang in Ausbildung und Beschäftigung. *Sozialer Fortschritt, 65*(6), 142–151.

Protsch, P. (2014). *Segmentierte Ausbildungsmärkte. Berufliche Chancen von Hauptschülerinnen und Hauptschülern im Wandel*. Opladen, Germany: Budrich UniPress.

Protsch, P., & Dieckhoff, M. (2011). What matters in the transition from school to vocational training in Germany – Educational credentials, cognitive abilities or personality? *European Societies, 13*(1), 69.91.

Protsch, P., Gerhards, C., & Mohr, S. (2017). *Welche Anforderungen stellen Betriebe an zukünftige Auszubildende mit mittlerem Schulabschluss? Stellenwert kognitiver und nichtkognitiver schulischer Leistungsmerkmale bei regional-beruflichen Rekrutierungsschwierigkeiten*. Bonn, Germany: BIBB.

Protsch, P., & Solga, H. (2016). The social stratification of the German VET system. *Journal of Education and Work, 29*(6), 637–661.

Risius, P., Malin, L., & Flake, R. (2017). *Ausbildung oder Studium? Wie Unternehmen Abiturienten bei der Berufsorientierung unterstützten können* (Studie 3/2017). Köln, Germany: Institut der deutschen Wirtschaft.

Roth, T. (2017). Interpersonal influences on education expectations: New evidence from Germany. *Research in Social Stratification and Mobility, 48*, 68–84.

Schnitzler, A., & Granato, M. (2016). Duale Ausbildung oder weiter zur Schule? Bildungspräferenzen von Jugendlichen in der 9. Klasse und wie sie sich ändern. *Berufsbildung in Wissenschaft und Praxis, 3*, 10–14.

Schoon, I., & Parsons, S. (2002). Teenage aspirations for future careers and occupational outcomes. *Journal of Vocational Behavior, 60*(2), 262–288.

Seibert, H. (2005). *Integration durch Ausbildung? Berufliche Platzierung ausländischer Ausbildungsabsolventen der Geburtsjahrgänge 1960 bis 1971*. Berlin, Germany: Logos.

Seibert, H., & Solga, H. (2005). Gleiche Chancen dank einer abgeschlossenen Ausbildung? Zum Signalwert von Ausbildungsabschlüssen bei ausländischen und deutschen jungen Erwachsenen. *Zeitschrift für Soziologie, 34*(5), 364–382.

Seibert, H., & Wydra-Somaggio, G. (2017). *Berufseinstieg nach der betrieblichen Ausbildung: Meist gelingt ein nahtloser Übergang* (IAB-Kurzbericht 20/2017). Nürnberg, Germany: Institut für Arbeitsmarkt- und Berufsforschung.

Seyfried, B. (2006). *Berufsausbildungsvorbereitung aus betrieblicher Sicht*. Bonn, Germany: BIBB.

Shackleton, J. R. (1995). *Training for employment in Western Europe and the United States*. Aldershot, England: Edward Elgar.

Solga, H. (2004). Ausgrenzungserfahrungen trotz Integration – Die Übergangsbiografien von Jugendlichen ohne Schulabschluss. In S. Hillmert & K. U. Mayer (Eds.), *Geboren 1964 und 1971 – Neuere Untersuchungen zu Ausbildungs- und Berufschancen in der Bundesrepublik Deutschland* (pp. 39–63). Wiesbaden, Germany: VS Verlag.

Solga, H. (2005). *Ohne Abschluss in die Bildungsgesellschaft*. Opladen, Germany: Barbara Budrich Verlag.

Solga, H. (2008). Lack of training – Employment opportunities of low-skilled persons from a sociological and microeconomic perspective. In K. U. Mayer & H. Solga (Eds.), *Skill formation – Interdisciplinary and cross-national perspectives* (pp. 173–204). New York, NY: Cambridge University Press.

Solga, H., & Konietzka. D. (1999). Occupational matching and social stratification. Theoretical insights and empirical observations taken from a German–German comparison. *European Sociological Review, 15*(1), 25–47.

Solga, H., & Menze, L. (2013). Der Zugang zur Ausbildung: Wie integrationsfähig ist das deutsche Berufsbildungssystem? *WSI Mitteilungen, 66*(1), 5–14.

Sørensen, A. B. (1977). The structure of inequality and the process of attainment. *American Sociological Review, 42*(6), 965–978.

Spence, M. A. (1974). *Market signaling*. Cambridge, MA: Harvard University Press.

Straits, B. C. (1998). Occupational sex segregation: The role of personal ties. *Journal of Vocational Behavior, 52*(2), 191–207.

Streeck, W. (1989). Skills and the limits of neo-liberalism. *Work, Employment and Society, 3*(1), 89–104.

Thurow, L. C. (1975). *Generating inequality*. New York, NY: Basic Books.

Tjaden, J. D., & Hunkler, C. (2017). The optimism trap: Migrants' educational choices in stratified education systems. *Social Science Research, 67*, 213–228.

Wegener, B. (1989). Vom Nutzen entfernter Bekannter. *Kölner Zeitschrift für Soziologie und Sozialpsychologie, 41*, 270–297.

Weißeno, S., Seeber, S., Kosanke, J.,& Stange, C. (2016). Development of mathematical competency in different German pre-vocational training programmes of the transition system. *Empirical Research in Vocational Education and Training,* 8:14.

Wicht, A., & Ludwig-Mayerhofer, W. (2014). The impact of neighborhoods and schools on young people's occupational aspirations. *Journal of Vocational Behavior, 85*(3), 298–308.

Wicht, A., & Nonnenmacher, A. (2017). Modeling spatial opportunity structures and youths' transitions from school to training. *Open Journal of Statistics, 7*(6), 1013–1038.

Wicht, A., Siembab, M., & Ludwig-Mayerhofer, W. (2017). Berufliche Aspirationen von Jugendlichen mit und ohne Migrationshintergrund. *Berufsbildung in Wissenschaft und Praxis, 4,* 10–13.

Higher Education and the Transition to Work

16

Julia-Carolin Brachem, Florian Aschinger, Gritt Fehring, Michael Grotheer, Sonja Herrmann, Marie Kühn, Uta Liebeskind, Andreas Ortenburger and Hildegard Schaeper

---

J.-C. Brachem (✉)
University of Vechta, Vechta, Germany
E-Mail: julia-carolin.brachem@uni-vechta.de

F. Aschinger
Bamberg University Library, Bamberg, Germany
E-Mail: florian.aschinger@uni-bamberg.de

G. Fehring · M. Grotheer · A. Ortenburger · H. Schaeper
DZHW – German Centre for Higher Education Research and Social Studies, Hanover, Germany
E-Mail: fehring@dzhw.eu

M. Grotheer
E-Mail: grotheer@dzhw.eu

A. Ortenburger
E-Mail: ortenburger@dzhw.eu

H. Schaeper
E-Mail: schaeper@dzhw.eu

S. Herrmann
Ludwig Maximilian University of Munich, Munich, Germany
E-Mail: sonja.herrmann@edu.lmu.de

M. Kühn
GESIS – Leibniz-Institute for the Social Sciences, Mannheim, Germany
E-Mail: marie.kuehn@gesis.org

U. Liebeskind
University of Siegen, Siegen, Germany
E-Mail: liebeskind@soziologie.uni-siegen.de

© Springer Fachmedien Wiesbaden GmbH, ein Teil von Springer Nature 2019
H.-P. Blossfeld and H.-G. Roßbach (eds.), *Education as a Lifelong Process*,
Edition ZfE 3, https://doi.org/10.1007/978-3-658-23162-0_16

Abstract

Within the conceptual framework of the German National Educational Panel Study (NEPS), data on higher education and the transition to work are collected by following about 18,000 students on their pathway from enrolment in the winter term 2010/2011 to the labor market (Starting Cohort First-Year Students). This article gives insights into methodological issues such as the study design, the challenges of web-based data collection, and survey participation. Furthermore, it describes the main research issues and gives an overview of the data collected so far, focusing on the measurement of subject-specific competencies, transitions (to/within higher education, to the labor market), learning environments in (pre-) doctoral programs, higher education graduates' employment situation and work characteristics, family planning, and the special survey program for teachers and teacher candidates. In addition, it gives an overview of educational trajectories within the student cohort.

Keywords

Higher education students · graduates · panel study · modes of data collection transitions · educational trajectories

16.1 Introduction

When the National Educational Panel Study (NEPS) was conceptualized in the 2000s, the German higher education system was facing several challenges: The Bachelor's/Master's system was newly introduced, the steering of higher education institutions (HEIs) and the curriculum development shifted from input orientation and teacher-centered education to an output-oriented student-centered approach, and the expansion of the private higher education sector and the diversification of HEIs began to alter the German higher education landscape. In addition, previous issues such as underinvestment in higher education, increasing heterogeneity of student populations, and the link between higher education and work continued to be a major concern for higher education policy and management (Mayer 2008; Liebeskind in press).

At the same time, empirical research lacked a comprehensive nationwide microdata base for analyzing higher education, its prerequisites, relevant decisions, and short- and long-term outcomes from a life-course perspective. Available data were restricted to particular transitions and stages within the higher education system without focusing on either competencies, learning environments, or the first years in the labor market. Panel data projects were restricted to particular Federal States, institutions, or fields of study. In addition to the lack of comprehensive data sources, little was known about the learning environments in HEIs and their impact on competence formation and higher education trajectories. The same was true for the impact that (generic) competencies have on the decisions and careers of higher education students and graduates. Moreover, a hitherto unfulfilled desideratum in German higher education research was to systematically collect nationwide data on teacher education and to shed light on (prospective) teachers' paths through higher education studies and their subsequent preparatory service, as well as on their entry into teaching positions and their first years as teachers.

Data collection in the NEPS Starting Cohort First-Year Students aimed to fill these gaps and thus pave the way for empirical research on the above-mentioned questions. The guiding research questions for setting up the sampling and data collection in the higher education stage centered on the overall issues in NEPS: competence acquisition and development in formal and nonformal/informal learning environments, educational decisions and transitions alongside their determinants and consequences, and monetary as well as nonmonetary returns to education. The Starting Cohort First-Year Students placed a special emphasis on developing a questionnaire to adequately measure learning environments in higher education (see Schaeper and Weiß 2016) and on developing a subject-specific competence test (see Lauterbach 2015). Both developments constituted an important novelty in higher education research: Hitherto, the implementation of items concerning learning environments at German HEIs was rare and lacked a coherent theoretical base. Subject-specific competence assessment across a broad variety of HEIs was completely new to higher education surveys in Germany. Unstandardized study programs and heterogeneous curricula even in study programs with identical names severely impeded the development of universally applicable test instruments (Zlatkin-Troitschanskaia et al. 2015). In cooperation with the WiwiKom project (see Förster et al. 2013), we made a first attempt to overcome these obstacles: We developed a competence test in business administration by adapting a test from a US- and Latin American context and applying it in a subsample of the First-Year Students Starting Cohort. The successful development and application of a subject-specific competence test is an important step in higher education competence measurement—last but not least for merely showing its feasibility (within certain boundaries) in the German higher education context.

After almost a decade of surveying the NEPS Starting Cohort First-Year Students, we can assess the extent to which data collection is succeeding in serving the originally formulated research goals (see Aschinger et al. 2011). It can be stated clearly that the Starting Cohort First-Year Students provides a rich database for analyzing pathways through and out of higher education in Germany and for addressing a broad range of research questions. For example, the cohort data allow us to describe learning environments during Bachelor's, Master's, and doctoral studies and to use these as predictors for educational decisions such as change of subject studied, dropout from higher education, as well as international or regional student mobility. Furthermore, the data provide determinants for educational and labor market decisions because the entry into higher education can now be analyzed empirically for all German Federal States and for the two main types of HEIs in Germany against the background of comprehensive life-course information. Thanks to an oversampling of teacher education students and to the development of a survey program specifically tailored to teacher training and the teaching profession, the educational careers and life courses of (prospective) teachers can now be investigated comprehensively.

Yet, some research objectives set at the beginning of the project have not been achieved: An assessment of domain-general cognitive abilities and domain-specific cognitive competencies in short measurement intervals could not be realized in either the First-Year Students Starting Cohort or in other cohorts. The potential to analyze competence development is therefore rather small, albeit the competence measures available in the First-Year Students Starting Cohort are valuable predictors for decisions, transitions, and educational outcomes. To assess subject-specific competencies in higher education, it was intended to collect self-report data on disciplinary competencies (cf. Sect. 17.2.1.1, first edition). This idea was abandoned because valid and reliable instruments were not available and a newly developed questionnaire did not show satisfactory psychometric properties.

Compared to the research goals outlined in Aschinger et al. (2011), some additional aspects were implemented in the research agenda of the Starting Cohort First-Year Students: The competence test in 2013 was designed as a complex mode effect study including four modes (for mode effect studies in NEPS competence testing, see Chap. 10, this volume): One group was invited to participate in an individual web-based test; another group was tested in a group setting with different modes—conventional paper-based assessment, paper-based assessment with digital pencils, and computer-based assessment. At the time of writing this chapter, the results of the mode effect study have yet to be published. Furthermore, the Starting Cohort First-Year Students regularly surveys panel members in a web-based mode. This implies that data collection has to deal more and more with rapidly changing habits of internet use. Therefore, NEPS is increasingly addressing the issue of collecting paradata and information on the interview setting in web-based surveys. In the Starting Cohort First-Year Students, especially the waves from 2016 onward provide promising data for research questions in the realm of online research.

In order to describe guiding ideas of data collection as well as the data available so far, we first address methodological issues such as the study design, challenges of web-based interviewing and testing, and panel attrition and selectivity in Sect. 16.2. We then sketch the main research questions actually pursued in the Starting Cohort First-Year Students over the past 8 years in Sect. 16.3. In Sect. 16.4, we present some key characteristics of the cohort's educational trajectories observed 5 years after having entered higher education. Finally, we draw a short conclusion in Sect. 16.5

16.2 Methodological Issues

16.2.1 Study Design

Since 2010/2011, data on higher education and the transition to the labor market have been collected within NEPS by observing a sample of higher education students longitudinally via surveys and competence tests.

The sample population consists of new entrants into higher education who enrolled at a German HEI (universities and equivalent institutions, colleges of art and music, universities of applied sciences) for the first time in the winter term 2010/2011 in order to study for their first degree.[1] The sample was drawn with a disproportionally stratified cluster sampling method with fields of study within institutions of higher education as primary sampling units. Fields of study within state-approved private HEIs and teacher education programs were oversampled. Within the selected clusters, all students were contacted[2] (see also Aschinger et al. 2011; cf. Sect. 17.3.1, first edition).

Data collection within the starting cohort consists of three components (cf. Sect. 17.3.2, first edition). The life course is updated in annual telephone interviews in spring when core concepts of the NEPS pillars (see Chaps. 4–9, this volume) are implemented as well. Questions that are specifically targeted in the Starting Cohort First-Year Students are integrated in biannually administered web-based surveys in autumn.[3] In addition, competence tests are carried out in several modes: In 2011, paper-and-pencil tests were administered in group settings at the participating HEIs. The competence test of 2013 included a mode experiment with individual web-based testing on the one hand and three different modes applied in a group setting on the other hand—conventional paper-based assessment, paper-based assessment with digital pencils (e-pen), and computer-based assessment (cf. Prussog-Wagner et al. 2013). Because of the high regional mobility of the Starting Cohort First-Year Students and its spatial dispersion, group-administered tests were replaced by individually administered tests from 2014 onward—beginning with the subject-specific competence test in business administration (see Sect. 16.3.2.1). For further information on data collection in the NEPS student cohort, see the study documentation on the internet.[4]

---

[1]With a few exceptions, the definition of the sample population excludes students who enrolled for a "Magister" or "Diplom" degree program and students at HEIs run by Federal Ministries or Federal States for members of their public services (cf. Zinn et al. 2017).

[2]Furthermore, the definition of the sample population has been expanded to include students who were not part of the sampled clusters, but had participated in the first wave of competence tests and first entered higher education in the winter term 2010/2011 (see Steinwede and Prussog-Wagner 2012, p. 11). For a more detailed description of the sampling strategy, see Aßmann et al. (2011, pp. 62–63).

[3]Until 2014, web-based surveys were conducted annually.

[4]https://www.neps-data.de/Portals/0/NEPS/Datenzentrum/Forschungsdaten/SC5/SC5_Overview_W1-10.pdf

16.2.2 Challenges of Web-Based Surveys and Web-Based Competence Tests

Web-based surveys have become a cost-effective means of interviewing target persons. However, this development also raises new challenges. First, web-based surveys achieve lower response rates than (computer-assisted) telephone interviews. In the Starting Cohort First-Year Students, around 58% participated in the web-based surveys in autumn 2012, 2013, and 2014 (see Table 16.1). However, the response rates for the telephone interviews, conducted about 6 months earlier, were more or less 10% higher. Second, more and more participants use device types other than the traditional computer, switch devices during the survey, and answer the survey in different settings (Bruijne and Wijnant 2014; Cook 2014; Lugtig and Toepoel 2016; Stapleton 2013). This is especially true for higher education students and graduates who are highly mobile. All these aspects lead to the question of how to motivate target persons to participate in web-based surveys, how to design surveys for mobile devices, and how to ensure data quality.

In the Starting Cohort First-Year Students, we tried to cope with these challenges by introducing new layout features. Until 2014, we presented our web-based surveys in a static visual layout designed for traditional computers and laptops/notebooks. We advised participants to take the survey on these devices, although we did not exclude respondents with mobile devices (smartphones, tablet computers). For the fifth web-based survey in 2016, we switched to a modernized and innovative visual layout. The aim was to provide participants with a functional design suitable for mobile devices (with small screens) as well, and to ensure a visual recognition effect and good data quality. To meet these requirements, the "infas Institute for Applied Social Sciences"

Table 16.1 Response status by wave (without final dropout in the following waves)

wave	response status						total	
	successful interview		temporary dropout		final dropout			
	N	%	N	%	N	%	N	%
1 2010/1011 (CATI)	17,910	100.00	0	0.00	0	0.00	17,910	100.00
1 2010/1011 (Competences)	5,949	33.22	11,961	66.78	0	0.00	17,910	100.00
2 2011 (CAWI)	12,273	68.53	5,591	31.22	46	0.26	17,910	100.00
3 2012 (CATI)	13,113	73.40	4,560	25.53	191	1.07	17,864	100.00
4 2012 (CAWI)	11,202	63.38	6,424	36.35	47	0.27	17,673	100.00
5 2013 (CATI)	12,694	72.02	4,616	26.19	316	1.79	17,626	100.00
5 2013 (Competences)	8,767	49.74	8,543	48.47	316	1.79	17,626	100.00
6 2013 (CAWI)	10,183	58.83	7,039	40.66	88	0.51	17,310	100.00
7 2014 (CATI)	9,547	65.92	4,484	30.96	451	3.11	14,482	100.00
7 2014 (Competences)	338	61.01	216	38.99	35	5.94	589	100.00
8 2014 (CAWI)	8,629	51.45	6,024	35.92	2,118	12.63	16,771	100.00
9 2015 (CATI)	10,096	68.90	4,321	29.49	236	1.61	14,653	100.00

Note: The numbers reported are calculated using the Scientific Use File 9.0.0 CohortProfile dataset.
Differences to the numbers reported in Zinn et al. (2017) are due to the definition of the categories reported.
Source: Scientific use file 9.0.0 NEPS Starting Cohort "First-Year Students" (doi:10.5157/NEPS:SC5:9.0.0).

developed a new questionnaire design with a dynamic layout that adapts to the screen size of the used device.

Although a mobile-optimized design offers chances to motivate participation, it also poses problems resulting from the smaller screen size of smartphones and tablet computers and the different way of entering data compared to traditional computers. Knowing that web-based surveys are completed on a range of different devices, they have to be rethought as mixed-device surveys, which makes question and item design a challenge (Link et al. 2014). Against this background, we had to take into account, on the one hand, that traditional grids are hardly suitable for small screens. On the other hand, we wanted to ensure data comparability between the different waves. Research on measurement differences provides mixed results. Especially when analyzing measurement error for certain item formats (e.g., open-ended questions, sliders) and response quality, conclusions seem to vary. Assuming higher break-off rates when the survey is not fully mobile optimized, in particular break-offs in grids (Mavletova and Couper 2015) and higher item nonresponse (Struminskaya et al. 2015), we finally decided to optimize the visual layout of all items in the panel. However, we chose not to use new item response formats such as sliders. Regarding item batteries, newly integrated batteries were designed as auto-forwarded single items, whereas batteries that had already been included in previous waves remained unchanged as traditional grids. As a consequence, respondents using mobile devices had to scroll answering questions in the traditional grid format.

As survey research indicates, the infrastructure used and the environment in which surveys take place affect to a certain extent the answers given (Mavletova and Couper 2013; Möhring and Schlütz 2010). Against this background, additional information on device types and survey settings can be useful in terms of survey management and monitoring and can increase data quality in the long run (Jocelyn et al. 2008; Kreuter 2013; Laflamme et al. 2008). Moreover, various research questions can be answered based on the additional data (e.g., share of mobile devices in web-based surveys, comparability of measurements, characteristics of mobile and nonmobile respondents, effects of different settings on data quality and survey dropout). Therefore, we started to collect additional data on the devices, operating systems, and web browsers used as well as on the settings in which the survey was completed (Prussog-Wagner et al. 2017).

The collection of data on device types can be realized in two ways. First, client-side information, transmitted via the participant's web browser and JavaScript, can be collected in the form of a user agent string (Couper and Singer 2013; Heerwegh 2004). Second, survey participants can be asked directly during the survey. For our web-based survey in 2016, we decided to gather information directly. The main reasons were that some devices, such as smartphones and tablet computers, are difficult to differentiate within the user agent string and that the storing of user agent strings requires informed consent from participants. In order to gather data as completely as possible on the device types used, we asked the question right at the beginning of the survey. Moreover, at the end of the survey, participants who had interrupted the survey were asked whether they had switched device and, if applicable, which different device types they had used. The questions concerning the used operating systems and web browsers were presented at the end of the survey as well. We also asked in which setting our target persons participated in the web-based survey (e.g., "at home," "on the move," "in the library/computer lab/office").

Considering this access-related data, 75.2% of all participants who finished the web-based questionnaire in 2016 ($N = 6,557$) started the survey on a traditional computer or on a laptop/notebook. Nearly one-quarter used mobile devices (19.3% smartphones, 5.2% tablet computers). The vast majority completed the survey "at home" (82.1%) or "in the library/computer lab/office" (10.1%). The proportion of participants using a smartphone or a tablet computer at home is surprisingly high (17.1% smartphones, 5.8% tablet computers).

As outlined in Sect. 16.2.1, web-based data collection was also used for competence testing. Web-based testing basically faces the same challenges as web-based interviewing: Respondents are mobile and tend to use mobile devices to access the testing. However, these challenges have to be met differently in the case of web-based testing. First, it is crucial to control the setting of the test situation to ensure comparability with test results from an interviewer-supported test scenario. Comparability depends to a large extent on a calm and undisturbed test situation and on the proper and controlled display of the test items. In line with this, participants in the web-based testing were asked to use a traditional computer or a laptop/notebook to complete the tests. In the 2017 competence test, the use of mobile devices was technically constrained using access-related paradata (for an overview of paradata in web-based surveys, see Callegaro 2013). Respondents who entered the test via mobile devices (smartphones, tablet computers) were asked to switch to a traditional computer or a laptop/notebook. If reluctant to switch, respondents with mobile devices could only proceed after requesting a PIN from the support team and using it when re-accessing the web-based testing. In addition to triggering the use of adequate (nonmobile) devices, the test setting was controlled by excluding some browser types in order to secure a full-screen display of the test, and by technically preventing temporal interruptions of the test. Second, the logging of the testing process is more important in web-based testing than in web-based interviewing. Detailed logging of web-based test completion is particularly important in mixed-mode test studies, because the adequate linking of test results requires information on the process of test completion when interviewer surveillance is lacking. Information on how the respondent worked through the test or on the device type and the web browser used provides important covariates for the test score estimation.

16.2.3 Participation

From a data quality point of view, it is important to understand survey participation and dropout and to determine possible sources of bias. During the recruitment (for the planning of the sampling, see Aßmann et al. 2011; for its realization, see Steinwede and Aust

Table 16.2 Response patterns

mode	response pattern											
	total		monotone all		non-monotone		monotone subdivided					
							response only		non-response only		m responses (0 < m < 9)	
	N	%	N	%	N	%	N	%	N	%	N	%
CATI	17,910	100.00	13,001	72.59	4,909	27.41	6,270	35.01	0	0.00	6,731	37.59
CAWI	17,910	100.00	13,213	73.77	4,697	26.23	4,042	22.57	2,339	13.06	6,620	36.96
all modes	17,910	100.00	6,460	36.07	11,450	63.93	3,261	18.21	0	0.00	3,199	17.86

Source: Scientific use file 9.0.0 NEPS Starting Cohort "First-Year Students" (doi:10.5157/NEPS:SC5:9.0.0).

2012), 31,082 higher education students provided valid contact information. The panel population, however, consists of those 17,910 respondents who took part in the first computer-assisted telephone interview (CATI) and who belong to the target population—both being prerequisites for staying in the panel study (Zinn et al. 2017).

A total of 69% of the respondents of the first CATI wave also took part in the first computer-assisted web interview (CAWI) and 33% took part in the first competence test. In the following CATI waves, the percentage of participants[5] varies between 73% in the third wave and 66% in the seventh wave.[6] Comparing CATI and CAWI participation within one year, the CAWI participation is generally lower. The lowest number of participants and the highest variation in participation rates can be found in the competence tests. Consistent with pertinent literature (cf. Groves et al. 2009; Schnell 2012), mode differences in response behavior can be observed in Table 16.1.

Looking at response patterns over the waves, the broad variety of patterns can be simplified by grouping them into monotone and nonmonotone patterns.[7] The response behavior in the first wave of the Starting Cohort First-Year Students tends to be monotone by mode, but nonmonotone overall. Table 16.2 shows the distribution of monotone and nonmonotone response patterns in the first nine waves of the cohort (see columns two and three), and more detailed information on the monotone response patterns (see the last three columns).

---

[5]The reported numbers do not reflect a comparison of the number of participants to the original sample population, but to the population of persons who could still participate in each wave excluding final dropouts.

[6]The low total number of respondents in the seventh wave is due to the structural dropout of all persons within the teacher training oversample in this wave. Additionally, in the seventh wave, only a subsample of economics students was asked to participate in the competence test (see Sect. 16.3.2.1).

[7]Monotone response patterns are patterns in which a respondent has either taken part in all analyzed waves or has taken part in all waves up to one point and dropped out in all later waves. Non-monotone response patterns contain both dropout waves and response waves that do not occur in the previously described temporal order (cf. Schnell 2012).

An analysis of panel attrition between the first and the second CATI wave identified self-reported intentions of dropping out of current studies, school-leaving grades, living alone, and the field of study as relevant predictors for availability in the second wave, as well as motivation and school grades as predictors of response given successful contact (Liebeskind and Vietgen 2017).

To account for a possible nonresponse bias due to selectivity, the scientific use files include nonresponse weights in addition to the design weights (Zinn et al. 2017). These nonresponse weights are calculated via several different modeling steps, correcting for nonresponse occurring in all stages of sampling, successful recruiting, and (non-)participation in further panel waves (Zinn et al. 2017).

There are several challenges in order to achieve high participation rates in the student cohort: First, the field access required the cooperation of the sampled HEIs. The institutions had to commit themselves to the NEPS project, and the teaching staff in the sampled study programs had to agree to open their lectures for the recruitment of target persons. Although field access via HEIs worked well in general, it turned out to be a bottleneck, especially regarding the recruitment of students at private HEIs, where we see much higher dropout rates from the gross sample to the first panel wave than in other strata (Zinn et al. 2017). Second, higher education students are less easy to contact than members of other populations. Students often provide their parents' home address, which might differ from their place of residence during the academic term. Higher education students tend to live in shared apartments, which is a challenge for identifying the eligible target person. Furthermore, students change flats frequently, for example, when sojourning abroad or changing to another HEI. Therefore, in order to achieve high participation rates in each wave, respondents are also contacted when sojourning abroad. If target persons could not be reached via the indicated addresses, these are validated at the residents' registration offices during field time. In addition to that, the survey institute does not limit the number of contact attempts. Persons who have not been contacted successfully for the current wave via telephone are asked again via (e-)mail to update their contact details in order to organize a telephone interview. Third, due to restricted financial resources, it was not possible to incentivize participation in the web-based surveys in the same way as for the telephone interviews. Whereas CATI participants received postpaid incentives (10 Euros), until now, CAWI participants have taken part in a lottery raffling prizes specially tailored for the student population.

16.3 Main Research Issues and Overview of Data Collected

16.3.1 Common Features

NEPS collects data from a life-course perspective. In this sense, respondents are surveyed within eight different stages of their educational biographies, which allows extensive research on educational transitions and trajectories. Within all stages, respondents' individual episodes and their various life spheres are recorded and updated (for further information, see Chaps. 1 and 2, this volume). Moreover, NEPS data provides longitudinal information on theoretical key dimensions such as competence development, learning environments, educational decisions, migration background, returns to education, and motivation and personality (for further information on the so-called "NEPS pillars," see Chaps. 4–9, this volume). This scientific concept forms the basis for the surveys in the Starting Cohort First-Year Students.

16.3.2 Specific Features

16.3.2.1 Subject-Specific Competence Test

Up to now, competence tests have been administered at three measurement points in the Starting Cohort First-Year Students. In the first wave, the domain-specific competencies mathematical literacy, reading literacy, and reading speed were tested; in the fifth wave, two domain-specific competencies (computer literacy, science literacy) as well as domain-general cognitive functions (perceptual speed, reasoning). Later on, in the seventh wave, a subject-specific competence test in business administration was conducted on a subsample of the student cohort. The results of this test should allow for the analysis of the interrelation of competences in business administration with other competence domains and the relevance of subject-specific competences for "employability" and other labor market outcomes.

As described in Aschinger et al. (2011; cf. Sect. 17.2.1.2, first edition), we followed a curriculum-oriented approach when developing the subject-specific test. In cooperation with the project "WiwiKom" (Förster et al. 2013), two foreign test instruments were translated and adapted to ensure the fit for German HEIs: (1) The EGEL (Exámenes Generales para el Egreso de la Licenciatura; Centro Nacional de Evaluación para la Educación Superior 2011), covering the business administration fields management and accounting; (2) the TUCE (Test of Understanding in College Economics; Walstad and Rebeck 2008), covering the areas of micro- and macroeconomics. Furthermore, an expert rating of the tasks and two developmental studies were administered in order to select the best items. The final test instrument consisted of 36 multiple-choice tasks in the fields of marketing, organization, financing, accounting, microeconomics, and macroeconomics (for an overview of the instrument development and the scaling results, see Lauterbach 2015).

The test in business administration was implemented for a subsample of 601 students in economics. This resulted in 338 valid cases that show different test results in terms of gender, first language, and educational background: On average, the students in the sample solved 19 out of 36 tasks correctly. Men performed significantly better than women, and native speakers did better than students with another first language than German. Moreover, if one of the students' parents had an academic degree, they performed slightly better than students with a lower educational background. Regarding the interrelations with the competence domains measured in the first wave, significant correlations could be observed between competencies in business administration and mathematical literacy ($r = 0.30$) as well as reading literacy ($r = 0.20$). Because 11 of the 36 test items require calculations, the stronger interrelation with mathematical literacy is not surprising. Besides the domain-specific competencies mathematical literacy and reading literacy, gender ($r = 0.33$) and migration background ($r = 0.46$) seemed to be comparatively strong predictors for competencies in business administration.[8]

Further analyses with respect to educational and occupational developments and outcomes are not yet feasible due to low case numbers in response to the relevant questions. Hopefully, responses in later waves and the potential use of imputation methods will fill this gap.

16.3.2.2 Transitions

Higher education students and graduates experience diverse transitions throughout their educational pathways: the transition from secondary to higher education, transitions within higher education, and the transition from higher education to the labor market (Grosemans and Kyndt 2017; Kyndt et al. 2017; Trigwell 2017).

According to Hussey and Smith (2010, p. 156), "a transition is a significant change in a student's life, self-concept and learning: a shift from one state of understanding, development and maturity to another." On the one hand, HEIs and labor market players can support these transitions and make them as easy as possible; on the other hand, transitions such as student dropout should be avoided. Therefore, it is important to understand the reasons for transitions.

The data of the Starting Cohort First-Year Students comprises information relevant for describing transition processes and explaining individual educational decision making. Thereby, transitions to higher education, transitions within higher education, and transitions to the labor market are addressed from a life-course perspective.

Regarding the transition to higher education, hurdles and assistance during the transition between different learning environments are recorded (for further information on life-course-specific learning environments, see Chap. 5, this volume). In the first telephone interview and web-based survey in 2011 shortly after the beginning of their studies, the panel members were asked how well prepared they felt for university in order to learn more about the match between acquired competencies and the demands of higher education. In addition, the participants had to answer whether they could take up their desired study program, how long they had to wait for it, and what family and friends think about their studies. To learn more about the assistance offered during the transition

---

[8]Due to incomplete data in the Scientific use file for the domains measured in the fifth wave (computer literacy, science literacy, perceptual speed, reasoning), the interrelations with competencies in business administration have not yet been analyzed.

process, students were asked whether the different learning environments offered information and advice.

Regarding the transitions within higher education, the data comprise information about changes of study majors, study programs, or HEIs; and about studying abroad, dropping out of university, and the transition to Master's programs. Questions concerning the transition to Master's programs have been an integral part of the interview program since the third web-based survey in 2013. Besides the preparation for Master's programs, entry requirements are examined as well as the question whether the current Master's program is a student's first choice and how supportive students perceive their personal environment. Moreover, Master students should specify how useful different personal or institutional sources of information had been for the decision to enter a Master's program. Furthermore, the offer, use, and quality of different information and qualification opportunities are observed.

Regarding the transition to the labor market, Master students and panel members who are no longer students receive, since the third web-based survey in 2013, questions concerning their prospective transition to the labor market as well as specific questions about their job search. In order to analyze the transitions from a retrospective point of view as well, employed persons have been given questions about their job search, the perceived job preparation, and employer measures for the career start since the fourth telephone interview in 2014.

The items used to capture the mentioned transition processes are self-developed, further developed, or adapted from existing studies on students' transition and information behavior, job search, job preparation, and career start (Grützmacher et al. 2011; Heine et al. 2010; Rehn et al. 2011).

In addition, the data of Starting Cohort First-Year Students includes information relevant for explaining transitions and educational decisions in the life course (for further information on educational decisions, see Chap. 6, this volume; cf. Sect. 17.2.3, first edition). For example, there is data available on students' academic and social integration (Dahm et al. 2016), student time resources and restrictions, educational aspirations, study-related expectancies and values, as well as cost-benefit considerations regarding doctoral studies.

All in all, the collected data might shed further light on individual transition processes between learning and working environments as well as on potential hurdles and deficits.

16.3.2.3 Learning Environments

In sociology but also in certain strands of psychology and educational science, it is widely acknowledged that the context in general and the learning environment in particular are important factors in decision making, social action, learning, and competence development. In contrast to the significance attached to the institutional and educational conditions, conceptual models and measurement instruments for HEIs as formal learning environments are rare (Schaeper and Weiß 2016). Therefore, coherent and theory-based questionnaires for assessing the learning environment, both in undergraduate or Master's education and in doctoral training, had to be developed (cf. Sect. 17.2.2, first edition).

In terms of Bronfenbrenner's (1979) ecological systems theory and his distinction between four system levels, the instrument focuses on the micro and meso system of the learning environment. Following research on the basic dimensions of process quality within schools (Klieme et al. 2006; Radisch et al. 2007), both questionnaires address three elements: structure (S), support (S), and challenge (C). The instrument designed to measure the learning environment in undergraduate and Master's programs additionally covers orientation (O) as a fourth dimension. In adopting this "SSCO" model, we chose a conceptual framework that guides the measurement of different learning environments in NEPS (cf. Bäumer et al. 2011; Chap. 5, this volume).

The questionnaire for assessing the quality of predoctoral programs was developed in cooperation with NEPS pillar "Education Processes in Life-Course-Specific Learning Environments." It consists of 11 subscales and 42 items that had been newly developed or selected and adapted from existing survey instruments (for a detailed account of the conceptual basis, the process of questionnaire construction, and psychometric properties, see Schaeper and Weiß 2016). Confirmatory factor analyses yielded acceptable results. Cronbach's alpha ranged from 0.85 for the scale "practice orientation" to 0.55 for the two-item scale "reproduction orientation." In addition to collecting data on the predoctoral learning environment as perceived by the students, we also gathered objective information by analyzing documents and statistics. This information related mainly to structural opportunities and restrictions of the degree programs, the HEI, and the local/regional context (Schaeper and Weiß 2016).

These comprehensive data on the learning environments in predoctoral study programs can be used, for example, to answer the question on which aspects of the learning environment impact on student outcomes and behaviors most, or whether the effect of the learning environment differs depending on students' characteristics.

To measure the perceived conditions for academic development during doctoral training, we adapted an instrument developed by de Vogel et al. (2017) and shortened it in collaboration with the authors. The questionnaire consists of 11 subscales each containing 3 items. The structural characteristics (S) refer to the continuity of supervision, the intensity of supervision, and the reliability and feasibility of the thesis topic. The support dimension (S) is represented by instrumental and informational support available in the academic environment, emotional support, assistance in building academic networks, and help in developing career perspectives. Within the challenge dimension (C), the focus is on the subdimensions participation in academic discourse, collaborative research, interdisciplinarity, and internationality. In view of the diverse ways of earning a doctoral degree, the instrument had to be suitable for all contexts of doctoral training (e.g., participants in structured doctoral programs, research assistants, scholarship holders, external candidates).

The instrument was applied for the first time in the web-based survey in 2016. A total of 526 doctoral candidates, who mostly started their doctoral training less than 2 years ago, participated in this panel wave. The data analysis suggests that all 11 subdimensions have been measured reliably ($0.75 \leq \alpha_c \leq 0.92$). Moreover, the results of a second-order confirmatory factor analysis provided evidence for the multidimensional structure of the conceptual model.

Given the reliability and validity of the instrument, the data can be used to analyze the impact of the perceived learning environment during doctoral training on degree completion or dropout as well as on career intentions and future occupational careers within or outside academia.

16.3.2.4 Employment Situation and Work Characteristics

A long-term perspective on individual employment histories is an important issue, especially in the higher stages of NEPS, because transitions to the labor market, employment trajectories, and specific employment situations illustrate the labor market outcomes of education. A long-term perspective is especially important in the Starting Cohort First-Year Students, because the labor market entries of graduates frequently turn out to be sequential processes accompanied by further academic and vocational training throughout graduates' working lives (Briedis et al. 2016).

Even if for some graduates, labor market entries take a few months and longer, in comparison to graduates of vocational training (Grotheer 2010), their unemployment rates are rather low (Euler et al. 2018). Therefore, specific job-related measures are much more informative regarding higher education graduates than the general prospects of labor market participation.

NEPS Starting Cohort First-Year Students applied a broad definition of "employment": Besides the main categories of paid employment, self-employment, civil service, and military, also practical activities throughout one's studies (e.g., internships, traineeships) and episodes with an educational focus after graduation (e.g., internships for a second state examination) are considered. In addition, information on marginal employment, temporary work, and all kinds of atypical work is covered.

Besides the general employment status of the target persons, a wide range of information on the contractual and business-related characteristics as well as on qualification demands is collected within the longitudinal recording of employment episodes via yearly telephone interviews. This includes, for example, information on contract types (permanent, fixed-term), working hours (contractual, actual), earnings (only for nontemporary jobs), and the detailed occupational status. Furthermore, the economic sector, the size, and the location of the employer are specified as well as employers' job-related requirements and the training offered at work. Whereas this information has been recorded for every employment episode since the winter term 2010/2011, other aspects are observed only after graduation (e.g., relationship between employment and former studies, learning opportunities, job tasks regarding qualification requirements and the variety, autonomy, and holistic nature of tasks. Besides this, further information on job characteristics (such as job adequacy and job satisfaction) has been collected in the CAWI waves since 2016. Regarding the transitions to the labor market, detailed information on job search, job preparation, and employer measures for the career start is provided within the CATI waves (see also Sect. 16.3.2.2).

The detailed recording of employment episodes allows us to analyze transitions to the labor market, participation in the labor market, and occupational mobility on the labor market for higher education students and graduates.

16.3.2.5 Family Planning

It is well known that family-related decision making is associated with educational choices and the educational level attained. Regarding highly educated persons, certain changes of status, such as marriage or the birth of the first child, occur later (Cygan-Rehm and Maeder 2013; Marini 1984). Moreover, childlessness is more prevalent among higher education graduates than among the rest of the population (Kreyenfeld and Konietzka 2017; Schaeper et al. 2017).

The data on the Starting Cohort First-Year Students comprises not only detailed (event history) data on children but also information about family planning and family-related attitudes. The latter were gathered in a telephone interview in spring 2018, at a time when most of the target persons were either advanced in their studies or had already left higher education and entered the labor market. The items applied originate from the German Family Panel "pairfam" (Thönnissen et al. 2017).

On the one hand, the panel members were asked how many children they would like to have altogether, assuming ideal circumstances ("idealistic family planning"). On the other hand, they should specify how many children they will probably have altogether, thinking realistically about having children ("realistic family planning"). Whereas idealistic family planning reflects a person's general family orientation, realistic family planning is directly connected to a person's environment and the associated opportunities and restrictions (Huinink et al. 2008). Furthermore, in terms of cost-benefit considerations, participants should indicate how strongly they expect or worry that different things may occur (e.g., getting new ideas, not accomplishing professional goals) because of having children ("Value of Children"). The Value of Children concept assumes that a life with children involves individual costs and benefits that can be assigned to the dimensions stimulation, affect, esteem, and comfort (Nauck 2001).

Taking into account additional panel information (e.g., educational choices, importance of areas of life, work–life conflict), the collected data might shed further light on family-related attitudes and the process of family formation among higher education students and graduates.

16.3.2.6 Special Survey Program for Teachers and Teacher Candidates

Because Starting Cohort First-Year Students places special emphasis on (prospective) teachers as a key profession for the quality of school education, teacher education students were oversampled considerably (see Sect. 16.2.1). The sample consists of around 5,500 teacher candidates (Wave 1) and covers the entire range of teacher training programs in all German Federal States. Thanks to a grant from the Federal Ministry of Education and Research, it was possible to continue monitoring the whole sample of teacher education students from 2014 onward for at least 3.5 years and to include survey instruments specifically aimed at (prospective) teachers.

The primary research interest of this "Panel of Teacher Education Students" ("*Lehramtsstudierenden-Panel*"; LAP) is to analyze and explain teachers' professional competencies and educational practices. In developing these competencies, the preparatory service is considered to play a decisive role. Therefore, the LAP project pays special attention to this second stage of teacher training that combines practical training at schools with theoretical reflection, and measures relevant aspects of this particular learning environment. The instrument focuses on the support dimension of the abovementioned SSCO model of learning environments (see Sect. 16.3.2.3 and Chap. 5, this volume), but also addresses the dimensions challenge and orientation.

The measurement of teachers' professional competencies is informed by the multidimensional competence model of Baumert and Kunter (2006) that includes both cognitive and noncognitive aspects and distinguishes between professional knowledge, attitudes and beliefs, motivational orientations, and self-regulation. For several reasons, it was not possible to collect data on professional knowledge. However, we used self-reports to measure attitudes and beliefs (e.g., beliefs about teaching and learning, professional self-concept, beliefs regarding inclusive education, cultural beliefs), motivational orientations (e.g., motivation for choosing teacher education, enthusiasm for teaching, general teaching self-efficacy beliefs, self-efficacy beliefs regarding inclusive education, teaching in a multicultural context), and occupational self-regulation with a focus on the dimensions "work engagement" and "resilience."

The LAP project is based on the assumption that teachers' professional competencies are related to the quality of teaching, which, in turn, impacts on students' learning outcomes. One approach to assessing the quality of teaching is to use teachers' self-reports of their instructional practices (Kunter and Klusmann 2010). Following the SSCO model, we consider classroom management ("structure"), constructive support ("support"), and cognitive activation ("challenge") to be central dimensions of instructional quality (Klieme et al. 2006). Therefore, we collected self-reported data on selected aspects of these dimensions (e.g., disturbance and monitoring, individualized instruction, cognitively activating instruction).

To measure the constructs that are specifically targeted at (prospective) teachers, we selected items from existing survey instruments that have been proved to be reliable and valid (Kauper et al. 2012; Kunter et al. 2016; Max-Planck-Institut für Bildungsforschung 2010). Together with the data from the basic survey program of NEPS Starting Cohort First-Year Students, this information significantly increases the potential for research on teacher education and the teaching profession. Due to the encompassing survey program and the longitudinal approach following teacher education students right from the beginning of their studies until well into their professional careers, the database opens up the opportunity to address a broad range of research issues—from the choice of the teaching profession and different stages of teacher training to professional competencies, practices, and well-being.

16.4 First-Year Students of the Winter Term 2010/2011: Educational Trajectories of the Cohort

In the following, we present an overview of educational trajectories within the NEPS Starting Cohort First-Year Students. To display complete trajectories for the first 4.5 years after entering higher education in 2010, only sample members who took part in the fifth CATI wave in 2015 were included (about 10,000 persons). Higher education students at universities (see Fig. 16.1) and universities of applied sciences (see Fig. 16.2) were examined separately, on the basis of the tertiary institution reported in the first wave.

The overview focuses on the following educational states: (1) studying for a Master's degree, (2) studying for a Bachelor's degree, (3) studying for other academic degrees (e.g., first state examination), (4) completing a (vocational) training, (5) dependent employment and self-employment, (6) other employment-related activities (e.g., internship, traineeship), (7) other states. For students reporting parallel states within one month, the lower-numbered state was prioritized. Thus, if a Master's program and any other concurrent state were reported, the Master's program is displayed; if a Bachelor's program and a concurrent employment were reported, the Bachelor's program is mapped. Because the purpose of the figures is to display the trajectories of target persons in the student cohort, the percentages shown are unweighted.

Due to the definition of the sample population, all surveyed persons are initially first-year students at a tertiary institution. Whereas only a small proportion of the sample passes into employment or (vocational) training within the first 2 years, up to 95% of the first-year students in the sample were still studying at a HEI by the end of the second year.

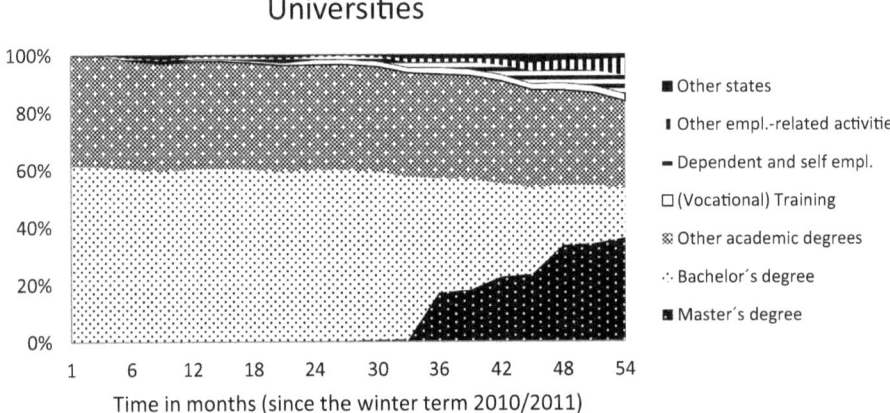

Fig. 16.1 Educational trajectories of higher education students at universities. *Note* The analysis is based on the tertiary institution reported in the first wave. *Source* Scientific use file 9.0.0 NEPS Starting Cohort "First-Year Students" (https://doi.org/10.5157/neps:sc5:9.0.0)

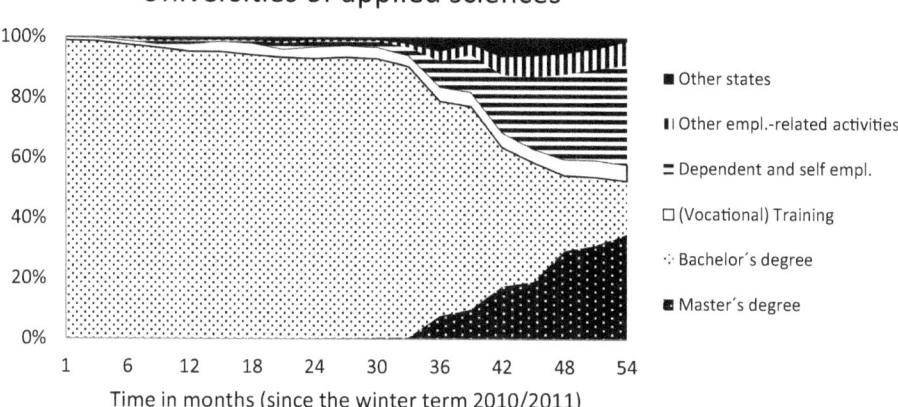

Fig. 16.2 Educational trajectories of higher education students at universities of applied sciences. *Note* The analysis is based on the tertiary institution reported in the first wave. *Source* Scientific use file 9.0.0 NEPS Starting Cohort "First-Year Students" (https://doi.org/10.5157/neps:sc5:9.0.0)

3 years (6 semesters) after entering higher education, a rising proportion of surveyed persons reported enrollment in Master's programs. At the end of the observation period, the proportion of Master's students is approximately 35% for students at universities and universities of applied sciences. However, Fig. 16.1 also contains degree programs for first state examinations ("other academic degrees") that, on average, last longer than Bachelor's programs (Autorengruppe Bildungsberichterstattung 2014) and usually lead to a subsequent internship and not to a Master's program. There is still a proportion of 30% studying for a first state examination at the end of the observation period (38% in the beginning). Fading out this group, one can see that the proportion of transitions into a Master's program after finishing a Bachelor's program is much higher at universities than at universities of applied sciences. This finding is in line with the findings of other studies (e.g., Rehn et al. 2011).

The share of transitions into doctoral training is still below 1% at the end of this observation period (not shown separately in the figures).

Other differences between the trajectories of first-year students at universities and universities of applied sciences become visible regarding the transitions to the labor market. After an average duration of study (6 semesters), the proportion of reported employment episodes rises from approximately 10% after 36 months to over 40% at the end of the observation period for target persons at universities of applied sciences. In the subsample of target persons at universities, the share of persons reporting an employment and no ongoing higher education episode lies well below 15%, even after 4.5 years. Again, leaving out target persons studying for a first state examination, the share of persons reporting an employment episode lies below 20%, which is obviously a smaller share compared to target persons at universities of applied sciences.

At the end of the observation period, there is still a proportion of about 17% of Bachelor's students. However, this does not necessarily reflect longer durations of study, because changes of fields of study or HEIs are not displayed in the figures.

Figure 16.3 shows the duration until target persons in NEPS Starting Cohort First-Year Students receive their first undergraduate degree. Only the first reported undergraduate degrees were considered in the analysis—that is, Bachelor's degrees, diplomas, first state examinations, and Magister degrees. Postgraduate degrees such as Master's degrees or Ph.Ds were excluded.

The analysis shows that students enrolled at universities of applied sciences graduate slightly faster than students at universities. Half of the students from universities of applied sciences graduate after 3.4 years (or after almost 7 semesters), whereas students from universities graduate about one semester later. Dropouts or other kinds of study interruptions were not taken into account.

To further examine which factors might influence the time a student needs to obtain the first undergraduate degree, an explorative Cox regression analysis was conducted. A Cox regression allows us to investigate how specified factors influence the rate of a particular event happening. The dependent variable in the following analysis is the time a

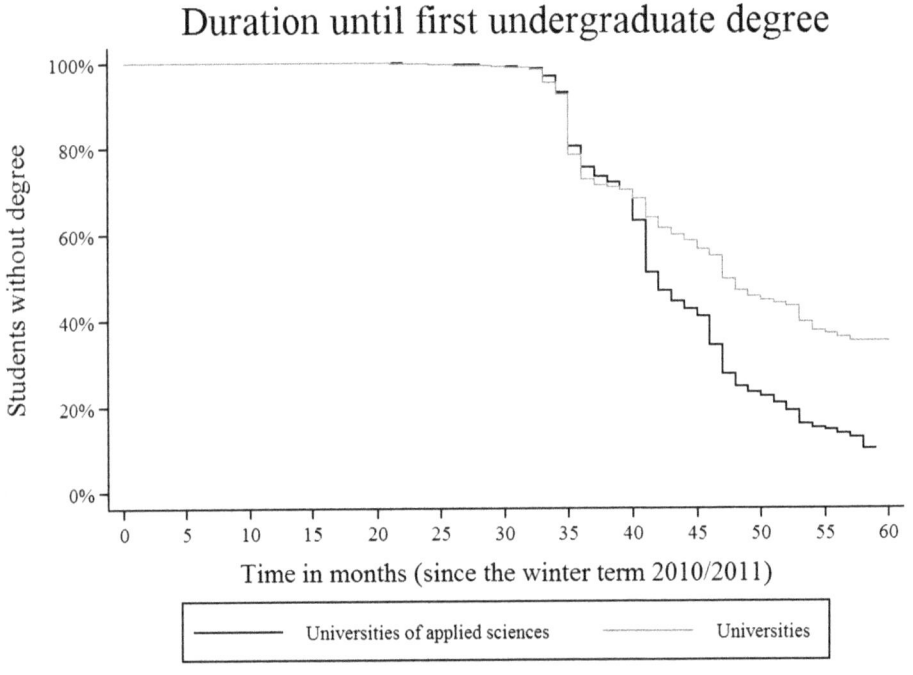

Fig. 16.3 Time needed to obtain the first undergraduate degree (Kaplan–Meier survival estimates). *Source* Scientific use file 9.0.0 NEPS Starting Cohort First-Year Students (https://doi.org/10.5157/neps:sc5:9.0.0)

student needs from the beginning of a study program to the completion of the first undergraduate degree. Students who did not receive a degree until the date of the last interview (right-censored observations) were included in the analysis as well. The analysis has an explorative function and is limited to the NEPS Starting Cohort First-Year Students. Hence, no conclusions regarding the total student population can be made and no significance levels are reported.

Various variables considered to be relevant for the duration were included such as gender, age, migration background, father's highest school leaving qualification, information on overall working hours per week,[9] and on minor children (under 18 years) living in the household. Furthermore, the average overall grade in the school leaving certificate (GPA), the field of study, information on enrollment in a teacher education program, as well as the specific type of HEI were included.

Table 16.3 shows the unweighted results of the analysis. Please note that the hazard ratios are exponentiated coefficients. Hence, values smaller than one indicate negative effects on the duration until the first undergraduate degree is obtained (dependent variable). Due to data and modeling requirements, potentially time varying covariates (e.g., age, working hours, minor children living in the household) were restricted to information from the first wave and are treated as if they were invariant.

The explorative analysis shows that in comparison to male students, female students have a higher probability of graduating successfully, that is, of obtaining an undergraduate degree. The age of the target person has a slightly negative effect on the completion rate, which means that every additional year of life lowers the probability of receiving an academic degree. In comparison to German students, students with a migration background have a lower probability of completing an undergraduate degree program. Compared to students whose fathers have a low general school leaving qualification, students whose fathers achieved an average school leaving qualification have a higher completion rate. Students with highly qualified fathers have only a slightly higher completion rate. The amount of working hours during studies shows neither a negative nor a positive effect. However, when minor children (under 18 years) are living in a student's household, the completion rate decreases. Regarding the performance and tertiary education variables, the model shows that the lower a student's GPA, the lower her or his completion rate. In comparison to students studying humanities or arts, students enrolled in business, law, or social sciences are less likely to obtain an undergraduate degree, whereas students enrolled in science, technology, engineering, or mathematics are more likely to attain an undergraduate degree. Students enrolled in teacher education programs have a lower completion rate than other students. Finally, students attending a university have a lower completion rate than students from universities of applied sciences. However, as university students are overrepresented in the sample, this effect might be overestimated.

---

[9]Students who reported not to be employed at all or who were employed before they started their degree were set to zero working hours. Students who were currently employed but did not give any information on working hours were excluded from the analysis.

Table 16.3 Factors influencing the time needed to obtain the first undergraduate degree (Cox regression)

	Hazard ratio
Gender (Ref.: male)	1.27
Age	0.99
Migration background (Ref.: no migration background)	0.84
Father: Highest general school leaving qualification (Ref.: low)	
Middle	1.26
High	1.09
Working hours	1.00
Minor children in household (Ref.: no children)	0.62
GPA	0.89
Field of study (Ref.: humanities, arts)	
Business, law, social sciences	0.88
STEM	1.09
Medicine, health sciences	0.17
Enrollment in teacher education program	0.47
Type of HEI (Ref.: University of applied sciences)	0.77
LR Chi^2	260.97
No. of observations	7763
No. of failures	1101

Note Duration until first degree (dep. var.); exponentiated coefficients
Source Scientific use file 9.0.0 NEPS Starting Cohort "First-Year Students" (https://doi.org/10.5157/neps:sc5:9.0.0)

16.5 Conclusion

In this article we provided an overview of NEPS Starting Cohort First-Year Students—its study design, main research issues, and the data available to the scientific community. We described the overall study design and the challenge of maintaining participation in a panel survey of higher education students. We highlighted some focal points shaping the last years of data collection such as the development of an instrument for measuring learning environments in higher education including doctoral studies, the implementation of questionnaire modules on teacher education and the teaching profession, the development of a subject-specific competence test, and the implementation of a layout for web-based surveys suitable for mobile devices such as smartphones and tablet computers. Finally, we presented some key findings regarding educational trajectories and the duration of studies.

At present, the members of NEPS Starting Cohort First-Year Students are either on the threshold of taking up employment after graduation or they are in their early professional careers. This new stage in the life course of the panel members calls for further developing the survey program and including specific work-related constructs such as the requirements of highly qualified work (e.g., knowledge work) and the employment situation of teachers (e.g., cooperation with colleagues). Such contextual data will make it possible to examine labor market outcomes of higher education graduates in more detail and to better understand career decisions.

Altogether, we can conclude that the NEPS Starting Cohort First-Year Students provides an excellent and unique database for analyzing educational processes in German higher education and its outcomes in a comprehensive life-course perspective. The cohort's data allows us to scrutinize individual pathways through higher education and beyond within an interdisciplinary theoretical framework. The highly integrated survey program of the NEPS Starting Cohorts (see Chaps. 11–17, this volume) opens up the potential for cohort comparisons, especially with the NEPS Starting Cohorts "9th Grade" and "Adults." Being a nationwide study on individual trajectories in and beyond higher education in Germany including competence testing and different theoretical as well as disciplinary perspectives, the NEPS Starting Cohort First-Year Students makes a substantial expansion of German educational data available to empirical research on higher education and its outcomes.

References

Aschinger, F., Epstein, H., Müller, S., Schaeper, H., Vöttiner, A., & Weiß, T. (2011). Higher education and the transition to work. In H.-P. Blossfeld, H. G. Rossbach, & J. von Maurice (Eds.), *Education as a lifelong process: The German National Educational Panel Study (NEPS)* (pp. 267–282). Wiesbaden, Germany: VS Verlag für Sozialwissenschaften.

Aßmann, C., Steinhauer, H. W., Kiesl, H., Koch, S., Schönberger, B., Müller-Kuller, A., Rohwer, G., Rässler, S., & Blossfeld, H.-P. (2011). Sampling designs of the National Educational Panel Study: Challenges and solutions. In H.-P. Blossfeld, H. G. Rossbach, & J. von Maurice (Eds.), *Education as a lifelong process: The German National Educational Panel Study (NEPS)* (pp. 51–65). Wiesbaden, Germany: VS Verlag für Sozialwissenschaften.

Autorengruppe Bildungsberichterstattung (Ed.). (2014). Bildung in Deutschland 2014: Ein indikatorengestützter Bericht mit einer Analyse zur Bildung von Menschen mit Behinderungen. Bielefeld, Germany: W. Bertelsmann.

Bäumer, T., Preis, N., Roßbach, H.-G., Stecher, L., & Klieme, E. (2011). Education processes in life-course-specific learning environments. In H.-P. Blossfeld, H. G. Rossbach, & J. von Maurice (Eds.), *Education as a lifelong process: The German National Educational Panel Study (NEPS)* (pp. 87–101). Wiesbaden, Germany: VS Verlag für Sozialwissenschaften.

Baumert, J., & Kunter, M. (2006). Stichwort: Professionelle Kompetenz von Lehrkräften. *Zeitschrift für Erziehungswissenschaft, 9*(4), 469–520.

Briedis, K., Klüver, S., & Trommer, M. (2016). Zwischen Etablierung, Stabilisierung und Aufstieg: Berufliche Entwicklung der Hochschulabsolvent(inn)en 2009: Zweite Befragung des Prüfungsjahrgangs 2009 fünf Jahre nach dem Abschluss (Forum Hochschule No. 14/2016). Hannover, Germany.

Bronfenbrenner, U. (1979). *The ecology of human development: Experiments by nature and design*. Cambridge, MA: Harvard University Press.

Bruijne, M. de, & Wijnant, A. (2014). Mobile response in web panels. *Social Science Computer Review, 32*(6), 728–742.

Callegaro, M. (2013). Paradata in web surveys. In F. Kreuter (Ed.), *Improving surveys with paradata: Analytic uses of process information* (pp. 261–280). Hoboken, NJ: Wiley.

Centro Nacional de Evaluación para la Educación Superior. (2011). *Exámenes generales para el egreso de la licenciatura*. Mexico City: CENEVAL.

Cook, W. A. (2014). Is mobile a reliable platform for survey taking? Defining quality in online surveys from mobile respondents. *Journal of Advertising Research, 54*(2), 141–148.

Couper, M. P., & Singer, E. (2013). Informed consent for web paradata use. *Survey Research Methods, 7*(1), 57–67.

Cygan-Rehm, K., & Maeder, M. (2013). The effect of education on fertility: Evidence from a compulsory schooling reform. *Journal of Labor Economics, 25*, 35–48.

Dahm, G., Lauterbach, O., & Hahn, S. (2016). Measuring students' social and academic integration: Assessment of the operationalization in the National Educational Panel Study. In H.-P. Blossfeld, J. von Maurice, M. Bayer, & J. Skopek (Eds.), *Methodological issues of longitudinal surveys: The example of the National Educational Panel Study* (pp. 313–330). Wiesbaden, Germany: Springer VS.

de Vogel, S., Brandt, G., & Jaksztat, S. (2017). Ein Instrument zur Erfassung der Lernumwelt Promotionsphase. *Zeitschrift für empirische Hochschulforschung, 1*(1), 24–44.

Euler, T., Trennt, F., Trommer, M., & Schaeper, H. (2018). *Werdegänge der Hochschulabsolventinnen und Hochschulabsolventen 2005* (Forum Hochschule No. 1/2018). Hannover, Germany.

Förster, M., Zlatkin-Troitschanskaia, O., Brückner, S., & Hansen, M. (2013). WiwiKom: Modeling and measuring competencies in business and economics among students and graduates by adapting and further developing existing American and Mexican measuring instruments (TUCE/EGEL). In S. Blömeke & O. Zlatkin-Troitschanskaia (Eds.), *The German funding initiative "Modeling and Measuring Competencies in Higher Education": 23 research projects on engineering, economics and social sciences, education and generic skills of higher education students* (pp. 19–22). Berlin, Mainz, Germany: Humboldt Universität zu Berlin, Johannes Gutenberg Universität.

Grosemans, I., & Kyndt, E. (2017). Transition from higher education to the labour market. In E. Kyndt, V. Donche, K. Trigwell, & S. Lindblom-Ylänne (Eds.), *Higher education transitions: Theory and research* (pp. 209–218). New York, NY: Routledge.

Grotheer, M. (2010). Studienqualität, berufliche Einstiege und Berufserfolg von Hochschulabsolventinnen und Hochschulabsolventen - Eine Analyse der Arbeitsmarktchancen der Absolventenkohorten von 1997, 2001 und 2005. In Hochschul-Informations-System GmbH (Ed.), *Perspektive Studienqualität: Themen und Forschungsergebnisse der HIS-Fachtagung Studienqualität* (1st ed., pp. 244–262). Bielefeld, Germany: W. Bertelsmann Verlag.

Groves, R. M., Fowler, F. J., Couper, M. P., Lepkowski, J. M., Singer, E., & Tourangeau, R. (2009). *Survey methodology* (2nd ed.). Hoboken, NJ: Wiley.

Grützmacher, J., Ortenburger, A., & Heine, C. (2011). Studien- und Berufsperspektiven von Bachelorstudierenden in Deutschland: Übergangsverhalten, Studiengangsbewertungen und Berufsaussichten von Bachelorstudierenden im Wintersemester 2009/10. Hannover, Germany.

Heerwegh, D. (2004, June). *Uses of client side paradata in web surveys*. International symposium in honour of Paul Lazarsfeld, Brussels, Belgium.

Heine, C., Willich, J., & Schneider, H. (2010). Informationsverhalten und Entscheidungsfindung bei der Studien- und Berufswahl: Studienberechtigte 2008 ein halbes Jahr vor dem Erwerb der Hochschulreife (HIS:Forum Hochschule No. 1). Hannover, Germany.

Huinink, J., Schröder, T., & Boehnke, M. (2008). Kinderwunsch und Familiengründung: Die Bedeutung von Voraussetzungen und Entscheidungsgrundsätzen. In M. Feldhaus & J. Huinink (Eds.), *Neuere Entwicklungen in der Beziehungs- und Familienforschung: Vorstudien zum Beziehungs- und Familienpanel* (pp. 321–349). Würzburg, Germany: Ergon.

Hussey, T., & Smith, P. (2010). Transitions in higher education. *Innovations in Education and Teaching International, 47*(2), 155–164.

Jocelyn, W., Phillips, O., Baribeau, B., & Lévesquee, A. (2008). *Using paradata to manage nonresponse in the survey of labour and income dynamics.* Paper presented at the Statistics Canada Symposium "Data Collection: Challenges, Achievements and New Directions".

Kauper, T., Retelsdorf, J., Bauer, J., Rösler, L., Möller, J., & Prenzel, M. (2012). PaLea – Panel zum Lehramtsstudium: Skalendokumentation und Häufigkeitsauszählungen des BMBF-Projektes. 4. Welle, Juli 2010. Kiel, Germany.

Klieme, E., Lipowsky, F., Rakoczy, K., & Ratzka, N. (2006). Qualitätsdimensionen und Wirksamkeit von Mathematikunterricht: Theoretische Grundlagen und ausgewählte Ergebnisse des Projekts "Pythagoras". In M. Prenzel & L. Allolio-Näcke (Eds.), *Untersuchungen zur Bildungsqualität von Schule: Abschlussbericht des DFG-Schwerpunktprogramms* (pp. 127–146). Münster, Germany: Waxmann.

Kreuter, F. (Ed.). (2013). Improving surveys with paradata: Analytic uses of process information. Hoboken, NJ: Wiley.

Kreyenfeld, M., & Konietzka, D. (2017). Analyzing childlessness. In M. Kreyenfeld & D. Konietzka (Eds.), *Childlessness in Europe: Patterns, contexts, causes, and consequences* (pp. 3–13). Wiesbaden, Germany: Springer.

Kunter, M., Baumert, J., Leutner, D., Terhart, E., Seidel, T., Dicke, T., Holzberger, D., Kunina-Habenicht, O., Linninger, C., Lohse-Bossenz, H., Schulze-Stocker, F., & Stürmer, K. (2016). *Dokumentation der Erhebungsinstrumente der Projektphasen des BilWiss-Forschungsprogramms von 2009 bis 2016.* Frankfurt a. M., Germany: IQB.

Kunter, M., & Klusmann, U. (2010). Kompetenzmessung bei Lehrkräften: Methodische Herausforderungen. *Unterrichtswissenschaft, 38*(1), 68–86.

Kyndt, E., Donche, V., Trigwell, K., & Lindblom-Ylänne, S. (2017). Understanding higher education transitions. In E. Kyndt, V. Donche, K. Trigwell, & S. Lindblom-Ylänne (Eds.), *Higher education transitions: Theory and research* (pp. 306–319). New York, NY: Routledge.

Laflamme, F., Maydan, M., & Miller, A. (2008, August). *Using paradata to actively manage data collection survey process.* Joint Statistical Meetings, Denver, CO.

Lauterbach, O. (2015). Erfassung wirtschaftswissenschaftlicher Fachkompetenz von Studierenden in Startkohorte 5 des Nationalen Bildungspanels: Technischer Bericht (NEPS Working Paper No. 51). Bamberg, Germany: Leibniz Institute for Educational Trajectories, National Educational Panel Study.

Liebeskind, U. (in press). Institutionen der Hochschulbildung. In O. Köller, M. Hasselhorn, F. W. Hesse, K. Maaz, J. Schrader, H. Solga, K. Spieß, & K. Zimmer (Eds.), *Das Bildungswesen in Deutschland: Bestand und Potenziale.* Stuttgart, Germany: UTB.

Liebeskind, U., & Vietgen, S. (2017). Panelausfall in der Studierendenkohorte des Nationalen Bildungspanels: Analyse des Ausfallprozesses zwischen der ersten und zweiten telefonischen Befragung (NEPS Working Paper No. 70). Bamberg, Germany: Leibniz Institute for Educational Trajectories, National Educational Panel Study.

Link, M. W., Murphy, J., Schober, M. F., Buskirk, T. D., Hunter Childs, J., & Langer Tesfaye, C. (2014). Mobile technologies for conducting, augmenting and potentially replacing surveys: Executive summary of the AAPOR task force on emerging technologies in public opinion research. *Public Opinion Quarterly, 78*(4), 779–787.

Lugtig, P., & Toepoel, V. (2016). The use of PCs, smartphones, and tablets in a probability-based panel survey: Effects on survey measurement error. *Social Science Computer Review, 34*(1), 78–94.

Marini, M. M. (1984). The order of events in the transition to adulthood. *Social Education, 57,* 63–84.

Mavletova, A., & Couper, M. P. (2013). Sensitive topics in PC web and mobile web surveys: Is there a difference? *Survey Research Methods, 7*(3), 191–205.

Mavletova, A., & Couper, M. P. (2015). A meta-analysis of breakoff rates in mobile web surveys. In D. Toninelli, R. Pinter, & Pedraza, de, Pablo (Eds.), *Mobile research methods: Opportunities and challenges of mobile research methodologies* (pp. 81–98). London, England: Ubiquity Press.

Max-Planck-Institut für Bildungsforschung. (2010). COACTIV-R: Eine Studie zum Erwerb professioneller Kompetenz von Lehramtsanwärtern während des Vorbereitungsdienstes: Dokumentation der Erhebungsinstrumente für den ersten und zweiten Messzeitpunkt. Unpublished document. Berlin, Germany.

Mayer, K. U. (2008). Das Hochschulwesen. In K. S. Cortina, J. Baumert, A. Leschinsky, L. Trommer, & K. U. Mayer (Eds.), *Rororo Sachbuch: Vol. 62339. Das Bildungswesen in der Bundesrepublik Deutschland: Strukturen und Entwicklungen im Überblick* (pp. 599–645). Reinbek, Germany: Rowohlt Taschenbuch Verlag.

Möhring, W., & Schlütz, D. (2010). *Die Befragung in der Medien- und Kommunikationswissenschaft: Eine praxisorientierte Einführung* (2nd ed.). Wiesbaden, Germany: VS Verlag für Sozialwissenschaften.

Nauck, B. (2001). Der Wert von Kindern für ihre Eltern: „Value of Children" als spezielle Handlungstheorie des generativen Verhaltens und von Generationenbeziehungen im interkulturellen Vergleich. *Kölner Zeitschrift für Soziologie und Sozialpsychologie, 53,* 407–435.

Prussog-Wagner, A., Weiß, T., Aust, F., & Weber, A. (2013). *Methodenbericht NEPS-Startkohorte 5: Kompetenztestung Haupterhebung. Sommer 2013. B57.* Bonn, Hannover, Germany: DZHW.

Prussog-Wagner, A., Weiß, T., & Turri, F. (2017). Methodenbericht NEPS Startkohorte 5: Online-Haupterhebung. Herbst 2016. B113. Bonn, Germany.

Radisch, F., Stecher, L., Klieme, E., & Kühnbach, O. (2007). Unterrichts- und Angebotsqualität aus Schülersicht. In H. G. Holtappels, E. Klieme, T. Rauschenbach, & L. Stecher (Eds.), *Ganztagsschule in Deutschland: Ergebnisse der Ausgangserhebung der „Studie zur Entwicklung von Ganztagsschulen" (StEG)* (pp. 227–260). Weinheim, Germany: Juventa.

Rehn, T., Brandt, G., Fabian, G., & Briedis, K. (2011). Hochschulabschlüsse im Umbruch: Studium und Übergang von Absolventinnen und Absolventen reformierter und traditioneller Studiengänge des Jahrgangs 2009 (HIS:Forum Hochschule No. 17). Hannover, Germany.

Schaeper, H., Grotheer, M., & Brandt, G. (2017). Childlessness and fertility dynamics of female higher education graduates in Germany. In M. Kreyenfeld & D. Konietzka (Eds.), *Childlessness in Europe: Patterns, contexts, causes, and consequences* (pp. 209–232). Wiesbaden, Germany: Springer.

Schaeper, H., & Weiß, T. (2016). The conceptualization, development, and validation of an instrument for measuring the formal learning environment in higher education. In H.-P. Blossfeld, J. von Maurice, M. Bayer, & J. Skopek (Eds.), *Methodological issues of longitudinal surveys: The example of the National Educational Panel Study* (pp. 267–290). Wiesbaden, Germany: Springer VS.

Schnell, R. (2012). *Survey-Interviews: Methoden standardisierter Befragungen.* Wiesbaden, Germany: VS Verlag für Sozialwissenschaften.

Stapleton, C. E. (2013). The smart(phone) way to collect survey data. *Survey Practice, 6*(2).

Steinwede, J., & Aust, F. (2012). Methodenbericht NEPS Startkohorte 5: CATI-Haupterhebung. Herbst 2010. B52. Bonn, Germany: infas.

Steinwede, J., & Prussog-Wagner, A. (2012). Methodenbericht NEPS Startkohorte 5: Kompetenztestung Haupterhebung. Frühjahr 2011. B53. Bonn, Germany: infas.

Struminskaya, B., Weyandt, K., & Bosnjak, M. (2015). The effects of questionnaire completion using mobile devices on data quality: Evidence from a probability-based general population panel. *Methods, data, analyses*, *9*(2), 261–292.

Thönnissen, C., Wilhelm, B., Alt, P., Fiedrich, S., & Walper, S. (2017). *Pairfam scales and instruments manual: Waves 1 to 8. Release 8.0.* Munich, Germany: LMU.

Trigwell, K. (2017). Transitions within the university. In E. Kyndt, V. Donche, K. Trigwell, & S. Lindblom-Ylänne (Eds.), *Higher education transitions: Theory and research* (pp. 103–112). New York, NY: Routledge.

Walstad, W., & Rebeck, K. (2008). The test of understanding of college economics. *American Economic Review: Papers & Proceedings*, *98*(2), 547–551.

Zinn, S., Steinhauer, H.-W., & Aßmann, C. (2017). *Samples, weights, and nonresponse: The student sample of the National Educational Panel Study (Wave 1 to 8)* (NEPS Survey Paper No. 18). Bamberg, Germany: Leibniz Institute for Educational Trajectories, National Educational Panel Study.

Zlatkin-Troitschanskaia, O., Shavelson, R., & Kuhn, C. (2015). The international state of research on measurement of competency in higher education. *Studies in Higher Education*, *40*(3), 393–411.

Adult Education and Lifelong Learning

Jutta Allmendinger, Corinna Kleinert, Reinhard Pollak, Basha Vicari, Oliver Wölfel, Agnieszka Althaber, Manfred Antoni, Bernhard Christoph, Katrin Drasch, Florian Janik, Ralf Künster, Marie-Christine Laible, Kathrin Leuze, Britta Matthes, Michael Ruland, Benjamin Schulz and Annette Trahms

Abstract

The adult stage (Stage 8) of the German National Educational Panel Study (NEPS) focuses on the adult working age population in Germany and serves, in many respects, as a capstone for the NEPS structure. Its main purpose is to collect data from Starting Cohort 6 (SC6, adults) on adult education, specifically on formal, nonformal, and informal further training; on competence endowment and its development over the life course; and on monetary and nonmonetary returns to initial and adult education in a life-course perspective. The data include a large number of theoretically derived determinants of adult education and competencies, as well as information on returns within and outside of the labor market. Detailed information on the learning environments at a workplace or in a household makes it possible to contextualize the returns to education. On the one hand, the SC6 data contain detailed retrospective information on education, labor market participation, and households; on the other hand, they provide yearly panel information from currently ten waves (as of May 2018). These rich data allow numerous analyses from a life-course perspective pertaining to sociological, economic, psychological, and developmental theories.

J. Allmendinger · A. Althaber · R. Künster · B. Schulz
WZB Berlin Social Science Center, Berlin, Germany
E-Mail: jutta.allmendinger@wzb.eu

A. Althaber
E-Mail: agnieszka.althaber@wzb.eu

R. Künster
E-Mail: ralf.kuenster@wzb.eu

B. Schulz
E-Mail: benjamin.schulz@wzb.eu

Keywords

Adult education · Further training · Competence development · Life-course Labor market · Panel study

---

C. Kleinert
Leibniz Institute for Educational Trajectories, Bamberg, Germany
E-Mail: corinna.kleinert@lifbi.de

R. Pollak (✉)
WZB Berlin Social Science Center and Freie Universität Berlin, Berlin, Germany
E-Mail: reinhard.pollak@wzb.eu

B. Vicari (✉) · O. Wölfel · M. Antoni · B. Christoph · M.-C. Laible · B. Matthes · A. Trahms
Institute for Employment Research (IAB) of the German Federal Employment Agency (BA),
Nürnberg, Germany
E-Mail: basha.vicari@iab.de

O. Wölfel
E-Mail: oliver.woelfel@iab.de

M. Antoni
E-Mail: manfred.antoni@iab.de

B. Christoph
E-Mail: bernhard.christoph@iab.de

M.-C Laible
E-Mail: marie-christine.laible@iab.de

B. Matthes
E-Mail: britta.matthes@iab.de

A. Trahms
E-Mail: annette.trahms@iab.de

K. Drasch
Friedrich-Alexander-University Erlangen-Nuremberg, Erlangen, Germany
E-Mail: katrin.drasch@fau.de

F. Janik
Oberbürgermeister der Stadt Erlangen, Erlangen, Germany
E-Mail: oberbuergermeister@stadt.erlangen.de

K. Leuze
Friedrich-Schiller Universität Jena, Jena, Germany
E-Mail: kathrin.leuze@uni-jena.de

M. Ruland
infas Institut für angewandte Sozialwissenschaft GmbH, Bonn, Germany
E-Mail: m.ruland@infas.de

17.1 Main Objectives

Both political and scientific debates have been stressing the growing societal importance of adult education and lifelong learning (European Commission 2017; German Council of Economic Experts 2017). This discussion is motivated by ongoing globalization, skill-biased technological change, digitalization, and the development of a knowledge society. As these structural changes are of crucial importance for the working lives of the population in (post-) industrialized countries, education is no longer an asset achieved in youth that remains of constant value during a long and stable employment career. Today, adults have to learn continuously to keep up with flexible requirements at the workplace and to be able to find employment in different and rapidly changing fields. Additionally, because the aging population in Germany is leading to a lack of skilled employees, lifelong learning becomes more important due to demographic changes. One way to meet this demand for skilled employees is through further education of adults. Thus, adult education and lifelong learning have become an integral part of current and future educational careers.

The *first objective* of Stage 8 of the National Educational Panel Study (NEPS) is to collect comprehensive high-quality data on adult education and lifelong learning—including data on the learning environments and decision-making processes leading to learning participation of adults. The NEPS adult stage is responsible for collecting data from Starting Cohort 6 (SC6, adults).[1] Due to the complexity of the research fields associated with lifelong learning, several choices had to be made: What kind of adult education should be covered—only job-related learning or private learning as well? What kind of training courses should be considered—only courses with physical attendance offered by certified providers or courses offered by any provider through any medium or platform? And what kinds of contents need to be covered—training of cognitive and/or noncognitive competencies or training of specific skills? The main topics chosen for the NEPS adult stage are presented in the following sections.

Lifelong learning is embedded in educational and occupational careers. On the one hand, participation in adult education depends, for example, on specific family arrangements, time constraints, and well-being; on the other hand, initial and adult education form occupational careers, family arrangements, well-being, and political participation later in life. Thus, the *second objective* of the NEPS adult stage is to collect complete and detailed data on the education, employment, and family histories of adults along with data on their subjective well-being, health, and political participation. SC6 data on the life-courses of individuals serve as background information for adult education,

---

[1] For details on Starting Cohort 6 (adults) see: https://www.neps-data.de/en-us/datacenter/dataanddocumentation/startingcohortadults.aspx. In 2018, respondents of Starting Cohort 4 are about 22 to 24 years old. From 2018 onward, they are being given the same core questionnaire for adults as the members of Starting Cohort 6.

and—equally importantly—as an outcome of educational investments at any previous point in the life-course. As the final stage in the overall study design, the NEPS adult stage provides information on the outcome of all educational efforts as well as information on continuing educational efforts during adulthood.

The *third objective* of the NEPS adult stage is to collect data on domain-specific and domain-general cognitive competencies during adulthood. So far, little is known about how competencies are acquired, distributed, and changed over the life-course (Allmendinger and von den Driesch 2015; Allmendinger and Leibfried 2003). SC6 data allow researchers to close this gap by gathering information not only on reading literacy and mathematical, natural sciences and computer skills but also on a person's interests, self-concept, and motivation. This enables analyses of the development of cognitive competencies over the life course combined with a simultaneous evaluation of returns to formal qualifications, competencies, and employment experiences.

Figure 17.1 summarizes the objectives of the NEPS adult stage within the context of the overlying NEPS structure. The theoretical model of NEPS is introduced in Chap. 1 of this volume. Figure 17.1 simply rephrases the six pillars representing this model and includes the adult stage objectives: The SC6 data collected in the NEPS adult stage enable researchers to study participation in adult education, including effects of learning environments, prior educational activities, migration backgrounds, and psychological aspects, as well as the decision-making processes that lead to participation in adult education. Moreover, this can be used to analyze effects of initial and adult education on

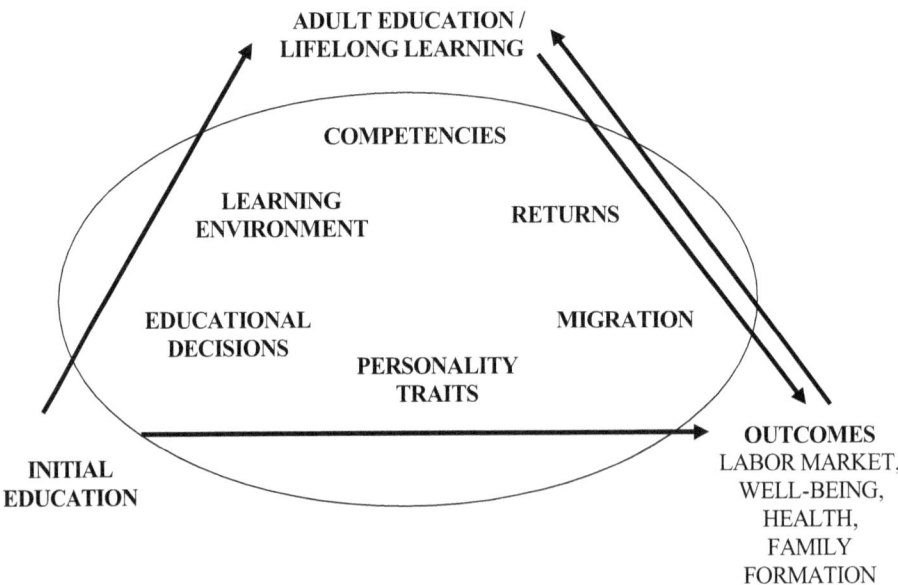

Fig. 17.1 Main research objectives of NEPS Stage 8. *Source* Own image

various outcomes, such as labor market participation and performance, well-being, and health. Finally, the development and the effects of competencies over the life course can be described and researchers can elaborate on this interrelation. Adopting a dynamic life-course perspective enables researchers to assess the extent to which previous competencies, learning environments, educational decisions, a person's migration background, and socioemotional traits (e.g., personality) reinforce educational participation, the development of competencies, and educational outcomes over time.

In order to achieve these objectives and to address more specific research questions from the six pillars of NEPS, the adult stage covers the population of all adults of working age regardless of their actual employment status. It introduces a number of innovative and unique elements to a large-scale panel study by:

- Combining economic, sociological, psychological, and educational sciences theories for a truly interdisciplinary approach to adult education and returns to education in a life-course perspective
- Developing and adjusting measures of various theoretical constructs for adult interviews—for example, measures of learning environments, social and cultural resources, migration-specific factors, and returns to education
- Introducing modularized measures of all dimensions of educational activities (formal, nonformal, and informal learning) and detailed measures of employment activities, job tasks, partnerships, and children over the entire life course
- Applying measures of various educational outcomes, including detailed information on labor market returns, subjective well-being, health, and social and political participation
- Repeatedly assessing the individual development of cognitive competencies in a representative adult sample, including various domain-specific assessments that can be compared with competence endowments in earlier stages of NEPS
- Introducing elements of data editing to the interview situation by applying the latest computer-assisted interview techniques in order to raise the quality and consistency of life-course data
- Enriching survey data with longitudinal administrative employment information from social security records—for example, data on earnings, labor market participation, and firm characteristics as well as on unemployment and participation in active labor market policy measures (for details, see Antoni et al. 2018)

17.2 Conceptual Framework and Research Questions

The research questions for the NEPS adult stage are based mainly on sociological and economic individual-level theories on education and labor market participation such as human capital theory, signaling theory, and a rational choice theory of educational decisions. These theoretical foundations are extended by approaches from educational sciences and developmental psychology. The latter are particularly important for understanding competence endowment and development over adulthood. The possibility of combining information on competence endowment and development with not only detailed schooling, training and employment trajectories but also personality traits, motivation, and attitudes makes the SC6 data a unique source for research in the social sciences. Moreover, it allows for the development of theoretical models explaining competence endowment.

17.2.1 The Life-Course Perspective on Educational Histories and Adult Education

The central *conceptual perspective* of the study is life-course research (Mayer 1990, 2009; see Chap. 2, this volume). This perspective perceives an individual's life course as a sequence of activities and events in various life domains and spheres (for examples, see *Aisenbrey and Fasang* 2017; *Brehm and Buchholz* 2014; *Struffolino et al.* 2016).[2] Life courses are understood as rule-based, dynamic characteristics of the social structure that affect numerous individuals and their social positions. Life courses are influenced by institutions in which individuals are embedded. Thus, life courses depend partly on individual decisions and intentional behavior and partly on unintentional outcomes of the individual's actions (for applications, see, e.g., *Bächmann and Gatermann* 2017; *Hägglund and Bächmann* 2017). Research on the life course theoretically and empirically analyzes the dynamics of the distribution of positions and the resources held by individuals in a society. This perspective allows for the simultaneous analysis of age, cohort, and period effects and thus accounts for "local interdependencies" of events and conditions (*Becker and Blossfeld* 2017; *Mayer and Huinink* 1990).

In particular, the timing and sequencing of education and training in occupational careers can be explored and linked with parallel activities in other life domains. With a life-course perspective, an adult's education embedded in that individual's life course can be analyzed in both work and private contexts. This makes it possible to explore the influence of employers and other (labor market) institutions, regional disparities, or the gender-specific impact of partners, children, and family arrangements in general. Moreover the effects of these factors on participation rates in adult education can be identified (for employer-specific effects, see *Ehlert* 2017; for regional-specific effects, see *Görlitz and Rzepka* 2017; *Rzepka and Tamm* 2016). Further, research questions on decision-making processes regarding participation in educational activities can be analyzed, including the importance of previous educational and occupational attainment and potential path dependencies (e.g., *Kramer and Tamm* 2018). Cumulative returns of adult

---

[2] All references in italics throughout this chapter refer to empirical research based on data of NEPS Starting Cohort 6 (SC6).

education over the life course for various labor market and non-labor-market-related outcomes can also be studied with the SC6 data.

The questionnaire is also based on concepts that capture salient historical changes in life-course patterns. The most comprehensive approach, individualization theory (Beck 1986), assumes that individuals are gaining greater control over their lives due to the process of modernization. Accordingly, they pursue a wider variety of life choices and life trajectories. This concept can be contrasted to various other, partly contradicting approaches to life course development such as pluralization (Zapf 1991), institutionalization (Kohli 1985), deinstitutionalization (Shanahan 2000), standardization (Kohli 1985), and destandardization (Modell et al. 1976). These concepts offer powerful and theoretically derived models for comparing the educational pathways of different cohorts. SC6 data from the NEPS adult stage enable researchers to empirically test these partially contradicting theories and compare the development of life-course patterns to overall developments in the labor market (for examples, see *Brzinsky-Fay and Solga* 2016; *Zimmermann and Konietzka* 2018).

Several changes in life-course patterns are already apparent. For example, the notion of "standard biographies" has lost empirical relevance (Buchmann 1989; Heinz 2003; Mayer et al. 2010). The traditional sequence of life stages—from education to work and from work to retirement—is gradually being expanded by more diverse patterns: Individuals may reenter education after periods of work, take sabbaticals, change occupations during their careers, or combine work and other activities in prolonged transitions into retirement (Jacob 2004).

The social sciences' view of life courses is supplemented by approaches from educational sciences and developmental psychology in which lifelong learning and competence development are central for understanding educational trajectories. These approaches imply that the development of competencies is subject to stage-specific dynamics. Thus for example, reading literacy is a domain-specific competence during school age, but it becomes a cross-curricular basic skill in vocational training, higher education, and an individual's career (Arnold et al. 2012). Therefore, an important open question is how basic competencies develop during adolescence and adulthood and how they influence the acquisition of domain-specific competencies in later life stages.

With the SC6 data, it is also possible to explore research questions focusing on, for example, educational participation, returns to education, changes in the importance of adult learning, and competence development during adulthood. To collect information on the different educational activities in which respondents have been engaged over their life courses, it is useful to distinguish these activities (for a detailed discussion, see Kleinert and Matthes 2009; Chap. 5, this volume). Education taking place in *formal* learning environments is institutionalized and often includes recognized certificates that strongly determine labor market chances in Germany (Damelang et al. 2015). Such formal educational activities are collected in the NEPS adult stage by applying retrospective questions covering the respondent's entire schooling and vocational training history. In order to cover educational activities in *nonformal* learning environments in adulthood—

institutionalized shorter training courses not leading to certificates—it is important to develop and implement a clear working definition of relevant nonformal education. It would be insufficient to include only courses that may be of importance for some projected return in later life. Instead, the strategy applied in NEPS is threefold: first, to ask for all forms of training in nonformal learning environments; second, to ask for the exact subject area; and third, to ask for the initial intention for participating in such a course (*Janik et al.* 2016).

Beyond participation rates in different population segments, little is known about *informal learning,* defined as learning processes that are organized by the individuals themselves (for a recent exception using NEPS SC6 data, see *Rüber and Bol* 2017). This is particularly true regarding the decisions that lead to these learning processes or their (cumulative) returns. Therefore, the NEPS adult stage collects information on informal educational activities in a standardized way. Because formal education programs are typically organized by an external provider and take a substantial amount of time, recall is comparatively easy. Nonformal and especially informal learning activities, however, may be rather short. Most importantly, informal learning activities maybe unintentional. Therefore, individuals have more difficulties in recalling nonformal learning over a longer time span (Dürnberger et al. 2011; Janik et al. 2016)—and we assume the same to be true for informal learning. Because the time span for recall is limited to the time between two panel waves, the panel structure of the survey is crucial to the collection of data on all forms of learning—be it formal, nonformal, or informal.

Unintentional learning is very important for several life-course outcomes and happens not only on the job but also while volunteering or during political engagement. Unfortunately, surveys cannot measure this form of learning directly. Therefore, the NEPS adult stage repeatedly asks respondents about their job tasks and their social and political participation to allow for the approximation of the effects of unintentional learning. In particular, changes in job tasks can be helpful to measure unintentional learning because they reflect a career development.

17.2.2 Competence Endowment and Development

A central aim of the NEPS project is to increase knowledge about competence endowment, development, distribution, and change over the course of an adult's life in Germany. The SC6 data enables a description of the distribution of competence endowments in different groups of the adult population (Wölfel et al. 2011) and an analysis of the developments and the factors triggering the acquisition of new skills (*Kramer and Tamm* 2018). Cognitive and noncognitive competencies are important determinants of labor market outcomes such as wages, job satisfaction, and unemployment (*Gnambs* 2017). Moreover, they are an important tool to cope with new challenges such as digitalization.

Determinants of the decline and loss of skills and competencies during adulthood can be detected with the SC6 data. Domain-specific cognitive competencies such as reading literacy and mathematics and their importance for educational success are well-researched in school, training, or higher education settings. However, little is known about these domain-specific competencies in combination with other employment-related skills that are acquired continuously beyond initial education. Thus, the questions whether domain-specific competencies remain relevant in occupational careers and how they interact with other skills remain to be answered.

Moreover, it is not yet clear how different competencies *cause* various outcomes in adult life courses. For example, competence endowment is expected to influence an adult's educational decisions and it may contribute to the returns to education beyond educational credentials—particularly with respect to employment-related returns. Repeated comprehensive measures of competencies, educational attainment, and vocational qualifications over the life course provide data not only on the importance of these constructs with respect to labor market returns, but also on how these constructs relate to each other. Moreover, the data enable the assessment of the changing relevance and interaction of competencies, credentials, and qualifications throughout an adult's career.

Prior to designing the measures of competencies in the NEPS adult stage, it was necessary to select competence domains that should be followed during adulthood. Three selection criteria were applied: First, the competencies should be relevant for a major part of the adult population and labor force. This first selection criterion is especially difficult with regard to the highly heterogeneous target group covered in the NEPS adult stage. Second, assessment of competencies should be valid and reliable (Kleinert 2005). Third, because it is impossible to select competencies in the NEPS adult stage independently of the other stages, the decision had to be based on a design overarching all stages of NEPS.

As illustrated in Chap. 4 of this volume, the NEPS adult stage (as well as the earlier educational stages) focuses on *cognitive competencies that are domain-specific during schooling but basic in adulthood*. It is undisputed that competencies such as reading, mathematical, scientific, and foreign-language literacy are necessary prerequisites for successful employment and active participation in society (Rychen and Salganik 2003). Taking the heterogeneous target group into account, it is important to adapt the existing student assessments to cover functional literacy. Thus, it is necessary first, to assess potential problems in adult daily life; second, to build tests measuring the full range of competence domains in the adult population; and third, to cover the dynamics of these competence domains over the adult life span.

The NEPS adult stage also focuses on measuring *skills connected to the employability* of adults. These skills are competencies that help adults find and maintain employment in different occupational fields under changing conditions. Due to these changes, different key competencies or metadisciplinary skills play an increasingly important role during adulthood. Therefore, the questionnaire inquiries about selected *noncognitive competencies* indirectly by self-assessment scales (see Chap. 9, this volume). Because educational processes throughout adulthood are mostly self-directed by specific interests, self-efficacy, self-regulation, and motivation, these concepts are included in the instrument—in addition to more stable personality traits such as the Big Five. Because social behavior and cooperation are considered important in adulthood, especially in occupational contexts, certain facets of social competencies, such as assertiveness or conflict-solving skills (Arnold et al. 2012), are included in the NEPS adult stage survey program.

The cognitive skill *literacy in information and communication technologies (ICT)* seems to be particularly important for many tasks in the employment context and in private life. On the one hand, ICT literacy has unique cognitive and technical aspects; on the other hand, it serves as a "tool" for applying other cognitive and social competencies (e.g., writing texts or communicating with others). Most important for the NEPS adult stage is the relevance of ICT skills for employment chances beyond specialized occupational fields. Finally, because these skills are highly relevant for lifelong learning processes, measures of *metacognition* are included in the survey. Metacognition includes knowledge, skills, and attitudes that enable strategic decision making when learning or thinking, as well as the ability to initiate, organize, and control active realization.

17.2.3 Learning Environments

Learning environments differ substantially for respondents in the NEPS adult stage, especially when compared to students and children in earlier educational stages. Whereas learning in all lower stages of NEPS takes place in the same predefined formal institutional contexts for the survey respondents (Chap. 5, this volume), the learning processes of adults occur in a multitude of different learning environments.

In Germany, numerous providers offer trainings or courses for adults in formal and nonformal environments. Examples for such providers are firms, state-founded institutions (e.g., adult education centers), state agencies (e.g., the Federal Employment Agency), chambers of commerce and crafts, higher education institutions, and a wide range of nongovernmental organizations (Kleinert and Matthes 2009). It is difficult to gain a complete picture of the relevant adult learning providers, particularly due to the country's federal structure. Programs vary considerably across federal states, and it is impossible to identify a coherent top-down approach to adult learning policy. Hence, because learning environments in the NEPS adult stage differ in their settings, standardized information from the adult learner's perspective needs to be collected to answer questions on the effects of the learning environment's structural characteristics on different educational outcomes.

The most important learning environment for adults is the *firm or workplace*. First, employers provide a substantial part of further education and training for employed adults in Germany (*Görlitz and Rzepka* 2017; Rosenbladt and Bilger 2008; *Rzepka and Tamm* 2016). Therefore they play a role in educational decision making, because they either encourage further training, hinder participation, or deny access. In general, large firms provide more training than small and medium-sized enterprises (SME). Whereas large firms often provide training themselves, SMEs turn to external providers. Furthermore, participation in formal adult training is strongly related to different types of employment (*Ehlert* 2017). Thus, individuals who are employed in small firms, in temporary jobs, or part-time are less likely to enroll in training.

Second, an important part of adult learning is learning on the job. This form of learning has received increasing attention from researchers because skill-biased technological change is altering the overall structure of a firm's organization and the composition of its workforce. These changes impact on an individual's need to invest in further training and to continue learning over the entire life span. Therefore, describing jobs in more detail than by mere job titles has become more relevant. The growing diversification of occupations makes it necessary to perform a proper identification of meaningful tasks profiles for occupations. Consequently, the NEPS adult stage developed a survey instrument on *job tasks* that provides detailed information on skill demands, learning possibilities, and learning conditions (*Matthes et al.* 2014). This instrument is based mainly on the theoretical considerations of Autor et al. (2003) who define a task as a unit that directly produces output either as goods or services. The authors distinguish between routine and nonroutine tasks, and between cognitive and manual tasks. In combination with the longitudinal data, the instrument provides a unique opportunity to answer a broad range of questions such as: How are job tasks, formal education, and competencies distributed in the adult population? Which factors determine under- and overqualification? How do job tasks change in changing labor markets, and what skills will be required in the future to guarantee stable employment careers?

Besides firms, *households* serve as an important learning environment for adults. Other household members, particularly the partner, may provide economic, cultural, social, or time resources for the investment in education or they may hinder participation by denying them. In this context, the analysis of family and household effects on adult learning participation can be particularly promising from a gender perspective. For example, research has shown that women, particularly mothers, participate less often in further training compared to men or women without children, but the dynamics leading to these differences have not yet been fully understood (Dieckhoff and Steiber 2011).

Alongside the structural information on adult education providers, firms, and households, an important feature of the NEPS adult stage is the provision of information on *specific characteristics* of adult learning courses. Based on a general model of how courses are conducted, including their atmosphere and the cognitive activation it triggers (see Chap. 5, this volume), data on three dimensions are collected for selected courses: First, the *structure* dimension measures the setting of a course and its internal design; second, the *support* dimension measures both the interaction patterns between participants and instructors and the interaction patterns among the participants themselves; and third, the cognitive *challenge dimension* measures the challenges participants face when taking the course. This detailed information about course characteristics can be used to analyze their effects on successful participation, on increases in skills or competencies, and on returns to adult educational investments.

17.2.4 Social Inequality and Educational Decisions Over the Life Course

As previously described, respondents of the NEPS adult stage are not institutionally required to make educational decisions at any specific point in time. Therefore research questions such as why adults engage in education and what types of education they choose or why adults refrain from education, are particularly interesting. Educational decisions can be based on rational decision-making processes, on heuristics taking limited information into account, or a mixture of the two. The SC6 data allow for tests of various theoretical approaches on educational decisions, the most prominent being rational choice theory (Erikson and Jonsson 1996), satisficing (Simon 1993), models of frame selection (Esser 2001), simple heuristics (Gigerenzer and Todd 1999), and further approaches such as bounded rationality (e.g., Brewer 1988; Chaiken and Trope 1999; for more details on these approaches, see Chaps. 6 and 8, this volume). Besides explaining educational decisions during adult age, retrospective educational data of SC6 is also well suited to study decisions earlier in life (for examples, see *Blossfeld et al.* 2015; *Buchholz and Schier* 2015; *Biewen and Tapalaga* 2017; *Weiss and Schindler* 2017).

To understand educational decisions, data on adults' work-related and non-work-related aspirations are crucial. For the analysis of work-related aspirations, information on attitudes toward labor force participation, working hours, workloads, family role models, division of domestic labor, and occupational career aspirations is essential. Likewise, for the understanding of education investments, information unrelated to the labor market, such as attitudes and aspirations regarding leisure activities, or measures of self-concept are needed. Predominantly, participation in adult education is understood as a means to meet aspirations or to live up to specific attitudes. Thus, theoretical models explaining educational participation of adults focus mainly on attitudes, benefits, and probabilities related to the expected returns to adult investment such as labor market returns (e.g., career outcomes) or returns to private interests.

Because the reasons behind educational decisions vary between different social groups (Boudon 1974; Breen and Goldthorpe 1997), the influence of relevant others is meaningful for the learning participation of adults. Members of different social groups have different attitudes and information, and their behaviors are affected by different economic, cultural, and social resources (for examples of earlier educational decisions, see *Braun and Stuhler* 2018; *Bukodi et al.* 2017; *Minello and Blossfeld* 2016). First, a lack of financial resources, for example to pay course fees or to offset opportunity costs, impacts on the likelihood of engaging in further education. Second, cultural resources, for example, previous educational achievements and competencies, significantly influence educational decisions. Third, social resources are needed to learn about educational offers, to gain active support from other course members, to acquire financial support, and to gain support within the household (e.g., to be able to allocate time to the course instead of the household). They also shape educational aspirations in general. Because of the competing explanations for the declining effect of social origin (Hillmert and Jacob

2005), studies on the social background of adults and the interplay of primary and secondary effects are valuable.

Optimal and actual timing of training participation throughout the life course are another important aspect of educational decisions. Information on time preferences gathered in NEPS allows investigations of decision making going beyond mere cost–benefit analyses. Unlike the lower stages covered in NEPS, the respondents of the NEPS adult stage do not necessarily participate in or prepare for imminent educational activities at the time they are being surveyed. Nevertheless, several indicators, measured for all respondents independent of the planning status of education or training activities, allow an analysis of processes leading to educational decisions. Therefore information is gathered on independent indicators such as educational aims, attitudes, and expectations; information on the motive of avoiding downward social mobility; and information on and knowledge of educational opportunities. Likewise, data is collected on the perceived benefits of educational investments, the perceived probabilities for a successful investment, and on the expected costs of participation in adult learning. Additionally, respondents are asked about their overall financial, cultural, and social resources, so that these determinants can be evaluated against possible educational decisions and their outcomes.

17.2.5 Special Target Groups: Migrants

Detailed knowledge of further education among adults with a migration background is scarce in Germany. At the same time, migrants and their descendants are a group that is often more in need of adult education because their educational background may be inadequate and/or their certificates are not transferable to the German education system or labor market. Thus, important objectives are to allow empirical investigations first, on migrants' competencies and their literacy in the German language; second, on their financial, educational, and ethnic resources; third, on their participation in further education; and fourth, on the returns to their educational and occupational investments.

For this purpose, the survey gathers detailed information on migration backgrounds up to the third generation. Respondents with a migration background are assessed in German language literacy like all respondents in the NEPS adult stage. In addition, they are asked about their native language, the languages used in the households where respondents grew up and in their current households, as well as the languages used at the workplace and during leisure time. Furthermore, the respondents' complete migration history, including what kind of legal status they had when they came to Germany, is surveyed. Additionally, migration-specific cultural and social capital, the effects of ethnically homogeneous or heterogeneous networks on the likelihood of participating in adult education, and the chances to succeed in different labor market segments are assessed. For example, SC6 data reveal that migrants commonly participate in formal and nonformal full-time education programs (*Söhn* 2016). Moreover, migrants have a higher risk of being overqualified, especially female migrants from an educationally disadvantaged family background (*Kracke* 2016). For a valid measure of human capital, respondents with a migration background are not merely asked to translate their educational degrees into equivalent German degrees. Rather, the two largest groups of migrants (migrants from Turkey and from the former Soviet Union) are invited to state their original degree's name (in Turkish or Russian), and asked whether this degree has been recognized by the German authorities. Furthermore, a translated questionnaire in Turkish or Russian is provided so that these two migration groups can be interviewed entirely in their mother tongue (for more details, see Chap. 7, this volume).

17.2.6 Returns to Education

Collecting information on returns to education is a main objective of the NEPS adult stage. Researchers are interested in the effects of education on wages or unemployment risks (e.g., Lauer and Steiner 2001), or on class outcomes, job prestige, or occupational mobility (e.g., Shavit and Müller 1998; Scherer 2005). For example, some studies focus on the effects of further training on wages or unemployment risks (Jenkins et al. 2003; *Kracke et al.* 2017; Kuckulenz 2007; *Rüber and Bol* 2017), whereas others address the influence on vertical or horizontal occupational mobility (Dieckhoff 2007; Wolter and Schiener 2009). These returns can be observed only after individuals have left initial education and belong to the active or passive labor force population. To address research questions on returns to education, it is essential to extend NEPS beyond student cohorts to the adult population.

For a number of reasons, SC6 data are better suited to analyze economic and occupational returns to education compared to data from most other existing adult surveys. First, the returns to different educational activities in different life periods can be analyzed, thus enabling clear temporal modeling. Second, detailed measures of educational degrees, fields of study, and adult education in formal, nonformal, and informal learning environments are provided, thereby surpassing the measures of existing data on education. Third, the data allow for a differentiation between returns to educational credentials and returns to competencies. Human capital theory (Becker 1964; Mincer 1974), signaling theory (Spence 1973), screening theory (Arrow 1973), and the job competition model (Thurow 1975) make different statements on the relevance of certificates and competencies for labor market success. However, because applications are usually based on the same limited qualification indicators, and competence measures are usually lacking (for exceptions, see Green and Riddell 2003; Tyler 2004), it has hardly been possible until now to compare these theories empirically. Fourth, with the respondent's informed consent, administrative social security information from the Institute for Employment Research (IAB) can be linked to the survey data (NEPS-SC6-ADIAB, see Antoni et al. 2018). Linking survey and administrative data has several advantages, specifically because administrative information on complete employment biographies and earnings as well as on establishment characteristics is available in the combined data, making more exhaustive analyses possible. Finally, the survey data contains detailed information on social origins, migration backgrounds, age, and gender that allows returns to educational degrees and competencies to be analyzed specifically for various well-defined subgroups of the population.

Educational achievement also contributes to explaining disparities in several life domains apart from work. For this reason, the concepts applied in NEPS to measure the returns to education go beyond questions of pure economic applicability. For example, the data allow the investigation of how education shapes competencies later in life, and how education and competencies affect social inclusion (*Jusri and Kleinert* 2018), political engagement, health, and subjective well-being. Analyzing social and political participation permits inferences not only on private but also on social returns to education. By including these external effects, a more comprehensive utility function underlying the decision to invest in human capital can be derived. Subjective well-being is included specifically because this measure contributes to a more holistic concept of social welfare returns to education compared to purely economic aspects of wealth (see Chapt. 8, this volume). Moreover, these dimensions are selected because they fulfill additional functions in the context of the NEPS adult stage. Whereas knowledge on social participation helps explain individual competence endowment, because competencies (in particular, social and personal) may be acquired in the context of voluntary activities (Gerzer-Sass et al. 2006; Kirchhöfer 2000), well-being is an important determinant of motivation and aspirations.

17.3 Methodological Aspects

17.3.1 Survey Design and Survey Modes

As described above, the main objectives of the NEPS adult stage are to provide data on (a) adult education and lifelong learning, (b) economic and noneconomic returns to education, and (c) the development of competencies over the life course. Because adult education is often not institutionalized, and learning can take place in almost any circumstance and period of life, the NEPS adult stage requires a sampling strategy that draws a sample from a broad target population at the individual level. Therefore, the SC6 population is defined as all adults of working age living in Germany irrespective of their labor force participation. To separate the target group from earlier stages in NEPS, only individuals are considered who are usually no longer enrolled in initial schooling; that is, who are at least 22 years old. Thus, the starting population (first wave in 2009) for the NEPS adult stage comprises adults born between 1944 and 1986 (aged 22–64 years in 2009). A description of the sampling methods of the NEPS adult stage is provided in Chap. 3 of this volume. The first wave of the NEPS adult stage in 2009 comprised three subsamples: (1) all respondents of the study *Working and Learning in a Changing World* (ALWA, for details, see Kleinert et al. 2011) who agreed to be contacted for further interviews (the ALWA study was conducted in 2007/2008 with adults born between 1956 and 1986); (2) an augmentation of older respondents born between 1944 and 1955; and (3) an additional refreshment with adults in the same age range as the original ALWA sample. In NEPS Wave 3 (2011), the entire sample was refreshed again.

In order to test domain-specific and domain-general competencies in the adult population, respondents are tested in one or two competence domains at regular intervals through self-administered tests. During these test waves, the respondent's life course since the last interview is updated and some additional short questions from other NEPS pillars are asked. Usually an interviewer visits the respondents in their homes, conducts the assessments, and carries out the computer-assisted personal interviews (CAPI). In waves in which no tests are administered, the life-course information is updated and questions provided by the pillars and the NEPS adult stage are surveyed. In these waves, the default mode is a computer-assisted telephone interview (CATI).

Overall, the survey modes are flexible, but also complex. When a telephone number is missing for a member of the sample, the individual is visited by interviewers in their home to ask about telephone numbers. If a respondent refuses to participate on the phone, a CAPI interview is conducted. Likewise, if a respondent refuses to welcome an interviewer into their home, a CATI interview is offered and the competence assessment is waived. Thus, a deliberate CATI/CAPI mix is offered in order to minimize nonresponse bias and panel attrition. The interviews last about 30 min when combined with competence assessments and at most 60 min in waves without assessments. The length of the competence tests varies between 30 and 60 min.

17.3.2 Questionnaire Design

Regardless of the survey mode, the interviews in the NEPS adult stage are always computer-assisted. Computer-assisted interviews provide numerous opportunities to enhance data quality and to conduct customized interviews due to almost unlimited filtering possibilities. The NEPS adult stage makes ample use of these possibilities (for a detailed description, see Drasch et al. 2016). Because a significant part of the yearly interviews is devoted to collecting or updating life-course information, the most important feature used is that of technical innovations in life-course instruments. To receive reliable and valid information, all subareas of the life course are recorded in independent longitudinal modules of schooling, vocational preparation, vocational training and higher education, military service, employment history, unemployment history, partners in the household, children, and parental leave. Thus, we explicitly allow for parallel episodes. This modular design guarantees adequate reporting of the entire life course in all its complexity.

Three technical strategies are combined to assist the respondents in remembering and anchoring their activities throughout time: First, interviewers can access information respondents had already given earlier in the interview to help them date other events correctly, for example, by reminding respondents of the date of graduation when asking for a date of relocation. Second, after the initial data collection, the consistency of dates across all modules is checked in a special data revision module. This consistency check is made by the interviewers with the help of special software during the interview, so that mistakes and problems can be corrected immediately with the help of the respondents. This step integrates immediate data editing into the survey, so that any inconsistencies that emerge can be clarified together with the respondents. These measures improve overall data quality and validity (Ruland et al. 2016). Other successful implementations of this design—for example, the German Life History Study (Hillmert et al. 2004) and the forerunner study of the NEPS adult stage, Working and Learning in a Changing World (ALWA) (Antoni et al. 2010; Kleinert et al. 2011)—have shown that the quality of data improves, and that significantly more episodes of education and unemployment are reported (Drasch and Matthes 2013). Third, Proactive Dependent Interviewing techniques are applied to collect life-course data as completely and consistently as possible (Trahms et al. 2016). Preloads are used to remind respondents of their answers from previous interviews, for example, on their employment or on their partner and children. These preloads are used primarily as cues to continue one or more episodes from one panel wave to the next.

17.4 Conclusion

This short overview has hopefully sparked the reader's interest in the theoretical approaches of the NEPS adult stage, the data generated within NEPS Starting Cohort 6, and the empirical studies that have analyzed these data so far. The three main objectives of Stage 8 are to provide rich data from a life-course perspective on adult education, on competencies, and on labor market and non-labor-market-related returns to educational investments. The data collected enable the testing of different theoretical models, and researchers of different disciplines and different research paradigms are invited to develop research questions that may be analyzed with the rich NEPS adult stage data on retrospective life courses. Furthermore, the design of the NEPS adult stage allows for the assessment of long-term developments because life-course data have been collected for a large range of birth cohorts. Thus, the data collection program provides detailed high-quality information on numerous aspects of the educational and employment trajectories and the transition between different stages of the life course and for specific population groups. This has already generated numerous empirical results and will certainly continue to do so in the future.

References

Aisenbrey, S., & Fasang, A. (2017). The interplay of work and family trajectories over the life course: Germany and the United States in comparison. *American Journal of Sociology, 122*, 1448–1484.

Allmendinger, J., & Driesch, E. von den (2015). Bildung in Deutschland. Elf Mythen—elf Tatsachen. In R. Hoffmann & C. Bogedan (Eds.), *Arbeit der Zukunft. Möglichkeiten nutzen—Grenzen setzen* (pp. 37–51). Frankfurt a.M., Germany: Campus Verlag.

Allmendinger, J., & Leibfried S. (2003). Education and the welfare state: The four worlds of competence production. *European Journal of Social Policy, 13*, 63–81.

Antoni, M., Bachbauer, N., Eberle, J., & Vicari, B. (2018). NEPS-SC6-Erhebungsdaten verknüpft mit administrativen Daten des IAB (NEPS-SC6-ADIAB 7515) FDZ-Datenreport, 02/2018. Nürnberg, Germany.

Antoni, M., Drasch, K., Kleinert, C., Matthes, B., Ruland, M., & Trahms, A. (2010). *Working and learning in a changing world. Part I: Overview of the study - March 2011* (Second, updated version) *FDZ Methodenreport 05/2010*. Nürnberg, Germany: IAB.

Arnold, K.-H., Lindner-Müller, C., & Riemann, R. (2012). *Erfassung sozialer Kompetenz bei Kindern und Erwachsenen* (NEPS Working Paper 7). Bamberg, Germany: Leibniz-Institut für Bildungsverläufe, Nationales Bildungspanel.

Arrow, K. J. (1973). Higher education as a filter. *Journal of Public Economics, 2*, 193–216.

Autor, D. H., Levy, F., & Murnane, R. J. (2003). The skill content of recent technological change: An empirical exploration. *The Quarterly Journal of Economics, 118*, 1279–1333.

Bächmann, A.-C., & Gatermann, D. (2017). The duration of family-related employment interruptions: The role of occupational characteristics. *Journal for Labour Market Research, 50*, 143–160.

Beck, U. (1986). Risikogesellschaft. Auf dem Weg in eine andere Moderne. Frankfurt a. M., Germany: Suhrkamp.

Becker, G. S. (1964). Human capital. A theoretical and empirical analysis with special reference to education. New York, NY: Columbia University Press.

Becker, R., & Blossfeld, H. P. (2017). Entry of men into the labour market in West Germany and their career mobility (1945–2008). *Journal for Labour Market Research, 50*, 113–130.

Biewen, M., & Tapalaga, M. (2017). Life-cycle educational choices in a system with early tracking and "second chance" options. *Economics of Education Review, 56*, 80–94.

Blossfeld, P. N., Blossfeld, G. J., & Blossfeld, H.-P. (2015). Educational expansion and inequalities in educational opportunity: Long-term changes for East and West Germany. *European Sociological Review, 31*, 144–160.

Boudon, R. (1974). Education, opportunity, und social inequality. Changing prospects in western society. New York, NY: Wiley.

Braun, S. T., & Stuhler, J. (2018). The transmission of inequality across multiple generations: Testing recent theories with evidence from Germany. *The Economic Journal, 128*, 471–916.

Breen, R., & Goldthorpe, J. H. (1997). Explaining educational differentials: Towards a formal rational action theory. *Rationality and Society, 9*, 275–305.

Brehm, U., & Buchholz, S. (2014). Is there a wrong time for a right decision? The impact of the timing of first births and the spacing of second births on women's careers. *Zeitschrift für Familienforschung, 26*, 269–301.

Brewer, M. B. (1988). A dual process model of impression formation. In T.-K. Srull & R. S. Wyer (Eds.), *Advances in social cognition; Vol. 1. A dual process model of impression formation* (pp. 1–36). Hillsdale, NJ: Erlbaum.

Brzinsky-Fay, C., & Solga, H. (2016). Compressed, postponed, or disadvantaged? School-to-work-transition patterns and early occupational attainment in West Germany. *Research in Social Stratification and Mobility, 46*, 21–36.

Buchholz, S., & Schier, A. (2015). New game, new chance? Social inequalities and upgrading secondary school qualifications in West Germany. *European Sociological Review, 31*, 603–615.

Buchmann, M. (1989). *The script of life in modern society: Entry into adulthood in a changing world.* Chicago, IL: University of Chicago Press.

Bukodi, E., Eibl, F., Buchholz, S., Marzadro, S., Minello, A., Wahler, S., & Schizzerotto, A. (2017). Linking the macro to the micro: A multidimensional approach to educational inequalities in four European countries. *European Societies.* Advance online publication.

Chaiken, S., & Trope, Y. (1999). *Dual-process theories in social psychology.* New York, NY: Guilford Press.

Damelang, A., Schulz, F., & Vicari, B. (2015). Institutionelle Eigenschaften von Berufen und ihr Einfluss auf berufliche Mobilität in Deutschland. *Schmollers Jahrbuch, 135*, 307–333.

Dieckhoff, M. (2007). Does it work? The effect of continuing training on labour market outcomes: A comparative study of Germany, Denmark, and the United Kingdom. *European Sociological Review, 23*, 295–308.

Dieckhoff, M., & Steiber, N. (2011). A re-assessment of common theoretical approaches to explain gender differences in continuing training participation. *British Journal of Industrial Relations, 49*, s135–s157.

Drasch, K., & Matthes, B. (2013). Improving retrospective life course data by combining modularized self-reports and event history calendars. Experiences from a large scale survey. *Quality & Quantity, 47*, 817–838.

Drasch, K., Kleinert, C., Matthes, B., & Ruland, M. (2016). Why do we collect data on educational histories over the life course the way we do? Core questionnaire design decisions in starting cohort 6 adults. In H.-P. Blossfeld, J. von Maurice, M. Bayer, & J. Skopek (Eds.), *Methodological Issues of Longitudinal Surveys* (pp. 331–347). Wiesbaden, Germany: Springer VS.

Dürnberger, A., Drasch, K., & Matthes, B. (2011). Kontextgestützte Abfrage in Retrospektiverhebungen. Ein kognitiver Pretest zu Erinnerungsprozessen bei Weiterbildungsereignissen. *Methoden, Daten, Analysen, 5*, 3–35.

Ehlert, M. (2017). Who benefits from training courses in Germany? Monetary returns to non-formal further education on a segmented labour market. *European Sociological Review.* Advance online publication.

Erikson, R., & Jonsson, J. O. (1996). Explaining class inequality in education: The Swedish case. In R. Erikson & J. O. Jonsson (Eds.), *Can education be equalized? The Swedish case in comparative perspective* (pp. 1–63). Oxford, England: Westview.

Esser, H. (2001). *Soziologie. Spezielle Grundlagen. Band 6: Sinn und Kultur.* Frankfurt a. M., Germany: Campus.

European Commission (2017). *White paper on the future of Europe. Reflections and scenarios for the EU27 by 2025.* Brussels, Belgium: Author.

German Council of Economic Experts (2017). *Annual Report 2017/18: Towards a Forward-Looking Economic Policy.* Berlin, Germany: Author.

Gerzer-Sass, A., Reupold, A., & Nußhart, C. (2006). *LisU-Projekt Kompetenznachweis Lernen im sozialen Umfeld.* München, Germany: Deutsches Jugendinstitut.

Gigerenzer, G., Todd, P.M., & The ABC Research Group. (1999). *Simple heuristics that make us smart.* New York, NY: Oxford University Press.

Gnambs, T. (2017). Human capital and reemployment success: The role of cognitive abilities and personality. *Journal of Intelligence, 5*, 9.

Görlitz, K., & Rzepka, S. (2017). Regional training supply and employees' training participation. *The Annals of Regional Science, 59*, 281–296.

Green, D. A., & Riddell, W. C. (2003). Literacy and earnings: An investigation of the interaction of cognitive and non-cognitive attributes in earnings generation. *Labour Economics, 10*, 165–184.

Hägglund, A. E., & Bächmann, A.-C. (2017). Fast lane or down the drain? Does the occupation held prior to unemployment shape the transition back to work? *Research in Social Stratification and Mobility, 49*, 32–46.

Heinz, W. R. (2003). From work trajectories to negotiated careers: The contingent life-course. In T. M. Jeylan & M. J. Shanahan (Eds.), *Handbook of the life-course* (pp. 185–204). New York, NY: Kluwer Academic.

Hillmert, S., & Jacob, M. (2005). Institutionelle Strukturierung und inter-individuelle Variation. Zur Entwicklung herkunftsbezogener Ungleichheiten im Bildungsverlauf. *Kölner Zeitschrift für Soziologie und Sozialpsychologie, 57*, 414–442.

Hillmert, S., Künster, R., Spengemann, P., & Mayer, K. U. (2004). *Projekt 'Ausbildungs- und Berufsverläufe der Geburtskohorten 1964 und 1971 in Westdeutschland'. Dokumentationshandbuch*. Berlin, Germany: Max-Planck-Institut für Bildungsforschung.

Jacob, M. (2004). *Mehrfachausbildung in Deutschland: Karriere, Collage, Kompensation?* Wiesbaden, Germany: VS Verlag für Sozialwissenschaften.

Janik, F., Wölfel, O., & Trepesch, M. (2016) Measurement of further training activities in life-course studies. In H.-P. Blossfeld, J. von Maurice, M. Bayer, & J. Skopek (Eds.), *Methodological Issues of Longitudinal Surveys* (pp. 385–397). Wiesbaden, Germany: Springer VS.

Jenkins, A., Vignoles, A., Wolf, A., & Galindo-Rueda, F. (2003). The determinants and labour market effects of lifelong learning. *Applied Economics, 35*, 1711–1721.

Jusri, R., & Kleinert, C. (2018). Haben höher Gebildete mehr Sozialkapital? Ungleichheit im Zugang zu sozialen Netzwerkressourcen. *Sozialer Fortschritt, 67*, 249–268.

Kirchhöfer, D. (2000). *Informelles Lernen in alltäglichen Lebensführungen. Chance für berufliche Kompetenzentwicklung* (QUEM-report 66). Berlin, Germany: Arbeitsgemeinschaft Qualifikations-Entwicklungs-Management, Geschäftsstelle der Arbeitsgemeinschaft Betriebliche Weiterbildungsforschung e. V.

Kleinert, C. (2005). Unscharf: Was sind denn eigentlich berufliche Kompetenzen? *IAB Forum, 2*, 28–31.

Kleinert, C., & Matthes, B. (2009). *Data in the field of adult education and lifelong learning: Present situation, improvements and challenges* (RatSWD Working Paper 91). Berlin, Germany: RatSWD.

Kleinert, C., Matthes, B., Antoni, M., Drasch, K., Ruland, M., & Trahms, A. (2011). ALWA - New life course data for Germany. *Schmollers Jahrbuch, 131*, 625–634.

Kohli, M. (1985). Die Institutionalisierung des Lebenslaufs. Historische Befunde und theoretische Argumente. *Kölner Zeitschrift für Soziologie und Sozialpsychologie, 37*, 1–29.

Kracke, N. (2016). Unterwertige Beschäftigung von AkademikerInnen in Deutschland: Die Einflussfaktoren Geschlecht, Migrationsstatus und Bildungsherkunft und deren Wechselwirkungen. *Soziale Welt, 67*, 177–204.

Kracke, N., Reichelt, M., & Vicari, B. (2017). Wage losses due to overqualification: The role of formal degrees and occupational skills. *Social Indicators Research*. Advance online publication.

Kramer, A., & Tamm, M. (2018). Does learning trigger learning throughout adulthood? Evidence from training participation of the employed population. *Economics of Education Review, 62*, 82–90.

Kuckulenz, A. (2007). *Studies on continuing vocational training in Germany* (ZEW Economic Studies 37). Mannheim, Germany: Physica.

Lauer, C., & Steiner, V. (2001). Germany. In C. Harmon, I. Walker, & N. Westergaard-Nielsen (Eds.), *Education and earnings in Europe: A cross country analysis of the returns to education* (pp. 102–128). Cheltenham, England: Edward Elgar.

Matthes, B., Christoph, B., Janik, F., & Ruland, M. (2014). Collecting information on job tasks - an instrument to measure tasks required at the workplace in a multi-topic survey. *Journal for Labour Market Research, 47*, 273–297.

Mayer, K. U. (1990). Lebensverläufe und sozialer Wandel: Anmerkungen zu einem Forschungspro- gramm. In K.-U. Mayer (Ed.), *Lebensverläufe und sozialer Wandel* (Kölner Zeitschrift für Soziologie und Sozialpsychologie: Sonderheft 31, 7–21). Opladen, Germany: Westdeutscher Verlag.

Mayer, K. U. (2009). New directions in life-course research. *Annual Review of Sociology, 35*, 493–514.

Mayer, K. U., Grunow, D., & Nitsche, N. (2010). Mythos Flexibilisierung? *Kölner Zeitschrift für Soziologie und Sozialpsychologie, 62*, 369–402.

Mayer, K. U., & Huinink, J. (1990). Age, period, and cohort in the study of the life-course. A comparison of classical A-P-C-Analyses with event history analyses or farewell to LEXIS? In.

Mincer, J. (1974). *Schooling, experience and earnings*. New York, NY: Columbia University Press.

Minello, A., & Blossfeld, H.-P. (2016). From parents to children: The impact of mothers' and fathers' educational attainments on those of their sons and daughters in West Germany. *British Journal of Sociology of Education, 38*, 686–704.

Modell, J., Furstenberg, F., & Hershberg, T. (1976). Social change and transitions to adulthood in historical perspective. *Journal of Family History, 1*, 7–32.

Rosenbladt, B. von, & Bilger, F. (2008). Weiterbildungsverhalten in Deutschland. Band 1. Berichtssystem Weiterbildung und Adult Education Survey 2007. Bielefeld, Germany: Bertelsmann.

Rüber, I. E., & Bol, T. (2017). Informal learning and labour market returns: Evidence from German panel data. *European Sociological Review, 33*, 765–778.

Ruland, M., Drasch, K., Künster, R., Matthes, B., & Steinwede, A. (2016). Data-revision module - a beneficial tool to support autobiographical memory in life-course studies. In H.-P. Blossfeld, J. von Maurice, M. Bayer, & J. Skopek (Eds.), *Methodological issues of longitudinal surveys* (pp. 367–384). Wiesbaden, Germany: Springer VS.

Rychen, D. S., & Salganik, L. H. (2003). A holistic model of competency. In D. S. Rychen & L. H. Salganik (Eds.), *Key competencies for a successful life and a well-functioning society* (pp. 41–62). Göttingen, Germany: Hogrefe & Huber.

Rzepka, S., & Tamm, M. (2016). Local employer competition and training of workers. *Applied Economics, 48*, 3307–3321.

Scherer, S. (2005). Patterns of labour market entry – Long wait or career stability? *Sociology, 31*, 645–672.

Shanahan, M. J. (2000). Pathways to adulthood in changing societies: Variability and mechanisms in the life-course perspective. *Annual Review of Sociology, 26*, 667–692.

Shavit, Y., & Müller, W. (Eds.). (1998). *From school to work: A comparative study of educational qualifications and occupational destinations*. Oxford, England: Clarendon.

Simon, H. A. (1993). Homo rationalis. Die Vernunft im menschlichen Leben. Frankfurt, Germany: Campus.

Söhn, J. (2016). Back to school in a new country? The educational participation of adult immigrants in a life-course perspective. *Journal of International Migration and Integration, 17*, 193–214.

Spence, M. (1973). Job market signaling. *Quarterly Journal of Economics, 87*, 355–374.

Struffolino, E., Studer, M., & Fasang, A. E. (2016). Gender, education, and family life courses in East and West Germany: Insights from new sequence analysis techniques. *Advances in Life Course Research, 29*, 66–79.

Thurow, L. C. (1975). *Generating inequality.* New York, NY: Basic Books.
Trahms, A., Matthes, B., & Ruland, M. (2016). Collecting life-course data in a panel design. Why and how we use proactive dependent interviewing. In H.-P. Blossfeld, J. von Maurice, M. Bayer, & J. Skopek (Eds.), *Methodological issues of longitudinal surveys* (pp. 367–384). Wiesbaden, Germany: Springer VS.
Tyler, J. H. (2004). Basic skills and the earnings of dropouts. *Economics of Education Review, 23,* 221–235.
Weiss, F., & Schindler, S. (2017). EMI in Germany: Qualitative differentiation in a tracked education system. *American Behavioral Scientist, 61,* 74–93.
Wölfel, O., Christoph, B., Kleinert, C., & Heineck, G. (2011). Grundkompetenzen von Erwachsenen: Gelernt ist gelernt? *IAB-Kurzbericht 05/2011.* Nürnberg, Germany.
Wolter, F., & Schiener, J. (2009). Einkommenseffekte beruflicher Weiterbildung. *Kölner Zeitschrift für Soziologie und Sozialpsychologie, 61,* 90–117.
Zapf, W. (1991). The role of innovation in modernization theory. *International Review of Sociology New Series, 3,* 83–94.
Zimmermann, O., & Konietzka, D. (2018). Social disparities in destandardization: Changing family life course patterns in seven European countries. *European Sociological Review, 34,* 64–78.

Data Protection Issues in the National Educational Panel Study

Antonia Schier, Meike Bender, Tobias Koberg, Brigitte Bogensperger, Sonja Gruner, David Schiller, Jutta von Maurice and Henriette Engelhardt-Wölfler

Abstract

In an information- and knowledge-based society, data protection plays a significant role. Basically, it has to ensure the right to informational self-determination codified in the individual's right to decide whether to disclose or not disclose her or his personal data. Recent decades have seen a strong growth in the awareness of data

---

A. Schier (✉) · M. Bender · T. Koberg · B. Bogensperger · J. von Maurice
Leibniz Institute for Educational Trajectories, Bamberg, Germany
E-Mail: antonia.schier@lifbi.de

M. Bender
E-Mail: meike.bender@lifbi.de

T. Koberg
E-Mail: tobias.koberg@lifbi.de

B. Bogensperger
E-Mail: brigitte.bogensperger@lifbi.de

J. von Maurice
E-Mail: jutta.von-maurice@lifbi.de

S. Gruner
Würzburg, Germany

D. Schiller
GESIS – Leibniz-Institute for the Social Sciences, Cologne, Germany
E-Mail: david.schiller@gesis.org

H. Engelhardt-Wölfler
University of Bamberg, Bamberg, Germany
E-Mail: henriette.engelhardt-woelfler@uni-bamberg.de

© Springer Fachmedien Wiesbaden GmbH, ein Teil von Springer Nature 2019
H.-P. Blossfeld and H.-G. Roßbach (eds.), *Education as a Lifelong Process*,
Edition ZfE 3, https://doi.org/10.1007/978-3-658-23162-0_18

protection issues in the social sciences. The German National Educational Panel Study (NEPS) was established to collect survey data on educational processes and competence development for the scientific community. Its complex multicohort sequence design harbors several challenges for data protection: The legal regulations, the longitudinal design, the different populations under study, the varying collection modes and the sampling procedure all need to be considered from the perspective of data protection when collecting, processing, and disseminating data. Appropriate procedures and clear structures are essential. These can be developed only in a close cooperation between social scientists and data protection experts. Besides the design of the study, the recent introduction of the General Data Protection Regulation of the European Union and the institutional transformation of the research project German National Educational Panel Study at the Otto Friedrich University of Bamberg into the Leibniz Institute for Educational Trajectories are also accompanied by alterations and challenges for data protection.

Keywords

Data protection · Social sciences · Education · Panel study

18.1 Introduction

Data protection is one of the most important acceptance factors for the development of modern information- and knowledge-based societies (Bizer 2007). A survey by the Allensbach Institute for Public Opinion Research in 2009, however, indicates that more than 60% of the German population worries about insufficient data protection; more than one-half of the respondents (52%) even say that they have become more cautious when asked to give data about themselves (Institut für Demoskopie Allensbach 2009). At the same time, more and more data are being produced, stored, and processed as a result of new technical advances. In the course of the rapidly expanding bulk of data, we hear about misuse of data, data leaks, identity theft, or illegal video surveillance in the media almost every day. Newspaper articles or broadcasts on these topics have become part of our daily lives. Although these incidents (e.g., violation of privacy by spying on employee data) do not extend into the field of scientific research, they reveal the importance of data protection in all areas of modern life.

For scientific (empirical) research, the collection and use of data is essential. Therefore, data protection issues in data collection and data use have to be a major priority in the research projects planned and conducted by all scientific disciplines. Consequently, advances in scientific research go hand in hand with advances in data protection. However, decisive progress in this area requires a detailed discussion of problems and their possible solutions as well as a close cooperation between scientific researchers and data protection experts. Recent decades have seen an ongoing discussion on the needs of data collection and data use in scientific contexts and on data protection issues. This process has led to, for example, modified Data Protection Acts and court decisions specifying data protection regulations and recently to new European legislation. After years of discussion, the General Data Protection Regulation (GDPR) of the European Union (EU) was adopted and became enforceable on May 25, 2018. This affects data protection regulations in science as well and requires adjustments for data protection of NEPS. There is also a growing awareness of these issues in the social sciences, as can be seen in the publication of data protection concepts for social research projects (see Frick et al. 2010) and continuous research on statistical disclosure control (Hundepool et al. 2010; Ichim and Franconi 2010; Shlomo et al. 2010). Especially the new legislation of the EU and its implementation are a subject of both discussion and the literature of institutions for data collection in social sciences (e.g. RatSWD, ADM).[1] Besides the new legislation, changes in the institutional setting of the NEPS occurred. The Leibniz Institute for Educational Trajectories at the Otto Friedrich University of Bamberg (LIfBi) was founded in 2014. The induction of LIfBi into the Leibniz Association ensures a stable and long-term future for NEPS.

A challenge for data protection of NEPS is its design. NEPS was set up to collect longitudinal data on educational processes and competence development. Its research goals and the complex multicohort sequence design harbor several challenges for data protection. This chapter outlines these data protection challenges and corresponding procedural-organizational stipulations within NEPS. It describes the kinds of data in social research, the consequences of the multicohort sequence design for data protection issues, and the legal regulations. This then serves as a background to focus on the implementation of data protection in the areas of data collection, data preparation, and data dissemination. Data protection in the sense of protecting data from getting lost, for example, by making copies of it or storing it in a secure environment, is not the focus of attention here.

18.2 Survey Data in the Social Sciences

The legal foundation for data protection in Germany and the EU has changed. Since May 25, 2018 the GDPR applies. This regulation is in force directly in all countries of the European Union. Because of some opening clauses, national governments can issue additional rules: thus national supplements are possible, but not mandatory. In Germany a national supplement, the Datenschutz–Anpassungs- und -Umsetzungsgesetz EU (DSAnpUG-EU) and the new German Federal Data Protection Act (Bundesdatenschutzgesetz-neu, BDSG-neu) was adopted and came into force on May 25, 2018 as well.[2] The German Federal Data Protection Act (Bundesdatenschutzgesetz, BDSG) expired on this date. The aim is to protect the individual's personal rights. As Article 1 (1) GDPR states:

---

[1] A detailed discussion of challenges in regard to the GDPR and its implementation in the NEPS goes beyond the constraints of this article.

[2] The new German Federal Data Protection Act (Bundesdatenschutzgesetz-neu, BDSG-neu) is Article 1 of the Datenschutz-Anpassungs- und -Umsetzungsgesetz EU (DSAnpUG-EU).

This Regulation lays down rules relating to the protection of natural persons with regard to the processing of personal data and rules relating to the free movement of personal data. The Regulation protects fundamental rights and freedoms of natural persons and in particular their right to the protection of personal data.

This right to privacy also includes the right to informational self-determination. It derives from Article 8 (1) of the Charter of Fundamental Rights of the European Union (GRCh): "Everyone has the right to the protection of personal data concerning him or her." The right to informational self-determination guarantees the protection of the individual from unregulated disclosure and utilization of personal data.

According to the legal definition in Article 4 (1) GDPR, *personal data* is defined as follows: "For the purposes of this Regulation 'personal data' means any information relating to an identified or identifiable natural person ('data subject')." On the one hand, the scope of protection accordingly covers personal data allowing a direct identification of a natural person (e.g., via name, personal picture, address, phone number, or social insurance number). On the other hand, it also refers to person-related data. That kind of data does not allow a clear or immediate identification of the respondent via "direct identifiers" but via additional information derived from other data sources (e.g., information given by friends, the media, etc.) and via the combination of several single pieces of information (e.g., combination of occupation, place of residence, and migration background; Häder 2009; Metschke and Wellbrock 2000).

In the field of social science, the units of analysis are individuals. Therefore, gathering data about individuals is a fundamental need for social research. It is also the basis for statistical methodology that successively develops new statistical models designed to explain social phenomena, changes in society, or human development. However, social scientists are not interested in specific individuals but in representatives of populations under study. The aim is not to assess individual characteristics, but to obtain generalizable results. As a consequence, statistical analyses in social science do not require the identity of single individuals, and there is no need to work with personal data. It is sufficient to work with survey data.

Survey data is a dataset belonging to individuals who have participated in a survey. Main characteristics of survey data are, first, that each individual in the dataset is defined by a unique code such as an ID (the code itself should not allow a direct connection to an individual; instead, it should be a real alias). Second, the entity of data in the dataset belonging to a single individual should not allow any reidentification of the person. Methods of pseudonymization and anonymization are necessary to meet this requirement (see Sect. 18.5). In general, survey data needs to be of high quality if one is to obtain significant and reliable results. The basis for high data quality is especially a reasonable deduction of questions, a good operationalization of constructs, a well-constructed sampling design, an adequate data collection process, and a high and representative response rate.

Survey data are essential for making substantial progress in social research. The freedom of science is guaranteed by Article 13 GRCh: "The arts and scientific research shall be free of constraint. Academic freedom shall be respected." As Metschke and Wellbrock (2000) point out, this freedom of science may collide with general personal rights in data collection. The challenge for social science is to find an acceptable compromise between realizing the freedom of science and guaranteeing general personal rights (Häder 2009; Metschke and Wellbrock 2000). Meeting both scientific requirements and data protection regulations is the general guideline for all activities within NEPS.

18.3 Data Protection Challenges in the Complex Multicohort Sequence Design

NEPS is one of the largest longitudinal studies ever started in the field of education. More than 60,000 target persons of different age groups are being questioned and tested on a regular basis (see Chap. 1, this volume). Its multicohort sequence design is quite challenging, not only for the scientific researchers developing the methods and instruments but also for the project coordination staff of NEPS and the data-collecting institutes implementing the data collection procedures. The ways of accessing respondents, the recruiting processes for different target groups, and the processes of field work had to be specified. Data protection has highest priority in all these aspects. The interplay between the main legal regulations, the implications of the longitudinal design, the different ages of the populations under study, the varying data collection modes (each connected with different procedures to gain consent to participate), and the hierarchical structure of data have crucial implications for data protection:

- Before setting up a data collection process within NEPS in a specified substudy, it is necessary to clarify the legal regulations. These differ depending on the context of the data collection. For example, recruiting students for NEPS in schools requires different processes compared to recruiting participants via register-based data (see Sect. 18.4).
- One important characteristic of NEPS is its longitudinal design. Whereas respondents are contacted only once in cross-sectional studies, NEPS follows all target persons for years. To approach our target persons in subsequent panel waves, NEPS needs to ask the respondents for contact data (i.e., name, address, e-mail address, telephone number). For the already established NEPS starting cohorts, the NEPS has decided not to store the contact information at the LIfBi in Bamberg, but to store it—strictly separated from the survey data—at one of the data-collecting institutes (see Sect. 18.5).
- Managing different cohorts from newborns to adults is a big and difficult task from a data protection perspective. First of all, we had to clarify responsibilities for giving consent to participate in different populations. Whereas asking adults for their participation is quite uncomplicated, the situation becomes more complex when minors are included in a sample. Here the interplay between parental consent and the child's consent had to be clarified taking the age of the child into account (see Sect. 18.5).

- Furthermore, a variety of data collection modes are used ranging from written questionnaires and competence tests (paper-and-pencil as well as technology-based), across interviews in a face-to-face or telephone mode, to online surveys. The way of asking for consent needed to be adjusted to the way of contacting the respondent. Of course, this also needs to be taken into account when providing participants with further information about current issues in the study at a later date (see Sect. 18.5).
- In addition, the reference to institutions such as schools or Kindergartens in the sampling procedure in some NEPS cohorts has implications for data protection concepts. These institutions themselves are worthy units of protection. When generating, for example, survey data for the scientific community, the aspect "additional information" (e.g., participant X attended school Y or Kindergarten Y) plays an important role and needs to be considered (see Sect. 18.6).

Altogether, many aspects need to be discussed when handling data collection in the multicohort sequence design of NEPS. Certainly, when conflicts emerge between data protection issues and scientific requirements, the staff of NEPS are highly committed to data protection regulations and cooperate closely with data protection experts in developing good solutions. Such a commitment also strengthens the respondents' confidence that needs to remain positive over the course of such a large-scale project.

18.4 Legal Regulations

NEPS has to consider various legal regulations for data collection, data handling, and data dissemination. Since 1 January 2014, NEPS is situated at the Leibniz Institute for Educational Trajectories (LIfBi). According to the joint funding through the Federal Republic of Germany and the federal states, the Federal Commissioner for Data Protection and Freedom of Information is the supervisory authority of the LIfBi.

The legal basis of data collection is quite complex. In general, NEPS data is collected by professional data-collecting institutes (see Chap. 1, this volume). Until May 25, 2018, these institutes were bound by the BDSG, and the Commissioners for Data Protection in the federal states in which the institutes are registered were responsible for controlling their operations (independent of the individual study commissioned). When starting the collaboration between NEPS and these institutes, the schedule of responsibilities and the compliance with data protection issues in data collection and data transfer had to be regulated carefully. A special case of jurisdiction in Germany is data collection in the school context (e.g., data collection in the 5th- and 9th-grade starting cohorts). In each of the 16 federal states, the particular Ministry of Education inspects the instruments, materials (e.g., information given about data protection to the participants), and the data collection procedures with regard to their content and data protection aspects. Here, priority is given to the respective Education Act (*Schulgesetz*). In many cases, however, the Ministries of Education refer to the Data Protection Act of their particular federal state.

When engaging in the verification process required for data collection in the school context, the Ministries of Education in the 16 federal states are in close contact with the LIfBi. Negotiations focus on finding appropriate solutions for all 16 federal states in order to avoid as far as possible any distortions due to federal-state-specific adjustments to instruments, materials, and procedures.

As a result of the processes described, the NEPS team is continuously optimizing instruments, materials, and procedures in compliance with data protection aspects. Many appropriate solutions have been found for difficult data protection issues (e.g., in the area of analyses of the underlying population). Since May 25, 2018, the GDPR and the BDSG-neu applies. Because of the dominant role of the GDPR for the LIfBi, and in order to restrict the following discussion to central aspects, we shall refer to this law when explaining the collection, processing, and utilization of NEPS data.

18.5 Data Collection Process

Participants in NEPS are selected through random samples that differ between the six starting cohorts (see Chap. 3, this volume). Data collection, processing, and utilization are regulated by Article 6 GDPR. This states that collecting, processing, and utilizing personal data is allowed only if a law or a different legal regulation allows or provides it, or if concerned persons agree to it. In the case of NEPS, there is no law obliging people to participate in the study; rather, it is every single person's own and free decision. Paragraph 1 cl. 1 BDSG-neu therefore legitimizes the survey process. Peoples' consent to participate is needed; collecting, processing, and using personal data against a person's will is not permitted.

Freedom of decision also means that everybody can determine the way in which and the extent to which their personal data is processed (Metschke and Wellbrock 2000). It is therefore essential for people to be able to estimate the full consequences of their participation in NEPS before giving their consent.

Article 12 GDPR stipulates that information must be given in a transparent way. Article 13 clarifies which information has to be given when asking people for their consent to participate in a survey. First, they need to be informed about the purpose of the data processing. Second, the receivers of their personal data have to be named. Third, the possibility of refusing consent has to be indicated explicitly. And, last but not least, people need to be informed about the consequences of refusing their consent—because participation in the NEPS is voluntary, nobody needs to fear any disadvantages by refusing. In addition, it is statutory for people to also be informed about their right to withdraw their given consent at any time. Basically, on the one hand, information about the study needs to be adequate and sufficient enough to ensure a valid consent. On the other hand, every individual should be able to understand it regardless of their education background. Realizing both requirements is quite a balancing act for NEPS.

According to Article 9 (1) GDPR, there is a set of data requiring special treatment when processing it. Data belonging to this set addresses "racial or ethnic origin, political opinions, religious or philosophical beliefs, or trade-union membership, and the processing of genetic data, biometric data for the purpose of uniquely identifying a natural person, data concerning health or data concerning a natural person's sex life or sexual orientation." Disclosure of such data could have especially harmful results for individuals. According to this regulation, NEPS is allowed to collect this kind of data only if the participants agree, and if their agreement refers explicitly to this kind of data. To answer the most current and important research questions on education and competence development in Germany, it is absolutely essential to collect data on peoples' migration background, the languages they speak—both indicators of "racial and ethnic origin"— and data about their religious life (see Chap. 7, this volume). Taken together, such sensitive data can be collected and used for scientific research; however, great care is needed.

Generally, the information given to the participants is the basic element for their consent, and this is absolutely obligatory for researchers. Insofar, "informed consent" frames the data processing process. However, panel studies are not static but develop over years. New research topics could evolve that were not covered by the original consent. In that case, researchers have to ask for consent again later on—should that be possible. Another option would be to formulate the declarations of consent in a broader way right from the start when recruiting participants at the beginning of the study—this procedure is more compatible with scientific working methods. In the end, it is peoples' individual and free decision whether they accept the more broadly formulated declaration of consent or not (Metschke and Wellbrock 2000). One big advantage of the panel design of our study is that we always stay in close contact with our participants. Therefore, we can easily inform them about a new main focus or about new developments in questioning should that be required.

Up to now, the written form of consent was the preferred form. Article 32 of the GDPR states that consent should be given by a clear affirmative act establishing a freely given, specific, informed and unambiguous indication of the data subject's agreement to the processing of personal data relating to him or her, such as by a written statement, including by electronic means, or an oral statement. This could include … another statement or conduct which clearly indicates in this context the data subject's acceptance of the proposed processing of his or her personal data.

In NEPS, we ask our target persons to sign a declaration of consent whenever possible. Depending on the institutional context and mode of survey, consent is obtained in different forms. For example, we also obtain consent orally in telephone interviews (and document the given consent in the data set), by sending back paper-and-pencil questionnaires via mail, or by an opt-in-option in online surveys.

Because NEPS is analyzing education across the entire life course and competence development from birth to adult life, our target persons are of different ages and many of them are minors (under 18 years). Basically, parents are responsible for their minor children. In NEPS, we always ask the parents to permit their minor child's participation in the study (see also Brocks 2009). Of course, we also need to respect the child's will, and we need to accept her or his decision not to participate despite the parents' consent—participation in our study is also voluntary for the children involved. Apart from that, GRCh grants every child the same basic rights as an adult, and consequently also the right to informational self-determination. In order to fulfill that legal condition, we also ask minor children to give explicit consent. Generally, this consent is valid and effective only if the individual has the ability to form a rational judgment about the issue, and this also includes understanding the consequences of the consent. Unfortunately, the different laws connected to data protection do not define an age limit for this. Ideally, one should check each potential participant's ability to make a rational judgment. Of course, this is not possible for the large number of persons in our sample. Moreover, there are no objective criteria to support such a procedure. For these reasons, a general guideline is favored. For example, according to German Criminal Law, minor children are assumed to be of age at 14 years. Thus, we ask children aged 14 years or older to give consent in addition to their parents' consent, and assume that, at this age, they are able to foresee the consequences of their participation in NEPS. In school-based studies, consent cannot be obtained based on the exact age, thus the NEPS standard for asking students to give consent is first applied in Grade 9. Because NEPS consists of several waves, we need the participants' contact information so that we can reach them and question them again some months or years later. The GDPR provides a strict separation between contact data that allows a clear identification of a natural person (such as name, address, telephone number, and e-mail address), and the data disclosed during the survey. In other words, direct identifiers, which would make it easy to reidentify participants' data, have to be separated from the survey data as soon as possible.

In conclusion, many data protection aspects need to be considered during the process of recruiting respondents for NEPS who will be questioned several times. One particular concern is to ensure that all the above-mentioned aspects are transferred into clear procedures that are implemented in all information letters or forms used in the data collection process.

18.6 Data Preparation and Data Dissemination

After completing the data collection in each wave, the data-collecting institutes send the data in a pseudonymized form to LIfBi. Article 4 no. 5 GDPR stipulates that "'pseudonymization' means the processing of personal data in such a manner that the personal data can no longer be attributed to a specific data subject without the use of additional information, provided that such additional information is kept separately and is subject to technical and organizational measures to ensure that the personal data are not attributed to an identified or identifiable natural person." According to this, the code should be constructed in such a way that nobody will be able to reidentify a participant by the code. At the same time, a persistent identification code per participant is needed because it is essential for a panel study such as the NEPS to be able to match participants' data from one wave to that from another wave. Taken together, for the already established NEPS starting cohorts, no direct identifiers will be delivered to LIfBi. Cutting of "those direct identifiers" within the data-collecting institutes and delivering only pseudonymized data to NEPS already fulfils a first important step toward anonymization. As a result, NEPS deals only with survey data.

When the survey data arrives at the LIfBi, the codes used by the data-collecting institutes are replaced by new ones; the new codes are the ones given to the scientific community. After that step, data anonymization—one of the most important legal requirements for data dissemination—data editing, and data documentation can start.

Even survey data have to be checked for their disclosure risk. The anonymization concept applied to NEPS data follows two principles: First, disclosing respondents should be impossible. Second, a high utility of the data should be maintained. Different expressions are used to describe the levels of anonymization: Formal anonymization is achieved by dropping direct identifiers. Absolute anonymization lowers the disclosure risk to zero. However, this simultaneously reduces the data utility to zero as well. Therefore, the most important level of anonymization is factually anonymous data.

Article 26 of the GDPR states that:the principles of data protection should apply to any information concerning an identified or identifiable natural person. Personal data which have undergone pseudonymisation, which could be attributed to a natural person by the use of additional information should be considered to be information on an identifiable natural person. To determine whether a natural person is identifiable, account should be taken of all the means reasonably likely to be used, such as singling out, either by the controller or by another person to identify the natural person directly or indirectly. To ascertain whether means are reasonably likely to be used to identify the natural person, account should be taken of all objective factors, such as the costs of and the amount of time required for identification, taking into consideration the available technology at the time of the processing and technological developments. The principles of data protection should therefore not apply to anonymous information, namely information which does not relate to an identified or identifiable natural person or to personal data rendered anonymous in such a manner that the data subject is not or no longer identifiable.

This definition is oriented toward the principle of the above comparativeness; it meets not only the individuals' right to informational self-determination but also ensures data utility for scientific research. Techniques of creating (factually) anonymized data are summarized under the term statistical disclosure control (see bullet point "*Statistical data protection*"). In the field of data dissemination, anonymization techniques are only one part of the entire data protection concept.

Within NEPS, setting up a comfortable and secure data access is guided by a portfolio approach (Lane et al. 2008). Five different approaches are combined to protect the collected data and the respondents' identity. Strategies for data protection accordingly include organizational, legal, statistical, informational, and technical data protection.

- *Organizational data protection.* According to the NEPS mission, the data it collects should be available only for scientific use. Commercial institutions or private persons should not gain access. Prior to allowing access to the data or transmitting it to somebody, the staff at the NEPS Research Data Center at the LIfBi screen the potential data user's status and check whether she or he is connected to a university or a noncommercial scientific research organization. Access to the data is conditional on the user belonging to the scientific community. Furthermore, the user is requested to present her or his research project to the NEPS staff so that they may confirm the scientific interest.
- *Legal data protection.* Our principal task is to assure compliance with the legal regulations when giving researchers access to our data. The data users therefore are provided with data protection and data security information when asking for data access. In addition, they have to sign a contract regulating important aspects of these issues.
- *Statistical data protection.* Using techniques of statistical data protection means modifying the data in a way that guarantees the respondents' privacy. The aim is to create factually anonymous data that guarantee privacy while simultaneously offering a high level of data utility. In the field of social science, research on statistical data protection is an ongoing project. The methods can be subsumed under the expression *statistical disclosure control*. A wide range of modifications can be used to alter the data by, for example, aggregating the original data (e.g., no detailed country of birth, but only an indicator "Germany/Abroad"), adding noise to it (e.g., modifying the values of variables by defined methods), or synthesizing the original data (Hundepool et al. 2010; Rubin 1993). The results of analyses can also be altered by techniques of statistical disclosure control in order to protect the respondents' privacy. The required methods depend mainly on the technical form of data access (see bullet point "*Technical data protection*") and on the disclosure risks of the data. Generating factually anonymous data in the context of a longitudinal survey is much more challenging than working with cross-sectional data. To evaluate the disclosure risk in a dataset, it is necessary to check all variables and combinations of variables. Furthermore, the possibilities of accessing additional information have to be taken into account. In longitudinal surveys, data is collected in multiple waves and data from new waves is merged with data from the existing ones. Therefore, no final check for disclosure risk can be performed, because the kind of data to be collected in the following waves is still unknown. Due to the increasing number of longitudinal surveys, there is a growing need for more research on this topic. Finding appropriate methods of statistical disclosure control for longitudinal surveys is absolutely essential.
- *Informational data protection.* Good research principally depends on good education. Accordingly, the NEPS staff offer a special training program to data users. The program includes lessons on the complex panel design of NEPS and the resulting data structure as well as lessons on data protection and data security. One main objective of the program is to provide researchers with sufficient information about secure scientific research. Another major ambition is to provide extensive documentation, including detailed information about data protection and anonymization measures. Beyond this, the full spectrum of (meta-)information and documentation minimizes the risk of possibly unintentional and unauthorized data usage.

- *Technical data protection.* The data collected within NEPS is digital data. Technical data protection in the form of hard- and software solutions is therefore essential. Two different fields of data protection can be distinguished here: data storage and data dissemination. Concerning data storage, the staff set up a server system based on an autonomous structure in which data is protected against both data loss and attacks from outside. In matters of data dissemination, NEPS wants to offer comfortable data access to researchers. Depending on the form of data access, appropriate technical data protection methods need to be installed—the level of technical data protection principally corresponds to the level of statistical data protection. When analyzing high-detail data, researchers need to work within the LIfBi building. There are two workrooms equipped with special computers that, for example, do not allow data to be copied and that are not connected to the Internet. Thus, a more detailed version of the data required can be offered to researchers there. Another form of data access is via a secure remote access (RemoteNEPS). Scientists connect their own computer to the LIfBi server system. The data is located within a so-called data enclave in which it is not possible to copy or store data on the researcher's own computer. The major difference to data access via the workrooms for scientific researchers in the LIfBi building is that the data enclave does not allow us to control what users are doing in front of their desktops. Consequently, the data offered via remote access is less detailed. In general, the lowest level of technical data protection is realized in a downloadable Scientific Use File (SUF) offered to the scientific community. In this case, after the data has left the LIfBi, there is no longer any chance of controlling the data flow of the files. The Download SUF therefore contain less detailed data compared to data files offered via the other techniques of data access.

NEPS has been set up to collect and disseminate educational data to the scientific community. In addition, it has to secure the data of all participants. The portfolio approach builds up a high-level multidimensional data protection system that still allows extensive data use for researchers.

18.7 Conclusion

In terms of data protection, the biggest challenge emerging from the complex multi-cohort sequence design of NEPS is how to handle the collection, preparation, and dissemination of data appropriately. The procedures developed within NEPS meet not only the requirements of the decisive data protection regulations—in particular, that of the respondents' privacy—but also the fundamental scientific need for high data utility. Altogether, data protection ranks high within NEPS and the LIfBi. It is therefore a pivotal task for the LIfBi that frames all the activities of the scientists and nonscientific staff working together within NEPS.

References

Bizer, J. (2007). Modernisierung des Datenschutzes: Vier Säulen des Datenschutzes. Datenschutz und Datensicherheit, 31, 264–266.

Brocks, H. (2009). Praxishandbuch Schuldatenschutz (2nd ed.). Kiel, Germany: Unabhängiges Landeszentrum für Datenschutz.

Frick, J. R., Goebel, J., Haas, H., Krause, P., Sieber, I., & Engelmann, M. (2010). Verfahren für den Datenschutz beim Zugang zu den SOEP-Daten innerhalb und außerhalb des DIW Berlin. Retrieved from http://www.diw.de/documents/dokumentenarchiv/17/diw_01.c.347090.de/soep_datenschutzverfahren.pdf.

Häder, M. (2009). Der Datenschutz in den Sozialwissenschaften: Anmerkungen zur Praxis sozialwissenschaftlicher Erhebungen und Datenverarbeitung in Deutschland (Working Papers No. 90). Berlin, Germany: Rat für Sozial- und Wirtschaftsdaten.

Hundepool, A., Domingo-Ferrer, J., Franconi, L., Giessing, S., Lenz, R., Nylor, J., Schulte Nordholt, E., Seri, G., & De Wolf, P.-P. (2010). Handbook on statistical disclosure control. Retrieved from http://neon.vb.cbs.nl/casc/SDC_Handbook.pdf.

Ichim, D., & Franconi, L. (2010). Strategies to achieve SDC harmonisation at European level: Multiple countries, multiple files, multiple surveys. In J. Domingo-Ferrer & E. Magkos (Eds.), Privacy in statistical databases (pp. 284–296). Berlin, Germany: Springer.

Institut für Demoskopie Allensbach. (Ed.). (2009). Zu wenig Datenschutz? Die meisten sind mit persönlichen Daten vorsichtiger geworden (Allensbacher Berichte Nr. 6). Retrieved from http://www.ifdallensbach.de/pdf/prd_0906.pdf.

Lane, J., Heus, P., & Mulcahy, T. (2008). Data access in a cyber world: Making use of cyberinfrastructure. Transactions on Data Privacy, 1, 2–16.

Metschke, R., & Wellbrock, R. (2000). Datenschutz in Wissenschaft und Forschung. Berlin, Germany: Verwaltungsdruckerei Berlin.

Rubin, D. B. (1993). Discussion: Statistical disclosure limitation. Journal of Official Statistics, 9, 461–468.

Shlomo, N., Tudor, C., & Groom, P. (2010). Data swapping for protecting census tables. In J. Domingo-Ferrer & E. Magkos (Eds.), Privacy in statistical databases (pp. 41–51). Berlin, Germany: Springer.

19 The Research Data Center: Making National Educational Panel Study Data Available for Research

Daniel Fuß and Knut Wenzig

Abstract

The Leibniz Institute for Educational Trajectories (LIfBi) aims to promote longitudinal analyses in educational research by providing a data infrastructure with the National Education Panel Study (NEPS) at its core. The survey, test, and context information collected so far across the six NEPS starting cohorts already offers a unique empirical basis to the scientific community in Germany and abroad. In order to exploit the enormous research potential of NEPS, extensive data preparation and documentation, flexible modes of data access, and proper assistance in handling the complex data are required. A crucial aspect here is user friendliness, with data security and data protection playing equally important roles. The LIfBi Research Data Center has developed several work processes and tools to meet the respective requirements and to enable both broad and secure usage of NEPS data.

Keywords

Data edition · Data access · Documentation · User service · Data usage

D. Fuß (✉)
Leibniz Institute for Educational Trajectories, Bamberg, Germany
E-Mail: daniel.fuss@lifbi.de

K. Wenzig
DIW Berlin, Berlin, Germany
E-Mail: kwenzig@diw.de

19.1 Introduction

According to its association statute, the Leibniz Institute for Educational Trajectories (LIfBi) aims to promote longitudinal studies in educational research in Germany by providing fundamental, transregional, and internationally significant scientific, research-based infrastructure for educational research—especially by overseeing and implementing the National Educational Panel Study (NEPS). Its fundamental task is to make high-quality NEPS data on educational processes and competence development from early childhood to late adulthood available to the national and the international scientific community. Following a combination of arguments regarding costs, the pursuit of scientific progress, and the responsibility for the survey participants, a broad dissemination of the collected and prepared data was defined as a funding condition right from the start of NEPS. The approach of building up large-scale research data infrastructures with free access corresponds to several science policy recommendations, together with the demand for a good scientific practice of acknowledging the necessary efforts and services: "Successful operators of a research infrastructure that inspire new research topics and whose data are used to achieve research results that win international recognition should not, in terms of reputation, be left behind the users of this infrastructure who are successful in research with these data" (German Council of Science and Humanities 2011, p. 82).

A large part of the responsibility for establishing and developing the data infrastructure at LIfBi lies with the Research Data Center (RDC, *Forschungsdatenzentrum*). The RDC was installed as a separate unit from the very beginning. Its key challenge is to ensure a maximum of data usability and user friendliness without disregarding the strict requirements of data security and the complexity of NEPS data. This data complexity originates from a panel survey design that comprises annual and even semiannual interviews and competence tests in six different starting cohorts—newborns, kindergarten children, 5th-graders, 9th-graders, first-year students, and adults—with an initial sample size of more than 60,000 target respondents supplemented by information from about 40,000 relevant context persons such as parents, teachers, and heads of institutions (see Chap. 1, this volume). The issue of data security refers to the basic requirement of guaranteeing confidentiality protection for the—partly underage—survey respondents and their individual microdata by a combination of several strategies including statistical disclosure control (see Chap. 18, this volume). The mandate to release the data immediately after preparation to the scientific community—without a sheltered period of own elaboration in "primary" research—constitutes another aspect of the challenge. Last but not least, it is a particular task to coordinate and process the different contributions from the contracted field institutes, the involved units at LIfBi, and the partners of the nationwide

NEPS consortium (see Chap. 1, this volume) in order to establish a research data infrastructure. Within this general framework the core activities of the RDC are:

- *Data edition*: that is, user-friendly preparation of NEPS survey data for scientific analyses
- *Data dissemination*: that is, timely provision of NEPS Scientific Use Files via secure data access
- *Data documentation*: that is, well-structured material for a comprehensive understanding of the data
- *User service*: that is, individual advice and support for researchers plus regular training courses

In a broader context, NEPS represents an integral part of the national research data infrastructure. Already in 2012, the RDC became an accredited research data center of the German Data Forum (*Rat für Sozial- und WirtschaftsDaten*, RatSWD) and member of the Standing Committee Research Data Infrastructure (*Ständiger Ausschuss Forschungsdateninfrastruktur*, FDI). As such, it operates according to the RatSWD/FDI standard principles for providing transparent access to high-quality research data for scientific purposes. An obligatory monitoring and evaluation process every year as well as a complaints office for data users ensures that the required criteria are permanently met (German Data Forum 2018). Because the committee also plays a crucial role in initiating and implementing standards for the collection, storage, provision and quality of research data, the RDC's active participation contributes to the further development and strategic establishment of secondary data in the scientific community.

This chapter takes a look at the four areas that are RDC's primary responsibility. It illustrates the procedures implemented to facilitate good scientific practice with NEPS data by reconciling the survey complexity and information extent on the one side with a convenient and proper data usage on the other. The role of *RemoteNEPS* as an innovative data access option and an important component of LIfBi's data security concept is particularly emphasized in this context and described in more detail. Another focus is on achievements with regard to the infrastructural goals as mentioned at the beginning. This "output dimension" covers both the reached state of the NEPS database as well as the extent of its utilization by scientists. The final section offers a brief insight into current efforts and future challenges to further improve the empirical infrastructure for educational research. The present article summarizes a couple of more detailed descriptions of NEPS procedures that are published in a common volume and recommended for further reading—the issues to be addressed are large-scale data editing (Bela 2016), string coding (Munz et al. 2016), metadata management (Wenzig et al. 2016), disclosure risks and anonymization methods (Koberg 2016), remote data processing (Skopek et al. 2016a), and the RDC's work in general (Skopek et al. 2016b; see also Fuß et al. 2016).

19.2 Data Edition

The preparation of huge collections of empirical information embedded in a panel design of six parallel survey samples requires systematic and collaborative efforts of data editing. After the field institutes deliver the raw material, the work sequence includes interlinked processes of data inspection, cleaning, consolidation, integration, coding, enrichment, anonymization, and quality testing before a Scientific Use File can be added to the NEPS research data infrastructure and made available to the professional public. Each step demands a high degree of care to satisfy the quality standards with regard to both the usability of complex data and compliance with data protection legislation.

The RDC has established two *guiding principles* for the compilation of NEPS Scientific Use Files. The first refers to the paradigm of unaltered data. All editing steps are set up in a way that the original information is not changed or lost. Thus, the full research potential of the data is preserved as far as possible throughout the entire process. The second principle refers to the paradigm of integrated data. Whereas the original material partly contains several hundreds of separate data files for a single starting cohort, the respective Scientific Use Files reduce this amount to a manageable size. This is achieved by merging and harmonizing wave-specific survey information into issue-specific panel, spell, and other longitudinal datasets. It is assumed that for the vast majority of researchers, it is more comfortable and reliable to start their analyses from already integrated datasets than to pool together the necessary information from scattered source data themselves.

To further facilitate researchers' work with NEPS Scientific Use Files, the *data structure* is similar across waves and starting cohorts. A number of clearly defined and documented conventions provide for homogeneous variable names and labels. The same applies for missing codes and file names. Each Scientific Use File consists of multiple data files representing different types of content and different data formats. A cohort profile dataset and suitable identifier variables in all other datasets—especially for the target respondent ("ID_t") and the measurement point ("wave")—guarantee the linkability of information. Given the complexity of NEPS data and the multicohort sequence design, these efforts to attain consistency are essential to reduce the burden of data management facing the researcher. If a user is familiar with the composition of one specific Scientific Use File, she or he will instantly recognize the data structure of any other NEPS starting cohort.

The RDC's *data preparation* procedures take place in a multi-editor environment. All NEPS Scientific Use Files are created by using a Stata syntax that is constantly refined and adjusted to upcoming survey waves and new data specifications. The modularly built script follows a uniform logic for the six starting cohorts to ensure continuous and consistent data processing. It integrates all editing steps from the initial raw material to the bilingually labeled Scientific Use File and implements a series of control loops and plausibility checks. To illustrate the extent: The script for the current Scientific Use File of Starting Cohort 4 (version 9.1.0) includes almost 30,000 Stata command lines.

The whole workflow is safeguarded by a version control system that records who has changed what and for which reason in a syntax element. As a result, the preparation of each NEPS Scientific Use File remains traceable at any point in time because it is being documented with such high precision.

A routine task to enhance usability is data enrichment by generating additional variables and datasets. Such variables are primarily the result of coding answers to open questions in the survey. A lot of information from NEPS respondents comes to the RDC in such a string format. The text entries on occupations, branches, vocational trainings, courses of study, educational attainments, and so forth pass through an elaborated and semiautomated process of coding—that is, the assignment of a numerical code from a selected category scheme to the string information. These numerical codes are then used to derive several standard classification variables. For instance, the primary coding of all occupational information in NEPS is based on a comprehensive and fine-grained database of the German Federal Employment Agency (DKZ 2010). The DKZ codes, in turn, constitute the basis for socioeconomic status and prestige variables that are provided by default in the NEPS Scientific Use Files (KldB 2010, ISCO-08, ISEI-08, SIOPS-08, CAMSIS-08, MPS, EGP; see Munz et al. 2016). Other generated variables refer to the level of education (ISCED, CASMIN, Years of Education), the school type (Bayer et al. 2014), and the migration background (Olczyk et al. 2016), or they provide indices with regard to personality traits (Müller et al. 2016), self-concept (Wohlkinger et al. 2016) and further scales. Some datasets consist almost exclusively of generated variables. This applies to life history information that is condensed from several spell files into a few simple-to-use datasets, such as "Biography," "Education," or "Children," as well as to the "Weights" dataset with generated weighting factors (Steinhauer et al. 2016; Zinn et al. 2017).

Across the entire data edition process, *quality assurance* is an essential element. Beyond the already mentioned consistency checks inherent to the data preparation script, the broad dissemination of a beta version of the Scientific Use File grants extra time for intense control and revision. The beta phase involves all NEPS staff members as well as "external" data users who are willing to inspect the preliminary data and to provide feedback to the RDC. The strategy has proven to be an effective measure to identify and resolve bugs before a data package finally gets published. Subsequently detected errors are documented in the so-called "Release Notes" that come along with each Scientific Use File. These up-to-date notes contribute to a higher data quality as they point the user to potential problems and, if possible, offer tips for troubleshooting.

19.3 Data Dissemination

Huge efforts are made to disseminate NEPS data with as much analytical power as possible while guaranteeing confidentiality protection for the survey respondents and their individual microdata. All released NEPS data are de facto anonymous data. The RDC's routinely employed *anonymization procedures* concentrate on the manual inspection of open text entries for potential threats of re-identification and the statistical modification of sensitive information in terms of aggregation, top- or bottom-coding, and so forth. Part of this strategy is to create different data versions with varying levels of modification to limit the risk of statistical disclosure. It applies the general principle: the higher the level of data modification, the stronger the anonymization and the lower the risk of re-identification. At the same time, however, this decreases the information content for analyses. The data versions, in turn, correspond to different access modes that can be distinguished by the control over data usage.

- *Download*: The classical modus of data access is the secure download from the NEPS website after personal login. Due to the low ability to influence the users' data handling, the download data version features the highest degree of anonymization.
- *Remote*: LIfBi offers an innovative remote desktop technology called RemoteNEPS. This allows researchers to access sensitive survey information from their own computers. The lesser degree of anonymization in the remote data version is possible because all content remains under the physical control of the LIfBi. To give an example, context information from schools and kindergartens or the Federal State label ("*Bundeslandkennung*") in the starting cohorts of schools and higher education institutions are only available within this server environment.
- *On-site*: Access to the least anonymized on-site data version is linked to a guest stay in Bamberg. Specifically equipped workstations in the data security rooms at LIfBi and a personal check-in/check-out system provide for a maximum controlled physical and technical environment. Information that is exclusively accessible in the on-site data version refers mainly to fine-grained regional indicators and uncoded text entries.

The concept of differently anonymized data versions and corresponding dissemination modes is completed by so-called *Semantic Data Structure Files*. They fully reflect the data structure of a Scientific Use File with all variables and labels included. However, they do not contain data rows. The structure files are absolutely anonymous and publicly available. Interested persons can freely download them for a first exploration before signing a contract to use the real data. For a better orientation, all relevant labels are provided with anonymization suffixes (_D, _R, _O). For instance, a variable with modified values in the download version, but full information in the remote version is suffixed once with _D for the anonymized content and once with _R for the unaltered content in the remote version. A detailed documentation of applied anonymization procedures together with a list of affected variables is published with each Scientific Use File.

The dissemination of NEPS data via *RemoteNEPS* plays a particular role. RemoteNEPS has been implemented as a system for remote data processing to fill the gap between the download option with full access to restricted data and the on-site option with restricted access to full data. Unlike "remote execution" or "job submission" solutions,

RemoteNEPS uses a virtual desktop technology.[1] Based on a visual representation of the data, the researcher can run its analyses directly from her or his own computer without any time delay. All data operations are carried out on servers within the LIfBi building. A transfer of files from this "data enclave" to the local storage medium or vice versa is possible only through an export or import request and after manual review and approval by the RDC staff. Thus, RemoteNEPS facilitates flexible access to rather sensitive NEPS data in full compliance with national and international standards of data safety.

When working with the remote version, the average gain of information compared to the download version is much larger than the average loss of information compared to the on-site data version. In fact, RemoteNEPS offers almost the full NEPS data spectrum (Koberg and Stark 2016). In combination with the flexibility regarding time and place of accessing it—RemoteNEPS technically requires an updated browser and a stable internet connection—and the saved costs for an on-site stay in Bamberg, this dissemination modus supports a more elaborated examination of available NEPS data and, hence, a better quality of research findings. Since we started the remote desktop service in 2009 as one of the first research data providers in Germany, the use of RemoteNEPS has increased continuously up to nearly 10,000 sessions of about 100 min on average in 2017. Another reason for the popularity of RemoteNEPS is the provision of a powerful research environment for data users. The advantages range from the availability of up-to-date NEPS data and the equipment with current and freely usable software packages (Stata, R, SPSS, Libre Office, etc.) to the setting up of shared project folders for efficient collaborative work and the permanent storage of syntax and transferred results for backup and reproducibility.

Logging on to the RemoteNEPS server system requires a biometric authentication via individual keystroke behavior when entering a specific phrase. The procedure ensures that only authorized persons have access to sensitive data. Prerequisite for the registration of the biometric profile is a written consent and the attendance of user training. The latter serves not only to inform researchers about the use of RemoteNEPS, but also to raise awareness of certain aspects of data protection and data security. Further safety measures consist in the signing of a supplemental agreement to prohibit any image recording from the desktop as well as in the automatic control of user rights and expiration dates to avoid unauthorized access to the data. RemoteNEPS is therefore deeply embedded in the portfolio approach of the so-called "five safes" (Desai et al. 2016; Lane et al. 2008): safe people (trained users), safe projects (supplemental agreement), safe data (anonymized survey information), safe setting (protected data enclave with personalized access), and safe outputs (direct export control of any output file).

---

[1]Whereas remote access solutions such as RemoteNEPS allow users to see the research data and to browse them, remote execution solutions typically do not. Remote execution works via queries and result files. This means that syntax files are sent by the researcher to the data-retaining institution, and the analysis is then initiated there on the data server. After necessary data protection controls, the output is returned to the researcher.

19.4 Data Documentation

Comprehensive data documentation is as essential for the user friendliness and usability of the NEPS research infrastructure as a careful data edition and a flexible data access. Detailed explanations and easy-to-use tools contribute to both the establishment of a community of well-informed users in terms of "safe people" and the successful dealing with the quantity and complexity of NEPS data. Intense efforts are being made to implement a documentation concept that follows some basic principles:

- *Consistency*: The application of a uniform and logical system of conventions for naming variables and datasets across waves and starting cohorts ensures clarity and orientation within the entire NEPS data portfolio.
- *Findability*: All Scientific Use Files are equipped with a standard set of reports; that is, documentation is divided by topic. A hierarchical structure with cohort-specific "Data Manuals" at the top makes sure that searched information can be found easily and quickly (see Fig. 19.1).
- *Relevance*: As documentation should be as up-to-date as possible, most materials are updated on the website with every new release of a Scientific Use File. A few reports are even permanently adapted, such as the release notes. The range of documentation is being expanded and improved constantly, not least through exchange of information and at the suggestion of NEPS data users.
- *Bilinguality*: In order to facilitate international research with the data, all variable and value labels are offered in English and German. The most important reports are available in either English or both languages as well.

Generating the majority of documentation materials is the responsibility of the Research Data Center. To meet the above requirements, it uses a *metadata database*. The relational

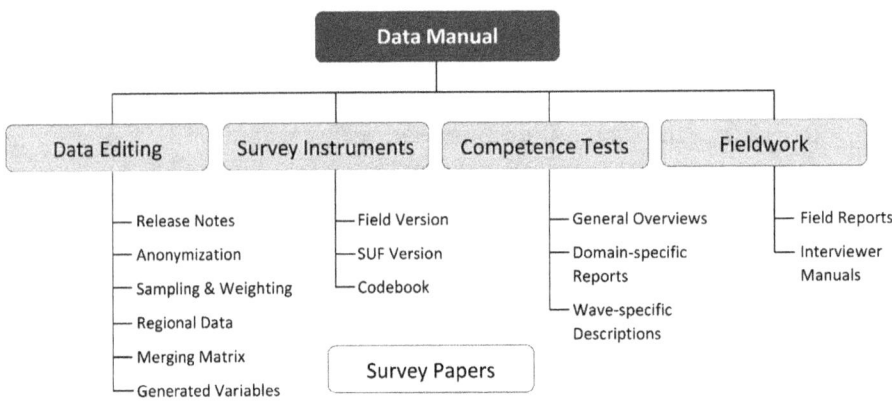

Fig. 19.1 NEPS data documentation. *Source* Own image

SQL database enables efficient storing of all relevant metadata on NEPS studies, instruments, items, and answer schemes in a systematic fashion. Based on a full transfer of information from the questionnaires, the central database initially functions as a tool for metadata control and management. Because many items are deployed repeatedly across the panel waves and starting cohorts, the abundance of metadata has to be administered in a way that links, deduplicates, reuses, and presents all relevant information including interviewer and filtering instructions, attribution to (sub)constructs, references to sources, and so forth. The database also functions as direct origin for the definition of data structures in the Scientific Use Files, the assignment of variable names and value labels, the creation of codebooks and other reports, and the feeding of an interactive exploration tool called NEPSplorer. Finally, the database functions as an interface for translating metadata into English. In sum, the central maintenance of NEPS metadata in one database ensures a high documentation utility because every change becomes effective in a synchronous and consistent way in all derived materials.[2]

Whereas several reports—for instance, on fieldwork and interview setting, competence testing and scaling, sampling and weighting, anonymization, or regional indicators—provide detailed information on specific issues, the more general *data manuals* are intended to assist researchers in getting started with the data. These manuals are of particular importance. Their primary focus on practical aspects such as panel progress and sample development, data structure and editing conventions, identifiers and merging procedures designates them as a first guide for dealing with the corresponding starting cohort. Systematic links to all other materials also make them a central reference document. Because the NEPS study constitutes a steadily growing research data infrastructure due to its ongoing panel design, the accompanying documentation is also dynamic in terms of regular updates and extensions. All manuals, reports, release notes, survey papers, and further documents are published instantly on the website.

19.5 User Service

The criteria of the German Data Forum mentioned above specify not only flexible data access and comprehensive data documentation but also a far-reaching service for data users. In the case of the RDC at LIfBi, the offered services range from contract and authorization management to user trainings and individual advice via telephone hotline and email ticket system. The latter is also important for processing researchers' import and export requests when using RemoteNEPS. Beyond these classical support activities, various aids and tools are provided by the RDC for a convenient and proper handling of

---

[2]It should be noted that the test booklets for the NEPS competence measurements are not accessible within the scope of the data documentation. This is mainly to protect the test instruments for further use in the panel. Inspection is possible, but only upon request and subject to conditions.

the complex NEPS database. All services are available online and described in detail on our German and English website at www.neps-data.de.

Regular user training and data workshops are a key feature of our service. These 1–2-day events are held about eight times a year in Bamberg and another three to five times at other locations in Germany and abroad. The courses provide basic knowledge on the NEPS study, its theoretical and methodological framework, the data portfolio and access options, the data structure of NEPS Scientific Use Files, and best practice solutions for browsing and merging information from different datasets. Some modules have a particular focus on either a certain starting cohort or a certain topic or a methodological challenge—for example, the use of weights and competence test scores. An overall objective is the sensitization of researchers to the terms and conditions of NEPS data usage, especially to issues of privacy and data protection. As noted earlier, course participation is obligatory for data users who want to enroll in the biometric authentication system for gaining access to the secure server environment of RemoteNEPS. Within the strategy to further promote NEPS data to an international audience, the RDC is also involved in data presentations at international scientific events such as conferences or summer schools. Once a year, the Leibniz Institute for Educational Trajectories organizes its own international *NEPS Conference* at the Bamberg site. This series of conferences brings together scientists from different disciplines and at different stages of their academic careers to discuss ongoing projects and current findings in educational research. Empirical analyses on all NEPS-related topics are presented in paper and poster sessions accompanied by keynote lectures from recognized experts and an informal round table exchange of ideas and suggestions with staff of the RDC.

Another important element of the user service refers to the supply of tools to facilitate the work with NEPS data. The *NEPSplorer* has already been mentioned as a metadata-based documentation and exploration tool. This web application performs a full text search through the German and English survey instruments of all released Scientific Use Files with the exception of competence tests. In addition to variable names and labels, information on the use of each item (starting cohort, wave, instrument), on corresponding response categories and univariate statistics, on the exact question phrase and interviewer instruction, on sources of literature and affiliation to higher-level (sub)constructs, and so forth can be retrieved and—depending on the users' requirements—stored in a personal watch list. The tool is particularly suitable for a quick access to the NEPS survey program in order to gain a first impression of the availability of the data of interest. It supports the search by keywords with several filter options, but also the search along a hierarchically structured concept tree. The tool is being developed and extended constantly by new functions to further improve its user friendliness on the one hand and to meet the growing complexity of the data on the other. The same applies to the so-called *NEPStools*, a free-to-use collection of specific Stata commands that is created and made available by the RDC. The package includes some programs—ado files—to simplify the handling of NEPS data. As an example, the "nepsmiss" command automatically recodes all of the numeric missing values from a Scientific Use File (−97, −98, etc.) into Stata's extended missing values (.a, .b, etc.) with correctly recoded value labels. Another example is the "infoquery" command that displays additional attributes of a variable such as the complete question text and the initial variable name in the instrument. The NEPStools are easy to install from the RDC's repository through Stata's built-in installation mechanism.

The combination of six starting cohorts and two school reform studies, different types of information, multiple informants, a broad range of covered topics, various survey modes, and the longitudinal design makes the NEPS database a highly attractive, but also very complex source of empirical research in the field of education and beyond. It is therefore a major concern and challenge to prepare these data in a well-structured, traceable, and user-friendly way while preserving the highest possible level of detail. At the end of the day, the success of these briefly presented efforts by the RDC, and by the NEPS as a whole, is measured by the use of the data made available for research.

19.6 The NEPS Data Portfolio and Data Usage

A timely provision is crucial for researchers to tap the full data's analytical potential; and, consequently, it is one of the accreditation criteria of the RatSWD for research data centers. The rule for NEPS is to provide the data to the scientific community as soon as possible—without any foot-dragging due to an "internal research privilege" for members of the NEPS team. Our general aim is to publish the data no later than 18 months after the fieldwork has finished. This time limit includes a data inspection and review phase for which the RDC releases a beta version of the Scientific Use File to the NEPS network and interested data users.[3]

The publication of NEPS Scientific Use Files follows a *cumulative strategy*; that is, the latest release replaces all former releases. Every time the data of a new survey wave are prepared or data bugs in previous waves are corrected, the existing Scientific Use File for the respective starting cohort is extended or updated by these data and released as a new version. An incremented numerical code clearly identifies the data version by informing about the number of survey waves (first digit), major updates (second digit), and minor updates (third digit). This version number is incorporated into the name of the Scientific Use File as well as its data file names and its digital object identifier (DOI). The persistent assignment of a unique DOI serves three main purposes: First, it indicates the relevant NEPS starting cohort and the data version of the Scientific Use File. Second, it directs to a landing page at the NEPS web portal with details about the data package

---

[3]Given the complexity of NEPS data and the time-consuming processes of establishing efficient data editing workflows, the 18-month criterion turned out to be overambitious during the first years.

Table 19.1 NEPS Scientific Use Files (December 31, 2017), Source: Own table

Starting cohort	Digital object identifier	Release date	Datasets	Variables
SC1—Early Childhood	doi:10.5157/NEPS:SC1:4.0.0	2017-08-10	17	3,496
SC2—Kindergarten	doi:10.5157/NEPS:SC2:6.0.0	2017-12-08	20	4,387
SC3—Grade 5	doi:10.5157/NEPS:SC3:7.0.0	2017-12-21	19	5,553
SC4—Grade 9	doi:10.5157/NEPS:SC4:9.1.0	2017-09-29	38	6,932
SC5—1st-Year Students	doi:10.5157/NEPS:SC5:9.0.0	2017-06-23	30	3,657
SC6—Adults	doi:10.5157/NEPS:SC6:8.0.0	2017-10-13	33	2,696
TH—Thuringia[a]	doi:10.5157/NEPS:TH:2.0.0	2014-12-03	5	1,821
BW—Baden-Wuerttemb[a]	doi:10.5157/NEPS:BW:3.1.0	2016-10-26	4	1,549

[a]The two federal-state-specific school-reform studies in Thuringia and Baden-Wuerttemberg with two respectively three cross-sectional survey waves were finalized in 2011 respectively 2013. The Thuringia study investigated the effects of a curriculum change between 2010 and 2011. The G8/G9 study in Baden-Wuerttemberg analyzed the effect of a reduction in school years in *Gymnasium*

and the data access options. Third, it enables researchers to cite the utilized NEPS data version in their publications in a precise way, which, in turn, is an essential requirement in the context of good scientific practice.[4]

Table 19.1 displays the data versions of NEPS Scientific Use Files available by the end of 2017 with corresponding DOI, release date, and two indicators for the amount of data. At that time, the NEPS research data inventory comprised 48 survey waves with more than 30,000 variables distributed across six ongoing panel cohorts and two completed school reform studies. Differences between the panel cohorts are mainly due to varying field starts (e.g., later beginning of the newborn cohort), varying intervals between the survey waves (e.g., semiannual data collections in the 9th-grade cohort), varying survey designs (e.g., inclusion of context persons in both school cohorts), and varying survey programs (e.g. detailed life-history calendar data in the adult cohort). As a basic rule, we recommend NEPS users to work with the most current data version of a Scientific Use File because it contains the latest data and a smaller risk of data errors. However, all former versions of a Scientific Use File are listed and available on our website at www.neps-data.de under the label "NEPS Data Portfolio."

Within a period of 6 years since the first NEPS data release in December 2011, an extraordinarily rich database for empirical research on educational trajectories and competence development over the life course has been established—a database that is growing continuously as further survey waves of all panel cohorts are already conducted, or in

---

[4]By default, all released NEPS Scientific Use Files are registered at dalra, the German registration agency for social and economic data, and thereby indexed with a DOI code (Wenzig 2012).

the field, or in preparation. For the NEPS data portfolio, this means an average provision rate of six new Scientific Use Files per year supplemented by updates if necessary.

Access to NEPS data is free of charge, but limited to the purpose of research and to members of the scientific community alone. Interested researchers are requested to conclude a data use agreement with LIfBi in which they provide a brief description of the intended project and a specification of the expected duration of data usage. For each project, a separate data use agreement is needed, whereby several researchers are usually participating in one project. By signing the agreement, they commit themselves to strict data protection guidelines that forbid any attempt at reidentification, passing on any data without permission, or using the data for other purposes than the specified research objective. In case of violation of these rules, severe penalties are prescribed in the contract (e.g., monetary penalty, proscription, exclusion from further data usage). As a key element of NEPS legal data protection (see Chap. 18, this volume), the data use agreement obligates all users to handle the data in a secure and confidential way. With the approval of an application, the RDC grants the necessary access authorizations that entitle the data recipient and all other involved persons to work with the full portfolio of NEPS Scientific Use Files.

The continuous growth of the data portfolio has been accompanied by a steady rise in *data usage*, indicating a great demand for longitudinal data on educational processes from early childhood to late adulthood. Figure 19.2 depicts this development, starting in summer 2011 when the first NEPS Scientific Use File was released.

The top graph shows the number of data users—without multiple counting of researchers who are assigned to more than one NEPS project—and how it has risen by at least 200 persons from year to year. In 2017, there were even 318 newly registered scientists and young researchers. At the end of that year, the cumulated total was over 1,600 NEPS data users. The graph at the bottom signals a considerable proportion of users from research institutions outside of Germany. The international NEPS community

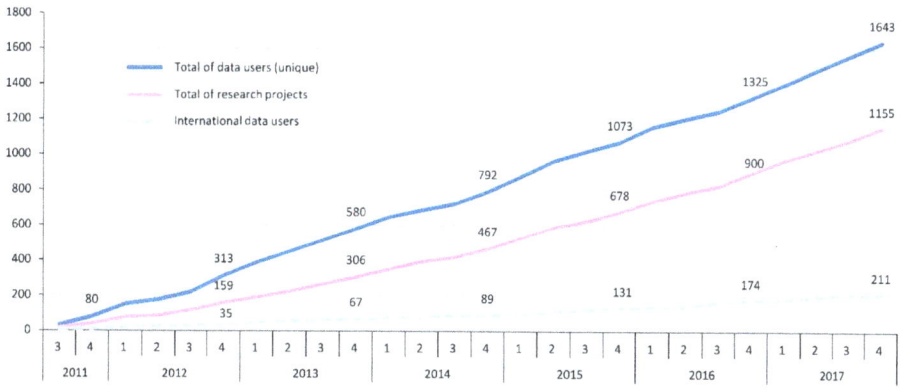

Fig. 19.2 NEPS data usage statistics (2011–2017). *Source* Own image

accounts for about 13% of all data users bringing together researchers from 25 countries such as the United Kingdom, Italy, Switzerland, Austria, the Netherlands, and other European countries; but also from the United States, China, Australia, Russia, Japan, and India. Finally, the graph in the middle represents the increase of research projects based on NEPS data. The total number has already exceeded the mark of 1,000 projects. At the moment, about 20 new data use agreements are submitted on average per month, with a tendency to rise and a significant share of proposals for academic qualification. Out of the 587 active research endeavors at the end of 2017, there were 152 dissertation projects (25.9%), 40 habilitation projects (6.8%), and 36 bachelor or master projects (6.1%). A closer look at the project descriptions reveals a great variety of involved disciplines and a broad spectrum of addressed research questions ranging from learning processes to issues of educational decision making, labor market, migration, social mobility, and family up to international comparisons, methodological modeling, and educational reporting.[5] In this regard, the Priority Program "Education as a Lifelong Process. Analyzing Data of the National Educational Panel Study (NEPS)" of the German Research Foundation (DFG) should be mentioned. The program has been initiated with the explicit aim of promoting the widespread scientific use of NEPS data in the national and international scientific community. It was set up in 2012, coordinated by Hans-Peter Blossfeld and Sabine Weinert. In the course of three funding phases (2012–2014, 2015–2017, 2018–2019), a total of more than 30 interdisciplinary research projects were devoted to studying competence development over the life course, or using the NEPS database for other substantive analyses, or dealing with important methodological issues.[6]

The scientific value of a large-scale research data infrastructure such as NEPS is measured not only according to the amount of data usage, but also, and more importantly, by the output in terms of *scholarly publications*. Up to and including 2017, the NEPS bibliography lists almost 250 empirical articles in academic journals, edited volumes, and monographs. This number underestimates the actual output, because not all users reliably inform LIfBi about their publications and, despite intense monitoring by LIfBi, not all relevant articles might therefore have been identified. Apart from this lack of information, it can be noted that all six panel cohorts and the two school reform studies are represented in the research outcomes. The majority of these works utilized the Scientific Use Files of either the "oldest" starting cohort of adults (SC6) or the most diverse—in terms of educational transitions—starting cohort of 9th-graders (SC4). NEPS data on several starting cohorts are also being used as part of the biennially published National Report on Education in Germany. In order to motivate further publications and to honor excellent scientific work carried out on the basis of NEPS data, the LIfBi gives out a competitive publication award during the annual NEPS conferences.

---

[5]A sorted list of all NEPS-based projects is available on the NEPS website (https://www.neps-data.de).
[6]Please refer to the SPP website for further information (https://spp1646.neps-data.de).

The first award was granted to Edele and Stanat (2015). One year later, the article by Fabian Ochsenfeld (2016) was selected by an interdisciplinary jury as the best NEPS publication among all nominations.

19.7 Outlook

It can be assumed that the use of NEPS data will continue to intensify in the future. On the one hand, the analytical potential of the Scientific Use Files available to date is still far from exhausted. Especially in an international context, there are still many application possibilities. In addition, the increasing visibility of the data within the scientific discourse will further promote the demand for reuse. On the other hand, the NEPS database grows continuously with each new survey wave of the six current starting cohorts. Apart from this "natural" increase in information due to the panel design, there are additional data enrichments—or they are in preparation—for extending the NEPS research data infrastructure:

- *Regional data*: Upon individual request, the RDC enriches the microdata of NEPS survey participants with macrolevel data from several external sources (e.g., official statistics), provided that the data users' self-compiled regional indicators meet certain requirements and a suitable link variable (e.g. municipality key) is available. The merged datasets are provided exclusively in the RemoteNEPS environment.
- *Paradata*: One of the upcoming goals is to strengthen methodological approaches, especially in the context of computer-assisted test execution and computer-assisted telephone interviews, by preparing and providing additional log and process data. Detailed response times and response sequences are intended as a starting point for the release of such paradata.
- *Administrative data*: In collaboration with the Research Data Center of the Institute for Employment Research (IAB) in Nuremberg, the provision of NEPS data of Starting Cohort 6 – Adults combined with administrative data from the Federal Employment Agency (BA) has been established and recently made available to the entire scientific community.[7] Data are linked on an individual level and on the basis of respondents' explicit consent. The general aim is to broaden the existing portfolio of combined NEPS and administrative data by including further starting cohorts in the process of record linkage to BA data and by intensifying the efforts to augment NEPS data with administrative information within the school context.

---

[7]The data package is hosted at the IAB (http://fdz.iab.de/en/FDZ_Individual_Data/NEPS-SC6-ADIAB.aspx).

A second big issue of immediate relevance for the future work of the RDC and the provision of NEPS data is the close networking with other data providers or research data centers and with the scientific community. Activities in this area have a strong focus on further improving the user friendliness of the data service, on intensifying the exchange with and among data users, and on conducting own research projects around the establishment and use of research data infrastructures:

- *Educational Research Data Alliance (VerbundFDB)*: The main concern of the partners involved in this network is the expansion of data services for educational research.[8] In this context, the RDC is particularly engaged in the field of data documentation in central information portals including the harmonization of study metadata.
- *NEPSforum*: Increased visibility of NEPS data is also a key objective of the recently launched online discussion platform. The so-called NEPSforum extends the existing dialogue between RDC and data users. On the one hand, questions, answers, comments, and so forth are completely transparent and can therefore be viewed by anybody at any time. On the other hand, the forum enables a direct exchange within the scientific community. In cooperation with other data providers, the goal is to further develop the tool and open it up as a comprehensive interaction medium.
- *Accompanying research*: Current and future research projects of RDC staff members address several topics such as decision-making mechanisms with regard to the use and citation of secondary data in educational research, ways to standardize the semantic indexing of data at the level of concepts, variables or indicators for improving discoverability, information quality in survey and administrative data, participants' consent to link data from external sources, effects of different data modifying anonymization techniques, and processes of computer-assisted coding of occupations. Most of these projects are being carried out or planned in cooperation with other research data centers.

Making NEPS data available for research: that is the main task of the RDC at LIfBi. This poses significant challenges, because the survey design with several panel cohorts pursued in parallel creates a very complex database. In order to ensure qualified and confident data handling, careful preparation and dissemination of the database needs to be supplemented by various measures of user support. The release of almost 40 NEPS Scientific Use Files in less than 10 years and the wide use of this empirical basis in hundreds of research projects testifies to the achievements of the RDC and all other units involved at the LIfBi and the NEPS network institutions. Because the user-friendly provision of large-scale data collections is an issue that the National Educational Panel Study has in common with other infrastructure operators, the benefits of joint efforts are obvious. With the general aim of

---

[8]Details are provided on the website of the alliance (https://www.forschungsdaten-bildung.de).

safeguarding and continuously improving the availability of research data for the national and international scientific community, the RDC participates actively in cooperation projects with other research data centers and in interinstitutional committees such as the Standing Committee Research Data Infrastructure, the Educational Research Data Alliance, or the Research Data Working Group of the Leibniz Association.

References

Bayer, M., Goßmann, F., & Bela, D. (2014). *NEPS Technical Report: Generated school type variable t723080_g1 in Starting Cohorts 3 and 4* (NEPS Working Paper No. 46). Bamberg, Germany: Leibniz Institute for Educational Trajectories, National Educational Panel Study.

Bela, D. (2016). Applied large-scale data editing. In H.-P. Blossfeld, J. von Maurice, M. Bayer, & J. Skopek (Eds.), *Methodological issues of longitudinal surveys: The example of the National Educational Panel Study* (pp. 649–667). Wiesbaden, Germany: Springer VS.

Desai, T., Ritchie, F., & Welpton, R. (2016). *Five Safes: Designing data access for research* (Economics Working Paper Series 1601). Bristol, England: University of the West of England.

Edele, A., & Stanat, P. (2015). The role of first-language listening comprehension in second-language reading comprehension. *Journal of Educational Psychology.* Advance online publication. https://doi.org/10.1037/edu0000060.

Fuß, D., von Maurice, J., & Roßbach, H.-G. (2016). A unique research data infrastructure for educational research and beyond: The National Educational Panel Study. *Journal of Economics and Statistics, 236*(4), 517–528. https://doi.org/10.1515/jbnst-2015-1021.

German Council of Science and Humanities [Wissenschaftsrat]. (2011). *Recommendations on research infrastructures in humanities and social sciences.* Retrieved from http://www.wissenschaftsrat.de/download/archiv/10465-11_engl.pdf.

German Data Forum [Rat für Sozial- und WirtschaftsDaten]. (2018). *The German Data Forum (RatSWD) and Research Data Infrastructure: Status Quo and Quality Management. RatSWD Output 1 (6).* Berlin, Germany: German Data Forum (RatSWD). Retrieved from https://doi.org/10.17620/02671.30.

Koberg, T. (2016). Disclosing the National Educational Panel Study. In H.-P. Blossfeld, J. von Maurice, M. Bayer, & J. Skopek (Eds.), *Methodological issues of longitudinal surveys: The example of the National Educational Panel Study* (pp. 691–708). Wiesbaden, Germany: Springer VS.

Koberg, T., & Stark, K. (2016). *Measuring information reduction caused by anonymization methods in NEPS Scientific Use Files* (NEPS Working Paper No. 65). Bamberg, Germany: Leibniz Institute for Educational Trajectories, National Educational Panel Study.

Müller, D., Linberg, T., Bayer, M., Schneider, T., & Wohlkinger, F. (2016). Measuring personality traits of young children: Results from a NEPS pilot study. In H.-P. Blossfeld, J. von Maurice, M. Bayer, & J. Skopek (Eds.), *Methodological issues of longitudinal surveys: The example of the National Educational Panel Study* (pp. 169–180). Wiesbaden, Germany: Springer VS.

Munz, M., Wenzig, K., & Bela, D. (2016). String coding in a generic framework. In H.-P. Blossfeld, J. von Maurice, M. Bayer, & J. Skopek (Eds.), *Methodological issues of longitudinal surveys: The example of the National Educational Panel Study* (pp. 709–726). Wiesbaden, Germany: Springer VS.

Lane, J., Heus, P., & Mulcahy, T. (2008). Data access in a cyber world: Making use of cyberinfrastructure. *Transactions on Data Privacy, 1,* 2–16.

Ochsenfeld, F. (2016). Preferences, constraints, and the process of sex segregation in college majors: A choice analysis. *Social Science Research, 56*, 117–132. https://doi.org/10.1016/j.ssresearch.2015.12.008.

Olczyk, M., Will, G., & Kristen, C. (2016, June). *Immigrants in the NEPS: Identifying generation status and group of origin* (NEPS Survey Paper No. 4). Bamberg, Germany: Leibniz Institute for Educational Trajectories, National Educational Panel Study.

Skopek, J., Koberg, T., & Blossfeld, H.-P. (2016a). RemoteNEPS: An innovative research environment. In H.-P. Blossfeld, J. von Maurice, M. Bayer, & J. Skopek (Eds.), *Methodological issues of longitudinal surveys: The example of the National Educational Panel Study* (pp. 611–626). Wiesbaden, Germany: Springer VS.

Skopek, J., Wenzig, K., Bela, D., Koberg, T., Munz, M., & Fuß, D. (2016b). Data dissemination, documentation, and user support. In H.-P. Blossfeld, J. von Maurice, M. Bayer, & J. Skopek (Eds.), *Methodological issues of longitudinal surveys: The example of the National Educational Panel Study* (pp. 597–609). Wiesbaden, Germany: Springer VS.

Steinhauer, H. W., Zinn, S., & Aßmann, C. (2016). Weighting panel cohorts in institutional contexts. In H.-P. Blossfeld, J. von Maurice, M. Bayer, & J. Skopek (Eds.), *Methodological issues of longitudinal surveys: The example of the National Educational Panel Study* (pp. 39–62). Wiesbaden, Germany: Springer VS.

Wenzig, K. (2012). *NEPS-Daten mit DOIs referenzieren.* (RatSWD Working Paper No. 202). Berlin, Germany: Rat für Sozial- und Wirtschaftsdaten.

Wenzig, K., Matyas, C., Bela, D., Barkow, I., & Rittberger, M. (2016). Management of metadata: An integrated approach to structured documentation. In H.-P. Blossfeld, J. von Maurice, M. Bayer, & J. Skopek (Eds.), *Methodological issues of longitudinal surveys: The example of the National Educational Panel Study* (pp. 627–647). Wiesbaden, Germany: Springer VS.

Wohlkinger, F., Bayer, M., & Ditton, H. (2016). Measuring self-concept in the NEPS. In H.-P. Blossfeld, J. von Maurice, M. Bayer, & J. Skopek (Eds.), *Methodological issues of longitudinal surveys: The example of the National Educational Panel Study* (pp. 181–193). Wiesbaden, Germany: Springer VS.

Zinn, S., Steinhauer, H. W., & Aßmann, C. (2017). *Samples, weights, and nonresponse: The student sample of the National Educational Panel Study (wave 1 to 8)* (NEPS Survey Paper No. 18). Bamberg, Germany: Leibniz Institute for Educational Trajectories, National Educational Panel Study.

Glossary of Institutions in the German Education System

Child care/day care (*Kindertagesbetreuung*)	Day-care establishment for children younger than 3 years of age, for example, institutional day care as part of the child and youth welfare services (Kinder- und Jugendhilfe) in either the private or public sector (Kindertageseinrichtungen); also nonfamilial day care by childminders (Kindertagespflege) (KMK 2010a)
Kindergarten	Preschool establishment for children aged 3–6 years as part of the child and youth welfare services (Kinder- und Jugendhilfe) in either the public or private sector (not part of the school system) (KMK 2010a)
Elementary school (Grundschule)	Compulsory school for all children aged 6 years and above. It extends over four grades, except in Berlin and Brandenburg (six grades) (KMK 2010a)
Special school (Förderschule/ Sonderschule/ Schule für Behinderte/ Förderzentrum)	School providing education for those whose development cannot be promoted adequately at mainstream schools on account of disability (KMK 2010a)
Secondary schools (Schulen im Sekundarbereich)	After elementary school, the German educational system tracks students into different types of secondary schools. The system varies throughout Germany because each federal state (Land) decides its own educational policies. In general, German secondary education includes four main types of school: the Hauptschule, the Realschule, the Gymnasium, and the Gesamtschule. Furthermore, several federal states (Länder) have new kinds of schools that combine the courses of education provided at Hauptschule and Realschule in curricular and organizational respects (KMK 2010b)

	• Hauptschule: Type of school at lower secondary level providing a basic general education. Compulsory for all students not attending a different type of secondary school, usually comprising Grades 5–9 (KMK 2010a) • Realschule: Type of school at lower secondary level, usually comprising Grades 5–10. Provides a more extensive general education and the opportunity to go on to courses of education at upper secondary level that lead to vocational or higher education entrance qualifications (e.g., Abitur) (KMK 2010a) • Gymnasium: Type of school covering both lower and upper secondary level (Grades 5–13 or 5–12) and providing an in-depth general education aiming toward the general higher education entrance qualification (Abitur), which can, however, also be obtained at other types of school such as the Gesamtschule. In the past, most Länder were converting gradually from a 9-year to an 8-year Gymnasium course of education. Currently, some of these countries are moving back to an 9-year course. The upper Gymnasium level (gymnasiale Oberstufe) comprises Grades 11–13 or 10–12, depending on the Land and the type of school (KMK 2010a) • Gesamtschule: Type of school at lower secondary level offering several courses of education leading to different qualifications. It takes the form of either a cooperative Gesamtschule or an integrated Gesamtschule. In the cooperative type, students are taught in classes grouped according to the different qualifications available, whereas in the integrated type, students are placed in courses grouped according to level of proficiency for a number of core subjects, but taught together as a year group for all other subjects. A Gesamtschule can also encompass the upper secondary level (KMK 2010a)
Vocational gymnasium (Berufliches Gymnasium)	Type of educational institution at upper secondary level offering a 3-year course of education in both the general education subjects taught at upper Gymnasium level (gymnasiale Oberstufe) and career-oriented subjects such as business and technology. It also leads to the general higher education entrance qualification (Abitur). Examples are vocational schools of economics or technical grammar schools (KMK 2010a)
Apprenticeship (Lehre)	Young people trained in Germany's dual system have an apprenticeship contract with a company in which they receive practical training. The contract basically stipulates the duration of training and the payment the apprentice receives. While the content of training apprentices receive at the workplace is highly regulated, the learning environment provided by companies may differ considerably

Glossary of Institutions in the German Education System

Vocational education and training, VET (Berufsausbildung)	In Germany, VET denotes the formal training young people receive below the university (tertiary) level. It typically focuses on a specific occupation and is completed with a certificate that often is recognized nationally due to the strong regulation of training content in many occupations. VET can take place either in the dual system or in specific educational institutions.
	System of VET in which young people take part in practical training in companies with parallel theoretical and specialist education in vocational schools. Practical training takes place typically on 3–4 days a week, with 1–2 days spent in school. Alternatively, education in schools may take place by way of block release
Dual system of vocational training (Duales Ausbildungssystem)	System of VET in which young people take part in practical training in companies with parallel theoretical and specialist education in vocational schools. Practical training takes place typically on 3–4 days a week, with 1–2 days spent in school. Alternatively, education in schools may take place by way of block release
Prevocational transition system (Übergangssystem)	A system of training courses that are supposed to provide young people who have not yet entered VET with skills that may enhance their "trainability." Courses typically last 9–12 months and do not lead to recognized vocational certificates; some courses offer the possibility for young people to acquire general educational certificates that they were unable to obtain in secondary school. In some cases, the training received may be recognized later on by firms as fulfilling some of the requirements of formal training
Vocational academy (Berufsakademie)	Tertiary education institution in some federal states (Länder), offering courses of academic training combined with practical in-company professional training following the principle of the dual system (KMK 2010a)
Universities and equivalent higher education institutions (Universitäten und vergleichbare Hochschulen)	Universities (Universitäten) and equivalent institutions of higher education include the traditional universities as well as universities of technology (Technische Hochschulen) that specialize in natural and engineering sciences, colleges of education (Pädagogische Hochschulen, College of education), which still exist only in Baden-Wuerttemberg, and theological colleges (Theologische Hochschulen) (KMK 2003)
Colleges of art and music (Kunst- und Musikhochschulen)	Colleges of art and music are higher education institutions offering teaching and research in fine art, design, music, drama, media, film, and television. Admission conditions often differ from those at universities because student admission is often granted on the basis of proven talent or aptitude tests (DAAD/HIS 2010)

College of education (Pädagogische Hochschule)	Type of higher education institution in Baden-Wuerttemberg, equivalent in status to the universities, offering courses of study for teaching careers at elementary level and certain teaching careers at lower secondary level. In specific cases, the colleges of education also offer study courses for educational and pedagogic professions outside the school sector (KMK 2010a)
Universities of applied sciences (Fachhochschulen)	Type of higher education institution established in the 1970s with the particular function of providing application-oriented teaching and research, particularly in engineering, business, administration, social services, computer sciences, and design (KMK 2010a)
Providers offering training or courses of adult learning (Anbieter für Weiterbildung)	In Germany, training or courses of adult learning are offered by various providers, for example, firms (the most important group), state-founded institutions such as Volkshochschule (adult education centers), state agencies such as the Federal Employment Agency, chambers of commerce and crafts, and a wide range of nongovernmental organizations.

References

DAAD/HIS (2010). Wissenschaft weltoffen. http://www.wissenschaft-weltoffen.de/glossar/index_html?lang=en. Accessed 10 Nov 2010.

KMK (2003). The Education System in the Federal Republic of Germany 2002. A description of responsibilities, structures and developments in education policy for the exchange of information in Europe. Bonn: Secretariat of the Standing Conference of the Ministers of Education and Cultural Affairs of the Länder in the Federal Republic of Germany.

KMK (2010a). Glossary on education. Institutions, examinations, qualifications, titles and other specialist terms. Bonn. http://www.kmk.org/fileadmin/doc/Dokumentation/Glossary_dt_engl.pdf. Accessed 11 Nov 2010.

KMK (2010b). The Education System in the Federal Republic of Germany 2008. A description of responsibilities, structures and developments in education policy for the exchange of information in Europe. Bonn.http://www.kmk.org/fileadmin/doc/Dokumentation/Bildungswesen_en_pdfs/secondary.pdf. Accessed 11 Nov 2010.

GPSR Compliance

The European Union's (EU) General Product Safety Regulation (GPSR) is a set of rules that requires consumer products to be safe and our obligations to ensure this.

If you have any concerns about our products, you can contact us on

ProductSafety@springernature.com

In case Publisher is established outside the EU, the EU authorized representative is:

Springer Nature Customer Service Center GmbH
Europaplatz 3
69115 Heidelberg, Germany